New England in U.S. Government Publications, 1789–1849

New England in U.S. Government Publications, 1789–1849

An Annotated Bibliography

SUZANNE M. CLARK

Bibliographies and Indexes in American History, Number 36

Greenwood Press
Westport, Connecticut • London

Library of Congress Cataloging-in-Publication Data

Clark, Suzanne M.
  New England in U.S. government publications, 1789–1849 : an
annotated bibliography / Suzanne M. Clark.
    p.   cm.—(Bibliographies and indexes in American history,
ISSN 0742–6828 ; no. 36)
  Includes bibliographical references and index.
  ISBN 0–313–28128–9 (alk. paper)
    1. New England—History—Sources—Bibliography.   2. Government
publications—United States—Bibliography.   I. Title.   II. Series.
Z1251.E1C58   1998
[F8]
016.974—dc21   98–10085

British Library Cataloguing in Publication Data is available.

Copyright © 1998 by Suzanne M. Clark

Library of Congress Catalog Card Number: 98–10085
ISBN: 0–313–28128–9
ISSN: 0742–6828

First published in 1998

Greenwood Press, 88 Post Road West, Westport, CT 06881
An imprint of Greenwood Publishing Group, Inc.

Printed in the United States of America

The paper used in this book complies with the
Permanent Paper Standard issued by the National
Information Standards Organization (Z39.48–1984).

10 9 8 7 6 5 4 3 2 1

In memory of my father, Erwin Walter Clark

CONTENTS

ACKNOWLEDGMENTS

I would like to thank the people whose efforts greatly contributed to the publication of this work. First and foremost, I would like to express my deepest appreciation to Richard L. Vogt, whose encouragement and support were unwavering from beginning to end. It is a pleasure to acknowledge a strong sense of gratitude to Roger Clark for patiently and perseveringly editing the manuscript. I also owe a special debt of gratitude to Daryl Purvee, for her excellent work as my research assistant.

In the preparation of this work, which began in 1991 and continued until 1996, many libraries were visited and consulted. I would particularly like to thank the staff at the government publications departments at the Bailey/Howe Library, University of Vermont, and the Hamilton Library, University of Hawaii at Manoa, for their continued encouragement, support, and assistance.

I would also like to take this opportunity to acknowledge the financial assistance of the University of Vermont and the READEX/ALA/GODORT/ Catharine J. Reynolds Award, both of which helped make the publication of this work possible.

S.M.C.

INTRODUCTION

"I have but one lamp by which my feet are guided, and that is the lamp of my experience. I know of no way of judging the future but by the past." (Patrick Henry)

This bibliography provides references to New England and New Englanders in United States government publications from 1789 through 1849. The period from 1789 to 1849 covers the growth and history of the United States from the first Congress, through the War of 1812, the Mexican War, and the territorial expansion of the United States. It traces the origin of many of the social, fiscal and foreign policies that were instrumental in the development of the country and whose consequences still affect us today. It encompasses the development of the postal system and the Treasury Department, the distribution of the public lands, the exploration of the west, systems of defense and fortifications, boundary disputes, the annexation of Texas, and the origin of the divisive differences between the South and the North over tariffs and slavery. In New England, issues such as the Dorr rebellion, the Canadian border dispute, surveys of canals and harbors, the wool and fishing industries, and militia claims from the War of 1812 were topics of particular sectional interest. During these first thirty congresses, the United States government published and distributed a wealth of primary and secondary source material documenting these historical events and issues. Historians researching the history of New England states and peoples can find a variety of information in these publications on New England topics and concerns. Speeches from New England Representatives and Senators also offer their views and the views of their constituents on the sectional and national issues of the day.

There is a demonstrable need for a government documents bibliography of New England references. The state series by the Committee on New England Bibliography, including *Connecticut: A Bibliography of Its History* (1986), *Maine: A Bibliography of Its History* (1983), *Massachusetts: A Bibliography of Its History* (1976), *New Hampshire: A Bibliography of Its History* (1979), *Rhode*

Island: A Bibliography of Its History (1983), and *Vermont: A Bibliography of Its History* (1983), and their update *New England: Additions to the Six State Bibliographies* (1989), are the most exhaustive bibliographies of historical literature on the New England states. They expressly exclude government documents to limit their sources to books, pamphlets, and magazine and journal articles. Citations in other New England bibliographies are few, and by no means indicate the breadth and scope of resources available for scholarly research. No other indexes have been published that detail government publications pertaining to a particular state. The bibliography, *Mormons and Mormonism in U.S. Government Documents* (1989), by Susan Fales and Chad Flake, looks at government publications on the subject of Mormonism, and was useful as a model for this project.

Infrequent utilization of federal publications is generally a result of the difficulty, perceived and actual, in identifying and locating the material. Peter Hernon, in his book *Use of Government Publications by Social Scientists*, found evidence of the perception that government documents are difficult to access and frequently underutilized. A combination of familiarity with document collections and the perseverance to struggle through volumes with poor and inconsistent indexing is required. My research validated the difficulties. Many index entries in the congressional debates were incorrect or out of alphabetical order, and congressmen with the same, or similar, last names were confused. Names and subjects were indexed regardless of the substance of the entry. Major historical figures had hundreds of entries for each Congress, with little or no subject classification. These hurtles are part of the reason researchers are reluctant to tackle government publications. This bibliography is intended to provide a guide that will ease and benefit the research process and open a vast new body of primary and secondary source material that has previously been neglected.

SCOPE

The scope of this work was defined to include any references in published government documents by and to the New England states, covering Connecticut, Maine, Massachusetts, New Hampshire, Rhode Island, and Vermont. Speeches by congressmen from these states, memorials and petitions voicing the opinion of the people of these states, and congressional and executive reports, documents, and references specifically about the states and their concerns are included.

Due to the volume of material available, speeches in the congressional debates are only indexed and included if they are greater than approximately one thousand words. In general, speeches of this length have substance and content that represent more than just a brief remark. This criterion was relaxed for smaller states where not as much was published on various topics and for individuals that were relatively underrepresented in the proceedings of Congress. This criterion was also relaxed if the content was considered particularly important and when the topic was discussed more fully at another date. References to, or speeches by, New Englanders while they are serving in a national office or capacity, are intentionally excluded as these individuals and their speeches or messages represent the nation, not their home state or the specific interests of that state. For example, speeches by John Quincy Adams while he served as President are excluded. The speeches and papers of these major national figures are frequently covered in other detailed and comprehensive bibliographies on the individuals.

All congressional and executive branch reports and documents included in the *American State Papers* and the U.S. Serial Set about the New England states, or representing the opinions of the people of those states, were included regardless of length. Publications indexed within these series include Presidential messages, department or agency reports, congressional reports on legislation considered during each Congress, reports from congressional investigations, annual reports from federal executive agencies, surveys, research publications, and selected reports of nongovernmental agencies.

References to maps are excluded unless they are part of larger New England reports or documents. The user is encouraged to use the *CIS U.S. Serial Set Index: Index and Carto-Bibliography of Maps*, edited by Donna Koepp, for a detailed and comprehensive index of maps published during this period.

SOURCES EXAMINED

The major series of government publications and sources of the period were examined, including the *Annals of Congress*, the *Register of Debates*, the *Congressional Globe*, the *American State Papers* and U.S. Serial Set, the *Public Statutes at Large*, and the CIS microfiche sets for the *U.S. Senate Executive Documents and Reports*, the *U.S. Congressional Committee Hearings*, and the *U.S. Congressional Committee Prints*. It was the intent that the collections indexed are owned by major depository libraries throughout the United States, and therefore readily accessible at many locations. In general, these series are indexed individually and unevenly through a variety of indexes, and required a detailed review of the sources to locate and retrieve relevant cites. Among the computer and printed indexes utilized were the *CIS Masterfile*, the *U.S. Serial Set Index*, and the indexes printed with the *Annals of Congress*, the *Register of Debates* and the *Congressional Globe*. When indexes were unavailable, the sources were physically examined for references page by page. The majority of sources reviewed were located at the University of Vermont and the University of Hawaii at Manoa. Other collections utilized were at the Vermont Department of Libraries, the Connecticut State Library, Middlebury College, and Colorado State University at Fort Collins.

The *Register of Debates* and *Congressional Globe* both index congressional speeches for the 23rd through 25th Congress and frequently duplicate each other. Speeches that duplicate, or closely approximate each other, are primarily indexed from the *Congressional Globe*, with a reference to the *Register of*

Debates, including the title of the speech in the *Register* and the page numbers. Entries indicate if the speech is exactly the same or a variation. Citations from both the *Congressional Globe* and the *Register of Debates* that are not duplicated, and which are only located in one of the sources, are indexed individually with their own entries.

During my examination and cross-checking of references at several different libraries, I discovered that more than one edition of the *Congressional Globe* had been distributed between the 24th and 28th Congresses. I specifically identified different editions for the 24th Congress, 1st Session, Appendix, the 24th Congress, 2nd Session, Appendix, the 25th Congress, 3rd Session, and the 28th Congress, 1st Session. Some of these volumes were identifiable as a "New Series," as indicated on the verso of the title page, but others were not identifiable and had no information as to the edition being used. I was unable to find any documentation of these different editions in Schmeckebier's *Government Publications and Their Use*, or other various guides to government documents. This bibliography cites the sources as used and available at the University of Vermont. As one of the oldest depositories in the country and as one of the New England states, its seems most likely that other New England libraries would have received these same editions and also that most researchers of New England history would be using these libraries. When page numbers in citations in this bibliography do not correspond to page numbers in these volumes of the *Congressional Globe*, the user should refer to the index in the volume itself, as well as use the date and title of the debate, to ascertain the corresponding page numbers.

ARRANGEMENT AND STYLE

The arrangement of the publication is chronological, by Congress and Session within each state. Within each Session, the citations are arranged alphabetically by the congressional speakers, followed by the U.S. House and U.S. Senate reports and documents, which are arranged alphabetically by title. The citation style uses a combination of Garner and Smith's *The Complete Guide to Citing Government Documents* and the citation style used in Fales and Flake's Mormon bibliography. The major changes from *The Complete Guide to Citing Government Documents* were to include the full name of the Congressman in the *Congressional Globe*, *Annals of Congress*, and *Register of Debate* citations, and to include the Congress and Session, and publisher and publishing date in the Serial Set citations. Each entry includes uniform bibliographic data appropriate to the source, accompanied by a brief abstract. In cases where the names varied, the *Biographical Directory of the United States Congress, 1774-1989 (Bicentennial Edition)* was used as the authority.

One advantageous feature of this bibliography is that cross-references to duplicate publications and speeches within the various publications indexed are provided. Besides enabling the user to be aware of the duplication of material, it offers an alternative location for material unavailable from one of the sources.

Frequently the public laws are printed in both the *Public Statutes at Large* and the *Annals of Congress.* Speeches made during the 23rd through 25th Congress are duplicated between the *Register of Debates* and *the Congressional Globe.* House and Senate reports and documents are printed by both houses of Congress and occasionally also published in the congressional debates publications. Citations cross-referencing duplicate reports and documents among the *American State Papers* and the U.S. Serial Set are referred to in the short form adopted by the CIS indexes, with a cross reference to the appropriate entry within this bibliography where the complete bibliographic citation may be found. The short form for *American State Papers*, for example, would use Mil.aff.584 (23-1) ASP 020 to refer to the *American State Papers: Military Affairs*, Document number 584, 23rd Congress, 1st Session, in volume number 20 of the *American State Papers*. The CIS short form for a U.S. Serial Set report or document, would use S.doc.489 (23-1) 243 to refer to Senate Document number 489, 23rd Congress, 1st Session, in Serial Set volume number 243. Most documents librarians and users of government documents are familiar with this form of citation.

New England in government publications can be a fascinating topic to explore. The style of writing and the expressions of the day make for an interesting and entertaining exploration of New England history. Topics of debate in the early years of history of the United States over the tariffs and protectionism, the value of public assistance to the needy, the sovereign rights of native peoples, and the role of the government in the lives of the people are still relevant and current issues in Congress. It is hoped that this book will benefit scholars by indicating the breadth and scope of resources available for scholarly research, negating the need for familiarity with document collections and the perseverance to struggle through volumes with poor and inconsistent indexing. It will open an important body of primary and secondary source material that has been previously neglected. It makes available in one location, in a consistently organized fashion, a reference source that can be easily consulted to ascertain federally published sources on New England.

CONNECTICUT

1ST CONGRESS, 1ST SESSION

1. Huntington, Benjamin (Conn.). "Duties on Imports," *Annals of Congress.* 1st Cong., 1st Sess. (15 May 1789) pp. 350-351. Objects to extending the revenue beyond the needs of the public debt.

2. Sherman, Roger (Conn.). "Department of Foreign Affairs," *Annals of Congress.* 1st Cong., 1st Sess. (17 June, 18 June 1789) pp. 491-492; 537-538. Addresses the right of the President to appoint and remove officers. Maintains that the power necessary to appoint is also necessary to remove, implying the advice and consent of the Senate.

3. Sherman, Roger (Conn.). "Duties on Imports," *Annals of Congress.* 1st Cong., 1st Sess. (9 May 1789) pp. 303-306; 316-317. Supports raising revenue to pay the Revolutionary War debts by means of duties rather than direct taxes. Discusses duties on distilled spirits and the advantages of the proposal over duties controlled by the individual states.

4. Wadsworth, Jeremiah (Conn.). "Duties on Imports," *Annals of Congress.* 1st Cong., 1st Sess. (23 June 1789) pp. 589-590. Remarks on the British and French trade and reciprocity with America.

5. Wadsworth, Jeremiah (Conn.). "Treasury Department," *Annals of Congress.* 1st Cong., 1st Sess. (20 May 1789) pp. 389-391. Supports the former Superintendent of Finance, and denounces the Board of Treasury as confused and disordered; advocates having a Secretary of the Treasury.

1ST CONGRESS, 2ND SESSION

6. Sherman, Roger (Conn.). "Public Credit," *Annals of Congress.* 1st Cong., 2nd Sess. (9 Feb., 23 Feb., 12 Apr. 1790) pp. 1156-1158; 1317-1318; 1523-

1525. Supports honoring debts by funding the debt at par; advocates the assumption of state debts; addresses objections of equality and constitutionality.

7. Wadsworth, Jeremiah (Conn.). "Public Credit," *Annals of Congress.* 1st Cong., 2nd Sess. (16 Feb., 1 Apr. 1790) pp. 1237-1239; 1513-1515. Opposes the plan to fund the domestic debt by exchanging depreciated securities for new interest-bearing bonds at face value; discusses the assumption of state debts as it would affect Connecticut.

1ST CONGRESS, 3RD SESSION

[no references]

2ND CONGRESS, 1ST SESSION

[no references]

2ND CONGRESS, 2ND SESSION

8. Wadsworth, Jeremiah (Conn.). "Military Establishment," *Annals of Congress.* 2nd Cong., 2nd Sess. (2 Jan. 1793) pp. 773-777. Opposes reducing the military establishment; maintains that regular troops are superior and cheaper than a militia. Recounts the history of the Indian hostilities and militia disgraces.

3RD CONGRESS, 1ST SESSION

9. Hillhouse, James (Conn.). "Commerce of the United States," *Annals of Congress.* 3rd Cong., 1st Sess. (25 Jan. 1794) pp. 314-322. Opposes restricting trade with Great Britain. Maintains that Great Britain's restrictions are no greater than those for other nations and that the proposed measures will not produce the desired effect; discusses and dismisses the political considerations of supporters.

10. Swift, Zephaniah (Conn.). "Non-Intercourse with Great Britain," *Annals of Congress.* 3rd Cong., 1st Sess. (14 Apr. 1794) pp. 576-582. Opposes prohibiting commercial intercourse between the U.S. and Great Britain as an ineffectual means to obtain the desired results, and as a measure leading to war.

11. Swift, Zephaniah (Conn.). "Sequestration of British Debts," *Annals of Congress.* 3rd Cong., 1st Sess. (28 Mar. 1794) pp. 552-556. Opposes seizing private and public debts for reprisal. Maintains that it would be a violation of the Laws of Nations, destroy the country's credit among other nations, and amount to a declaration of war.

12. Tracy, Uriah (Conn.). "Commerce of the United States," *Annals of Congress.* 3rd Cong., 1st Sess. (24 Jan. 1794) pp. 293-302. Objects to the proposal to restrict commerce so as to withdraw trade from Britain and give it to France. Contends that the proposal will stagnate trade and cause unemployment for questionable benefits; compares benefits of trade under Great Britain and France.

13. Wadsworth, Jeremiah (Conn.). "Tobacco and Sugar Duties," *Annals of Congress.* 3rd Cong., 1st Sess. (19 May 1794) pp. 704-705. Supports a duty on refined sugar; opposes the proposed duty on snuff.

14. "An Act to Provide for Placing Buoys on Certain Rocks off the Harbor of New London, and in Providence River, and other Places," *Statutes at Large,* Vol. I (5 Apr. 1794) p. 353. Also printed in the *Annals of Congress* (3rd Cong., 1st Sess.) Appendix, p. 1430.

3RD CONGRESS, 2ND SESSION

15. Hillhouse, James (Conn.). "Public Debt," *Annals of Congress.* 3rd Cong., 2nd Sess. (18 Feb. 1795) pp. 1237-1239. Maintains that it is unnecessary, improper, and unjust to change the terms of the agreement for the remaining non-subscribing creditors; contends that it would operate unfairly upon those who complied with the earlier provisions and would weaken the confidence of the people in the government.

16. Tracy, Uriah (Conn.). "The Public Debt," *Annals of Congress.* 3rd Cong., 2nd Sess. (6 Feb. 1795) pp. 1191-1195. Supports continuing the excise tax on loaf sugar for a long enough trial to ensure that the tax would not injure the manufacturer and would produce revenue. Reviews the reactions to the excise tax in Philadelphia and New York.

4TH CONGRESS, 1ST SESSION

17. Coit, Joshua (Conn.). "American Seamen," *Annals of Congress.* 4th Cong., 1st Sess. (28 Mar. 1796) pp. 802-803; 812. Opposes the provisions to provide relief against the impressment of American seamen; maintains that the proof of citizenship is too loose to be effective.

18. Coit, Joshua (Conn.). "Execution of British Treaty," *Annals of Congress.* 4th Cong., 1st Sess. (22 Apr. 1796) pp. 1140-1153. Supports the treaty. Addresses the various articles of the treaty and the objections and merits of each. Maintains that rejecting the treaty would lead to war.

19. Coit, Joshua (Conn.). "Loan to the City of Washington," *Annals of Congress.* 4th Cong., 1st Sess. (31 Mar. 1796) pp. 826-827. Opposes the loan.

20. Coit, Joshua (Conn.). "Treaty with Great Britain," *Annals of Congress.* 4th Cong., 1st Sess. (22 Mar. 1796) pp. 654-660. Discusses the treaty-making power, and the related powers and privileges of the House, President, and Senate; maintains that the House has the right to exercise discretion over appropriations.

21. Goodrich, Chauncey (Conn.). "Treaty with Great Britain," *Annals of Congress.* 4th Cong., 1st Sess. (24 Mar. 1796) pp. 717-725. Analyzes the treaty-making power as granted by the Constitution; maintains that the House has no controlling power.

22. Griswold, Roger (Conn.). "Execution of British Treaty," *Annals of Congress.* 4th Cong., 1st Sess. (26 Apr. 1796) pp. 1176-1183. Addresses the provisions of the treaty of 1783 that have not been executed, the settlement of disputes, and the regulation of trade between the U.S. and the British colonies.

23. Hillhouse, James (Conn.). "Debt Due Bank of the United States," *Annals of Congress.* 4th Cong., 1st Sess. (12 Apr. 1796) pp. 936-938. Reviews the state of the public debt. Maintains that revenues are exceeding expenditures; proposes a means of paying the debt.

24. Hillhouse, James (Conn.). "Intercourse with the Indians," *Annals of Congress.* 4th Cong., 1st Sess. (9 Apr. 1796) pp. 898-899. Defends the rights and titles of the Indians to their lands.

25. Hillhouse, James (Conn.). "Treaty with Great Britain," *Annals of Congress.* 4th Cong., 1st Sess. (22 Mar. 1796) pp. 660-676. Discusses the treaty-making power as defined by the Constitution; maintains that a treaty made by the President and ratified by the Senate has the binding force of law, but that the House authorizes the appropriations to enact treaties and is entitled to request information.

26. Smith, Nathaniel (Conn.). "Execution of British Treaty," *Annals of Congress.* 4th Cong., 1st Sess. (29 Apr. 1796) pp. 1264-1273. Addresses the controversial articles of the treaty, the treaty-making power of the House, and the consequences of rejection. Maintains that even if the House had the authority to reject the treaty, honor and interest would require them to ratify the treaty.

27. Smith, Nathaniel (Conn.). "Treaty with Great Britain," *Annals of Congress.* 4th Cong., 1st Sess. (9 Mar., 6 Apr. 1796) pp. 452-457; 769-771. Opposes requesting papers from the President concerning the treaty; maintains that the House does not have the constitutional authority to judge the merits of the treaty.

28. Swift, Zephaniah (Conn.). "Execution of British Treaty," *Annals of Congress.* 4th Cong., 1st Sess. (16 Apr. 1796) pp. 1015-1024. Discusses the treaty-making power and the duty of the Legislature to make the necessary appropriation. Maintains that the treaty is reasonable, honorable, and beneficial in the adjustment of past disputes and the commercial advantages granted.

29. Tracy, Uriah (Conn.). "Execution of British Treaty," *Annals of Congress.* 4th Cong., 1st Sess. (27 Apr. 1796) pp. 1213-1227. Gives a general review of the provisions and articles of the treaty and addresses opponents' arguments. Expounds at length on the ninth article, regarding United States land held by British subjects, as it would affect the State of North Carolina and the lands once claimed by the Earl of Grenville.

30. Tracy, Uriah (Conn.). "Treaty with Great Britain," *Annals of Congress.* 4th Cong., 1st Sess. (7 Mar. 1796) pp. 612-621. Objects to the call for papers regarding the treaty and to denying appropriations necessary to enforce its provisions; discusses the history and intents of the treaty-making power. Maintains that the House has no treaty-making power, and that it has a constitutional obligation to appropriate moneys to enforce treaty provisions.

4TH CONGRESS, 2ND SESSION

31. Swift, Zephaniah (Conn.). "Additional Revenue," *Annals of Congress.* 4th Cong., 2nd Sess. (19 Jan. 1797) pp. 1915-1916. Supports direct taxes apportioned according to the number of inhabitants in each state.

32. "Claims to Land in Luzerne County, Pennsylvania," *American State Papers: Public Lands*, Vol. I (Doc. 36) p. 79. (ASP 028). Petition of Connecticut charter landowners in Luzerne County requests fair treatment by the State of Pennsylvania, which has reversed its decision of the act confirming their titles.

5TH CONGRESS, 1ST SESSION

33. Dana, Samuel W. (Conn.). "Impeachment of William Blount," *Annals of Congress.* 5th Cong., 1st Sess. (6 July 1797) pp. 452-453. Discusses impeachment for offenses that do not violate official duty, and the status of members of the Legislature as civil officers.

34. Griswold, Roger (Conn.). "Answer to the President's Speech," *Annals of Congress.* 5th Cong., 1st Sess. (23 May 1797) pp. 93-94. Addresses proposed measures concerning foreign relations with France.

5TH CONGRESS, 2ND SESSION

35. "Breach of Privilege," *Annals of Congress.* 5th Cong., 2nd Sess. (30 Jan., 1 Feb., 2 Feb., 6 Feb., 7 Feb., 8 Feb., 9 Feb., 12 Feb. 1798) pp. 955; 959; 961-962; 966-968; 969; 970-980; 981-1000; 1000-1029. Reports of the attack of

Matthew Lyon (Vt.) upon Roger Griswold (Conn.) and introduction of a resolution calling for Lyon's expulsion from the House. Includes a letter from Matthew Lyon responding to the accusation; report of the Committee of Privileges detailing the course of events and supporting the above resolution, brief statements by Samuel W. Dana (Conn.) and Nathaniel Chipman (S-Vt.), correction of printed account of Samuel W. Dana, Matthew Lyon's defense, brief remarks by Christopher G. Champlin (R.I.) and William Shepard (Mass.), et al. and letter from Nathaniel Chipman (S-Vt.), debate on the impropriety of extending the power of expulsion (the vote for expulsion, which failed, two-thirds not concurring), and a complete transcript of the testimony taken at the trial (including testimony of David Brooks [N.Y.], Hezekiah L. Hosmer [N.Y.], Samuel W. Dana [Conn.], Joshua Coit [Conn.], Chauncey Goodrich [Conn.], Nathaniel Chipman [S-Vt.], Joseph B. Varnum [Mass.], and Matthew Lyon's defense statement).

36. "Case of Griswold and Lyon," *Annals of Congress.* 5th Cong., 2nd Sess. (16 Feb., 23 Feb. 1798) pp. 1036-1040; 1040-1043; 1063-1068. Debates the resolution that Roger Griswold and Matthew Lyon be expelled for violent and disorderly behavior; debate on the resolution that they promise not to commit any act of violence upon each other again.

37. "Case of Griswold and Lyon," *Annals of Congress.* 5th Cong., 2nd Sess. (20 Feb. 1798) pp. 1048-1058. Evidence gathered by the Committee of Privileges on the resolution that Roger Griswold and Matthew Lyon be expelled for violent and disorderly behavior committed in the House. Includes testimony from Peleg Sprague (N.H.), William Shepard (Mass.), and William Gordon (N.H.). Also printed as Misc.103 (5-2) ASP 037 (entry **60**).

38. "Fracas in the House," *Annals of Congress.* 5th Cong., 2nd Sess. (15 Feb. 1798) p. 1034. Account of Roger Griswold's attack on Matthew Lyon.

39. Allen, John (Conn.). "Foreign Intercourse," *Annals of Congress.* 5th Cong., 2nd Sess. (18 Jan. 1798) pp. 854-856. Calls for unity and reason in the debate instead of tactics intended to destroy the confidence of the people in their government.

40. Allen, John (Conn.). "Protection of Trade," *Annals of Congress.* 5th Cong., 2nd Sess. (20 Apr. 1798) pp. 1476-1488. Supports defensive action against France's depredations. Discusses the ineffectiveness of previous negotiations and the implications of peace in Europe.

41. Allen, John (Conn.). "Punishment of Crime," *Annals of Congress.* 5th Cong., 2nd Sess. (5 July 1798) pp. 2093-2101. Supports the principles of the Sedition Act; cites examples from speeches and publications.

42. Coit, Joshua (Conn.). "Breach of Privilege," *Annals of Congress.* 5th Cong., 2nd Sess. (12 Feb. 1798) p. 1020. Testimony on the case of Matthew Lyon (Vt.) assaulting Roger Griswold (Conn.).

43. Coit, Joshua (Conn.). "Foreign Intercourse," *Annals of Congress.* 5th Cong., 2nd Sess. (28 Feb. 1798) pp. 1098-1101. Supports fixing the salaries of ministers; contends that the President has a right to appoint ministers and send them where deemed necessary.

44. Dana, Samuel W. (Conn.). "Abrogation of Treaty with France," *Annals of Congress.* 5th Cong., 2nd Sess. (6 July 1798) pp. 2123-2124. Supports a preamble to the act repealing the treaties with France that states the facts justifying this measure.

45. Dana, Samuel W. (Conn.). "Breach of Privilege," *Annals of Congress.* 5th Cong., 2nd Sess. (12 Feb. 1798) pp. 1018-1020. Testimony in the case of Matthew Lyon assaulting Roger Griswold.

46. Dana, Samuel W. (Conn.). "Foreign Intercourse," *Annals of Congress.* 5th Cong., 2nd Sess. (19 Jan. 1798) pp. 883-885. Supports the power of the Executive to appoint foreign ministers and opposes the proposed reduction of ministers to Europe.

47. Dana, Samuel W. (Conn.). "Protection of Commerce," *Annals of Congress.* 5th Cong., 2nd Sess. (2 July 1798) pp. 2075-2076. Supports the authorization of private armed vessels to capture pirating ships.

48. Dana, Samuel W. (Conn.). "Protection of Trade," *Annals of Congress.* 5th Cong., 2nd Sess. (20 Apr. 1798) pp. 1501-1505. Requests the House to unite in supporting the measures to resist French depredations upon commerce.

49. Dana, Samuel W. (Conn.). "Provisional Army," *Annals of Congress.* 5th Cong., 2nd Sess. (8 May, 14 May, 16 May 1798) pp. 1637; 1704-1705; 1757-1758. Supports a volunteer corps that would be available for emergencies.

50. Dana, Samuel W. (Conn.). "Punishment of Crime," *Annals of Congress.* 5th Cong., 2nd Sess. (5 July 1798) pp. 2111-2113. Supports punishing conspiracies against the government; discusses freedom of the speech and press under these circumstances.

51. Dana, Samuel W. (Conn.). "Relations with France," *Annals of Congress.* 5th Cong., 2nd Sess. (27 Mar. 1798) pp. 1330-1331. Advocates that merchant vessels arm themselves for self-defense against French depredations.

52. Edmond, William (Conn.). "Protection of Commerce," *Annals of Congress.* 5th Cong., 2nd Sess. (26 May, 2 July 1798) pp. 1822-1824; 2077-2078. Discusses the depredations of France on American commerce. Maintains that negotiation is no longer realistic; supports the right of private-armed vessels to carry arms for self-defense.

53. Goodrich, Chauncey (Conn.). "Breach of Privilege," *Annals of Congress.* 5th Cong., 2nd Sess. (12 Feb. 1798) pp. 1020-1022. Testimony in the case of Matthew Lyon assaulting Roger Griswold.

54. Goodrich, Chauncey (Conn.). "Foreign Intercourse," *Annals of Congress*. 5th Cong., 2nd Sess. (26 Jan. 1798) pp. 931-941. Opposes the right of the House to determine the number and grade of the public ministers; maintains that privilege is included within the Executive's power. Addresses opponents' arguments.

55. Griswold, Roger (Conn.). "Foreign Intercourse," *Annals of Congress*. 5th Cong., 2nd Sess. (22 Jan. 1798) pp. 890-893. Supports the Executive's right and need to appoint ministers.

56. Smith, Nathaniel (Conn.). "Direct Taxes," *Annals of Congress*. 5th Cong., 2nd Sess. (30 May 1798) pp. 1844-1846. Supports taxing the value of land and houses separately.

57. Smith, Nathaniel (Conn.). "Evidence in Contested Elections," *Annals of Congress*. 5th Cong., 2nd Sess. (5 Dec. 1797) pp. 684-685. Advocates establishing regulations on taking evidence for contested elections.

58. Smith, Nathaniel (Conn.). "Foreign Intercourse," *Annals of Congress*. 5th Cong., 2nd Sess. (19 Jan. 1798) pp. 867-869. Supports the executive authority to appoint foreign ministers and to assign them to certain locations.

59. "Breach of Privileges," *American State Papers: Miscellaneous*, Vol. I (Doc. 103) pp. 166-173. (ASP 037). Report of the Committee of Privileges details the course of events of the assault and supporting consideration of the resolution calling for Lyon's expulsion from the House. Includes testimony taken at the trial from David Brooks (N.Y.), Hezekiah L. Hosmer (N.Y.), Samuel W. Dana (Conn.), Joshua Coit (Conn.), Chauncey Goodrich (Conn.), Nathaniel Chipman (Vt.), and Joseph B. Varnum (Mass.). Also printed in the *Annals of Congress* (5th Cong., 2nd Sess.) "Breach of Privilege," pp. 961-962, 1009-1025.

60. "Breach of Privileges," *American State Papers: Miscellaneous*, Vol. I (Doc. 104) pp. 174-178. (ASP 037). Depositions taken on the assault upon Roger Griswold; includes those from Peleg Sprague (N.H.), William Shepard (Mass.), and William Gordon (N.H.). Also printed in the *Annals of Congress* (5th Cong., 2nd Sess.) "Case of Griswold and Lyon," pp. 1048-1058 (entry **37**).

5TH CONGRESS, 3RD SESSION

61. Brace, Jonathan (Conn.). "Intercourse with France," *Annals of Congress*. 5th Cong., 3rd Sess. (24 Jan. 1799) pp. 2771-2773. Supports the suspension of trade between the U.S. and France until the French cease their commercial depredations.

62. Brace, Jonathan (Conn.). "Usurpation of Executive Authority," *Annals of Congress*. 5th Cong., 3rd Sess. (11 Jan. 1799) pp. 2631-2634. Supports the punishment of any person interfering in disputes between the U.S. and a foreign country.

63. Dana, Samuel W. (Conn.). "Capture of French Vessels," *Annals of Congress.* 5th Cong., 3rd Sess. (20 Feb. 1799) pp. 2942-2944. Advocates resisting the maritime violence of France in order improve the prospects of negotiation.

64. Dana, Samuel W. (Conn.). "Impeachment of William Blount," *Annals of Congress.* 5th Cong., 3rd Sess. (21 Dec. 1798) pp. 2474-2475. Objects to requiring the accused to appear in person since the sentence doesn't affect his person or his property.

65. Dana, Samuel W. (Conn.). "Usurpation of Executive Authority," *Annals of Congress.* 5th Cong., 3rd Sess. (27 Dec. 1798; 10 Jan. 1799) pp. 2499-2500; 2614-2617. Supports the punishment of unauthorized individuals who interfere in disputes between the U.S. and foreign countries.

66. Edmond, William (Conn.). "Impeachment of William Blount," *Annals of Congress.* 5th Cong., 3rd Sess. (21 Dec. 1798) pp. 2482-2483. Advocates proceeding with the prosecution regardless of Blount's personal attendance.

67. Edmond, William (Conn.). "Usurpation of Executive Authority," *Annals of Congress.* 5th Cong., 3rd Sess. (9 Jan., 11 Jan. 1799) pp. 2597-2599; 2645-2647. Remarks on preventing individuals from interfering with the executive authority in disputes between the U.S. and a foreign country.

68. Smith, Nathaniel (Conn.). "Usurpation of Executive Authority," *Annals of Congress.* 5th Cong., 3rd Sess. (27 Dec., 28 Dec. 1798) pp. 2519-2521; 2543-2545. Supports legislation to guard against interference of individuals in negotiations with a foreign government.

6TH CONGRESS, 1ST SESSION

69. Dana, Samuel W. (Conn.). "Breach of Privilege," *Annals of Congress.* 6th Cong., 1st Sess. (28 Jan. 1800) pp. 490-494. Remarks on the letter from Mr. Randolph (Va.) appealing to the President; discusses the tone of the letter, the reason for appeal to the President, and the offending words used in debate.

70. Edmond, William (Conn.). "Breach of Privilege," *Annals of Congress.* 6th Cong., 1st Sess. (28 Jan. 1800) pp. 482-483. Remarks concerning the letter from Mr. Randolph (Va.) who made an appeal to the President.

71. Tracy, Uriah (Conn.). "Breach of Privilege," *Annals of Congress.* 6th Cong., 1st Sess. (5 Mar. 1800) pp. 85-88. Remarks on lies that were published in the *Aurora* respecting the official conduct of members of the Senate.

72. "An Act to Establish the District of Kennebunk, and to Annex Lyme to New London, and to Alter the District of Bermuda Hundred and City Point; and Therein to Amend the Act Intituled 'An Act to Regulate the Collection of Duties on Imports and Tonnage'," *Statutes at Large*, Vol. II (10 May 1800) pp. 68-69. Also printed in the *Annals of Congress* (6th Cong., 1st Sess.) Appendix, pp. 1509-1510.

73. "An Act to Provide for Rebuilding the Lighthouses at New London; for the Support of a Lighthouse at Clark's Point; for the Erection and Support of a Lighthouse at Wigwam Point, and for Other Purposes," *Statutes at Large*, Vol. II (29 Apr. 1800) pp. 57-58. Also printed in the *Annals of Congress* (6th Cong., 1st Sess.) Appendix, p. 1497.

74. "An Act to Authorize the President of the United States to Accept, for the United States, a Cession of Jurisdiction of the Territory West of Pennsylvania, Commonly Called the Western Reserve of Connecticut," *Statutes at Large*, Vol. II (28 Apr. 1800) pp. 56-57. Also printed in the *Annals of Congress* (6th Cong., 1st Sess.) Appendix, pp. 1495-1496.

75. "Connecticut Western Reserve," *American State Papers: Public Lands*, Vol. I (Doc. 51) pp. 94-98. (ASP 028). Report supports the cession of jurisdiction of the territory west of Pennsylvania, commonly called the Western Reserve of Connecticut. Provides a detailed outline of the grants and legislative acts concerning the boundaries of Connecticut and jurisdiction of the land.

6TH CONGRESS, 2ND SESSION

76. Dana, Samuel W. (Conn.). "Sedition Act," *Annals of Congress*. 6th Cong., 2nd Sess. (21 Jan. 1801) pp. 923-925. Supports the Sedition Act and the punishment of slander and lies against the government.

77. Griswold, Roger (Conn.). "Sedition Act," *Annals of Congress*. 6th Cong., 2nd Sess. (21 Jan. 1801) pp. 920-921. Supports the provisions of the Sedition Act as necessary and constitutional.

78. "An Act for Erecting Lighthouses on New Point Comfort, and on Smith's Point, in the State of Virginia, and on Faulkner's Island in Long Island Sound, in the State of Connecticut, and for Placing Buoys in Naraganset Bay," *Statutes at Large*, Vol. I (3 Mar. 1801) p. 125. Also printed in the *Annals of Congress* (6th Cong., 2nd Sess.) Appendix, pp. 1576-1578.

7TH CONGRESS, 1ST SESSION

79. Dana, Samuel W. (Conn.). "French Spoliations," *Annals of Congress*. 7th Cong., 1st Sess. (13 Mar. 1802) pp. 1005-1006, 1011-1012. Supports an inquiry into the claims against the French.

80. Dana, Samuel W. (Conn.). "Impost Duties," *Annals of Congress.* 7th Cong., 1st Sess. (25 Jan. 1802) pp. 459-460. Comments on the "silent" legislators, who support the repeal of internal taxes without reducing the impost, but will not debate the issue.

81. Dana, Samuel W. (Conn.). "Internal Taxes," *Annals of Congress.* 7th Cong., 1st Sess. (22 Mar. 1802) pp. 1070-1073. Supports the use of internal taxes to pay the public debt; addresses opponents' arguments.

82. Dana, Samuel W. (Conn.). "Judiciary System," *Annals of Congress.* 7th Cong., 1st Sess. (1 Mar. 1802) pp. 887-933. Exhaustive analysis opposes the proposed repeal of the Judiciary Act of 1801; discusses the legislative history of the act, the political influence, document No.8 (an official declaration of facts concerning the business of the courts), supporters' objections, constitutionality, and consequences if passed.

83. Dana, Samuel W. (Conn.). "Naval Appropriations," *Annals of Congress.* 7th Cong., 1st Sess. (17 Apr. 1802) pp. 1201-1202. Supports the requested appropriations.

84. Goddard, Calvin (Conn.). "Judiciary System," *Annals of Congress.* 7th Cong., 1st Sess. (24 Feb. 1802) pp. 721-734. Opposes repealing the existing judiciary system and returning to the former system. Maintains that the existing system offers speedier justice. Discusses the constitutional question; establishes that the Judiciary is not a subordinate branch of the government. Addresses the dangers of judges dependent upon the Legislature for office or salaries.

85. Griswold, Roger (Conn.). "Debt of the United States," *Annals of Congress.* 7th Cong., 1st Sess. (13 Apr. 1802) pp. 1169-1170, 1176-1177. Supports paying the debt when due while ample funds are available.

86. Griswold, Roger (Conn.). "Disbursement of Public Moneys," *Annals of Congress.* 7th Cong., 1st Sess. (1 May 1802) pp. 1255-1267. Objects to the report on the disbursement of public moneys; maintains that the report is erroneous, with a political bias, and that the minority members had no input. Discusses major errors concerning the expense of moving the Executive office to Washington, and the accounts of the War and Navy Departments.

87. Griswold, Roger (Conn.). "Internal Revenues," *Annals of Congress.* 7th Cong., 1st Sess. (25 Jan. 1802) pp. 450-451. Desires clarification from the Sec. of the Treasury concerning the costs incurred in collecting internal taxes.

88. Griswold, Roger (Conn.). "Internal Taxes," *Annals of Congress.* 7th Cong., 1st Sess. (18 Mar. 1802) pp. 1037-1042. Supports retaining all the internal taxes, including the carriage tax; recommends modifications to decrease the expense of collection. Analyzes expenditures and revenues of the government; praises the previous administration.

89. Griswold, Roger (Conn.). "Northwestern Territory," *Annals of Congress.* 7th Cong., 1st Sess. (30 Mar. 1802) pp. 1104-1105. Opposes Legislative interference into the authority of the territorial legislatures.

90. Hillhouse, James (Conn.). "Judiciary System," *Annals of Congress.* 7th Cong., 1st Sess. (15 Jan. 1802) pp. 108-110. Supports the repeal of the Judiciary Act, but not by the unconstitutional action that would remove a judge.

91. Tallmadge, Benjamin (Conn.). "Judiciary System," *Annals of Congress.* 7th Cong., 1st Sess. (1 Mar. 1802) pp. 935-949. Opposes the proposed repeal of the Judiciary Act as unconstitutional and inexpedient. Discusses the judiciary system as established by the Constitution, and the separation of powers that does not allow the Legislature to interfere; addresses objections to the current act.

92. Tracy, Uriah (Conn.). "Internal Taxes," *Annals of Congress.* 7th Cong., 1st Sess. (31 Mar. 1802) pp. 236-244. Supports internal taxes; maintains that they are necessary to meet the public exigencies and to pay the national debt, and that the obstacles of collection have been surmounted. Examines expenses and revenues; makes general observations on internal taxes versus duties on imports.

93. Tracy, Uriah (Conn.). "Judiciary System," *Annals of Congress.* 7th Cong., 1st Sess. (12 Jan. 1802) pp. 51-58. Opposes the repeal of the Judiciary Act; gives a legislative history on the formation of the judiciary system; presents objections to the repeal. Maintains that the repeal offers no advantageous substitute and that it is essential for the Judiciary to be independent of the Executive and the Legislature.

7TH CONGRESS, 2ND SESSION

94. Dana, Samuel W. (Conn.). "Cession of Louisiana to France," *Annals of Congress.* 7th Cong., 2nd Sess. (6 Jan., 11 Jan. 1803) pp. 336-337; 352-353, 358-359. Supports the request of information from the President concerning the cession of Louisiana to France.

95. Goddard, Calvin (Conn.). "Cession of Louisiana to France," *Annals of Congress.* 7th Cong., 2nd Sess. (11 Jan. 1803) pp. 361-363. Supports the request for official documents concerning the cession of Louisiana to France.

96. Griswold, Roger (Conn.). "Cession of Louisiana to France," *Annals of Congress.* 7th Cong., 2nd Sess. (11 Jan. 1803) pp. 352, 354-356. Presents and defends resolution requesting information from the President concerning the cession of Louisiana to France.

97. Griswold, Roger (Conn.). "Sale of Bank Stock," *Annals of Congress.* 7th Cong., 2nd Sess. (3 Mar. 1803) pp. 666-668. Contends that the Commissioners had no authority to sell the bank stock.

98. Griswold, Roger (Conn.). "Sinking Fund," *Annals of Congress.* 7th Cong., 2nd Sess. (2 Mar. 1803) pp. 614-620, 633-640. Speech and resolution on the need to inquire into the accounts and proceedings of the Sinking Fund, and to determine if the required amount has been paid towards the public debt; discusses questionable and objectionable aspects of their activities and accounts.

99. Hillhouse, James (Conn.). "Petition of William Marbury and Others," *Annals of Congress.* 7th Cong., 2nd Sess. (28 Jan. 1803) pp. 37-38. Advocates allowing the journals of the Senate to be used as evidence of appointments of justices of the peace.

100. Smith, John C. (Conn.). "Memorial of United States Judges," *Annals of Congress.* 7th Cong., 2nd Sess. (27 Jan. 1802) pp. 435-436. Advocates following proper procedure regarding the petitions of the judges on their salaries.

101. Tracy, Uriah (Conn.). "Petition of William Marbury and Others," *Annals of Congress.* 7th Cong., 2nd Sess. (28 Jan. 1802) pp. 40-44. Supports the petitioners' request for an extract from the *Executive Journals* of the Senate to be used as testimony confirming their appointments.

8TH CONGRESS, 1ST SESSION

102. Baldwin, Simeon (Conn.). "Virginia Contested Election," *Annals of Congress.* 8th Cong., 1st Sess. (1 Mar. 1804) pp. 1082-1085. Opposes the decision of the Committee of Elections that Thomas Lewis was not, and Andrew Moore was, entitled to a seat. Objects to the mode of taking evidence, the qualifications of voters, and the neglect of the petitioner to give proper notice.

103. Dana, Samuel W. (Conn.). "Amendment to the Constitution," *Annals of Congress.* 8th Cong., 1st Sess. (7 Dec. 1803) pp. 672-673. Opposes the proposed amendment to elect the President and the Vice President separately; discusses abolishing the office of the Vice President.

104. Dana, Samuel W. (Conn.). "Official Conduct of Judge Chase," *Annals of Congress.* 8th Cong., 1st Sess. (7 Jan. 1804) pp. 867-871. Maintains that the resolution to inquire into the conduct of Judge Chase is improper as no charge has been made specifying a subject of inquiry.

105. Goddard, Calvin (Conn.). "Amendment to the Constitution," *Annals of Congress.* 8th Cong., 1st Sess. (8 Dec. 1803) pp. 712-718. Objects to the amendment to elect separately the President and Vice President. Contends that the provisions of the Constitution have worked well, and that the proposed amendment will be ineffective against corruption and will increase the power of the Chief Executive. Addresses the Senate amendments to the resolution.

106. Goddard, Calvin (Conn.). "The Louisiana Treaty," *Annals of Congress.* 8th Cong., 1st Sess. (24 Oct. 1803) pp. 390-391, 410-412. Questions the owner of the title to Louisiana; maintains that the treaty at St. Ildefonso was a promise, not a title; requests information documenting that France had an incontestable title to transfer.

107. Goddard, Calvin (Conn.). "Salaries of Certain Officers," *Annals of Congress.* 8th Cong., 1st Sess. (21 Nov. 1803) pp. 604-612. Opposes the proposed salaries. Discusses the salary act of 1799. Addresses objections to the bill, targeting the salaries of the Attorney General and the Secretary of the Treasury. General salary remarks and comparisons.

108. Griswold, Roger (Conn.). "Amendment to the Constitution," *Annals of Congress.* 8th Cong., 1st Sess. (6 Dec., 8 Dec. 1803) pp. 646-648, 660-662; 744-752. Contends that the resolution to separately elect the President and Vice President did not pass the Senate with a constitutional majority. Maintains that the amendment diminishes the rights of the small states, encourages corruption, and interferes with a proven system.

109. Griswold, Roger (Conn.). "The Louisiana Treaty," *Annals of Congress.* 8th Cong., 1st Sess. (24 Oct., 25 Oct. 1803) pp. 403-406; 459-465. Supports the request for information on the title in order to pass laws for governing the territory. Maintains that it is a violation of the Constitution and the treaty-making power to promise to admit a foreign nation and people as a state into the Union, and that it is also a violation of the Constitution to allow France and Spain duty advantages in the ports of the ceded territory.

110. Griswold, Roger (Conn.). "Official Conduct of Judge Chase," *Annals of Congress.* 8th Cong., 1st Sess. (5 Jan. 1804) pp. 809-810, 812-813. Contends that facts are needed to justify an inquiry into the conduct of Judge Chase.

111. Hillhouse, James (Conn.). "Amendment to the Constitution," *Annals of Congress.* 8th Cong., 1st Sess. (23 Nov., 1 Dec., 2 Dec. 1803) pp. 89-90; 129-130; 189-192. Opposes the proposed amendment to elect the President and Vice President separately; maintains that the current system allows the two principal officers to be checks upon each other.

112. Smith, John C. (Conn.). "Amendment to the Constitution," *Annals of Congress.* 8th Cong., 1st Sess. (28 Oct. 1803) pp. 538-540. Opposes the proposed amendment respecting the election of President and Vice President; discusses the effect of the amendment on the small states and the office of Vice President.

113. Smith, John C. (Conn.). "Georgia Militia Claims," *Annals of Congress.* 8th Cong., 1st Sess. (3 Feb. 1804) pp. 974-975. Remarks on the liability of the government for state militia called into service; questions whether Georgia was already compensated for claims when compensated for the ceded territory.

114. Tracy, Uriah (Conn.). "Amendment to the Constitution," *Annals of Congress.* 8th Cong., 1st Sess. (2 Dec. 1803) pp. 159-180. Opposes the proposed amendment to elect separately the President and Vice President. Maintains that it would sacrifice the rights of the small states and upset the balance of power. Discusses the last election, the need for the amendment, the elective process and the procedural difficulties of the proposed process.

115. Tracy, Uriah (Conn.). "The Louisiana Treaty," *Annals of Congress.* 8th Cong., 1st Sess. (3 Nov. 1803) pp. 53-58. Objects to the treaty as unconstitutional; maintains that the President and Senate do not have the power to promise to admit a new foreign state into the Union without the consent of the old partners. Discusses the treaty making power and the power to transfer or introduce a state.

8TH CONGRESS, 2ND SESSION

116. Dana, Samuel W. (Conn.). "Georgia Claims," *Annals of Congress.* 8th Cong., 2nd Sess. (1 Feb. 1805) pp. 1129-1138. Defends the actions of the Committee of Claims concerning the Georgia claims. Maintains that the objective is compromise; presents an historical account of the land transactions; discusses opponents' objections.

117. Goddard, Calvin (Conn.). "District of Columbia," *Annals of Congress.* 8th Cong., 2nd Sess. (9 Jan. 1805) pp. 943-946. Opposes receding the District of Columbia; discusses the necessity, constitutionality, and history of the cession.

118. Griswold, Roger (Conn.). "District of Columbia," *Annals of Congress.* 8th Cong., 2nd Sess. (8 Jan. 1805) pp. 911-914. Opposes receding the District of Columbia as unconstitutional and inexpedient; addresses the need for a permanent seat of government.

119. Griswold, Roger (Conn.). "Preservation of Peace," *Annals of Congress.* 8th Cong., 2nd Sess. (6 Dec. 1804) pp. 764-765, 766-767. Questions provisions of the bill concerning the authorization of the use of the militia to execute the laws of a particular state.

9ᵀᴴ CONGRESS, 1ˢᵀ SESSION

120. Dana, Samuel W. (Conn.). "Detachment of Militia," *Annals of Congress.* 9th Cong., 1st Sess. (27 Jan. 1806) pp. 405-408. Maintains that the proposed force would be ineffective, inadequate, and injurious to the state militias.

121. Dana, Samuel W. (Conn.). "Foreign Aggressions," *Annals of Congress.* 9th Cong., 1st Sess. (29 Mar. 1806) pp. 895-906. Proposes a legal means of defense of American coasts and ports. Discusses the legality and precedence of establishing territorial jurisdiction to extend various distances from the shore, according to the nature of the coasts.

122. Hillhouse, James (Conn.). "Trade with St. Domingo," *Annals of Congress.* 9th Cong., 1st Sess. (20 Dec. 1805) pp. 35-36. Objects to prohibiting trade; prefers armed defense.

123. Tallmadge, Benjamin (Conn.). "Detachment of Militia," *Annals of Congress.* 9th Cong., 1st Sess. (27 Jan. 1806) pp. 398-401. Adamantly objects to the proposed bill as a "military farce" achieving no special purpose and having a negative effect upon the state militias.

124. "An Act for Erecting Certain Lighthouses in the State of Massachusetts; for Building a Beacon, or Pier, at Bridgeport, in the State of Connecticut; and for Fixing Buoys in Pamplico Sound, in the State of North Carolina," *Statutes at Large*, Vol. II (21 Apr. 1806) p. 406. Also printed in the *Annals of Congress* (9th Cong., 1st Sess.) Appendix, pp. 1292-1293.

9ᵀᴴ CONGRESS, 2ᴺᴰ SESSION

125. "Collection Districts," *Annals of Congress.* 9th Cong., 2nd Sess. (4 Feb. 1807) pp. 455-456. Reprint of the report opposed to granting the petitions to form a new collection district that includes Stonington and Groton, in Connecticut, and Pawcatuck, in Rhode Island. Also printed as Finance 263 (9-2) ASP 010.

126. "Fees of Officers of State Courts," *Annals of Congress.* 9th Cong., 2nd Sess. (24 Oct. 1806) Appendix, pp. 1156-1159. Response to the fees authorized and allowed by statute. Maintains that sums actually paid exceed the statute; supplies information on actual compensation practices.

127. "New Haven Memorial," *Annals of Congress.* 9th Cong., 2nd Sess. (7 Feb. 1806) Appendix, pp. 909-910. Memorial addresses the British depredations and aggressions upon commerce; requests vigorous and permanent measures to protect property and defend commercial rights.

128. Dana, Samuel W. (Conn.). "Coast Survey," *Annals of Congress.* 9th Cong., 2nd Sess. (15 Dec. 1806) pp. 151-152, 152-153. Remarks and resolution to survey the coasts of the United States to within twenty leagues from the shore.

129. Dana, Samuel W. (Conn.). "Duty on Salt," *Annals of Congress.* 9th Cong., 2nd Sess. (13 Jan. 1807) pp. 312-319. Maintains that he would prefer a reduction of the duty instead of repeal, but that is not an alternative. Debates the connection of the repeal of the salt duty with continuing the Mediterranean fund; discusses the implications and revenue of that fund.

130. Dana, Samuel W. (Conn.). "National Defence," *Annals of Congress.* 9th Cong., 2nd Sess. (21 Feb. 1807) pp. 598-603, 605-606. Supports the fortification of ports and harbors along the Atlantic coast; desires a foundation of systematic appropriations for a permanent means of defense. Maintains that after the expenses of securing the western frontiers the use of surplus funds for securing the Atlantic frontier is only just.

131. Dana, Samuel W. (Conn.). "Non-Importation Act," *Annals of Congress.* 9th Cong., 2nd Sess. (15 Dec. 1806) pp.156-157, 158. Favors giving the President the power to suspend the act.

132. Dwight, Theodore (Conn.). "Importation of Slaves," *Annals of Congress.* 9th Cong., 2nd Sess. (31 Dec. 1806) pp. 240-242. Advocates that importing slaves be a capital offense.

133. Dwight, Theodore (Conn.). "Punishment of Certain Crimes," *Annals of Congress.* 9th Cong., 2nd Sess. (14 Jan. 1807) pp. 322-327. Opposes the proposed amendment to punish citizens for committing crimes against the United States in foreign countries. Maintains that the law is absurd and a form of judicial tyranny, and that it needs to define the crimes to be punished.

134. Moseley, Jonathan O. (Conn.). "Importation of Slaves," *Annals of Congress.* 9th Cong., 2nd Sess. (31 Dec. 1806) pp. 233-235. Supports the death penalty for importing slaves as an effective measure to stop the trafficking.

135. Moseley, Jonathan O. (Conn.). "National Defence," *Annals of Congress.* 9th Cong., 2nd Sess. (4 Feb. 1807) pp. 435-437. Supports authorizing the President to utilize other armed vessels in addition to, or in connection with, gunboats.

136. Pitkin, Timothy (Conn.). "Importation of Slaves," *Annals of Congress.* 9th Cong., 2nd Sess. (18 Dec. 1806) pp. 185-188, 188-189. Addresses the sections of the bill concerning forfeited slaves and the penalties and forfeitures of vessels engaged in importing them.

137. Tallmadge, Benjamin (Conn.). "Importation of Slaves," *Annals of Congress.* 9th Cong., 2nd Sess. (31 Dec. 1806) pp. 232-233. Strong remarks in support of the death penalty for importing slaves.

138. "Collection Districts," *American State Papers: Finance*, Vol. II (Doc. 263) p. 226. (ASP 010). Report opposes granting the petition to form a new collection district including Stonington and Groton, in Connecticut, and Pawcatuck, in Rhode Island. Also printed in the *Annals of Congress*. (9th Cong., 2nd Sess.) pp. 455-456.

10TH CONGRESS, 1ST SESSION

139. Dana, Samuel W. (Conn.). "Additional Army," *Annals of Congress*. 10th Cong., 1st Sess. (6 Apr., 7 Apr. 1808) pp. 1991-2006; 2052-2053. Supports additional men for garrison duty and military stations. Questions the time limit of the bill and the intended country it is directed against. Lengthy discussion of relations with Great Britain, covering the *Chesapeake*, impressment, the embargo, and the chance of war. Suggests alternative uses for the money.

140. Dana, Samuel W. (Conn.). "American Seamen," *Annals of Congress*. 10th Cong., 1st Sess. (9 Jan. 1808) pp. 1380-1384. Proposes a resolution to require ships or vessels enjoying the privileges of the United States to have some proportion of seamen having U.S. citizenship. Maintains that this would protect and encourage American seamen.

141. Dana, Samuel W. (Conn.). "Attack on the Frigate *Chesapeake*," *Annals of Congress*. 10th Cong., 1st Sess. (5 Nov. 1807) pp. 809-810. Remarks on the importance of the attack and the need for an inquiry.

142. Dana, Samuel W. (Conn.). "Fortifications and Gunboats," *Annals of Congress*. 10th Cong., 1st Sess. (10 Dec., 11 Dec. 1807) pp. 1121-1125; 1165-1167. Advocates giving the President discretionary power to build additional gunboats; generally discusses the efficacy of gunboats.

143. Dana, Samuel W. (Conn.). "Military Establishment," *Annals of Congress*. 10th Cong., 1st Sess. (17 Feb. 1808) pp. 1625-1626, 1635-1636. Supports more information on the requested troops - whether infantry, riflemen, or cavalry.

144. Dana, Samuel W. (Conn.). "Naval Appropriations," *Annals of Congress*. 10th Cong., 1st Sess. (9 Nov. 1807) pp. 826-828. Supports appropriations to cover expenses already incurred.

145. Dana, Samuel W. (Conn.). "Philadelphia Memorial," *Annals of Congress*. 10th Cong., 1st Sess. (15 Dec. 1807) pp. 1186-1187. Requests that serious consideration be given to the memorial against the non-importation act.

146. Hillhouse, James (Conn.). "Amendments to the Constitution," *Annals of Congress*. 10th Cong., 1st Sess. (12 Apr. 1808) pp. 332-358. Introduces and proposes various amendments to guard against ambition and favoritism. Proposes to shorten the term of the President and Representatives to one year, and Senators to three years, to appoint the President from the Senate by lot and abolish the office of V.P, and to require approval from the Senate and House for appointments to office. Generally discusses the different kinds of government.

147. Hillhouse, James (Conn.). "Case of Mr. John Smith, Senator from Ohio," *Annals of Congress.* 10th Cong., 1st Sess. (9 Apr. 1808) pp. 266-279. Defends Senator Smith from his alleged participation in the conspiracy of Aaron Burr against the United States. Maintains that the suspicions are easily explained when his conversations and confessions are taken together; compares to the trial of William Blount.

148. Moseley, Jonathan O. (Conn.). "Additional Army," *Annals of Congress.* 10th Cong., 1st Sess. (6 Apr. 1808) pp. 1977-1979. Opposes raising the additional military force until it is needed for the defense of the country.

149. Sturges, Lewis B. (Conn.). "Maryland Contested Election," *Annals of Congress.* 10th Cong., 1st Sess. (12 Nov. 1807) pp. 877-879. Defends the report of the Committee of Elections as to fact and constitutionality; discusses the power of the states to add qualifications of the elected onto those of the Constitution.

150. Tallmadge, Benjamin (Conn.). "Additional Army," *Annals of Congress.* 10th Cong., 1st Sess. (6 Apr. 1808) pp. 1979-1985. Supports the additional force as necessary for defense in the present hostile state of the world; addresses objections, including those to standing armies and military establishments.

151. Tallmadge, Benjamin (Conn.). "Arming the Militia," *Annals of Congress.* 10th Cong., 1st Sess. (4 Dec. 1807) pp. 1053-1054. Opposes the bill as too broad and inexpedient; briefly discusses earlier legislation to arm and discipline the militia.

152. Tallmadge, Benjamin (Conn.). "Removal of the Seat of Government," *Annals of Congress.* 10th Cong., 1st Sess. (8 Feb. 1808) pp. 1584-1592. Supports moving the seat of government from Washington to Philadelphia. Addresses constitutionality and expediency; discusses the history and problems of establishing the seat of government in Washington; addresses objections against moving.

153. "An Act for Erecting a Lighthouse on the South Point of the Island of Sapelo, and for Placing Buoys and Beacons in the Shoals of the Inlet Leading to the Town of Darien, and Near the Entrance of Ipswich Harbor, near Plymouth Harbor, before the Harbor of Nantucket, and on the Island of Tuckanuck, at or near the Entrance of Connecticut River, and near the Entrance of Great Egg Harbor River," *Statutes at Large,* Vol. II (17 Mar. 1808) p. 476. Also printed in the *Annals of Congress* (10th Cong., 1st Sess.) Appendix, p. 2843.

10TH CONGRESS, 2ND SESSION

154. Dana, Samuel W. (Conn.). "Naval Establishment," *Annals of Congress.* 10th Cong., 2nd Sess. (10 Jan. 1809) pp. 1046-1047. Supports equipping naval frigates.

155. Dana, Samuel W. (Conn.). "Preparation for War," *Annals of Congress.* 10th Cong., 2nd Sess. (30 Jan., 31 Jan. 1809) pp. 1232-1235, 1238-1240; 1264-1266. Opposes the embargo and a war with Great Britain and France; maintains that there is no rebellion in the northern states.

156. Dana, Samuel W. (Conn.). "Repeal of the Embargo," *Annals of Congress.* 10th Cong., 2nd Sess. (2 Feb. 1809) pp. 1321-1328. Opposes the embargo, submission, and war with France or Great Britain. Discusses the idea of the secession of any state from the Union; maintains that a state has the freedom to refuse to act in aid of an act of Congress that they believe to be unconstitutional.

157. Goodrich, Chauncey (Conn.). "Enforcement of the Embargo," *Annals of Congress.* 10th Cong., 2nd Sess. (17 Dec. 1808) pp. 241-249. Opposes further provisions to enforce the embargo; maintains that the embargo is not accomplishing its objectives towards Britain, and that it has had disastrous effects in the United States. Discusses the restraints placed on the coasting trade.

158. Hillhouse, James (Conn.). "Disbursement of Public Moneys," *Annals of Congress.* 10th Cong., 2nd Sess. (13 Feb. 1809) pp. 347-352. Remarks and resolution for further regulations to check on the disbursement of public moneys. Gives examples of improper disbursements by the Secretary of War concerning General Wilkinson.

159. Hillhouse, James (Conn.). "The Embargo," *Annals of Congress.* 10th Cong., 2nd Sess. (21 Nov., 29 Nov. 1808) pp. 20-28; 161-175. Defends his resolution to repeal the embargo. Discusses the effects of the embargo and the possibility of a non-intercourse law. Contends that the repeal would not mean war. Lengthy discussion of the "spirit and policy of '76" and the cause of the present situation.

160. Hillhouse, James (Conn.). "Enforcement of the Embargo," *Annals of Congress.* 10th Cong., 2nd Sess. (21 Dec. 1808, 7 Jan. 1809) pp. 282-298; 315-318. Maintains that the embargo is radically wrong, and that the proposed bill is arbitrary, oppressive, and unconstitutional. Provides a sectional analysis.

161. Hillhouse, James (Conn.). "Non-Intercourse," *Annals of Congress.* 10th Cong., 2nd Sess. (20 Feb. 1809) pp. 424-436. Opposes the act as unenforceable, inefficient, oppressive and injurious. Discusses foreign relations and public sentiment; maintains that the act would destroy commerce and involve the country in war.

162. Hillhouse, James (Conn.). Speech in Answer to Mr. Giles on the Embargo, *Annals of Congress.* 10th Cong., 2nd Sess. (2 Dec. 1808) Supplementary Speeches, pp. 1577-1581. Clarifies his position on the Senate resolution in 1806 and the British Orders in Council, as connected with act of Parliament imposing a tax.

163. Moseley, Jonathan O. (Conn.). "Enforcing the Embargo," *Annals of Congress.* 10th Cong., 2nd Sess. (5 Jan. 1809) pp. 1019-1022. Opposes the proposed provisions to enforce the embargo as arbitrary, oppressive, odious, detestable, vexatious, unconstitutional, exceptionable, dangerous, and ruinous.

164. Moseley, Jonathan O. (Conn.). "Repeal of the Embargo," *Annals of Congress.* 10th Cong., 2nd Sess. (3 Feb. 1809) pp. 1332-1334. Supports an immediate repeal.

165. Pitkin, Timothy (Conn.). "Additional Military Force," *Annals of Congress.* 10th Cong., 2nd Sess. (28 Jan. 1809) pp. 1214-1229. Opposes raising the additional force. Discusses the embargo and its intended and actual effect on Britain and France; discusses the reasons an additional force is wanted, and concludes that it is for an offensive war, to which he objects.

166. Sturges, Lewis B. (Conn.). "Enforcing the Embargo," *Annals of Congress.* 10th Cong., 2nd Sess. (5 Jan. 1809) pp. 995-1001. Objects to enforcing the embargo, particularly as it applies to the coasting trade. Discusses the objectionable sections of the bill.

167. Tallmadge, Benjamin (Conn.). "Additional Military Force," *Annals of Congress.* 10th Cong., 2nd Sess. (27 Jan. 1809) pp. 1192-1207. Opposes raising the army of fifty thousand men whose officers are to be appointed by the President. Discusses who is requesting the army, its use and destination, the objects of the army, and the means to accomplish these objects.

168. Tallmadge, Benjamin (Conn.). "Enforcing the Embargo," *Annals of Congress.* 10th Cong., 2nd Sess. (27 Dec. 1808) pp. 931-934. Objects to the proposed measures to enforce the embargo. Maintains that the bill is dangerous and defective, would destroy the coasting trade, and would give unlimited power to the Executive to enforce the measure.

169. Tallmadge, Benjamin (Conn.). "Repeal of the Embargo," *Annals of Congress.* 10th Cong., 2nd Sess. (2 Feb. 1809) pp. 1304-1305. Supports a speedy decision to repeal the embargo.

11TH CONGRESS, 1ST SESSION

170. Dana, Samuel W. (Conn.). "Doctrine of Libels," *Annals of Congress.* 11th Cong., 1st Sess. (25 May 1809) pp. 78-80, 83-84. Discusses the status of libel cases prosecuted in Connecticut.

171. Dana, Samuel W. (Conn.). "Naval Establishment," *Annals of Congress.* 11th Cong., 1st Sess. (22 June 1809) pp. 386-387, 390-391. Remarks that it is unnecessary to have gunboats laid up in readiness.

172. Dana, Samuel W. (Conn.). "Non-Intercourse," *Annals of Congress.* 11th Cong., 1st Sess. (23 June, 26 June, 27 June 1809) pp. 409-411; 419-420, 445-446; 452-457. Various remarks contending that a nation whose commerce is excluded for acts of outrage should likewise have its armed vessels excluded from U.S. ports, but that there is no longer any reason to exclude British armed vessels. Opposes this system of commercial restriction and its inconsistency with government policy.

173. Dana, Samuel W. (Conn.). "Vote of Approbation," *Annals of Congress.* 11th Cong., 1st Sess. (29 May 1809) pp. 135-141. Supports commending the President for his conduct towards opening intercourse with Great Britain and the resolution of the controversy over the Chesapeake. Discusses when approbations are appropriate.

174. Pitkin, Timothy (Conn.). "Naval Establishment," *Annals of Congress.* 11th Cong., 1st Sess. (22 June 1809) pp. 382-383, 389-390. Objects to continued funding of gunboats as expensive, ineffective and unnecessary.

175. Tallmadge, Benjamin (Conn.). "Fortifications," *Annals of Congress.* 11th Cong., 1st Sess. (8 June 1809) pp. 252-253. Supports repairing or completing fortifications as necessary to defend the ports and harbors of the United States.

11TH CONGRESS, 2ND SESSION

176. Dana, Samuel W. (Conn.). "Conduct of the British Minister," *Annals of Congress.* 11th Cong., 2nd Sess. (19 Dec. 1809) pp. 762-783. Opposes the resolution as unwarranted. Discusses the powers of a minister, particularly Mr. Erskine, to negotiate and conclude arrangements for his government.

177. Dana, Samuel W. (Conn.). "Detachment of Militia," *Annals of Congress.* 11th Cong., 2nd Sess. (7 Feb., 8 Mar., 19 Mar. 1810) pp. 1381, 1382-3; 1521-1522, 1525; 1569-1570, 1571. Various remarks concerning the means of drafting the militia and the propriety of sending a militia out of the jurisdiction of the United States. Maintains that the militia is a domestic force for domestic defense. Discusses the proposed distribution of arms.

178. Dana, Samuel W. (Conn.). "Reduction of the Army and Navy," *Annals of Congress.* 11th Cong., 2nd Sess. (16 Apr. 1810) pp. 1876-1878. Remarks on the officers of the additional military force and the availability of the regular troops.

179. Dana, Samuel W. (Conn.). "Reduction of the Navy," *Annals of Congress.* 11th Cong., 2nd Sess. (25 Apr. 1810) pp. 1985-1986. Opposes the proposed reduction.

180. Dana, Samuel W. (Conn.). "Torpedo Experiment," *Annals of Congress.* 11th Cong., 2nd Sess. (23 Mar. 1810) pp. 1625-1627. Opposes the experiment as contributing nothing new.

181. Hillhouse, James (Conn.). "Privileges of Foreign Ministers," *Annals of Congress.* 11th Cong., 2nd Sess. (8 Dec. 1809) pp. 509-510. Opposes the bill giving the President the legislative power to remove foreign ministers as unnecessary and redundant.

182. Moseley, Jonathan O. (Conn.). "Detachment of Militia," *Annals of Congress.* 11th Cong., 2nd Sess. (19 Mar. 1810) pp. 1577-1580. Opposes the bill to raise a volunteer corps that is neither militia nor military; maintains that there is no reason to expect war; addresses objections to its utility in times of peace.

183. Pitkin, Timothy (Conn.). "Commercial Intercourse," *Annals of Congress.* 11th Cong., 2nd Sess. (18 Apr. 1810) pp. 1888-1890. Opposes the proposed increased duties on trade between the U.S. and Great Britain and France and their dependencies.

184. Pitkin, Timothy (Conn.). "Conduct of the British Minister," *Annals of Congress.* 11th Cong., 2nd Sess. (28 Dec. 1809) pp. 964-987. Objects to the resolution to support the President's dismissal of the British minister, Francis Jackson, as improper and a conditional declaration of war against Great Britain. Reviews the papers and correspondence concerning the alleged offense against the Sec. of State and of Mr. Erskine's agreement.

185. Pitkin, Timothy (Conn.). "Detachment of Militia," *Annals of Congress.* 11th Cong., 2nd Sess. (19 Mar. 1810) pp. 1566-1569. Opposes the proposal to furnish arms to the volunteering militia; maintains that it is a duty of a freeman to furnish himself with arms.

186. Pitkin, Timothy (Conn.). "Foreign Relations," *Annals of Congress.* 11th Cong., 2nd Sess. (30 Apr. 1810) pp. 2018-2020. Requests information from the President on the status of relations between the U.S. and Great Britain and France.

187. Pitkin, Timothy (Conn.). "General Wilkinson," *Annals of Congress.* 11th Cong., 2nd Sess. (3 Apr. 1810) pp. 1728-1731. Favors an inquiry into the conduct of General James Wilkinson.

188. Sturges, Lewis B. (Conn.). "American Navigation Act," *Annals of Congress.* 11th Cong., 2nd Sess. (19 Jan. 1810) pp. 1226-1231. Opposes the navigation act as a commercial measure and as a coercive measure to compel Great Britain to redress the wrongs she has inflicted. Maintains that the act would destroy the commerce of the country and, like the non-importation law and the embargo, be ineffectual against Great Britain.

189. Tallmadge, Benjamin (Conn.). "Conduct of the British Minister," *Annals of Congress.* 11th Cong., 2nd Sess. (1 Jan. 1810) pp. 1049-1064. Opposes the resolution concerning the British minister, Francis Jackson, who was dismissed for insulting the Sec. of State. Maintains that the President has control over foreign ministers, and that the resolution would lead to a war for which the country is not prepared.

190. Tallmadge, Benjamin (Conn.). "Torpedo Experiment," *Annals of Congress.* 11th Cong., 2nd Sess. (26 Mar. 1810) pp. 1630-1631. Opposes the experiment.

11ᵀᴴ CONGRESS, 3ᴿᴰ SESSION

191. Dana, Samuel W. (Conn.). "Question of Order," *Annals of Congress.* 11th Cong., 3rd Sess. (2 Jan. 1811) pp. 67-70. Remarks on the breach of confidence when Timothy Pickering (Mass.) disclosed confidential correspondence in the Senate. Discusses the circumstances and suggests amending the rules of procedure.

192. Goodrich, Chauncey (Conn.). "Question of Order," *Annals of Congress.* 11th Cong., 3rd Sess. (2 Jan. 1811) pp. 81-82. Objects to censuring Timothy Pickering (Mass.) for disclosing confidential information in the Senate.

193. Moseley, Jonathan O. (Conn.). "Apportionment of Representation," *Annals of Congress.* 11th Cong., 3rd Sess. (19 Dec. 1810) pp. 419-421. Supports delaying the bill until the census returns are completed; favors the current ratio of apportionment.

194. Pitkin, Timothy (Conn.). "Apportionment of Representation," *Annals of Congress.* 11th Cong., 3rd Sess. (14 Dec. 1810) pp. 406-408, 422-423. Advocates that the ratio be determined when the census returns are completed. Supports a ratio that would maintain a minimum of each state's current representation, as well as allow the size of the House to gradually increase with the population.

195. Pitkin, Timothy (Conn.). "General Wilkinson," *Annals of Congress.* 11th Cong., 3rd Sess. (18 Dec. 1810) pp. 448-449. Remarks on how General Wilkinson illegally obtained public money.

196. Pitkin, Timothy (Conn.). "Orleans Territory," *Annals of Congress.* 11th Cong., 3rd Sess. (14 Jan. 1811) pp. 518-520. Questions the westward boundary of the Territory of Orleans and the proposed new state.

197. Sturges, Lewis B. (Conn.). "Apportionment of Representation," *Annals of Congress.* 11th Cong., 3rd Sess. (17 Dec. 1810) pp. 416-418. Advocates postponing consideration of the bill until the census returns are completed and the actual fractions can be calculated on proposed ratios. Maintains that a large ratio would benefit the large states at the expense of the small ones.

198. Sturges, Lewis B. (Conn.). "Commercial Intercourse," *Annals of Congress.* 11th Cong., 3rd Sess. (9 Feb. 1811) pp. 946-948. Supports the repeal of the Non-Intercourse Act; discusses the validity of the provisions of the law revived May 1810.

199. Tallmadge, Benjamin (Conn.). "Bank of the United States," *Annals of Congress.* 11th Cong., 3rd Sess. (23 Jan. 1811) pp. 779-786. Supports renewing the charter of the bank. Maintains that Congress has the constitutional power to renew the present charter; presents arguments defending his position.

12TH CONGRESS, 1ST SESSION

200. Law, Lyman (Conn.). "Naval Establishment," *Annals of Congress.* 12th Cong., 1st Sess. (21 Jan. 1812) pp. 895-899. Supports repairing older ships and building ten additional frigates. Maintains that it is in the interest and security of the U.S. to lay the foundations of a navy.

201. Pitkin, Timothy (Conn.). "British Intrigues," *Annals of Congress.* 12th Cong., 1st Sess. (6 Mar. 1812) pp. 1181-1182. Disclaims knowledge of any connection of Vermont or Massachusetts with the British government or of a separation from the Union.

202. Pitkin, Timothy (Conn.). "Rules and Orders," *Annals of Congress.* 12th Cong., 1st Sess. (23 Dec. 1811) pp. 577-581. Opposes the proposed rule of the House concerning debate of the main question after an affirmative decision of the previous question.

203. Pitkin, Timothy (Conn.). "Volunteer Corps," *Annals of Congress.* 12th Cong., 1st Sess. (11 Jan. 1812) pp. 745-749. Maintains that Congress can only call for the militia for the purposes detailed in the Constitution and cannot, therefore, send the militia beyond the limits of the U.S. for foreign conquest or offensive war.

204. Tallmadge, Benjamin (Conn.). "Assistant Secretaries of War," *Annals of Congress.* 12th Cong., 1st Sess. (1 May 1812) pp. 1371-1373. Opposes the proposed structural changes as unnecessary, expensive, and obstructive to the functioning of the War Department.

205. Tallmadge, Benjamin (Conn.). "The Militia," *Annals of Congress.* 12th Cong., 1st Sess. (3 Feb. 1812) pp. 1013-1018. Opposes the bill to class and arm the militia. Examines its constitutionality, previous militia laws, and various sections of the bill. Maintains that the law is unconstitutional and imposes on the authority of the states.

206. Tallmadge, Benjamin (Conn.). "Petitions for Repeal of the Embargo," *Annals of Congress.* 12th Cong., 1st Sess. (11 May 1812) pp. 1417-1418. Supports the petitions.

207. "An Act to Alter the Times of Holding the District Courts, within and for the District of Connecticut," *Statutes at Large*, Vol. II (6 Feb. 1812) p. 676. Also printed in the *Annals of Congress* (12th Cong., 1st Sess.) Appendix, p. 2235.

208. "Protection to Manufactures," *American State Papers: Finance*, Vol. II (Doc. 370) p. 553. (ASP 010). Petition requests that duties be paid on imported wire as it is now being manufactured in the United States in the towns of Simsbury and Winchester, Connecticut.

12TH CONGRESS, 2ND SESSION

209. "Refusal to Furnish Militia," *Annals of Congress.* 12th Cong., 2nd Sess. (6 Nov. 1812) Appendix, pp. 1295-1310. Correspondence between the Dept. of War and the Governors of Massachusetts and Connecticut. Connecticut objects to furnishing their quota as none of the contingencies enumerated in the Constitution allowing for a calling forth the militia have taken place; they also object to placing the militia under the immediate command of an officer of the army of the United States. Same as Mil.aff.115 (12-2) ASP 016 (entry **217**).

210. Law, Lyman (Conn.). "Additional Military Force," *Annals of Congress.* 12th Cong., 2nd Sess. (5 Jan. 1813) pp. 536-540. Opposes raising the additional standing army, as it would be injurious to the militia and unnecessary and inadequate to meet the objectives.

211. Moseley, Jonathan O. (Conn.). "Additional Military Force," *Annals of Congress.* 12th Cong., 2nd Sess. (2 Jan. 1813) pp. 482-486. Opposes the proposed twelve-month additional force of 20,000 men as inadequate to the proclaimed objective of conquering the British provinces in America. Briefly discusses the war.

212. Pitkin, Timothy (Conn.). "Additional Military Force," *Annals of Congress.* 12th Cong., 2nd Sess. (4 Jan. 1813) pp. 521-533. Objects to the necessity of the measure. Maintains that since Britain removed the Orders in Council and the blockades, that the primary reason for continuing the war is over impressments. Discusses impressments and obligations to U.S. nationals in British territory and visa versa.

213. Pitkin, Timothy (Conn.). "Loan Bill," *Annals of Congress.* 12th Cong., 2nd Sess. (26 Jan. 1813) pp. 902-907. Opposes the bill as it does not limit the rate of interest and no funds are provided for the repayment of the money to be borrowed. Discusses the public finances and debt.

214. Pitkin, Timothy (Conn.). "Pay of the Army," *Annals of Congress.* 12th Cong., 2nd Sess. (21 Nov. 1812) pp. 179-180. Maintains that enlisting minors without the consent of the master or guardian infringes on state laws.

215. Tallmadge, Benjamin (Conn.). "Additional Military Force," *Annals of Congress.* 12th Cong., 2nd Sess. (7 Jan. 1813) pp. 631-648. Discusses the Orders in Council, impressment of American seamen, and the attack upon the Chesapeake as causes of the war. Opposes the proposed bill as useless, inefficient, inexpedient, anti-republican, increasing executive patronage, and very expensive. Discusses the benefits and practicality of conquering Canada.

216. Tallmadge, Benjamin (Conn.). "Arming the Militia," *Annals of Congress.* 12th Cong., 2nd Sess. (28 Jan. 1813) pp. 923-926. Objects to the bill to arm and class the militia. Maintains that citizens are legally required to equip themselves and that money already appropriated has been unevenly distributed and is still available.

217. "Refusal of the Governors of Massachusetts and Connecticut to Furnish Their Quotas of Militia," *American State Papers: Military Affairs,* Vol. I (Doc. 115) pp. 321-326. (ASP 016). First page numbered as '319'. Also printed in the *Annals of Congress* (12th Cong., 2nd Sess.) "Refusal to Furnish Militia," Appendix, pp. 1295-1310 (entry **209**). See entry **209** for abstract.

13TH CONGRESS, 1ST SESSION

218. Pitkin, Timothy (Conn.). "Distribution of Arms," *Annals of Congress.* 13th Cong., 1st Sess. (15 June 1813) pp. 158-159, 160-161. Supports an inquiry into the law for arming and equipping the militia; maintains that the intent of the law was to distribute the arms in equal proportions to each state.

13TH CONGRESS, 2ND SESSION

219. Law, Lyman (Conn.). "Blue Lights," *Annals of Congress.* 13th Cong., 2nd Sess. (24 Jan. 1814) pp. 1123-1125. Supports an inquiry into the blue lights near New London harbor, said to be signaling the enemy.

220. Moseley, Jonathan O. (Conn.). "Blue Lights," *Annals of Congress.* 13th Cong., 2nd Sess. (24 Jan. 1814) pp. 1125-1126. Supports an inquiry into the blue lights near New London harbor, said to be signaling the enemy.

221. Pitkin, Timothy (Conn.). "The Loan Bill," *Annals of Congress.* 13th Cong., 2nd Sess. (10 Feb. 1814) pp. 1285-1298. Opposes the bill; maintains that the vast expenditures and loans would be for the conquest of Canada, the advantages of which would not counterbalance the expenses. Discusses the public finances since the war and the increase in the public debt.

222. Pitkin, Timothy (Conn.). "Supplemental Journal - Embargo," *Annals of Congress.* 13th Cong., 2nd Sess. (11 Dec. 1813) pp. 2042-2046. Opposes the embargo; discusses its effects and operation upon the enemy and upon the country.

13TH CONGRESS, 3RD SESSION

223. "Relative Powers of the General and State Governments over the Militia," *Annals of Congress.* 13th Cong., 3rd Sess. (28 Feb. 1815) Appendix, pp. 1744-1795. Report of the Committee on Military Affairs supports the conduct of the Dept. of War relative to the powers of the general and state governments over the militia. Majority of the report is a response from the Sec. of the Dept. of War objecting to the resistance of the States of Massachusetts, Connecticut, and Rhode Island to furnish their quota of the militia. Includes correspondence between the Dept. of War and the Governors of those states. Addresses the objections of the Governors. Same as Mil.aff.142 (13-3) ASP 016 (entry **227**).

224. Daggett, David (Conn.). "Militia of the United States," *Annals of Congress.* 13th Cong., 3rd Sess. (16 Nov. 1814) pp. 70-77. Opposes a conscription of the militia to constitute part of the regular army. Maintains that it is unconstitutional and oppressive, and that the state governments will not lend their aid to carry it into effect.

225. Law, Lyman (Conn.). "Tax Bills," *Annals of Congress.* 13th Cong., 3rd Sess. (17 Dec. 1814) pp. 939-950. Opposes the proposed taxes; maintains that they are to be applied to a war which the people do not support. Discusses the causes and status of the war.

226. Moseley, Jonathan O. (Conn.). "Militia Draughts," *Annals of Congress.* 13th Cong., 3rd Sess. (9 Dec. 1814) pp. 830-833. Opposes a military conscription as unconstitutional, odious, tyrannical and oppressive.

227. "Relative Powers of the General and State Governments over the Militia," *American State Papers: Military Affairs,* Vol. I (Doc. 142) pp. 603-623. (ASP 016). Also printed in the *Annals of Congress* (13th Cong., 3rd Sess.) Appendix, pp. 1744-1795 (entry **223**). See entry **223** for abstract.

14TH CONGRESS, 1ST SESSION

228. Dana, Samuel W. (Conn.). "Amendment to the Constitution," *Annals of Congress.* 14th Cong., 1st Sess. (20 Mar. 1816) pp. 221-223. Objects to electors and to districting the United States.

229. Dana, Samuel W. (Conn.). "Compensation Bill," *Annals of Congress.* 14th Cong., 1st Sess. (14 Mar. 1816) pp. 201-202. Supports increasing the compensation of members of Congress.

230. Tallmadge, Benjamin (Conn.). "Post Office Bill," *Annals of Congress.* 14th Cong., 1st Sess. (2 Mar. 1816) pp. 1123-1125. Supports closing post offices and not delivering the mail on the Sabbath.

231. "An Act concerning the Entry of Vessels at the Ports of Middletown and Plymouth," *Statutes at Large*, Vol. III (24 Apr. 1816) p. 299. Also printed in the *Annals of Congress* (14th Cong., 1st Sess.) Appendix, p. 1854.

232. "Amendments to the Constitution of the United States Proposed by Massachusetts and Connecticut, and Rejected by Ohio," *American State Papers: Miscellaneous*, Vol. II (Doc. 397) pp. 282-283. (ASP 038). Resolutions of the State of Ohio oppose assorted proposed amendments concerning taxes, admission of states into the Union, embargoes, commercial intercourse, declaration of war, eligibility to Congress or civil office, and the number of terms a President may serve.

14TH CONGRESS, 2ND SESSION

233. Daggett, David (Conn.). "Internal Improvements," *Annals of Congress.* 14th Cong., 2nd Sess. (26 Feb. 1817) pp. 165-171. Opposes using public money on internal improvements as unconstitutional and inexpedient; discusses constitutional authority.

15TH CONGRESS, 1ST SESSION

234. Williams, Thomas S. (Conn.). "Uniform Bankrupt Law," *Annals of Congress.* 15th Cong., 1st Sess. (19 Feb. 1818) pp. 977-981. Supports equal distribution of the property of a bankrupt, the bankrupt then to be exempt from further liability to his creditors; advocates a uniform system throughout the United States.

15TH CONGRESS, 2ND SESSION

235. "Connecticut Asylum," *Annals of Congress.* 15th Cong., 2nd Sess. (1 Mar. 1819) pp. 1427-1428. Debate over aid to the asylum for the deaf and mute.

236. Pitkin, Timothy (Conn.). "Military Appropriation Bill," *Annals of Congress.* 15th Cong., 2nd Sess. (8 Jan. 1819) pp. 480-482. Opposes appropriations to construct military roads. Maintains that it would allow the Executive to make roads without permission of the state or the landowners.

237. Williams, Thomas S. (Conn.). "Seminole War," *Annals of Congress.* 15th Cong., 2nd Sess. (6 Feb. 1819) pp. 1077-1088. Reaffirms that only Congress has the right to declare and judge the causes of war. Maintains that Jackson usurped these powers and violated the Constitution when he entered a neutral nation and captured its forts without the consent of the Legislature or without grounds of necessity. Discusses the illegal trial and execution of Arbuthnot and Ambrister.

238. "An Act in Behalf of the Connecticut Asylum for the Deaf and Dumb," *Annals of Congress.* 15th Cong., 2nd Sess. (3 Mar. 1819) Appendix, p. 2513.

239. "Deaf and Dumb Asylum of Connecticut," *American State Papers: Miscellaneous,* Vol. II (Doc. 467) p. 545. (ASP 038). Report supports the petition for assistance of money or land to be applied toward the instruction of deaf and mute persons; asylum instructs deaf and mute people from all parts of the country, qualifies teachers for other schools which may be established, and is the first attempt of its kind. Same as H.doc.142 (15-2) 24 (entry **240**).

240. U.S. House. [Report on the Deaf and Dumb Asylum of Connecticut]. 15th Cong., 2nd Sess. (H.Doc.142). [Washington: E. De Krafft, 1819]. 2 pg. (Serial Set 24). Same as Misc.467 (15-2) ASP 038. See entry **239**.

16ᵀᴴ CONGRESS, 1ˢᵀ SESSION

241. "Prohibition of Slavery in Missouri," *Annals of Congress.* 16th Cong., 1st Sess. (18 Jan. 1820) Appendix, pp. 2457-2463. Memorial and resolutions of citizens of Hartford and vicinity oppose the further extension of slavery in the United States; maintain that Congress has the power to determine the terms for admission to the Union. Same as Misc.481 (16-1) ASP 038 (entry **248**).

242. "Protection to Manufactures," *Annals of Congress.* 16th Cong., 1st Sess. (10 Jan. 1820) Appendix, pp. 2307-2311. Memorial from Middletown requests that duties be imposed upon imported fabrics, especially wool and cotton, in order to protect American manufactures; maintains that revenue would not be harmed, as the higher duties would counterbalance the reduced quantity of imports. Same as Finance 568 (16-1) ASP 011 (entry **249**).

243. Dana, Samuel W. (Conn.). "Admission of Maine and Missouri," *Annals of Congress.* 16th Cong., 1st Sess. (14 Jan. 1820) pp. 117-118. Contends that the admission of the two states should be considered in two separate bills.

244. Edwards, Henry W. (Conn.). "Admission of Missouri," *Annals of Congress.* 16th Cong., 1st Sess. (21 Feb. 1820) pp. 1440-1450. Addresses the constitutional issues of admitting new states into the Union; analyzes treaty obligations to Missouri; discusses slavery and the hostility between the northern and southern states.

245. Foot, Samuel A. (Conn.). "Revision of the Tariff," *Annals of Congress.* 16th Cong., 1st Sess. (28 Apr. 1820) pp. 2135-2136. Opposes the revisions as injurious to agriculture and commerce.

246. Foot, Samuel A. (Conn.). "Savannah Sufferers," *Annals of Congress.* 16th Cong., 1st Sess. (6 Apr. 1820) pp. 1804-1805. Opposes granting relief as unconstitutional.

247. Stevens, James (Conn.). "Admission of Missouri," *Annals of Congress.* 16th Cong., 1st Sess. (2 Mar. 1820) pp. 1583-1586. Implores that sectional differences be laid aside; advocates a compromise of allowing slavery to continue in Missouri, but forbidding the future importation of any more slaves.

248. "Prohibition of Slavery in Missouri," *American State Papers: Miscellaneous,* Vol. II (Doc. 481) pp. 572-574. (ASP 038). Same as "Prohibition of Slavery in Missouri," *Annals of Congress,* 16th Cong., 1st Sess. (18 Jan. 1820) Appendix, pp. 2457-2463. See entry **241**.

249. "Protection to Manufactures," *American State Papers: Finance,* Vol. III (Doc. 568) pp. 452-454. (ASP 011). Same as "Protection to Manufactures," *Annals of Congress,* 16th Cong., 1st Sess. (10 Jan. 1820) Appendix, pp. 2307-2311. See entry **242**.

16TH CONGRESS, 2ND SESSION

250. Foot, Samuel A. (Conn.). "Admission of Missouri," *Annals of Congress.* 16th Cong., 2nd Sess. (13 Feb. 1821) pp. 1145-1146. Opposes the unconditional admission of Missouri.

251. Foot, Samuel A. (Conn.). "Pay of Army Officers," *Annals of Congress.* 16th Cong., 2nd Sess. (15 Feb. 1821) pp. 1170-1173. Supports standardizing the pay of officers in the army as economically feasible and just. Specifically addresses the salary of the President of the Military Academy at West Point.

252. Foot, Samuel A. (Conn.). "Reduction of Salaries," *Annals of Congress.* 16th Cong., 2nd Sess. (21 Feb. 1821) pp. 1211-1214. Advocates retrenchment and the reduction of salaries of civil and departmental officers; disapproves of the rate at which expenses in executive departments have increased since the war concluded.

253. Tomlinson, Gideon (Conn.). "Admission of Missouri," *Annals of Congress.* 16th Cong., 2nd Sess. (12 Feb. 1821) pp. 1094-1102. Opposes the clause in the Missouri constitution excluding free colored persons from entering the state as unconstitutional. Discusses the viability of an amendment providing that the legislature would never pass any law enacting this clause.

254. Tomlinson, Gideon (Conn.). "Reduction of the Army," *Annals of Congress.* 16th Cong., 2nd Sess. (20 Jan. 1821) pp. 912-925. Supports the reduction of the army; maintains that the country cannot afford to support the current force, and that it is unnecessary in times of peace. Discusses the status of the country's finances, alternative means of raising revenue, and the need for retrenchment.

255. U.S. House. *Memorial of the Chamber of Commerce of the City of New Haven.* 16th Cong., 2nd Sess. (H.Doc.4). Washington: Gales & Seaton, 1820. 4 pg. (Serial Set 48). Memorial opposes increasing duties for the alleged protection of manufactures; maintains that it will operate unequally, diminish foreign commerce, decrease navigation, and promote smuggling.

17TH CONGRESS, 1ST SESSION

256. "General Wooster," *Annals of Congress.* 17th Cong., 1st Sess. (18 Jan. 1822) pp. 745-746. Resolution to erect a monument to the memory of General David Wooster, who fell on June 17, 1777, at Danbury, Conn., while defending his country.

257. Burrows, Daniel (Conn.). "Apportionment Bill," *Annals of Congress.* 17th Cong., 1st Sess. (2 Feb. 1822) pp. 881-883. Advocates a ratio of 1:39,000.

258. Edwards, Henry W. (Conn.). "Apportionment Bill," *Annals of Congress.* 17th Cong., 1st Sess. (31 Jan. 1822) pp. 864-865. Supports a ratio of 1:38,000; advocates a ratio that would not reduce the number of representatives from any state.

259. Tomlinson, Gideon (Conn.). "Exchange of Stocks," *Annals of Congress.* 17th Cong., 1st Sess. (22 Mar. 1822) pp. 1348-1352. Advocates waiting to sell the stocks until the war loan of 1813 becomes due in 1825 and 1826, and then selling stock for the portion of the debt that the government cannot meet.

260. "Application of Connecticut for a Grant," *American State Papers: Public Lands,* Vol. III (Doc. 340) p. 501. (ASP 030). Resolution supports Maryland's just appropriation of public land for the purpose of education.

17TH CONGRESS, 2ND SESSION

261. Burrows, Daniel (Conn.). "New Tariff Bill," *Annals of Congress.* 17th Cong., 2nd Sess. (30 Jan. 1823) pp. 767-770. Supports protective tariffs to encourage domestic industry.

18TH CONGRESS, 1ST SESSION

262. "Memorial of Merchants, &c., of Connecticut," *Annals of Congress.* 18th Cong., 1st Sess. (19 Jan. 1824) Appendix, pp. 3124-3128. Memorial requests increased tariffs on woolens, fine cottons, and iron, and protection from foreign competition. Same as H.doc.36 (18-1) 94 (entry **267**).

263. "Remonstrance of the New Haven Chamber of Commerce," *Annals of Congress.* 18th Cong., 1st Sess. (27 Feb. 1824) Appendix, pp. 3150-3155. Memorial opposes increasing duties; maintains that a large majority of citizens oppose an increase and that it will operate unequally and unjustly. Discusses the implications for bar iron and coal in particular. Same as H.doc.96 (18-1) 97 (entry **268**).

264. Foot, Samuel A. (Conn.). "Surveys for Roads and Canals," *Annals of Congress.* 18th Cong., 1st Sess. (10 Feb. 1824) pp. 1463-1467. Opposes the internal improvements as unconstitutional, inexpedient, and violating the rights of state governments.

265. Foot, Samuel A. (Conn.). "The Tariff Bill," *Annals of Congress.* 18th Cong., 1st Sess. (12 Apr. 1824) pp. 2296-2309. Supports free and unrestricted trade; maintains that the proposed protective tariff would operate at the expense of agriculture and commerce. Addresses the British policy, earlier tariffs, and the provisions of the bill.

266. Tomlinson, Gideon (Conn.). "The Tariff Bill," *Annals of Congress.* 18th Cong., 1st Sess. (11 Feb., 13 Feb., 24 Mar. 1824) pp. 1483-1484; 1506-1512; 1900-1903. Opposes the proposed additional duty on imported distilled spirits as particularly injurious to the eastern states and destructive of the West India trade. Discusses the importation of distilled spirits from the West India islands, including statistics.

267. U.S. House. *Memorial of Sundry Manufacturers, Mechanics, and Friends to National Industry, of the State of Connecticut.* 18th Cong., 1st Sess. (H.Doc.36). Washington: Gales & Seaton, 1824. 7 pg. (Serial Set 94). Same as "Memorial of Merchants, &c., of Connecticut," *Annals of Congress,* 18th Cong., 1st Sess. (19 Jan. 1824) Appendix, pp. 3124-3128. See entry **262**.

268. U.S. House. *Remonstrance of the Chamber of Commerce of New Haven, against the Tariff Bill.* 18th Cong., 1st Sess. (H.Doc.96). Washington: Gales & Seaton, 1824. 7 pg. (Serial Set 97). Same as "Remonstrance of the New Haven Chamber of Commerce," *Annals of Congress,* 18th Cong., 1st Sess. (10 Feb. 1824) Appendix, pp. 3150-3155. See entry **263**.

18TH CONGRESS, 2ND SESSION

[no references]

19TH CONGRESS, 1ST SESSION

269. Edwards, Henry W. (Conn.). "Amendment to the Constitution," *Register of Debates.* 19th Cong., 1st Sess. (29 Mar. 1826) pp. 381-383. Contends that the amendment to limit the number of terms of the President is unnecessary.

270. Ingersoll, Ralph I. (Conn.). "Amendment of the Constitution," *Register of Debates.* 19th Cong., 1st Sess. (6 Mar. 1826) pp. 1532-1541. Opposes dividing the country into electoral districts, and preventing Congress from deciding the election when a majority is not achieved. Maintains that the proposed amendments would be destructive to the small states and in opposition to the principles of the Constitution.

271. Ingersoll, Ralph I. (Conn.). "Judiciary System," *Register of Debates.* 19th Cong., 1st Sess. (17 Jan. 1826) pp. 1014-1018. Supports extending the judicial system to the new states in the west and south. Addresses objections.

272. "An Act to Alter the Times of Holding the Circuit Courts of the United States for the District of New York, and the April Term of the Circuit Court for the District of Connecticut," *Statutes at Large*, Vol. IV (13 May 1826) p. 161. Also printed in the *Register of Debates* (19th Cong., 1st Sess.) Appendix, p. xiii.

273. "On the Expediency of Establishing a Navy Yard on the River Thames, in Connecticut," *American State Papers: Naval Affairs*, Vol. II (Doc. 297) p. 637. (ASP 024). Report that it is not expedient to establish the yard at this time.

274. U.S. House. *Post Route - Litchfield to Norfolk, Con.* 19th Cong., 1st Sess. (H.Rpt.163). [Washington: 1826]. 1 pg. (Serial Set 142). Report opposes granting the petitions for the discontinuance of a post route from Litchfield to Norfolk.

19TH CONGRESS, 2ND SESSION

275. Ingersoll, Ralph I. (Conn.). "British Colonial Trade," *Register of Debates.* 19th Cong., 2nd Sess. (28 Feb. 1827) pp. 1486-1490. Discusses proposed trade restrictions with Britain and the effect on West India trade; supports only those restrictions that parallel Britain's restrictions on American vessels.

276. Tomlinson, Gideon (Conn.). "British Colonial Trade," *Register of Debates.* 19th Cong., 2nd Sess. (26 Feb., 2 Mar. 1827) pp. 1419-1433; 1501-1503. Supports the proposed regulations that would close American ports against trade with British colonies unless Britain agrees to an arrangement similar to that negotiated in 1824. Provides a history of the legislation of Great Britain concerning trade with her colonies.

277. "An Act concerning the Entry of Vessels at the Port of Fairfield, in Connecticut," *Statutes at Large*, Vol. IV (22 Feb. 1827) p. 206. Also printed in the *Register of Debates* (19th Cong., 2nd Sess.) Appendix, p. iv.

20ᵀᴴ CONGRESS, 1ˢᵀ SESSION

278. Foot, Samuel A. (Conn.). "Case of Abraham Ogden," *Register of Debates.* 20th Cong., 1st Sess. (8 Feb. 1828) pp. 268-270. Opposes the claim for the relief of Abraham Ogden and others for the loss of a vessel and subsequent delay.

279. Foot, Samuel A. (Conn.). "Delaware Breakwater," *Register of Debates.* 20th Cong., 1st Sess. (19 Mar. 1828) pp. 462-464. Supports the construction of a breakwater at the mouth of the Delaware Bay to protect the coasting trade. Protests against more appropriations for fortifications and artificial harbors.

280. Foot, Samuel A. (Conn.). "Powers of the Vice President," *Register of Debates.* 20th Cong., 1st Sess. (11 Feb., 12 Feb. 1828) pp. 278-279; 325-326. Supports amending or expunging the rules of the Senate to authorize the presiding officer to call a person to order.

281. Ingersoll, Ralph I. (Conn.). "Case of Marigny D'Auterive," *Register of Debates.* 20th Cong., 1st Sess. (22 Jan. 1828) pp. 1068-1071. Opposes the relief of Marigny D'Auterive for the impressment of a slave into military service.

282. Ingersoll, Ralph I. (Conn.). "Tariff Bill," *Register of Debates.* 20th Cong., 1st Sess. (2 Apr. 1828) pp. 2123-2131. Supports the American system, but opposes the bill as oppressing the agricultural interest it is supposed to sustain. Discusses the effect of specific duties on the West India trade.

283. U.S. House. *Letter from the Secretary of War, Transmitting a Report of the Survey of the Harbor of Black Rock, in the State of Connecticut.* 20th Cong., 1st Sess. (H.Doc.52). Washington: Gales & Seaton, 1828. 8 pg. (Serial Set 170). Report of the survey of the Harbor of Black Rock with recommendations and estimate of expenses to erect a beacon necessary for safe navigation.

284. U.S. House. *Memorial of Sundry Inhabitants of the Counties of Windham and Tolland, State of Connecticut, Praying for the Aid of Government in the Cultivation of the Mulberry Tree and of Silk.* 20th Cong., 1st Sess. (H.Doc.159). Washington: Gales & Seaton, 1828. 6 pg. (Serial Set 172). Resolutions and memorial asking for government aid; briefly describes the silk industry.

285. U.S. House. *Statement of the Clerk of the District Court of Connecticut, Showing the Amount of Fees Received by the Marshal, in 1827.* 20th Cong., 1st Sess. (H.Doc.131). Washington: Gales & Seaton, 1828. 3 pg. (Serial Set 172).

20TH CONGRESS, 2ND SESSION

286. Ingersoll, Ralph I. (Conn.). "Occupancy of the Oregon River," *Register of Debates.* 20th Cong., 2nd Sess. (7 Jan. 1829) pp. 187-189. Supports extending American criminal and civil jurisdiction through the territory and also supports erecting and maintaining forts.

287. "An Act to Allow a Salary to the Marshal of the District of Connecticut," *Statutes at Large*, Vol. IV (6 Jan. 1829) p. 330. Also printed in the *Register of Debates* (20th Cong., 2nd Sess.) Appendix, p. 54.

21ST CONGRESS, 1ST SESSION

288. Ellsworth, William W. (Conn.). "Ardent Spirits in the Navy," *Register of Debates.* 21st Cong., 1st Sess. (26 Feb. 1830) pp. 588-589. Supports controlling intemperance in the navy and questions the daily ration of distilled spirits.

289. Ellsworth, William W. (Conn.). "Judge Peck," *Register of Debates.* 21st Cong., 1st Sess. (7 Apr. 1830) pp. 746-747, 749-750. Supports impeaching Judge Peck for arresting and imprisoning a citizen who commented on one of his opinions.

290. Ellsworth, William W. (Conn.). "The Judiciary Bill," *Register of Debates.* 21st Cong., 1st Sess. (16 Feb. 1830) pp. 568-571. Objects to the proposed system that would increase the number of Supreme Court judges. Desires a uniform and permanent system that separates the duties of the circuit courts from the judges of the Supreme Court.

291. Foot, Samuel A. (Conn.). "Mr. Foot's Resolution," *Register of Debates.* 21st Cong., 1st Sess. (20 May 1830) pp. 438-447. Supports an inquiry into the condition of the public lands. Defends against claims of hostility to the west. Responds to comments from other Senators. Reviews the status of the public lands and the provisions for their sale. Maintains that the sales of the public lands ought to be limited to those already in the market. Also discusses the power of the President to make appointments to and removals from office.

292. Huntington, Jabez W. (Conn.). "Judge Peck," *Register of Debates.* 21st Cong., 1st Sess. (7 Apr. 1830) pp. 750-753. Opposes impeaching Judge Peck for misdemeanors in office. Maintains that the judge did have the power to imprison and disbar Mr. Lawless for his article.

293. Huntington, Jabez W. (Conn.). "The Judiciary Bill," *Register of Debates.* 21st Cong., 1st Sess. (16 Feb. 1830) pp. 560-568. Opposes the proposed judiciary system that would increase the number of Supreme Court judges. Discusses the necessity for the bill and the remedies proposed. Advocates dividing the states into judicial circuits where the Supreme Court would function only as an appellate court.

294. Huntington, Jabez W. (Conn.). "Removal of the Indians," *Register of Debates.* 21st Cong., 1st Sess. (18 May 1830) Omitted Speeches, pp. 5-18. Opposes the removal of the Indians to lands west of the Mississippi River. Maintains that past treaties are valid and that the Indians have title to their lands. Provides a summary of previous practice, legislation, and treaties by Great Britain and the U.S. with the Indians that recognize their sovereignty.

295. Ingersoll, Ralph I. (Conn.). "Diplomatic Expenses," *Register of Debates.* 21st Cong., 1st Sess. (10 Feb. 1830) pp. 556-557, 558. Objects to the contention that the requested sum required for ministers and diplomatic agents was no more than that appropriated under the former administration for foreign missions.

296. Ingersoll, Ralph I. (Conn.). "Duty on Salt," *Register of Debates.* 21st Cong., 1st Sess. (20 May 1830) pp. 1120-1121. Supports reducing the duty on molasses and on coarse salt. Maintains that the majority of imported salt is refined and used only by the rich.

297. Ingersoll, Ralph I. (Conn.). "West Point Academy," *Register of Debates.* 21st Cong., 1st Sess. (21 Jan. 1830) pp. 551-552. Demonstrates that the requested information concerning the military academy has already been reported to the House.

298. Young, Ebenezer (Conn.). "The Tariff," *Register of Debates.* 21st Cong., 1st Sess. (7 May 1830) pp. 896-902. Supports the protective system as reducing the price of domestic manufactured articles and increasing that of agriculture, benefiting both the agriculturist and consumer. Illustrates by example the effects of protection.

299. U.S. House. *Farmington and Hampshire Canal Company.* 21st Cong., 1st Sess. (H.Rpt.341). [Washington: 1830]. 2 pg. (Serial Set 201). Statement of the Connecticut River Company opposes the Farmington and Hampshire and Hampden canals; maintains that the river route would be best mode of transportation. Reviews the improvements to the navigation of the Connecticut River and objections to the canals.

300. U.S. House. *Letter from the Secretary of War, Transmitting a Survey and Estimate for the Improvement of the Harbor of Westbrook, in the State of Connecticut.* 21st Cong., 1st Sess. (H.Doc.124). [Washington: Duff Green, 1830]. 4 pg. (Serial Set 198). Report and estimates support forming an artificial harbor at Westbrook, which lies equidistant along the Long Island

Sound between New Haven and New London and would offer great convenience and safe shelter. Accompanying map and plans not included with printed report.

301. U.S. House. *Letter from the Secretary of War, Transmitting a Copy of a Report of the Engineer Appointed to Make a Survey of the River Thames in the State of Connecticut.* 21st Cong., 1st Sess. (H.Doc.125). [Washington: Duff Green, 1830]. 7 pg. (Serial Set 198). Report indicates that improved navigation would benefit the coasting trade and whale fisheries; discusses previous attempts to improve the river and recommends a course of action with cost estimates and relevant statements.

302. U.S. House. *Statement of the Petition of the Farmington, and Hampshire and Hampden, Canals.* 21st Cong., 1st Sess. (H.Rpt.221). [Washington: 1830]. [10 pg.]. (Serial Set 200). Petition requests aid to complete the canal to Northampton, Massachusetts. Reviews the current status of the canals and the benefits of completing them. Discusses the support of the other New England states that want to extend the canal through the valley of the Connecticut River to Canada. Includes supporting statement of the Agent of the Companies on their petition, and "Answer to the Remonstrance of the Agent of the Connecticut River Company."

303. U.S. Senate. *Memorial of Inhabitants of Sharon, Connecticut, Praying that Government Would Extend its Protection over Certain Indian Tribes, &c.* 21st Cong., 1st Sess. (S.Doc.101). [Washington: 1830]. 3 pg. (Serial Set 193). Memorial opposes the treatment of the Indians in Georgia, particularly the Cherokees, in their projected removal; maintains that they have no choice but removal or submission to laws that deny their rights as free citizens.

304. U.S. Senate. *Memorial of Sundry Citizens of Farmington, Connecticut, Praying that the Indians May Be Protected in Their Just Rights, &c.* 21st Cong., 1st Sess. (S.Doc.74). [Washington: 1830]. 4 pg. (Serial Set 193). Memorial maintains that the Indians have the rights of soil and sovereignty until voluntarily surrendered and that the removal of any Indian nation by force or dishonorable means is an act of oppression and injustice.

21ST CONGRESS, 2ND SESSION

305. Huntington, Jabez W. (Conn.). "Insolvent Debtors," *Register of Debates.* 21st Cong., 2nd Sess. (22 Feb. 1831) pp. 780-781. Supports offering assistance to debtors.

22ND CONGRESS, 1ST SESSION

306. Ellsworth, William W. (Conn.). "Apportionment Bill," *Register of Debates.* 22nd Cong., 1st Sess. (18 Jan. 1832) pp. 1578-1580. Supports a ratio of 1:48,000.

307. Ellsworth, William W. (Conn.). "Bank of the United States," *Register of Debates.* 22nd Cong., 1st Sess. (1 Mar. 1832) pp. 1957-1959. Supports the Bank of the United States and the investigation into the charges of corruption and improper conduct.

308. Ellsworth, William W. (Conn.). "Case of Samuel Houston," *Register of Debates.* 22nd Cong., 1st Sess. (8 May 1832) pp. 2839-2846. Discusses Samuel Houston assaulting a member of the House. Maintains that the House has the power to punish for assaults committed out of doors on a member for speech or debate representing the sentiments of his constituents.

309. Ellsworth, William W. (Conn.). "Chickasaw Treaty," *Register of Debates.* 22nd Cong., 1st Sess. (7 Feb. 1832) pp. 1754-1757. Supports an inquiry into an 1830 treaty with the Chickasaw Indians in which the commissioners exceeded their powers.

310. Ellsworth, William W. (Conn.). "Revolutionary Pensions," *Register of Debates.* 22nd Cong., 1st Sess. (28 Mar. 1832) pp. 2277-2282. Supports extending the pension benefits to those who served for nine or six months in either the continental or state militia troops.

311. Foot, Samuel A. (Conn.). "Apportionment Bill," *Register of Debates.* 22nd Cong., 1st Sess. (5 Mar. 1832) pp. 510-513. Objects to the present and proposed mode of apportioning representatives as unequal, unjust, and unconstitutional. Proposes apportioning the extra members to those states with the largest underrepresented fractions.

312. Foot, Samuel A. (Conn.). "Expenses of Courts," *Register of Debates.* 22nd Cong., 1st Sess. (2 Apr. 1832) pp. 679-684. Supports the appropriations for expenses of the courts. Discusses the expenses of the Jackson administration compared to those of the Adams administration. Recommends abolishing the offices of Second Auditor and Comptroller. Discusses the report of the Committee on Retrenchment.

313. Foot, Samuel A. (Conn.). "Pensions," *Register of Debates.* 22nd Cong., 1st Sess. (11 May 1832) pp. 920-927. Supports increasing the coverage of the act of 1828 to provide for state troops, volunteers, and militia who were called into service by Congress during the Revolutionary War. Discusses the number of soldiers affected. Responds to remarks on providing for the militia; defends the militia of the eastern states. Addresses objections from the South.

314. Huntington, Jabez W. (Conn.). "Bank of the United States," *Register of Debates.* 22nd Cong., 1st Sess. (2 Jan., 28 Feb. 1832) pp. 1517-1520; 1912-

1917. Supports referring the memorial to re-charter the bank to the Committee of Ways and Means. Opposes the resolution to appoint a committee to examine the affairs of the bank. Addresses some of the charges against the bank; maintains that they are unsubstantiated.

315. Huntington, Jabez W. (Conn.). "Chickasaw Treaty," *Register of Debates.* 22nd Cong., 1st Sess. (1 Feb. 1832) pp. 1700-1706. Supports requesting information concerning the circumstances of the negotiation of the 1830 treaty with the Chickasaw tribe. Addresses objections to the inquiry.

316. Huntington, Jabez W. (Conn.). "Minimum Duties," *Register of Debates.* 22nd Cong., 1st Sess. (21 Jan. 1832) pp. 1612-1615. Responds to objectionable comments about protectionists, "manufacturing gamblers," and the benefits of protectionism to New England.

317. Huntington, Jabez W. (Conn.). "Wiscasset Collector," *Register of Debates.* 22nd Cong., 1st Sess. (28 Mar. 1832) pp. 2273-2275. Supports pursuing the investigation into the charges against the Wiscasset collector; maintains that only Congress has the power to perform a full and complete investigation.

318. Storrs, William L. (Conn.). "Wiscasset Collector," *Register of Debates.* 22nd Cong., 1st Sess. (10 Apr. 1832) pp. 2463-2475. Maintains that the House has a duty to investigate into the charges against the Wiscasset collector. Discusses the impeachment power as delegated by the Constitution to the House and the responsibilities of the power. Questions the motivations and politics of those opposed to the inquiry; addresses opponents' arguments.

319. Young, Ebenezer (Conn.). "Revolutionary Pensions," *Register of Debates.* 22nd Cong., 1st Sess. (3 Apr. 1832) pp. 2359-2365. Opposes the exclusion of pensions from those who possess property above a certain amount. Maintains that it would be impractical to administer and that the country still owes the soldiers for the original payments that were not fulfilled.

320. "An Act Authorizing the Secretary of the Treasury to Permit a Wharf to be Built near the Site of the Lighthouse on Stratford Point, in the State of Connecticut," *Statutes at Large,* Vol. IV (15 June 1832) pp. 530-531. Also printed in the *Register of Debates* (22nd Cong., 1st Sess.) Appendix, p. xvii.

321. "Application of Connecticut for a More Perfect Organization of the Militia of the United States," *American State Papers: Military Affairs,* Vol. IV (Doc. 493) p. 807. (ASP 019).

322. "On the Claims of Connecticut for the Services of the Militia of That State During the War of 1812-'15," *American State Papers: Military Affairs,* Vol. IV (Doc. 514) pp. 876-933. (ASP 019). Report of the Secretary of War on the claims of Connecticut for services and expenses incurred by her militia during the War of 1812. Includes relevant correspondence among the Sec. of

War, Governor Smith of Connecticut, and Brigadier General Cushing. The statement of claims from Connecticut, detailing expenses incurred for the pay of troops, transportation, munitions, and contingent expenses is presented along with the Treasury Department's response of the allowable and disallowed expenses.

323. "Report, Plan, and Estimate for the Construction of Fort Griswold, in the State of Connecticut," *American State Papers: Military Affairs*, Vol. IV (Doc. 494) pp. 807-810. (ASP 019). Report on the projected new Fort Griswold for the defense of the Thames River; includes description of the Fort Griswold currently occupying the site, plan of the projected fort, and extensive estimates.

324. U.S. House. *Letter from the Secretary of War, Transmitting a Report of a Survey of the Harbor of Westbrook, in the Town of Saybrook, in the State of Connecticut.* 22nd Cong., 1st Sess. (H.Doc.86). Washington: Duff Green, 1832. 5 pg. (Serial Set 218). Report and estimates support improving the harbor at Westbrook. Reprints an earlier report (H.doc.124 (21-1) 198). Accompanying drawings and map not included with printed report.

325. U.S. House. *Letter from the Secretary of War, Transmitting a Report on the Examination of the Hampshire and Hampden and Farmington Canal.* 22nd Cong., 1st Sess. (H.Doc.113). Washington: Duff Green, 1832. 7 pg. (Serial Set 219). Favorable report on the examination of the route of the canals. Describes the routes and the status of the construction; provides estimates of necessary expenses. Discusses the benefits of the proposed improvements.

326. U.S. House. *Memorial of a Committee of the Citizens of Hartford, Connecticut, Against Rechartering the Bank of the United States.* 22nd Cong., 1st Sess. (H.Doc.107). Washington: Duff Green, 1832. 2 pg. (Serial Set 219). Memorial and resolutions detail objections to the bank. Same as S.doc.56 (22-1) 213 (entry **332**).

327. U.S. House. *Memorial of Merchants and Other Citizens of Hartford, Conn. in Favor of a Renewal of the Charter of the Bank of the United States.* 22nd Cong., 1st Sess. (H.Doc.108). Washington: Duff Green, 1832. 6 pg. (Serial Set 219). Brief memorial including five pages of memorialists' names.

328. U.S. House. *Memorial of the Hartford Fire Insurance Company, for a Renewal of the Charter of the Bank of the United States.* 22nd Cong., 1st Sess. (H.Doc.112). Washington: Duff Green, 1832. 1 pg. (Serial Set 219).

329. U.S. House. *Petition of the President and Directors of the Thames Bank, Praying for a Renewal of the Charter of the United States' Bank.* 22nd Cong., 1st Sess. (H.Doc.164). Washington: Duff Green, 1832. 1 pg. (Serial Set 219).

330. U.S. House. *Resolutions of Inhabitants of Waterbury upon the Subject of the Tariff.* 22nd Cong., 1st Sess. (H.Doc.260). Washington: Duff Green, 1832. 1 pg. (Serial Set 221). Resolutions support the protective tariff.

331. U.S. House. *Resolutions of the General Assembly of the State of Connecticut, upon the Subject of the Tariff.* 22nd Cong., 1st Sess. (H.Doc.282). Washington: Duff Green, 1832. 2 pg. (Serial Set 221). Resolutions support continuing the existing protective policy.

332. U.S. Senate. *Memorial and Resolutions Adopted at a Meeting of Sundry Citizens of Hartford, Connecticut, Adverse to the Renewal of the Charter of the Bank of the United States.* 22nd Cong., 1st Sess. (S.Doc.56). Washington: Duff Green, 1832. 2 pg. (Serial Set 213). Same as H.doc.107 (22-1) 219. See entry **326.**

333. U.S. Senate. *Memorial of the Bank of Windham County, in Windsor, Connecticut, Praying that the Charter of the Bank of the United States May Be Renewed, &c.* 22nd Cong., 1st Sess. (S.Doc.86). Washington: Duff Green, 1832. 1 pg. (Serial Set 213).

334. U.S. Senate. *Resolutions of a Meeting of the Citizens of Norwalk, Connecticut, in Favor of the Protective System, &c.* 22nd Cong., 1st Sess. (S.Doc.165). Washington: Duff Green, 1832. 2 pg. (Serial Set 214).

335. U.S. Senate. *Resolutions of a Meeting of the Inhabitants of Fairfield County, Connecticut, Remonstrating against the Adoption of the Tariff System Proposed by the Secretary of the Treasury, &c.* 22nd Cong., 1st Sess. (S.Doc.164). Washington: Duff Green, 1832. 2 pg. (Serial Set 214). Resolutions oppose altering the tariff of 1828 and the protective policy it supports.

336. U.S. Senate. *Resolutions Passed at a Meeting of the Inhabitants of Sharon, Connecticut, in Favor of the Protective System, &c.* 22nd Cong., 1st Sess. (S.Doc.169). Washington: Duff Green, 1832. 1 pg. (Serial Set 214). Resolutions support the current protective tariff and address the South's threat to dissolve the Union if the present system is continued.

337. U.S. Senate. *Resolutions Passed at a Meeting of the Citizens of New Canaan, Fairfield County, Connecticut, in Favor of the Protective System.* 22nd Cong., 1st Sess. (S.Doc.175). Washington: Duff Green, 1832. 2 pg. (Serial Set 214). Resolutions support the constitutionality and benefits of the protective system, deplore the unstable legislation on tariffs, and address the South's threat to dissolve the Union.

22ND CONGRESS, 2ND SESSION

338. Ellsworth, William W. (Conn.). "The Tariff Bill," *Register of Debates.* 22nd Cong., 2nd Sess. (14 Jan. 1833) pp. 1022-1034. Opposes the reduction of protective tariffs as premature, hasty, and unequal. Maintains that the real cause of the bill is the discontent of South Carolina. Reviews past legislation on the protective policy and the effects on both the North and the South.

339. Ingersoll, Ralph I. (Conn.). "Bank of the United States," *Register of Debates.* 22nd Cong., 2nd Sess. (13 Feb. 1833) pp. 1714-1716. Supports a quick decision as to future of the bank; opposes selling the bank stock in the public market.

340. Ingersoll, Ralph I. (Conn.). "The Tariff," *Register of Debates.* 22nd Cong., 2nd Sess. (10 Jan. 1833) pp. 977-990. Opposes reducing protective duties on imports. Discusses the effects of the measure on revenue, the current and future finances of the country, the wisdom of using the public lands for revenue, and specific provisions of the bill.

341. Young, Ebenezer (Conn.). "The Tariff Bill," *Register of Debates.* 22nd Cong., 2nd Sess. (28 Jan. 1833) pp. 1413-1424. Opposes reducing protective duties as capricious, partial and arbitrary, and operating against the interests of New England. Discusses the manufacturing industry, their alleged enormous profits, and the effect of the bill on manufacturers.

342. U.S. House. *Memorial of Citizens of Litchfield County, Connecticut, against the Bill to Reduce the Duties on Imports.* 22nd Cong., 2nd Sess. (H.Doc.98). Washington: Duff Green, 1832. 2 pg. (Serial Set 234). Memorial opposes amending the protective tariff acts as devastating to those who have extensive interests invested under what was considered a settled policy of legislation. Same as S.doc.67 (22-2) 230 (entry **343**).

343. U.S. Senate. *Memorial of Sundry Citizens of Connecticut, in Favor of the Protective System, &c.* 22nd Cong., 2nd Sess. (S.Doc.67). Washington: Duff Green, 1832. 2 pg. (Serial Set 230). Same as H.doc.98 (22-2) 234. See entry **342.**

23RD CONGRESS, 1ST SESSION

344. Ellsworth, William W. (Conn.). "Bank Reports," *Register of Debates.* 23rd Cong., 1st Sess. (27 May 1834) pp. 4265-4266, 4270. Supports printing the majority and minority reports of the committee together. Defends the printers.

345. Ellsworth, William W. (Conn.). "The Deposites and United States Bank," *Congressional Globe.* 23rd Cong., 1st Sess. (27 Mar. 1834) pp. 270-271. Opposes the removal of the deposits, the substitute of the State banks for the Bank of the United States, and a metallic currency. Much longer version of this speech is reported in the *Register of Debates,* "Public Deposites.", pp. 3259-3271; this version discusses in more detail the conduct of the Executive, the power of removal, the condition of the country, and the effects of the removal of the deposits.

346. Foot, Samuel A. (Conn.). "Connecticut Memorial," *Register of Debates.* 23rd Cong., 1st Sess. (17 Feb. 1834) pp. 2724-2725. Presents and supports petitions from Hartford and the Connecticut River Banking Company requesting that the deposits be restored and the bank be re-chartered.

347. Foot, Samuel A. (Conn.). "Proceedings at New Haven," *Register of Debates.* 23rd Cong., 1st Sess. (24 Feb. 1834) pp. 2773-2774. Presents and supports resolutions from a meeting in New Haven in favor of re-chartering the Bank of the United States and restoring to that bank the public deposits.

348. Huntington, Jabez W. (Conn.). "Kentucky Election," *Register of Debates.* 23rd Cong., 1st Sess. (5 Dec. 1833) pp. 2154-2157. Questions the right of Mr. T.P. Moore to take a seat in the House. Discusses the validity of his certificate and credentials. Reviews possible precedents.

349. Huntington, Jabez W. (Conn.). "Memorials from Banks in Connecticut," *Register of Debates.* 23rd Cong., 1st Sess. (24 Feb. 1834) pp. 2771-2773. Presents and supports resolutions and memorials from the Bank of Hartford, the Phoenix Bank of Hartford, and several banks of Norwich, Conn., in favor of restoring the public deposits and re-chartering the Bank of the United States or establishing another national bank. Describes the character of the memorialists.

350. Huntington, Jabez W. (Conn.). "Removal of the Deposites," *Congressional Globe.* 23rd Cong., 1st Sess. (24 Jan., 28 Jan. 1834) pp. 125-126; 132-133. Defends the actions of the Bank of the United States and supports actions of Congress to restore the deposits. Addresses the reasons given for the withdrawal of the deposits. Longer version of this speech printed in the *Register of Debates*, "The Deposite Question," (23 Jan. 1834) pp. 2510-2537.

351. Smith, Nathan (Conn.). "Public Distress," *Register of Debates* 23rd Cong., 1st Sess. (24 Feb. 1834) pp. 656-662. Presents petitions and resolutions from New Haven and Hartford describing the distress caused by the removal of the deposits and praying that the bank be re-chartered. Supports the character of the petitioners and their petitions. Discusses the true reasons behind the removal of the deposits and the experiment of returning to a hard money system.

352. Smith, Nathan (Conn.). "Tolland County (Conn.) Memorial," *Register of Debates.* 23rd Cong., 1st Sess. (18 June 1834) pp. 2024-2025. Supports the memorialists and their memorial praying for the deposits to be restored and the bank to be re-chartered.

353. Tomlinson, Gideon (Conn.). "Lyme (Conn.) Memorial," *Register of Debates.* 23rd Cong., 1st Sess. (12 June 1834) pp. 1997-1998. Supports the memorialists and their memorial praying for the restoration of the public deposits and the re-chartering of the Bank of the United States.

354. Tomlinson, Gideon (Conn.). "Public Distress," *Register of Debates.* 23rd Cong., 1st Sess. (5 Mar. 1834) pp. 807-809. Supports the character of the memorialists and their memorials from various banks in Norwich, Conn., requesting a restoration of the public deposits and the establishment of a national bank or a renewal of the charter of the Bank of the United States.

355. Tomlinson, Gideon (Conn.). "Public Distress," *Register of Debates.* 23rd Cong., 1st Sess. (19 Mar. 1834) pp. 1005-1006. Presents memorial from Bridgeport, Conn., remonstrating against the removal of the deposits. Describes the town and its economy.

356. Tomlinson, Gideon (Conn.). "Windham County (Conn.) Memorial," *Register of Debates.* 23rd Cong., 1st Sess. (23 June 1834) pp. 2065-2066. Supports the memorialists and their memorial asking for a restoration of the public deposits and the re-chartering of the bank.

357. "On Application for the Erection of a Monument to the Memory of Captain Nathan Hale, of the Revolution," *American State Papers: Military Affairs*, Vol. V (Doc. 584) pp. 357-358. (ASP 020). Report acknowledges that Captain Hale's brave deeds entitle him to be remembered by such a monument, but that there is no precedence to support it; reprint of memorial from citizens of Coventry, Conn. describes his Revolutionary War activities. Same as S.doc.489 (23-1) 243 (entry **376**).

358. U.S. House. *Memorial of Citizens of Hartford County, in Relation to the Currency.* 23rd Cong., 1st Sess. (H.Doc.508). [Washington: Gales & Seaton, Print., 1834]. 14 pg. (Serial Set 259). Memorial blames the derangement of the currency and other economic calamities upon the current policy towards the Bank of the United States. Includes 13 pages of names of memorialists.

359. U.S. House. *Memorial of Citizens of Newtown, Connecticut, on the Currency.* 23rd Cong., 1st Sess. (H.Doc.379). [Washington: Gales & Seaton, Print., 1834]. 3 pg. (Serial Set 258). Memorial asks to restore the public deposits and re-charter the Bank of the United States; maintains that the withdrawal of the deposits was unauthorized and calculated to enlarge the power of the Executive. Names of memorialists included. Same as S.doc.491 (23-1) 243 (entry **372**).

360. U.S. House. *Memorial of Inhabitants of New London County, Asking a Recharter of the United States Bank.* 23rd Cong., 1st Sess. (H.Doc.476). [Washington: Gales & Seaton, Print., 1834]. 6 pg. (Serial Set 259). Memorial asks to restore the deposits and re-charter the Bank of the United States. Same as S.doc. 438 (23-1) 243 (entry **368**), but includes names of memorialists.

361. U.S. House. *Memorial of Inhabitants of Norwich, Connecticut, in Favor of Rechartering the Bank of the United States.* 23rd Cong., 1st Sess. (H.Doc.94). [Washington: Gales & Seaton, Print., 1834]. 4 pg. (Serial Set 256). Memorial asks to restore the deposits and re-charter the bank. Includes names of memorialists.

362. U.S. House. *Memorial of Inhabitants of Stafford County, Approving of the Removal of the Public Deposites, and against Rechartering the Bank of the United States.* 23rd Cong., 1st Sess. (H.Doc.334). [Washington: Gales & Seaton, Print., 1834]. 2 pg. (Serial Set 257). Memorial includes names of memorialists.

363. U.S. House. *Memorial of Inhabitants of the County of Windham, in Favor of a Restoration of the Public Deposites, and the Establishment of a National Bank.* 23rd Cong., 1st Sess. (H.Doc.471). [Washington: Gales & Seaton, Print., 1834. 3 pg. (Serial Set 259). Memorial blames the widespread problems with the economy on the ruinous policy of the Executive towards the Bank of the United States. Same as S.doc.469 (23-1) 243 (entry **371**).

364. U.S. House. *Memorial of Inhabitants of the Town of Windham, in Favor of a Restoration of the Public Deposites.* 23rd Cong., 1st Sess. (H.Doc.474). [Washington: Gales & Seaton, 1834]. 2 pg. (Serial Set 259). Memorial asks to restore the deposits and re-charter the Bank of the United States.

365. U.S. House. *Memorial of the Banks in the City of Norwich, Connecticut, in Relation to the Present Distress, and in Favor of a National Currency.* 23rd Cong., 1st Sess. (H.Doc.129). [Washington: Gales & Seaton, 1834]. 2 pg. (Serial Set 256). Memorial supports renewing the charter of the Bank of the United States or establishing a new national bank. Same as S.doc.146 (23-1) 240 (entry **375**), but with two additional documents.

366. U.S. House. *Proceedings of a Public Meeting of Inhabitants of Windham, in Favor of Rechartering the Bank of the United States.* 23rd Cong., 1st Sess. (H.Doc.472). [Washington: Gales & Seaton, Print., 1834]. 2 pg. (Serial Set 259). Resolutions support restoring the deposits and re-chartering the bank. Reprinted in S.doc.470 (23-1) 243 (entry **374**).

367. U.S. House. *Resolutions Adopted at a Meeting of Citizens of Newhaven, Connecticut, in Relation to the Currency.* 23rd Cong., 1st Sess. (H.Doc.127). [Washington: Gales & Seaton, Print., 1834]. 9 pg. (Serial Set 256). Resolutions support restoring the public deposits to the Bank of the United States and re-chartering that institution. Includes eight pages of names and occupations of supporting citizens. Resolutions without names also presented as S.doc.113 (23-1) 239 (entry **378**).

368. U.S. Senate. *Memorial from the Citizens of Lyme, Connecticut, against the Removal of the Deposites, and in Favor of the Recharter of the Bank of the United States.* 23rd Cong., 1st Sess. (S.Doc.438). Washington: Duff Green, 1834. 2 pg. (Serial Set 243). Same as H.doc.476 (23-1) 259 (entry **360**), but without the names of the memorialists.

369. U.S. Senate. *Memorial of About Three Hundred and Eighty of the Inhabitants of Bridgeport, Connecticut, against the Removal of the Deposites from the Bank of the United States.* 23rd Cong., 1st Sess. (S.Doc.191).

Washington: Duff Green, 1834. 1 pg. (Serial Set 240). Brief memorial blames the disastrous state of the economy on the removal of the deposits.

370. U.S. Senate. *Memorial of About Three Hundred of the Inhabitants of Hartford, Complaining of the Distresses of the Community, and Praying Relief Therefrom.* 23rd Cong., 1st Sess. (S.Doc.117). Washington: Duff Green, 1834. 2 pg. (Serial Set 239). Memorial supports restoring the public deposits and re-chartering the Bank of the United States as the most effective means of obtaining relief.

371. U.S. Senate. *Memorial of Inhabitants of Windham County, Connecticut, in Favor of Restoring the Deposites, and of Rechartering the Bank of the United States.* 23rd Cong., 1st Sess. (S.Doc.469). Washington: Duff Green, 1834. 3 pg. (Serial Set 243). Same as H.doc.471 (23-1) 259. See entry **363**.

372. U.S. Senate. *Memorial of the Inhabitants of Newtown, Fairfield County, Connecticut, against the Measures of the Executive in Removing the Deposites from the Bank of the United States, &c.* 23rd Cong., 1st Sess. (S.Doc.491). Washington: Duff Green, 1834. 4 pg. (Serial Set 243). Same as H.doc.379 (23-1) 258. See entry **359**.

373. U.S. Senate. *Memorial of the Inhabitants of Tolland County, Connecticut, for the Restoration of the Deposites, and Renewal of the Charter of the Bank of the United States.* 23rd Cong., 1st Sess. (S.Doc.448). Washington: Duff Green, 1834. 9 pg. (Serial Set 243). Memorial includes eight pages of names of memorialists.

374. U.S. Senate. *Memorial of the Inhabitants of Windham County, Connecticut, for a Restoration of the Deposites, and Recharter of the Bank of the United States.* 23rd Cong., 1st Sess. (S.Doc.470). Washington: Duff Green, 1834. 3 pg. (Serial Set 243). Memorial and resolutions in support of the bank; resolutions are a reprint of H.doc.472 (23-1) 259 (entry **366**).

375. U.S. Senate. *Memorial of the Officers of the Banks in Norwich, Connecticut, for Relief from the Prevailing Distress, and for the Establishment of a National Bank.* 23rd Cong., 1st Sess. (S.Doc.146). Washington: Duff Green, 1834. 1 pg. (Serial Set 240). Memorial supports renewing the charter of the Bank of the United States or establishing a new national bank.

376. U.S. Senate. [Report on Requested Monument to Honor of Capt. Nathan Hale]. 23rd Cong., 1st Sess. (S.Doc.489). Washington: Duff Green, 1834. 3 pg. (Serial Set 243). Same as Mil.aff.584 (23-1) ASP 020. See entry **357**.

377. U.S. Senate. *Resolution of the Connecticut River Banking Company, in Favor of Rechartering the Bank of the United States.* 23rd Cong., 1st Sess. (S.Doc.116). Washington: Duff Green, 1834. 1 pg. (Serial Set 239). Maintains that restoring the deposits would provide relief from the distress of the country and that re-chartering the bank would re-establish commercial confidence.

378. U.S. Senate. *Resolutions of About Nine Hundred of the Citizens of New Haven, Conn., Attributing the Distresses of the Community to the Removal of the Deposites from the Bank of the United States, and Asking Their Restoration* 23rd Cong., 1st Sess. (S.Doc.113). Washington: Duff Green, 1834. 1 pg. (Serial Set 239). Resolutions to restore the deposits to the Bank of the United States and to renew the charter of that institution. Same resolutions as H.doc.127 (23-1) 256 (entry **367**), but without the names of the supporting citizens.

379. U.S. Senate. *Resolutions of Citizens of Norwich, Connecticut, Opposed to the Removal of the Public Deposites from the Bank of the United States.* 23rd Cong., 1st Sess. (S.Doc.144). Washington: Duff Green, 1834. 2 pg. (Serial Set 240). Resolutions support restoring the public deposits and re-chartering the bank.

23RD CONGRESS, 2ND SESSION

380. Jackson, Ebenezer Jr. (Conn.). "Baltimore and Washington Railroad," *Register of Debates.* 23rd Cong., 2nd Sess. (18 Feb. 1835) pp. 1419-1422. Supports the completion of the road as beneficial to the country; contends that the company should terminate the road where they judge best.

381. Jackson, Ebenezer Jr. (Conn.). "Harbor Bill," *Register of Debates.* 23rd Cong., 2nd Sess. (26 Feb. 1835) pp. 1505-1506. Supports appropriations to deepen the channel at the mouth of the Connecticut River.

382. Trumbull, Joseph (Conn.). "Harbor Bill," *Register of Debates.* 23rd Cong., 2nd Sess. (26 Feb. 1835) pp. 1504-1505. Supports the bill to deepen the channel at the mouth of the Connecticut River; remarks on the results of the survey and the benefits to be derived from the improvement.

383. Young, Ebenezer (Conn.). "Captain Nathan Hale," *Register of Debates.* 23rd Cong., 2nd Sess. (12 Jan. 1835) pp. 981-982. Supports the Coventry, Conn., petition for the erection of a monument to the memory of Captain Nathan Hale.

384. U.S. House. *Letter from the Secretary of the Treasury, Transmitting Information Relative to Sites Purchased for a Warehouse and Custom-houses, and the Sale of Public Grounds.* 23rd Cong., 2nd Sess. (H.Doc.24). [Washington]: Gales & Seaton, [1834] 1 pg. (Serial Set 272). Provides for building custom-houses at Newburyport, New Bedford, New London, Middletown, and New York; for selling land purchased for a customhouse at Mobile; for selling timber on land at Sandy Hook; and for a warehouse at Baltimore.

24TH CONGRESS, 1ST SESSION

385. "Captain Nathan Hale," *Congressional Globe*. 24th Cong., 1st Sess. (6 Jan., 17 Feb. 1836) pp. 73, 191. Brief debate and remarks on the petition to erect a monument in honor of Captain Nathan Hale, of the Revolutionary Army. Includes remarks by Andrew T. Judson (Conn.). Jan. 6th remarks printed in *Register of Debates*, "Captain Nathan Hale," pp. 2134-2135.

386. Haley, Elisha (Conn.). "Death of Hon. Zalmon Wildman," *Congressional Globe*. 24th Cong., 1st Sess. (14 Dec. 1835) p. 22. Remarks on the death of the Hon. Zalmon Wildman, Representative from Connecticut.

387. Judson, Andrew T. (Conn.). "Naval Service Bill," *Register of Debates*. 24th Cong., 1st Sess. (7 Apr. 1836) pp. 3204-3205. Supports appropriations to improve the navy yard at Pensacola.

388. Judson, Andrew T. (Conn.). "New York Relief Bill," *Congressional Globe*. 24th Cong., 1st Sess. (8 Mar. 1836) p. 237. Supports relief for sufferers of the fire in New York, and defends the mercantile class. Almost the same remarks printed in the *Register of Debates*, "Sufferers by Fire in New York," pp. 2711-2712.

389. Niles, John M. (Conn.). "Captain Nathan Hale," *Congressional Globe*. 24th Cong., 1st Sess. (1 Feb. 1836) pp. 156-157. Remarks on petitions of citizens of Connecticut that a monument be erected to the memory of Captain Nathan Hale of the Revolutionary Army; biographical information given. Same remarks printed in the *Register of Debates*, "Nathan Hale," pp. 323-325.

390. Niles, John M. (Conn.). "Cumberland Road," *Congressional Globe, Appendix*. 24th Cong., 1st Sess. (26 Feb. 1836) pp. 165-166. Supports the continuation of appropriations for the Cumberland Road; contends that the government has supported this road for over thirty years and is committed to its completion. Same remarks printed in the *Register of Debates*, "Cumberland Road," pp. 4635-4638.

391. Niles, John M. (Conn.). "Fortification Bill," *Congressional Globe, Appendix*. 24th Cong., 1st Sess. (13 May 1836) pp. 434-437. Supports the bill authorizing the erection of new fortifications. Discusses the surplus in the Treasury and the need to enlarge and extend the system of defense of towns and harbors, including Fort Trumbull. Discusses recommendations of the Sec. of War. Same speech printed in the *Register of Debates*, "Fortifications," (12 May 1836) pp. 1435-1446.

392. Niles, John M. (Conn.). "Fortification Bill," *Register of Debates*. 24th Cong., 1st Sess. (24 May 1836) pp. 1559-1563. Responds to Sen. Davis (Mass.). Defends the need for fortifications as essential for national defense; discusses the importance of the militia system, the influence of politics on the militia, and the role of railroads in the defense system.

393. Niles, John M. (Conn.). "Gold and Silver for Public Lands," *Congressional Globe.* 24th Cong., 1st Sess. (23 Apr. 1836) pp. 390-392. Opposes the distribution bill that would divide funds among the states derived from the public lands; discusses the surplus in the Treasury and the general state of public finances. Also printed in the *Register of Debates*, "Specie Payments," pp. 1263-1266, 1268-1269.

394. Niles, John M. (Conn.). "Incendiary Publications," *Register of Debates.* 24th Cong., 1st Sess. (13 Apr. 1836) pp. 1156, 1157-1159, 1163-1165. Various remarks opposed to the bill restricting delivery of publications touching the subject of slavery; proposes a less restrictive amendment. Maintains that the bill would paralyze mail delivery and be impossible to execute. Responds to remarks of Sen. Calhoun (S.C.).

395. Niles, John M. (Conn.). "Independence of Texas," *Congressional Globe.* 24th Cong., 1st Sess. (13 June 1836) pp. 546-547. Presents petitions from the Legislature of Connecticut favoring the independence of Texas; supports the patriotism of the petitioners but contends it is premature to act. Also printed in the *Register of Debates*, "Recognition of Texas," pp. 1759-1763.

396. Niles, John M. (Conn.). "Independence of Texas," *Congressional Globe, Appendix.* 24th Cong., 1st Sess. (1 July 1836) p. 529. Supports a qualified recognition of the independence of Texas; contends that it is premature to unqualifiedly recognize her independence until there is reasonable grounds to believe it can be sustained. Same speech printed in the *Register of Debates*, "Texas," pp. 1916-1918.

397. Niles, John M. (Conn.). "Land Distribution Bill," *Congressional Globe, Appendix.* 24th Cong., 1st Sess. (28 Apr. 1836) pp. 359-365. Opposes the bill to distribute the proceeds from the sale of the public lands among the states as unconstitutional, unjust and inexpedient. Addresses remarks of Sen. Clay regarding the security of the public revenues in the deposit banks. Discusses the financial view of the measure and state of the Treasury. Same speech printed in the *Register of Debates*, "Land Bill," pp. 1318-1338.

398. Niles, John M. (Conn.). "Northern Boundary of Ohio," *Congressional Globe, Appendix.* 24th Cong., 1st Sess. (1 Apr. 1836) pp. 310-311. Supports admitting Michigan into the Union according to her rights under the ordinance of 1787; maintains that her proceedings were legal and authorized by the Legislative Council of the territory. Addresses objections. Same speech printed in the *Register of Debates*, "Admission of Michigan," (30 Mar. 1836) pp. 1015-1019.

399. Niles, John M. (Conn.). Remarks on the Deposit Banks, *Congressional Globe.* 24th Cong., 1st Sess. (6 Apr. 1836) p. 326. Maintains that the distributed surplus is temporary; discusses the removal of funds from the Bank of the United States to the deposit banks. Same remarks printed in the *Register of Debates*, "Revolutionary Pensions," pp. 1097-1099.

400. Niles, John M. (Conn.). Remarks on the Petition of David Melville, *Congressional Globe*. 24th Cong., 1st Sess. (15 Apr. 1836) pp. 361-362. Disfavors the petition of David Melville, a customs officer who was removed from office. Maintains that the removal was legal, fair and reasonable; opposes the principle of perpetuity of office. Same speech printed in *Register of Debates*, "Removal of David Melville," pp. 1179-1182.

401. Niles, John M. (Conn.). "Slavery in the District of Columbia," *Congressional Globe, Appendix*. 24th Cong., 1st Sess. (17 Feb. 1836) pp. 114-115. Defends the character and policy of Pres. Andrew Jackson. Same remarks printed in the *Register of Debates*, "National Defence," pp. 560-563.

402. Niles, John M. (Conn.). "Slavery in the District of Columbia," *Congressional Globe, Appendix*. 24th Cong., 1st Sess. (15 Feb. 1836) pp. 117-123. Opposes Mr. Calhoun's resolution against the reception of abolition petitions as unconstitutional and inexpedient. Majority of speech addresses misapprehensions about public sentiment in the North concerning slavery. Discusses the power of government over slavery, slavery in the District, abolitionists in Conn., and the right to petition. Same speech printed in the *Register of Debates*, "Slavery in the District of Columbia," pp. 512-531.

403. Niles, John M. (Conn.). "Sufferers by New York Fire," *Congressional Globe*. 24th Cong., 1st Sess. (13 Jan. 1836) pp. 98-99. Supports granting relief through extending credit for duties; addresses the constitutionality of special legislation.

404. Tomlinson, Gideon (Conn.). "Obituary," *Congressional Globe*. 24th Cong., 1st Sess. (8 Dec. 1835) p. 11. Remarks on the death of Nathan Smith, Senator from Connecticut. Also printed in the *Register of Debates*, "Death of Mr. Smith," pp. 4-5.

405. U.S. House. *Monument to the Memory of Captain Hale*. 24th Cong., 1st Sess. (H.Rpt.171). [Washington]: Blair & Rives, Printers, [1836]. 3 pg. (Serial Set 293). Select Committee report supports erecting the petitioned monument to honor Captain Nathan Hale; reviews the circumstances of his death.

406. U.S. House. *Petition of the Selectmen, Mayor, and Aldermen of Norwich, Praying that the City of Norwich Be Made a Port of Entry, &c.* 24th Cong., 1st Sess. (H.Doc.36). [Washington: Blair & Rives, Printers, 1835]. 4 pg. (Serial Set 287). Petition includes description of Norwich; describes how the change in trade from foreign to domestic has made the previous relation with the port of entry at New London unsatisfactory.

407. U.S. House. *Resolutions of the General Assembly of Connecticut*. 24th Cong., 1st Sess. (H.Doc.288). [Washington]: Blair & Rives, Printers, [1836]. 2

pg. (Serial Set 292). Resolutions to recognize Texas as a free, sovereign, and independent nation.

408. U.S. Senate. *Memorial of Sundry Citizens of Connecticut, That a Monument be Erected to the Memory of Captain Nathan Hale, a Martyr in the Cause of American Independence.* 24th Cong., 1st Sess. (S.Doc.108). Washington: Gales & Seaton, 1836. 4 pg. (Serial Set 280). Reprints earlier memorial found in S.doc.489 (23-1) 243 (entry **377**); reprint of acts of the General Assembly of Connecticut passed in 1776 regarding independence from Great Britain.

409. U.S. Senate. [Report on the Recognition of the Independence of Texas]. 24th Cong., 1st Sess. (S.Doc.406). Washington: Gales & Seaton, 1836. 3 pg. (Serial Set 284). Report responds to the resolutions of the Legislature of Connecticut concerning recognition of the independence of Texas; reviews policy in respect to new powers and means of recognition. Recommends waiting until Texas has demonstrated that it has a successful civil government.

24ᵀᴴ CONGRESS, 2ᴺᴰ SESSION

410. Ingham, Samuel (Conn.). "Connecticut Militia Claims," *Congressional Globe, Appendix.* 24th Cong., 2nd Sess. (Feb. 1837) pp. 225-226. Supports payment of the claim of the State of Connecticut for services rendered by her militia during the late war. Includes history of the services of the militia and of the claim. Speech also printed in the *Register of Debates*, "Army Appropriation Bill," pp. 1950-1953.

411. Ingham, Samuel (Conn.). "Fortifications at New London, &c.," *Congressional Globe, Appendix.* 24th Cong., 2nd Sess. (24 Feb. 1837) pp. 223-224. Supports appropriations already approved for the construction of fortifications at New London and at the mouth of the Connecticut River. Describes the areas and their military importance. Speech also printed in *Register of Debates*, "Fortification Bill," pp. 1920-1925.

412. Niles, John M. (Conn.). "Admission of Michigan into the Union," *Congressional Globe, Appendix.* 24th Cong., 2nd Sess. (2 Jan., 3 Jan. 1837) pp. 82-83. Maintains that the condition providing for the admission of Michigan into the Union has been complied with; the people have given their assent to the boundary. Discusses the power of the people in government. Speech also printed in *Register of Debates*, "Admission of Michigan," (4 Jan. 1837) pp. 285-290.

413. Niles, John M. (Conn.). "Duty on Foreign Coal," *Congressional Globe, Appendix.* 24th Cong., 2nd Sess. (24 Feb. 1837) pp. 241-245. Supports reducing the duties on coal; maintains that it is not protective of the domestic coal interest, but an unnecessary and burdensome tax which targets the poor.

Discusses the duty in respect to the compromise act of 1833; responds to remarks of Mr. Webster. Speech also printed in the *Register of Debates*, "Reduction of the Tariff," pp. 939-948, 953-954, 956-957, 962-965.

414. Niles, John M. (Conn.). "On the Expunging Resolution," *Congressional Globe, Appendix*. 24th Cong., 2nd Sess. (14 Jan. 1837) pp. 125-127. Supports expunging from the *Journal* the impeachment resolution of March 1834, which arraigned, tried and condemned Pres. Jackson. Maintains that the act was unconstitutional and could establish dangerous precedent. Speech also printed in *Register of Debates*, "Expunging Resolution," (13 Jan. 1837) pp. 408-416.

415. Niles, John M. (Conn.). "Papers of Mr. Madison," *Register of Debates*. 24th Cong., 2nd Sess. (20 Feb. 1837) pp. 862-864. Questions the purpose of purchasing the manuscripts. Opposes publishing the works at the public expense and by the authority of Congress as an unauthorized assumption of power.

416. Niles, John M. (Conn.). "Recission of the Treasury Order," *Congressional Globe, Appendix*. 24th Cong., 2nd Sess. (22 Dec. 1836) pp. 31-36. Supports the Treasury order as a temporary measure to address the sales of the public lands and to check speculation. Maintains that the order is legal, and that it is not the cause of the present crisis, which is inherent in the banking system and the paper currency. Discusses the evils of a paper currency and the right of Congress to regulate the currency of the country. Speech also printed in the *Register of Debates*, "Treasury Circular," pp. 104-120.

417. Niles, John M. (Conn.). "Unexpended Balances of Appropriations," *Congressional Globe, Appendix*. 24th Cong., 2nd Sess. (28 Dec. 1836) p. 43. Remarks on the deposit act and the allegedly false character assigned to it as a distribution bill to dispose of the surplus revenue among the states. Prefers the money to be distributed among the states than to remain in the Treasury and with the deposit banks. Speech also printed in the *Register of Debates*, "Unexpended Appropriations," pp. 162-165.

418. Toucey, Isaac (Conn.). "Admission of Michigan," *Congressional Globe, Appendix*. 24th Cong., 2nd Sess. (24 Jan. 1837) pp. 184-186. Maintains that Michigan became a state when her constitution was accepted and her state government ratified and confirmed. Contends that the boundaries prescribed have received the requested assent. Addresses objections. Speech also printed in the *Register of Debates*, "Admission of Michigan," pp. 1444-1451.

419. "Claim of Connecticut for a Balance Due for Military Services of the Militia of That State During the War of 1812-'15," *American State Papers: Military Affairs*, Vol. VI (Doc. 707) p. 984. (ASP 021). Same as H.doc.57 (24-2) 302 (entry **420**).

420. U.S. House. *Resolution of the Legislature of Connecticut, Instructing Their Senators and Requesting Their Representatives to Obtain Payment of*

Balance Due for Military Service, &c. During the Late War. 24th Cong., 2nd Sess. (H.Doc.57). [Washington]: Blair & Rives, Printers, [1836]. 1 pg. (Serial Set 302). Same as Mil.aff.707 (24-2) ASP 021 (entry **419**).

421. U.S. Senate. *Petition of the Inhabitants of Norwich, Connecticut, for a Repeal of the Duty on Coal.* 24th Cong., 2nd Sess. (S.Doc.30). Washington: Gales and Seaton, 1837. 4 pg. (Serial Set 297). Petition to repeal the duty on coal; maintains that the supply would increase, resulting in lower prices and greater availability. Includes names of petitioners.

422. U.S. Senate. [Report on Memorials Praying for a Repeal of the Duty on Foreign Coal]. 24th Cong., 2nd Sess. (S.Doc.102). Washington: Gales and Seaton, 1837. 12 pg. (Serial Set 298). Report supports memorials from Boston, Mass. and Norwich, Conn.; reviews historical duties on coal and objections to the duty; maintains that it is not wanted for revenue nor retained as a protection of the domestic coal trade.

25TH CONGRESS, 1ST SESSION

423. Niles, John M. (Conn.). "Making Public Officers Depositories," *Congressional Globe, Appendix.* 25th Cong., 1st Sess. (20 Sept. 1837) pp. 61-66. Supports the bill that would employ federal officers to assist in the keeping and disbursement of the revenue. Discusses and dismisses the alternatives of a national bank or the state deposit banks. Maintains that the proposed Sub-Treasury system is practical and simple, free from moneyed influence, and would separate the government from the banks. Addresses objections. Summary of speech in *Congressional Globe*, pp. 44-45. Same speech printed in the *Register of Debates*, "Sub-Treasury Bill," pp. 105-122.

424. Niles, John M. (Conn.). "Making Public Officers Depositories," *Congressional Globe, Appendix.* 25th Cong., 1st Sess. (23 Sept. 1837) pp. 193-195. Replies to Sen. King's (Ga.) responses to his earlier speech on the Sub-Treasury; discusses the disastrous effects of the Bank of the United States, and the reasons assigned by the President in his Message for the present state of the economy. Same speech printed in the *Register of Debates*, "Sub-Treasury Bill," pp. 236-243.

425. Niles, John M. (Conn.). Remarks on the District Banks, *Congressional Globe.* 25th Cong., 1st Sess. (11 Oct. 1837) p. 125. Supports forcing the banks to resume payment and pay their debts.

426. Toucey, Isaac (Conn.). "Deposite Law," *Congressional Globe.* 25th Cong., 1st Sess. (29 Sept. 1837) pp. 88-89. Remarks on the proposed fourth installment of deposit with the states. Discusses the public finances and the current lack of surplus revenue. Same remarks printed in the *Register of Debates*, "Fourth Instalment Bill," pp. 1133-1135.

427. U.S. House. *Memorial of Inhabitants of New Haven, in the State of Connecticut, Praying for the Establishment of a National Bank.* 25th Cong., 1st Sess. (H.Doc.22). Washington: Thomas Allen, 1837. 2 pg. (Serial Set 311). Memorial maintains a national bank would allow the resumption of specie payments and an equalization of the exchanges.

25ᵀᴴ CONGRESS, 2ᴺᴰ SESSION

428. Niles, John M. (Conn.). "Deposite Act of 1836," *Congressional Globe, Appendix.* 25th Cong., 2nd Sess. (30 June 1838) pp. 456-458. Supports repealing the first twelve sections of the deposit act of 1836 as unequal and unjust. Majority of speech responds to comment by Sen. Clay (Ky.); gives a satirical biographical sketch of Clay's public life.

429. Niles, John M. (Conn.). "District Banks - Free Banking," *Congressional Globe, Appendix.* 25th Cong., 2nd Sess. (May 1838) pp. 312-316. Supports renewing the charters of the banks in the District of Columbia for a short time to allow them to close up their affairs and resume payment of notes. Discusses the status of banks in various states, the conduct and mismanagement of D.C. banks in 1834 to their present condition, and the free banking system.

430. Niles, John M. (Conn.). "Finances of the Government," *Congressional Globe, Appendix.* 25th Cong., 2nd Sess. (8 June 1838) pp. 378-379. Speech on the status of the Independent Treasury bill and the government's war upon the banks. Maintains that the resumption of the banks is not related to change in the policy of the administration or Congress.

431. Niles, John M. (Conn.). "Graduation of the Price of Public Lands," *Congressional Globe.* 25th Cong., 2nd Sess. (9 Apr. 1838) pp. 293-294. Proposes eight years as the minimum length of time land must remain on the market to determine it is of such inferior quality that the price should be reduced for it to sell.

432. Niles, John M. (Conn.). "Independent Treasury Bill," *Congressional Globe, Appendix.* 25th Cong., 2nd Sess. (13 Feb. 1838) pp. 114-124. Supports the Independent Treasury. Discusses the opposition to the measure and a proposed substitute measure, based upon the deposit bank system. Remarks on the Independent Treasury bill, demonstrating its practicability and greater safety and security; addresses objections against it. Detailed discussion of the banking system, its defects and present condition.

433. Niles, John M. (Conn.). "Mr. Calhoun's Resolutions," *Congressional Globe, Appendix.* 25th Cong., 2nd Sess. (6 Jan. 1838) pp. 39-41. Opposes the resolutions concerning the handling of petitions on slavery; discusses the growing influence of the abolitionists.

434. Niles, John M. (Conn.). "Mr. Clay's Resolution," *Congressional Globe, Appendix.* 25th Cong., 2nd Sess. (2 May, 25 May 1838) pp. 298-299; 341-343. Opposes the resolution concerning currency and bank notes. Maintains that the object is to renew the connection between the government and the banks, to the advantage of the banks, and that the resolution is uncalled for and designed to agitate the public. Discussion and history of banking policy.

435. Niles, John M. (Conn.). Remarks on Pension Payments, *Congressional Globe.* 25th Cong., 2nd Sess. (6 Feb. 1838) p. 165. Clarifies the pension payment procedures of deposit banks; advocates abandoning the deposit system.

436. Niles, John M. (Conn.). Remarks on Petitions for a National Bank, *Congressional Globe.* 25th Cong., 2nd Sess. (31 May 1838) pp. 419-420, 420-421. Maintains that the petition from Connecticut in support of a national bank did not emanate from both political parties. Discusses the Whig politics in Connecticut, particularly concerning the last election.

437. Niles, John M. (Conn.). Remarks on Suppression of Small Notes in the District, *Congressional Globe.* 25th Cong., 2nd Sess. (22 Dec. 1837) pp. 52-53. Supports suppressing the small notes; responds to Sen. Clay's comments on Treasury notes, the Independent Treasury and the national bank.

438. Niles, John M. (Conn.). "Resurrection Notes," *Congressional Globe, Appendix.* 25th Cong., 2nd Sess. (19 Apr. 1838) pp. 284-287. Supports preventing the issuing and circulation of currency purported to be created by the Bank of the United States. Maintains that Congress has the power and the duty to protect against this fraud and abuse of power.

439. Niles, John M. (Conn.). "Slavery in the District," *Congressional Globe.* 25th Cong., 2nd Sess. (18 Dec. 1837) p. 35. Supports the consideration of petitions for the abolition of slavery in the District of Columbia; discusses the Senate treatment of abolition petitions for the past two years.

440. Niles, John M. (Conn.). Speech on Connecticut Resolutions against the Sub-Treasury Bill, *Congressional Globe.* 25th Cong., 2nd Sess. (21 June 1838) pp. 466-470, 471-472. Discusses the authority and binding force of the doctrine of legislative instruction as applied to the actions of the Conn. Legislature. Includes lengthy response to the Legislature justifying his course of action. Maintains that the resolution is not obligatory upon the Senators, and that it has been politically motivated. Responds to comments of Sen. Crittenden (Ky.).

441. Niles, John M. (Conn.). "Suppression of Duelling," *Congressional Globe, Appendix.* 25th Cong., 2nd Sess. (29 Mar. 1838) pp. 226-227. Supports the bill for the prevention and punishment of dueling in the District of Columbia; maintains that sanction of duels growing out of the proceedings of Congress would impair the freedom and independence of that body.

442. Niles, John M. (Conn.). "Suppression of Small Notes in the District," *Congressional Globe, Appendix.* 25th Cong., 2nd Sess. (21 Dec. 1837) pp. 13-15. Supports eliminating small bills and compelling the banks of the District to redeem their notes and fulfill their obligations to the public.

443. Smith, Perry (Conn.). "Grant Lands for Rail Roads," *Congressional Globe, Appendix.* 25th Cong., 2nd Sess. (June 1838) pp. 437-438. Supports the appropriation of land to construct the New Albany and Mount Carmel Railroad in Illinois and Indiana. Maintains that the benefits of the railroad will profit the entire country and more than compensate the government for the value of the land.

444. Smith, Perry (Conn.). "The Independent Treasury Bill," *Congressional Globe, Appendix.* 25th Cong., 2nd Sess. (14 Feb. 1838) pp. 154-163. Supports a Sub-Treasury and the separation of the public money from the money and business of banks and individuals. Presents objections to making the banks depositories of the public money. Discusses the origins and policies of the Federal and Democratic parties.

445. Smith, Perry (Conn.). "Mr. Calhoun's Resolutions," *Congressional Globe, Appendix.* 25th Cong., 2nd Sess. (9 Jan. 1838) pp. 53-54. Opposes the resolution, which would prohibit the states, or their citizens, from discussing legislation concerning the expediency of slavery in the District.

446. Smith, Perry (Conn.). Remarks on Dueling, *Congressional Globe.* 25th Cong., 2nd Sess. (30 Mar., 5 Apr. 1838) pp. 278; 283. Supports a bill providing for punishment for those involved in the odious practice of dueling. Maintains that such a law is necessary to protect Representatives from the North from those of the South where dueling is an "institution."

447. Smith, Perry (Conn.). Remarks on the Sub-Treasury Bill, *Congressional Globe.* 25th Cong., 2nd Sess. (21 June 1838) pp. 470-471. Supports Sen. Niles' position on instructions received from the Connecticut Legislature to vote against the Sub-Treasury bill.

448. Toucey, Isaac (Conn.). "Independent Treasury," *Congressional Globe, Appendix.* 25th Cong., 2nd Sess. (23 June 1838) pp. 413-418. Supports the establishment of an Independent Treasury. Maintains that the country's distress is due to the expansion of the paper currency by the banks and that a national bank would perpetuate the problem. Recommends substituting a metallic currency for some portion of the paper currency and using coin in the fiscal operations of the government. Contends that an Independent Treasury would be a check upon excess in trade, banking, and speculation.

449. Toucey, Isaac (Conn.). "The Late Duel," *Congressional Globe, Appendix.* 25th Cong., 2nd Sess. (27 Apr. 1838) pp. 289-291. Defends the actions of the committee investigating the death of the Hon. Jonathan Cilley. Discusses the responsibilities and duties of the committee. Maintains that the House conferred upon the committee full power to investigate, and that the committee acted according to precedent. Reviews precedents. Summary of speech in *Congressional Globe*, pp. 337-338.

450. Whittlesey, Thomas T. (Conn.). "Neutrality Bill," *Congressional Globe*. 25th Cong., 2nd Sess. (24 Feb. 1838) p. 199. Supports the bill; defends its constitutionality and expediency. Discusses the power to seize property and prevent citizens from interfering in the affairs of other governments.

451. "On the Necessary Fortifications for the Defence of the Harbor of New London, Connecticut, and the Facilities for Establishing a Navy Yard at That Place," *American State Papers: Military Affairs*, Vol. VII (Doc. 748) pp. 764-767. (ASP 022). Correspondence concerning the status of appropriations for defense of the mouth of the Connecticut River and the harbor of New London; describes current fortifications.

452. U.S. House. *Letter from the Secretary of War, Transmitting a Copy of the Survey of the Harbor and Mouth of Connecticut River, &c.* 25th Cong., 2nd Sess. (H.Doc.252). [Washington: Thomas Allen, Print., 1838]. 10 pg., 1 map. (Serial Set 328). Report of the survey on the improvement of the harbor of Saybrook and the mouth of the Connecticut River. Describes area with estimates of cost of dredging and removal; maintains that it is a delicate and difficult venture. Includes map entitled "Map of the Mouth of the Connecticut River and Saybrook Harbour."

453. U.S. House. *Monument to the Memory of Capt. Nathan Hale.* 25th Cong., 2nd Sess. (H.Rpt.989). [Washington]: Thomas Allen, Print., [1838]. 4 pg. (Serial Set 336). Report supports erecting a monument to the memory of Captain Nathan Hale, of the Revolutionary Army; reviews his military history.

454. U.S. House. *Petition of Merchants of New Haven, Connecticut, Praying Congress to Pass a Law Allowing Collectors to Receive Notes of Specie-Paying Banks Which Issue Notes of Less than $5.* 25th Cong., 2nd Sess. (H.Doc.429). [Washington]: Thomas Allen, Print., [1838]. 2 pg. (Serial Set 331). Same as S.doc.481 (25-2) 319 (entry **460**), but does not include the names of petitioners.

455. U.S. House. *Resolutions of Legislature of Connecticut upon the Subject of Removal from Office.* 25th Cong., 2nd Sess. (H.Doc.442). [Washington: Thomas Allen, Print., 1838]. 1 pg. (Serial Set 331). Resolutions request an amendment of the Constitution concerning the power of appointment to, and removal from, office. Same as S.doc.489 (25-2) 319 (entry **461**).

456. U.S. House. *Resolutions of the Legislature of Connecticut, Protesting against the Resolution of the House of Representatives of the 21st of December Last, in Relation to Petitions, Memorials, &c., Touching the Abolition of Slavery, &c.* 25th Cong., 2nd Sess. (H.Doc.415). [Washington]: Thomas Allen, Print., [1838]. 2 pg. (Serial Set 330). Resolutions protest the resolution that all petitions, memorials, etc. relating to slavery be laid on the table with no further action as a denial of the right of petition.

457. U.S. House. *Resolutions of the Legislature of the State of Connecticut, for Indemnity for Losses Sustained by French Spoliations Prior to 1800.* 25th Cong., 2nd Sess. (H.Doc.414). [Washington: Thomas Allen, 1838]. 1 pg. (Serial Set 330).

458. U.S. Senate. *Memorial of a Number of Citizens of Hartford, Conn., Remonstrating against the Adoption of the Sub-Treasury Scheme.* 25th Cong., 2nd Sess. (S.Doc.185). Washington: Blair and Rives, 1838. 6 pg. (Serial Set 316). Includes six pages of names of memorialists.

459. U.S. Senate. *Petition of a Number of Merchants and Others, Citizens of Hartford County, Connecticut, Praying the Establishment of a National Bank.* 25th Cong., 2nd Sess. (S.Doc.462). Washington: Blair and Rives, 1838. 17 pg. (Serial Set 318). Includes 16 pages of names of petitioners.

460. U.S. Senate. *Petition of a Number of Merchants of New Haven, Connecticut, Praying the Repeal of the Law Which Prevents Collectors and Receivers from Taking in Payment the Bills of Such Banks As Have Issued Notes of a Less Denomination than Five Dollars, since the 4th July, 1836.* 25th Cong., 2nd Sess. (S.Doc.481). Washington: Blair and Rives, 1838. 2 pg. (Serial Set 319). Same as H.Doc.429 (25-2) 331 (entry **454**), but includes the names of the petitioners.

461. U.S. Senate. *Resolutions of the Legislature of Connecticut, to Obtain an Amendment of the Constitution of the United States, in Relation to the Power of Appointment to, and Removal from, Office.* 25th Cong., 2nd Sess. (S.Doc.489). Washington: Blair and Rives, 1838. 1 pg. (Serial Set 319). Same as H.doc.442 (25-2) 331 (entry **455**).

25TH CONGRESS, 3RD SESSION

462. Ingham, Samuel (Conn.). "Civil List Bill," *Congressional Globe.* 25th Cong., 3rd Sess. (15 Feb. 1839) p. 187. Opposes abolishing the Navy Board without making provision for the resulting changes to the service.

463. Niles, John M. (Conn.). "Fourth Installment of Deposit," *Congressional Globe.* 25th Cong., 3rd Sess. (13 Dec. 1838) p. 28. Maintains that the deposit act was intended as a means of disposing of a surplus in the Treasury, not for a distribution among the states. As there will be no surplus in the Treasury for the fourth installment, the states have no claim to this money.

464. Niles, John M. (Conn.). Remarks on the Treasury Report, *Congressional Globe.* 25th Cong., 3rd Sess. (27 Dec., 31 Dec. 1838) pp. 63; 77-78. Advocates printing additional copies of the Secretary's response to the resolutions of inquiry; contends that it should have as wide a distribution as the speech which originated the report and attacked the Secretary and the administration.

465. Niles, John M. (Conn.). "Salt Duty," *Congressional Globe, Appendix.* 25th Cong., 3rd Sess. (29 Jan. 1839) pp. 111-113. Supports revising the tariff so that duties of all articles considered primary necessities of life are dealt with together. Defends the 1813 vote of New England states against the salt duty. Rebuts charges that the policy of the Jackson administration was hostile to the interests of the eastern states.

466. Niles, John M. (Conn.). "United States Bank Bonds," *Congressional Globe, Appendix.* 25th Cong., 3rd Sess. (20 Dec. 1838) pp. 101-103. Supports an inquiry into the transactions of the Secretary of the Treasury and the Bank of the United States. Discusses the status of the government's war with the banks and public opinion of the Independent Treasury. Reprinted in the *Congressional Globe*, pp. 50-52.

467. Niles, John M. (Conn.). "United States Bank Bonds," *Congressional Globe, Appendix.* 25th Cong., 3rd Sess. (5 Jan. 1839) pp. 81-88. Responds to a request for information concerning the government and the sales of bonds of the Bank of the United States. Maintains that there has been no change in the policy of the administration concerning the deposit system and the Independent Treasury. Addresses the charges made against the Secretary of the Treasury and the President. Discusses the changing financial opinions and policies of Sen. Rives (Va.) at different periods of history.

468. Toucey, Isaac (Conn.). "Swartwout's Defalcation," *Congressional Globe, Appendix.* 25th Cong., 3rd Sess. (16 Jan. 1839) pp. 93-95. Opposed to a select committee to investigate Samuel Swartwout, late collector of the port of New York, for embezzlement. Discusses embezzlement under previous administrations and charges against the Secretary of the Treasury.

469. U.S. House. *Letter from the Secretary of the Treasury, Transmitting a Map of New Haven and Its Harbor, in the State of Connecticut.* 25th Cong., 3rd Sess. (H.Doc.202). [Washington: Thomas Allen, Print., 1839]. 1 pg., 1 map. (Serial Set 347). Map entitled "New Haven Harbour", an extract from the coast survey work.

470. U.S. Senate. *Report from the Secretary of War, in Compliance with a Resolution of the Senate, in Reference to the Expenditure of the Appropriation for Removal of the Sand Bar at the Mouth of the Connecticut River.* 25th Cong., 3rd Sess. (S.Doc.289). Washington: Blair and Rives, 1839. 2 pg. (Serial Set 342). Explains the status of the appropriation for the improvement of Saybrook Harbor, Connecticut; due to delays and miscommunications only a small portion of appropriated moneys was spent before it reverted to the surplus fund.

26TH CONGRESS, 1ST SESSION

471. Osborne, Thomas B. (Conn.). Remarks on the Death of the Hon. Thaddeus Betts (Conn.), *Congressional Globe.* 26th Cong., 1st Sess. (7 Apr. 1840) p. 309.

472. Smith, Perry (Conn.). "Death of the Hon. Thaddeus Betts," *Congressional Globe.* 26th Cong., 1st Sess. (7 Apr. 1840) p. 309. Remarks on the death of Thaddeus Betts, a Senator from Connecticut.

473. Smith, Perry (Conn.). "The District Banks," *Congressional Globe.* 26th Cong., 1st Sess. (15 June 1840) p. 466. Opposes incorporating the banks in the District of Columbia; maintains that Congress does not have the power to grant bank charters in either the states or the District.

474. Smith, Perry (Conn.). Remarks on the Abolition of Slavery, *Congressional Globe.* 26th, Cong., 1st Sess. (13 Feb. 1840) pp. 190-191. Objects to receiving the abolition petitions as their requests are unconstitutional and inexpedient. Contends that the abolitionists are aligned with the Federalists and that it is better that Negroes should remain slaves.

475. U.S. House. *Monument to Captain Nathan Hale.* 26th Cong., 1st Sess. (H.Rpt.713). [Washington: 1840]. 3 pg. (Serial Set 373). Report of the Select Committee supports erecting the monument to honor Captain Nathan Hale; reprints the 1836 report (H.rp.171 (24-1) 293 (entry **405**)) which reviews the circumstances of his death.

476. U.S. House. *Resolutions of the Legislature of Connecticut, upon the Subject of a National Foundry.* 26th Cong., 1st Sess. (H.Doc.55). [Washington]: Blair & Rives, Printers, [1840]. 2 pg. (Serial Set 364). Resolutions for the establishment of a foundry in the Housatonic valley; purported advantages are the inexhaustible beds of iron ore, waterpower, and available transportation to the seacoast and the interior. Same as S.Doc.32 (26-1) 355 (entry **477**).

477. U.S. Senate. *Resolutions of the General Assembly of Connecticut, in Favor of the Establishment of a National Foundry within that State.* 26th Cong., 1st Sess. (S.Doc.32). Washington: Blair and Rives, 1840. 2 pg. (Serial Set 355). Same as H.Doc.55 (26-1) 364. See entry **476**.

26TH CONGRESS, 2ND SESSION

478. Huntington, Jabez W. (Conn.). "Pre-emption Law," *Congressional Globe, Appendix.* 26th Cong., 2nd Sess. (7 Jan. 1841) pp. 36-38. Details objections to the proposed preemption bill. Addresses the class and qualifications of the settlers to be encouraged, the acts required of them to receive the land, the limits of the land being offered, the lack of protection against speculators, and the lack of a judicial tribunal. Comparison to the act of 1838.

479. Huntington, Jabez W. (Conn.). "Prospective Pre-emption Bill," *Congressional Globe, Appendix.* 26th Cong., 2nd Sess. (20 Jan. 1841) pp. 193, 194. Presents amendments to protect land with Indian titles, to limit preemption to land actually settled upon, and to establish rights when two or more persons have settled on the same quarter section.

480. Huntington, Jabez W. (Conn.). Speech on Dismissing Blair and Rives as Printers, *Congressional Globe.* 26th Cong., 2nd Sess. (9 Mar. 1841) pp. 243-245. Maintains that the Printer is an officer of the Senate, which makes him subject to removal, and that to dismiss him would not be a breach of contract.

481. Smith, Perry (Conn.). "Pre-emption Bill," *Congressional Globe, Appendix.* 26th Cong., 2nd Sess. (20 Jan. 1841) p. 196. Proclaims the advantages of preemption for society and the settlers.

482. U.S. House. *Letter from the Secretary of State, Transmitting an Abstract of the Returns of the Marshal of Connecticut, Showing the Number of Slaves in Said District, &c. &c.* 26th Cong., 2nd Sess. (H.Doc.90). [Washington: 1841]. 2 pg. (Serial Set 384). Clarifies that the return includes thirty-seven Negroes of the Amistad, a Spanish slave ship.

483. U.S. House. *Resolutions of the Legislature of Connecticut, Relative to the Disposition of the Proceeds of the Public Lands.* 26th Cong., 2nd Sess. (H.Doc.65). [Washington: 1840]. 1 pg. (Serial Set 383). Resolutions support distributing the proceeds of the public lands among the states and oppose any reduction in the prices of the lands.

484. U.S. Senate. [Memorial of Horatio Alden and Philura Alden, his Wife, Late Philura Deane, of Hartford, in Connecticut]. 26th Cong., 2nd Sess. (S.Doc.201). Washington: Blair & Rives, Printers, 1841. 8 pg. (Serial Set 378). Favorable report of the Committee on Revolutionary Claims to allow payment for expenses incurred by Silas Deane while commissioned as ambassador to France. Includes a copy of his contract, instructions, and commission.

27TH CONGRESS, 1ST SESSION

485. Huntington, Jabez W. (Conn.). "The Case of McLeod," *Congressional Globe, Appendix.* 27th Cong., 1st Sess. (11 June 1841) pp. 253-257. Discusses the affair of the Caroline and the individual responsibility of McLeod. Maintains that the affair was an act of the British government, not an obscure individual. Considers the rules of international law; defends the actions of the administration as just and in accordance to the acknowledged principles of international law.

486. Huntington, Jabez W. (Conn.). "Fiscal Bank," *Congressional Globe, Appendix.* 27th Cong., 1st Sess. (3 July 1841) pp. 358-361. Supports the proposed national bank and the right of Congress to establish offices of discount and deposit in the states without their consent. Discusses the authority of Congress to establish these branches, and the expediency of doing so if the authority exists.

487. Smith, Perry (Conn.). "Fiscal Bank," *Congressional Globe, Appendix.* 27th Cong., 1st Sess. (20 July 1841) pp. 239-243. Opposes the bill for a national bank. Responds to resolutions of the Conn. Legislature requesting him to support the bill. Demonstrates that Congress does not have the power to incorporate a bank. Discusses the effect of the bank on the currency, and the power of the government to interfere with the internal affairs of the states.

488. Smith, Perry (Conn.). Remarks on Relief for Mrs. Harrison, *Congressional Globe.* 27th Cong., 1st Sess. (24 June 1841) pp. 107-108. Objects to granting the relief; maintains that it would establish precedence and that others are more in need of this assistance.

489. Trumbull, Joseph (Conn.). "Bankrupt Law," *Congressional Globe.* 27th Cong., 1st Sess. (11 Aug. 1841) pp. 323-324. Opposes the proposed bill. Objects to provisions that include corporations, especially banks, in its scope, and that allow the debtor to control the creditor. Desires conformity with the act of 1800.

490. U.S. House. *Report of a Joint Select Committee of the State of Connecticut upon the Subject of the Public Domain.* 27th Cong., 1st Sess. (H.Doc.26). [Washington: Gales and Seaton, 1841]. 3 pg. (Serial Set 392). Report and resolutions maintain that the public land is the property of all the states, and that the proceeds should be distributed among the states in proportion to their population. Calculates available land. Same as S.doc.39 (27-1) 390 (entry **494**), without a transmittal note.

491. U.S. House. *Resolutions of the Legislature of Alabama, Responding to Resolutions of Connecticut, on the Protective Policy of the United States.* 27th Cong., 1st Sess. (H.Doc.12). [Washington: Gales & Seaton, 1841]. 2 pg. (Serial Set 392). Resolutions oppose the protective tariff that protects one portion of the states at the expense of the other; maintains that it provokes fierce and political animosities between the North and South.

492. U.S. Senate. *Resolutions of the General Assembly of Connecticut, in Favor of the Repeal of the Sub-Treasury Law, and of the Establishment of a National Bank.* 27th Cong., 1st Sess. (S.Doc.42). [Washington]: Thomas Allen, Print., [1841]. 2 pg. (Serial Set 390).

493. U.S. Senate. *Resolutions of the General Assembly of Connecticut, in Favor of the Establishment of a Protective Tariff* 27th Cong., 1st Sess. (S.Doc.40). [Washington]: Thomas Allen, Print., [1841]. 2 pg. (Serial Set 390).

494. U.S. Senate. *Resolutions of the General Assembly of Connecticut, in Relation to the Disposal of the Public Lands.* 27th Cong., 1st Sess. (S.Doc.39). [Washington]: Thomas Allen, Print., [1841]. 3 pg. (Serial Set 390). Same as H.Doc.26 (27-1) 392, with extra transmittal note. See entry **490**.

495. U.S. Senate. *Resolutions of the General Assembly of Connecticut, in Favor of So Amending the Constitution of the United States, As to Restrict the Eligibility of the President of the United States to a Single Term.* 27th Cong., 1st Sess. (S.Doc.41). [Washington: Thomas Allen, Print., 1841]. 1 pg. (Serial Set 390).

27ᵀᴴ CONGRESS, 2ᴺᴰ SESSION

496. Huntington, Jabez W. (Conn.). "The Apportionment Bill," *Congressional Globe.* 27th Cong., 2nd Sess. (25 May 1842) pp. 532-533. Reviews the apportionment bill of 1792; supports the proposed amendment concerning fractions as a principle consonant with previous apportionment legislation.

497. Huntington, Jabez W. (Conn.). "Apportionment Bill," *Congressional Globe, Appendix.* 27th Cong., 2nd Sess. (31 May 1842) pp. 490-493. Supports districting and the advantages of a uniform system; objects to each state regulating whether elections shall be by districts or general election. Discusses the constitutionality and expediency of the measure. Summary of speech in *Congressional Globe*, pp. 555-556.

498. Huntington, Jabez W. (Conn.). "Retrenchment and Reform," *Congressional Globe.* 27th Cong., 2nd Sess. (21 Mar. 1842) p. 341. Supports a protective tariff. Discusses free trade as practiced in England and France; supports the need to adjust the tariff to supply the necessary revenue for the government as well as to protect the industry of the country.

499. Smith, Perry (Conn.). "The Apportionment Bill," *Congressional Globe.* 27th Cong., 2nd Sess. (6 June 1842) p. 584. Remarks against the district system as unconstitutional and a usurpation of the rights of the states.

500. Smith, Perry (Conn.). "Bankrupt Act," *Congressional Globe, Appendix.* 27th Cong., 2nd Sess. (23 Jan. 1842) pp. 146-149. Opposes the bankrupt act and its retrospective operation as unconstitutional. Also maintains that it takes the legal rights of the creditor and bestows them upon the debtor.

501. Smith, Perry (Conn.). "Courts of the United States," *Congressional Globe, Appendix.* 27th Cong., 2nd Sess. (July 1842) pp. 645-647. Opposes the bill that would make foreign governments liable for their soldiers, who, in time of peace, kill a U.S. citizen. The act would encompass the Indian tribes, as well as independent nations. Maintains that it would be unconstitutional, and would give license to foreign soldiers to commit crimes against U.S. citizens.

502. Smith, Perry (Conn.). "Loan Bill," *Congressional Globe, Appendix*. 27th Cong., 2nd Sess. (11 Apr. 1842) pp. 292-296. Opposes the loan bill as a Whig bill designed to enrich one portion of the population and impoverish another. Discusses the public debt and expenses of government in the context of party politics; ascribes the present condition to the mismanagement and poor financial skills of Whig policies.

503. Smith, Perry (Conn.). "The Tariff Bill," *Congressional Globe*. 27th Cong., 2nd Sess. (27 Aug. 1842) pp. 952-953. Opposes the proposed protective tariff.

504. "An Act Explanatory of an Act Entitled, 'An Act to Constitute the Ports of Stonington, Mystic River, and Pawcatuck River, a Collection District'," *Statutes at Large*, Vol. V (16 Aug. 1842) p. 506.

505. "An Act to Authorize the Collector of the District of Fairfield to Reside in either of the Towns of Fairfield or Bridgeport," *Statutes at Large*, Vol. V (4 June 1842) pp. 489-490.

506. "An Act to Constitute the Ports of Stonington, Mystic River, and Pawcatuck River, a Collection District," *Statutes at Large*, Vol. V (3 Aug. 1842) pp. 499-50.

507. U.S. House. *Collector of Bridgeport*. 27th Cong., 2nd Sess. (H.Rpt.687). [Washington: 1842]. 1 pg. (Serial Set 409). Report supports allowing the collector of the district of Fairfield to reside in either Fairfield or Bridgeport.

508. U.S. House. *Monument to Captain Nathan Hale*. 27th Cong., 2nd Sess. (H.Rpt.783). [Washington: Thomas Allen, Print., 1842]. 2 pg. (Serial Set 410). Report of the Select Committee supports erecting a monument to honor Captain Nathan Hale; reviews his military career.

509. U.S. Senate. *Resolutions of the General Assembly of Connecticut, in Favor of the Repeal of the "Act to Appropriate the Proceeds of the Sales of the Public Lands, and to Grant Pre-emption Rights."* 27th Cong., 2nd Sess. (S.Doc.360). [Washington]: Thomas Allen, Print., [1842]. 2 pg. (Serial Set 399). Resolutions oppose the act as unconstitutional and of injurious tendency.

510. U.S. Senate. *Resolutions of the General Assembly of Connecticut, in Favor of the Repeal of the Bankrupt Law*. 27th Cong., 2nd Sess. (S.Doc.361). [Washington: Thomas Allen, Print., 1842]. 1 pg. (Serial Set 399).

511. U.S. Senate. *Resolutions of the General Assembly of Connecticut, in Favor of Abolishing the Military Academy at West Point*. 27th Cong., 2nd Sess. (S.Doc.363). [Washington]: Thomas Allen, Print., [1842]. 1 pg. (Serial Set 399).

512. U.S. Senate. *Resolutions of the General Assembly of Connecticut, in Favor of a Discriminating Tariff, and of Abolishing the Credit System*. 27th

Cong., 2nd Sess. (S.Doc.362). [Washington]: Thomas Allen, Print., [1842]. 2 pg. (Serial Set 399). Resolutions concerning the Compromise Act.

27ᵀᴴ CONGRESS, 3ᴿᴰ SESSION

513. Huntington, Jabez W. (Conn.). "Oregon Territory," *Congressional Globe.* 27th Cong., 3rd Sess. (24 Jan. 1843) p. 194. Contends that granting titles to land within the territory would be a violation of the stipulations of the treaty of 1818.

514. Smith, Perry (Conn.). "Fine on General Jackson," *Congressional Globe, Appendix.* 27th Cong., 3rd Sess. (20 Feb. 1843) pp. 220-222. Supports restoring the fine imposed on Jackson for an alleged contempt of court. Describes the necessity and propriety of Jackson's actions at New Orleans.

515. "An Act Altering the Times of Holding the Circuit Court of the United States for the District of Connecticut," *Statutes at Large*, Vol. V (24 Feb. 1843) p. 601.

516. U.S. House. *Wharf for the Custom-House, New London.* 27th Cong., 3rd Sess. (H.Rpt.214). [Washington: 1843]. 1 pg. (Serial Set 427). Report of the Committee on Commerce supports appropriations to build the wharf.

517. U.S. Senate. *Resolutions of the General Assembly of Connecticut, in Favor of Refunding to General Andrew Jackson, without Qualification, the Amount of a Fine Imposed on Him at New Orleans, in 1815.* 27th Cong., 3rd Sess. (S.Doc.24). [Washington: Thomas Allen, Print., 1843]. 1 pg. (Serial Set 414).

518. U.S. Senate. *Resolutions of the General Assembly of Connecticut, to Obtain Some Provision for Drilling and Disciplining the Officers of the Militia.* 27th Cong., 3rd Sess. (S.Doc.25). [Washington: Thomas Allen, Print., 1843]. 1 pg. (Serial Set 414).

519. U.S. Senate. *Resolutions of the General Assembly of Connecticut, in Favor of the Repeal of That Proviso in the Law for the Apportionment of Representatives Among the Several States According to the Sixth Census, Which Directs that the States Shall be Divided into Districts.* 27th Cong., 3rd Sess. (S.Doc.23). [Washington]: Thomas Allen, Print., [1843]. 3 pg. (Serial Set 414). Resolutions object on the grounds that the proviso is unconstitutional and a violation of the states' primary jurisdiction over elections.

28ᵀᴴ CONGRESS, 1ˢᵀ SESSION

520. Debate on the Qualifications of John Niles, *Congressional Globe.* 28th Cong., 1st Sess. (30 Apr. 1844) pp. 592-594. Debate on the proper means to ascertain that senator-elect John M. Niles (Conn.) is mentally competent to take his seat. Resolution passed for a select committee to inquire into his mental capacity. Discussion centers on the issues of constitutionality and precedence. Includes remarks from John Fairfield (Maine).

521. "Hon. John M. Niles," *Congressional Globe.* 28th Cong., 1st Sess. (16 May 1844) p. 636. Favorable report of the select committee inquiring into the mental capacity of John M. Niles (Conn.) that he be permitted to take his seat in the Senate.

522. Catlin, George S. (Conn.). "Report of the Committee of Elections," *Congressional Globe, Appendix.* 28th Cong., 1st Sess. (10 Feb. 1844) pp. 164-167. Supports the legality of the general ticket elections held in New Hampshire, Georgia, Mississippi, and Missouri. Maintains that it is unconstitutional and a violation of states' rights to mandate the district system. Summary of speech in *Congressional Globe*, pp. 263-265.

523. Huntington, Jabez W. (Conn.). "The Tariff," *Congressional Globe, Appendix.* 28th Cong., 1st Sess. (12 Feb, 13 Feb. 1844) pp. 737-741. Supports the protective tariff of 1842. Addresses the many objections of Senator Woodbury, N.H. Senator Huntington maintains that the tariff act of 1842 was a revenue act, which benefited the entire country, not just a very small class. Discusses the benefits of the 1842 tariff, the constitutional authority for protectionism, and the free trade policies of foreign governments. Summary of speech in *Congressional Globe*, pp. 269-270, 275-276.

524. Seymour, Thomas H. (Conn.). "Military Academy," *Congressional Globe.* 28th Cong., 1st Sess. (12 Mar. 1844) pp. 382-383. Opposes continuing appropriations for the academy. Maintains that the academy is unnecessary, prohibits a republican army, and has become an institution educating men for the pursuits of civil rather than military life.

525. Simons, Samuel (Conn.). "Committee on Maps and Charts," *Congressional Globe, Appendix.* 28th Cong., 1st Sess. (16 Mar. 1844) pp. 236-237. Supports appointing a standing committee of the House to superintend the printing and engraving of maps and charts. Discusses the frauds and abuses of the past.

526. Simons, Samuel (Conn.). "Insane Asylum," *Congressional Globe.* 28th Cong., 1st Sess. (11 May 1844) pp. 623-624. Opposes the bill providing for an insane asylum in the District of Columbia as completely inadequate and outmoded.

527. U.S. House. *Resolutions of the Legislature of Connecticut, Recommending Modifications of the Tariff Act of the Last Congress.* 28th Cong., 1st Sess. (H.Doc.32). [Washington]: Blair & Rives, Printers, [1843]. 2 pg. (Serial Set 441). Resolutions declare the last tariff act unequal and unjust;

request a tariff act which, when combined with other revenue, would meet the expenses of the government while showing no favoritism.

528. U.S. House. *Resolutions of the Legislature of Connecticut, Relating to French Spoliations Prior to the Year 1800.* 28th Cong., 1st Sess. (H.Doc.28). [Washington]: Blair & Rives, Print., [1843]. 2 pg. (Serial Set 441). Resolutions support the government's obligation to meet the claims.

529. U.S. Senate. *Memorial of a Number of Citizens of Connecticut, Praying the Ratification of a Treaty of Commerce and Navigation Between the United States and the Republic of Texas.* 28th Cong., 1st Sess. (S.Doc.177). Washington: Gales and Seaton, 1844. 2 pg. (Serial Set 434). Memorial lists advantages of commercial relations and mutual reciprocity; includes names of memorialists.

530. U.S. Senate. *Resolutions of the General Assembly of Connecticut, in Relation to an Adjustment of the Claims for Indemnity for French Spoliations Committed Prior to 1800.* 28th Cong., 1st Sess. (S.Doc.403). Washington: Gales and Seaton, 1844. 2 pg. (Serial Set 437). Report and resolutions support the claims; summarize the circumstances connected with the French spoliations. Same as H.doc.4 (28-2) 463 (entry **539**).

531. U.S. Senate. *Resolutions of the General Assembly of Connecticut, Adverse to the Annexation of Texas to the United States.* 28th Cong., 1st Sess. (S.Doc.402). Washington: Gales and Seaton, 1844. 1 pg. (Serial Set 437). Resolutions opposed to annexation as unconstitutional, a violation of the treaty with Mexico, and a stretch of executive privilege.

532. U.S. Senate. *Resolutions of the General Assembly of Connecticut, in Favor of the Establishment of a Protective Tariff, and of the Division of the Proceeds of the Sales of the Public Lands Among the States.* 28th Cong., 1st Sess. (S.Doc.404). Washington: Gales and Seaton, 1844. 1 pg. (Serial Set 437). Same as H.doc.3 (28-2) 463 (entry **538**).

28TH CONGRESS, 2ND SESSION

533. Huntington, Jabez W. (Conn.). "Annexation of Texas," *Congressional Globe, Appendix.* 28th Cong., 2nd Sess. (21 Feb., 22 Feb. 1845) pp. 397-402. Objects to the annexation of Texas. Maintains that it is unconstitutional to admit independent foreign governments into the Union, and that if it were, the territory should be acquired through the treaty-making power and then admitted as a state. Regardless of above issues, maintains that it would be inexpedient to annex Texas. Discusses the need for the additional territory and the issue of slavery in the territory.

534. Niles, John M. (Conn.). "Cumberland Road," *Congressional Globe.* 28th Cong., 2nd Sess. (22 Jan. 1845) pp. 171-172. Opposes appropriations to continue the road; maintains that it is a local road and that appropriations for internal improvements are unconstitutional.

535. Niles, John M. (Conn.). "Deposites of the Public Moneys," *Congressional Globe.* 28th Cong., 2nd Sess. (18 Dec. 1844) pp. 43-44. Supports requesting information from the Secretary of the Treasury on the public deposits.

536. Niles, John M. (Conn.). "Post Office Bill," *Congressional Globe, Appendix.* 28th Cong., 2nd Sess. (16 Jan. 1845) pp. 209-212. Supports the bill to reduce postage rates. Maintains that substantially decreased rates will increase the volume of mail, and thus increase revenue. Discusses similar system in England.

537. Simons, Samuel (Conn.). "Map of the United States," *Congressional Globe* 28th Cong., 2nd Sess. (30 Dec. 1844) p. 74. Supports the committee appointed to review maps and charts.

538. U.S. House. *Resolutions of the General Assembly of Connecticut, Relative to the Tariff.* 28th Cong., 2nd Sess. (H.Doc.3). [Washington]: Blair & Rives, Print., [1844]. 1 pg. (Serial Set 463). Resolutions support a protective tariff and dividing the proceeds from the public lands among the states. Same as S.doc.404 (28-1) 437 (entry **532**).

539. U.S. House. *Resolutions of the General Assembly of Connecticut, Relative to French Spoliations.* 28th Cong., 2nd Sess. (H.Doc.4). [Washington]: Blair & Rives, Print., [1844]. 2 pg. (Serial Set 463). Report and resolutions support the claims for indemnity for French spoliations committed prior to 1800; summarize the circumstances. Same as S.doc.403 (28-1) 437 (entry **530**).

29TH CONGRESS, 1ST SESSION

540. Dixon, James (Conn.). "Naturalization Laws," *Congressional Globe, Appendix.* 29th Cong., 1st Sess. (30 Dec. 1845) pp. 68-71. Opposes the proposed changes in the naturalization laws to extend the period of probation for foreigners and to prohibit foreigners from holding office under this government. Discusses the origin and history of the Native American Party. Summary of speech in *Congressional Globe*, pp. 116-117.

541. Dixon, James (Conn.). "Senator Webster," *Congressional Globe.* 29th Cong., 1st Sess. (10 Apr. 1846) pp. 649, 650. Supports allowing Mr. Webster to refute the charges against him as Secretary of State.

542. Dixon, James (Conn.). "The Tariff," *Congressional Globe, Appendix.* 29th Cong., 1st Sess. (30 June 1846) pp. 1061-1066. Supports the protective tariff of 1842 and its resultant prosperity. Includes detailed discussion of protectionism and its history. Maintains that the proposed reduction of tariffs would reduce revenue in the midst of a war. Demonstrates the beneficial effect of protectionism on wages.

543. Huntington, Jabez W. (Conn.). "Admission of Texas," *Congressional Globe.* 29th Cong., 1st Sess. (22 Dec. 1845) pp. 89-91. Opposes the admission of Texas on the basis of constitutionality and expediency. Maintains that the Connecticut resolutions on the topic represent the true sentiments of his constituents. Major objections to the admission are due to the procedure followed and the slavery provisions in the Texas Constitution.

544. Huntington, Jabez W. (Conn.). "Custom-House Officers," *Congressional Globe.* 29th Cong., 1st Sess. (5 Feb. 1846) p. 311. Supports the proposed changes in the compensation of customhouse officers.

545. Huntington, Jabez W. (Conn.). "Oregon Question," *Congressional Globe, Appendix.* 29th Cong., 1st Sess. (13 Apr. 1846) pp. 627-633. Discusses the annulment of the convention with Great Britain. Supports giving notice only if it is accompanied by the expressed desire of a just and amicable adjustment of the question. Considers the question of title and past arbitration efforts. Summary of speech in *Congressional Globe*, p. 660.

546. Huntington, Jabez W. (Conn.). "The Tariff Bill," *Congressional Globe.* 29th Cong., 1st Sess. (28 July 1846) pp. 1150-1151, 1158. Objects to the request of the Committee of Finance to be discharged from reporting back the amendments requested by the Senate, concerning graduating the tariff bill with reference to the tariff of 1842.

547. Huntington, Jabez W. (Conn.). "The Tariff," *Congressional Globe, Appendix.* 29th Cong., 1st Sess. (21 July 1846) pp. 1129-1130. Presents a memorial from New England manufacturers and dealers in paper, objecting to the proposed reduction of duties on paper and books. Gives overview of the paper industry, and the reasons opposed to reducing duties.

548. Huntington, Jabez W. (Conn.). "Texan Navy," *Congressional Globe.* 29th Cong., 1st Sess. (16 July 1846) pp. 1104-1105. Opposes incorporating the late Texan navy into the United States navy; maintains that it would interfere with the promotion of the officers.

549. Huntington, Jabez W. (Conn.). "The Warehouse Bill," *Congressional Globe.* 29th Cong., 1st Sess. (30 June 1846) pp. 1041-1042. Objects to the proposed warehouse system. Maintains that it would abolish the cash system and introduce an unjust credit system, reduce the revenue, and encourage excessive importation.

550. Niles, John M. (Conn.). "Admission of Texas," *Congressional Globe.* 29th Cong., 1st Sess. (22 Dec. 1845) p. 89. Supports admitting Texas into the Union; justifies his position, which is contrary to the resolutions of the Connecticut legislature.

551. Niles, John M. (Conn.). "Michigan Land Bill," *Congressional Globe.* 29th Cong., 1st Sess. (29 Apr. 1846) pp. 742-743. Opposes granting public land to Michigan to complete some roads and other projects of internal improvement.

552. Niles, John M. (Conn.). "National Defence," *Congressional Globe.* 29th Cong., 1st Sess. (16 Dec. 1845) pp. 54-55. Supports giving notification to Great Britain concerning the Oregon convention. Maintains that negotiation has failed, that the U.S. should extend its jurisdiction over its citizens in Oregon, and that the country should be preparing for the possibility of war.

553. Niles, John M. (Conn.). "The Oregon Question," *Congressional Globe, Appendix.* 29th Cong., 1st Sess. (19 Mar. 1846) pp. 552-556. Supports terminating the convention with Great Britain as the best means of bringing about a peaceful adjustment. Discusses the historical position of the government and the comparative claims of title. Summary of speech in *Congressional Globe,* pp. 526-527.

554. Niles, John M. (Conn.). "Post Office Appropriations," *Congressional Globe.* 29th Cong., 1st Sess. (7 June 1846) p. 943. Supports appropriations for steam mail service to Liverpool, England and Bremen.

555. Niles, John M. (Conn.). "Report of Commissioner of Patents," *Congressional Globe.* 29th Cong., 1st Sess. (18 Mar. 1846) pp. 519-520. Opposes increased expenditures of the Patent Office on agricultural statistics; maintains that its proceedings were without legal authority.

556. Niles, John M. (Conn.). "Steam Mail Transportation," *Congressional Globe, Appendix.* 29th Cong., 1st Sess. (15 June 1846) pp. 984-987. Supports the postal law passed last session reducing the postage rates. Presents and supports an amendment for appropriations for steam mail to Liverpool and to Cowes and Bremen; discusses commercial and military advantages.

557. Niles, John M. (Conn.). "The Tariff," *Congressional Globe.* 29th Cong., 1st Sess. (6 July 1846) pp. 1056-1057. Objects to the proposed reduction of the tariff; maintains that it discriminates against protection, will exhaust the treasury, and will discredit the government.

558. Niles, John M. (Conn.). "The Tariff," *Congressional Globe, Appendix.* 29th Cong., 1st Sess. (20 July 1846) pp. 881-890. Opposes the bill to reduce the tariff. Maintains that the bill is based upon unqualified free trade and the repudiation of the entire protective policy; discusses its general principles and details. Contends that it is a measure designed to favor the slave labor of the South, diverting industry to the cultivation of the soil. Discusses the bill's potential as a revenue measure, and its political aspects.

559. Niles, John M. (Conn.). "The Tariff," *Congressional Globe, Appendix.* 29th Cong., 1st Sess. (28 July 1846) pp. 890-891. Supports his motion to postpone further consideration of the tariff bill so that it might go before their constituents for consideration. Summary of speech in *Congressional Globe*, pp. 1156-1157.

560. Rockwell, John A. (Conn.). "Connecticut Resolutions," *Congressional Globe, Appendix.* 29th Cong., 1st Sess. (15 Dec. 1845) pp. 59-61. Protests the refusal of the House to print or refer to Committee resolutions from the Legislature of Connecticut against the admission of Texas into the Union. Discusses the resolutions and their concerns of constitutionality and slavery. Speech summarized in *Congressional Globe*, pp. 51-52.

561. Rockwell, John A. (Conn.). "Harbors and Rivers," *Congressional Globe.* 29th Cong., 1st Sess. (12 Mar. 1846) p. 495. Remarks on the topic of internal improvements, and the false distinction between improvements for harbors on the seaboard from harbors on rivers and lakes.

562. Rockwell, John A. (Conn.). "Oregon Question," *Congressional Globe, Appendix.* 29th Cong., 1st Sess. (16 Jan. 1846) pp. 126-131. Opposes the resolution to annul the convention with Great Britain; maintains that it would impede negotiation and lead towards war. Reviews the laws of Great Britain in relation to the territory, the proposed legislation of Congress, and the operations of the laws. Discusses the Hudson Bay Company. Introduces a resolution to authorize the Executive to give notice with a view to renewing negotiations. Appendix to speech includes brief statistics on the whaling industry and the text of the British Oregon Law. Brief summary of speech in the *Congressional Globe*, pp. 213-214.

563. Rockwell, John A. (Conn.). "The Tariff," *Congressional Globe, Appendix.* 29th Cong., 1st Sess. (n.d.) pp. 743-744. Excerpt from a speech maintaining that manufacturers have not, as a class, benefited by the protective policy. Discusses the fate of the cotton and woolen goods factories in Connecticut.

564. Rockwell, John A. (Conn.). "The Tariff," *Congressional Globe.* 29th Cong., 1st Sess. (26 June 1846) pp. 1034-1037. Opposes the proposed tariff changes; refutes the report of the Secretary of the Treasury and the reasons given to overturn the protective system. Demonstrates that protection has encouraged mechanical, rather than manufacturing industries, that the labor of the country has greatly benefited, and that the public at large, regardless of class or geography, has benefited by the protective policy.

565. Smith, Truman (Conn.). "Oregon Question," *Congressional Globe, Appendix.* 29th Cong., 1st Sess. (7 Feb. 1846) pp. 256-261. Discusses the notification of Great Britain of the annulment of the convention of 1827. Supports a qualified notice or modification that would allow for a just and equitable compromise. Discusses the history and character of the negotiations and the question of title. Summary of speech in *Congressional Globe*, p. 331.

566. U.S. House. *Resolutions of the Legislature of Connecticut, Relative to the State of Rhode Island.* 29th Cong., 1st Sess. (H.Doc.22). [Washington: Ritchie & Heiss, Printers, 1845]. 1 pg. (Serial Set 482). Resolutions support the actions of Rhode Island and object to the interference of other states in the exercise of her constitutional jurisdiction.

567. U.S. House. *Resolutions of the Legislature of Connecticut, Relative to the Distribution of the Decisions of the Supreme Court of the United States.* 29th Cong., 1st Sess. (H.Doc.23). [Washington: Ritchie & Heiss, Printers, 1845]. 1 pg. (Serial Set 482). Resolutions maintain that it is the duty of Congress to distribute the decisions.

568. U.S. House. *Resolutions of the Legislature of Connecticut, Relative to the Admission of New States into the Union, &c., &c.* 29th Cong., 1st Sess. (H.Doc.32). [Washington: Ritchie & Heiss, Printers, 1845]. 1 pg. (Serial Set 482). Resolutions maintain that Congress cannot admit new states not formed from the original territory, and that the annexation of a slaveholding territory is unconstitutional, a dangerous precedent, and destructive to the Union.

29TH CONGRESS, 2ND SESSION

569. Dixon, James (Conn.). "Extension of Slave Territory," *Congressional Globe, Appendix.* 29th Cong., 2nd Sess. (9 Feb. 1847) pp. 332-335. Opposes the extension of slavery into any territory acquired from Mexico. Discusses the origin of the Mexican War and its roots in the desire to perpetuate slavery by the annexation of Texas. Suggests that no territory be acquired while the North and South are so divided on this issue.

570. Huntington, Jabez W. (Conn.). "Army Bill," *Congressional Globe.* 29th Cong., 2nd Sess. (1 Feb. 1847) pp. 301-302. Opposes several provisos of the bill. Objects to the proposed appointment of officers of the volunteer forces by soldiers, and the proposed bounties that would create a debt that was indefinite in amount and duration.

571. Huntington, Jabez W. (Conn.). "Increase of the Army," *Congressional Globe.* 29th Cong., 2nd Sess. (22 Jan. 1847) p. 237. Opposes raising regiments of regular troops as unnecessary and a dangerous increase of the executive power; supports using a volunteer force.

572. Huntington, Jabez W. (Conn.). "Independent Treasury," *Congressional Globe.* 29th Cong., 2nd Sess. (21 Jan. 1847) pp. 219-220. Briefly remarks on the operations of the Independent Treasury.

573. Huntington, Jabez W. (Conn.). "The Loan Bill," *Congressional Globe.* 29th Cong., 2nd Sess. (25 Jan. 1847) pp. 250-251. Objects to the loan bill and the issue of Treasury notes; maintains that the loan could not be obtained under this bill.

574. Huntington, Jabez W. (Conn.). "Military Bill and Bounty Lands," *Congressional Globe*. 29th Cong., 2nd Sess. (13 Jan. 1847) p. 208. Supports removing any limitations on the grant of bounty lands to be used as an inducement to enlist.

575. Huntington, Jabez W. (Conn.). "Question of Privilege," *Congressional Globe*. 29th Cong., 2nd Sess. (13 Feb. 1847) p. 413. Supports the resolution to expel Mr. Ritchie for abusing the courtesy of the Senate by his misconduct and libelous activities.

576. Huntington, Jabez W. (Conn.). "The Ten Regiment Bill," *Congressional Globe*. 29th Cong., 2nd Sess. (8 Feb. 1847) pp. 347-348. Objects to the provision in the bill allowing the President to appoint officers when the Senate is in recess as unnecessary and inexpedient. Discusses the constitutional authority for the appointment of officers.

577. Niles, John M. (Conn.). "Memorial of the Society of Friends," *Congressional Globe*. 29th Cong., 2nd Sess. (23 Dec. 1846) pp. 70-71. Supports printing the petition of the Society of Friends for New England asking for the termination of the Mexican War.

578. Niles, John M. (Conn.). "War Steamers," *Congressional Globe*. 29th Cong., 2nd Sess. (15 Feb. 1847) p. 423. Opposes appropriations to enlarge the navy with steamers; contends that they are unnecessary for the war. Advocates the encouragement of private steamers.

579. Niles, John M. (Conn.). "Army Bill," *Congressional Globe*. 29th Cong., 2nd Sess. (20 Jan. 1847) p. 215. Opposes offering grants of the public land to induce enlistments; maintains that it is an unequal means of compensation.

580. Niles, John M. (Conn.). Remarks on Relief for Ireland, *Congressional Globe*. 29th Cong., 2nd Sess. (26 Feb. 1847) pp. 513-514. Opposes offering relief as an improper use of the public money; maintains that it would establish precedent, and that it is Great Britain's responsibility to provide relief for her own people.

581. Niles, John M. (Conn.). "The Tariff," *Congressional Globe*. 29th Cong., 2nd Sess. (7 Jan. 1847) pp. 129-130. Questions the wisdom of the last tariff act, which reduced income to a level inadequate to the demands of peace let alone those of war. Opposes providing for additional revenue exclusively by loans; recommends higher duties to meet the needs of war.

582. Niles, John M. (Conn.). "The Three Million Bill," *Congressional Globe*. 29th Cong., 2nd Sess. (27 Feb. 1847) pp. 529-533. Discusses the Mexican War - its origin, objects, and consequences. Addresses the likely acquisition of territory as a consequence of ending the war, and the question of slavery in the territory.

583. Rockwell, John A. (Conn.). "The Spirit Ration in The Navy," *Congressional Globe, Appendix.* 29th Cong., 2nd Sess. (27 Jan. 1847) pp. 262-266. Supports abolishing the spirit ration from the navy. Maintains that it is unnecessary and injurious. Supports his position with extensive documentation. Summary of speech in *Congressional Globe*, p. 274.

30TH CONGRESS, 1ST SESSION

584. Baldwin, Roger S. (Conn.). "The French Revolution," *Congressional Globe, Appendix.* 30th Cong., 1st Sess. (31 Mar. 1848) pp. 453-454. Opposes the resolution of congratulation to the French people; maintains that Congress would be interfering with the duties of the Executive in regard to foreign intercourse and that Congress is not authorized to speak for the American people in this matter.

585. Baldwin, Roger S. (Conn.). "Public Domain in Mexico," *Congressional Globe.* 30th Cong., 1st Sess. (24 Jan. 1848) pp. 231, 232-233. Supports the request to disclose information concerning the extent and value of the public domain in Mexico that can be ceded to the United States. Maintains that Mexico, like the United States, does not have the power to cede any portion of her territory without the consent of the people of that territory.

586. Baldwin, Roger S. (Conn.). "Territorial Government of Oregon," *Congressional Globe, Appendix.* 30th Cong., 1st Sess. (3 June 1848) pp. 702-705. Advocates the adoption of a territorial government and recognition of legislation enacted by the provisional government of Oregon prohibiting slavery in the territory. Discusses the power of Congress to legislate on slavery in the territories and the concept of slaves as property.

587. Baldwin, Roger S. (Conn.). "Territorial Government of Oregon," *Congressional Globe, Appendix.* 30th Cong., 1st Sess. (26 July 1848) pp. 1194-1195. Objects to including Oregon in the same bill for territorial organization as that of New Mexico and California. Supports Congress legislating the prohibition of slavery in the territories rather than conferring that authority on the territorial legislatures.

588. Baldwin, Roger S. (Conn.). "The War with Mexico," *Congressional Globe, Appendix.* 30th Cong., 1st Sess. (15 Mar. 1848) pp. 418-421. Opposes increasing the army in Mexico as the war is over. Objects to acquiring territory from Mexico that she does not have the right to cede, and that the U.S. does not have the right to acquire. Addresses the causes of the war and the boundary of western Texas. Summary of speech in *Congressional Globe*, pp. 468-469.

589. Dickinson, Rodolphus (Ohio). "Harbors and Rivers," *Congressional Globe, Appendix.* 30th Cong., 1st Sess. (8 Aug. 1848) pp. 1120-1122. Compares the Whig party of 1848 with the Federal party of 1812. Page 1121 contains excerpts from the Hartford Convention concerning the extension of slavery, admission of new states into the Union, and the naturalization of emigrants.

590. Dixon, James (Conn.). "The Mexican War," *Congressional Globe, Appendix.* 30th Cong., 1st Sess. (24 Jan. 1848) pp. 164-172. Demonstrates that the President of the United States unnecessarily and unconstitutionally began the war with Mexico. Maintains that the territory defended as U.S. territory was in reality Mexican soil and was never a part of Texas. Discusses the annexation of Texas and the western boundary issue. Summary of speech in *Congressional Globe,* pp. 227-230.

591. Niles, John M. (Conn.). "Annexation of Territory," *Congressional Globe.* 30th Cong., 1st Sess. (20 Dec. 1847) p. 55. Remarks on concluding the war and the annexation of territory from Mexico.

592. Niles, John M. (Conn.). "The Late Senator Huntington," *Congressional Globe.* 30th Cong., 1st Sess. (9 Dec. 1847) p. 15. Death announcement and eulogy of Senator Jabez W. Huntington (Conn.).

593. Niles, John M. (Conn.). "The Loan Bill," *Congressional Globe, Appendix.* 30th Cong., 1st Sess. (27 Mar. 1848) pp. 472-476, 477. Supports a direct loan instead of Treasury notes, and taxation instead of loans. Maintains that the finances are now in a sound condition as a result of the Independent Treasury. Discusses the finances of the country, past, present and future. Contends that the loan bill is inadequate to the needs of the Treasury due to a decline in revenue from exports. Summary of speech in *Congressional Globe,* p. 541.

594. Niles, John M. (Conn.). "Mexican Spoliations," *Congressional Globe.* 30th Cong., 1st Sess. (2 Feb. 1848) pp. 291-292. Supports the memorial of Philo B. Johnson, a Connecticut native who suffered personal and financial injustices when his vessel was seized.

595. Niles, John M. (Conn.). "The Mexican War," *Congressional Globe, Appendix.* 30th Cong., 1st Sess. (9 Feb. 1848) pp. 278-285. Supports resolving the war. Discusses the different views of the political parties with historical comparisons. Supports claiming Texas up to the Rio Grande, accepting New Mexico and California as indemnity, and withdrawing troops from other territory. Denounces the annexation of Mexico, giving cultural, political, legal and military reasons. Summary of speech in *Congressional Globe,* pp. 328-329.

596. Niles, John M. (Conn.). "Petitions and Memorials," *Congressional Globe.* 30th Cong., 1st Sess. (19 Jan. 1848) pp. 208-209. Supports the petition of Major Charles Larabee, a Connecticut citizen, concerning his pension.

597. Niles, John M. (Conn.). "Public Lands to Illinois," *Congressional Globe, Appendix.* 30th Cong., 1st Sess. (3 May 1848) pp. 534-535, 535-536, 537.

Objects to granting public lands to Illinois to make a railroad as unconstitutional and unjust; gives historical context of similar requests for internal improvement.

598. Niles, John M. (Conn.). "Reduction of Postage," *Congressional Globe, Appendix.* 30th Cong., 1st Sess. (21 June 1848) pp. 705-706. Supports the reduction of the postage. Discusses the success of a similar proposal in England, and the financial benefits to be obtained. Summary of speech in *Congressional Globe*, p. 862.

599. Niles, John M. (Conn.). Remarks on Resolutions of Connecticut Opposed to Slavery in the Territories, *Congressional Globe.* 30th Cong., 1st Sess. (20 Dec. 1847) pp. 51-52. Remarks on the resolutions. Niles maintains that Congress should not legislate on slavery in the territories - it should be left voluntary.

600. Niles, John M. (Conn.). Remarks on the Late Senator Fairfield, *Congressional Globe.* 30th Cong., 1st Sess. (27 Dec. 1847) p. 70. Remarks upon the life and character of the Hon. John Fairfield, Senator from Maine.

601. Niles, John M. (Conn.). "Temporary Occupation of Yucatan," *Congressional Globe, Appendix.* 30th Cong., 1st Sess. (9 May, 17 May 1848) pp. 608-613, 641-642. Opposes temporary military occupation of Yucatan to assist the white population in their war against the Indians. Maintains that the U.S. does not have the right to interfere in the domestic concerns of a foreign state or province, particularly as Mexico still claims jurisdiction over Yucatan. Discusses the Monroe doctrine and other doctrines governing foreign policy. Addresses the expediency, advantages, and consequences of the measure.

602. Niles, John M. (Conn.). "Territorial Government of Oregon," *Congressional Globe, Appendix.* 30th Cong., 1st Sess. (2 June 1848) pp. 696-699. Supports Congress prohibiting slavery in the territorial government. Maintains that the rights of property are state rights, created by state laws; discusses the concept of slaves as property. Supports retaining existing law and conditions as the basis of the legislation of the new territory. Summary of speech in *Congressional Globe*, pp. 811-812.

603. Niles, John M. (Conn.). "Territorial Government of Oregon," *Congressional Globe, Appendix.* 30th Cong., 1st Sess. (22 July 1848) pp. 1141, 1142. Advocates settling the slavery issue now. Maintains that leaving the door open to slavery would just create more problems later.

604. Niles, John M. (Conn.). "Territorial Government of Oregon," *Congressional Globe, Appendix.* 30th Cong., 1st Sess. (26 July 1848) pp. 1195-1201. Opposes admitting slavery into the territories, specifically Calif., N.M., and Oregon. Maintains that Congress should use its constitutional authority to decide the issue by passing a direct act to prohibit slavery. Reviews the history of slavery and its extension; examines the reasons for and against its extension; addresses the condition of slavery in the U.S. and the sectional issues involved.

605. Rockwell, John A. (Conn.). "The Amistad Case," *Congressional Globe, Appendix.* 30th Cong., 1st Sess. (8 Aug. 1848) pp. 1126-1130. Objects to the President's support of the claim of the Spanish government for reimbursement for the Negroes on board the Amistad, a Spanish slave ship. Reviews the history of the case and previous claims from the Spanish government; maintains that the claim was settled by the courts. Appendix includes relevant correspondence.

606. Rockwell, John A. (Conn.). "Deficient Appropriations," *Congressional Globe.* 30th Cong., 1st Sess. (1 Mar. 1848) pp. 404-407. Demonstrates the inaccuracies of the report of the Secretary of the Treasury on the public finances; maintains that the Secretary of the Treasury is incompetent to fill his position. Discusses the actual and estimated expenditures and revenues of the government.

607. Rockwell, John A. (Conn.). "Internal Improvements," *Congressional Globe, Appendix.* 30th Cong., 1st Sess. (11 Jan. 1848) pp. 104-107. Disproves statements in the President's message on the origin and history of the system of internal improvements. Using documentary evidence, analyzes internal improvement appropriations of different administrations; compares appropriations apportioned to the different sections of the country. Summary of speech in *Congressional Globe*, pp. 145-146.

608. Rockwell, John A. (Conn.). "The National Finances," *Congressional Globe, Appendix.* 30th Cong., 1st Sess. (27 June 1848) pp. 830-832. Responds to the report of the Committee on Public Expenditures on the report of the Secretary of the Treasury. Discusses continued inaccuracies. Proposes an official examination into the condition of the Treasury Department.

609. Rockwell, John A. (Conn.). "Obituary," *Congressional Globe.* 30th Cong., 1st Sess. (13 Dec. 1847) p. 20. Death announcement and eulogy of Senator Jabez W. Huntington (Conn.).

610. Rockwell, John A. (Conn.). "Revolutionary and Other Pensions," *Congressional Globe.* 30th Cong., 1st Sess. (11 May 1848) pp. 755-759. Demonstrates again the inaccuracies and inconsistencies of the report of the Secretary of the Treasury; addresses responses since he first brought this to the public's attention.

611. Smith, Truman (Conn.). "The Mexican War," *Congressional Globe, Appendix.* 30th Cong., 1st Sess. (2 Mar. 1848) pp. 383-393. Opposes the acquisition of the Mexican territory. Discusses the objects and purposes of the war with Mexico, the proposed treaty, and the moral and political considerations. Describes the character and resources of the territory to be annexed, with documentation from exploring expeditions. Summary of speech in *Congressional Globe*, pp. 415-417.

612. Smith, Truman (Conn.). "Rules of the House," *Congressional Globe*. 30th Cong., 1st Sess. (18 Dec. 1847) pp. 4-5. Remarks on the one-hour rule.

613. U.S. Senate. [Report of the Memorial of the Hartford Argillo Manufacturing Company]. 30th Cong., 1st Sess. (S.Rpt.224). Washington: Wendell and Van Benthuysen, 1848. 6 pg. (Serial Set 512). Report recommends "argillo" as a substitute for marble in public buildings; maintains that the variety of hue, coloring, brilliancy and luster are superior to marble. Includes report of the tests performed to ascertain its durability and general fitness for practical use.

614. U.S. Senate. *Resolutions of the Legislature of Connecticut, in Favor of a Railroad from Lake Michigan to the Pacific, on the Plan Proposed by Mr. Whitney*. 30th Cong., 1st Sess. (S.Mis.Doc.18). Washington: Tippin & Streeper, 1847. 2 pg. (Serial Set 511).

615. U.S. Senate. *Resolutions of the Legislature of Connecticut, in Relation to Slavery*. 30th Cong., 1st Sess. (S.Mis.Doc.15). Washington: Tippin & Streeper, 1848. 2 pg. (Serial Set 511). Resolutions ask that a provision excluding slavery be required for any future territory acquired or annexed by the United States.

30TH CONGRESS, 2ND SESSION

616. Baldwin, Roger S. (Conn.). "Law for California," *Congressional Globe*. 30th Cong., 2nd Sess. (1 Mar. 1849) pp. 629, 630-631. Supports his proposed amendment to extend the right of trial by jury and the writ of habeas corpus to the territories of New Mexico and California.

617. Baldwin, Roger S. (Conn.). "Slavery in the Territories," *Congressional Globe*. 30th Cong., 2nd Sess. (22 Jan.1849) p. 318. Brief remarks on the history of the legislation of Connecticut concerning fugitive slaves.

618. Niles, John M. (Conn.). "Civil and Diplomatic Bill," *Congressional Globe*. 30th Cong., 2nd Sess. (13 Feb. 1849) pp. 525-526. Opposes further appropriations for the City Hall building in Washington used by the courts; prefers to build a new structure rather than try and salvage the old one.

619. Niles, John M. (Conn.). "Department of the Interior," *Congressional Globe*. 30th Cong., 2nd Sess. (3 Mar. 1849) p. 671. Objects to establishing a Department of the Interior as an unnecessary and improper action.

620. Niles, John M. (Conn.). "Draining the Everglades of Florida," *Congressional Globe*. 30th Cong., 2nd Sess. (22 Dec. 1848) p. 87. Opposes the bill, which would grant the Everglades to the State of Florida. Maintains that a survey is necessary to ascertain the value and extent of the lands, and that a guarantee to drain the lands should be obtained from Florida.

621. Niles, John M. (Conn.). "Flogging in the Navy," *Congressional Globe.* 30th Cong., 2nd Sess. (12 Feb. 1849) pp. 510-511. Supports abolishing flogging in the navy; contends that it is a barbaric and unnecessary form of punishment.

622. Niles, John M. (Conn.). "John P. Baldwin," *Congressional Globe.* 30th Cong., 2nd Sess. (2 Jan. 1849) p. 133. Supports reimbursing John P. Baldwin for the destruction of the Spanish brig Gil Blas by a government officer; discusses rights of private property in war.

623. Niles, John M. (Conn.). "New Mexico and California," *Congressional Globe, Appendix.* 30th Cong., 2nd Sess. (28 Feb. 1849) pp. 285, 304-309. Opposes the extension of slavery into the territories. Responds to Senator Dickinson's (N.Y.) speech. Addresses the political aspects of the agitation, the alleged violation of the rights of the slave states, and the power of Congress to legislate over the territories and to delegate its legislative powers to the Executive.

624. Niles, John M. (Conn.). "Railroad across Isthmus of Panama," *Congressional Globe.* 30th Cong., 2nd Sess. (31 Jan. 1849) pp. 412-413. Opposes appropriations to construct the railroad across the isthmus. Maintains that Congress does not have the constitutional power, and that the advantages of the railroad would be minimal.

625. Niles, John M. (Conn.). "Reduced Rates of Postage," *Congressional Globe.* 30th Cong., 2nd Sess. (17 Jan. 1849) pp. 275, 276. Explains the amendment establishing a uniform postage rate for foreign mail; introduces amendments concerning domestic postage rates and the franking privilege.

626. Niles, John M. (Conn.). "Reduction of Postage," *Congressional Globe.* 30th Cong., 2nd Sess. (24 Jan. 1849) pp. 346, 346-347. Addresses arguments of opponents of the bill to reduce postage.

627. Niles, John M. (Conn.). "Reduction of the Rates of Postage," *Congressional Globe, Appendix.* 30th Cong., 2nd Sess. (2 Feb. 1849) pp. 81-86. Supports the bill to reduce the postage rates. Discusses the general and financial character and provisions of the bill. Maintains that the bill must be viewed in its entirety in order for the revenue to sustain the operations. Responds to speech of Senator Allen (Ohio) concerning principles of civil liberty.

628. Niles, John M. (Conn.). "The Reports of Debate," *Congressional Globe.* 30th Cong., 2nd Sess. (30 Jan. 1849) p. 396. Supports allowing Senators to review and correct reports of their remarks before publication.

629. Niles, John M. (Conn.). "Slavery in the Territories," *Congressional Globe.* 30th Cong., 2nd Sess. (22 Jan. 1849) pp. 316-317. Maintains that legislating on slavery in the territories does not interfere with states' rights; contends that the Union is strong.

630. Rockwell, John A. (Conn.). "Army Appropriation Bill," *Congressional Globe.* 30th Cong., 2nd Sess. (24 Jan. 1849) pp. 355-357. Analyzes the financial condition of the country and the report of the Secretary of the Treasury. Maintains that the expenditures are under-estimated, revenues are over-estimated, and that income will be insufficient to meet expenses.

631. Rockwell, John A. (Conn.). "Board to Settle Private Claims," *Congressional Globe.* 30th Cong., 2nd Sess. (9 Jan. 1849) p. 198. Objects to referring the bill to the Committee on the Judiciary; includes a synopsis of the history of the proposal.

632. Rockwell, John A. (Conn.). "Board to Settle Private Claims," *Congressional Globe.* 30th Cong., 2nd Sess. (19 Jan. 1849) pp. 304-306. Supports establishing a Board of Commissioners to adjudicate claims against the government. Answers objections to the bill, addressing the permanency and authority of the Board, rejected claims, and time limitations.

633. Rockwell, John A. (Conn.). "California and New Mexico," *Congressional Globe, Appendix.* 30th Cong., 2nd Sess. (17 Feb. 1849) pp. 231-236. Defends the Connecticut resolutions to exclude slavery from new territories. Demonstrates that Congress has the constitutional power to legislate on this subject, and that it has been repeatedly exercised since the adoption of the Constitution. Includes a history of slavery legislation in the territories. Addresses Virginia's response to the resolutions as inconsistent with past acts and opinions of her statesmen. Answers various arguments of advocates of slavery.

634. Rockwell, John A. (Conn.). "Claims against the United States," *Congressional Globe.* 30th Cong., 2nd Sess. (2 Jan. 1849) pp. 139-140. Supports establishing a Board of Commissioners to review claims against the government. Reviews systems of other countries, and the strengths and weaknesses of the present system. Briefly explains the provisions of the proposed bill.

635. Smith, Truman (Conn.). "Mexican Claims," *Congressional Globe.* 30th Cong., 2nd Sess. (2 Mar. 1849) p. 661. Supports making the appropriation to pay the claims which the board of commissioners determined as valid.

636. Smith, Truman (Conn.). "The Boundary Line," *Congressional Globe.* 30th Cong., 2nd Sess. (28 Feb. 1849) pp. 619-621. Opposes the President appointing a commissioner and surveyor for the Mexican boundary without the consent or knowledge of the Senate or House. Maintains that the President violated the rights of the House and the Constitution. Reviews precedence necessitating Congress to pass a law to create the office, fix the salary, and declare its tenure. Questions how these appointments can be paid without an appropriation.

MAINE

[For references to Maine before statehood, see Massachusetts]

16TH CONGRESS, 1ST SESSION

637. Debate on the Admission of Maine and Missouri, *Annals of Congress.* 16th Cong., 1st Sess. (13 Jan., 14 Jan., 17 Jan., 19 Jan., 20 Jan., 24 Jan., 25 Jan., 26 Jan., 27 Jan., 28 Jan., 1 Feb., 2 Feb., 3 Feb., 14 Feb., 15 Feb., 16 Feb. 1820) pp. 85-100; 101-118; 119-156; 159-200; 201-232; 234-236; 237-255; 259-275; 278-299; 300-311; 314-359; 360-361; 363; 374-388; 388-417; 418-424. Debate on the admission of Maine into the Union. Includes speeches and remarks by Prentiss Mellen (Mass.), James Burrill (R.I.), David Morril (N.H.), Harrison Otis (Mass.), and Samuel Dana (Conn.).

638. "Maine Bill," *Annals of Congress.* 16th Cong., 1st Sess. (28 Feb., 3 Mar. 1820) pp. 457-458; 471-472. Debate on the admission of Maine into the Union.

639. "Maine and Missouri," *Annals of Congress.* 16th Cong., 1st Sess. (28 Feb. 1820) pp. 1552-1555. Brief debate on connecting the admission of Maine into the Union with that of Missouri.

640. "State of Maine," *Annals of Congress.* 16th Cong., 1st Sess. (30 Dec. 1819) pp. 831-844. Debate on the admission of Maine into the Union and the representation of Maine in Congress. Includes speeches and remarks by John Holmes (Mass.), Arthur Livermore (N.H.), and Ezekiel Whitman (Mass.).

641. "An Act for the Admission of the State of Maine into the Union," *Statutes at Large*, Vol. III (3 Mar. 1820) p. 544. Also printed in the *Annals of Congress* (16th Cong., 1st Sess.) Appendix, p. 2554.

642. "An Act Establishing a Circuit Court within and for the District of Maine," *Statutes at Large*, Vol. III (30 Mar. 1820) pp. 554-555. Also printed in the *Annals of Congress* (16th Cong., 1st Sess.) Appendix, pp. 2565-2566.

643. "An Act for Apportioning the Representatives in the Seventeenth Congress, to Be Elected in the State of Massachusetts and Maine, and for Other Purposes," *Statutes at Large*, Vol. III (7 Apr. 1820) p. 555. Also printed in the *Annals of Congress* (16th Cong., 1st Sess.) Appendix, p. 2567.

644. U.S. House. *Petition of a Convention of the People of the District of Maine, Praying to Be Admitted into the Union As a Separate and Independent State, Accompanied with a Constitution for Said State.* 16th Cong., 1st Sess. (H.Doc.3). Washington: Gales & Seaton, 1819. 35 pg. (Serial Set 31). Brief petition with proposed constitution for adoption in town meetings.

645. U.S. House. *Representation of the Members of the House of Representatives from That Part of Massachusetts Hitherto Known As the District of Maine.* 16th Cong., 1st Sess. (H.Doc.82). Washington: Gales & Seaton, 1820. 4 pg. (Serial Set 36). Request for a speedy decision on the admission of Maine into the Union; election and legislation decisions are dependent upon verdict.

16TH CONGRESS, 2ND SESSION

646. "Memorial from Maine," *Annals of Congress.* 16th Cong., 2nd Sess. (19 Oct. 1820) Appendix, pp. 1493-1498. Opposes increasing duties; protecting manufacturers would be detrimental to commerce. Same as H.doc.23 (16-2) 48 (entry **650**).

647. Holmes, John (Maine). "Admission of Missouri," *Annals of Congress.* 16th Cong., 2nd Sess. (9 Dec. 1820) pp. 80-89. Supports the right of Missouri to prohibit free blacks and mulattos from settling in that state; maintains that neither the Constitution nor Congress has extended the "privileges and immunities" of citizenship to free blacks and mulattos, and that the privileges of citizenship are conferred or withheld by each state.

648. "Drawback System," *American State Papers: Finance*, Vol. III (Doc. 598) pp. 546-547. (ASP 011). Committee on Manufactures reports on petitions from Belfast, Maine and Richmond, Virginia, opposed to the abolition of drawbacks. Committee maintains that the petitioners are misinformed and have misrepresented the situation. Same as H.rp.7 (16-2) 57 (entry **652**).

649. "Remonstrance against an Increase of Duties on Imports," *American State Papers: Finance*, Vol. III (Doc. 596) pp. 540-543. (ASP 011). Memorial and report from Petersburg, Maine, opposes the tariff bill and the restrictive system as detrimental to the commercial and agricultural interests of the nation.

650. U.S. House. *Memorial of the Delegates from the Commercial and Agricultural Sections of the State of Maine.* 16th Cong., 2nd Sess. (H.Doc.23). Washington: Gales & Seaton, 1820. 8 pg. (Serial Set 48). Same as "Memorial from Maine," *Annals of Congress.* 16th Cong., 2nd Sess. (19 Oct. 1820) Appendix, pp. 1493-1498. See entry **646.**

651. U.S. House. *Memorial of the Merchants of Bath, State of Maine.* 16th Cong., 2nd Sess. (H.Doc.20). Washington: Gales & Seaton, 1820. 6 pg. (Serial Set 48). Memorial opposes the proposed tariff bill and the protection of the manufacturers at the expense of the commercial and agricultural classes.

652. U.S. House. *Report of the Committee on Manufactures, on Sundry Petitions, from Inhabitants of Belfast, Maine, and Richmond, Virginia, Relating to Drawback of Duties.* 16th Cong., 2nd Sess. (H.Rpt.7). [Washington: Gales & Seaton, 1821]. 4 pg. (Serial Set 57). Same as Finance 598 (16-2) ASP 011. See entry **648.**

17TH CONGRESS, 1ST SESSION

653. Herrick, Ebenezer (Maine). "Apportionment Bill," *Annals of Congress.* 17th Cong., 1st Sess. (2 Feb. 1822) pp. 894-896. Opposes an apportionment of Representatives by any assumed ratio; presents alternative proposal.

654. Hill, Mark L. (Maine). "The Bankrupt Bill," *Annals of Congress.* 17th Cong., 1st Sess. (5 Mar. 1822) pp. 1210-1212. Supports the bill; contends that it is constitutional and expedient.

655. Holmes, John (Maine). "Amendment to the Constitution," *Annals of Congress.* 17th Cong., 1st Sess. (14 Jan. 1822) pp. 94-95. Opposes the amendment to give the Senate appellate jurisdiction over judicial controversies.

656. Holmes, John (Maine). "Officers of the Customs," *Annals of Congress.* 17th Cong., 1st Sess. (18 Jan. 1822) pp. 132-133. Supports reducing the commissions of the collector of the port of New York; opposes paying officers more than a fair salary for the purpose of making them honest.

657. Holmes, John (Maine). "Officers of the Customs," *Annals of Congress.* 17th Cong., 1st Sess. (30 Jan. 1822) pp. 168-173. Supports reducing the percentage on the commissions of the collectors of the customs.

658. Whitman, Ezekiel (Maine). "Transactions at Pensacola," *Annals of Congress.* 17th Cong., 1st Sess. (17 Dec. 1821, 2 Jan. 1822) pp. 558-559; 611-612, 615-616. Supports requesting information from the Secretary of State relating to the controversy between General Jackson and Judge Fromentin.

659. Whitman, Ezekiel (Maine). "Transactions in Florida," *Annals of Congress.* 17th Cong., 1st Sess. (28 Feb. 1822) pp. 1156-1158. Justifies the need to further investigate the affair in Florida. Disapproves of the conduct of General Jackson, as Governor, towards the Spanish Commissioner.

660. Williamson, William D. (Maine). "Apportionment Bill," *Annals of Congress.* 17th Cong., 1st Sess. (28 Jan. 1822) pp. 812-813. Objects to a greater number of Representatives.

661. Williamson, William D. (Maine). "Exchange of Stocks," *Annals of Congress.* 17th Cong., 1st Sess. (21 Mar. 1822) pp. 1339-1341. Supports the exchange of loans of the U.S. payable in 1825-26 by a new stock to be created bearing a lower interest and payable in 1821-2-3.

662. "Application of Maine for a Grant of Land for the Purpose of Education," *American State Papers: Public Lands,* Vol. III (Doc. 347) p. 511. (ASP 030). Supports appropriations of public land for the purposes of education.

663. "Light-houses, &c.," *American State Papers: Commerce and Navigation,* Vol. II (Doc. 239) pp. 505-506. (ASP 015). Correspondence, report, and expense estimate in support of building a sea-wall between Smutty Nose Island and Cedar Island, part of the Isles of Shoals on the coast of N.H. and Maine.

17TH CONGRESS, 2ND SESSION

664. Holmes, John (Maine). "Amendment to the Constitution," *Annals of Congress.* 17th Cong., 2nd Sess. (13 Feb. 1823) pp. 228-234. Discusses an amendment respecting the election of President and Vice President; proposes own amendment providing for a contested election.

665. Lincoln, Enoch (Maine). "Pay of Certain Officers," *Annals of Congress.* 17th Cong., 2nd Sess. (22 Jan. 1823) pp. 664-666. Supports establishing certain offices by law, instead of by annual appropriations or per diem allowances.

666. "An Act Altering the Time of Holding the Circuit Court in the Districts of Maine (a) and New Hampshire (b)," *Statutes at Large,* Vol. III (3 Mar. 1823) pp. 773-774. Also printed in the *Annals of Congress* (17th Cong., 2nd Sess.) Appendix, p. 1400.

18TH CONGRESS, 1ST SESSION

667. Cushman, Joshua (Maine). "General Appropriation Bill," *Annals of Congress.* 18th Cong., 1st Sess. (13 Mar. 1824) pp. 1777-1780. Supports appropriations for the north portico of the President's house.

668. Holmes, John (Maine). "Amendments to the Constitution," *Annals of Congress.* 18th Cong., 1st Sess. (18 Mar. 1824) pp. 370-372. Remarks on the propriety of a congressional caucus in presidential elections.

669. Holmes, John (Maine). "Indian Fur Trade," *Annals of Congress.* 18th Cong., 1st Sess. (31 Mar. 1824) pp. 460-461. Opposes protecting trade with the northwestern Indians by establishing a military force in their territory without their consent.

670. Holmes, John (Maine). "Surveys for Roads and Canals," *Annals of Congress.* 18th Cong., 1st Sess. (21 Apr. 1824) pp. 541-558. Objects to surveys for internal improvements; addresses basis of claims of constitutional authority - regulating commerce, the consent of the States, the right to erect needed buildings, the military power, and the common defense and general welfare.

671. "Refunding Duties Paid while Castine Was in Possession of an Enemy," *American State Papers: Finance*, Vol. IV (Doc. 686) pp. 392-393. (ASP 012). Supports the refund of duties in accordance with the Supreme Court decision that exacting said bonds was illegal. Same as H.rp.29 (18-1) 105 (entry **673**).

672. U.S. House. *Memorial of the Merchants, &c. of Portland, against the Tariff Bill.* 18th Cong., 1st Sess. (H.Doc.71). Washington: Gales & Seaton, 1824. 5 pg. (Serial Set 96). Opposes the additional duties; maintains that they will destroy commerce, and, with it, the best revenue source of the government. Briefly reviews the advantages of commerce to the country.

673. U.S. House. *Report of the Committee of Ways and Means, on the Petition of Joshua Aubin, and Others, Merchants, Who Imported Goods into Castine, during the Late War, Accompanied with a Bill for Their Relief.* 18th Cong., 1st Sess. (H.Rpt.29). [Washington: 1824]. 2 pg. (Serial Set 105). Same as Finance 686 (18-1) ASP 012. See entry **671**.

18TH CONGRESS, 2ND SESSION

674. Lincoln, Enoch (Maine). "Niagara Sufferers," *Register of Debates.* 18th Cong., 2nd Sess. (19 Jan. 1825) pp. 272-274. Supports remuneration for losses for Niagara inhabitants who housed soldiers for the government but who were inadequately defended by these soldiers and subsequently invaded.

675. "An Act to Establish the City of Hudson and the City of Troy, in the State of New York, Bowdoinham, in the State of Maine, and Fairport, in the State of Ohio, Ports of Delivery, and to Abolish Topsham As a Port of Delivery," *Statutes at Large*, Vol. IV (3 Mar. 1825) p. 127. Also printed in the *Register of Debates* (18th Cong., 2nd Sess.) Appendix, p. 120.

676. U.S. House. *Memorial of a Committee Selected by the Merchants of Portland, in the State of Maine, on the Subject of Piracies Committed on the Commerce of the United States, in the West India Seas.* 18th Cong., 2nd Sess. (H.Doc.14). Washington: Gales & Seaton, 1824. 5 pg. (Serial Set 114). Requests protection from pirates, particularly upon the coasts of Cuba and Puerto Rico.

677. U.S. House. *Report of the Committee on Revolutionary Pensions on the Petition of Daniel Small, Elias Foss, Benjamin Day, and Harvey Libby, Praying an Extension of the Provisions of the Revolutionary Pension Acts.* 18th Cong., 2nd Sess. (H.Rpt.54). [Washington: 1825]. 3 pg. (Serial Set 122). Committee resolves that it cannot support the petition to extend the laws to everyone serving in the Revolutionary War, regardless of need.

19TH CONGRESS, 1ST SESSION

678. Chandler, John (Maine). "Prevention of Desertion," *Register of Debates.* 19th Cong., 1st Sess. (12 Jan. 1826) pp. 48-49. Discusses the character of enlisted men and the futility of the proposed measures to prevent desertion.

679. Herrick, Ebenezer (Maine). "Amendment of the Constitution," *Register of Debates.* 19th Cong., 1st Sess. (8 Mar. 1826) pp. 1554-1555. Proposes a constitutional amendment that Congress cannot propose amendments to the Constitution, uncalled for by the people, oftener than once in ten years.

680. Holmes, John (Maine). "The Judicial System," *Register of Debates.* 19th Cong., 1st Sess. (10 Apr., 11 Apr., 13 Apr. 1826) pp. 455-458; 483-488; 539-543. Supports increasing the number of Supreme Court judges, thereby increasing representation from the small states, and also requiring a greater unanimity of the judges in deciding questions. Addresses Senator Woodbury's (N.H.) arguments and proposal revising the duties of the various judges.

681. Holmes, John (Maine). "On the Panama Mission," *Register of Debates.* 19th Cong., 1st Sess. (14 Mar. 1826) pp. 263-276. Maintains that as there is great confusion as to the nature, character, and extent of the mission, and the powers and duties of the deputies to be sent, that it is best not to get involved.

682. Sprague, Peleg (Maine). "Massachusetts Claims," *Register of Debates.* 19th Cong., 1st Sess. (7 Apr. 1826) pp. 2110-2121. Supports the claims Massachusetts incurred while protecting herself from invasion; addresses objections based on doctrines and conduct of Massachusetts during the war.

683. Sprague, Peleg (Maine). "Mission to Panama," *Register of Debates.* 19th Cong., 1st Sess. (20 Apr. 1826) pp. 2410-2412. Objects to limiting the legitimate constitutional powers of the Executive to conduct a foreign mission.

684. Sprague, Peleg (Maine). "Revolutionary Officers," *Register of Debates.* 19th Cong., 1st Sess. (25 Apr. 1826) pp. 2559-2566. Supports the soldiers and the officers; maintains that earlier legislation is not comprehensive enough.

685. "Remission of Duties on Goods Imported into Castine, in Maine, whilst in Possession of the Enemy during the War of 1812-15," *American State Papers: Finance,* Vol. V (Doc. 734) p. 263. (ASP 013). Committee on Finance supports the claims, regardless of residence of the importer or owner of the goods, in accordance with the ruling of the Supreme Court.

686. U.S. House. *Improvement of the Navigation of the Kennebec River.* 19th Cong., 1st Sess. (H.Rpt.118). [Washington: Gales & Seaton, 1826]. 2 pg. (Serial Set 141). Supports the memorial to improve navigation of the Kennebec River and to connect it to the St. Lawrence. Maintains that this accomplishment would promote the commercial, defensive and naval operations of the government.

687. U.S. House. *Memorial of Sundry Inhabitants of the State of Maine [on an Observatory at Brunswick, Maine].* 19th Cong., 1st Sess. (H.Doc.35). Washington: Gales & Seaton, 1826. 4 pg. (Serial Set 133). Encourages the establishment of an observatory in the U.S. as critical to the interests of commerce; New Brunswick indicated as favorable location.

688. U.S. Senate. [Report on Providing for Surveys for Roads and Canals in Indiana and Maine]. 19th Cong., 1st Sess. (S.Doc.81). [Washington: Gales & Seaton, 1826]. 2 pg. (Serial Set 128). Supports the surveys of Indiana and Maine from national and military points of view.

19TH CONGRESS, 2ND SESSION

689. Holmes, John (Maine). "The Bankrupt Bill," *Register of Debates.* 19th Cong., 2nd Sess. (18 Jan., 23 Jan., 25 Jan., 27 Jan. 1827) pp.66-67; 80-81; 101-102; 151-153. Supports extending the benefits of the act to all classes of persons, not just merchants.

690. Holmes, John (Maine). "The Colonial Trade Bill," *Register of Debates.* 19th Cong., 2nd Sess. (21 Feb., 23 Feb. 1827) pp. 418-420; 450-451. Opposes passing a bill restricting trade with Great Britain until her ports are opened; contends that it will only force trade through Canada and that Britain's policy is obviously to build up her North American colonies at our expense.

691. Holmes, John (Maine). "Duty on Salt," *Register of Debates.* 19th Cong., 2nd Sess. (1 Feb. 1827) pp. 228-230. Opposes repealing the duty on salt on the grounds that it is necessary to protect the salt manufacturers and because it would destroy the bounty given to the fisheries.

692. Sprague, Peleg (Maine). "Internal Improvement," *Register of Debates.* 19th Cong., 2nd Sess. (20 Feb. 1827) pp. 1315-1317. Defends against aspersions cast on surveys to connect the Kennebec River and the St. Lawrence.

693. Sprague, Peleg (Maine). "Military Appropriation Bill," *Register of Debates.* 19th Cong., 2nd Sess. (21 Feb. 1827) pp. 1347-1351. Addresses the discrepancies of the condition of the Treasury as reported by the Secretary of the Treasury and the Committee of Ways and Means.

694. "An Act Authorizing the Establishment of an Arsenal in the Town of Augusta, in Maine," *Statutes at Large*, Vol. IV (3 Mar. 1827) p. 241. Also printed in the *Annals of Congress* (19th Cong., 2nd Sess.) Appendix, p. xxii.

695. "Relative to the Establishment of an Arsenal in Maine," *American State Papers: Military Affairs*, Vol. III (Doc. 345) p. 577. (ASP 018). Reports that the establishment of the arsenal is unnecessary due to the extensive arsenal at Watertown, near Boston. A small depot for emergencies could be established.

696. U.S. House. *Letter from the Secretary of War, Transmitting a Report of a Survey of Kennebec River, in the State of Maine.* 19th Cong., 2nd Sess. (H.Doc.103). Washington: Gales & Seaton, 1827. 6 pg. (Serial Set 152). Report of the survey of the pass of Lovejoy's narrows and recommendations for improvement. Accompanying plan not with report.

697. U.S. House. *Port Entry - Penobscot River.* 19th Cong., 2nd Sess. (H.Rpt.78). [Washington: 1827]. 2 pg. (Serial Set 159). Committee on Commerce reports against establishing a collection district and port of entry on the Penobscot River.

20ᵀᴴ CONGRESS, 1ˢᵀ SESSION

698. Anderson, John (Maine). "Tariff Bill," *Register of Debates.* 20th Cong., 1st Sess. (5 Mar. 1828) pp. 1772-1784. Opposes increasing duties to protect a few at the expense of many. Discusses effects of duties on hemp, duck cloth, distilled spirits and molasses as they concern the West Indies trade and Maine.

699. Parris, Albion K. (Maine). "Kenyon College," *Register of Debates.* 20th Cong., 1st Sess. (28 Mar. 1828) pp. 537-539. Supports grants of public land for the purposes of education as a benefit to all states.

700. Parris, Albion K. (Maine). "Surviving Officers of the Revolution," *Register of Debates.* 20th Cong., 1st Sess. (28 Jan. 1828) pp. 166-167. Advocates benefits for soldiers as well as officers.

701. Parris, Albion K. (Maine). "The Tariff Bill," *Register of Debates.* 20th Cong., 1st Sess. (8 May 1828) pp. 736-744. Discusses the proposed duties on molasses, iron, and hemp, and the repressive effects of the bill on the West Indies trade and the Maine shipping industry. Maintains that the bill unfairly targets Maine and the other New England states.

702. Sprague, Peleg (Maine). "Internal Improvements," *Register of Debates.* 20th Cong., 1st Sess. (14 Feb. 1828) pp. 1510-1512. Supports additional appropriations to remove obstructions at Lovejoy's narrows in the Kennebec River.

703. Sprague, Peleg (Maine). "The Tariff Bill," *Register of Debates.* 20th Cong., 1st Sess. (1 Apr. 1828) pp. 2054-2079. Opposes the tariff bill. Addresses duties on woolens, hemp, and molasses and the effect of the bill on ship building; contends that it would oppress navigation and commerce, destroy the West India trade, prostrate the fisheries and wound the navy.

704. "An Act to Provide for Opening and Making a Military Road in the State of Maine," *Statutes at Large*, Vol. IV (24 May 1828) pp. 303-304. Also printed in the *Register of Debates* (20th Cong., 1st Sess.) Appendix, p. xxxiii.

705. "Against Increase of Duties on Imports," *American State Papers: Finance*, Vol. V (Doc. 845) p. 846. (ASP 013). Objects to increasing duties and recommends that vessels enter coastwise without the payment of duties.

706. "Against Increase of Duties on Imports," *American State Papers: Finance*, Vol. V (Doc. 832) pp. 756-757. (ASP 013). Portland memorial opposes the proposed increase of duties as the purpose is not to raise revenue, but to discourage importation. Same as H.doc.91 (20-1) 171 (entry **713**).

707. "Aggressions on John Baker and Other Citizens of the United States by the Authorities of Great Britain in New Brunswick," *American State Papers: Foreign Relations*, Vol. VI (Doc. 473) pp. 838-855. (ASP 06). Documents relating to jurisdiction of the disputed territory on the Madawaska and the Aroostook, branches of the St. John; specifically addresses the case of John Baker, charged for sedition and obstructing the passage of the British mail.

708. "Correspondence Relative to the Arrest and Imprisonment of John Baker by the British Authorities of New Brunswick," *American State Papers: Foreign Relations*, Vol. VI (Doc. 498) pp. 1015-1020. (ASP 06). Correspondence between H. Clay, Secretary of State of the U.S. and Chas. R. Vaughan, Envoy Extraordinary and Minister Plenipotentiary of his Britannic Majesty, relative to the arrest of John Baker. Same as H.Doc.278 (20-1) 175 (entry **714**).

709. "Documents Accompanying the President's Message at the Opening of the First Session of the Twentieth Congress, Relating to the Imprisonment of John Baker, an American Citizen, by the British Authorities of New Brunswick.," *American State Papers: Foreign Relations*, Vol. VI (Doc. 457) pp. 630-637. (ASP 06). Official documents and correspondence relating to the case of John Baker, charged with sedition and obstructing the mail; case based on disputed territory claimed by U.S. and New Brunswick.

710. "Relative to a Further Appropriation for the Arsenal at Augusta, Maine," *American State Papers: Military Affairs*, Vol. III (Doc. 373) p. 793. (ASP 018). Report recommends the establishment of a larger arsenal in Maine, as the Watertown arsenal is now deemed to be useless to Maine in times of war. Same as S.doc.121 (20-1) 166 (entry **716**).

711. "Report from the State of Maine Relative to the Northeastern Boundary of That State," *American State Papers: Foreign Relations*, Vol. VI (Doc. 483) pp. 893-945. (ASP 06). Extensive report and accompanying documents; follows the chronological order of events and relevant treaties; implications for John Baker case. Same as S.doc.171 (20-1) 167 (entry **717**).

712. U.S. House. *Letter from the Secretary of War, Transmitting a Report of the Surveys of the Kennebec River, and of Contemplated Routes for Canals, Connected with the Waters of the Said Rivers.* 20th Cong., 1st Sess. (H.Doc.173). Washington: Gales & Seaton, 1828. 57 pg. (Serial Set 173). Reports of the various surveys in the States of Maine, New Hampshire, and Vermont. Surveys include: the Kennebec River, from its mouth to Augusta; the Brunswick Canal, to join the waters of Merrymeeting and Casco Bays (reviews three possible routes); Cobbisecontee Canal, to connect the waters of the Kennebec at Gardner, with those of the Androscoggin at Leeds; Ammonoosuck Canal, to unite the waters of the Connecticut with those of the Androscoggin; Oliverian Canal, to connect the waters of the Connecticut with those of the Pemigawasset or Merrimac; Sunapee Canal, to connect the Connecticut River with the Merrimac; Pasumpsic Canal, to unite the waters of the Connecticut with those of Lake Memphremagog; Montpelier Canal, to connect the waters of Lake Champlain with those of Connecticut River; Rutland Canal, to connect the town of Rutland, Vt. with the northern canal at Whitehall, N.Y.; and La Moille Canal, to connect Lake Memphremagog with Lake Champlain.

713. U.S. House. *Memorial of Merchants and Others, of Portland, in the State of Maine, against an Increase of Duty on Imported Hemp, Iron, Molasses, and Woollen Goods.* 20th Cong., 1st Sess. (H.Doc.91). Washington: Gales & Seaton, 1828. 5 pg. (Serial Set 171). Same as Finance 832 (20-1) ASP 013. See entry **706**.

714. U.S. House. *Message from the President of the United States Transmitting a Correspondence Between the Secretary of State and the Minister of His Britannic Majesty in Relation to the Arrest and Imprisonment of John Baker.* 20th Cong., 1st Sess. (H.Doc.278). Washington: Gales & Seaton, 1828. 18 pg. (Serial Set 175). Same as For.rel.498 (20-1) ASP06. See entry **708**.

715. U.S. House. Road - *Penobscot River to New Brunswick.* 20th Cong., 1st Sess. (H.Rpt.214). [Washington: 1828]. 2 pg. (Serial Set 178). Report of the Committee on Roads and Canals supports constructing a national road from the Penobscot River to the boundary line of New Brunswick.

716. U.S. Senate. [Report on the Arsenal at Augusta, Maine]. 20th Cong., 1st Sess. (S.Doc.121). [Washington: Duff Green, 1828]. 2 pg. (Serial Set 166). Same as Mil.aff.373 (20-1) ASP 018. See entry **710**.

717. U.S. Senate. [Report on the North-eastern Boundary of Maine]. 20th Cong., 1st Sess. (S.Doc.171). [Washington: Duff Green, 1828]. 126 pg. (Serial Set 167). Same as For.rel.483 (20-1) ASP 06. See entry **711**.

20TH CONGRESS, 2ND SESSION

718. "Military Road in the State of Maine," *Register of Debates.* 20th Cong., 2nd Sess. (28 Feb. 1829) p. 385. Debates the bill to construct a military road from Mars Hill, in Maine, through the disputed territory on the northern frontier

719. Holmes, John (Maine). "Executive Proceedings," *Register of Debates.* 20th Cong., 2nd Sess. (2 Feb. 1829) pp. 86-91. Supports acting on John J. Crittenden's nomination for an Associate Judge of the Supreme Court; maintains that to postpone the nomination to give the patronage to a future administration is against principle and constitutional duty, and a dangerous precedent.

720. Sprague, Peleg (Maine). "Drawback on Refined Sugar," *Register of Debates.* 20th Cong., 2nd Sess. (15 Dec. 1828) pp. 104-105. Opposes withholding the drawback; contends that it would prohibit exportation as the foreigners would not consent to pay increased costs.

721. Sprague, Peleg (Maine). "Tonnage Duty," *Register of Debates.* 20th Cong., 2nd Sess. (4 Feb. 1829) pp. 309-313. Supports repealing the tonnage duties upon ships and vessels; maintains that the means of collecting it is unequal. Addresses the various arguments in support of the duty.

722. U.S. House. *Message from the President of the United States, Transmitting the Information Required by a Resolution of the House of Representatives of the 5th Instant, in Relation to the Arrest and Trial, in the British Province of New Brunswick, of John Baker, a Citizen of the United States.* 20th Cong., 2nd Sess. (H.Doc.90). [Washington: Gales & Seaton, 1829]. 88 pg. (Serial Set 186). Correspondence between the U.S. and Great Britain, in relation to the said arrest, and to the encroachment by New Brunswick within the jurisdiction of the State of Maine at the Madawaska and Aroostook region.

723. U.S. Senate. [Report on Increasing Salaries of District Judges in Rhode Island, Maine, and South Carolina]. 20th Cong., 2nd Sess. (S.Doc.51). [Washington: Duff Green, 1829]. 1 pg. (Serial Set 181). Opposes an increase in compensation in these particular cases; recommends that the whole subject needs a general revision.

21ST CONGRESS, 1ST SESSION

724. Anderson, John (Maine). "The Tariff," *Register of Debates.* 21st Cong., 1st Sess. (11 Mar. 1830) pp. 605-608. Supports allowing a drawback on rum distilled in this country from foreign molasses and then exported to a foreign country. Maintains that the repeal of the drawback with the tariff of 1828 has not realized its intentions of helping the whiskey distiller.

725. Evans, George (Maine). "Removal of the Indians," *Register of Debates.* 21st Cong., 1st Sess. (18 May 1830) pp. 1037-1049. Supports respecting previous commitments made to the Indians; maintains that they should be treated as free and sovereign communities. Discusses relevant treaties and legislation in detail.

726. Holmes, John (Maine). "Executive Powers of Removal," *Register of Debates.* 21st Cong., 1st Sess. (28 Apr. 1830) pp. 385-396. Questions the authority of the President to remove officers and fill vacancies when the Senate is in recess; addresses executive power and patronage, and precedence.

727. Holmes, John (Maine). "Mr. Foot's Resolution," *Register of Debates.* 21st Cong., 1st Sess. (19 Jan., 19 Feb. 1830) pp. 27-29; 160-168. Supports Mr. Foot's resolution to acquire accurate information on the surveys and sales of public lands. Defends New England against charges of preventing settlements in the west by limiting the surveys and sales of the lands, of attempting to circumscribe territory and surrender privileges, and of withholding protection.

728. Holmes, John (Maine). "The Public Lands," *Register of Debates.* 21st Cong., 1st Sess. (30 Dec. 1829) pp. 5-6. Supports an inquiry into the value of the land and whether surveyors are required any longer; favors disclosure and opposes executive patronage.

729. Sprague, Peleg (Maine). "The Indians," *Register of Debates.* 21st Cong., 1st Sess. (17 Apr. 1830) pp. 343-357. Lengthy speech addresses the rights and duties of the U.S. with respect to the Indian tribes, specifically the Cherokees. Discusses treaties and legislation on the principles of the right of discovery, the powers conferred by the articles of the confederation, the confirmation of pre-existing treaties by the adoption of the Constitution, the renunciation of powers by the respective states, and the acts of the State of Georgia. Maintains that the U.S. is obligated to abide by its promises to the Indians, and that they should have the right to decide whether to move without interference.

730. Sprague, Peleg (Maine). "Mr. Foot's Resolution," *Register of Debates.* 21st Cong., 1st Sess. (3 Feb., 21 May 1830) pp. 119-128; 451-452. Defends New England against charges of hostility and injustice towards the West. Addresses the accusations, dating from the Continental Congress, as they relate to the disposition of the public lands. Later remarks re-affirm his former statements.

731. "Application of Maine for the Settlement and Payment of the Claims of Massachusetts for the Services of the Militia of That State during the War of 1812-'15," *American State Papers: Military Affairs,* Vol. IV (Doc. 448) pp. 367-369. (ASP 019). Maine requests payment of Massachusetts' claims; provides a brief history of previous actions and decisions on the claims. Same as S.doc.107 (21-1) 193 (entry **738**).

732. "Application of Maine that the Fortifications on the Penobscot Bay and River Be Repaired," *American State Papers: Military Affairs*, Vol. IV (Doc. 424) p. 250. (ASP 019).

733. "On the Erection and Repairing of Fortifications on the Penobscot Bay and River," *American State Papers: Military Affairs*, Vol. IV (Doc. 427) pp. 269-270. (ASP 019). Committee on Military Affairs reviews requests and decides that Mount Desert Island is much preferred as a site; presents a proposal for a fort opposite Bucksport.

734. U.S. House. *Contested Election.* 21st Cong., 1st Sess. (H.Rpt.88). [Washington: 1830]. [48 pg.]. (Serial Set 199). Report of the Committee on Elections denies the petition of Reuel Washburn, claiming a right to a seat in Congress in the place of James W. Ripley. Report includes copies of relevant documents, including extracts from the Constitution and laws of Maine.

735. U.S. House. *Message from the President of the United States, Transmitting a Copy of the Report on Survey Made of the Ship Channel of Penobscot River, &c. &c.* 21st Cong., 1st Sess. (H.Doc.82). [Washington: 1830]. 3 pg. (Serial Set 197). Report on survey of the ship channel from Whitehead to Bangor, with the recommended sites and costs for buoys. Accompanying plan not with report.

736. U.S. Senate. *Memorial of Inhabitants of Brunswick, Maine, Praying that the Southern Indians May Not Be Removed from Their Present Places of Abode, without Their Free Consent.* 21st Cong., 1st Sess. (S.Doc.92). [Washington: 1830]. 1 pg. (Serial Set 193). Supports the right of the Indians in Georgia, Mississippi, and Alabama, to self-government and to remain on their lands.

737. U.S. Senate. *Memorial of Inhabitants of Kennebunk, Maine, Praying that the Indians May Be Protected in Their Rights, and in the Possession of Their Lands, &c.* 21st Cong., 1st Sess. (S.Doc.96). [Washington: 1830]. 1 pg. (Serial Set 193).

738. U.S. Senate. [Report and Resolution of Maine in Support of Settlement of Claims of Massachusetts for Militia Services during War of 1812]. 21st Cong., 1st Sess. (S.Doc.107). [Washington: 1830. 4 pg. (Serial Set 193). Same as Mil.aff.448 (21-1) ASP 019. See entry **731**.

739. U.S. Senate. *Report of the Secretary of War, in Compliance to a Resolution of the Senate, Relative to the Erection of the Pier at Kennebunk.* 21st Cong., 1st Sess. (S.Doc.7). [Washington: Duff Green, 1829]. 13 pg. (Serial Set 192). Report on why repairs to the pier, for which Congress appropriated money at the last session, have not been completed; includes detailed account of expenditures on labor and materials.

21ST CONGRESS, 2ND SESSION

740. Evans, George (Maine). "Distribution of the Surplus Revenue," *Register of Debates.* 21st Cong., 2nd Sess. (1 Feb. 1831) pp. 550-555. Objects to printing more copies of the report on the distribution of the surplus revenue among the states, as it would imply that the House had sanctioned the doctrines contained in the report. Supports the constitutionality of appropriations for internal improvements but not the distribution of funds to the states for domestic uses.

741. Holmes, John (Maine). Speech on the Post Office Department, *Register of Debates.* 21st Cong., 2nd Sess. (4 Feb., 7 Feb., 11 Feb., 5 Mar. 1831) pp. 96-101; 103-109; 197-203; 338-340. Supports the inquiry into the management of the Post Office, particularly what Postmasters have been removed and why. Maintains that this information is necessary to determine if removals result from executive patronage or from retrenchment and economy.

742. "An Act to Alter the Times of Holding the District Courts of the United States for the Districts of Maine and Illinois, and Northern District of Alabama," *Statutes at Large*, Vol. IV (27 Jan. 1831) p. 434. Also printed in the *Register of Debates* (21st Cong., 2nd Sess.) Appendix, pp. 4-5.

743. U.S. House. *Inhabitants of Freeport - Remove the Indians.* 21st Cong., 2nd Sess. (H.Doc.89). Washington: Duff Green, 1831. 1 pg. (Serial Set 208). Supports the removal of the Indians as humane and just; contends that the Indians do not have a right to set up an independent government within a sovereign state without that state's consent.

744. U.S. House. *Memorial of the Inhabitants of Surry, State of Maine, Respecting the Removal of the Southern Indians.* 21st Cong., 2nd Sess. (H.Doc.138). Washington: Duff Green, 1831. 2 pg. (Serial Set 209-1). Supports removing the Indians to allow them their own government and to preserve them from annihilation.

745. U.S. Senate. *Memorial of Inhabitants of Vassalborough, Maine, Praying that Protection May Be Extended to the Indian Tribes by Congress, &c.* 21st Cong., 2nd Sess. (S.Doc.18). Washington: Duff Green, 1831. 4 pg. (Serial Set 203). Memorial supports protection for the Cherokees; reviews obligations of previous treaties and administrations and asks that they be honored.

22ND CONGRESS, 1ST SESSION

746. "Northeastern Boundary," *Register of Debates.* 22nd Cong., 1st Sess. (18 Jan. 1832) pp. 108-109. Debate on the resolution asking the President to communicate all correspondence about arrangements between the U.S. and Great Britain on the northeastern boundary and the selection of an arbiter.

747. "Official Corruption," *Register of Debates.* 22nd Cong., 1st Sess. (27 Mar. 1832) pp. 2252-2259. Debate on the resolution to inquire into the charges made against the collector of the port of Wiscasset, Maine. Includes brief remarks by George Evans (Maine), John Anderson (Maine), Isaac Bates (Mass.), and George Briggs (Mass.).

748. Anderson, John (Maine). "Claim of Mrs. Decatur," *Register of Debates.* 22nd Cong., 1st Sess. (3 Mar. 1832) pp. 2001-2004. Supports the claim to grant prize money to the representative, officers and crew of Commodore Decatur, for the capture and destruction of the frigate Philadelphia.

749. Anderson, John (Maine). "Official Corruption," *Register of Debates.* 22nd Cong., 1st Sess. (27 Mar. 1832) pp. 2255-2256. Supports having the Treasury Dept. investigate the charges against the Wiscasset collector.

750. Anderson, John (Maine). "The Tariff," *Register of Debates.* 22nd Cong., 1st Sess. (26 June 1832) pp. 3786-3789. Opposes giving a drawback to ships and steamboats on materials used in their construction; prefers a direct reduction of the duty on hemp, duck, and iron, to this indirect reduction.

751. Anderson, John (Maine). "Wiscasset Collector," *Register of Debates.* 22nd Cong., 1st Sess. (3 Apr. 1832) pp. 2351-2357. Objects to the House investigating the charges against the Wiscasset collector as it would establish a dangerous precedent; discusses and dismisses cases cited as precedent.

752. Evans, George (Maine). "Bank of the United States," *Register of Debates.* 22nd Cong., 1st Sess. (7 Mar. 1832) pp. 2045-2058. Opposes the proposed investigation of the bank. Contends that it is unnecessary as the valid charges have already been discussed, the other charges are frivolous, and the investigation will not elicit the desired information.

753. Evans, George (Maine). "Chickasaw Treaty," *Register of Debates.* 22nd Cong., 1st Sess. (3 Feb. 1832) pp. 1733-1741. Supports the disclosure of information on how Chickasaw territory was transferred to the U.S. and then to private citizens without the assent of Congress.

754. Evans, George (Maine). "The Tariff," *Register of Debates.* 22nd Cong., 1st Sess. (11 June 1832) pp. 3421-3453. Supports protectionism; addresses various arguments presented, the European system, and the effect of protective tariffs upon Southern interests.

755. Evans, George (Maine). "Wiscasset Collector," *Register of Debates.* 22nd Cong., 1st Sess. (30 Mar. 1832) pp. 2300-2311. Debates the merits of having the Treasury Dept. or the House investigate the conduct of the collector at Wiscasset, Maine, charged with extortion and solicitation to commit perjury; discusses the credibility of the witness.

756. Holmes, John (Maine). "Appropriation Bill - Colonial Trade," *Register of Debates.* 22nd Cong., 1st Sess. (9 Apr. 1832) pp. 740-761. Opposes the current

colonial trade arrangement, which discriminates in favor of British tonnage; describes the colonial trade and reviews the acts and effects of the policies of the administration.

757. Holmes, John (Maine). "The British Colonial Trade," *Register of Debates.* 22nd Cong., 1st Sess. (22 Dec. 1831) pp. 24-26. Remarks on the inequities that still remain for American trade with the West Indies.

758. Holmes, John (Maine). "Postages and the Post Office," *Register of Debates.* 22nd Cong., 1st Sess. (4 May 1832) pp. 885-899. Supports repealing the postage on newspapers; addresses various arguments, including foreign competition, lost revenue for the Post Office, inequality, and the potential abuse of influencing and corrupting the press.

759. Holmes, John (Maine). Remarks on Nomination of Mr. Van Buren as Minister to Great Britain, *Register of Debates.* 22nd Cong., 1st Sess. (25 Jan. 1832) pp. 1310-1313. Opposes the nomination and requests an investigation into Van Buren's involvement in the removal and resignation of several members of the President's cabinet.

760. Holmes, John (Maine). "The Tariff," *Register of Debates.* 22nd Cong., 1st Sess. (30 Jan, 1 Feb. 1832) pp. 194-221; 253-255. Supports the protective system; discusses the history and constitutionality of protective tariffs, maintaining that Congress has the power to lay and collect imposts; reviews the beneficial effects of the system; responds to the objections of the South.

761. Jarvis, Leonard (Maine). "Wiscasset Collector," *Register of Debates.* 22nd Cong., 1st Sess. (28 Mar., 14 Apr. 1832) pp. 2275-2276; 2504-2512. Remarks on the propriety of an investigation. Defends against remarks accusing him of politicizing the debate on the Wiscasset collector, charged with misdemeanors in office. Contends that those opposed to the administration have tried to bolster the credibility of the witness by referring to his political offices; defends the productivity of the customhouses in New England.

762. Sprague, Peleg (Maine). "Foreign Intercourse - Colonial Trade," *Register of Debates.* 22nd Cong., 1st Sess. (3 Apr. 1832) pp. 685-706. Discusses the disastrous agreement on colonial trade reached by the administration without the approval of the Senate. Discusses inequities; demonstrates the effects.

763. Sprague, Peleg (Maine). Speech on Determination of the Northeastern Boundary, *Register of Debates.* 22nd Cong., 1st Sess. (10 July 1832) pp. 1399-1412. Objects to adopting the boundary designated by the King of the Netherlands; discussion of the boundary includes lengthy list of maps from authentic and official sources supporting Maine's claim.

764. Sprague, Peleg (Maine). "The Tariff," *Register of Debates.* 22nd Cong., 1st Sess. (22 Mar. 1832) pp. 595-606. Supports reducing duties and modifying the tariff law of 1828. Demonstrates by documentary history that protective tariffs are constitutional; maintains that the issue is the extent of the protection and that primary regard should go to the interests of the laboring class.

765. "Application of Maine for a More Perfect and Uniform Organization of the Militia of the United States," *American State Papers: Military Affairs*, Vol. V (Doc. 522) pp. 5-6. (ASP 020).

766. "On the Construction of a Military Road from Mattanawcook to Mar's Hill, in Maine," *American State Papers: Military Affairs*, Vol. V (Doc. 527) pp. 11-13. (ASP 020). Report gives recommendations and estimates of alternative plans to complete the road from Mattanwcook to Houlton. Continuing the road from Houlton to Mar's Hill deemed unnecessary.

767. "On the Expediency of Erecting Fortifications on the Penobscot River and Bay, in Maine," *American State Papers: Military Affairs*, Vol. IV (Doc. 517) pp. 935-936. (ASP 019). Report that Mount Desert Island is the chosen site as Penobscot Bay is too large to realistically defend. Recommends establishing a fort opposite Bucksport, to be built after more expedient projects are done.

768. U.S. House. *Letter from the Secretary of State, Transmitting the Information Required by a Resolution of the House of Representatives, of the 26th of January, Instant, in Relation to Slaves Returned in the 5th Census, in Maine, Massachusetts, and Ohio.* 22nd Cong., 1st Sess. (H.Doc.84). Washington: Duff Green, 1832. 2 pg. (Serial Set 218). Letter gives names of official returning the slave, name and county of family to which slave belongs, and sex and approximate age of slave.

769. U.S. House. *Portland Marine Hospital.* 22nd Cong., 1st Sess. (H.Rpt.468). Washington: Duff Green, 1831. 1 pg. (Serial Set 228). Supports the petition from Portland, Maine, for the erection of a marine hospital in that city.

770. U.S. House. *Reduce Tariff.* 22nd Cong., 1st Sess. (H.Doc.183). Washington: Duff Green, 1832. 2 pg. (Serial Set 219). Resolutions of the State of Maine support reducing the tariff.

771. U.S. House. *Resolution of the Legislature of Maine, against Rechartering the Bank of the United States.* 22nd Cong., 1st Sess. (H.Doc.169). Washington: Duff Green, 1832. 1 pg. (Serial Set 219).

772. U.S. House. *Revolutionary Soldiers.* 22nd Cong., 1st Sess. (H.Doc.182). Washington: Duff Green, 1832. 2 pg. (Serial Set 219). Resolutions from Maine legislature to compensate officers and soldiers of the Revolutionary War not entitled to pensions under existing law.

773. U.S. Senate. "[Arbitration of U.S. and British Claims regarding the Northeastern Boundary of the U.S.]," *U.S. Senate Executive Documents and Reports.* [Washington: 1831]. (CIS microfiche 22-1-2). Confidential.

Documents transmitted by the President on the differences of opinion between the U.S. and Great Britain on the location of the northeastern boundary line.

774. U.S. Senate. "[Documents concerning the Northeastern Boundary of the U.S.]," *U.S. Senate Executive Documents and Reports.* [Washington: 1832]. (CIS microfiche 22-1-9). Confidential. Documents transmitted to the Senate include correspondence from the Governor of Maine, the Dept. of State, the President, the Minister from Great Britain, and the King of the Netherlands.

775. U.S. Senate. "Letter from the Charge D'Affaires of Great Britain to the Secretary of State, Communicating the Determination of His Majesty the King of Great Britain to Abide by the Decision of His Majesty the King of the Netherlands, on the Subject of the Boundary," *U.S. Senate Executive Documents and Reports.* [Washington: 1831]. (CIS microfiche 22-1-3). Confidential. Great Britain maintains that the arbitration decision should be taken as final and conclusive, as stipulated in the articles of the convention. Letter reviews the grounds and motives of her acceptance of the decision.

776. U.S. Senate. "[Northeast Boundary of U.S.]," *U.S. Senate Executive Documents and Reports.* [Washington: 1832]. (CIS microfiche 22-1-14). Confidential. Report of the Committee on Foreign Relations recommends that the Senate adopt a resolution advising the President to agree to the arbitration decision by the King of the Netherlands regarding the northeastern boundary.

777. U.S. Senate. "Northeastern Boundary," *U.S. Senate Executive Documents and Reports.* [Washington: 1832]. (CIS microfiche 22-1-18). Confidential. President transmits report of the State Department, with accompanying documents, relating to the northeastern boundary arbitration. Report discusses possible compensation to Maine for loss of territory should the boundary designated by the King of the Netherlands be established.

778. U.S. Senate. "[Settlement of the Northeastern Boundary of the U.S.]," *U.S. Senate Executive Documents and Reports.* [Washington: 1832]. (CIS microfiche 22-1-7). Confidential. Text of Senate resolution concerning U.S. response to arbiter's decision regarding the establishment of the northeastern boundary.

779. U.S. Senate. "[State of Maine Documents concerning Northeastern Boundary of the U.S.]," *U.S. Senate Executive Documents and Reports.* [Washington: 1832]. (CIS microfiche 22-1-8). Confidential. Copies of the Jan. 14 and 18, 1832 proceedings and resolutions of the Maine legislature opposed to the arbitration decision of the King of the Netherlands.

22ND CONGRESS, 2ND SESSION

780. Holmes, John (Maine). "Revenue Collection Bill," *Register of Debates.* 22nd Cong., 2nd Sess. (5 Feb. 1833) pp. 348-358. Debates who has the ultimate authority between Congress and a state. Question arises when South Carolina declares revenue laws passed by Congress as unconstitutional and passes laws intended to repeal them or make them inoperative within her limits. Maintains that when the Constitution was adopted, the states granted the right of ultimate decision to the general government.

781. Holmes, John (Maine). "Tariff," *Register of Debates.* 22nd Cong., 2nd Sess. (4 Jan. 1833) pp. 52-59. Favors requesting the Treasury Dept. to provide information on items "indispensable to national defense" that are proposed to be protected; discusses South Carolina's threat of nullification.

782. Jarvis, Leonard (Maine). "The Tariff Bill," *Register of Debates.* 22nd Cong., 2nd Sess. (31 Jan. 1833) pp. 1558-1564. Supports reducing the rates of duties so that revenue from protected articles would be reduced to zero; answers objections that sufficient revenue will not be raised by the bill and that it diminishes protection to home manufacturers.

783. Sprague, Peleg (Maine). "Reduction of Postage," *Register of Debates.* 22nd Cong., 2nd Sess. (31 Dec. 1832, 2 Jan. 1833) pp. 28-29, 32-34; 46-48. Supports reducing postage; considers it an unequal tax upon knowledge and information. Maintains that the Post Office Dept. should sustain itself and the resulting increased volume of mail would replace the lost revenue.

784. Sprague, Peleg (Maine). "The Tariff," *Register of Debates.* 22nd Cong., 2nd Sess. (25 Feb. 1833) pp. 745-749. Supports the bill as it would provide protection by a scheme of equal reduction; discusses tariffs on woolens and iron.

785. "An Act for Making Calais and Pembroke, in the State of Maine, Ports of Delivery," *Statutes at Large*, Vol. IV (5 Feb. 1833) p. 611. Also printed in the *Register of Debates* (22nd Cong., 2nd Sess.) Appendix, p. 5.

786. "On the Expediency of Completing the Military Road from Houlton to Mars Hill, in Maine," *American State Papers: Military Affairs*, Vol. V (Doc. 545) p. 156. (ASP 020). Report that the road is unnecessary.

787. "Statement of Fortifications in Maine, Their Location, Number of Men and Armament," *American State Papers: Military Affairs*, Vol. V (Doc. 539) pp. 127-128. (ASP 020). Report describes three military posts and the defenses of the northeastern section of the coast. Same as H.doc.24 (22-2) 233 (entry 789).

788. U.S. House. *Joseph Prescott* 22nd Cong., 2nd Sess. (H.Rpt.112). Washington: Duff Green, 1832. 1 pg. (Serial Set 236). Report of the Committee on Invalid Pensions on the claim of Joseph Prescott.

789. U.S. House. *Letter from the Secretary of War, Transmitting a Report in Relation to the Fortifications and Other Defences in the State of Maine.* 22nd

Cong., 2nd Sess. (H.Doc.24). Washington: Duff Green, 1832. 4 pg. (Serial Set 233). Same as Mil.aff.539 (22-2) ASP 020. See entry **787**.

23RD CONGRESS, 1ST SESSION

790. "Maine Petitions," *Register of Debates.* 23rd Cong., 1st Sess. (21 Feb., 22 Feb. 1834) pp. 616-636; 639-656. Presentation and debate over memorials and resolutions from Portland, Maine, deploring their financial situation and requesting the re-charter of the Bank of the U.S. or the establishment of a national bank. First day's debate includes remarks by Peleg Sprague (Me.), Ether Shepley (Me.), John Forsyth (Ga.), and Ezekiel F. Chambers (Md.). Second day's debates includes remarks by Daniel Webster (Mass.), John Forsyth (Ga.), Ezekiel Chambers (Md.), and Elias Kane (Ill.).

791. "Memorial from Bangor, Maine," *Register of Debates.* 23rd Cong., 1st Sess. (24 Feb. 1834) pp. 2762-2771. Debates the memorial from Bangor praying to either renew the charter of the Bank of the U.S. or establish another national bank. Includes remarks from Gorham Parks (Me.), John Reed (Mass.), and George Evans (Me.).

792. "State of Maine," *Congressional Globe.* 23rd Cong., 1st Sess. (3 Feb. 1834) pp. 148-149. Debates the resolutions of the State of Maine opposed to the re-chartering of the Bank of the U.S. and in support of the removal of the public deposits from the bank. Resolutions reprinted; remarks by Gorham Parks, Francis O.J. Smith, and George Evans. Different version of this debate printed in the *Register of Debates*, "Maine Resolutions," pp. 2570-2581.

793. Evans, George (Maine). "Gardiner (Me.) Memorial," *Register of Debates.* 23rd Cong., 1st Sess. (14 Apr. 1834) pp. 3640-3641. Supports the memorialists from Gardiner and Pittston, Maine, and their memorial in favor of a national bank.

794. Evans, George (Maine). "Gardiner (Me.) Memorial," *Register of Debates.* 23rd Cong., 1st Sess. (21 Apr. 1834) pp. 3715-3742. Maintains that the reasons of the Secretary of the Treasury for the removal of the public money are insufficient, and that a national bank is necessary. Examines the report of the Committee of Ways and Means; claims that it skirts the true questions. Reviews the reasons presented by the Secretary for the removal. Addresses issues of constitutional authority. Describes the distress of the country; defends the bank.

795. Evans, George (Maine). "The General Appropriation Bill," *Register of Debates.* 23rd Cong., 1st Sess. (1 May 1834) pp. 3892-3894. Remarks on the role and importance of various foreign ministers in negotiating treaties.

796. Evans, George (Maine). "Hallowell (Me.) Memorial," *Register of Debates.* 23rd Cong., 1st Sess. (26 May 1834) pp. 4256-4257. Supports the memorialists and their memorial asking for relief from financial distress through a national bank.

797. Evans, George (Maine). "Harbor Bill," *Register of Debates.* 23rd Cong., 1st Sess. (19 June 1834) pp. 4576-4577. Supports appropriations for surveys for internal improvements.

798. Evans, George (Maine). "Memorial from Bangor, Maine," *Register of Debates.* 23rd Cong., 1st Sess. (24 Feb. 1834) pp. 2767-2771. Defends the memorialists and their memorial asking for the re-chartering of the Bank of the U.S. or the establishment of another national bank. Maintains that the distress of the country is real, and that their memorial deserves proper respect.

799. Evans, George (Maine). "State of Maine," *Congressional Globe.* 23rd Cong., 1st Sess. (3 Feb. 1834) p. 149. Attempts to discredit the resolutions of the State of Maine and of Portland opposed to the Bank of the United States. Much longer version of remarks printed in the *Register of Debates*, "Maine Resolutions," pp. 2573-2580.

800. Parks, Gorham (Maine). Remarks on the Bangor Memorial, *Congressional Globe.* 23rd Cong., 1st Sess. (24 Feb. 1834) p. 195. Disagrees with the Bangor memorial praying for a re-charter of the Bank of the United States. Highlights the inconsistencies in the report and resolutions. Same speech printed in the *Register of Debates*, "Memorial from Bangor, Maine," pp. 2762-2765.

801. Parks, Gorham (Maine). "State of Maine," *Congressional Globe.* 23rd Cong., 1st Sess. (3 Feb. 1834) p. 148. Remarks on resolutions from Maine in support of the removal of the deposits, and opposed to renewing the charter of the Bank of the U.S.; reprint of resolutions included. Same remarks printed in the *Register of Debates*, "Maine Resolutions," pp. 2570-2571.

802. Shepley, Ether (Maine). "The Deposite Question," *Register of Debates.* 23rd Cong., 1st Sess. (14 Jan. 1834) pp. 233-251. Supports the President and Secretary of the Treasury in removing the deposits. Discusses allegations concerning assumption of power, the removal of the previous Secretary, the supervisory relationship of the President to the Secretary, the power of the Secretary, and the authority to withdraw money from the Treasury. Accuses the bank of precipitating the economic distress by its actions.

803. Shepley, Ether (Maine). "Hallowell (Me.) Memorial," *Register of Debates.* 23rd Cong., 1st Sess. (30 Apr. 1834) pp. 1561-1562. Remarks on the Whig tendencies of the inhabitants of Kennebec, Maine.

804. Shepley, Ether (Maine). "Maine Memorial," *Register of Debates.* 23rd Cong., 1st Sess. (10 Apr. 1834) pp. 1287-1288. Presents and supports a memorial from Gardiner and Pittston which states their financial distress and advocates a bank to regulate the money concerns of the country.

805. Shepley, Ether (Maine). "Maine Petitions," *Register of Debates.* 23rd Cong., 1st Sess. (21 Feb. 1834) pp. 618-620, 632. Opposes the memorials and resolutions presented by Sen. Sprague. Maintains that Congress and the Bank of the U.S. are responsible for the financial distress of the country.

806. Shepley, Ether (Maine). Remarks on Resolutions from Citizens of Portland on the Bank of the U.S., *Congressional Globe.* 23rd Cong., 1st Sess. (3 Feb. 1834) pp. 146-147. Remarks on resolutions from citizens of Portland opposed to the removal of the deposits; maintains that the resolutions passed by the Legislature of Maine supporting the removing of deposits and opposing the renewal of the charter represents the true opinion of the people. Different version of these remarks printed in the *Register of Debates*, pp. 442-443.

807. Shepley, Ether (Maine). Remarks on Trade with the West Indies, *Register of Debates.* 23rd Cong., 1st Sess. (22 Jan. 1834) pp. 333-335. Presents statistics on exports to the West Indies, British West Indies, and British American colonies; describes the manner of that trade.

808. Shepley, Ether (Maine). "Restoration of the Deposites," *Register of Debates.* 23rd Cong., 1st Sess. (2 June 1834) pp. 1851-1858. Supports the actions of the President and Secretary of the Treasury in removing the deposits. Discusses whether the bank was guilty of misconduct; maintains that the bank has the power to derange the business concerns of the country and that she used her power to aide in causing the distresses of the country. Discusses the bank's influence upon the State banks and on equalizing the exchanges.

809. Smith, Francis O. J. (Maine). Further Remarks on the Resolutions from the Citizens of Portland on the Bank of the United States, *Congressional Globe.* 23rd Cong., 1st Sess. (17 Mar. 1834) pp. 247-248. Responds to a communication from one of the petitioners who provides explanations concerning the petition that Mr. Smith earlier attacked. Mr. Smith defends his earlier remarks. The communication and Mr. Smith's remarks are also printed in the *Register of Debates*, "Portland Resolutions," pp. 3014-3017.

810. Smith, Francis O. J. (Maine). "State of Maine," *Congressional Globe.* 23rd Cong., 1st Sess. (3 Feb. 1834) pp. 148-149. Discounts the resolutions opposed to the removal of the deposits from the bank. Remarks also printed in the *Register of Debates*, "Maine Resolutions," pp. 2571-2573.

811. Sprague, Peleg (Maine). "Augusta (Me.) Memorial," *Register of Debates.* 23rd Cong., 1st Sess. (2 June 1834) pp. 1838-1839. Supports the memorialists and the memorial remonstrating against removing the public deposits.

812. Sprague, Peleg (Maine). "Bath (Me.) Memorial," *Register of Debates.* 23rd Cong., 1st Sess. (3 Apr. 1834) pp. 1243-1244. Presents and supports their memorial seeking a renewal of the charter of the Bank of the U.S. or the establishment of another bank which could stabilize the currency.

813. Sprague, Peleg (Maine). "Boston Memorial," *Register of Debates*. 23rd Cong., 1st Sess. (18 Mar. 1834) pp. 982-983. Supports the memorialists and their memorial protesting against the removal of the deposits.

814. Sprague, Peleg (Maine). "Hallowell (Me.) Memorial," *Register of Debates*. 23rd Cong., 1st Sess. (30 Apr. 1834) pp. 1559-1561, 1562-1563. Supports the memorialists and their memorials asking for relief from economic distress through a national bank. Responds to remarks from Sen. Shepley regarding the Whig tendencies of the inhabitants of Kennebec, Maine.

815. Sprague, Peleg (Maine). "Maine Memorials," *Register of Debates*. 23rd Cong., 1st Sess. (13 Mar. 1834) pp. 942-943. Presents memorials from Eastport and Lubec, Maine, opposed to removing public deposits and the course of the Executive.

816. Sprague, Peleg (Maine). "Maine Petitions," *Register of Debates*. 23rd Cong., 1st Sess. (21 Feb. 1834) pp. 616-618, 620-623, 623-626, 627, 632-633. Presents and supports memorials and resolutions from Portland, Maine, requesting the re-charter of the United States Bank, or the establishment of a national bank. Defends the character of the memorialists and their claim that their financial distress was caused by the removal of the deposits. Responds to Sen. Shepley's charges that Congress and the bank caused their distress.

817. Sprague, Peleg (Maine). "New Jersey Petitions," *Register of Debates*. 23rd Cong., 1st Sess. (11 Mar. 1834) pp. 870-872, 873-874, 875-876. Rebuts Sen. Forsyth's (Ga.) claim that opponents of the administration were happy that the administration had tried the experiment of removing the deposits as it had greatly injured the reputation of the administration.

818. Sprague, Peleg (Maine). "Protest," *Congressional Globe*. 23rd Cong., 1st Sess. (17 Apr. 1834) pp. 317-318. Objects to President Jackson's protest against the Senate resolutions expressing disapprobation with the Executive seizing the public deposits. Appalled at Jackson's claim that all executive power is vested in him, that the Constitution gives him possession of the public money and public property. Longer version of speech printed in the *Register of Debates*, "President's Protest," pp. 1340-1345.

819. Sprague, Peleg (Maine). "Removal of the Deposites," *Register of Debates*. 23rd Cong., 1st Sess. (29 Jan., 3 Feb., 5 Feb. 1834) pp. 380-397; 443-444; 480. Deplores the accumulating power of the Executive, occurring at the expense of Congress and the Judiciary. Reviews President Jackson's encroachments upon the authority of the other branches of government. Discusses the veto power and the power of removal. Reviews the circumstances of removing the deposits and other acts against the Bank of the U.S. . Defends the Portland memorialists and their resolution for a restoration of the deposits. Evaluates the reasons presented by the Secretary of the Treasury for removing the deposits.

820. Sprague, Peleg (Maine). "Reports on the Post Office," *Register of Debates.* 23rd Cong., 1st Sess. (11 June 1834) pp. 1985-1986, 1992-1993. Advocates printing many copies of the report; defends the majority report.

821. Sprague, Peleg (Maine). "Trade with the West Indies," *Register of Debates.* 23rd Cong., 1st Sess. (3 Jan. 1834) pp. 139-140. Presents statistics on the condition of trade with the British colonies and the British West Indies.

822. Sprague, Peleg (Maine). "West India Trade," *Register of Debates.* 23rd Cong., 1st Sess. (28 Jan. 1834) pp. 373-375. Remarks on the trade between the U.S. and the British and foreign West India ports and the British North American colonies; gives statistics of exports and tonnage.

823. "An Act for the Repair of the Mars Hill Military Road, in the State of Maine," *Statutes at Large*, Vol. IV (30 June 1834) p. 716. Also printed in the *Register of Debates* (23rd Cong., 1st Sess.) Appendix, p. 338.

824. "On Claim of Officers, Non-Commissioned Officers, and Privates of the Army for Losses Sustained by the Burning of Hancock Barracks, in Maine," *American State Papers: Military Affairs*, Vol. V (Doc. 557) pp. 241-242. (ASP 020). Petition not supported. Same as H.rp.112 (23-1) 260 (entry **831**).

825. U.S. House. *Letter from the Secretary of War, Transmitting a Report and Survey of the Harbor of Portland, in the State of Maine.* 23rd Cong., 1st Sess. (H.Doc.491). [Washington: Gales & Seaton, Print., 1834]. 5 pg.; 2 pg. maps and profiles. (Serial Set 259). Report of the survey with estimates. Includes map of Portland Harbor, Maine, and profiles of the proposed harbor and breakwater.

826. U.S. House. *Marine Hospital - Portland, Maine.* 23rd Cong., 1st Sess. (H.Rpt.151). [Washington: 1834]. 1 pg. (Serial Set 260). Same report as issued during the 22nd Congress (H.rp.468 (22-1) 228 (entry **769**)), supporting the erection of a marine hospital in Portland.

827. U.S. House. *Memorial of Inhabitants of Bangor, Maine, on the Subject of the Present Deranged State of the Money Market.* 23rd Cong., 1st Sess. (H.Doc.125). [Washington: Gales & Seaton, Print., 1834]. 7 pg. (Serial Set 256). Proceedings of meeting and memorial. Supports re-chartering the Bank of the U.S., with modifications and restrictions, or the establishment of a new national banking institution for the deposit of the public money. Memorial same as S.doc.111 (23-1) 239 (entry **835**), but includes the names of the memorialists.

828. U.S. House. *Memorial of Inhabitants of Bath, Maine, in Relation to the Currency.* 23rd Cong., 1st Sess. (H.Doc.250). [Washington: Gales & Seaton, Print., 1834]. 4 pg. (Serial Set 257). Same as S.doc.240 (23-1) 240 (entry **836**), but with the names of the memorialists.

829. U.S. House. *Memorial of Inhabitants of Eastport, Maine, in Relation to the Currency.* 23rd Cong., 1st Sess. (H.Doc.171). [Washington: Gales &

Seaton, Print., 1834]. 2 pg. (Serial Set 256). Memorial for relief from present financial condition. Same as S.doc.169 (23-1) 240 (entry **840**), but with the names of the memorialists.

830. U.S. House. *Memorial of Inhabitants of Lubec, Maine, in Favor of Rechartering the Bank of the United States.* 23rd Cong., 1st Sess. (H.Doc.172). [Washington: Gales & Seaton, Print., 1834]. 2 pg. (Serial Set 256). Supports the restoration of the deposits and the re-chartering of the Bank of the United States. Same as S.doc.170 (23-1) 240 (entry **837**), but with names of memorialists.

831. U.S. House. *Officers - Hancock Barracks.* 23rd Cong., 1st Sess. (H.Rp.112). [Washington: 1834]. 1 pg. (Serial Set 260). Request of petition for losses sustained by the burning of Hancock Barracks is denied. Same as Mil.aff.557 (23-1) ASP 020 (entry **824**).

832. U.S. House. *Proceedings and Memorial Adopted at a Meeting of Inhabitants of Hallowell, in Relation to the Currency.* 23rd Cong., 1st Sess. (H.Doc.475). [Washington: Gales & Seaton, Print., 1834]. 9 pg. (Serial Set 259). Opposes the removal of the deposits from the U.S. Bank and advocates a national bank. Memorial same as S.doc.317 (31-1) 241 (entry **843**), but with names and occupations of the memorialists.

833. U.S. House. *Resolutions Adopted at a Meeting of Citizens of Portland, upon the Subject of the Present Depression of Trade, and the Embarrassments in the Money Market.* 23rd Cong., 1st Sess. (H.Doc.74). [Washington: Gales & Seaton, Print., 1834. 3 pg. (Serial Set 255). Resolutions on the need to restore the deposits of the Bank of the United States, opposed to cash payment for duties, and for improvement of the financial climate. Same as S.doc.69 (23-1) 239 (entry **844**), but with additional letter from the President of Exchange Bank, Portland.

834. U.S. House. *Resolutions of the Legislature of Maine, in Relation to the Removal of the Public Deposites, from the Bank of the United States.* 23rd Cong., 1st Sess. (H.Doc.75). [Washington: Gales & Seaton, 1834]. 2 pg. (Serial Set 255). Resolutions oppose re-chartering the bank and support the removal of the public deposits from the bank. Same as S.doc.68 (23-1) 239 (entry **845**).

835. U.S. Senate. *Memorial and Resolutions of the People of Bangor, Maine, Opposed to the Measures of the Executive in Removing the Public Deposites from the Bank United States.* 23rd Cong., 1st Sess. (S.Doc.111). Washington: Duff Green, 1834. 5 pg. (Serial Set 239). Same as H.doc.125 (23-1) 256, but without the names of the memorialists. See entry **827**.

836. U.S. Senate. *Memorial from the Inhabitants of Bath, Maine, Opposed to the Removal of the Deposites from the Bank of the United States.* 23rd Cong., 1st Sess. (S.Doc.240). Washington: Duff Green, 1834. 1 pg. (Serial Set 240).

Same as H.doc.250 (23-1) 257 (entry **828**), but without the names of the memorialists.

837. U.S. Senate. *Memorial of Inhabitants of Lubec, Maine, for a Restoration of the Deposites to the Bank of the United States.* 23rd Cong., 1st Sess. (S.Doc.170). Washington: Duff Green, 1834. 2 pg. (Serial Set 240). Same as H.doc.172 (23-1) 256 but without the names of the memorialists. See entry **830**.

838. U.S. Senate. *Memorial of Inhabitants of Portland, Maine, Complaining of the Pecuniary Distresses of the Community, and Praying to Be Relieved Therefrom.* 23rd Cong., 1st Sess. (S.Doc.112). Washington: Duff Green, 1834. 1 pg. (Serial Set 239). Plea for measures that will restore the economy.

839. U.S. Senate. *Memorial of Seth Pitts, in Opposition to the Bank of the United States, and Stating that He Had Signed a Memorial in Its Favor without Being Aware of It.* 23rd Cong., 1st Sess. (S.Doc.418). Washington: Duff Green, 1834. 1 pg. (Serial Set 242). Describes circumstances under which he mistakenly signed a petition in favor of the Bank of the United States.

840. U.S. Senate. *Memorial of Sundry Inhabitants of Eastport, Maine, Praying for Relief from Present Distresses of the Community, &c.* 23rd Cong., 1st Sess. (S.Doc.169). Washington: Duff Green, 1834. 1 pg. (Serial Set 240). Same as H.doc.171 (23-1) 256 (entry **829**), but without the names of the memorialists.

841. U.S. Senate. *Memorial of the Inhabitants of Augusta, Maine, against the Removal of the Deposites, and in Favor of the Recharter of the Bank of the United States.* 23rd Cong., 1st Sess. (S.Doc.410). Washington: Duff Green, 1834. 7 pg. (Serial Set 242). Memorial blames the removal of the deposits for the present calamity; five pages of names of memorialists.

842. U.S. Senate. *Memorial of the Inhabitants of Gardiner and Pittston, Maine, in Favor of a Bank of the United States, &c.* 23rd Cong., 1st Sess. (S.Doc.268). Washington: Duff Green, 1834. 1 pg. (Serial Set 241). Supports the bank as indispensable to a sound uniform currency and successful commerce.

843. U.S. Senate. *Memorial of the Legal Voters of Hallowell, Maine, for the Adoption of Such Measures As Will Give Relief.* 23rd Cong., 1st Sess. (S.Doc.317). Washington: Duff Green, 1834. 2 pg. (Serial Set 241). Same as H.doc.475 (23-1) 259, excluding the names of memorialists. See entry **832**.

844. U.S. Senate. *Resolutions Adopted at a Meeting of the Citizens of Portland, Maine, Relative to Present Embarrassments in Commercial Transactions; the Necessity of Restoring the Deposites to the Bank of the United States; and Expressing an Opinion against the Change from the Credit to the Cash Payment for Duties, &c.* 23rd Cong., 1st Sess. (S.Doc.69). Washington: Duff Green, 1834. 3 pg. (Serial Set 239). Same as H.doc.74 (23-1) 255, without the letter from the Exchange Bank, Portland. See entry **833**.

845. U.S. Senate. *Resolutions of the Legislature of Maine, against Rechartering the Bank of the United States, &c.* 23rd Cong., 1st Sess. (S.Doc.68). Washington: Duff Green, 1834. 1 pg. (Serial Set 239). Same as H.doc.75 (23-1) 255. See entry **834**.

23RD CONGRESS, 2ND SESSION

846. "Northeastern Boundary," *Register of Debates.* 23rd Cong., 2nd Sess. (24 Dec., 27 Dec. 1834) pp. 850-876. Debate on resolutions from Massachusetts requesting the President to disclose communications between the U.S. government and Great Britain, and the U.S. government and Maine, since the rejection of the advisory opinion of the King of the Netherlands. Includes brief speeches by Levi Lincoln (Mass.), Gorham Parks (Me.), George Evans (Me.), and Frances O.J. Smith (Me). Different version of this debate printed in the *Congressional Globe*, pp. 74-77.

847. Evans, George (Maine). "Election of the Printer to the House," *Register of Debates.* 23rd Cong., 2nd Sess. (10 Feb. 1835) pp. 1263-1265. Remarks on the House resolution for the election of a printer; favors a ballot election.

848. Evans, George (Maine). "Northeastern Boundary," *Register of Debates.* 23rd Cong., 2nd Sess. (24 Dec. 1834) pp. 857-862, 872-874. Supports the resolutions from Massachusetts requesting communications between the U.S. government and Great Britain, and the U.S. government and Maine, concerning the northeastern boundary. Addresses Mr. Parks' (Maine) and Mr. Smith's objections. Reviews the history of the separation of Maine from Massachusetts. Maintains that the boundary question is of national interest, rather than Maine's alone. Shorter version of these speeches in *Congressional Globe*, pp. 75, 77.

849. Jarvis, Leonard (Maine). "General Appropriation Bill," *Congressional Globe.* 23rd Cong., 2nd Sess. (28 Jan. 1835) p. 178. Remarks on the necessity for reform in the customhouse system; introduces an amendment to allow customhouse officers to transfer to districts when requisite.

850. Parks, Gorham (Maine). "Northeastern Boundary," *Register of Debates.* 23rd Cong., 2nd Sess. (24 Dec. 1834) pp. 854-857. Objects to the Massachusetts resolutions requesting information on communications between the U.S. government and Great Britain, and the government and Maine, on the status of the northeastern boundary. Maintains that Massachusetts is interfering in Maine's affairs. Also printed in the *Congressional Globe*, pp. 74-75.

851. Shepley, Ether (Maine). "French Spoliations," *Congressional Globe.* 23rd Cong., 2nd Sess. (17 Dec., 22 Dec. 1834) pp. 45; 54-56. Remarks and speech support the claims for spoliations made upon American commerce by France prior to 1800; uses published documents to document the history and validity of the claims. Same remarks and speech printed in the *Register of Debates,* "French Spoliations," pp. 23-24; 36-44.

852. Smith, Francis O. J. (Maine). "Northeastern Boundary," *Congressional Globe.* 23rd Cong., 2nd Sess. (24 Dec. 1834) pp. 75-76, 77. Remarks oppose the resolution requesting the President to disclose any communication between the U.S. government and Great Britain since the rejection of the advisory opinion of the King of the Netherlands; advocates support for the Executive. Also printed in the *Register of Debates,* "Northeastern Boundary," pp. 870-872, 874-875.

853. Smith, Francis O. J. (Maine). "Post Office Department," *Congressional Globe.* 23rd Cong., 2nd Sess. (14 Feb. 1835) pp. 246-247. Opposes printing extra copies of the report on the condition of the Post Office Department. Same remarks printed in *Register of Debates,* "Post Office Reports," pp. 1371-1374.

854. Smith, Francis O. J. (Maine). "Post Office Reports," *Register of Debates.* 23rd Cong., 2nd Sess. (14 Feb. 1835) pp. 1382-1385. Defends the Postmaster General and the current administration against attack; maintains that publishing the reports would be an unnecessary extravagance and overburden the mails.

855. U.S. House. *Letter from the Secretary of War, Transmitting the Report of a Reconnoissance [sic] of a Road through the Northern Frontier of the State of Maine.* 23rd Cong., 2nd Sess. (H.Doc.144). [Washington: Gales & Seaton, Print., 1835]. 14 pg.; 1 map. (Serial Set 274). Report of a survey from Augusta to the Canadian frontier, following the Kennebec River to West Forks, then north to the border; report supports connecting the inland frontier of Maine with its principal rivers for the military and commercial advantages. Map is titled "The Kennebec River and Adjacent Country Shewing the Routes Examined for a Road from Augusta to the Canada Line in the Direction of Quebec."

856. U.S. House. *Message from the President of the United States, Transmitting Information in Relation to the Establishment and Settlement of the Northeastern Boundary of the United States.* 23rd Cong., 2nd Sess. (H.Doc.62). [Washington: Gales & Seaton, Print., 1835]. 2 pg. (Serial Set 272). President Jackson responds that while the settlement of the northeastern boundary is in progress it would be against the public interest to disclose further communications between the U.S. and Great Britain.

857. U.S. House. *Proceedings of a Meeting of Merchants of Portland, Maine, in Relation to the Erection of a Breakwater in Portland Harbor.* 23rd Cong., 2nd Sess. (H.Doc.155). [Washington: Gales & Seaton, Print., 1835]. 1 pg. (Serial Set 274). Meeting with resolutions that it is expedient and desirable to erect a breakwater on Stanford's Ledge in Portland harbor.

24ᵀᴴ CONGRESS, 1ˢᵀ SESSION

858. Debate on Maine's Resolutions concerning Abolition Proceedings in the Non-slaveholding States, *Congressional Globe.* 24th Cong., 1st Sess. (8 Apr. 1836) pp. 335-338. Debate on Maine's resolutions that maintain that the power of regulating slavery belongs to each state. Discusses abolition publications and anti-slavery societies, including the Maine Abolition Society. Includes remarks by John Ruggles (Maine.). Debate also printed in the *Register of Debates*, "Maine Resolutions," pp. 1109-1120.

859. Evans, George (Maine). "Failure of Fortification Bill," *Congressional Globe, Appendix.* 24th Cong., 1st Sess. (28 Jan. 1836) pp. 542-548. Details the causes and circumstances of the failure of the fortification bill of the last session, particularly regarding the $3,000,000 appropriation and the animosity between the House and the Senate. Same speech, with additional notes, printed in the *Register of Debates*, "Fortification Bill of Last Session," pp. 2414-2435. Summary of speech in *Congressional Globe*, pp.151-152.

860. Evans, George (Maine). "Navy Appropriations," *Congressional Globe, Appendix.* 24th Cong., 1st Sess. (15 Mar. 1836) pp. 548-553. Supports appropriations to pay seamen and for improvements and repairs in the navy yards, including the navy yard at Portsmouth. Lengthy rebuttal, with statistics, to South Carolina's claim that disbursements favored the North. Same speech printed in the *Register of Debates*, "Naval Service Bill," pp. 2780-2799. Summary of speech in *Congressional Globe*, pp. 256-257.

861. Fairfield, John (Maine). "Post Office Department," *Register of Debates.* 24th Cong., 1st Sess. (31 May 1836) pp. 4112-4114. Opposes establishing an express mail system at triple the postage rate; maintains that few would benefit.

862. Fairfield, John (Maine). Remarks on a Bill to Amend the Charter of the Potomac Fire Insurance Company, *Congressional Globe.* 24th Cong., 1st Sess. (25 June 1836) pp. 585-586. Provides brief information on the charter, organization and past operations of the company. Same remarks printed in the *Register of Debates*, "Potomac Fire Insurance Company," pp. 4489-4490.

863. Jarvis, Leonard (Maine). "Maritime Defenses," *Congressional Globe, Appendix.* 24th Cong., 1st Sess. (4 Apr. 1836) pp. 265-271. Supports appropriations for the naval yards; addresses objections, including number of yards, expenses incurred, and the specific yards at Portsmouth and Pensacola. Responds to charges of inequality of expenditures to the advantage of the North. Same speech printed in the *Register of Debates*, "Naval Service Bill," pp. 3097-3117. Summary of speech in *Congressional Globe*, p. 319.

864. Jarvis, Leonard (Maine). "Slavery in the District of Columbia," *Register of Debates.* 24th Cong., 1st Sess. (6 Jan. 1836) pp. 2135-2136. Presents a resolution that the House not entertain the subject of the abolition of slavery in the District. Also presents a supporting resolution from Augusta, Maine, objecting to the non-slaveholding states interfering in the subject of slavery.

865. Parks, Gorham (Maine). "Public Deposits," *Congressional Globe, Appendix.* 24th Cong., 1st Sess. (22 June 1836) pp. 461-462. Opposes the bill to distribute the public money among the states to be deposited in the state treasuries; claims that the effect would be an eventual increase of the tariff, that money would be diverted from defense and fortifications, and that the navy would be neglected. Projects the effects upon Maine. Same speech printed in the *Register of Debates*, "Public Deposites," pp. 4372-4376.

866. Ruggles, Benjamin (Maine). "Fortifying the Maritime Frontier," *Congressional Globe, Appendix.* 24th Cong., 1st Sess. (21 May 1836) pp. 365-369. Supports appropriations for fortifications along the Maritime frontier, particularly on the Kennebec and Penobscot rivers. Addresses Maine's vulnerability, the benefit to the South of protecting the shipping industry of Maine, and the potential influence on negotiations of the northeastern boundary if Maine is perceived as properly fortified. Same speech printed in the *Register of Debates*, "Fortification Bill," (19 May 1836) pp. 1490-1503.

867. Shepley, Ether (Maine). "Gold and Silver for Public Lands," *Congressional Globe.* 24th Cong., 1st Sess. (23 Apr. 1836) p. 392. Blames the Bank of the U.S. for the problems with the currency and the fluctuations and speculations in business. Slightly different version of remarks printed in the *Register of Debates*, "Specie Payments," pp. 1272-1273.

868. Shepley, Ether (Maine). "National Defense: the Administration," *Congressional Globe, Appendix.* 24th Cong., 1st Sess. (18 Feb. 1836) pp. 115-116. Brief remarks on a variety of topics, including the status of the Treasury, influencing elections, and the Senate. Same remarks printed in the *Register of Debates*, "National Defence," pp. 572-575.

869. Shepley, Ether (Maine). "Northeastern Boundary of Maine," *Congressional Globe, Appendix.* 24th Cong., 1st Sess. (23 Mar. 1836) p. 181. Defers comment on the resolutions of Massachusetts respecting the northeastern boundary of Maine until the Legislature of Maine has commented.

870. Shepley, Ether (Maine). Remarks on Charges against Samuel Gwin, *Congressional Globe.* 24th Cong., 1st Sess. (1 June 1836) p. 518. Supports printing testimony disproving the charges made against Samuel Gwin; provides a history of Senate action. Slightly different version of remarks printed in the *Register of Debates*, "B.F. Curry and Samuel Gwin," pp. 1662-1664.

871. Smith, Francis O. J. (Maine). "Bank of the United States," *Congressional Globe.* 24th Cong., 1st Sess. (22 Mar. 1836) p. 278. Supports consideration of the bill to repeal the 14th section of the bank charter regarding whether bills of the bank are receivable in payment for public lands. Same remarks also printed in the *Register of Debates*, "United States Bank," pp. 2924-2926.

872. Smith, Francis O. J. (Maine). "Documentary History of the Revolution," *Congressional Globe, Appendix*. 24th Cong., 1st Sess. (16 Apr. 1836) pp. 280-281. Opposed to appropriations to fulfill the contract with Messrs. Clarke and Force for the *Documentary History of the American Revolution*. Discusses the contract and original memorial agreement. Same speech printed in the *Register of Debates*, "General Appropriation Bill," pp. 3290-3296.

873. Smith, Francis O. J. (Maine). "Harbor Bill," *Congressional Globe, Appendix*. 24th Cong., 1st Sess. (24 June 1836) pp. 508-510. Supports two harbor bills, one for construction and improvement of harbors partially completed, the other for works not yet commenced. Maintains that both bills are equally meritorious; blames the expenditures devoted towards this type of improvements on the act of 1824 which appropriated money for surveys of new works. Same speech printed in the *Register of Debates*, "Improvement of Harbors," pp. 4466-4471.

874. Smith, Francis O. J. (Maine). "Portsmouth Navy-Yard," *Congressional Globe, Appendix*. 24th Cong., 1st Sess. (10 Feb. 1836) pp. 81-82. Supports appropriations for construction and repairs at the navy yard at Portsmouth, New Hampshire. Same speech printed in the *Register of Debates*, "Naval Appropriation Bill," pp. 2512-2515.

875. Smith, Francis O. J. (Maine). "Post Office Department," *Congressional Globe*. 24th Cong., 1st Sess. (19 May 1836) p. 476. Defends the checks and balances in the selection of the Auditor of the Post Office Dept. Same remarks printed in the *Register of Debates*, "Post Office Department," pp. 3780-3781.

876. Smith, Francis O. J. (Maine). "Public Deposits," *Congressional Globe, Appendix*. 24th Cong., 1st Sess. (21 June 1836) pp. 498-499. Objects to separating the deposit bill into two bills; one to provide for depositing a portion of the public money with the local banking corporations and one to provide for depositing another portion of the public funds with the state governments. Contends that both serve to dispose on deposit the surplus money of the federal government. Same speech printed in the *Register of Debates*, "The Deposite Bill," (20 June 1836) pp. 4342-4346.

877. Smith, Francis O. J. (Maine). "Tariff of Postages," *Congressional Globe, Appendix*. 24th Cong., 1st Sess. (31 May 1836) pp. 426-427. Favors reducing the postage rates; addresses various arguments presented; reviews revenues and expenses of the Post Office Department. Same speech printed in the *Register of Debates*, "Post Office Department," pp. 4108-4111.

878. "Application of Maine for Liberal Appropriations by Congress for the Defences of the Country," *American State Papers: Military Affairs*, Vol. VI (Doc. 673) pp. 404-405. (ASP 021). Maine pleads for fair share of appropriations to establish necessary fortifications.

879. U.S. House. *Marine Hospital - Portland, Maine.* 24th Cong., 1st Sess. (H.Rpt.85). [Washington]: Blair & Rives, Printers, [1836]. 2 pg. (Serial Set 293). Report supports the erection of the hospital; same report as given in 23rd Congress (H.rp.151 (23-1) 260 (entry **826**)) and 22nd Congress (H.rp.468 (22-1) 228 (entry **769**)).

880. U.S. House. *Memorial of the Physicians of the City of Portland, Maine, Relative to the Erection of a Marine Hospital at Said City.* 24th Cong., 1st Sess. (H.Doc.68). [Washington: Blair & Rives, Printers, 1836]. 2 pg. (Serial Set 288). Memorial supports the erection of the hospital, but demonstrates the need for one more extensive than that planned, and for matching appropriations.

881. U.S. Senate. *Report from the Secretary of War, Relative to the Improvement of the Harbor of East Thomaston, Maine.* 24th Cong., 1st Sess. (S.Doc.75). Washington: Gales & Seaton, 1836. 5 pg. (Serial Set 280). Report of a survey to select a site for a breakwater in the harbor. Report agrees with the projected position, form and dimensions of the contemplated breakwater, but doubts the adequacy of the protection it would offer. Drawing that accompanied the original report not included.

882. U.S. Senate. *Resolutions of the Legislature of Maine, Relative to the Mode of Electing the President and Vice President of the United States.* 24th Cong., 1st Sess. (S.Doc.323). Washington: Gales & Seaton, 1836. 1 pg. (Serial Set 282). Resolutions support a constitutional amendment to prevent future elections of the President by the House, and the Vice President by the Senate; recommend that each state have an equal voice in the election.

883. U.S. Senate. *Resolutions of the Legislature of Maine, in Favor of Liberal Appropriations for the Defences of the Country.* 24th Cong., 1st Sess. (S.Doc.322). Washington: Gales & Seaton, 1836. 3 pg. (Serial Set 282). Describes the State of Maine and the current status of its defenses; resolutions support increased fortifications.

884. U.S. Senate. *Resolutions of the Legislature of Maine, Disapproving of Any Interference with the Subject of Slavery in Any of the States by the General Government.* 24th Cong., 1st Sess. (S.Doc.296). Washington: Gales & Seaton, 1836. 1 pg. (Serial Set 282). Resolutions declare that the power of regulating slavery belongs to each state, that Maine has decided against slavery, and that other states should not interfere in that decision.

24TH CONGRESS, 2ND SESSION

885. "Northeastern Boundary," *Congressional Globe.* 24th Cong., 2nd Sess. (22 Feb. 1837) pp. 197-198. Report of the Committee on Foreign Affairs against Maine's claim for reimbursement of money paid to John and Phineas Harford for expenses incurred over the disputed boundary.

886. Dana, Judah (Maine). "Admission of Michigan into the Union," *Congressional Globe, Appendix.* 24th Cong., 2nd Sess. (2 Jan., 3 Jan. 1837) pp. 70-71. Supports admitting Michigan into the Union as she has met all the conditions required of her; discusses the disputed boundary between Michigan and Ohio and the validity of the convention that assented to the terms of admission. Speech also printed in the *Register of Debates*, "Admission of Michigan," (2 Jan. 1837) pp. 223-226.

887. Dana, Judah (Maine). "On the Expunging Resolution," *Congressional Globe, Appendix.* 24th Cong., 2nd Sess. (12 Jan., 13 Jan. 1837) pp. 86-87. Supports expunging the resolution which violated President Jackson's right to a full, fair and impartial trial and could be considered as establishing precedence. Discusses the power of impeachment and maintains that the Senate improperly assumed jurisdiction; defends Jackson. Speech also printed in the *Register of Debates*, "Expunging Resolution," pp. 391-396.

888. Dana, Judah (Maine). "To Limit the Sales of the Public Lands," *Congressional Globe, Appendix.* 24th Cong., 2nd Sess. (24 Jan. 1837) pp. 127-128. Supports limiting the sales of the public lands to actual settlers; maintains that it would control speculation while reducing the revenue. Briefly discusses the disposition of the surplus revenue, and the northeastern boundary dispute. Speech also printed in the *Register of Debates*, "Public Lands," pp. 551-553.

889. Fairfield, John (Maine). "Case of R.M. Whitney," *Register of Debates.* 24th Cong., 2nd Sess. (15 Feb. 1837) pp. 1768-1773. Testimony presented.

890. Fairfield, John (Maine). "Public Deposites," *Congressional Globe, Appendix.* 24th Cong., 2nd Sess. (2 Mar. 1837) pp. 228-229. Defends his testimony in the case of Reuben M. Whitney. Also printed in the *Register of Debates*, "Civil and Diplomatic Appropriation Bill," pp. 2139-2141.

891. Jarvis, Leonard (Maine). "Navy Appropriation Bill," *Register of Debates.* 24th Cong., 2nd Sess. (2 Feb., 23 Feb. 1837) pp. 1564-1565; 1901-1902. Opposes the proposed appropriations for the exploring expedition and for launching the ship Pennsylvania.

892. Smith, Francis O. J. (Maine). "Interest on Advances during Revolutionary War," *Congressional Globe, Appendix.* 24th Cong., 2nd Sess. (16 Dec. 1836) pp. 27-28. Opposes paying interest on the claim of Colonel A.W. White as it would establish precedence for all past and future claims against the government. Speech also printed in the *Register of Debates*, "Colonel Anthony W. White," pp. 1109-1112.

893. Smith, Francis O. J. (Maine). "Refunding Certain Duties on Salt Destroyed," *Congressional Globe, Appendix.* 24th Cong., 2nd Sess. (14 Jan. 1837) pp. 90-92. Supports refunding duties paid upon salt destroyed by a flood. Supports remitting duties on imports destroyed when they are in their original imported state, there is no suspicion of fraud, and the goods could not have been covered by ordinary insurance. Offers precedents. Speech also printed in the *Register of Debates*, "N. and L. Dana," pp. 1388-1396.

894. Smith, Francis O. J. (Maine). "West Point Academy," *Congressional Globe, Appendix.* 24th Cong., 2nd Sess. (28 Feb. 1837) pp. 249-250. Opposes appropriations for a building to protect the cadets while exercising and drilling. Maintains that the cadets are pampered at the public expense. Speech also printed in the *Register of Debates*, "West Point Academy," pp. 2072-2075.

895. U.S. House. *Message from the President of the United States, Transmitting a Copy of a Letter from the Governor of the State of Maine, Claiming the Reimbursement of Certain Moneys Paid to John and Phineas R. Harford Out of the Treasury of That State.* 24th Cong., 2nd Sess. (H.Doc.125). [Washington]: Blair & Rives, Printers, [1837]. 3 pg. (Serial Set 303). Resolutions and report from Maine for claims for money paid to John and Phineas Harford for losses incurred as a result of the disturbance at Madawaska.

896. U.S. House. *Petition of Sundry Citizens of Portland and Vicinity, for a Repeal of the Duty Imposed upon Coal.* 24th Cong., 2nd Sess. (H.Doc.106). [Washington]: Blair & Rives, Printers, [1837]. 1 pg. (Serial Set 303).

897. U.S. House. *Report from the Secretary of War, in Compliance with a Resolution of the Senate, with Reports of Certain Surveys Made in the State of Maine.* 24th Cong., 2nd Sess. (H.Doc.143). [Washington]: Blair & Rives, Printers, [1837]. 1 pg., 6 maps. (Serial Set 303). Correspondence to report the surveys; maps and profiles include surveys of the Kennebec and Androscoggin River and Winthrop Pond. Same as S.doc.226 (24-2) 299 (entry **898**).

898. U.S. Senate. *Report from the Secretary of War, in Compliance with a Resolution of the Senate, with Reports of Certain Surveys Made in the State of Maine.* 24th Cong., 2nd Sess. (S.Doc.226). Washington: Gales and Seaton, 1837. 1 pg., 6 maps. (Serial Set 299). Same as H.doc.143 (24-2) 303. See entry **897**.

25TH CONGRESS, 1ST SESSION

899. Carter, Timothy J. (Maine). Remarks on Reimbursement for Property Lost in Military Service, *Congressional Globe.* 25th Cong., 1st Sess. (13 Oct. 1837) p. 138. Supports reimbursement for horses lost while in the service of the military; also supports the Tennessee volunteers. Same speech printed in the *Register of Debates*, "Remuneration for Losses in the Florida Campaigns," pp. 1538-1540.

900. Fairfield, John (Maine). "Postpone the Fourth Instalment [*sic*] with the States," *Congressional Globe.* 25th Cong., 1st Sess. (22 Sept. 1837) pp. 58-59. Opposes the deposit act of 1836 and supports the postponement of the fourth installment; maintains that the deposit act was not a contract. Same speech printed in the *Register of Debates*, "Fourth Instalment [*sic*] Bill, pp. 756-760.

901. Smith, Francis O. J. (Maine). "Postponement of Fourth Instalment [*sic*]," *Congressional Globe, Appendix*. 25th Cong., 1st Sess. (23 Sept. 1837) pp. 315-316. Supports a repeal or a postponement of the fourth installment. Maintains that the deposit act was not a contract with legal or moral obligations and was not intended as a distribution bill. Summary of speech in *Congressional Globe*, pp. 65-66. Same speech printed in the *Register of Debates*, "Fourth Instalment Bill," pp. 772-780.

902. U.S. House. *Message from the President of the United States, Transmitting the Information Required by the Resolution of the House of the 13th Instant, upon the Subject of the Northeastern Boundary of the United States*. 25th Cong., 1st Sess. (H.Doc.31). Washington: Thomas Allen, 1837. 32 pg. (Serial Set 311). Correspondence between the Governor of Maine and the government of the U.S., and between the U.S. and Great Britain, on the subject of alleged aggressions by the British authorities and the northeastern boundary.

25TH CONGRESS, 2ND SESSION

903. "Death of Hon. Jonathan Cilley," *Congressional Globe*. 25th Cong., 2nd Sess. (28 Feb. 1838) pp. 200-202. Debates resolution to investigate the death of Jonathan Cilley, Representative from Maine, who was killed in a duel.

904. "Duelling [*sic*] Report," *Congressional Globe*. 25th Cong., 2nd Sess. (7 May, 10 May 1838) pp. 353-356; 358-359. Further debate on the printing and acceptance of the report investigating the death of Jonathan Cilley (Maine).

905. "The Late Duel," *Congressional Globe*. 25th Cong., 2nd Sess. (21 Apr., 23 Apr., 24 Apr., 26 Apr., 27 Apr., 28 Apr., 1 May, 2 May 1838) pp. 320-321; 321-323; 324-325; 334; 337-338; 341-342; 342-344; 349-350; 350-351. Debate concerning the printing and reception of the report of the Committee of Investigation into the late duel and the death of Jonathan Cilley (Maine). Includes brief remarks by Isaac Toucey (Conn.), John Fairfield (Maine), Isaac Fletcher (Vt.), George Briggs (Mass.), Samuel Cushman (N.H.), John Quincy Adams (Mass.), George Grennell (Mass.), and Joseph Tillinghast (R.I.).

906. "Report of the Duelling [*sic*] Committee," *Congressional Globe*. 25th Cong., 2nd Sess. (25 Apr. 1838) pp. 326-333. Debate on the report of the investigation. Includes report, correspondence and related materials. Report concludes that the causes of the duel were related to the proceedings of the House; presents resolutions to expel involved members.

907. Buchanan, James (Pa.). "Northeastern Boundary," *Congressional Globe, Appendix*. 25th Cong., 2nd Sess. (18 June 1838) pp. 382-387. Opposes the bill directing the President to survey the disputed northeastern boundary line of the

U.S. Concerned that it would terminate pending negotiations and start a war. Examines the northwest angle of Nova Scotia to ascertain the true boundary of the territory. Discusses the negotiations with Great Britain. Maintains that Maine has transcended its legitimate power, and has no more right to control the negotiation than any other state.

908. Cilley, Jonathan (Maine). "Relations with Mexico and Great Britain," *Congressional Globe, Appendix.* 25th Cong., 2nd Sess. (5 Jan. 1838) pp. 35-36. Objects to the Chairman of the Committee on Foreign Affairs remarks that the U.S. should be mild in pressing the settlement of the northeastern boundary while the present difficulties exist between the British government and Canada. Maintains that now is the time to assert our just rights.

909. Cilley, Jonathan (Maine). "Suppression of Indian Hostilities," *Congressional Globe, Appendix.* 25th Cong., 2nd Sess. (23 Jan. 1838) pp. 78-80. Supports appropriations for the suppression of Indian hostilities in Florida and Georgia; deplores the current practice of idolizing the Indian at the expense of the defenseless citizens; discusses the Indian character.

910. Elmore, Franklin H. (S.C.). "The Late Duel," *Congressional Globe, Appendix.* 25th Cong., 2nd Sess. (24 Apr. 1838) pp. 277-279. Discusses the investigation into the causes leading to the death of the Hon. Jonathan Cilley. Defends the committee against charges of irregularity, unparliamentary procedure, and exceeding authority. Discusses the privileges of the House; reviews precedence. Maintains that the committee had the authority to examine witnesses, submit arguments, and recommend final action to the House.

911. Evans, George (Maine). Announcement of the Death of the Hon. T.J. Carter, *Congressional Globe.* 25th Cong., 2nd Sess. (14 Mar. 1838) pp. 239-240. Announces the death of Timothy J. Carter, a Representative from Maine; remarks on character.

912. Evans, George (Maine). "Northeastern Boundary," *Congressional Globe.* 25th Cong., 2nd Sess. (7 Feb. 1838) p. 168. Introduces and supports a bill to provide for surveying the northeastern boundary according to the provisions of the treaty of 1783.

913. Evans, George (Maine). "The Northeastern Boundary," *Congressional Globe, Appendix.* 25th Cong., 2nd Sess. (29 May 1838) pp. 521-523. Discusses the proposed renewed negotiations for surveying and establishing the northeastern boundary. Analyses the "original American proposition"; particularly objects to using a new principle in surveying which deviates from the true north. Discusses Great Britain's proposed modifications; reviews original objections offered by the Secretary of State. Maintains that the proposal is objectionable and dangerous and does not have the endorsement of the Maine.

914. Fairfield, John (Maine). "Death of the Hon. Jonathan Cilley," *Congressional Globe*. 25th Cong., 2nd Sess. (26 Feb. 1838) p. 199. Announces the death of Jonathan Cilley, Representative from Maine; remarks.

915. Fairfield, John (Maine). "The Late Duel," *Congressional Globe*. 25th Cong., 2nd Sess. (28 Apr. 1838) p. 343. Supports the committee inquiring as to whether any breach of privilege of the House was committed regarding the duel, which killed the Hon. Jonathan Cilley.

916. Fairfield, John (Maine). "Northeastern Boundary Question," *Congressional Globe, Appendix*. 25th Cong., 2nd Sess. (8 Mar. 1838) pp. 196-203. Supports a bill to survey, mark, and erect monuments upon the boundary line of 1783. Provides a lengthy history of the diplomatic efforts preceding this proposal; condemns the efforts of the Adams administration and approves those of the Jackson and Van Buren administrations.

917. Fairfield, John (Maine). "Northeastern Boundary," *Congressional Globe, Appendix*. 25th Cong., 2nd Sess. (29 May 1838) pp. 334-335. Clarifies a proposal offered to the British government to open negotiations authorizing the exploration and survey of the boundary.

918. Fairfield, John (Maine). Remarks on the Investigation into the Duel Which Killed Hon. Jonathan Cilley, *Congressional Globe*. 25th Cong., 2nd Sess. (23 Apr. 1838) pp. 321-322. Defends the investigating committee and the printing of their report; maintains that the committee has not exceeded their authority.

919. Foster, Henry A. (N.Y.). "Duel Reports," *Congressional Globe, Appendix*. 25th Cong., 2nd Sess. (24 Apr. 1838) pp. 551-552. Supports printing the report of the committee investigating the death of the Hon. Jonathan Cilley (Maine). Maintains that the committee did not violate any rules of the House. Responds to remarks of Mr. Slade (Vt.) concerning the excitement of the people.

920. Howard, Benjamin C. (Md.). "Northeastern Boundary," *Congressional Globe, Appendix*. 25th Cong., 2nd Sess. (29 May 1838) pp. 387-389. Supports the decision not to reimburse Maine for remuneration made to individuals in compensation for losses experienced. Maintains that the opinion of the legislature of a single state should not be considered obligatory; a proper claim should be furnished. Discusses the role of Maine in negotiations and the questionable propriety of resolutions passed by her legislature. Contends that the government of the U.S. has sole authority to adjust the boundary. Advocates an amicable negotiation; reviews the status of negotiations.

921. Menefee, Richard H. (Ky.). "Duel Reports," *Congressional Globe, Appendix*. 25th Cong., 2nd Sess. (24 Apr. 1838) pp. 552-555. Objects to the proceedings and report of the committee investigating the death of the Hon. Jonathan Cilley (Maine). Maintains that the actions of the committee were irregular and unauthorized and therefore the report should not be printed.

Reviews the relevant rules of the House. Discusses public sentiment and the influence of party politics on the proceedings.

922. Naylor, Charles (Pa.). "The Duel Reports," *Congressional Globe, Appendix.* 25th Cong., 2nd Sess. (28 Apr. 1838) pp. 340-341. Opposes the proceedings of the committee investigating the death of Jonathan Cilley. Maintains that the committee violated the Constitution, disregarded rules of the House, and was partisan in its inquiry. Reviews the House rules concerning members who are involved in an inquiry. Recommends that the names of members involved in the inquiry be stated. Addresses opponents' arguments.

923. Ruggles, John (Maine). "Death of the Hon. T.J. Carter," *Congressional Globe.* 25th Cong., 2nd Sess. (15 Mar. 1838) p. 241. Announces the death of Timothy J. Carter, a Representative from Maine; remarks on career and character.

924. Smith, Francis O. J. (Maine). "British Aggressions," *Congressional Globe, Appendix.* 25th Cong., 2nd Sess. (5 Jan. 1838) pp. 96-97. Deplores the continued nonresolution of the northeastern boundary situation, particularly since a citizen of Maine is unjustly imprisoned in a foreign jail by the British government; hopes that similar aggressions in Niagara against New York, along with those against Maine, will stimulate a resolution of the issue.

925. Williams, Reuel (Maine). "Death of the Hon. Jonathan Cilley," *Congressional Globe.* 25th Cong., 2nd Sess. (26 Feb. 1838) pp. 199-200. Announces the death of Jonathan Cilley, a Representative from Maine; remarks on career and character.

926. Williams, Reuel (Maine). "District Banks," *Congressional Globe.* 25th Cong., 2nd Sess. (11 May 1838) pp. 367-368. Opposes the renewal of the charters of the banks in the District of Columbia.

927. Williams, Reuel (Maine). "Northeastern Boundary," *Congressional Globe, Appendix.* 25th Cong., 2nd Sess. (14 May 1838) pp. 324-330. Presents a bill to provide for running and marking the northeastern boundary line according to the treaty of 1783. Provides a history of the efforts of the government to settle the boundary line by negotiation, and documentation of the British desire to substitute a conventional line. Also supplies background information supporting Maine's claim for the treaty line of 1783 as the true boundary.

928. Williams, Reuel (Maine). "Northeastern Boundary," *Congressional Globe, Appendix.* 25th Cong., 2nd Sess. (18 June 1838) pp. 396-398. Defends Maine's desire to mark and survey the boundary line according to the treaty of 1783; maintains that they are not taking the law into their own hands, that they have exhausted all other means of negotiation, and that the proposed commission of exploration and survey will accomplish nothing useful.

929. Williams, Reuel (Maine). Remarks on a Hospital in the District of Columbia, *Congressional Globe.* 25th Cong., 2nd Sess. (2 Jan. 1838) pp. 70-71. Supports a hospital to house the insane of the District as well as soldiers, seamen, and others who have come to the District to petition Congress for relief.

930. U.S. House. *Death of Mr. Cilley - Duel.* 25th Cong., 2nd Sess. (H.Rpt.825). [Washington]: Thomas Allen, Print., [1838]. 182 pg. (Serial Set 336). Complete report of the Committee of Investigation on the death of Jonathan Cilley (Maine) as it relates to the maintenance of the privileges of the House. Presents the facts and circumstances, testimony of the witnesses, and relevant documents and correspondence. Recommends that various involved individuals be expelled for breach of privileges.

931. U.S. House. *Letter from the Secretary of War, Transmitting a Report of a Survey of Kennebec River, &c.* 25th Cong., 2nd Sess. (H.Doc.94). [Washington]: Thomas Allen, Print., [1838]. 9 pg., 1 map. (Serial Set 325). Report, plan and estimates of the survey to ascertain the practicability and probable cost of improving the navigation of the Kennebec River between Augusta and Lovejoy's narrows. Includes map, titled "Chart of Kennebeck River from Augusta to Gardiner." Same as S.doc.114 (25-2) 315 (entry **948**).

932. U.S. House. *Maine - Legislature - Fortifications.* 25th Cong., 2nd Sess. (H.Doc.363). [Washington]: Thomas Allen, Print., [1838]. 2 pg. (Serial Set 330). Resolutions on the importance of building fortifications to defend Maine's frontiers. Same resolutions as S.doc.422 (25-2) 318 (entry **944**).

933. U.S. House. *Marine Hospital, Maine.* 25th Cong., 2nd Sess. (H.Rpt.82). [Washington]: Thomas Allen, Print., [1837]. 4 pg. (Serial Set 333). Reports legislative history of past efforts; supportive arguments given; reprint of earlier report (H.rp.468 (22-1) 228, entry **769**) and petition of physicians (H.doc.68 (24-1) 288, entry **880**).

934. U.S. House. *Memorial of Inhabitants of Cumberland and Oxford Counties, Maine, Praying for an Appropriation for the Survey of Crooked and Androscoggin Rivers, &c.* 25th Cong., 2nd Sess. (H.Doc.280). [Washington]: Thomas Allen, Print., [1838]. 2 pg. (Serial Set 328). Supports a survey for a canal between the Crooked and Androscoggin Rivers, which would then connect the Portland harbor to the frontiers of New Hampshire and Maine; also advocates a military fortification and depot on the frontier at that point.

935. U.S. House. *Memorial of Inhabitants of Newark, New Jersey, In Relation to the Death of the Honorable Jonathan Cilley.* 25th Cong., 2nd Sess. (H.Doc.198). [Washington]: Thomas Allen, Print., [1838]. 1 pg. (Serial Set 327). Memorial requests that a prompt investigation and necessary action be taken concerning the death of Jonathan Cilley.

936. U.S. House. *Memorial of Jabez Mowry and Sixty-Four Others, Inhabitants of Lubec, Maine, Praying Congress to Make Inquiry into the Existing State of the Trade with the British Colonies under the Proclamation of the President of the United States Made the 5th Day of October, 1830.* 25th Cong., 2nd Sess. (H.Doc.151). [Washington]: Thomas Allen, Print., [1838]. 2 pg. (Serial Set 327). Request that Great Britain opens all her colonial ports to U.S. vessels, just as the U.S. accordingly opened her ports under the act of May 29, 1930.

937. U.S. House. *Memorial of Levi Cutter and 204 Others, Inhabitants of Portland, Maine, for the Establishment of a Marine Hospital at Portland.* 25th Cong., 2nd Sess. (H.Doc.288). [Washington: Thomas Allen, Print., 1838]. 1 pg. (Serial Set 328). Memorial supports building the hospital.

938. U.S. House. *Message from the President of the United States, Transmitting Documents in Relation to the Claims of the State of Maine, and the Northeastern Boundary.* 25th Cong., 2nd Sess. (H.Doc.380). [Washington: Thomas Allen, Print., 1838]. 9 pg. (Serial Set 330). Documents on the northeastern boundary include Maine's request to run a line according to the treaty of 1783, thereby declaring its views and intentions on the boundary; also includes correspondence between the U.S. and Britain on establishing a joint commission to survey the line. Documents on claims are submitted for reimbursement to Maine for money paid to Ebenezer Greely (census taker) and John Baker, and others, for compensation for losses. Same as S.doc.451 (25-2) 318 (entry **947**).

939. U.S. House. *Message from the President of the United States, Transmitting the Information Required by a Resolution of the House of Representatives of the 9th Instant, in Relation to the Imprisonment of Mr. Greely, at Frederickton, in the British Province of New Brunswick, &c.* 25th Cong., 2nd Sess. (H.Doc.126). [Washington]: Thomas Allen, Print., [1838]. 49 pg. (Serial Set 326). Documents and correspondence on the case of Mr. Greely, a citizen of Maine, imprisoned for taking a census in the Madawaska and Aroostook region; also includes documents and correspondence on the jurisdiction of the disputed territory.

940. U.S. House. *Message of the Governor, and Resolutions of the Legislature of the State of Maine, upon the Subject of the Northeastern Boundary, &c.* 25th Cong., 2nd Sess. (H.Doc.354). [Washington]: Thomas Allen, Print., [1838]. 7 pg. (Serial Set 330). Response of the Governor to correspondence on the northeastern boundary and the request for the sense of Maine in regard to establishing a conventional line. Governor and Maine oppose establishing a conventional line and remain committed to the treaty line of 1783. Same as S.doc.424 (25-2) 318 (entry **945**).

941. U.S. House. *Petition of Citizens of the City of Portland, Maine, for a Law Establishing a Uniform System of Bankruptcy in the United States.* 25th Cong.,

2nd Sess. (H.Doc.132). [Washington]: Thomas Allen, Print., [1838]. 3 pg. (Serial Set 326). Petition includes two pages of names of petitioners.

942. U.S. House. *Petition of Inhabitants of Portland, Maine, against a Sub-Treasury, and for a National Bank.* 25th Cong., 2nd Sess. (H.Doc.388). [Washington]: Thomas Allen, Print., [1838]. 1 pg. (Serial Set 330).

943. U.S. House. *Resolutions of the Legislature of the State of Maine, in Relation to the Commercial Intercourse Between the United States and the British Provinces of Nova Scotia and New Brunswick.* 25th Cong., 2nd Sess. (H.Doc.355). [Washington]: Thomas Allen, Print., [1838]. 2 pg. (Serial Set 330). Requests that ports in Nova Scotia and New Brunswick be opened to U.S. vessels since U.S. ports are open to their vessels. Same resolution as S.doc.423 (25-2) 318 (entry **950**).

944. U.S. Senate. *Message from the Governor, and Resolutions of the Legislature, of Maine, in Relation to the Fortifications on the Frontiers of That State.* 25th Cong., 2nd Sess. (S.Doc.422). Washington: Blair and Rives, 1838. 2 pg. (Serial Set 318). Same resolutions as H.doc.363 (25-2) 330. See entry **932**.

945. U.S. Senate. *Message from the Governor, and Resolutions of the Legislature, of Maine, in Relation to the Northeastern Boundary of That State.* 25th Cong., 2nd Sess. (S.Doc.424). Washington: Blair and Rives, 1838. 7 pg. (Serial Set 318). Same as H.doc.354 (25-2) 330. See entry **940**.

946. U.S. Senate. *Message from the President of the United States, Transmitting All the Correspondence Between the United States and Great Britain on the Subject of the Northeastern Boundary, in Compliance with a Resolution of the Senate.* 25th Cong., 2nd Sess. (S.Doc.319). Washington: Blair and Rives, 1838. 33 pg. (Serial Set 317). Correspondence between the Secretary of State and the British Envoy Extraordinary and Minister Plenipotentiary on the northeastern boundary of Maine; also includes status report of Secretary of State to Governor of Maine asking the sense of that state.

947. U.S. Senate. *Message from the President of the United States, Transmitting a Communication from the Governor of Maine in Relation to the Northeastern Boundary, and the Claims of Ebenezer S. Greely, John Baker, and Others.* 25th Cong., 2nd Sess. (S.Doc.451). Washington: Blair and Rives, 1838. 9 pg. (Serial Set 318). Same as H.doc.380 (25-2) 330. See entry **938**.

948. U.S. Senate. *Report from the Secretary of War, in Compliance with a Resolution of the Senate of the 20th December Last, with a Report of the Survey of Kennebec River.* 25th Cong., 2nd Sess. (S.Doc.114). Washington: Blair & Rives, Printers, 1838. 9 pg., 1 map. (Serial Set 315). Same as H.Doc.94 (25-2) 325. See entry **931**.

949. U.S. Senate. [Report on the Investigation of John Ruggles, Senator from Maine]. 25th Cong., 2nd Sess. (S.Doc.377). Washington: Blair and Rives, 1838. 69 pg. (Serial Set 317). Report on the investigation of John Ruggles, accused of requesting a percentage of a patent for a lock in return for using his influence to procure a contract with the Post Office to use said locks. Includes testimony. Committee finds there is no satisfactory evidence to sustain the charges.

950. U.S. Senate. *Resolutions of the Legislature of Maine, in Relation to the Commercial Intercourse Between the United States and the British Provinces of Nova Scotia and New Brunswick.* 25th Cong., 2nd Sess. (S.Doc.423). Washington: Blair and Rives, 1838. 2 pg. (Serial Set 318). Same resolutions as H.doc.355 (25-2) 330. See entry **943**.

25TH CONGRESS, 3RD SESSION

951. Debate on the Maine Boundary Controversy, *Congressional Globe.* 25th Cong., 3rd Sess. (2 Mar. 1839) pp. 224-225. Debate in the Senate over the bill giving the President additional powers to defend the disputed territory.

952. "Maine Boundary Question," *Congressional Globe, Appendix.* 25th Cong., 3rd Sess. (26 Feb., 27 Feb. 1839) pp. 210-214, 226-233; 256-259. Debates on the difficulties between Maine and New Brunswick. Discusses the question of title to the disputed territory, Great Britain's claim of exclusive jurisdiction, and the actions of Maine in sending her land agent into the disputed territory to expel the trespassers. Includes remarks by Daniel Webster (Mass.), John Davis (Mass.), Reuel Williams (Maine), George Evans (Maine), John Quincy Adams (Mass.), Levi Lincoln (Mass.), Caleb Cushing (Mass.), Horace Everett (Vt.), and John Ruggles (Maine).

953. "Maine Boundary Question," *Congressional Globe, Appendix.* 25th Cong., 3rd Sess. (1 Mar. 1839) pp. 308-315. Debate on the resolutions of the Committee on Foreign Relations, particularly on the resolution concerning the obligation of the federal government to support Maine if she precipitates a war on her own authority. Includes remarks by John Davis (Mass.), Reuel Williams (Maine) and Daniel Webster (Mass.).

954. "Maine Boundary," *Congressional Globe.* 25th Cong., 3rd Sess. (28 Feb., 1 Mar., 2 Mar. 1839) pp. 218-219; 221-222; 227-229. Report of the Committee on Foreign Affairs in relation to the controversy between Maine and New Brunswick over the disputed Madawaska and Aroostook region. Report is accompanied by a bill giving the President additional powers for the defense of disputed territory. Summary of the debate on the proposed bill; selected speeches printed in the *Congressional Globe, Appendix.*

955. Message from the President on the Maine Boundary Controversy, *Congressional Globe*. 25th Cong., 3rd Sess. (26 Feb. 1839) pp. 209-210. Message from the President concerning the controversy between Maine and New Brunswick over the Madawaska and Aroostook region; declares that the government will defend Maine's rights if New Brunswick attempts to enforce her claim of exclusive jurisdiction.

956. "Northeastern Frontier," *Congressional Globe*. 25th Cong., 3rd Sess. (27 Feb. 1839) p. 213. Message from the President enclosing a memorandum of agreement between Mr. Fox, the British minister, and Mr. Forsyth, Secretary of State, to temporarily settle the difficulties between Maine and New Brunswick over the Madawaska and Aroostook region.

957. Resolutions on the Maine Boundary Controversy, *Congressional Globe*. 25th Cong., 3rd Sess. (28 Feb. 1839) p. 216. Text of the resolutions from the Committee on Foreign Relations concerning the difficulties between Maine and New Brunswick over the Madawaska and Aroostook region.

958. Benton, Thomas H. (Mo.). "Maine Boundary Question," *Congressional Globe, Appendix*. 25th Cong., 3rd Sess. (1 Mar. 1839) p. 311. Opposes the resolution clarifying the position of the general government if Maine should precipitate a war. Maintains that the resolution is unconstitutional and that the government was created for the common defense.

959. Biddle, Richard (Pa.). "Maine Boundary Question," *Congressional Globe, Appendix*. 25th Cong., 3rd Sess. (1 Mar. 1839) pp. 259-261. Cautions against false movement. Maintains that the matter of jurisdiction is of incidental and temporary importance and that the U.S. does not have an indisputable case. Reviews diplomatic correspondence to demonstrate that remissiveness has given credibility to the British claim of exclusive jurisdiction.

960. Brown, Bedford (N.C.). "Maine Boundary Question," *Congressional Globe, Appendix*. 25th Cong., 3rd Sess. (1 Mar. 1839) pp. 312-313. Supports the resolution by the Committee on Foreign Relations. Contends that Maine has no right to use military force to possess the disputed territory and that only the general government has the authority to settle controversies with foreign governments.

961. Buchanan, James (Pa.). "Maine Boundary Question," *Congressional Globe, Appendix*. 25th Cong., 3rd Sess. (26 Feb. 1839) pp. 211-212. Supports the actions of Maine. Maintains that Great Britain does not have exclusive jurisdiction over the disputed territory and that Maine did not violate any rights by sending her land agent to expel the trespassers. Regrets that Maine did not notify the government of New Brunswick as to her purpose in sending an armed force to the Aroostook.

962. Buchanan, James (Pa.). "Maine Boundary Question," *Congressional Globe, Appendix*. 25th Cong., 3rd Sess. (1 Mar. 1839) pp. 309-310. Supports the resolutions of the Committee on Foreign Relations that deny the right of the British government to exclusive jurisdiction over the disputed territory, justify the conduct of Maine, pledge the forces of the country to protect the property, and define the country's position if British forces are withdrawn.

963. Buchanan, James (Pa.). "Maine Boundary Question," *Congressional Globe, Appendix.* 25th Cong., 3rd Sess. (1 Mar. 1839) p. 314. Supports the resolutions by the Committee on Foreign Relations that Maine has no right to exclusive possession of the disputed territory and that the government is under no constitutional obligation to support her if she takes possession of the territory on her own.

964. Clay, Henry (Ky.). "Maine Boundary Question," *Congressional Globe, Appendix.* 25th Cong., 3rd Sess. (26 Feb. 1839) pp. 212-213. Supports the title of the State of Maine to the disputed territory. Regrets that no prior notification was given to the government of New Brunswick or the U.S. as to the expedition to expel the trespassers. Concerned that Maine should draw the entire Union into a war without their consent.

965. Clay, Henry (Ky.). "Maine Boundary Question," *Congressional Globe, Appendix.* 25th Cong., 3rd Sess. (1 Mar. 1839) pp. 309-310, 315. Supports the position that the U.S. will respond with force if Britain persists in asserting her claim to exclusive jurisdiction. Also supports the resolution clarifying the position of the government if Maine should precipitate a war on her own.

966. Evans, George (Maine). "Maine Boundary Question," *Congressional Globe, Appendix.* 25th Cong., 3rd Sess. (26 Feb. 1839) pp. 226-228. Defends the actions of Maine. Contends that the President underrates the imminent danger of relations with Great Britain. Discusses the British claim of exclusive jurisdiction and the repeated indignities Maine has suffered under this assumed claim. Describes the state and history of the controversy in the Madawaska and Aroostook region. Approves of the President's proposal to leave the adjustment of the controversy to the governments of Maine and New Brunswick.

967. Evans, George (Maine). "The Maine Boundary Question," *Congressional Globe, Appendix.* 25th Cong., 3rd Sess. (1 Mar. 1839) pp. 274-277. Defends the bill giving the President additional power to defend the disputed territory. Responds to Mr. Biddle's (Pa.) arguments against the bill. Maintains that the measure will preserve the peace. Reviews the increasing aggressions of the British government in asserting exclusive jurisdiction. Applauds the government for supporting Maine's rights.

968. Fillmore, Millard (N.Y.). "Maine Boundary Question," *Congressional Globe, Appendix.* 25th Cong., 3rd Sess. (1 Mar. 1839) pp. 281-282. Objects to the bill giving the President additional power to defend the disputed territory because it does not provide for the defense of the northern frontier. Maintains that if war erupts, it will not be confined to the frontier of Maine.

969. Howard, Benjamin C. (Md.). "Maine Boundary Question," *Congressional Globe, Appendix.* 25th Cong., 3rd Sess. (1 Mar. 1839) pp. 261-263. Refutes Mr. Biddle's (Pa.) claim that the administration of Gen. Jackson acquiesced to Britain's claim of exclusive jurisdiction. Maintains that there are no documents to indicate that the British government was misled. Supports the bill to give the President additional power to defend the disputed territory. Discusses the consequences of refusing to pass the bill. Contends that there is no time or disposition for negotiation. Addresses opponents' arguments.

970. Legare, Hugh S. (S.C.). "Maine Boundary Question," *Congressional Globe, Appendix.* 25th Cong., 3rd Sess. (1 Mar. 1839) pp. 282-283. Supports the bill giving the President additional power to defend the disputed territory. Maintains that the bill is not a war measure, but rather is calculated to avert war. Supports Maine's claim of jurisdiction.

971. Menefee, Richard H. (Ky.). "Maine Boundary Question," *Congressional Globe, Appendix.* 25th Cong., 3rd Sess. (1 Mar. 1839) pp. 280-281. Supports giving the President additional power to defend the disputed territory. Refutes Great Britain's claim of exclusive jurisdiction. If negotiation is discontinued and arms substituted, supports using force to defend the country.

972. Norvell, John (Mich.). "Maine Boundary Question," *Congressional Globe, Appendix.* 25th Cong., 3rd Sess. (1 Mar. 1839) p. 310. Opposes the resolution stating that if Maine precipitates a war on her own then the federal government is under no obligation to support her. Maintains that the Constitution provides that the federal government must protect a state from foreign invasion.

973. Pickens, Francis W. (S.C.). "Maine Boundary Question," *Congressional Globe, Appendix.* 25th Cong., 3rd Sess. (26 Feb. 1839) pp. 231-232. Supports preserving the peace. Advocates strong military movements to prevent conflict. Discusses other points of difficulty between the U.S. and Great Britain concerning the right of property in persons.

974. Pickens, Francis W. (S.C.). "Maine Boundary Question," *Congressional Globe, Appendix.* 25th Cong., 3rd Sess. (1 Mar. 1839) pp. 298-300. Objects to the bill giving the President additional power to defend the disputed territory. Responds to remarks of Mr. Legare (S.C.), Mr. Menefee (Ky.), and Mr. Biddle (Pa.). Objects to the precedent of allowing a standing army to be created by executive discretion. Advocates negotiation. Discusses Britain's claim for exclusive jurisdiction. Maintains that Sir John Harvey misconceived his instructions. Addresses the issue with Britain regarding slaves as property.

975. Preston, William C. (S.C.). "Maine Boundary Question," *Congressional Globe, Appendix.* 25th Cong., 3rd Sess. (1 Mar. 1839) p. 312. Supports the resolution stating that if Maine starts a war on her own the federal government is under no obligation to support her. Maintains that Maine has no right to use military force to occupy the disputed territory until the boundary is settled.

976. Rives, William C. (Va.). "Maine Boundary Question," *Congressional Globe, Appendix.* 25th Cong., 3rd Sess. (1 Mar. 1839) pp. 313-314. Supports the resolutions by the Committee on Foreign Relations; maintains that they assert the rights of Maine and also indicate her duty in relation to withdrawing her military force from the disputed territory.

977. Ruggles, John (Maine). "Maine Boundary Question," *Congressional Globe, Appendix.* 25th Cong., 3rd Sess. (27 Feb. 1839) pp. 258, 259. Remarks support Maine in defending her territory against British aggressions at the Madawaska and Aroostook region.

978. Sergeant, John (Penn.). "Maine Boundary Question," *Congressional Globe, Appendix.* 25th Cong., 3rd Sess. (26 Feb. 1839) p. 232. Supports the actions of Maine and the Executive. Refutes Britain's claim to exclusive jurisdiction. Advocates a speedy settlement.

979. Smith, Francis O. J. (Maine). "Maine Boundary Question," *Congressional Globe, Appendix.* 25th Cong., 3rd Sess. (2 Mar. 1839) pp. 278-280. Supports appropriations to protect the rights of the citizens of Maine; describes the rights of the state and the position in which she now stands in defense of her claim of exclusive jurisdiction over the Aroostook country, now under dispute.

980. Southard, Samuel L. (N.J.). "Maine Boundary Question," *Congressional Globe, Appendix.* 25th Cong., 3rd Sess. (1 Mar. 1839) pp. 310-311. Supports the resolution stating that if Maine precipitates a war on her own then the federal government is under no obligation to support her. Maintains that if the foreign army is withdrawn, as indicated in the resolution, then Maine is not being invaded and therefore has no constitutional guarantee of support.

981. Williams, Reuel (Maine). "Boundary of Maine," *Congressional Globe.* 25th Cong., 3rd Sess. (25 Feb. 1839) pp. 204-205. Discusses the misrepresentations of Maine's defense of the disputed Aroostook region by the *National Intelligencer.* Claims that it was neither a "hasty measure" nor a political party issue.

982. Williams, Reuel (Maine). "Maine Boundary Question," *Congressional Globe, Appendix.* 25th Cong., 3rd Sess. (26 Feb.; 27 Feb., 1 Mar. 1839) pp. 213-214; 256-257; 308, 312. Various brief speeches support Maine's defense of the disputed territory in the Madawaska and Aroostook region.

983. Williams, Reuel (Maine). "Salt Duties, Fishing Bounties, and Allowances," *Congressional Globe, Appendix.* 25th Cong., 3rd Sess. (29 Jan. 1839) pp. 73-75. Opposes the bill to repeal salt duties and fishing bounties; questions why it is limited to salt and why the West first moved the repeal when they have their own supply of salt; defends the fishing bounty.

984. U.S. House. *Disturbance in Maine.* 25th Cong., 3rd Sess. (H.Rpt.314). [Washington]: Thomas Allen, Print., [1839]. 7 pg. (Serial Set 352). Report of the Committee on Foreign Affairs on the disturbances upon the disputed Aroostook River. Recommends giving the President power to call in any military forces needed and encourages negotiation to end the dispute.

985. U.S. House. *Message from the President of the United States, upon the Subject of the Present State of Affairs Between the State of Maine and the British Province of New Brunswick.* 25th Cong., 3rd Sess. (H.Doc.222). [Washington]: Thomas Allen, Print., [1839]. [50 pg.]. (Serial Set 348). Documents and correspondence from the Governor of Maine, Secretary of State, and British representatives on several disputes in the Madawaska and Aroostook region. This report is a longer version of S.doc.270 (25-3) 341 (entry **988**), with a slightly different arrangement.

986. U.S. House. *Military Works - Northeast Frontier.* 25th Cong., 3rd Sess. (H.Doc.218). [Washington]: Thomas Allen, Print., [1839]. 2 pg. (Serial Set 348). Committee on Military Affairs recommends appropriation of $100,000 for erection of proper defenses for the frontier of the State of Maine.

987. U.S. Senate. *Documents Relating to the Defence of the Northeastern Frontier of the United States.* 25th Cong., 3rd Sess. (S.Doc.251). Washington: Blair and Rives, 1839. 4 pg. (Serial Set 340). Reports on the expediency of constructing fortifications on the maritime frontier of Maine, particularly at Portland harbor, at the entrance of Kennebec River, and at the Narrows of the Penobscot River.

988. U.S. Senate. *Message from the President of the United States, in Relation to the Dispute Between the State of Maine and the British Province of New Brunswick.* 25th Cong., 3rd Sess. (S.Doc.270). Washington: Blair and Rives, 1839. 32 pg. (Serial Set 341). Documents and correspondence from the Governor of Maine, Secretary of State, and British representatives on several disputes in the Madawaska and Aroostook region. This report is an abbreviated version of H.doc.222 (25-3) 348 (entry **985**).

989. U.S. Senate. *Message from the President of the United States, Transmitting Additional Documents in Relation to the Dispute Between the State of Maine and the British Province of New Brunswick.* 25th Cong., 3rd Sess. (S.Doc.271). Washington: Blair and Rives, 1839. 8 pg. (Serial Set 341). Further documents on the disputed Madawaska and Aroostook territory; memorandum from Great Britain of the terms upon which an agreement could be reached.

990. U.S. Senate. *Message from the President of the United States, in Compliance with a Resolution of the Senate, in Relation to the Northeastern Boundary.* 25th Cong., 3rd Sess. (S.Doc.141). Washington: Blair and Rives,

1839. 1 pg. (Serial Set 339). Pres. Van Buren reports that no further official communications have passed between the two governments since last reported.

991. U.S. Senate. *Petition of a Number of Citizens of Kittery, Maine, against the Repeal of the Duty on Salt, and against Abolishing the Bounty Allowed to Owners of Fishing Vessels.* 25th Cong., 3rd Sess. (S.Doc.259). Washington: Blair and Rives, 1839. 2 pg. (Serial Set 341).

992. U.S. Senate. *Report from the Secretary of War, in Compliance with a Resolution of the Senate, in Reference to the Defence of the Frontier of Maine.* 25th Cong., 3rd Sess. (S.Doc.35). Washington: Blair and Rives, 1839. 16 pg. (Serial Set 339). Report of the military reconnaissance of the frontier of Maine with recommendations for better defense; observations on the topographical features of the reconnaissance. Accompanying map not included with report.

993. U.S. Senate. [Report on the Difficulties on the Northeastern Frontier of the United States]. 25th Cong., 3rd Sess. (S.Doc.272). Washington: Blair and Rives, 1839. 2 pg. (Serial Set 341). Resolutions of the Committee on Foreign Relations regarding the dispute in the Madawaska and Aroostook region.

26THCONGRESS, 1ST SESSION

994. Correspondence on the Maine Boundary Controversy, *Congressional Globe.* 26th Cong., 1st Sess. (23 Jan. 1840) pp. 134-138. Copies of a portion of the correspondence on the movement of British troops in the disputed region. Includes letters between A. Vail (Acting Sec. of State), John Fairfield (Governor of Maine), John Forsyth (Sec. of State), and Henry S. Fox (British Minister).

995. "The Maine Boundary," *Congressional Globe.* 26th Cong., 1st Sess. (17 Jan. 1840) pp. 126-127. Debate on the resolution to ask the President for any correspondence in relation to the Maine boundary or jurisdiction of the disputed territory. Includes remarks by John Ruggles (Maine) and John Davis (Mass.).

996. "Military and Naval Preparations on Our Northern Frontier," *Congressional Globe.* 26th Cong., 1st Sess. (1 Apr. 1840) p. 298. Report from the Secretary of War on the movement of British troops in the disputed territory.

997. "Northeastern Boundary," *Congressional Globe.* 26th Cong., 1st Sess. (29 Jan. 1840) pp. 151-152. Additional correspondence between the Sec. of State and the British minister at Washington on the movements of British troops in the disputed Madawaska and Aroostook territory. Also printed in S.doc.129 (26-1) 357 (entry **1028**).

998. "Northeastern Boundary," *Congressional Globe.* 26th Cong., 1st Sess. (9 Mar. 1840) pp. 248-250. Additional correspondence from the Governor of

Maine and between the Sec. of State and the British minister on the movement of British troops in the disputed territory.

999. "Northeastern Boundary," *Congressional Globe.* 26th Cong., 1st Sess. (26 Mar. 1840) pp. 291-292. Further correspondence between the British minister and the Secretary of State on the Madawaska and Aroostook controversy. Same as S.doc.319 (26-1) 359 (entry **1029**).

1000. "Northeastern Boundary," *Congressional Globe.* 26th Cong., 1st Sess. (14 Apr. 1840) pp. 322-324. Report of the Committee on Foreign Relations on the state of the pending negotiation on the northeastern boundary. Report also printed as S.doc.382 (26-1) 359 (entry **1032**). Debate includes remarks by John Ruggles (Maine).

1001. "Northeastern Boundary," *Congressional Globe.* 26th Cong., 1st Sess. (29 June 1840) pp. 491-492. President transmits two letters between the Sec. of State and the British Envoy regarding the negotiations and the report of the British survey; as the British survey differs from the line claimed by the U.S., the President proposes an American survey. Same as S.doc.580 (26-1) 361 (entry **1030**).

1002. "A Preamble and Joint Resolutions in Relation to the Northeastern Boundary," *Congressional Globe.* 26th Cong., 1st Sess. (10 Apr. 1840) p. 318. Reprint of resolutions adopted by Indiana that supports the action taken by Maine in defense of the disputed Madawaska and Aroostook region. Also printed in S.doc.371 (26-1) 359 (entry **1035**) and H.doc.223 (26-1) 368 (entry **1021**).

1003. "Resolves Relating to the Northeastern Boundary," *Congressional Globe.* 26th Cong., 1st Sess. (10 Apr. 1840) p. 318. Reprint of resolutions that support their defense of the disputed territory; requests Congress to establish the line of the treaty of 1783. Same as H.doc.189 (26-1) 366 (entry **1025**) and S.doc.370 (26-1) 359 (entry **1038**).

1004. Clay, Henry (Ky.). "Northeastern Boundary," *Congressional Globe.* 26th Cong., 1st Sess. (14 Apr. 1840) pp. 323-324. Remarks on the report of the Committee on Foreign Relations on the northeastern boundary. Advocates negotiation; maintains that the government alone has the right of arbitration.

1005. Clifford, Nathan (Maine). "Appropriation Bill," *Congressional Globe, Appendix.* 26th Cong., 1st Sess. (24 Apr. 1840) pp. 469-476. Speech on the history and policies of the political parties in the U.S. from the framing of the Constitution to the present.

1006. Clifford, Nathan (Maine). "New Jersey Election," *Congressional Globe, Appendix.* 26th Cong., 1st Sess. (10 Jan., 11 Jan. 1840) pp. 204-210. Discusses the resolution to refer all the documents and testimony relating to the New Jersey disputed election to the Committee of Elections. Statement of the Clerk of the House given; discussion of election laws of New Jersey. Maintains that the House has the power to ascertain its own members, and that an executive of a state appointing a member of either branch of Congress is a presumptive evidence of right. Introductory remarks in the *Congressional Globe*, p. 115.

1007. Evans, George (Maine). "The Public Printing," *Congressional Globe*. 26th Cong., 1st Sess. (13 May 1840) p. 392. Recommends establishing a government printing office.

1008. Evans, George (Maine). Remarks on Continuing the Documentary History of the American Revolution, *Congressional Globe*. 26th Cong., 1st Sess. (7 May 1840) pp. 384-385. Supports appropriations honoring the contract for the publication of the *Documentary History of the American Revolution*. Summarizes the circumstances and the importance of the work.

1009. Evans, George (Maine). Remarks on the Civil and Diplomatic Bill, *Congressional Globe*. 26th Cong., 1st Sess. (23 Apr. 1840) p. 353. Remarks on expenditures; defends votes for appropriations for fortifications, and debates the executive power over appropriations.

1010. Evans, George (Maine). "Treasury Notes," *Congressional Globe, Appendix*. 26th Cong., 1st Sess. (24 Mar. 1840) pp. 839-844. Reluctantly supports the bill; claims that the Treasury deficit is not temporary but permanent, and that a permanent remedy should be applied. Supports this by demonstrating that revenues of former years have not been sufficient to meet disbursements. Summary of speech in *Congressional Globe*, p. 285.

1011. Lowell, Joshua A. (Maine). "Independent Treasury," *Congressional Globe, Appendix*. 26th Cong., 1st Sess. (27 May, 28 May 1840) pp. 488-496. Supports an Independent Treasury. Compares the present banking system with an Independent Treasury, finding the Independent Treasury constitutional (the banking system is not) and greatly superior for convenience and security. Favors a hard currency, as originally contemplated by the Constitution. Presents a history of the Bank of the U.S. and its role in the currency problems; addresses objections to the measure. Summary in *Congressional Globe*, pp. 426-427.

1012. Parris, Virgil (Maine). "Cumberland Road," *Congressional Globe, Appendix*. 26th Cong., 1st Sess. (11 Feb. 1840) pp. 423-424. Opposes appropriations for the Cumberland road as unconstitutional. Demonstrates that the government has fulfilled its obligations towards the compact made with the western states regarding public land proceeds to be applied to roads leading to and through them. Summary of speech in *Congressional Globe*, p. 185.

1013. Ruggles, John (Maine). "The Maine Boundary," *Congressional Globe*. 26th Cong., 1st Sess. (17 Jan. 1840) p. 126. Supports requesting correspondence concerning the Maine boundary; questions the motives of the commissioners appointed to survey the country and report to the British government.

1014. Ruggles, John (Maine). "Northeastern Boundary," *Congressional Globe*. 26th Cong., 1st Sess. (13 Apr. 1840) pp. 322-323. Briefly remarks on the report of the Committee on Foreign Relations concerning the northeastern boundary. Maintains that Great Britain will never submit to the true boundary until the U.S. takes a strong stand.

1015. Smith, Albert (Maine). Remarks on the Maine Boundary Question, *Congressional Globe*. 26th Cong., 1st Sess. (9 Apr. 1840) p. 312. Argues that Maine's actions defending the Aroostook region were not rash and indiscreet.

1016. Williams, Reuel (Maine). "Fugitives from Justice," *Congressional Globe*. 26th Cong., 1st Sess. (11 Mar. 1840) p. 259. Briefly reviews Georgia's demands for the master and mate of a vessel who unknowingly transported a slave.

1017. Williams, Reuel (Maine). "Naval Appropriations," *Congressional Globe*. 26th Cong., 1st Sess. (11 July 1840) p. 521. Supports appropriations for the gradual improvement of the navy.

1018. U.S. House. *Message from the President of the United States, Transmitting the Information Required by the Resolution of the House of Representatives of the 9th Ultimo, in Relation to the Arrangement Entered into Between the Governor of Maine and the Lieutenant Governor of New Brunswick, in the Month of March Last, &c., &c.* 26th Cong., 1st Sess. (H.Doc.169). [Washington]: Blair & Rives, Printers, [1840]. 22 pg. (Serial Set 366). Copy of the arrangement entered into through the mediation of Major General Scott, together with copies of the instructions given to General Scott, and all correspondence with him relating to the controversy between the State of Maine and the Province of New Brunswick.

1019. U.S. House. *Message from the President of the United States, Transmitting a Communication from the Secretary of State, upon the Subject of the Boundary Between the United States and the British Province of New Brunswick, Called for by a Resolution of the House of Representatives of the 9th Instant.* 26th Cong., 1st Sess. (H.Doc.134). [Washington]: Blair & Rives, Printers, [1840]. 1 pg. (Serial Set 365). Secretary of State reports that no action has been taken concerning a topographical survey or exploration of the disputed territory; nor has the accuracy of the British topographical survey been tested.

1020. U.S. House. *Resolutions of Citizens of Prospect, Maine, in Favor of Fortifying Penobscot Bay.* 26th Cong., 1st Sess. (H.Doc.227). [Washington: Blair & Rives, Printers, 1840]. 2 pg. (Serial Set 368).

1021. U.S. House. *Resolutions of the General Assembly of Indiana, concerning the Northeastern Boundary.* 26th Cong., 1st Sess. (H.Doc.223). [Washington:

Blair & Rives, Printers, 1840]. 2 pg. (Serial Set 368). Indiana adopts resolutions passed by Ohio in support of action taken by Maine in defense of the disputed Madawaska and Aroostook region. Same as S.doc.371 (26-1) 359 (entry **1035**). Also printed in the *Congressional Globe*, p. 318 (entry **1002**).

1022. U.S. House. *Resolutions of the Legislature of Maine, in Relation to an Appropriation for the Purchase of "Repeating Arms Manufactured by Mighill Nutting of Portland, Maine, After They Shall Have Been Approved by the War Department."* 26th Cong., 1st Sess. (H.Doc.175). [Washington: Blair & Rives, Printers, 1840]. 2 pg. (Serial Set 366). Resolutions support the appropriation for repeating arms.

1023. U.S. House. *Resolutions of the Legislature of Maine, Relating to the French Spoliations Prior to September, 1800.* 26th Cong., 1st Sess. (H.Doc.233). [Washington: 1840]. 1 pg. (Serial Set 368). Resolution supports claims. Same as S.doc.366 (26-1) 359 (entry **1033**), without the Governor's note.

1024. U.S. House. *Resolutions of the Legislature of Maine, Relative to the Repeal of the Act Giving a Bounty to Vessels Engaged in the Fisheries.* 26th Cong., 1st Sess. (H.Doc.209). [Washington]: Blair & Rives, Printers, [1840]. 1 pg. (Serial Set 368). Resolutions opposed to the repeal. Same as S.doc.369 (26-1) 359 (entry **1037**), without the note from the Governor.

1025. U.S. House. *Resolutions of the Legislature of the State of Maine, in Relation to the Northeastern Boundary.* 26th Cong., 1st Sess. (H.Doc.189). [Washington]: Blair & Rives, Printers, [1840]. 2 pg. (Serial Set 366). Resolutions support their defense of the disputed territory; request Congress to establish the line of the treaty of 1783. Same as S.doc.370 (26-1) 359 (entry **1038**). Also printed in the *Congressional Globe*, p. 318 (entry **1003**).

1026. U.S. House. *Settlement of the Claim of Maine for Militia Services.* 26th Cong., 1st Sess. (H.Rpt.566). [Washington: Blair & Rives, Printers, 1840]. 4 pg. (Serial Set 372). Report supports Maine's claims, incurred while maintaining her jurisdiction at the Aroostook vicinity; describes the circumstances of the disturbance. Same as S.doc.419 (26-1) 359 (entry **1031**).

1027. U.S. Senate. *Message from the President of the United States, Communicating, in Compliance with a Resolution of the Senate, Copies of Correspondence in Relation to the Northeastern Boundary and the Jurisdiction of the Disputed Territory; and Also, in Relation to the Establishment of Military Posts in the State of Maine.* 26th Cong., 1st Sess. (S.Doc.107). Washington: Blair and Rives, 1840. 66 pg. (Serial Set 356). Includes a report and documents from the Secretary of State, and a report from the Secretary of War. Correspondence dates from 1838 to 1840.

1028. U.S. Senate. *Message from the President of the United States, Communicating Additional Correspondence in Relation to the Adjustment of* *the Northeastern Boundary, and the Occupation of the Disputed Territory.* 26th Cong., 1st Sess. (S.Doc.129). Washington: Blair and Rives, 1840. 4 pg. (Serial Set 357). Also printed in the *Congressional Globe,* pp. 151-152 (entry **997**). See entry **997** for abstract.

1029. U.S. Senate. *Message from the President of the United States, Communicating Additional Correspondence in Relation to the Adjustment of the Northeastern Boundary, and the Occupation of the Disputed Territory.* 26th Cong., 1st Sess. (S.Doc.319). Washington: Blair and Rives, 1840. 7 pg. (Serial Set 359). Also printed in the *Congressional Globe,* pp. 291-292 (entry **999**). See entry **999** for abstract.

1030. U.S. Senate. *Message from the President of the United States, in Relation to the Adjustment of the Northeastern Boundary.* 26th Cong., 1st Sess. (S.Doc.580). Washington: Blair and Rives, 1840. 5 pg. (Serial Set 316). Also printed in the *Congressional Globe,* pp. 491-492 (entry **1001**). See entry **1001** for abstract.

1031. U.S. Senate. [Report on Claim of State of Maine for Services of Her Militia in the Protection of the Northeastern Frontier in 1839]. 26th Cong., 1st Sess. (S.Doc.419). Washington: Blair and Rives, 1840. 4 pg. (Serial Set 359). Same as H.rp.566 (26-2) 372. See entry **1026**.

1032. U.S. Senate. [Report on Correspondence Relating to the Disputed Territory on Our Northeastern Frontier]. 26th Cong., 1st Sess. (S.Doc.382). Washington: Blair and Rives, 1840. 2 pg. (Serial Set 359). Committee on Foreign Relations defers from making a report until the British commissioners complete their survey of the disputed territory.

1033. U.S. Senate. *Resolution of the Legislature of Maine, on the Subject of Making Provision for French Spoliations Prior to 1800.* 26th Cong., 1st Sess. (S.Doc.366). Washington: Blair and Rives, 1840. 1 pg. (Serial Set 359). Resolution supports the claims. Same as H.doc.233 (26-1) 368 (entry **1023**), with additional note from the Governor.

1034. U.S. Senate. *Resolutions Adopted at a Meeting of the Citizens of Frankfort, Maine, in Favor of the Construction of Fortifications on the Penobscot River.* 26th Cong., 1st Sess. (S.Doc.549). Washington: Blair and Rives, 1840. 2 pg. (Serial Set 360).

1035. U.S. Senate. *Resolutions of the General Assembly of Indiana, in Relation to the Northeastern Boundary.* 26th Cong., 1st Sess. (S.Doc.371). Washington: Blair and Rives, 1840. 2 pg. (Serial Set 359). Same as H.doc.223 (26-1) 368. See entry **1021**. Also printed in the *Congressional Globe,* p. 318 (entry **1002**).

1036. U.S. Senate. *Resolutions of the Legislature of Maine, in Favor of the Passage of a Bankrupt Law.* 26th Cong., 1st Sess. (S.Doc.365). Washington: Blair and Rives, 1840. 2 pg. (Serial Set 359).

1037. U.S. Senate. *Resolutions of the Legislature of Maine, Adverse to the Repeal or Modification of the Law Giving a Bounty to Vessels Engaged in the Fisheries.* 26th Cong., 1st Sess. (S.Doc.369). Washington: Blair and Rives, 1840. 2 pg. (Serial Set 359). Same as H.doc.209 (26-1) 368 (entry **1024**), with additional note from the Governor.

1038. U.S. Senate. *Resolutions of the Legislature of Maine, in Relation to the Adjustment of the Northeastern Boundary, and the Occupation of the Disputed Territory.* 26th Cong., 1st Sess. (S.Doc.370). Washington: Blair and Rives, 1840. 2 pg. (Serial Set 359). Same as H.doc.189 (26-1) 366. See entry **1025**. Also printed in the *Congressional Globe*, p. 318 (entry **1003**).

1039. U.S. Senate. *Two Messages from the President of the United States, Communicating Additional Correspondence in Relation to the Adjustment of the Northeastern Boundary, and the Occupation of the Disputed Territory.* 26th Cong., 1st Sess. (S.Doc.266). Washington: Blair and Rives, 1840. 14 pg. (Serial Set 358). Reprint of correspondence in S.doc.129 (26-1) 357 (entry **1028**) on troop movements; also letters and depositions received since testifying that the British troops are moving in the disputed area, and the subsequent correspondence between the Secretary of State and the British minister.

26TH CONGRESS, 2ND SESSION

1040. "Indiana Canal Lands and Northeastern Boundary of the United States," *Congressional Globe*. 26th Cong., 2nd Sess. (22 Feb. 1841) pp. 199-200. Debate over appropriations to provide for an exploration and survey of part of the northeastern boundary line of the United States. Includes remarks by Nathan Clifford (Maine).

1041. "Northeastern Boundary," *Congressional Globe*. 26th Cong., 2nd Sess. (8 Jan. 1841) pp. 91-92. Debate on a resolution to obtain copies of debates in British Parliament concerning the northeastern U.S. boundary. Includes brief remarks by Daniel Webster (Mass.).

1042. Anderson, Hugh J. (Maine). "Fortifications of the United States for the Year 1841," *Congressional Globe*. 26th Cong., 2nd Sess. (1 Mar. 1841) p. 221. Opposes the proposed appropriations; contends that it ignores the War Department's recommendation for a fort at the mouth of the Penobscot River and is generally inadequate in its support of Maine fortifications.

1043. Anderson, Hugh J. (Maine). "Pension Act of 1837," *Congressional Globe, Appendix*. 26th Cong., 2nd Sess. (30 Dec. 1840) pp. 32-33. Favors repealing the navy pension act of 1837; discusses the abuses of the acts and the history of its passage.

1044. Clifford, Nathan (Maine). "Indiana Canal Lands and Northeastern Boundary of the United States," *Congressional Globe*. 26th Cong., 2nd Sess. (22 Feb. 1841) pp. 199-200. Remarks on the position of Maine regarding the survey and exploration of the boundary. While Maine did not request the survey, advocates the necessary appropriations.

1045. Evans, George (Maine). "Treasury Note Bill," *Congressional Globe, Appendix*. 26th Cong., 2nd Sess. (18 Jan. 1841) pp. 234-242. Supports issuing Treasury notes to meet the obligations of the government; discusses the state of the Treasury, and the status of various revenues and expenses of the government, including pensions, the Seminoles, and the branches of service.

1046. Williams, Reuel (Maine). "Navy Pensions," *Congressional Globe*. 26th Cong., 2nd Sess. (23 Dec. 1840) p. 49. Supports reducing the number of people eligible to collect a navy pension.

1047. Williams, Reuel (Maine). "Pursers in the Navy," *Congressional Globe*. 26th Cong., 2nd Sess. (23 Dec. 1840) p. 49. Briefly remarks on the bill to establish the pay and privileges of pursers.

1048. Williams, Reuel (Maine). "Repeal of the Independent Treasury," *Congressional Globe*. 26th Cong., 2nd Sess. (20 Feb. 1841) pp. 197-198. Remarks on his responsibility and duty to the Legislature of Maine.

1049. U.S. House. *Maine - Militia Services*. 26th Cong., 2nd Sess. (H.Rpt.78). [Washington: 1841]. 3 pg. (Serial Set 388). Supports the claims of the State of Maine for the services of her militia in the protection of the northeastern frontier at Aroostook River in 1839.

1050. U.S. House. *Memorial from Inhabitants of Bucksport, in the State of Maine, Praying for a Permanent Revenue, and Correction of Abuses in Affairs of Government*. 26th Cong., 2nd Sess. (H.Doc.67). [Washington: 1841]. 4 pg. (Serial Set 383). Memorial supports a permanent revenue, and objects to executive patronage regarding public offices. Names of memorialists included.

1051. U.S. Senate. *Resolutions of the Legislature of Maine, in Favor of the Repeal of the Independent Treasury Bill, and the Establishment of a National Bank; an Increase of the Tariff; and the Distribution of the Proceeds of the Sales of the Public Lands*. 26th Cong., 2nd Sess. (S.Doc.202). Washington: Blair and Rives, 1841. 2 pg. (Serial Set 378).

27ᵀᴴ CONGRESS, 1ˢᵀ SESSION

1052. Allen, Elisha H. (Maine). "Bankrupt Bill," *Congressional Globe., Appendix*. 27th Cong., 1st Sess. (Aug. 1841) pp. 477-479. Supports establishing a uniform system of bankruptcy as necessary and expedient. Reviews the constitutional authority. Examines the principles of the measure and its probable effects on the public interest. Addresses opponents' arguments.

1053. Allen, Elisha H. (Maine). "Bankrupt Law," *Congressional Globe.* 27th Cong., 1st Sess. (12 Aug. 1841) pp. 330-331. Supports the bankrupt law as constitutional and expedient.

1054. Clifford, Nathan (Maine). "Distribution and Pre-emption Bill," *Congressional Globe.* 27th Cong., 1st Sess. (29 June, 30 June 1841) pp. 127-129; 130. Opposes distributing proceeds from the public lands and then making up the deficit by duties on luxuries; contends that it is unconstitutional and inexpedient, and that the proposed duties are inadequate for the purpose.

1055. Clifford, Nathan (Maine). "Post Office Department," *Congressional Globe.* 27th Cong., 1st Sess. (24 Aug. 1841) pp. 375-376. Opposes using Treasury funds to assist the Post Office; comments on the high number of removals from office.

1056. Evans, George (Maine). Remarks on the Loan Bill, *Congressional Globe.* 27th Cong., 1st Sess. (17 July 1841) p. 218. Supports the loan.

1057. Fessenden, William P. (Maine). "Bankrupt Bill," *Congressional Globe, Appendix.* 27th Cong., 1st Sess. (11 Aug. 1841) pp. 469-471. Supports the bill to establish a uniform system of bankruptcy throughout the U.S.; contends that it is a measure of critical relief, benefiting creditors as well as debtors. Maintains that Congress has the right to legislate on this subject; discusses the provisions of the bill. Summary of speech in *Congressional Globe*, p. 323.

1058. Fessenden, William P. (Maine). "The Fortification Bill," *Congressional Globe.* 27th Cong., 1st Sess. (15 July 1841) p. 205. Supports appropriations for fortifications; discusses the reasons Forts Preble and Scammel (Portland Harbor) are not included.

1059. Fessenden, William P. (Maine). Remarks on the Sub-Treasury, *Congressional Globe.* 27th Cong., 1st Sess. (22 June 1841) p. 89. Supports repealing the Sub-Treasury law; maintains that it is odious and dangerous.

1060. Littlefield, Nathaniel S. (Maine). "Post Office Department," *Congressional Globe.* 27th Cong., 1st Sess. (25 Aug. 1841) p. 384. Supports a loan to enable the Post Office Dept. to pay the mail contractors; also comments negatively about the removals and appointments of postmasters.

1061. Littlefield, Nathaniel S. (Maine). Remarks on Appropriations for Fortifications, *Congressional Globe.* 27th Cong., 1st Sess. (19 July 1841) pp. 227-228. Supports the fortification bill, even though defenses of Maine are neglected. Discusses efforts to amend the bill to include fortifications of Portland harbor; deplores the McLeod affair and the actions of the current administration that are responsible for the country's present financial situation.

1062. U.S. House. *Resolutions of the Legislature of Alabama, Responsive to Those of South Carolina on the Subject of Controversy Between the States of Maine and Georgia.* 27th Cong., 1st Sess. (H.Doc.11). Washington: Gales & Seaton, 1841. 2 pg. (Serial Set 392). Copy of the report and resolutions concerning the failure of Maine to surrender Daniel Philbrook and Edward Kilbron, who were charged with stealing a slave and transporting him to Maine.

1063. U.S. Senate. *Resolutions of the Legislature of Maine, in Favor of Making Provision for Indemnification for French Spoliations Committed Prior to the Year 1800.* 27th Cong., 1st Sess. (S.Doc.31). [Washington]: Thomas Allen, Print., [1841]. 2 pg. (Serial Set 390). Resolutions and report support the claims.

1064. U.S. Senate. *Resolutions of the Legislature of Maine, in Favor of So Amending the Constitution of the United States, As to Restrict the Eligibility of the President to a Single Term.* 27th Cong., 1st Sess. (S.Doc.30). [Washington]: Thomas Allen, Print., [1841]. 1 pg. (Serial Set 390).

27ᵀᴴ CONGRESS, 2ᴺᴰ SESSION

1065. Allen, Elisha H. (Maine). "Northeastern Boundary," *Congressional Globe, Appendix.* 27th Cong., 2nd Sess. (25 July 1842) pp. 803-805. Responds to the agreement between the ministers of the U.S. and Great Britain for a settlement of the northeastern boundary. Includes a brief history of events; defends Maine's position regarding the British aggressions.

1066. Allen, Elisha H. (Maine). "The Tariff Bill," *Congressional Globe, Appendix.* 27th Cong., 2nd Sess. (11 July 1842) pp. 862-866. Supports the protective, American system over free trade; maintains that those advocating free trade are working towards the interests of the British government. Discusses various protective duties and their effects.

1067. Clifford, Nathan (Maine). "Apportionment Bill," *Congressional Globe, Appendix.* 27th Cong., 2nd Sess. (28 Apr. 1842) pp. 347-350. Opposes giving Congress the power to regulate elections for Representatives; maintains that it is an encroachment on states' rights. Provides a brief history of states' rights regarding elections; discusses the expediency of the measure.

1068. Clifford, Nathan (Maine). Remarks on Appropriations to Continue the Survey of the Northeastern Boundary, *Congressional Globe.* 27th Cong., 2nd Sess. (8 Apr. 1842) p. 403. Supports further appropriations to continue the survey; contends that the miles to be surveyed were greater than estimated.

1069. Clifford, Nathan (Maine). "The Tariff Bill," *Congressional Globe, Appendix.* 27th Cong., 2nd Sess. (July 1842) pp. 669-678. Opposes the distribution of the proceeds of the public lands and the proposed tariff increases as extravagant and unequal. Addresses the effect of the measure on the economy; reviews the history of tariff policies, detailing those of the administrations of Jackson, Van Buren, and Adams. Advocates restricting tariffs solely to the purpose of revenue, not to protect, retaliate, or prohibit.

1070. Evans, George (Maine). "The Little Tariff," *Congressional Globe.* 27th Cong., 2nd Sess. (23 June 1842) pp. 668-669. Supports postponing for one month the operation of the provisions of the Compromise Act that would come into effect on the 1st of July, relating to the tariff and land distribution.

1071. Evans, George (Maine). "Loan Bill," *Congressional Globe.* 27th Cong., 2nd Sess. (5 Apr. 1842) pp. 385-386. Portion and summary of speech support the extension of the loan of 1841 plus an additional loan of five million. Discusses the provisions of the bill and the condition of the Treasury; advocates maximum flexibility to enable the Secretary of the Treasury to obtain the best terms.

1072. Evans, George (Maine). "The Navy Appropriation Bill," *Congressional Globe.* 27th Cong., 2nd Sess. (14 June 1842) pp. 624-625. Opposes an amendment to define and limit the number of officers in the navy; maintains that such important legislation respecting the organization of the navy should not be suddenly brought up in an appropriation bill.

1073. Evans, George (Maine). "Proposed Board of Exchequer," *Congressional Globe.* 27th Cong., 2nd Sess. (10 Jan. 1842) pp. 110-111. Supports the proposed Board to establish a good currency, remedy the exchanges and keep the public money. Addresses the pros and cons of the plan, and concludes that it is the best solution presented to meet the present emergency.

1074. Evans, George (Maine). Remarks on the Loan Bill and Treasury Notes, *Congressional Globe.* 27th Cong., 2nd Sess. (31 Aug. 1842) pp. 975-976. Supports using Treasury notes as a temporary remedy to the embarrassments of the government.

1075. Evans, George (Maine). Remarks on the Treasury Note Bill, *Congressional Globe.* 27th Cong., 2nd Sess. (19 Jan. 1842) pp. 146-147. Reluctantly supports the bill because of the demands of the Treasury and the necessity of the case; reviews the condition of the Treasury and anticipated revenues and expenditures.

1076. Evans, George (Maine). "Retrenchment and Reform," *Congressional Globe.* 27th Cong., 2nd Sess. (17 Mar., 18 Mar. 1842) pp. 327-328; 335-336. Summary of speeches reviews the expenditures and revenues of the government and the financial condition of the country. Maintains that the retrenchments of the past administration were merely postponements, and that Congress should address more effective ways of raising revenue than retrenchment.

1077. Evans, George (Maine). "The Tariff Bill," *Congressional Globe, Appendix.* 27th Cong., 2nd Sess. (25 July 1842) pp. 751-754. Supports the bill; discusses the general principles and necessity for the measure. Maintains that government has always met its revenue demands through commerce; defends the distribution of the proceeds of the public lands to the states. Summary of speech in *Congressional Globe*, pp. 786-787.

1078. Evans, George (Maine). "The Tariff Bill," *Congressional Globe.* 27th Cong., 2nd Sess. (26 July 1842) pp. 791-792. Answers some objections to statements made in earlier speech.

1079. Evans, George (Maine). "The Tariff Bill," *Congressional Globe, Appendix.* 27th Cong., 2nd Sess. (5 Aug. 1842) pp. 794-796. Defends the Whig administration that had to cope with the debts and policies of the previous administration. Discusses proposed measures to raise revenue; compares duties to those of 1828. Summary of speech in *Congressional Globe*, pp. 850-851.

1080. Fessenden, William P. (Maine). "Army Appropriation Bill," *Congressional Globe, Appendix.* 27th Cong., 2nd Sess. (31 May 1842) pp. 733-736. Opposes reducing the size of the army. Maintains that a necessary number of men are needed to garrison the military posts along the frontiers, to keep up a military spirit and to preserve a standard of discipline. The situation is not comparable to European countries, or to the army manpower needs of 1821. Summary of speech in *Congressional Globe*, p. 559.

1081. Fessenden, William P. (Maine). "Treasury Note Bill," *Congressional Globe.* 27th Cong., 2nd Sess. (11 Jan. 1842) pp. 118-119. Supports issuing Treasury notes; explains his reversal of opinion. Addresses the possibility of a loan, the constitutionality and the expediency.

1082. Lowell, Joshua A. (Maine). "Army Appropriation Bill," *Congressional Globe, Appendix.* 27th Cong., 2nd Sess. (30 May 1842) pp. 444-448. Opposes reducing the military establishment; maintains that a standing army adequate to protect the public property and to repel invasion is necessary. Discusses current difficulties with Great Britain that also make this an improper time to attempt reduction. Presents a brief history of the origin of the dispute over the Madawaska and Aroostook territory, with the progress, and termination of the various negotiations. Summary of speech in *Congressional Globe*, pp. 553-554.

1083. Lowell, Joshua A. (Maine). "British Colonial Trade," *Congressional Globe, Appendix.* 27th Cong., 2nd Sess. (9 June 1842) pp. 474-480. Discusses memorials and resolutions received regarding the trade. Reviews the several conventions, acts and orders by which commerce with Great Britain and her colonies has been regulated, maintaining that Great Britain has always kept her advantage; proposes notice and complaint of dissatisfaction to Great Britain rather than this rash and hasty bill.

1084. Randall, Benjamin (Maine). "Contested Election in Maine," *Congressional Globe.* 27th Cong., 2nd Sess. (16 Mar. 1842) p. 323. Opposes the resolutions to investigate the contested election of Joshua A. Lowell.

1085. Williams, Reuel (Maine). "Naval Appropriation Bill," *Congressional Globe.* 27th Cong., 2nd Sess. (17 June 1842) p. 645. Remarks on various items of naval expenditure. Opposes additional ships of war in commission; questions the requested appropriations for the home squadron.

1086. Williams, Reuel (Maine). "Navy Appropriation Bill," *Congressional Globe, Appendix.* 27th Cong., 2nd Sess. (14 June 1842) pp. 486-487. Supports decreasing the number of officers in the navy. Historical comparisons and statistics demonstrate how the number of naval officers has increased to excessive proportions and that reducing the number would not be harmful to the service. Summary of speech in *Congressional Globe*, p. 625.

1087. Williams, Reuel (Maine). "Pursers in the Navy," *Congressional Globe.* 27th Cong., 2nd Sess. (9 Aug. 1842) p. 865. Supports regulating the pay of pursers in the navy.

1088. Williams, Reuel (Maine). "The Tariff Bill," *Congressional Globe.* 27th Cong., 2nd Sess. (27 Aug. 1842) p. 957. Explains why he will vote for the bill though he opposes it and finds it particularly harmful to Maine.

1089. "An Act to Extend the Collection District of Wiscasset," *Statutes at Large*, Vol. V (31 Aug. 1842) p. 578.

1090. "An Act to Provide for the Settlement of the Claims of the State of Maine for Services of Her Militia," *Statutes at Large*, Vol. V (13 June 1842) p. 490.

1091. U.S. House. *John Campbell.* 27th Cong., 2nd Sess. (H.Rpt.425). [Washington: 1842]. 1 pg. (Serial Set 408). Report of the Committee on Invalid Pensions against the petition of John Campbell.

1092. U.S. House. *Letter from the Secretary of War, Transmitting the Information Required by a Resolution of the House of Representatives of the 8th Instant, respecting Estimates of the Cost of a Military Road in the State of Maine. &c.* 27th Cong., 2nd Sess. (H.Doc.78). [Washington: 1842]. 3 pg. (Serial Set 402). Report of estimates to construct military roads from the mouth of the Little Machias to Fort Fairfield, and from Fort Kent to the Aroostook and onward to the state road in Masadis.

1093. U.S. House. *Memorial of Inhabitants of Portland, on the Subject of the Colonial Trade with Great Britain.* 27th Cong., 2nd Sess. (H.Doc.68). [Washington: 1842]. 3 pg. (Serial Set 402). Contends that reciprocity of trade with Great Britain's colonies does not exist due to prohibition of some products, higher taxes, and limited open ports; requests a review of the arrangement respecting the commercial intercourse with the British colonies.

1094. U.S. House. *Message from the President of the United States, in Reply to the Resolution of the House of Representatives of the 21st Instant, in Relation to the Negotiation Between the United States and Great Britain, upon the Subject of the Northeastern Boundary of the State of Maine.* 27th Cong., 2nd Sess. (H.Doc.109). [Washington: 1842]. 1 pg. (Serial Set 402). Pres. Tyler reports that he cannot make communications public without danger to the public interest.

1095. U.S. House. *Militia Claims of Maine.* 27th Cong., 2nd Sess. (H.Rpt.363). [Washington: 1842]. 5 pg. (Serial Set 408). Supports claims of Maine for the services of her militia in 1839 for the defense of the northeastern frontier. Committee adopts and reprints earlier report, printed as H.rpt.566 (26-1) 372 (entry **1026**) and S.doc.419 (26-1) 359 (entry **1031**).

1096. U.S. House. *Report of a Joint Select Committee of the Legislature of the State of Maine, upon the Subject of the Northeastern Boundary of the Said State, &c.* 27th Cong., 2nd Sess. (H.Doc.66). [Washington: 1842]. 3 pg. (Serial Set 402). Supports continuing the military road existing from Mattanawcook to Houlton onwards to the Madawaska settlements on the St. John River. Same as S.doc.84 (27-2) 396 (entry **1103**).

1097. U.S. House. [Report on the Contested Election of Joshua A. Lowell]. 27th Cong., 2nd Sess. (H.Rpt.285). [Washington: 1842]. 119 pg. (Serial Set 407). Committee of Elections resolves that Joshua A. Lowell is entitled to his seat as a member of the House. Includes testimony and statements relative to his election, a defense by Lowell, copies of various election acts from the State of Maine, and voting statistics. Pagination skips from page 1 to page 17.

1098. U.S. House. *Resolutions of the Legislature of Maine, in Favor of Repealing the Act for the Distribution of the Proceeds of the Sales of the Public Lands.* 27th Cong., 2nd Sess. (H.Doc.172). [Washington: 1842]. 2 pg. (Serial Set 404).

1099. U.S. House. *Resolutions of the Legislature of Maine, Relative to the Defence of the Seacoast and Inland Frontier of That State.* 27th Cong., 2nd Sess. (H.Doc.171). [Washington: 1842]. 2 pg. (Serial Set 404). Resolutions request Congress to appropriate money for the defense of the State of Maine.

1100. U.S. House. *Resolution of the Legislature of the State of Maine, in Relation to Fixing the Time for the Choice of Electors of President and Vice President.* 27th Cong., 2nd Sess. (H.Doc.183). [Washington: 1842]. 1 pg. (Serial Set 404). Requires all states to hold elections for the electors on the same day.

1101. U.S. House. *Resolutions of the Legislature of the State of Maine, in Relation to the British Colonial Trade.* 27th Cong., 2nd Sess. (H.Doc.184). [Washington: 1842]. 2 pg. (Serial Set 404). Resolutions request equity and reciprocity in trade with Great Britain's colonies.

1102. U.S. Senate. *Resolutions of the General Assembly of Maine, Rescinding Certain Resolutions Adopted March 18, 1840, in Favor of the Passage of a General Bankrupt Law.* 27th Cong., 2nd Sess. (S.Doc.85). [Washington: Thomas Allen, Print., 1842]. 1 pg. (Serial Set 396).

1103. U.S. Senate. *Resolutions of the General Assembly of Maine, to Procure an Appropriation for the Construction of a Military Road in That State.* 27th Cong., 2nd Sess. (S.Doc.84). [Washington]: Thomas Allen, Print., [1842]. 3 pg. (Serial Set 396). Same as H.doc.66 (27-2) 402. See entry **1096.**

27TH CONGRESS, 3RD SESSION

1104. "The British Treaty and the Red Lines," *Congressional Globe.* 27th Cong., 3rd Sess. (5 Jan. 1843) pp. 119-121. Continues the debate correcting a printed report of a debate concerning the French map of 1784 from Mr. Jefferson's collection and Dr. Franklin's alleged map. Questions the validity of the maps and whether the red line indicates the northeastern boundary of the U.S. or the French boundary from when Canada belonged to France.

1105. "The Red Lines Again," *Congressional Globe.* 27th Cong., 3rd Sess. (18 Jan. 1843) pp. 169-171. Continues the discussion on the earlier printed report of the debate concerning the red lines on the maps.

1106. Remarks on the Northeastern Boundary Line, *Congressional Globe.* 27th Cong., 3rd Sess. (4 Jan. 1843) p. 111. Various remarks correcting a report of an earlier debate concerning the red line on Dr. Franklin's alleged map and the old French map of 1784 from Mr. Jefferson's collection.

1107. Evans, George (Maine). "Petersburg Railroad Company," *Congressional Globe.* 27th Cong., 3rd Sess. (23 Jan. 1843) pp. 187-188. Supports exempting the company from the duty on railroad iron laid by Dec. 1843.

1108. Evans, George (Maine). Remarks on Treasury Notes, *Congressional Globe.* 27th Cong., 3rd Sess. (2 Mar. 1843) p. 380. Supports the amendment to allow all outstanding Treasury notes to be entitled to interest; maintains that public finances make it impossible to redeem any of outstanding notes this year.

1109. Evans, George (Maine). "Retrenchment, Economy, and Government Resources," *Congressional Globe.* 27th Cong., 3rd Sess. (24 Feb. 1843) p. 281. Remarks on the state of the economy; contends that the want of a sound currency of uniform value is the problem, and that the passage of the last tariff law revived the government's credit.

1110. Fessenden, William P. (Maine). Remarks on the Bankrupt Law, *Congressional Globe.* 27th Cong., 3rd Sess. (29 Dec. 1842) p. 99. Supports the bankrupt law; maintains that it was designed for the benefit of creditors. Responds to remarks of other speakers.

1111. Williams, Reuel (Maine). "British Treaty," *Congressional Globe, Appendix.* 27th Cong., 3rd Sess. (19 Aug. 1842) pp. 53-56. Impassioned speech opposes the ratification of the Treaty of Washington. Maintains that Maine does not support the boundary decisions; includes the report of the commissioners of Maine and their objections.

1112. "An Act Declaring Robbinston in the State of Maine, to Be a Port of Delivery," *Statutes at Large*, Vol. V (3 Mar. 1843) p. 609.

1113. "An Act to Change the Place of Holding the Circuit and District Courts in the District of Maine," *Statutes at Large*, Vol. V (15 Feb. 1843) p. 600.

1114. "An Act to Repeal an Act Entitled "An Act to Extend the Collection District of Wiscasset"," *Statutes at Large*, Vol. V (3 Mar. 1843) p. 612.

1115. U.S. House. *Refund General Jackson's Fine.* 27th Cong., 3rd Sess. (H.Doc.105). [Washington: 1843]. 1 pg. (Serial Set 420). Supports refunding the fine and interest incurred in the alleged contempt of the authority of Judge Hall. Same as S.Doc.114 (27-3) 415 (entry **1122**).

1116. U.S. House. *Resolution of the Legislature of Maine, in Relation to the Post Office Department.* 27th Cong., 3rd Sess. (H.Doc.154). [Washington: 1843]. 1 pg. (Serial Set 422). Resolutions oppose paying letter postage on newspapers addressed with an individual's name.

1117. U.S. House. *Resolution of the Legislature of the State of Maine, Relating to the Bankrupt Act.* 27th Cong., 3rd Sess. (H.Doc.118). [Washington: 1843]. 1 pg. (Serial Set 421). Resolutions favor the repeal of the law. Same as S.doc.128 (27-3) 415 (entry **1121**).

1118. U.S. House. *Resolutions of the Legislature of Maine, in Favor of Amos Kendall.* 27th Cong., 3rd Sess. (H.Doc.193). [Washington: 1843]. 2 pg. (Serial Set 422). Supports Amos Kendall, Postmaster General of the U.S., for withholding his official sanction to the claim of Stockton & Stokes.

1119. U.S. House. *Resolutions of the Legislature of Maine in Relation to the Military Academy at West Point.* 27th Cong., 3rd Sess. (H.Doc.155). [Washington: 1843]. 1 pg. (Serial Set 422). Supports abolishing the military academy at West Point.

1120. U.S. Senate. [Report on Claims for the Schooner Martha, of Eastport, Maine]. 27th Cong., 3rd Sess. (S.Doc.49). [Washington]: Thomas Allen, Print., [1843]. 1 pg. (Serial Set 414). Opposes granting the claim for fishing bounty.

1121. U.S. Senate. *Resolutions of the Legislature of Maine, in Favor of the Repeal of the Bankrupt Law.* 27th Cong., 3rd Sess. (S.Doc.128). [Washington]: Thomas Allen, Print., [1843]. 1 pg. (Serial Set 415). Same as H.doc.118 (27-3) 421 (entry **1117**).

1122. U.S. Senate. *Resolutions of the Legislature of Maine, in Favor of Refunding to General Andrew Jackson, the Amount of a Fine Imposed on Him in 1815.* 27th Cong., 3rd Sess. (S.Doc.114). [Washington: Thomas Allen, Print., 1843]. 1 pg. (Serial Set 415). Same as H.doc.105 (27-3) 420. See entry **1115**.

28TH CONGRESS, 1ST SESSION

1123. Dunlap, Robert P. (Maine). "The Tariff," *Congressional Globe, Appendix.* 28th Cong., 1st Sess. (1 May 1844) pp. 408-410. Calls for a bipartisan investigation of the problem. Opposes, on the basis of constitutionality, a largely productive tariff, contributions to the states from the general government, and the distribution of public lands proceeds by Congress. Summary of remarks in *Congressional Globe*, p. 599.

1124. Evans, George (Maine). "The Compromise Act," *Congressional Globe.* 28th Cong., 1st Sess. (18 Jan. 1844) pp. 163-164. Claims that the proposed bill to gradually reduce duties, which originated in the Senate, is in reality a revenue bill, and as such it is unconstitutional for the Senate to act upon it.

1125. Evans, George (Maine). "Duties on Railroad Iron," *Congressional Globe.* 28th Cong., 1st Sess. (7 June 1844) p. 695. Supports the remission of duties on railroad iron.

1126. Evans, George (Maine). "Stolen Treasury Notes," *Congressional Globe.* 28th Cong., 1st Sess. (23 May 1844) p. 655. Supports payment of canceled Treasury notes stolen from the customhouse at New Orleans; maintains that individuals who received them in good faith should receive payment.

1127. Evans, George (Maine). "The Tariff," *Congressional Globe, Appendix.* 28th Cong., 1st Sess. (22 Jan., 23 Jan. 1844) pp. 353-363. Discusses Mr. McDuffie's bill to gradually reduce the rates of duties to the standard of the Compromise Act. Addresses opponents' arguments regarding raising the whole revenue for the government on imposts, the tariff law of 1842 as protectionist legislation, the value of internal commerce, the effect of low duties, and the unequal and burdensome results of the tariff law of 1842. Discusses the cotton duty. Summary of remarks in *Congressional Globe*, pp. 176-177, 180-181.

1128. Evans, George (Maine). "The Tariff," *Congressional Globe, Appendix.* 28th Cong., 1st Sess. (6 Feb., 7 Feb. 1844) pp. 708-715. Replies to Mr. McDuffie's second speech on the tariff. Addresses controversies over inductive reasoning, the tariff act of 1842 and the effect of previous protectionist legislation, advantages of dividing this country into three separate confederations, comparative industry of different sections of the Union, and the effects of the South separating from the Union. Summary of speech in *Congressional Globe*, pp. 231-233, 236-237.

1129. Fairfield, John (Maine). "Edward Kennard," *Congressional Globe.* 28th Cong., 1st Sess. (11 Jan. 1844) p. 135. Supports relief for the fine paid by Edward Kennard, Captain of the ship *Pactolus,* for an improper certificate of registry.

1130. Fairfield, John (Maine). Remarks on French Spoliations Prior to 1800, *Congressional Globe.* 28th Cong., 1st Sess. (12 Feb. 1844) pp. 266-268. Supports the report and resolutions of Maine to honor the claims of those who suffered by French captures and spoliations from 1793 to 1800. Contends that after 18 reports from Congress, of which 14 were favorable, Congress needs to resolve the issue. Provides a brief history of the claims and negotiations.

1131. Fairfield, John (Maine). "United States Schooner Grampus," *Congressional Globe, Appendix.* 28th Cong., 1st Sess. (13 May 1844) pp. 433-434. Supports claims for remuneration to the officers and crew of the ship-of-war Adams, destroyed by fire Sept. 1814. Gives history of events and responds to arguments of the opposition.

1132. Hamlin, Hannibal (Maine). "Army Appropriation Bill," *Congressional Globe, Appendix.* 28th Cong., 1st Sess. (15 Apr. 1844) pp. 504-509. Addresses the acts of the Federal party, or Whigs, focusing on the 27th Congress. Discusses the bankrupt law, distribution of the sales of the public lands, the U.S. Bank, the increase of the tariff, and the assumption of state debts. Maintains that the Whig party is responsible for increasing public expenditure, creating a public debt, and squandering the public money to support a political press. Summary of speech in *Congressional Globe*, pp. 538-539.

1133. Hamlin, Hannibal (Maine). "Presidential Election," *Congressional Globe, Appendix.* 28th Cong., 1st Sess. (15 May 1844) pp. 434-435. Supports the bill to hold the presidential election on the same day throughout the U.S.; maintains that the Constitution gives Congress the power to fix on a particular day, though not the place and manner. Summary of speech in *Congressional Globe*, p. 634.

1134. Hamlin, Hannibal (Maine). "Rules of the House," *Congressional Globe, Appendix.* 28th Cong., 1st Sess. (5 Jan. 1844) pp. 28-29. Opposes the adoption of the 21st rule, prohibiting the reception of abolition petitions. Maintains that the right of petition is guaranteed by the Constitution. Summary of speech in *Congressional Globe*, p. 110.

1135. Severance, Luther (Maine). "Abolition Petitions," *Congressional Globe, Appendix.* 28th Cong., 1st Sess. (16 Feb. 1844) pp. 591-594. Supports the abolition petitions and the abolishment of slavery in the District of Columbia. Addresses the power of the states to legislate to abolish slavery, slaves as private property, insanity of colored persons in the North, crime committed by free colored persons, interracial marriages, and the benefits of abolition in the District. Summary of speech in *Congressional Globe*, pp. 294-295.

1136. Severance, Luther (Maine). "The Tariff," *Congressional Globe, Appendix.* 28th Cong., 1st Sess. (3 May 1844) pp. 715-720. Supports protectionism and the tariff law of 1842. Discusses the laboring poor in England, demonstrating that the protecting policy is not the cause of poverty in England. Maintains that protection to manufactures is not at the expense of commerce. Opposes "incidental protection" and "democratic tariffs." Analyzes proposed reduced duties; discusses the national debt.

1137. "An Act Relating to the Port of Entry in the District of Passamaquoddy, in the State of Maine," *Statutes at Large,* Vol. V (31 May 1844) p. 658.

1138. U.S. House. *Bangor, Maine - Port of Entry.* 28th Cong., 1st Sess. (H.Rpt.123). [Washington: Blair & Rives,. Printers, 1844]. 2 pg. (Serial Set 445). Supports petitions to establish Bangor as a port of entry. Petitions included.

1139. U.S. House. *Dry Docks.* 28th Cong., 1st Sess. (H.Rpt.394). [Washington]: Blair & Rives, Print., [1844]. [6 pg.]. (Serial Set 446). Objects to granting petitions to erect dry docks at Kittery, Maine and Philadelphia. Includes lists of ships and vessels using the navy yard at Gosport and Boston from June/July 1833-June/July 1843. Minority report supports a dry dock at Philadelphia.

1140. U.S. House. *Fortification - Penobscot River.* 28th Cong., 1st Sess. (H.Rpt.333). [Washington]: Blair & Rives, Printers, [1844]. 1 pg. (Serial Set 445). Report on the status of the erection of the fortification upon the Penobscot River, near Bucksport. As negotiations for the purchase of the site not yet concluded, further appropriations are unnecessary for the next fiscal year.

1141. U.S. House. *Resolutions of the Legislature of Maine, Relative to French Spoliations.* 28th Cong., 1st Sess. (H.Doc.148). [Washington]: Blair & Rives, Print., [1844]. 2 pg. (Serial Set 442). Resolutions support claims for French spoliations prior to 1800.

1142. U.S. House. *Resolutions of the Legislature of Maine, Relative to the British Colonial Trade.* 28th Cong., 1st Sess. (H.Doc.237). [Washington]: Blair & Rives, Print., [1844]. 1 pg. (Serial Set 443). Resolutions to review and rescind the existing arrangements of trade. Same as S.doc. 246 (28-1) 434 (entry **1144**), with additional note from the Governor.

1143. U.S. House. *Resolutions of the Legislature of Maine, Asking the Passage of a Law to Make Uniform the Time for the Election of President and Vice President of the United States throughout the Country.* 28th Cong., 1st Sess. (H.Doc.205). [Washington: Blair & Rives, Printers, 1844]. 1 pg. (Serial Set 443). Same as S.doc.244 (28-1) 434 (entry **1146**).

1144. U.S. Senate. *Resolutions of the Legislature of the State of Maine, in Relation to the British Colonial Trade.* 28th Cong., 1st Sess. (S.Doc.246).

Washington: Gales and Seaton, 1844. 1 pg. (Serial Set 434). Resolutions to review and rescind the existing arrangement of trade. Same as H.doc.237 (28-1) 443 (entry **1142**), but without note from the Governor.

1145. U.S. Senate. *Resolutions of the Legislature of the State of Maine, in Favor of Repealing the Laws of States or Territories Which Render Persons of Color Liable to Arrest and Imprisonment and to Be Sold for Jail Fees.* 28th Cong., 1st Sess. (S.Doc.245). Washington: Gales and Seaton, 1844. 1 pg. (Serial Set 434). Resolutions to protect free colored citizens.

1146. U.S. Senate. *Resolutions of the Legislature of the State of Maine, in Favor of Fixing a Day for the Election of Electors for President and Vice President of the United States.* 28th Cong., 1st Sess. (S.Doc.244). Washington: Gales and Seaton, 1844. 1 pg. (Serial Set 434). Same as H.doc.205 (28-1) 443 (entry **1143**).

28TH CONGRESS, 2ND SESSION

1147. Cary, Shepard (Maine). "Annexation of Texas," *Congressional Globe, Appendix.* 28th Cong., 2nd Sess. (9 Jan. 1845) pp. 61-62. Supports the annexation as beneficial to the North and West, as well as the South. Maintains that the annexation would not be palatable to the Whigs in any form; discusses the Whig party and its alliance with the abolition parties of the North.

1148. Cary, Shepard (Maine). "Military Academy," *Congressional Globe.* 28th Cong., 2nd Sess. (14 Feb. 1845) pp. 289-290. Objects to the West Point Academy, which he contends eliminates the possibility of promotion to enlisted soldiers; maintains that a military academy is not necessary to educate officers.

1149. Cary, Shepard (Maine). "Oregon Bill," *Congressional Globe, Appendix.* 28th Cong., 2nd Sess. (1 Feb. 1845) pp. 159-162. Supports the bill to establish a territorial government in Oregon. Majority of speech discusses the Treaty of Washington and the true position of Maine; maintains that Maine never assented to the treaty. Discusses the indemnities stipulated; includes extracts from his report in the Senate of Maine concerning the treaty.

1150. Cary, Shepard (Maine). "Reduction and Graduation of the Public Lands," *Congressional Globe.* 28th Cong., 2nd Sess. (4 Feb. 1845) pp. 240-241. Supports the bill to reduce and graduate the price of the public lands in favor of actual settlers; maintains that it would preclude speculators while enabling citizens to settle upon the public domain and to become independent freeholders and useful members of society. Compares the situation to that of Maine.

1151. Cary, Shepard (Maine). Remarks on the Independent Treasury Bill, *Congressional Globe.* 28th Cong., 2nd Sess. (21 Dec. 1844) pp. 60-61. Remarks on the Whig party and their reversal of opinion regarding the safekeeping of the public money after the failure of the State banks as depositories.

1152. Evans, George (Maine). "The New States of Iowa and Florida," *Congressional Globe.* 28th Cong., 2nd Sess. (1 Mar. 1845) pp. 380-381. Opposes the admission of Florida as a slavery state; discusses treatment of free blacks entering the southern states and the psychology of the abolitionists

1153. Fairfield, John (Maine). "Admission of Florida and Iowa," *Congressional Globe.* 28th Cong., 2nd Sess. (1 Mar. 1845) p. 378. Supports the admission of Florida. Maintains that Congress can only insist that the constitution and form of government is "republican" and cannot interfere with the details, even potentially objectionable provisions regarding slavery.

1154. Hamlin, Hannibal (Maine). "Annexation of Texas," *Congressional Globe.* 28th Cong., 2nd Sess. (23 Jan. 1845) p. 182. Supports the annexation as beneficial to both the North and the South; advocates the spirit of compromise.

1155. Hamlin, Hannibal (Maine). "Question of Privilege," *Congressional Globe.* 28th Cong., 2nd Sess. (16 Jan. 1845) pp. 145-146. Supports an act that would justify the expulsion of a member for dueling; contends that it would save lives and protect freedom of debate in the House.

1156. Hamlin, Hannibal (Maine). Remarks on the Oregon Bill, *Congressional Globe.* 28th Cong., 2nd Sess. (30 Jan. 1845) p. 223. Supports exercising jurisdiction over the Oregon territory; suggests amending the bill so as to leave the boundaries indefinite, a lesson learned after a similar joint occupation of territory with Great Britain in Maine.

1157. Severance, Luther (Maine). "Annexation of Texas," *Congressional Globe, Appendix.* 28th Cong., 2nd Sess. (15 Jan. 1845) pp. 367-371. Opposes the annexation as unconstitutional and unjust to Mexico. Presents a detailed history of negotiations with Mexico and the efforts of the U.S. to obtain a cession of Texas from Mexico. Discusses the slavery issue, the territory included in the Louisiana Purchase, boundaries, and opponents' arguments. Summary of speech in *Congressional Globe*, pp. 141-142.

1158. Severance, Luther (Maine). "Territorial Government for Oregon," *Congressional Globe.* 28th Cong., 2nd Sess. (31 Jan. 1845) p. 227. Opposes the extension of the federal government over the Oregon territory; contends that the best policy would be to let things alone until necessary.

1159. U.S. House. *Letter from the Secretary of the Navy, Transmitting a Report of Officers and Engineers Relative to the Properties and Advantages of a Dry Dock, &c.* 28th Cong., 2nd Sess. (H.Doc.163). [Washington]: Blair & Rives, Printers, [1845]. 79 pg. (Serial Set 466). Report on the examinations of the navy yards at Kittery and Pensacola to ascertain whether dry docks could be constructed at those locations and at what cost. Compares the relative properties and advantages of dry docks and the different kinds of floating docks.

1160. U.S. House. *Resolutions of the Legislature of Maine, Relative to the Annexation of Texas and the Occupation of Oregon.* 28th Cong., 2nd Sess. (H.Doc.112). [Washington]: Blair & Rives, Print., [1845]. 2 pg. (Serial Set 465). Resolutions support the annexation of Texas and the occupation of the Oregon territory.

1161. U.S. Senate. *Resolutions of the General Assembly of Maine, in Favor of Making Indemnity for French Spoliations Committed Prior to 1800.* 28th Cong., 2nd Sess. (S.Doc.120). Washington: Gales and Seaton, 1845. 2 pg. (Serial Set 456).

29TH CONGRESS, 1ST SESSION

1162. Evans, George (Maine). "Issue of Treasury Notes," *Congressional Globe.* 29th Cong., 1st Sess. (17 July 1846) p. 1109. Supports issuing the Treasury notes, but questions how the payment of these notes will be met; briefly discusses the condition of the Treasury.

1163. Evans, George (Maine). "The Oregon Question," *Congressional Globe, Appendix.* 29th Cong., 1st Sess. (9 Mar., 10 Mar. 1846) pp. 572-579. Opposes the proposal to notify Great Britain of the intention to annul the treaty for the joint occupation of the Oregon territory; questions the validity of U.S. title to the territory; examines the basis of the claim. Speech printed almost in entirety in *Congressional Globe*, pp. 467-470, 475-478.

1164. Evans, George (Maine). "Sub-Treasury," *Congressional Globe.* 29th Cong., 1st Sess. (31 July 1846) p. 1172. Opposes the Sub-Treasury as restricting imports and commerce, diminishing prospects for making successful loans, and restricting business operations of the country.

1165. Evans, George (Maine). "The Tariff," *Congressional Globe.* 29th Cong., 1st Sess. (14 July, 21 July 1846) pp. 1090-1093, 1097-1098; 1124. Supports the tariff of 1842 and the restoration of the public credit through the uniform revenue it has raised; demonstrates through figures from the Secretary of the Treasury that the present bill would not raise a sufficient amount of revenue.

1166. Fairfield, John (Maine). "Augmentation of the Navy," *Congressional Globe, Appendix.* 29th Cong., 1st Sess. (27 Jan. 1846) pp. 289-292. Supports appropriations to build and equip additional steam vessels of war; addresses conflicts with Mexico and disputes with Britain over the northeastern boundary, fishing rights, navigation of the St. John, and the Oregon question. Maintains that these appropriations would afford the country with some security against sudden attacks. Summary of speech in *Congressional Globe*, pp. 251-253.

1167. Fairfield, John (Maine). "Duty on Salt," *Congressional Globe.* 29th Cong., 1st Sess. (24 Mar. 1846) p. 539. Opposes the repeal and justifies the fishing bounty.

1168. Fairfield, John (Maine). "Northeastern Boundary," *Congressional Globe, Appendix.* 29th Cong., 1st Sess. (10 Apr. 1846) pp. 621-623. Responds to Webster's statement that Maine was satisfied with the Treaty of Washington; Fairfield maintains that Maine submitted to the treaty as a matter of necessity, but was never satisfied with it. He provides excerpts representing public sentiment; claims that the compensations received by Maine are over-estimated. Slightly briefer version of speech in *Congressional Globe*, pp. 644-646.

1169. Fairfield, John (Maine). Remarks on Changing the Distribution of Duties Among the Naval Bureaus, *Congressional Globe.* 29th Cong., 1st Sess. (8 Apr. 1846) p. 625. Supports and defends the proposed changes.

1170. Fairfield, John (Maine). Remarks on the Oregon Question, *Congressional Globe.* 29th Cong., 1st Sess. (10 Mar. 1846) p. 474. Contends that the conventions of 1817 and 1828 do not provide precedent for arbitration regarding the Oregon territory as Maine was a question of boundary while Oregon is a question of title.

1171. Fairfield, John (Maine). "The Texan Navy," *Congressional Globe.* 29th Cong., 1st Sess. (9 July, 29 July 1846) pp. 1073; 1162-1163. Opposes the bill allowing officers in the Texan navy to be transferred to the navy of the U.S. with their present ranks; maintains that it is an infringement of constitutional rights and unjust to the officers of the navy.

1172. Hamlin, Hannibal (Maine). "Contested Election from Florida," *Congressional Globe.* 29th Cong., 1st Sess. (20 Jan. 1846) pp. 222-224. Defends the decision that William H. Brockenbrough was entitled to a seat in the House and that E. Carrington Cabell was not; reviews the election laws of Florida and the facts of the case.

1173. Hamlin, Hannibal (Maine). "The Graduation Bill," *Congressional Globe.* 29th Cong., 1st Sess. (9 July 1846) p. 1072. Supports offering the lands at graduated prices to actual settlers only; contends that it would be just, equal, and of lasting benefit to the whole country.

1174. Hamlin, Hannibal (Maine). "The Post Office," *Congressional Globe.* 29th Cong., 1st Sess. (24 Apr. 1846) p. 724. Various remarks favor reduced rates of postage and the abolishment of the franking privilege.

1175. Hamlin, Hannibal (Maine). Speech on the Oregon Question, *Congressional Globe.* 29th Cong., 1st Sess. (12 Jan. 1846) pp. 186-189. Supports terminating the convention with Great Britain. Maintains that it is the duty of government to protect its citizens. Addresses concerns of war and commercial considerations; supports building a railroad to the Pacific coast.

1176. Hamlin, Hannibal (Maine). "Two Regiments of Riflemen," *Congressional Globe.* 29th Cong., 1st Sess. (23 Mar. 1846) pp. 534-535. Various brief remarks concerning a bill to increase forces by the addition of two new regiments of riflemen.

1177. Sawtelle, Cullen (Maine). "The Oregon Debate," *Congressional Globe.* 29th Cong., 1st Sess. (27 Jan. 1846) pp. 249-250. Supports notifying Great Britain that the convention concerning the territory of Oregon shall be annulled in twelve months. Opposed to "compromise" in the manner in which Maine was "compromised" to satisfy Great Britain; defends the character of the North.

1178. Severance, Luther (Maine). "Harbors and Rivers," *Congressional Globe, Appendix.* 29th Cong., 1st Sess. (13 Mar. 1846) pp. 489-492. Supports appropriations to remove obstructions on the tide waters of the Kennebec River, thereby making the U.S. arsenal at Augusta more accessible. Maintains that Ogden vs. Gibbons gave the general government jurisdiction over waters. Discusses the policy of internal improvements and free trade.

1179. Severance, Luther (Maine). "Mexican War," *Congressional Globe, Appendix.* 29th Cong., 1st Sess. (28 May 1846) pp. 683-687. Supports a vote of thanks to General Zachary Taylor and his men for their gallantry upon the Rio Grande. Acknowledges the necessity of military academies. Main focus of speech opposes the war, documenting the dispute over the Texan border and maintaining that no treaties with Mexico or Spain gave us the right to the Rio Grande as the boundary. Summary of speech in *Congressional Globe*, p. 879.

1180. Severance, Luther (Maine). "The Tariff," *Congressional Globe, Appendix.* 29th Cong., 1st Sess. (27 June 1846) pp. 702-708. Supports protectionism and the tariff of 1842 and opposes the proposed amendments; detailed analysis disagrees with the report of the Secretary of the Treasury and the anticipated effects of the tariff upon the revenue.

1181. U.S. House. *Custom-House at Castine.* 29th Cong., 1st Sess. (H.Rpt.438). [Washington]: Ritchie & Heiss, Print., [1846]. 1 pg. (Serial Set 489). Report supports purchasing the remainder of the customhouse at Castine and making the necessary repairs.

1182. U.S. House. *Custom-House at Eastport.* 29th Cong., 1st Sess. (H.Rpt.581). [Washington]: Ritchie & Heiss, Print., [1846]. 3 pg. (Serial Set 490). Supports the petition requesting an appropriation for the purchase of a site and erection of a new customhouse in Eastport. Includes letter from the collector of Eastport.

1183. U.S. House. *Message from the President of the United States, Transmitting Correspondence Between This Government and Great Britain, within the Last Two Years, in Relation to the "Washington Treaty," and to the Free Navigation of the River St. John, and to the Disputed Territory Fund; in Compliance with the Resolution of the House of Representatives of 19th*

December Last. 29th Cong., 1st Sess. (H.Doc.110). [Washington]: Ritchie & Heiss, Printers, [1846]. 78 pg. (Serial Set 483). Includes correspondence relating to the third, fourth, and fifth articles of the Treaty of Washington, dealing with free navigation, land claims, and the disputed territory fund respectively.

29ᵀᴴ CONGRESS, 2ᴺᴰ SESSION

1184. Evans, George (Maine). "The Loan Bill," *Congressional Globe.* 29th Cong., 2nd Sess. (25 Jan. 1847) pp. 249-250. Rather than raising loans by issuing Treasury notes, prefers to adopt the tariff policy of 1841 and restore the system destroyed in 1846.

1185. Evans, George (Maine). Remarks on the Treasury Note and Loan Bill, *Congressional Globe.* 29th Cong., 2nd Sess. (26 Jan. 1847) pp. 257, 259-260. Proposes and defends an amendment to restrict the ability of the Secretary of the Treasury to redeem the notes.

1186. Evans, George (Maine). "The Three Million Bill," *Congressional Globe.* 29th Cong., 2nd Sess. (23 Feb. 1847) pp. 480-482. Opposes the appropriation of three million dollars to resolve the war with Mexico. Compares this bill with one discussed last session, maintaining that the earlier one was a treaty for limits and boundaries, not for the acquisition of new territory; discusses the origin and causes of the war and various propositions for its termination.

1187. Fairfield, John (Maine). "Relief for Ireland," *Congressional Globe, Appendix.* 29th Cong., 2nd Sess. (27 Feb. 1847) pp. 430-431. Opposes granting relief. Maintains that Congress does not have the power to give away money that was raised to defray the expenses of the government to another totally different purpose, one not authorized by the Constitution.

1188. Hamlin, Hannibal (Maine). "Increase of the· Army," *Congressional Globe.* 29th Cong., 2nd Sess. (4 Jan. 1847) pp. 110-111. Supports the supplies of men and money necessary for the war, but advocates changing the organization from that of a standing army to that of volunteers enlisted for five years' service, or for the war, and officered by men of their own choice.

1189. Hamlin, Hannibal (Maine). Remarks on Establishing the Territory of Oregon, *Congressional Globe.* 29th Cong., 2nd Sess. (16 Jan. 1847) pp. 195-198. Objects to the extension of slavery in any territory subsequently acquired and made a part of the Union. Maintains that Congress should pass a declaratory act against slavery, thereby preventing new states from establishing slavery; discusses precedence and constitutionality of such an act.

1190. Sawtelle, Cullen (Maine). Remarks on a Change in the Collection District of Belfast, *Congressional Globe.* 29th Cong., 2nd Sess. (20 Feb. 1847)

p. 470. Opposes the creation of a new district, composed of a part of the district at Belfast; also objects to making Bangor a separate port of entry.

1191. Severance, Luther (Maine). "The Mexican War," *Congressional Globe, Appendix*. 29th Cong., 2nd Sess. (4 Feb. 1847) pp. 282-289. Opposes the Mexican War. Maintains that it does not exist by the act of Mexico, but rather is a war of conquest, promoted to acquire territory for the purpose of establishing slavery. Gives history of the origin of the war and provides detailed discussion of the boundaries, with extensive references to relevant maps.

1192. "An Act Creating a Collection District in Maine, and Constituting Bangor, in Said District, a Port of Entry and Delivery," *Statutes at Large*, Vol. IX (3 Mar. 1847) pp. 183-184.

1193. U.S. Senate. *Report of the Secretary of the Treasury, on the Propriety of Establishing a Marine Hospital in Maine*. 29th Cong., 2nd Sess. (S.Doc.13). Washington: Ritchie & Heiss, 1847. 2 pg. (Serial Set 494). Opposes the establishment of the hospital until there are funds to provide for maintenance.

30TH CONGRESS, 1ST SESSION

1194. Bradbury, James W. (Maine). Announcement of the Death of the Hon. John Fairfield, *Congressional Globe*. 30th Cong., 1st Sess. (27 Dec. 1847) p. 70. Announces the death of John Fairfield, Senator from Maine; remarks on career and character.

1195. Bradbury, James W. (Maine). "Territorial Government of Oregon," *Congressional Globe, Appendix*. 30th Cong., 1st Sess. (26 July 1848) pp. 1191-1194. Opposes the bill concerning the territorial government in Oregon, California and New Mexico. Primarily objects to the non-resolution of the slavery issue. Maintains that Congress has the power to determine the issue; gives legislative precedents and judicial interpretations to support his position. Addresses the supposed antagonism of the North to the South.

1196. Hamlin, Hannibal (Maine). "Territorial Government of Oregon," *Congressional Globe, Appendix*. 30th Cong., 1st Sess. (22 July 1848) pp. 1145-1148. Opposes the bill, which includes the territories of Oregon, California, and New Mexico, maintaining it would guarantee and perpetuate slavery in the new territories. Advocates Congress retaining freedom in territories without slavery and retaining slavery in territories where it is already established. Summary of speech in *Congressional Globe*, p. 989.

1197. Hammons, David (Maine). "Death of Senator Fairfield," *Congressional Globe*. 30th Cong., 1st Sess. (27 Dec. 1847) p. 72. Announces the death of the Hon. John Fairfield, Senator from Maine; remarks on career and character.

1198. Niles, John M. (Conn.). Remarks on Funeral Arrangements for the Hon. John Fairfield, *Congressional Globe*. 30th Cong., 1st Sess. (28 Dec. 1847) p. 73.

1199. Smart, Ephraim K. (Maine). "Oregon Bill," *Congressional Globe*. 30th Cong., 1st Sess. (28 Mar. 1848) pp. 545-548. Opposes the extension of slavery into the territories. Addresses arguments concerning the ordinance of 1787, and the jurisdiction of Congress over the territories. Claims that the Mexican War was fought to defend Texas, not to acquire territory. Contends that the South would benefit as much as the North by preserving the territory from Mexico as free. Compares the population and land area of the free states versus the slave states; concludes that there is a greater necessity for additional free territory.

1200. Wiley, James S. (Maine). "Territorial Indemnity," *Congressional Globe, Appendix*. 30th Cong., 1st Sess. (16 May 1848) pp. 552-555. Supports the acquisition of New Mexico and Upper California as indemnity for the injuries incurred from the war with Mexico. Maintains that the acquisition has public support, is constitutional, and the only source for repayment. Describes the value of the territory and the resources of New Mexico and California.

1201. "An Act to Change the Time of Holding the Terms of the Circuit Court of the United States in the District of Maine," *Statutes at Large*, Vol. IX (11 Aug. 1848) p. 282.

1202. "An Act to Make Bangor a Port of Entry for Ships or Vessels Coming from and beyond the Cape of Good Hope," *Statutes at Large*, Vol. IX (25 July 1848) p. 251.

1203. U.S. House. *Citizens of Elliottsville, Maine*. 30th Cong., 1st Sess. (H.Rpt.660). [Washington: 1848]. 1 pg. (Serial Set 526). Opposes the petition's request to appropriate the public lands to aid in the extinction of slavery.

1204. U.S. Senate. *Memorial of Nathan Cummings and Others, Citizens of the United States, and Owners of Lands within the Former Limits of the State of Maine, Which Were Given Up, by the Treaty of Washington, to Great Britain, Praying the Adoption of Some Mode of Relief to Indemnify Them against Loss*. 30th Cong., 1st Sess. (S.Mis.Doc.91). Washington: Tippin & Streeper, 1848. 3 pg. (Serial Set 511). Requests relief from duties due to the U.S. on timber and lumber produced from lands formerly part of Maine.

1205. U.S. Senate. *Message from the President of the United States, Communicating a Report from the Secretary of the Navy in Relation to the Construction of Floating Dry Docks at Pensacola, Philadelphia, and Kittery*. 30th Cong., 1st Sess. (S.Exec.Doc.11). Washington: Wendell and Van Benthuysen, 1847. 152 pg. (Serial Set 505). Presents the plans and inventions for consideration, with explanations and specifications, for each of the proposed locations. Includes report of the board of experts assembled to judge the plans and the opinion of the chief of the Bureau of Yards and Docks. Includes reprint of H.doc.163 (28-2) 466 (entry **1159**) discussing the relative properties and advantages of a dry dock and of the different kinds of floating docks.

1206. U.S. Senate. *Petition of Citizens of Maine and Massachusetts, Praying that Lumber Manufactured in New Brunswick, from Timber Grown in Maine, May Be Admitted into the United States Free of Duty.* 30th Cong., 1st Sess. (S.Mis.Doc.90). Washington: Tippin & Streeper, 1848. 2 pg. (Serial Set 511). Supports eliminating the duty as lumber from Maine must be transported to New Brunswick via the Aroostook and Saint John Rivers in rough logs and timber for processing and shipment out of Saint John.

1207. U.S. Senate. *Resolutions of the Legislature of Maine, in Favor of a Railroad from Lake Michigan to the Pacific, on the Plan Proposed by Mr. Whitney.* 30th Cong., 1st Sess. (S.Mis.Doc.5). Washington: Tippin & Streeper, 1848. 2 pg. (Serial Set 511). Resolutions support granting Asa Whitney the right to construct the railroad and pledge the public lands along the line.

30TH CONGRESS, 2ND SESSION

1208. Hamlin, Hannibal (Maine). "Corps of Sappers and Miners," *Congressional Globe.* 30th Cong., 2nd Sess. (1 Mar. 1849) pp. 633-634. Supports allowing the discharge of those whom desire from this corps who were recruited to learn civil engineering, but instead fought in the Mexican War at great loss.

1209. Hamlin, Hannibal (Maine). "Naval Appropriation Bill," *Congressional Globe.* 30th Cong., 2nd Sess. (2 Mar. 1849) p. 648. Objects to restoring officers in the Marine Corps.

1210. Hamlin, Hannibal (Maine). "Reduction of Postage," *Congressional Globe.* 30th Cong., 2nd Sess. (19 Jan. 1849) pp. 300-301. Advocates that all mail should contribute to support the mail system; supports low postage rates and opposes the franking privilege and free postage for newspapers.

1211. Smart, Ephraim K. (Maine). "Army Appropriation Bill," *Congressional Globe.* 30th Cong., 2nd Sess. (24 Jan. 1849) pp. 350-355. Addresses the expediency and justice of legislating upon slavery in the territories. Demonstrates that the free states furnished their full share of money and men to carry on the war with Mexico, and so ought to have their proportional share of free land. Opposes the proposed 35 degree 30 minute line; maintains that the people inhabiting the territories are opposed to slavery, and that the government promised the people of Mexico a free government.

1212. U.S. House. *Collection District, East Thomaston, Maine.* 30th Cong., 2nd Sess. (H.Rpt.113). [Washington: 1849]. 1 pg. (Serial Set 545). Report against the establishment of a collection district at East Thomaston.

1213. U.S. Senate. *Memorial of Jesse E. Dow, in Relation to the Route to the Pacific, via Tehuantepec, over a Plank Road.* 30th Cong., 2nd Sess. (S.Mis.Doc.56). Washington: Tippin & Streeper, 1848. 3 pg. (Serial Set 533). Memorialist claims that he is the original proposer of a central railroad from the Mississippi valley to the Pacific Ocean; proposes a temporary route from Pensacola, across the isthmus of Tehauantepec, to run to the Atlantic in connection with the chain of railroads already complete.

MASSACHUSETTS

1ST CONGRESS, 1ST SESSION

1214. Ames, Fisher (Mass.). "Amendments to the Constitution," *Annals of Congress.* 1st Cong., 1st Sess. (14 Aug. 1789) pp. 720-721. Advocates one representative for every forty thousand inhabitants.

1215. Ames, Fisher (Mass.). "Department of Foreign Affairs," *Annals of Congress.* 1st Cong., 1st Sess. (16 June, 18 June 1789) pp. 473-477; 538-543. Discusses the constitutionality of the power of removal from office; maintains that the power is delegated to the President alone.

1216. Ames, Fisher (Mass.). "Duties on Imports," *Annals of Congress.* 1st Cong., 1st Sess. (14 Apr., 28 Apr. 1789) pp. 132-135, 136; 228-229. Opposes the proposed high duties on molasses as unequal; discusses the potential impact on fishing and trade with the West Indies.

1217. Ames, Fisher (Mass.). "Duties on Imports," *Annals of Congress.* 1st Cong., 1st Sess. (9 May 1789) pp. 296-300, 309-311. Discusses the disadvantages of high duties; supports duties that are only sufficient to meet the revenue needs of the government. Addresses opponents' arguments.

1218. Ames, Fisher (Mass.). "Duties on Imports," *Annals of Congress.* 1st Cong., 1st Sess. (15 May 1789) pp. 352-354. Opposes a time limitation clause.

1219. Ames, Fisher (Mass.). "Duties on Tonnage," *Annals of Congress.* 1st Cong., 1st Sess. (5 May 1789) pp. 253-256. Opposes reducing duties on tonnage as necessary to protect and encourage American navigation.

1220. Ames, Fisher (Mass.). "Judiciary," *Annals of Congress.* 1st Cong., 1st Sess. (29 Aug. 1789) pp. 806-808. Supports a judiciary as prescribed by the

Constitution. Discusses the relationship between the state and the federal courts.

1221. Ames, Fisher (Mass.). "Permanent Seat of Government," *Annals of Congress.* 1st Cong., 1st Sess. (4 Sept. 1789) pp. 868-870, 871-874. Supports having the seat of government on the Susquehanna; demonstrates its superior centrality, accessibility, and safety.

1222. Ames, Fisher (Mass.). "Treasury Department," *Annals of Congress.* 1st Cong., 1st Sess. (25 June 1789) pp. 595-597. Supports the proposed reporting responsibilities of the Secretary of the Treasury as valuable and safe from abuse.

1223. Gerry, Elbridge (Mass.). "Amendments to the Constitution," *Annals of Congress.* 1st Cong., 1st Sess. (8 June 1789) pp. 444-447. Supports delaying consideration of amendments until the proper time; endorses the importance of the amendments and the need for a discussion in the Committee of the Whole.

1224. Gerry, Elbridge (Mass.). "Amendments to the Constitution," *Annals of Congress.* 1st Cong., 1st Sess. (15 Aug. 1789) pp. 736-738. Opposes an amendment that binds representatives to obey their constituents' instructions.

1225. Gerry, Elbridge (Mass.). "Compensation of Members," *Annals of Congress.* 1st Cong., 1st Sess. (6 Aug. 1789) pp. 680-682, 682-683. Supports an allowance sufficient to hire men of abilities and to compensate them for leaving their businesses and occupations.

1226. Gerry, Elbridge (Mass.). "Department of Foreign Affairs," *Annals of Congress.* 1st Cong., 1st Sess. (16 June, 17 June, 18 June, 19 June 1789) pp. 472-473; 501-505; 534-537; 573-576. Discusses the constitutional basis of the power of removal. Advocates vesting the power in the President, with the advice and consent of the Senate.

1227. Gerry, Elbridge (Mass.). "Duties on Imports," *Annals of Congress.* 1st Cong., 1st Sess. (27 Apr., 28 Apr., 9 May, 12 May 1789) pp. 211-212; 229-230; 314-315; 332-335. Various remarks oppose high duties, particularly on molasses. Maintains that the proposed duty on molasses is oppressive.

1228. Gerry, Elbridge (Mass.). "Judiciary," *Annals of Congress.* 1st Cong., 1st Sess. (31 Aug. 1789) pp. 827-829. Supports establishing the federal judiciary as specified in the Constitution; discusses the relationship between the federal and state judiciary systems.

1229. Gerry, Elbridge (Mass.). "Treasury Department," *Annals of Congress.* 1st Cong., 1st Sess. (20 May 1789) pp. 384-389. Supports a Board of Treasury to conduct the affairs of the Treasury Department; addresses the advantages and disadvantages of the Board versus a single officer.

1230. Gerry, Elbridge (Mass.). "Treasury Department," *Annals of Congress.* 1st Cong., 1st Sess. (25 June 1789) pp. 601-602, 603-604. Warns against vesting too much power in the Secretary of the Treasury.

1231. Goodhue, Benjamin (Mass.). "Duties on Imports," *Annals of Congress.* 1st Cong., 1st Sess. (27 Apr. 1789) pp. 209-210. Opposes the proposed duty on molasses.

1232. Sedgwick, Theodore (Mass.). "Department of Foreign Affairs," *Annals of Congress.* 1st Cong., 1st Sess. (16 June, 18 June 1789) pp. 460-461; 520-523. Discusses the power of appointment and removal; maintains that the power of removal is constitutionally vested in the President.

1233. Sedgwick, Theodore (Mass.). "Permanent Seat of Government," *Annals of Congress.* 1st Cong., 1st Sess. (3 Sept. 1789) pp. 846-848. Opposes locating the seat of government at the Susquehanna and the Potomac; favors Philadelphia as the temporary seat.

1234. Thatcher, George (Mass.). "Duties on Imports," *Annals of Congress.* 1st Cong., 1st Sess. (28 Apr. 1789) pp. 214-216. Opposes a duty on molasses as unreasonable and partial in its operation; maintains that molasses is a necessity of life in the eastern states, and the raw material for an important manufacture.

1235. Thatcher, Samuel (Mass.). "Contested Election," *Annals of Congress.* 1st Cong., 1st Sess. (22 May 1789) pp. 403-404. Remarks on whether Mr. William Smith (S.C.) meets the citizenship requirements to have a seat in the House.

1236. "Cessions from New York and Massachusetts," *American State Papers: Public Lands*, Vol. I (Doc. 2) pp. 7-8. (ASP 028). Recommends ascertaining the meridian lines of the eastern boundary of the cessions.

1237. "Ship-building and Manufactures," *American State Papers: Finance*, Vol. I (Doc. 4) pp. 10-11. (ASP 09). Petition from tradesmen and manufacturers of Boston asking for assistance to promote manufacturing and shipbuilding.

1ST CONGRESS, 2ND SESSION

1238. Ames, Fisher (Mass.). "Public Credit," *Annals of Congress.* 1st Cong., 2nd Sess. (9 Feb. 1790) pp. 1153-1155. Opposes discriminating between foreign and domestic creditors.

1239. Ames, Fisher (Mass.). "Public Credit," *Annals of Congress.* 1st Cong., 2nd Sess. (15 Feb. 1790) pp. 1216-1223. Opposes Madison's proposal to discriminate between original holders of securities and subsequent purchasers. Maintains that there is not a debt against the public, in favor of the original holders, and that discrimination would be impartial, unjust, impracticable, expensive, and tend towards corruption and confusion. Maintains that the subsequent purchasers are protected by contract.

1240. Ames, Fisher (Mass.). "Public Credit," *Annals of Congress.* 1st Cong., 2nd Sess. (18 Feb. 1790) pp. 1290-1291. Supports honoring encumbered obligations and funding the public debt.

1241. Ames, Fisher (Mass.). "Public Credit," *Annals of Congress.* 1st Cong., 2nd Sess. (26 Feb. 1790) pp. 1368-1373. Supports the federal government assuming the state debts. Demonstrates the justice and sound policy behind the assumption; addresses objections.

1242. Ames, Fisher (Mass.). "Public Credit," *Annals of Congress.* 1st Cong., 2nd Sess. (11 Mar., 13 Mar. 1790) pp. 1427-1435; 1439-1442. Speeches support funding the debt as proposed by the Secretary of the Treasury. Fisher examines the measures proposed by the Secretary, including the proposal to make the debt irredeemable; compares it to similar operations to fund public debt in Great Britain.

1243. Ames, Fisher (Mass.). "Public Debt," *Annals of Congress.* 1st Cong., 2nd Sess. (25 May 1790) pp. 1600-1613. Lengthy speech supports the assumption of the state debts. Addresses objections that have been presented.

1244. Gerry, Elbridge (Mass.). "Public Credit," *Annals of Congress.* 1st Cong., 2nd Sess. (10 Feb. 1790) pp. 1175-1179. Opposes discriminating between the foreign and domestic debt. Addresses arguments of opponents; demonstrates that American independence was not principally established by foreign loans.

1245. Gerry, Elbridge (Mass.). "Public Credit," *Annals of Congress.* 1st Cong., 2nd Sess. (18 Feb. 1790) pp. 1279-1287. Opposes discriminating between the original and assigned holders of public securities. Discusses the losses sustained by the soldiers, the nature of public securities as a species of stock and property subject to public opinion, and precedents for discriminating. Addresses positions of those supporting discrimination.

1246. Gerry, Elbridge (Mass.). "Public Credit," *Annals of Congress.* 1st Cong., 2nd Sess. (23 Feb., 25 Feb. 1790) pp. 1324-1326; 1348-1352, 1360-1362. Remarks support the federal government assuming the state debts. Maintains that the debts are those of the United States, and that the assumption is constitutional and necessary to preserve the peace of the Union.

1247. Gerry, Elbridge (Mass.). "Public Credit," *Annals of Congress.* 1st Cong., 2nd Sess. (13 Mar. 1790) pp. 1442-1448. Maintains that the propositions for modifying the debt would be unacceptable to the creditors. Discusses the contract between the U.S. and its creditors, and measures necessary for justice; reviews the revenues and expenses of government.

1248. Gerry, Elbridge (Mass.). "Public Debt," *Annals of Congress.* 1st Cong., 2nd Sess. (24 July 1790) pp. 1702-1710. Addresses objections to the federal government assuming the state debts. Discusses the conduct of Massachusetts relative to the debts, the effect of the measure, and the alleged benefits Massachusetts received from the war.

1249. Gerry, Elbridge (Mass.). "Seat of Government," *Annals of Congress.* 1st Cong., 2nd Sess. (6 July 1790) pp. 1666-1667. Supports Baltimore as the seat of government and opposes the Potomac.

1250. Goodhue, Benjamin (Mass.). "Public Credit," *Annals of Congress.* 1st Cong., 2nd Sess. (16 Feb., 23 Feb. 1790) pp. 1239-1240; 1319-1320. Supports the assumption of the state debts.

1251. Sedgwick, Theodore (Mass.). "Officers of the Navy," *Annals of Congress.* 1st Cong., 2nd Sess. (24 June 1790) pp. 1650-1651. Opposes granting the memorial of the officers as it would establish a precedent that the country cannot afford.

1252. Sedgwick, Theodore (Mass.). "Public Credit," *Annals of Congress.* 1st Cong., 2nd Sess. (10 Feb., 15 Feb. 1790) pp. 1169-1170; 1205-1208. Objects to James Madison's proposal to fund the domestic debt by discriminating between original holders and subsequent purchasers of the securities.

1253. Sedgwick, Theodore (Mass.). "Public Credit," *Annals of Congress.* 1st Cong., 2nd Sess. (24 Feb., 1 Mar., 12 Apr. 1790) pp. 1332-1338; 1388-1389; 1525-1526. Supports the federal government assuming debts incurred by the states during the Revolution. Maintains that Congress is authorized to assume the debts; presents arguments in support of the measure.

1254. Sedgwick, Theodore (Mass.). "Public Debt," *Annals of Congress.* 1st Cong., 2nd Sess. (30 Mar. 1790) pp. 1490-1493. Responds to North Carolina's arguments for opposing the federal government's assumption of the state debts.

1255. Sedgwick, Theodore (Mass.). "Public Debt," *Annals of Congress.* 1st Cong., 2nd Sess. (25 May, 29 July 1790) pp. 1614-1616; 1715-1716. Maintains that the assumption of the state debts should be provided for before establishing funds to preserve the public credit.

1256. "An Act Authorizing the Secretary of the Treasury to Finish the Lighthouse on Portland Head, in the District of Maine," *Statutes at Large,* Vol. I (10 Aug. 1790) p. 184. Also printed in the *Annals of Congress* (1st Cong., 2nd Sess.) Appendix, p. 2301.

1257. "Eastern Boundary," *American State Papers: Foreign Relations,* Vol. I (Doc. 40) pp. 90-99. (ASP 01). Documents and correspondence relative to the boundary between Maine, then a part of Massachusetts, and Nova Scotia, now called New Brunswick, along the St. Croix. Includes letters from the Governors of Massachusetts, Nova Scotia, and New Brunswick, the report and correspondence of the Secretary for Foreign Affairs, and other documentation.

1258. "Eastern Boundary," *American State Papers: Foreign Relations*, Vol. I (Doc. 41) p. 99. (ASP 01). Message from the President and resolution of Massachusetts relative to the eastern boundary of Massachusetts (now Maine) and Canada.

1259. "Eastern Boundary," *American State Papers: Foreign Relations*, Vol. I (Doc. 42) p. 100. (ASP 01). Report and suggestions support resolving the dispute as soon as possible.

1ST CONGRESS, 3RD SESSION

1260. Ames, Fisher (Mass.). "Bank of the United States," *Annals of Congress.* 1st Cong., 3rd Sess. (3 Feb. 1791) pp. 1903-1909. Supports establishing a Bank of the United States. Endorses the doctrine of implied power, maintaining that Congress may exercise powers not expressly granted by the Constitution.

1261. Gerry, Elbridge (Mass.). "Bank of the United States," *Annals of Congress.* 1st Cong., 3rd Sess. (7 Feb. 1791) pp. 1945-1954. Supports the constitutionality of establishing a national bank. Addresses objections to the measure; maintains that one should consider the objects for which the Constitution was established in its administration. Applies the rules of interpretation of Judge Blackstone.

1262. Sedgwick, Theodore (Mass.). "Bank of the United States," *Annals of Congress.* 1st Cong., 3rd Sess. (4 Feb. 1791) pp. 1910-1914. Supports establishing a Bank of the United States; discusses the constitutional powers authorizing the bank.

1263. Sedgwick, Theodore (Mass.). "Duties on Spirits," *Annals of Congress.* 1st Cong., 3rd Sess. (6 Jan. 1791) pp. 1849-1850. Favors duties on spirits to raise revenue.

1264. "Fisheries," *American State Papers: Commerce and Navigation*, Vol. I (Doc. 5) pp. 8-22. (ASP 014). Comprehensive report on the cod and whale fishing industries in the United States, addressing their history, progress, and present status. Specific attention to identifying measures that aid the industries, and in determining what relief is necessary. Statistics of the cod and whale fisheries in the U.S., Mass., and abroad, and relevant correspondence included.

2ND CONGRESS, 1ST SESSION

1265. Ames, Fisher (Mass.). "Apportionment Bill," *Annals of Congress.* 2nd Cong., 1st Sess. (19 Dec. 1791) pp. 254-262. Objects to the proposed apportionment plan as unjust, unequal, and contrary to the principles of the Constitution. Demonstrates the deficiencies of the plan and the advantages of an alternative plan.

1266. Ames, Fisher (Mass.). "Cod Fisheries," *Annals of Congress.* 2nd Cong., 1st Sess. (3 Feb. 1792) pp. 367-374. Supports proposed drawback of the duty paid on salt used in exporting dried fish; maintains that it will promote the national wealth, the national safety, and be more just. Presents a financial overview of the salt duty under the present practice.

1267. Ames, Fisher (Mass.). "John Torrey," *Annals of Congress.* 2nd Cong., 1st Sess. (8 Nov. 1791) pp. 160-164. Supports the petition of Major John Torrey. Maintains that Torrey, who died in Nov. 1783, was eligible for the promised half-pay, as the war ended in April 1783.

1268. Gerry, Elbridge (Mass.). "Cod Fisheries," *Annals of Congress.* 2nd Cong., 1st Sess. (3 Feb. 1792) pp. 375-378. Supports a drawback on the salt duty paid on exported fish to give encouragement to the fishing industries.

1269. Gerry, Elbridge (Mass.). "Publication of the Debates," *Annals of Congress.* 2nd Cong., 1st Sess. (19 Apr. 1792) pp. 563-565. Supports his resolution to publish full and accurate accounts of the debates of the House.

1270. Gerry, Elbridge (Mass.). "Ratio of Representation," *Annals of Congress.* 2nd Cong., 1st Sess. (10 Nov., 15 Nov. 1791) pp. 168-169; 190-191. Favors the ratio of one to thirty thousand.

1271. Sedgwick, Theodore (Mass.). "Additional Supplies," *Annals of Congress.* 2nd Cong., 1st Sess. (8 Mar. 1792) pp. 437-440. Supports receiving opinions from the Secretary of the Treasury concerning the public finances.

1272. Sedgwick, Theodore (Mass.). "Apportionment Bill," *Annals of Congress.* 2nd Cong., 1st Sess. (19 Dec. 1791) pp. 271-273. Remarks on the proposed one to thirty thousand ratio.

1273. Sedgwick, Theodore (Mass.). "Post Office Bill," *Annals of Congress.* 2nd Cong., 1st Sess. (7 Dec. 1791) pp. 239-241. Remarks on the authority of the Executive to establish post roads.

1274. Thatcher, George (Mass.). "Post Office Bill," *Annals of Congress.* 2nd Cong., 1st Sess. (2 Feb. 1792) pp. 358-361. Debates whether the mail from Boston should go to Exeter, then Portsmouth, or Portsmouth then Exeter.

1275. "Manufacturer's Marks," *American State Papers: Commerce and Navigation,* Vol. I (Doc. 9) p. 48. (ASP 014). Responds to petition from Boston in support of allowing manufacturers to have exclusive rights to marks designating their wares; establishes jurisdiction according to boundaries of trade.

2ND CONGRESS, 2ND SESSION

1276. Ames, Fisher (Mass.). "The President's Speech," *Annals of Congress.* 2nd Cong., 2nd Sess. (21 Nov. 1792) pp. 715-722. Supports the Secretary of the Treasury forming a plan for the Sinking Fund to pay off the public debt. Addresses objections to the Secretary framing the system and preparing and reporting financial plans.

1277. Sedgwick, Theodore (Mass.). "Pay of the Late Army," *Annals of Congress.* 2nd Cong., 2nd Sess. (14 Jan. 1793) pp. 813-814. Supports discussing a means to compensate patriots from the late army for their services.

3RD CONGRESS, 1ST SESSION

1278. Ames, Fisher (Mass.). "Commerce of the United States," *Annals of Congress.* 3rd Cong., 1st Sess. (27 Jan. 1794) pp. 328-349. Lengthy speech opposes the proposed measures to advance the trade and navigation of the United States. Addresses the current status of trade, the market, the restrictions and prohibitions, and the state of navigation. Discusses in detail the trade with Britain and the British West Indies.

1279. Dexter, Samuel (Mass.). "Commerce of the United States," *Annals of Congress.* 3rd Cong., 1st Sess. (23 Jan., 14 Mar. 1794) pp. 272-274; 508-510. Opposes the resolutions retaliating against Britain; contends that her treatment of America was no different than her treatment of other nations.

1280. Dexter, Samuel (Mass.). "Non-Intercourse with Great Britain," *Annals of Congress.* 3rd Cong., 1st Sess. (11 Apr. 1794) pp. 585-592. Opposes the resolutions as useless and injurious. Maintains that negotiations should be exhausted before commercial intercourse is prohibited and other measures taken to avenge the condemnations of our vessels in the West Indies.

1281. Foster, Dwight (Mass.). "Commerce of the United States," *Annals of Congress.* 3rd Cong., 1st Sess. (31 Jan. 1794) pp. 413-417. Reviews the principle arguments for and against the resolutions to restrict commerce with Great Britain.

1282. Goodhue, Benjamin (Mass.). "Commerce of the United States," *Annals of Congress.* 3rd Cong., 1st Sess. (16 Jan. 1794) pp. 243-245. Opposes the proposed restrictive laws affecting trade with Great Britain.

1283. Lyman, William (Mass.). "Commerce of the United States," *Annals of Congress.* 3rd Cong., 1st Sess. (14 Mar. 1794) pp. 520-521. Favors the proposed restrictions on commerce with Great Britain as a just and temperate defense.

1284. Sedgwick, Theodore (Mass.). "Commerce of the United States," *Annals of Congress.* 3rd Cong., 1st Sess. (14 Mar. 1794) pp. 512-520. Opposes the proposed discrimination against Great Britain intended to compel her to relax her commercial restrictions. Maintains that Britain's policies are not discriminatory towards the U. S., and that such retaliatory measures are not in the interests of America. Discusses the probable consequences and their tendency towards war.

1285. Sedgwick, Theodore (Mass.). "Indemnity for Spoliations," *Annals of Congress.* 3rd Cong., 1st Sess. (15 May 1794) pp. 691-692. Supports indemnity for the sufferers but opposes obtaining indemnity by confiscating British property.

1286. Sedgwick, Theodore (Mass.). "National Defence," *Annals of Congress.* 3rd Cong., 1st Sess. (12 Mar. 1794) pp. 500-504. Resolutions and speech defend raising a standing army in preparation for a possible war; maintains that it would afford the most protection with the least expense.

1287. Sedgwick, Theodore (Mass.). "Non-Intercourse with Great Britain," *Annals of Congress.* 3rd Cong., 1st Sess. (10 Apr. 1794) pp. 566-570. Objects to prohibiting trade between the United States and Great Britain. Maintains that negotiation should first be attempted to obtain redress for injuries; contends that the proposed measures would tend to war, preclude negotiation, and be more injurious to the U.S. than Britain.

1288. Sedgwick, Theodore (Mass.). "On the State of the Treasury," *Annals of Congress.* 3rd Cong., 1st Sess. (28 Feb. 1794) pp. 469-473, 474. Remarks on the state of the public finances; explains the select committee's report to authorize the President to borrow one million dollars if necessary.

1289. "An Act for Erecting a Lighthouse on the Island of Saguin in the District of Maine, and for Erecting a Beacon and Placing Three Buoys at the Entrance of Saint Mary's River, in the State of Georgia," *Statutes at Large*, Vol. I (19 May 1794) pp. 368-369. Also printed in the *Annals of Congress* (3rd Cong., 1st Sess.) Appendix, p. 1447.

3RD CONGRESS, 2ND SESSION

1290. Ames, Fisher (Mass.). "President's Speech," *Annals of Congress.* 3rd Cong., 2nd Sess. (26 Nov. 1794) pp. 920-932. Supports the President's opposition to self-created societies or other groups of men intended to obstruct the laws. Provides a brief history of the destructive influence of such clubs in Europe; offers examples of actions of self-created societies in the United States.

1291. Ames, Fisher (Mass.). "Public Debt," *Annals of Congress.* 3rd Cong., 2nd Sess. (16 Jan. 1795) pp. 1104-1114. Supports establishing an efficient and permanent plan to pay off the public debt. Desires to use the revenues to pay the principle as well as the interest; reviews the status of income and expenditures.

1292. Ames, Fisher (Mass.). "Thanks to General Wayne," *Annals of Congress.* 3rd Cong., 2nd Sess. (4 Dec. 1794) pp. 963-965. Supports a vote of appreciation.

1293. Dexter, Samuel (Mass.). "President's Speech," *Annals of Congress.* 3rd Cong., 2nd Sess. (27 Nov. 1794) pp. 935-939. Opposes self-created societies that vilify and misrepresent the government and its laws. Maintains that such clubs abuse their right of freedom of expression; discusses their influence in the Whisky Insurrection.

1294. Sedgwick, Theodore (Mass.). "Public Debt," *Annals of Congress.* 3rd Cong., 2nd Sess. (5 Feb. 1795) pp. 1175-1182. Supports continuing the proposed taxes in order to reduce the public debt. Enumerates reasons why the debt should be reduced; discusses the Sinking Fund.

1295. "Claims of Nathaniel Appleton, Commissioner of Loans for the State of Massachusetts, for Office Rent, Fuel, and Candles, and the Loss of a House," *American State Papers: Claims,* (Doc. 61) p. 147. (ASP 036). Report supports compensating Nathaniel Appleton for losses incurred while saving the public property from destruction by fire.

1296. "Remission of Duties," *American State Papers: Finance,* Vol. I (Doc. 74) p. 320. (ASP 09). Report responds to petition from Boston giving qualified support of remission of duties on goods destroyed by fire or accident.

4ᵀᴴ CONGRESS, 1ˢᵀ SESSION

1297. "Contested Election," *Annals of Congress.* 4th Cong., 1st Sess. (30 Mar. 1796) pp. 822-825. Reprint of the petition and documents concerning the alleged unfair election and return of Joseph Bradley Varnum to the House and debate over the course of action to be taken.

1298. Ames, Fisher (Mass.). "Execution of British Treaty," *Annals of Congress.* 4th Cong., 1st Sess. (28 Apr. 1796) pp. 1239-1263. Passionate speech supports Jay's Treaty and opposes the House's attempt to block appropriations for enforcing it. Discusses the House's role in the treaty-making power, and the obligations a treaty imposes on the President, Senate, House and nation. Addresses some of the provisions of the treaty and the effects of rejection.

1299. Ames, Fisher (Mass.). "Naval Armament," *Annals of Congress.* 4th Cong., 1st Sess. (7 Apr. 1796) pp. 882-883. Favors keeping up a naval force.

1300. Foster, Dwight (Mass.). "Execution of British Treaty," *Annals of Congress.* 4th Cong., 1st Sess. (26 Apr. 1796) pp. 1172-1173. Supports Jay's Treaty as right, proper, advisable, and advantageous.

1301. Freeman, Nathaniel, Jr. (Mass.). "Treaty with Great Britain," *Annals of Congress.* 4th Cong., 1st Sess. (16 Mar. 1796) pp. 584-588. Supports the request for the Executive papers concerning the treaty and supports the authority of the House to decide whether or not to grant an appropriation to carry a treaty into effect.

1302. Goodhue, Benjamin (Mass.). "Execution of British Treaty," *Annals of Congress.* 4th Cong., 1st Sess. (18 Apr. 1796) pp. 1053-1059. Supports Jay's Treaty. Focuses on the advantageous commercial aspects of the treaty, including the article relative to the West India trade. Discusses major objections to the treaty and the results if the House refuses to carry it into effect.

1303. Lyman, Samuel (Mass.). "Execution of British Treaty," *Annals of Congress.* 4th Cong., 1st Sess. (15 Apr. 1796) pp. 987-990. Supports the treaty as constitutional and commercially advantageous.

1304. Lyman, Samuel (Mass.). "Treaty with Great Britain," *Annals of Congress.* 4th Cong., 1st Sess. (14 Mar. 1796) pp. 530-532. Contends that only if a treaty is unconstitutional does the House have the right to exercise Legislative discretion as to carrying it into operation.

1305. Lyman, William (Mass.). "Treaty with Great Britain," *Annals of Congress.* 4th Cong., 1st Sess. (16 Mar. 1796) pp. 601-609. Supports requesting papers from the Executive concerning the treaty and supports the House's authority to participate in the treaty-making process when those treaties infringe on its specific legislative powers. Provides an historical review of recognition of the House's authority. Briefly addresses other arguments and objections.

1306. Reed, John (Mass.). "Treaty with Great Britain," *Annals of Congress.* 4th Cong., 1st Sess. (17 Mar. 1796) pp. 609-612. Supports the House's discretionary rights to judge the treaty as to its constitutionality and the propriety of making appropriations.

1307. Sedgwick, Theodore (Mass.). "Case of Robert Randall," *Annals of Congress.* 4th Cong., 1st Sess. (6 Jan. 1796) pp. 216-218. Testimony on all he knows about the transactions of Randall and Whitney.

1308. Sedgwick, Theodore (Mass.). "Debt Due Bank United States," *Annals of Congress.* 4th Cong., 1st Sess. (12 Apr. 1796) pp. 916-921. Discusses the bank and its debts; reviews the status of the finances and obligations of the nation.

1309. Sedgwick, Theodore (Mass.). "Intercourse with the Indians," *Annals of Congress.* 4th Cong., 1st Sess. (9 Apr. 1796) pp. 900-901. Supports the rights of the Indians to their land.

1310. Sedgwick, Theodore (Mass.). "Treaty with Great Britain," *Annals of Congress.* 4th Cong., 1st Sess. (11 Mar. 1796) pp. 514-530. Discusses the treaty-making power and the rights of the House in this department. Reviews the authority to form treaties, the extent of the power, the intent of the Constitution at the time it was deliberated on and ratified, and the construction given from the commencement of the government. Presents various passages from the *Debates and Proceedings of the Convention of Virginia.*

1311. "An Act Authorizing the Erection of a Lighthouse on Baker's Island, in the State of Massachusetts," *Statutes at Large*, Vol. I (8 Apr. 1796) p. 452. Also printed in the *Annals of Congress* (4th Cong., 2nd Sess.) Appendix, p. 2889.

1312. "An Act Authorizing the Erection of a Lighthouse on Cape Cod, in the State of Massachusetts," *Statutes at Large*, Vol. I (17 May 1796) p. 464. Also printed in the *Annals of Congress* (4th Cong., 2nd Sess.) Appendix, p. 2904.

1313. "Contested Election of Joseph B. Varnum, a Representative from Massachusetts," *American State Papers: Miscellaneous*, Vol. I (Doc. 80) p. 145. (ASP 037). Report on the contested election requests instructions on how to proceed.

1314. "Extra Tonnage Duty on Vessels Entering Kennebunk River," *American State Papers: Commerce and Navigation*, Vol. I (Doc. 33) p. 343. (ASP 014). Considers a petition requesting permission to charge duty on vessels passing by a pier erected through private expense. While Congress does not refund expenses for local improvements, it gives the Legislature of Massachusetts the authority to impose a tonnage duty to defray the expenses.

4ᵀᴴ CONGRESS, 2ᴺᴰ SESSION

1315. "Buoys in Boston Harbor," *Annals of Congress.* 4th Cong., 2nd Sess. (6 Feb. 1797) p. 2076. Brief debate on the request of the Chamber of Commerce of Boston to place buoys in Boston Harbor.

1316. "Contested Election," *Annals of Congress.* 4th Cong., 2nd Sess. (19 Jan., 25 Jan., 26 Jan. 1797) pp. 1913; 1984; 1986-1987. Report of the Committee of Elections declares Varnum to have been duly elected; revision and acceptance of the report.

1317. Ames, Fisher (Mass.). "Accommodation of the President," *Annals of Congress.* 4th Cong., 2nd Sess. (27 Feb. 1797) pp. 2317-1218. Brief remarks support the proposed appropriations for the President to establish a suitable household.

1318. Ames, Fisher (Mass.). "Address to the President," *Annals of Congress.* 4th Cong., 2nd Sess. (14 Dec. 1796) pp. 1625-1629. Supports President Washington, his *Farewell Address*, and the response of the committee assigned to answer to the President's Speech.

1319. Ames, Fisher (Mass.). "Address to the President," *Annals of Congress*. 4th Cong., 2nd Sess. (15 Dec. 1796) pp. 1641-1645, 1648-1651. Defends the national character and dignity of the United States. Contends that Americans are more free and enlightened citizens than those of other nations. Maintains that the U.S. should be united in its actions against France, and that France has no interest in causing a war.

1320. Lyman, William (Mass.). "Direct Taxes," *Annals of Congress*. 4th Cong., 2nd Sess. (18 Jan. 1797) pp. 1905-1908. Objects to direct, or land, taxes as impolitic, unequal, and discouraging to land cultivation. Favors selectively increasing duties.

1321. Varnum, Joseph B. (Mass.). "Direct Taxes," *Annals of Congress*. 4th Cong., 2nd Sess. (16 Jan. 1797) pp. 1879-1885. Supports using imposts and excises to raise revenue rather than land taxes. Discusses and opposes the three modes of levying direct taxes proposed in the Secretary's report. Reviews the receipts and expenditures of the government and concludes that an additional tax is unnecessary and inexpedient at this time.

1322. "An Act Providing for Certain Buoys, to Be Placed in and near the Harbor of Boston," *Statutes at Large*, Vol. I (3 Mar. 1797) p. 516. Also printed in the *Annals of Congress* (4th Cong., 2nd Sess.) Appendix, p. 2963.

5ᵀᴴ CONGRESS, 1ˢᵀ SESSION

1323. Otis, Harrison Gray (Mass.). "Answer to the President's Speech," *Annals of Congress*. 5th Cong., 1st Sess. (23 May 1797) pp. 103-108. Supports the President's address. Maintains that given the nature of the conflict between France and the U.S., the complaints should be officially stated, negotiation attempted, and the Executive given the right to prepare for the defense of the nation should negotiations fail.

1324. Otis, Harrison Gray (Mass.). "Defensive Measures," *Annals of Congress*. 5th Cong., 1st Sess. (8 June 1797) pp. 268-270. Supports arming merchant vessels for self-defense.

1325. Sewall, Samuel (Mass.). "Answer to the President's Speech," *Annals of Congress*. 5th Cong., 1st Sess. (26 May, 1 June 1797) pp. 159-168; 220-221. Maintains that the House should support the President and his intention to provide for the defense of the country as the best way to avoid hostilities. Indignant at the rejection of Mr. Pinckney as minister; defends the conduct of the government in maintaining its neutrality. Opposes the proposed amendments.

5ᵀᴴ CONGRESS, 2ᴺᴰ SESSION

1326. Foster, Dwight (Mass.). "Additional Revenue," *Annals of Congress.* 5th Cong., 2nd Sess. (7 May 1798) pp. 1614-1615. Opposes permanent land taxes.

1327. Otis, Harrison Gray (Mass.). "Alien Enemies," *Annals of Congress.* 5th Cong., 2nd Sess. (22 May, 19 June, 21 June 1798) pp. 1790-1791; 1986-1989; 2016-2020. Supports giving discretionary power to the President over aliens that he may ensure the public safety. Discusses whether the right of expulsion can be exercised by the general government without infringing upon the right of admission, which is reserved to the individual states. Demonstrates the need for precautions. Refutes speech of Livingston (N.Y.).

1328. Otis, Harrison Gray (Mass.). "Breach of Privilege," *Annals of Congress.* 5th Cong., 2nd Sess. (9 Feb. 1798) pp. 987-990. Supports a resolution calling for Matthew Lyon's expulsion from the House after his attack upon Roger Griswold (Conn.).

1329. Otis, Harrison Gray (Mass.). "Direct Taxes," *Annals of Congress.* 5th Cong., 2nd Sess. (30 May 1798) pp. 1842-1843. Supports taxes upon houses.

1330. Otis, Harrison Gray (Mass.). "Foreign Intercourse," *Annals of Congress.* 5th Cong., 2nd Sess. (2 Mar. 1798) pp. 1145-1159. Supports the President's foreign trade policies; details advantages gained by treaties with France, Great Britain, Spain, Portugal, and Prussia. Maintains that it is the House's moral obligation to support executive appointments with reasonable appropriations. Discusses executive power of appointment and executive patronage.

1331. Otis, Harrison Gray (Mass.). "Protection of Trade," *Annals of Congress.* 5th Cong., 2nd Sess. (20 Apr. 1798) pp. 1488-1494. Supports defending the country, including property at sea as well as on land. Briefly reviews the history of the U.S. protecting its commerce and the power of granting convey. Maintains that France will not permit free American commerce; discusses the balance of trade with Britain and France.

1332. Otis, Harrison Gray (Mass.). "Provisional Army," *Annals of Congress.* 5th Cong., 2nd Sess. (8 May, 16 May 1798) pp. 1641-1644; 1732-1736. Defends the right of the President to raise an army in case of a declaration of war, an invasion, or imminent danger of an invasion. Discusses and dismisses the militia as an alternative to an army. Addresses opponents' arguments.

1333. Otis, Harrison Gray (Mass.). "Punishment of Crime," *Annals of Congress.* 5th Cong., 2nd Sess. (10 July 1798) pp. 2145-2151. Justifies the punishment of conspiracies against the government, including speaking, writing, or publishing of a licentious or seditious nature. Maintains that freedom of speech and press does not apply under these circumstances.

1334. Otis, Harrison Gray (Mass.). "Relations with France," *Annals of Congress.* 5th Cong., 2nd Sess. (13 Mar. 1798) pp. 1260-1262. Favors protecting commerce against French depredations.

1335. Otis, Harrison Gray (Mass.). "Seditious Practices," *Annals of Congress.* 5th Cong., 2nd Sess. (16 June 1798) pp. 1959-1962. Establishes that the Constitution authorizes restricting and expelling seditious aliens when necessary for the country's defense.

1336. Parker, Isaac (Mass.). "Foreign Intercourse," *Annals of Congress.* 5th Cong., 2nd Sess. (23 Jan. 1798) pp. 908-910. Supports the executive privilege to appoint and assign foreign officers; maintains that the balance of powers in republican governments will prevent misuse of this privilege.

1337. Reed, John (Mass.). "Foreign Intercourse," *Annals of Congress.* 5th Cong., 2nd Sess. (5 Mar. 1798) pp. 1202-1207. Opposes the amendment to restrict the executive power to appoint foreign ministers by reducing appropriations. Discusses representative government, the advantages of political intercourse, and the doctrine of appropriations as intended by the Constitution.

1338. Sewall, Samuel (Mass.). "Foreign Intercourse," *Annals of Congress.* 5th Cong., 2nd Sess. (26 Jan. 1798) pp. 941-945. Defends the executive power to make appointments to office, including those of foreign ministers. Maintains that the House does not have the right to refuse an executive request for appropriations for foreign ministers.

1339. Sewall, Samuel (Mass.). "Provisional Army," *Annals of Congress.* 5th Cong., 2nd Sess. (24 Apr., 8 May 1798) pp. 1527-1529; 1634-1637. Supports giving the President the power to raise an army if deemed necessary. Maintains that it is constitutional, expedient, and important to be prepared for defense.

1340. Sewall, Samuel (Mass.). "Seditious Practices," *Annals of Congress.* 5th Cong., 2nd Sess. (16 June 1798) pp. 1957-1959; 1971. Maintains that Congress has the constitutional right to take whatever measures are necessary to preserve peace and tranquillity, and therefore has the power to expel dangerous and seditious aliens from the country.

1341. Sewall, Samuel (Mass.). "Sick and Disabled Seamen," *Annals of Congress.* 5th Cong., 2nd Sess. (10 Apr. 1798) pp. 1386-1387; 1389-1390. Opposes the bill; maintains that relief for seamen should be a public charity and that seamen should not be taxed for the relief of foreign sailors.

1342. Shepard, William (Mass.). "Case of Griswold and Lyon," *Annals of Congress.* 5th Cong., 2nd Sess. (20 Feb. 1798) pp. 1052-1053. Testimony on the events that occurring during the assault.

1343. Thatcher, George (Mass.). "Foreign Intercourse," *Annals of Congress.* 5th Cong., 2nd Sess. (27 Feb. 1798) pp. 1113-1116. Objects to using appropriations to restrict the executive power to appoint ministers as unconstitutional; addresses opponents' arguments.

1344. Thatcher, George (Mass.). "Georgia Limits," *Annals of Congress.* 5th Cong., 2nd Sess. (23 Mar. 1798) pp. 1310-1311. Objects to permitting slavery in the new territory.

1345. Varnum, Joseph B. (Mass.). "Additional Revenue," *Annals of Congress.* 5th Cong., 2nd Sess. (7 May 1798) pp. 1627-1630. Objects to making the proposed direct tax a permanent tax. Calculates the revenue from duties. Maintains that the expenses for fortifications and munitions are temporary.

1346. Varnum, Joseph B. (Mass.). "Direct Taxes," *Annals of Congress.* 5th Cong., 2nd Sess. (30 May 1798) pp. 1843-1844. Opposes direct taxes as operating unequally.

1347. Varnum, Joseph B. (Mass.). "Provisional Army," *Annals of Congress.* 5th Cong., 2nd Sess. (16 May 1798) pp. 1739-1740. Opposes the proposed provisional army as unconstitutional and ineffectual.

1348. "An Act Declaring the Consent of Congress to an Act of the Commonwealth of Massachusetts," *Statutes at Large*, Vol. I (27 Mar. 1798) p. 546. An act for upkeep and repair of a pier at the mouth of the Kennebunk River. Also printed in the *Annals of Congress* (5th Cong., 2nd Sess.) Appendix, p. 3716.

1349. "An Act Establishing an Annual Salary for the Surveyor of the Port of Gloucester," *Statutes at Large*, Vol. I (14 July 1798) p. 596. Also printed in the *Annals of Congress* (5th Cong., 2nd Sess.) Appendix, p. 3776.

1350. "An Act for Erecting a Lighthouse at Gay-head, on Martha's Vineyard; and for Other Purposes," *Statutes at Large*, Vol. I (16 July 1798) p. 697. Also printed in the *Annals of Congress* (5th Cong., 2nd Sess.) Appendix, p. 3789.

5TH CONGRESS, 3RD SESSION

1351. Otis, Harrison Gray (Mass.). "Augmentation of the Navy," *Annals of Congress.* 5th Cong., 3rd Sess. (11 Feb. 1799) pp. 2874-2878. Supports increasing the size of the navy; maintains that the navy is an essential component of the defense system. Addresses objections concerning effectiveness, necessity and finance.

1352. Otis, Harrison Gray (Mass.). "Intercourse with France," *Annals of Congress.* 5th Cong., 3rd Sess. (22 Jan. 1799) pp. 2742-2745. Supports maintaining trade with France's colonies; discusses the implications of a rebellion.

1353. Otis, Harrison Gray (Mass.). "Uniform Bankruptcy," *Annals of Congress.* 5th Cong., 3rd Sess. (15 Jan. 1799) pp. 2674-2676. Supports a uniform bankrupt act. Illustrates the weakness of the present situation; maintains that the proposed legislation will benefit both creditor and debtor.

1354. Otis, Harrison Gray (Mass.). "Usurpation of Executive Authority," *Annals of Congress.* 5th Cong., 3rd Sess. (28 Dec. 1798, 17 Jan. 1799) pp. 2523-2528; 2692-2696. Speeches support a resolution to restrain individual citizens from negotiating with France on behalf of the United States; maintains that it is necessary for the defense of the country.

1355. Sewall, Samuel (Mass.). "Impeachment of William Blount," *Annals of Congress.* 5th Cong., 3rd Sess. (21 Dec. 1798) pp. 2472-2473, 2483-2485. Supports a law stating the consequences when a person impeached fails to appear before the Senate after being summoned; maintains that according to the principles of common law Blount must be present before his trial can take place.

1356. Sewall, Samuel (Mass.). "Intercourse with France," *Annals of Congress.* 5th Cong., 3rd Sess. (23 Jan. 1799) pp. 2754-2757. Supports a bill to suspend trade between the U.S. and places under the authority of the French Republic.

1357. "An Act to Erect a Beacon on Boon Island," *Statutes at Large*, Vol. I (2 Mar. 1799) p. 790. Also printed in the *Annals of Congress* (5th Cong., 3rd Sess.) Appendix, p. 3939.

6ᵀᴴ CONGRESS, 1ˢᵀ SESSION

1358. Otis, Harrison Gray (Mass.). "Breach of Privilege," *Annals of Congress.* 6th Cong., 1st Sess. (27 Jan. 1800) pp. 467-473. Demonstrates how Mr. Randolph's (Va.) letter deviates from the customary mode of writing to the President; examines the justification of Mr. Randolph's complaint for a breach of privilege and concludes that there is insufficient evidence.

1359. Otis, Harrison Gray (Mass.). "Reduction of the Army," *Annals of Congress.* 6th Cong., 1st Sess. (9 Jan. 1800) pp. 301-308. Objects to reducing the size of the army. Addresses the principle objection of expense. Maintains that the army is necessary and expedient, and that the militia is a poor alternative. Considers the army one link in the chain of national defense.

1360. Sewall, Samuel (Mass.). "Breach of Privilege," *Annals of Congress.* 6th Cong., 1st Sess. (27 Jan. 1800) pp. 452-458. Reviews his reasons for concurring with the report concerning the letters of the President and Mr. Randolph (Va.). Maintains that there was insufficient evidence to support the charge.

1361. Thatcher, George (Mass.). "Petition of Free Blacks," *Annals of Congress.* 6th Cong., 1st Sess. (3 Jan. 1800) pp. 240-241. Supports a petition opposed to slavery.

1362. "An Act to Establish the District of Kennebunk, and to Annex Lyme to New London; and to Alter the District of Bermuda Hundred and City Point; and Therein to Amend the Act Intituled 'An Act to Regulate the Collection of Duties on Imports and Tonnage'," *Statutes at Large,* Vol. II (10 May 1800) pp. 68-69. Also printed in the *Annals of Congress* (6th Cong., 1st Sess.) Appendix, pp. 1509-1510.

1363. "An Act to Provide for Rebuilding the Lighthouse at New London; for the Support of a Lighthouse at Clark's Point; for the Erection and Support of a Lighthouse at Wigwam Point, and for Other Purposes," *Statutes at Large,* Vol. II (29 Apr. 1800) pp. 57-58. Provides for lighthouses at Clark's Point, in New Bedford, Massachusetts, and at Wigwam Point, in Gloucester, Massachusetts. Also provides for buoys at Buzzard's Bay, in Massachusetts. Also printed in *Annals of Congress* (6th Cong., 1st Sess.) Appendix, p. 1497.

1364. "Application for Pecuniary Aid to Prosecute a Claim against the British Government," *American State Papers: Claims,* (Doc. 111) p. 226. (ASP 036). Application and denial of the petition for assistance to obtain the balance due for supplies furnished to British troops during the Revolutionary War.

1365. "Armory at Springfield," *American State Papers: Military Affairs,* Vol. I (Doc. 37) pp. 130-132. (ASP 016). Report on the expenditures of the national armory at Springfield, Mass.; includes recommendations for improvement.

6TH CONGRESS, 2ND SESSION

1366. Otis, Harrison Gray (Mass.). "Reduction of Artillery," *Annals of Congress.* 6th Cong., 2nd Sess. (16 Dec. 1800) pp. 825-829. Opposes the resolution to reduce the size of the artillery. Demonstrates that the artillery was meant to be part of the permanent army. Addresses necessity, expense, the militia as an alternative, and other objections.

1367. Otis, Harrison Gray (Mass.). "Sedition Act," *Annals of Congress.* 6th Cong., 2nd Sess. (22 Jan. 1801) pp. 952-958. Supports reenacting the Sedition Act. Defends the principles of the act, addresses objections, reviews cases prosecuted under it. Maintains that the press could ultimately be responsible for overturning the government of this country.

1368. "An Act Making the Port of Biddeford and Pepperrelborough, and the Port of New Bedford, in Massachusetts, Ports of Entry for Ships or Vessels, Arriving from the Cape of Good Hope, and from Places beyond the Same," *Statutes at Large,* Vol. II (25 Feb. 1801) p. 101.

1369. "An Act to Augment the Salaries of the District Judges in the Districts of Massachusetts, New York, New Jersey, Delaware and Maryland, Respectively," *Statutes at Large*, Vol. I (3 Mar. 1801) p. 121. Also printed in the *Annals of Congress* (6th Cong., 2nd Sess.) Appendix, p. 1572.

1370. "An Act to Provide for the Erection and Support of a Lighthouse on Cape Page, at the Northeasterly Part of Martha's Vineyard," *Statutes at Large*, Vol. II (30 Jan. 1801) pp. 88-89. Also printed in the *Annals of Congress* (6th Cong., 2nd Sess.) Appendix, pp. 1533-1534.

7TH CONGRESS, 1ST SESSION

1371. Bacon, John (Mass.). "Apportionment Bill," *Annals of Congress.* 7th Cong., 1st Sess. (4 Jan. 1802) pp. 370-372. Favors the ratio of apportionment of 1:33,000. Addresses and dismisses arguments for increasing the representation.

1372. Bacon, John (Mass.). "Judiciary System," *Annals of Congress.* 7th Cong., 1st Sess. (17 Feb. 1802) pp. 558-564. Demonstrates the constitutionality and expediency of abolishing the late circuit courts and establishing the present circuit courts; maintains that Congress has the power to repeal a law instituting an office.

1373. Cutler, Manasseh (Mass.). "Judiciary System," *Annals of Congress.* 7th Cong., 1st Sess. (1 Mar. 1802) pp. 862-867. Objects to repealing the judiciary law as unconstitutional. Maintains that the intent of the Constitution was to establish an independent Judiciary to serve as a check against the Legislative and Executive branches.

1374. Eustis, William (Mass.). "Judiciary System," *Annals of Congress.* 7th Cong., 1st Sess. (2 Mar. 1802) pp. 953-956. Requests that the judiciary law not be repealed until amendments are approved to improve the old system that would be restored and which is allowed to be defective.

1375. Hastings, Seth (Mass.). "Judiciary System," *Annals of Congress.* 7th Cong., 1st Sess. (1 Mar. 1802) pp. 880-887. Opposes repealing the law establishing the new judiciary system. Maintains that the repeal would be an unconstitutional violation of the judiciary power and inexpedient. Presents supporting arguments and addresses opponents' objections.

1376. Mason, Jonathan (Mass.). "Judiciary System," *Annals of Congress.* 7th Cong., 1st Sess. (8 Jan. 1802) pp. 31-35. Maintains that repealing the judiciary law would be a violation of the Constitution and not expedient. Contends that the Constitution intends appointments of judges to be permanent and independent of the Legislative and Executive branches.

1377. Varnum, Joseph B. (Mass.). "Judiciary System," *Annals of Congress.* 7th Cong., 1st Sess. (3 Mar. 1802) pp. 971-981. Supports the repeal of the judiciary law as constitutional; maintains that Congress has the right to repeal any law which it has passed. Demonstrates the intent of the Constitution by examining the original states' judiciary systems and comparing them to the national Judiciary. Addresses opponents' arguments.

7TH CONGRESS, 2ND SESSION

1378. Bacon, John (Mass.). "District of Columbia," *Annals of Congress.* 7th Cong., 2nd Sess. (9 Feb. 1803) pp. 496-498. Supports the retrocession of the District of Columbia.

1379. Bacon, John (Mass.). "Importation of Certain Persons," *Annals of Congress.* 7th Cong., 2nd Sess. (7 Feb. 1803) pp. 467-469. Objects to a bill prohibiting the importation or admission of people of color into the ports of certain states as unconstitutional and discriminatory.

1380. Eustis, William (Mass.). "Navy Yards and Docks," *Annals of Congress.* 7th Cong., 2nd Sess. (19 Jan. 1803) pp. 405-407. Opposes the proposed docks and navy yards at the Eastern Branch area of the Tyber River (Tiber).

1381. Mason, Jonathan (Mass.). "Mississippi Question," *Annals of Congress.* 7th Cong., 2nd Sess. (23 Feb. 1803) pp. 142-146. Supports the resolutions declaring the right of the United States to the free navigation of the Mississippi River and authorizing the President to take possession of New Orleans.

1382. Thatcher, Samuel (Mass.). "Importation of Arms," *Annals of Congress.* 7th Cong., 2nd Sess. (17 Jan. 1803) pp. 391-393. Opposes eliminating the duty on imported arms; maintains that it would destroy arms manufacturing in the U.S., operate unequally among the states, and that there is no great demand.

1383. "An Act Authorizing the Sale of a Piece of Land, Parcel of the Navy Yard Belonging to the United States, in Charlestown, in the State of Massachusetts, to the Proprietors of the Salem Turnpike Road and Chelsea Bridge Corporation," *Statutes at Large*, Vol. II (10 Feb. 1803) p. 199. Also printed in the *Annals of Congress* (7th Cong., 2nd Sess.) Appendix, p. 1557.

1384. "An Act for Erecting a Lighthouse at the Entrance of Penobscot Bay, or Any Other Place in Its Vicinity, that May Be Deemed Preferable by the Secretary of the Treasury," *Statutes at Large*, Vol. II (3 Mar. 1803) p. 228. Also printed in the *Annals of Congress* (7th Cong., 2nd Sess.) Appendix, p. 1592.

1385. "An Act to Make Beaufort and Passamaquoddy, Ports of Entry and Delivery; to Make Easton and Tiverton, Ports of Delivery; and to Authorize the Establishment of a New Collection District on Lake Ontario," *Statutes at Large*, Vol. II (3 Mar. 1803) pp. 228-229. Also printed in the *Annals of Congress* (7th Cong., 2nd Sess.) Appendix, pp. 1592-1593.

1386. "Discriminating Duties and Ship Building," *American State Papers: Commerce and Navigation*, Vol. I (Doc. 69) p. 509. (ASP 014). Memorial from Newburyport opposes a proposed repeal of the discriminating duties.

1387. "Indemnity to a Postmaster for His Expenses in Defending a Vexatious Prosecution," *American State Papers: Claims*, (Doc. 143) p. 285. (ASP 036). Report against granting the petition for relief of Boston postmaster.

1388. "Survey of the Harbor of Nantucket," *American State Papers: Commerce and Navigation*, Vol. I (Doc. 74) pp. 526-527. (ASP 014). Report recommends a survey of the harbor with recommendations for improvement; includes petition from Nantucket requesting aid to form a channel.

8ᵀᴴ CONGRESS, 1ˢᵀ SESSION

1389. Adams, John Quincy (Mass.). "Amendment to the Constitution," *Annals of Congress.* 8th Cong., 1st Sess. (29 Nov. 1803) pp. 117-120. Remarks on the proposed amendment altering the rules of the election of the President and Vice President. Discusses federate and popular principles.

1390. Adams, John Quincy (Mass.). "The Louisiana Treaty," *Annals of Congress.* 8th Cong., 1st Sess. (3 Nov. 1803) pp. 65-68. Supports the treaty. Answers objections concerning the power of Congress to ratify the treaty and the questions about the legal possession of the territory.

1391. Eustis, William (Mass.). "Amendment to the Constitution," *Annals of Congress.* 8th Cong., 1st Sess. (8 Dec. 1803) pp. 705-707, 771-775. Remarks on the proposed amendment regarding the election of the President and Vice President. Supports designating the Pres. and Vice President on distinct ballots, and allowing the House to choose from five candidates when there is no choice by the electors.

1392. Eustis, William (Mass.). "Georgia Claims," *Annals of Congress.* 8th Cong., 1st Sess. (7 Mar. 1804) pp. 1119-1121. Supports the decision of the Committee to compensate the land claims in question without investigating the circumstances of the acts of the Georgia Legislature. Desires the issue closed.

1393. Eustis, William (Mass.). "Louisiana Territory," *Annals of Congress.* 8th Cong., 1st Sess. (28 Feb. 1804) pp. 1057-1059. Supports a bill to provide for a temporary government for the territory. Maintains that the people of the territory are not prepared to exercise the full rights of citizenship.

1394. Eustis, William (Mass.). "Official Conduct of Judge Chase," *Annals of Congress.* 8th Cong., 1st Sess. (7 Jan. 1804) pp. 857-859. Advocates establishing a committee to inquire into the official conduct of Judge Chase.

1395. Eustis, William (Mass.). "Salaries of Certain Officers," *Annals of Congress.* 8th Cong., 1st Sess. (21 Nov. 1803) pp. 596-598, 599. Supports the salaries established in 1799; maintains that current salaries are inadequate.

1396. Hastings, Seth (Mass.). "Amendment to the Constitution," *Annals of Congress.* 8th Cong., 1st Sess. (28 Oct. 1803) pp. 535-536. Objects to altering the proposed mode of electing the President and Vice President as unnecessary and inexpedient.

1397. Hastings, Seth (Mass.). "Salaries of Certain Officers," *Annals of Congress.* 8th Cong., 1st Sess. (21 Nov. 1803) pp. 587-589. Opposes augmenting the proposed salaries; maintains that it is economically unnecessary and that they are sufficient to attract and retain suitable candidates.

1398. Pickering, Timothy (Mass.). "Amendment to the Constitution," *Annals of Congress.* 8th Cong., 1st Sess. (2 Dec. 1803) pp. 195-199. Opposes altering the mode of electing the President and Vice President. Maintains that the public will represent a superficial view of the subject; reviews the origination of the constitutional mode of election; addresses the impact of the amendment on the small states.

1399. Pickering, Timothy (Mass.). "The Louisiana Treaty," *Annals of Congress.* 8th Cong., 1st Sess. (3 Nov. 1803) pp. 44-47. Objects to the treaty as containing stipulations that cannot be executed. Questions the security of the title to Louisiana, and the right of France to cede it.

1400. Taggart, Samuel (Mass.). "Amendment to the Constitution," *Annals of Congress.* 8th Cong., 1st Sess. (8 Dec. 1803) pp. 727-735. Objects to amending the Constitution for any reason, including for the purpose of altering the means of electing the President and Vice President. Questions the support of the designating principle and its consequences if passed. Considers the resolution as passed by the Senate as even more objectionable.

1401. Taggart, Samuel (Mass.). "Salaries of Certain Officers," *Annals of Congress.* 8th Cong., 1st Sess. (21 Nov. 1803) pp. 584-587. Supports the proposed salaries. Objects to the amendment introduced by Mr. Eustis (Mass.).

1402. Thatcher, Samuel (Mass.). "Amendment to the Constitution," *Annals of Congress.* 8th Cong., 1st Sess. (28 Oct., 8 Dec. 1803) pp. 536-538; 737-742. Remarks and speech oppose the proposed amendments to alter the mode of electing the President and Vice President. Maintains that the changes would be detrimental to the smaller states, impinging upon their rights, and ultimately damaging the foundations of the Union.

1403. Thatcher, Samuel (Mass.). "The Louisiana Treaty," *Annals of Congress.* 8th Cong., 1st Sess. (24 Oct., 25 Oct. 1803) pp. 396-397; 454-456. Requests clear proof of title to Louisiana. Objects to the treaty as unconstitutional and damaging to the trade of the eastern states.

1404. Thatcher, Samuel (Mass.). "State Balances," *Annals of Congress.* 8th Cong., 1st Sess. (17 Jan. 1804) pp. 901-902. Opposes expunging the debts still owed by some states for the costs of the Revolutionary War. Presents supporting arguments.

1405. Varnum, Joseph B. (Mass.). "Salaries of Certain Officers," *Annals of Congress.* 8th Cong., 1st Sess. (21 Nov. 1803) pp. 589-591. Supports allowing the salaries of 1799.

1406. "Inequality of the Allowances to Fishing Vessels," *American State Papers: Commerce and Navigation,* Vol. I (Doc. 79) p. 535. (ASP 014). Report, in response to petition from Gloucester, Mass., that it is inexpedient to alter the mode of distributing the bounty to fishing vessels.

1407. "Pier in Barnstable Bay," *American State Papers: Commerce and Navigation,* Vol. I (Doc. 90) p. 573. (ASP 014). Report denies the petition for aid to construct the pier.

1408. "Survey of the Harbor of Nantucket," *American State Papers: Commerce and Navigation,* Vol. I (Doc. 77) pp. 533-534. (ASP 014). Report of the survey with recommendations for improvement and estimated expenses.

1409. "Survey of the Harbor of Nantucket," *American State Papers: Commerce and Navigation,* Vol. I (Doc. 78) pp. 534-535. (ASP 014). Unfavorable report on the petition and survey of Nantucket harbor; contends that the recommended improvements are problematical.

8TH CONGRESS, 2ND SESSION

1410. Eustis, William (Mass.). "Armed Merchant Vessels," *Annals of Congress.* 8th Cong., 2nd Sess. (13 Dec. 1804) pp. 814-815. Supports arming merchant vessels trading with the West India islands.

1411. Eustis, William (Mass.). "Georgia Claims," *Annals of Congress.* 8th Cong., 2nd Sess. (30 Jan. 1805) pp. 1057-1060. Supports the resolution to compensate claimants as an equitable compromise. Demonstrates that the New England claimants had no knowledge of the fraud or of the rescinding act when they made their purchases.

1412. Eustis, William (Mass.). "Navy Yards, &c.," *Annals of Congress.* 8th Cong., 2nd Sess. (24 Jan. 1805) pp. 1009-1010. Presents and supports resolution to establish a navy yard nearer to the ocean to receive and repair ships of war.

1413. Taggart, Samuel (Mass.). "District of Columbia," *Annals of Congress.* 8th Cong., 2nd Sess. (9 Jan. 1805) pp. 930-937. Objects to the motion to recede the District of Columbia. Addresses the possible consequences of the permanency or removal of the seat of government, the constitutionality, and the effect on the civil and political rights of its citizens.

1414. Thatcher, Samuel (Mass.). "District of Columbia," *Annals of Congress.* 8th Cong., 2nd Sess. (9 Jan. 1805) pp. 929-930. Opposes the motion to recede the District of Columbia.

1415. "An Act Declaring Cambridge, in the State of Massachusetts, to Be a Port of Delivery," *Statutes at Large*, Vol. II (11 Jan. 1805) p. 310. Also printed in the *Annals of Congress* (8th Cong., 2nd Sess.) Appendix, p. 1660.

1416. "Land Claims in the Mississippi Territory," *American State Papers: Public Lands*, Vol. I (Doc. 108) pp. 215-218. (ASP 028). Report of the Committee of Claims on the land claims in Mississippi; includes statement of claims from citizens of Massachusetts and from the New England Mississippi Land Company. Brief history of the circumstances and claims; recommends a settlement as in the best interests of the United States.

9TH CONGRESS, 1ST SESSION

1417. Adams, John Quincy (Mass.). "Ex-Bashaw of Tripoli," *Annals of Congress.* 9th Cong., 1st Sess. (1 Apr. 1806) pp. 211-224. Opposes the proposed relief of Hamet Caramalli, ex-Bashaw of Tripoli. Maintains that the report of the Committee is inaccurate. Offers an exhaustive and documented review of the true nature of the contract and the events that transpired.

1418. Adams, John Quincy (Mass.). "Privileges of Foreign Minister," *Annals of Congress.* 9th Cong., 1st Sess. (3 Mar. 1806) pp. 145-161. Explains the principles and motives upon which the bill was based. Reviews the privileges of foreign ministers as they relate to the laws of nations and as the Constitution. Explains why the bill allows the President to expel a minister when the crime is personal misconduct, but it is necessary for the concurrence of Congress when the crime is national differences. Addresses objections.

1419. Bidwell, Barnabas (Mass.). "Importation of Slaves," *Annals of Congress.* 9th Cong., 1st Sess. (4 Feb. 1806) pp. 435-438. Supports a duty on the importation of slaves as the only preventive measure available to Congress until 1808. Presents and defends an amendment that would permanently prohibit slavery after 1808.

1420. Bidwell, Barnabas (Mass.). "Non-Importation of Goods from Great Britain," *Annals of Congress.* 9th Cong., 1st Sess. (8 Mar. 1806) pp. 650-660. Reviews the complaints against Great Britain and the measures taken to resolve them. Maintains that agriculture and commerce are inseparably connected with a mutual interest in resolving the dispute; establishes that the Constitution provides for the common defense of all classes of citizens.

1421. Chandler, John (Mass.). "Non-Importation of Goods from Great Britain," *Annals of Congress.* 9th Cong., 1st Sess. (14 Mar. 1806) pp. 788-790. Supports total non-importation. Maintains this would be the most effectual means of obtaining redress.

1422. Cook, Orchard (Mass.). "Trade with St. Domingo," *Annals of Congress.* 9th Cong., 1st Sess. (28 Feb. 1806) pp. 525-530. Supports augmenting the navy in order to protect commerce. Maintains that prosperity depends upon commerce; that commerce is entitled to equal protection, and that the non-importation act will be ineffective. Addresses opponents' arguments.

1423. Crowninshield, Jacob (Mass.). "Non-Importation of Goods from Great Britain," *Annals of Congress.* 9th Cong., 1st Sess. (5 Mar., 12 Mar. 1806) pp. 552-555; 750-760. Supports prohibiting the importation of British goods unless America's sailors are released and her ships restored. Maintains that it is not a war measure. Reviews the events leading to the measure and the need to protect citizens and commerce; reviews the status of trade with Great Britain.

1424. Quincy, Josiah (Mass.). "Defence of Ports and Harbors," *Annals of Congress.* 9th Cong., 1st Sess. (15 Apr. 1806) pp. 1030-1042. Supports regular appropriations toward the defense of the ports and harbors of the country. Discusses the importance of commercial cities to the country; reviews the utility of fortifications as a means of defense. Demonstrates that moneys have been available for the security of the South and the Southwest, and that fairness demands equal consideration of the interests of the North and East.

1425. Quincy, Josiah (Mass.). "Detachment of Militia," *Annals of Congress.* 9th Cong., 1st Sess. (27 Jan. 1806) pp. 403-405. Objects to repealing the previous law; maintains that the proposed revisions would decrease the power of the Executive to defend the country.

1426. Varnum, Joseph B. (Mass.). "Organization of the Militia," *Annals of Congress.* 9th Cong., 1st Sess. (18 Apr. 1806) pp. 1069-1075. Maintains that there is no immediate need to augment the army. Contrasts the weak situation of the country at the start of the Revolutionary War to its present strength in terms of numbers, organization and supplies. Table compares militia and defense status of the various states. Describes status of the Massachusetts militia.

1427. "An Act Declaring the Town of Jersey, in the State of New Jersey, to Be a Port of Delivery; and for Erecting a Lighthouse on Wood Island, or Fletcher's Neck, in the State of Massachusetts," *Statutes at Large,* Vol. II (8 Mar. 1806) p. 355. Also printed in the *Annals of Congress* (9th Cong., 1st Sess.) Appendix, p. 1233.

1428. "An Act for Erecting Certain Lighthouses in the State of Massachusetts; for Building a Beacon, or Pier, at Bridgeport, in the State of Connecticut; and for Fixing Buoys in Pamplico Sound, in the State of North Carolina," *Statutes* *at Large*, Vol. II (21 Apr. 1806) p. 406. Also printed in the *Annals of Congress* (9th Cong., 1st Sess.) Appendix, pp. 1292-1293.

1429. "An Act to Provide for Lighthouses in Long Island Sound; and to Declare Roxbury, in the State of Massachusetts, to Be a Port of Delivery," *Statutes at Large*, Vol. II (22 Jan. 1806) p. 349. Also printed in the *Annals of Congress* (9th Cong., 1st Sess.) Appendix, pp. 1225-1226.

1430. "Extension of Patent Rights," *American State Papers: Miscellaneous*, Vol. I (Doc. 207) p. 453. (ASP 037). Report denies the petition from Salem, Mass. for an extension of patent rights.

1431. "Further Encouragement to Fishing Vessels at Nantucket," *American State Papers: Commerce and Navigation*, Vol. I (Doc. 111) pp. 666-667. (ASP 014). Report against the petition requesting relief from customhouse expenses incurred by whaling vessels that lighten their loads in a different collection district in order to negotiate Nantucket harbor.

1432. "Protecting Duties," *American State Papers: Finance*, Vol. II (Doc. 242) p. 171. (ASP 010). Report against the petition of manufacturers in Massachusetts for an increased duty on imported iron hollowware.

1433. "Protection to the Fisheries," *American State Papers: Commerce and Navigation*, Vol. I (Doc. 112) p. 667. (ASP 014). Memorial from Barnstable and Plymouth requests an increased duty or a total prohibition on foreign fish.

1434. "Public Lands in Mississippi," *American State Papers: Public Lands*, Vol. I (Doc. 114) pp. 252-255. (ASP 028). Petitions and correspondence on the land claims; includes a petition from the New England Mississippi Land Company requesting a settlement of their claims.

1435. "Reimbursement of the Cost of Two Piers Erected in Merrimack River," *American State Papers: Claims*, (Doc. 167) p. 314. (ASP 036). Report against the petition from Newburyport for reimbursement of money expended to erect the piers.

9TH CONGRESS, 2ND SESSION

1436. "Boston Memorial," *Annals of Congress.* 9th Cong., 2nd Sess. (20 Jan. 1806) Appendix, pp. 890-899. Memorial objects to the interference of Great Britain with American trade and requests action towards resolution of the problems. Details examples of depredation and the principles assumed by Great Britain which act against U.S. commerce.

1437. Memorial from Newburyport to the Secretary of State, *Annals of Congress.* 9th Cong., 2nd Sess. ([no date]) Appendix, pp. 819-822. Memorial protests foreign depredations against their property on the high seas; requests indemnification for past losses and protection from future aggressions.

1438. "Salem Memorial," *Annals of Congress.* 9th Cong., 2nd Sess. (Feb. 1806) Appendix, pp. 899-908. Memorial addresses the British aggressions; discusses the new principles directing the British Admiralty, and their effect on the rights to trade of neutrals. Supports measures defend commerce and redress wrongs.

1439. "Table of the Fees and Compensation of Several Officers, as Regulated and Established in the Commonwealth of Massachusetts, by an Act of the Legislature Passed on the 13th of February, 1796, and (being Temporary) Continued by Another Act Passed in May, 1798," *Annals of Congress.* 9th Cong., 2nd Sess. (20 Nov. 1806) Appendix, pp. 1149-1153. List of fees allowed to officers of the courts and others in Massachusetts for various services.

1440. Cook, Orchard (Mass.). "National Defence," *Annals of Congress.* 9th Cong., 2nd Sess. (21 Feb. 1807) pp. 592-596. Impassioned support of a permanent general appropriation to protect the ports and harbors.

1441. Hodge, Michael (Mass.). Protest Against the Robbery of the Brig Lucretia, *Annals of Congress.* 9th Cong., 2nd Sess. (2 Dec. 1805) Appendix, pp. 820-822. Notarized claim and protest against the owners, captains, officers and crew of the brig Andromeda for the robbery of the brig Lucretia.

1442. Quincy, Josiah (Mass.). "Duty on Salt," *Annals of Congress.* 9th Cong., 2nd Sess. (12 Jan., 13 Jan. 1807) pp. 291-293, 295-296; 299-300, 300-306. Remarks support his proposal of a partial repeal of the salt tax combined with repeals on other necessary articles. Speech demonstrates the impolicy of a total repeal of the tax. Discusses the nature, extent, and importance of the salt manufacture. Maintains that the salt tax is a capitation tax and a property tax. Total abolition of the tax would be unequal and partial in its relief in respect to the classes and to the geographic regions of the country.

1443. Quincy, Josiah (Mass.). "National Defence," *Annals of Congress.* 9th Cong., 2nd Sess. (13 Feb. 1807) pp. 490-493. Opposes the proposed appropriations for New York harbor. Favors regular appropriations for the general defense that are apportioned by the Executive rather than individual and solitary applications that result in dividing the common interests.

1444. Quincy, Josiah (Mass.). "National Defence," *Annals of Congress.* 9th Cong., 2nd Sess. (23 Feb. 1807) pp. 611-615. Demonstrates the necessity for fortifications as preparation against aggressions that are bound to happen to a prosperous nation in the midst of martial nations. Maintains that expense should not be the issue due to the importance of the goal and the surplus available.

1445. Quincy, Josiah (Mass.). "Writ of Habeas Corpus," *Annals of Congress.* 9th Cong., 2nd Sess. (19 Feb. 1807) pp. 565-568. Supports an inquiry into the status of the writ and any additional provisions it requires for enforcement.

10TH CONGRESS, 1ST SESSION

1446. "Boston Memorials," *Annals of Congress.* 10th Cong., 1st Sess. (14 Dec. 1807) pp. 1172-1177. Debate on the Boston petitions praying for a modification or repeal of the embargo.

1447. Adams, John Quincy (Mass.). "Case of Mr. John Smith, Senator from Ohio," *Annals of Congress.* 10th Cong., 1st Sess. (8 Apr., 9 Apr. 1808) pp. 237-265; 317-321. Responds to the objections of Mr. Smith's counsel. Addresses concerns of 1) jurisdiction and the power of expulsion, 2) written vs. oral testimony, with a review of the practice of the English House of Commons, and 3) the accuracy and validity of the facts of the case. Detailed review of the testimony and course of events leading to the charges. States reasons supporting the resolution to expel Sen. Smith.

1448. Bacon, Ezekiel (Mass.). "Arming the Militia," *Annals of Congress.* 10th Cong., 1st Sess. (4 Dec. 1807) pp. 1040-1046. Opposes the resolution whereby the general government would arm and equip the militia. Maintains that the measure is impolitic and inconsistent with the general principles of liberty and the Constitution, and that it would be unequal in its operation upon the states who have already achieved different levels of preparedness.

1449. Bacon, Ezekiel (Mass.). "Death of Mr. Crowninshield," *Annals of Congress.* 10th Cong., 1st Sess. (15 Apr. 1808) p. 2172. Death announcement and resolutions for Jacob Crowninshield, Representative from Massachusetts.

1450. Bacon, Ezekiel (Mass.). "Foreign Relations," *Annals of Congress.* 10th Cong., 1st Sess. (18 Feb. 1808) pp. 1645-1647. Maintains that it is not the duty of the House to remind the Executive to supply information on the state of foreign relations.

1451. Bacon, Ezekiel (Mass.). "General Wilkinson," *Annals of Congress.* 10th Cong., 1st Sess. (7 Jan., 11 Jan., 13 Jan. 1808) pp. 1351-1352; 1391-1393; 1454-1455, 1455-1456. Various remarks object to the House requesting an inquiry into the charges against General Wilkinson; maintains that the House does not have the constitutional power to complete an inquiry. Briefly reviews the progress of the resolution.

1452. Cook, Orchard (Mass.). "Fortifications and Gunboats," *Annals of Congress.* 10th Cong., 1st Sess. (9 Dec. 1807) pp. 1094-1098. Supports more equally apportioning defense moneys between gunboats and ships of war. Maintains that a navy and its ships of war are an indispensable means of protection and defense and that gunboats are still unproved.

1453. Crowninshield, Jacob (Mass.). "Fortifications and Gunboats," *Annals of Congress.* 10th Cong., 1st Sess. (8 Dec., 9 Dec., 10 Dec. 1807) pp. 1069-1070; 1088-1089; 1141-1144. Various remarks support gunboats. Defends their abilities and benefits as part of a system of defense, citing examples of their utility. Addresses the issue of expense in terms of comparison with frigates, labor, and the status of the Treasury.

1454. Livermore, Edward St. Loe (Mass.). "Embargo," *Annals of Congress.* 10th Cong., 1st Sess. (29 Feb. 1808) pp. 1698-1703. Opposes the proposed bill, which would prevent commerce among the border states and their neighboring countries. Maintains that the operation of the bill would harm the citizens of the U.S. and not affect the intended foreign nations. Discusses the mutually dependent relationship between commerce and agriculture. Maintains that the bill is unnecessary, oppressive, and would encourage speculation.

1455. Livermore, Edward St. Loe (Mass.). "Embargo," *Annals of Congress.* 10th Cong., 1st Sess. (18 Mar. 1808) pp. 1850-1854. Introduces a resolution to discontinue the embargo of trade with Great Britain. Discusses the economic consequences of the loss of trade on the United States. Maintains that the embargo is not injurious to Great Britain and that France is the nation that should be addressed.

1456. Livermore, Edward St. Loe (Mass.). "General Wilkinson," *Annals of Congress.* 10th Cong., 1st Sess. (13 Jan. 1808) pp. 1452-1454. Supports requesting the President to inquire into the conduct of General Wilkinson; maintains that such a request is reasonable and constitutional.

1457. Livermore, Edward St. Loe (Mass.). "Military Courts," *Annals of Congress.* 10th Cong., 1st Sess. (8 Mar., 9 Mar. 1808) pp. 1750-1751; 1758-1760. Opposes the proposed bill. Maintains that the bill is unnecessary and was introduced to address the particular case of General Wilkinson.

1458. Quincy, Josiah (Mass.). "Attack on the Frigate *Chesapeake*," *Annals of Congress.* 10th Cong., 1st Sess. (5 Nov. 1807) pp. 805-807. Supports his resolution requesting an official investigation into the circumstances of the attack on the Chesapeake.

1459. Quincy, Josiah (Mass.). "Boston Memorials," *Annals of Congress.* 10th Cong., 1st Sess. (14 Dec. 1807) pp. 1174-1176. Endorses the Boston petition requesting a modification or repeal of the embargo. Maintains that the petitioners have a right to have their petition heard and referred to committee.

1460. Quincy, Josiah (Mass.). "Defence of Ports and Harbors," *Annals of Congress.* 10th Cong., 1st Sess. (16 Dec. 1807) pp. 1195-1204. Supports allowing the maximum possible appropriation to protect the ports and harbors. Maintains that the sum indicated by the Secretary of War is insufficient and that gunboats alone are inadequate. Discusses the need for defense measures.

1461. Quincy, Josiah (Mass.). "Foreign Relations," *Annals of Congress.* 10th Cong., 1st Sess. (14 Mar. 1808) pp. 1830-1838. Supports his proposed resolution requesting official information on foreign relations with France. Reviews official information pertaining to France that has been given to the

House since the Ninth Congress. Maintains that the House's information is deficient and that the Executive has information that it has not communicated.

1462. Quincy, Josiah (Mass.). "Fortifications and Gunboats," *Annals of Congress.* 10th Cong., 1st Sess. (10 Dec. 1807) pp. 1137-1141. Objects to gunboats as the principle means of defending the harbors. Maintains that gunboats are abhorred by seamen and are inadequate in deep-water harbors. Addresses the importance and necessity of a navy.

1463. Quincy, Josiah (Mass.). "Maryland Contested Election," *Annals of Congress.* 10th Cong., 1st Sess. (16 Nov. 1807) pp. 906-909. Supports the report. Examines the powers of the States and the federal government pertaining to elections. Maintains that a state does not have the right to increase the number of qualifications of office seekers.

1464. Quincy, Josiah (Mass.). "Operation of the Embargo," *Annals of Congress.* 10th Cong., 1st Sess. (11 Apr. 1808) pp. 2070, 2071-2073, 2075-2076. Various remarks support his proposed resolution to investigate the hardships to the fishing industry caused by the embargo. Maintains that the fishing industry is unique, and that although it is unprofitable to the fisherman it is very important to the nation that it be encouraged.

1465. Quincy, Josiah (Mass.). "Suspension of the Embargo," *Annals of Congress.* 10th Cong., 1st Sess. (19 Apr. 1808) pp. 2199-2211. Supports authorizing the President to suspend the embargo. Maintains that the Executive's power should not be restricted by the occurrence of various contingencies, and that when the embargo is suspended it should be totally, not partially, repealed. Reviews the need to repeal the embargo.

1466. Upham, Jabez (Mass.). "Additional Army," *Annals of Congress.* 10th Cong., 1st Sess. (21 Mar. 1808) pp. 1861-1868. Objects to raising an additional army without evidence to demonstrate the need. Maintains that he would support a standing army in times of war. Illustrates the previous inconsistencies of those recommending war measures. Discusses the necessity and propriety of a request for more information from the President.

1467. Upham, Jabez (Mass.). "General Wilkinson," *Annals of Congress.* 10th Cong., 1st Sess. (12 Jan. 1808) pp. 1422-1424. Opposes the House inquiring into the misconduct of General Wilkinson; maintains that the House does not have that authority and that it would encroach upon the rights of the Judiciary.

1468. Varnum, Joseph B. (Mass.). "The Militia," *Annals of Congress.* 10th Cong., 1st Sess. (19 Jan. 1808) pp. 1484-1486. Opposes the bill to class the militia as unnecessary, disastrous, and conflicting with systems already established by various state constitutions. Describes the Massachusetts militia.

1469. "An Act for Erecting a Lighthouse on the South Point of the Island of Sapelo, and for Placing Buoys and Beacons in the Shoals of the Inlet Leading to the Town of Darien, and near the Entrance of Ipswich Harbor, near Plymouth Harbor, before the Harbor of Nantucket, and on the Island of Tuckanuck, and or near the Entrance of Connecticut River, and near the Entrance of Great Egg Harbor River," *Statutes at Large*, Vol. II (17 Mar. 1808) p. 470. Also printed in the *Annals of Congress* (10th Cong., 1st Sess.) Appendix, p. 2843.

1470. "An Act to Change the Name of the District of Biddleford and Pepperelborough, in Massachusetts, to That of Saco," *Statutes at Large*, Vol. II (15 Dec. 1807) p. 451. Also printed in the *Annals of Congress* (10th Cong., 1st Sess.) Appendix, p. 2814.

1471. "An Act to Make Plymouth, in North Carolina, a Port of Entry; to Change the Name of the District of Nanjemoy to That of St. Mary's, and to Make Augusta, in the District of Maine, a Port of Delivery," *Statutes at Large*, Vol. II (25 Apr. 1808) p. 497. Also printed in the *Annals of Congress* (10th Cong., 1st Sess.) Appendix, pp. 2867-2868.

1472. "Embargo," *American State Papers: Commerce and Navigation*, Vol. I (Doc. 129) p. 727. (ASP 014). Report against the petition of sundry inhabitants of Boston to export fish that would perish under the restrictions of the embargo.

10TH CONGRESS, 2ND SESSION

1473. "Collectorship of Boston," *Annals of Congress.* 10th Cong., 2nd Sess. (25 Jan. 1809) pp. 1173-1183. Debate over Mr. Quincy's (Mass.) charge and subsequent motion maintaining that the President abused his power to fill public offices by not accepting the resignation of Benjamin Lincoln in order to hold the post of collectorship of the port of Boston and Charlestown in reserve for Henry Dearborn. Quincy was the only yea vote.

1474. "Massachusetts Memorial," *Annals of Congress.* 10th Cong., 2nd Sess. (27 Feb. 1809) pp. 1538-1539. Debate on the motion to print the memorial, which criticizes the acts of the government, particularly the embargo.

1475. "Presidential Election," *Annals of Congress.* 10th Cong., 2nd Sess. (31 Jan., 2 Feb., 6 Feb. 1809) pp. 1241-1242; 1302-1303; 1376-1377. Debate on the reception of several memorials from Massachusetts objecting to the method of the late election of the electors of President and Vice President.

1476. "Remonstrance of Massachusetts," *Annals of Congress.* 10th Cong., 2nd Sess. (27 Feb. 1809) pp. 444-450. Presentation and text of the memorial from Massachusetts advocating a repeal of the embargo laws. Reviews complaints; dismisses alternative measures, advocates negotiation with Britain. Same as Com.nav.142 (10-2) ASP 014 (entry **1499**).

1477. Bacon, Ezekiel (Mass.). "Collectorship of Boston," *Annals of Congress.* 10th Cong., 2nd Sess. (25 Jan. 1809) pp. 1178-1181. Opposes Mr. Quincy's (Mass.) resolution concerning the question over filling the position of Collector of Boston. Maintains that the President's conduct was proper.

1478. Bacon, Ezekiel (Mass.). "Defensive Maritime War," *Annals of Congress.* 10th Cong., 2nd Sess. (27 Jan. 1809) pp. 1189-1191. Introduces and supports his resolution to authorize defensive resistance against aggressions.

1479. Bacon, Ezekiel (Mass.). "Extra Session," *Annals of Congress.* 10th Cong., 2nd Sess. (20 Jan. 1809) pp. 1132-1138. Accuses Rep. Quincy (Mass.) of agitating the people and provoking the dissolution of the Union. Discusses the embargo and its historical use as a precautionary measure and means of coercion. Agrees that it should be limited to a finite period and that our national defenses should be improved.

1480. Bacon, Ezekiel (Mass.). "Foreign Relations," *Annals of Congress.* 10th Cong., 2nd Sess. (29 Nov. 1808) pp. 557-571. Responds point by point to Mr. Quincy's (Mass.) remarks; defends the report of the select committee. Maintains that Mr. Quincy has exaggerated the inequality of the measure and the destitute circumstances of the people.

1481. Bacon, Ezekiel (Mass.). "Preparation for War," *Annals of Congress.* 10th Cong., 2nd Sess. (1 Feb. 1809) pp. 1270-1277. Opposes the resolution to repeal the embargo in June. Maintains that there is no benefit to be gained by waiting, and that announcing the declaration of war months in advance is not good strategy. Rather than authorize general reprisals, advocates defensive resistance and restitution only when attacked first.

1482. Cook, Orchard (Mass.). "Preparation for War," *Annals of Congress.* 10th Cong., 2nd Sess. (31 Jan. 1809) pp. 1248-1251. Opposes the proposed date of the repeal of the embargo. Proposes an alternative plan that substitutes defensive arming and discriminatory duties.

1483. Livermore, Edward St. Loe (Mass.). "Enforcing the Embargo," *Annals of Congress.* 10th Cong., 2nd Sess. (5 Jan. 1809) pp. 1002-1019. Opposes the bill as destroying commerce, disregarding private rights and liberties, and violating the Constitution. Provides a detailed, sectional analysis of the bill; discusses the constitutionality, precedents, and consequences.

1484. Lloyd, James (Mass.). "Additional Duties," *Annals of Congress.* 10th Cong., 2nd Sess. (24 Feb. 1809) pp. 438-443. Opposes additional duties on imported goods. Cites authorities to demonstrate that even if war occurred, additional duties are unnecessary and would harm commerce and diminish revenue.

1485. Lloyd, James (Mass.). "The Embargo," *Annals of Congress.* 10th Cong., 2nd Sess. (21 Nov., 25 Nov. 1808) pp. 29-35; 131-138. Supports repealing the embargo. Addresses its effect upon security to navigation, upon France and Great Britain, and upon the United States. Maintains that the embargo has only been harmful to America. Second speech addresses opponents' arguments and the effect of the embargo on Great Britain and the states, particularly Massachusetts.

1486. Lloyd, James (Mass.). "Enforcement of the Embargo," *Annals of Congress.* 10th Cong., 2nd Sess. (19 Dec. 1808) pp. 249-256. Opposes further enforcing the embargo. Objects to various provisions; demonstrates their effects. Maintains that Congress does not have the power to enact these regulations and prohibitions that violate the principles of the Constitution.

1487. Lloyd, James (Mass.). "Non-Intercourse," *Annals of Congress.* 10th Cong., 2nd Sess. (21 Feb. 1809) pp. 414-423. Opposes the bill that would prohibit trade between the United States and Great Britain and France. Maintains that it would be a declaration of war for which the country is not prepared. Advocates war against France, as the first aggressor, which would in turn cause Britain to be more accommodating.

1488. Pickering, Timothy (Mass.). "The Embargo," *Annals of Congress.* 10th Cong., 2nd Sess. (30 Nov. 1808) pp. 175-194. Supports repealing the embargo; advocates negotiation. Considers the traditions of impressing seamen and restricting trade of neutrals in time of war. Documents the risk to trade since the French decrees and British Orders in Council and projects the risk if the embargo is lifted. Reviews the circumstances leading to the embargo; maintains that the British Orders in Council were not the cause.

1489. Pickering, Timothy (Mass.). "Enforcement of the Embargo," *Annals of Congress.* 10th Cong., 2nd Sess. (21 Dec. 1808) pp. 276-282. Opposes further enforcing the embargo. Reviews the causes of the embargo; maintains that it should never have been imposed and only complies with the wishes of France.

1490. Quincy, Josiah (Mass.). "Additional Military Force," *Annals of Congress.* 10th Cong., 2nd Sess. (30 Dec. 1808) pp. 960-963. Maintains that the House surrendered its control over commerce to the Executive when the embargo law was passed.

1491. Quincy, Josiah (Mass.). "Collectorship of Boston," *Annals of Congress.* 10th Cong., 2nd Sess. (25 Jan. 1809) pp. 1173-1175, 1181-1182. Introduces and defends a resolution to inquire into the President's delay in accepting General Lincoln's resignation. Charges the President with abusing his power to fill public offices by holding the position for Henry Dearborn.

1492. Quincy, Josiah (Mass.). "Extra Session," *Annals of Congress.* 10th Cong., 2nd Sess. (19 Jan., 20 Jan. 1809) pp. 1105-1117; 1138-1145, 1164-1166. Opposes the bill to continue commercial restrictions until May. Examines the difference between the original reasons given for the adoption of the embargo and the reasons given for its continuance. Maintains that it was the intention of the administration to deceive, and that the embargo was intended as a permanent coercive measure and as the sole support of maritime rights. Defends against opponents' criticism.

1493. Quincy, Josiah (Mass.). "Foreign Relations," *Annals of Congress.* 10th Cong., 2nd Sess. (28 Nov., 7 Dec. 1808) pp. 534-547; 754-767. Opposes the report of the Committee of Foreign Relations recommending continuance of the embargo laws. Discusses the concept of submission, the embargo's effect on the people of New England, its constitutionality and public sentiment. Examines the assertions of the report; addresses opponents' arguments and reactions, including Mr. Bacon's (Mass.). Maintains that the embargo is directly subservient to the edicts of Great Britain and France, unconstitutional, opposes Nature, fails as a means of coercion, and operates unequally.

1494. Story, Joseph (Mass.). "Foreign Relations," *Annals of Congress.* 10th Cong., 2nd Sess. (17 Jan. 1809) pp. 1090-1092. Denounces Mr. Canning's letter claiming that the offer to repeal the embargo was not authorized.

1495. Taggart, Samuel (Mass.). "Foreign Relations," *Annals of Congress.* 10th Cong., 2nd Sess. (17 Dec. 1808) pp. 865-886. Opposes the embargo and the proposed measures to further restrict trade with Great Britain and France. Examines the embargo in respect to its constitutionality and its ability to influence the intended nations. Maintains that it has not preserved ships, seamen, or property, and that it has failed as a means of coercion. Discusses the effect of the embargo upon the country.

1496. Upham, Jabez (Mass.). "Foreign Relations," *Annals of Congress.* 10th Cong., 2nd Sess. (15 Dec. 1808) pp. 857-861. Declares that the embargo was intended as a permanent measure by which to destroy the commerce. Maintains that the embargo cannot be enforced, particularly among the northern states, and that there is no difference between it and submission.

1497. "Instructions of Massachusetts to Her Delegation in Congress to Procure a Repeal of the Embargo Laws," *American State Papers: Commerce and Navigation,* Vol. I (Doc. 131) pp. 728-729. (ASP 014). Report and resolutions request the repeal of the embargo; discuss the effects of the embargo and suggest alternative measures.

1498. "Protection to Manufactures," *American State Papers: Finance,* Vol. II (Doc. 285) p. 306. (ASP 010). Petition from twine and line manufacturers of Massachusetts requests an increase of duties on those articles.

1499. "Remonstrance of Massachusetts against the Embargo Laws," *American State Papers: Commerce and Navigation,* Vol. I (Doc. 142) pp. 776-778. (ASP 014). Memorial advocates a repeal of the embargo laws. Reviews complaints; dismisses alternative measures of non-intercourse and arming merchantmen; contends that accommodation with France would be impossible, but that negotiations with Britain could restore harmony. Also printed in the *Annals of Congress* (10th Cong., 2nd Sess.) pp. 444-450 (entry **1476**).

11TH CONGRESS, 1ST SESSION

1500. "Contested Election," *Annals of Congress.* 11th Cong., 1st Sess. (8 June, 12 June, 13 June, 21 June, 24 June, 28 June 1809) pp. 238-239; 266-267; 268; 361-363; 417-418; 461-462. Debates over the contested election between William Baylies and Charles Turner, Jr. Includes a brief description of the election, and portions of the report of the committee deciding against Baylies. See Misc. 266 (11-1) ASP 038 (entry **1504**) for complete report and supporting documents by the two parties.

1501. Cutts, Richard (Mass.). "Naval Establishment," *Annals of Congress.* 11th Cong., 1st Sess. (22 June 1809) pp. 387-389. Defends gunboats.

1502. Livermore, Edward St. Loe (Mass.). "Non-Intercourse," *Annals of Congress.* 11th Cong., 1st Sess. (21 June, 26 June 1809) pp. 373-376; 431-434. Remarks on a resolution regarding the non-intercourse act. Maintains that although the act no longer applies to Great Britain since she has withdrawn the Orders in Council, it should still operate against France. Concerned about jeopardizing negotiations with Great Britain.

1503. "Contested Election of William Baylies, a Representative from Massachusetts," *American State Papers: Miscellaneous*, Vol. II (Doc. 264) p. 1. (ASP 038). Briefly describes the circumstances of the election; decision postponed to allow Baylies to prepare his case.

1504. "Contested Election of William Baylies, a Representative from Massachusetts," *American State Papers: Miscellaneous*, Vol. II (Doc. 266) pp. 7-11. (ASP 038). Report of the committee against William Baylies and for Charles Turner, Jr.; includes supporting documents by the two parties.

11TH CONGRESS, 2ND SESSION

1505. "Yazoo Land Claims," *Annals of Congress.* 11th Cong., 2nd Sess. (14 Dec. 1809) pp. 729-738. Debate on the memorial of the Directors of the New England Land Company praying that Congress speedily examine and adjust their claim. Includes remarks by Ezekiel Bacon (Mass.), Samuel W. Dana (Conn.), Edward St. Loe Livermore (Mass.), and Timothy Pitkin (Conn.).

1506. Bacon, Ezekiel (Mass.). "Detachment of Militia," *Annals of Congress.* 11th Cong., 2nd Sess. (10 Mar. 1810) pp. 1502-1503, 1514-1517. Supports allowing a volunteer detachment of militia to be ordered outside the jurisdiction of the United States if they have previously agreed to that stipulation.

1507. Cutts, Richard (Mass.). "American Navigation Act," *Annals of Congress.* 11th Cong., 2nd Sess. (19 Jan. 1810) pp. 1231-1234. Supports the proposed act and its commercial restrictions; maintains that, unlike the non-intercourse act which was evaded and partial, this act could operate effectually.

1508. Livermore, Edward St. Loe (Mass.). "American Navigation Act," *Annals of Congress.* 11th Cong., 2nd Sess. (10 Jan. 1810) pp. 1190-1193. Opposes the sections of the bill that would further regulate commerce; supports the part that repeals the non-intercourse act.

1509. Livermore, Edward St. Loe (Mass.). "Commercial Intercourse," *Annals of Congress.* 11th Cong., 2nd Sess. (18 Apr. 1810) pp. 1903-1904, 1917-1926. Opposes the bill as a continuance of the non-intercourse act and embargo policy; maintains that it is impolitic, unjust, and encourages smuggling. Clarifies and demonstrates that the non-intercourse act has not been in force respecting Great Britain since the act expired in June.

1510. Livermore, Edward St. Loe (Mass.). "Conduct of the British Minister," *Annals of Congress.* 11th Cong., 2nd Sess. (27 Dec. 1809, 2 Jan. 1810) pp. 909-911; 1069-1088. Remarks and speech oppose the resolution concerning the conduct of the Executive. Maintains that the President had a constitutional right to exercise his powers, and that the resolution is calculated to create dissension. Analyzes the correspondence as to the alleged offensive remarks, reviews the events. Discusses the implications of passing the resolution.

1511. Livermore, Edward St. Loe (Mass.). "Relations with Spain," *Annals of Congress.* 11th Cong., 2nd Sess. (28 Feb. 1810) pp. 1466-1468. Introduces and supports his resolution requesting the President to provide information concerning relations with Spain.

1512. Pickman, Benjamin, Jr. (Mass.). "American Navigation Act," *Annals of Congress.* 11th Cong., 2nd Sess. (8 Jan., 23 Jan. 1810) pp. 1163-1164; 1284-1288. Various remarks support excluding armed ships of Great Britain and France from United States waters, but not the importation of their goods. Replies to opponents' arguments, briefly reviews actions of prior restrictive laws, and discusses the consequences of the proposed act.

1513. Quincy, Josiah (Mass.). "Conduct of the British Minister," *Annals of Congress.* 11th Cong., 2nd Sess. (28 Dec. 1809) pp. 942-958. Opposes the resolution that states that the insinuations of Francis Jackson about the President's conduct were insolent and indecorous. Provides a minute analysis of all parts of the correspondence in which the insulting idea was said to be asserted. Maintains that the charge has no basis.

1514. Upham, Jabez (Mass.). "Conduct of the British Minister," *Annals of Congress.* 11th Cong., 2nd Sess. (1 Jan. 1810) pp. 1032-1049. Opposes the resolution approving the conduct of the President respecting the British minister, Francis Jackson. Demonstrates that there is no evidence that Mr.

Jackson made the alleged insult. Maintains that passing the resolution would be inexpedient and a conditional declaration of war with Great Britain.

1515. Wheaton, Laban (Mass.). "American Navigation Act," *Annals of Congress.* 11th Cong., 2nd Sess. (29 Jan. 1810) pp. 1333-1341. Opposes the bill to further regulate commerce with Great Britain and France. Compares it to the non-importation, embargo, and non-intercourse laws. Advocates peace as the most expedient course. Addresses opponents' arguments and the political characteristics of the bill.

1516. Wheaton, Laban (Mass.). "Conduct of the British Minister," *Annals of Congress.* 11th Cong., 2nd Sess. (20 Dec. 1809) pp. 789-795. Opposes the resolution to express approval of the presidential actions concerning the British minister, Mr. Jackson. Maintains that he cannot find evidence of the alleged insult, and that even if he had, he could not approve the subsequent actions. Briefly reviews the correspondence and the consequences of the President's actions; explores the possibility of war.

1517. "An Act to Allow the Benefit of Drawback on Merchandise Transported by Land Conveyance from Newport to Boston, and from Boston to Newport, in Like Manner as if the Same Were Transported Coastwise," *Statutes at Large*, Vol. II (25 Apr. 1810) p. 578. Also printed in the *Annals of Congress* (11th Cong., 2nd Sess.) Appendix, pp. 2541-2542.

1518. "An Act to Erect a Lighthouse at the Entrance of Scituate Harbor, a Stone Column on a Spit of Sand at the Entrance into Boston Harbor, and a Beacon on Beach Point near Plymouth Harbor in the State of Massachusetts; a Light at the Entrance of Bayou St. John into Lake Ponchartrain, and Two Lights on Lake Erie, and for Beacons and Buoys near the Entrance of Beverly Harbor," *Statutes at Large*, Vol. II (1 May 1810) pp. 611-612. Also printed in the *Annals of Congress* (11th Cong., 2nd Sess.) Appendix, pp. 2589-2590.

1519. "Armory and Arsenal at Springfield," *American State Papers: Military Affairs*, Vol. I (Doc. 94) pp. 255-256. (ASP 016). Report certifies that the armory is well conducted and the muskets manufactured within the past year are of good quality.

1520. "Claims for Services and Expenses in Assisting to Enforce the Embargo Laws in Massachusetts, in 1809," *American State Papers: Claims*, (Doc. 213) pp. 382-383. (ASP 036). Committee of Claims reports to grant the petition of Charles Bean. Describes the circumstances of the case.

11ᵀᴴ CONGRESS, 3ᴿᴰ SESSION

1521. "Middlesex Canal," *Annals of Congress.* 11th Cong., 3rd Sess. (15 Jan. 1811) pp. 551-555. Memorial from the proprietors of the Middlesex Canal requesting government assistance is presented. Describes the canal, its history and potential benefits. Memorial also printed in Misc. 285 (11-3) ASP 038 (entry **1534**).

1522. Bigelow, Abijah (Mass.). "Commercial Intercourse," *Annals of Congress.* 11th Cong., 3rd Sess. (26 Feb. 1811) pp. 1057-1061. Supports repealing the commercial restrictions of May 1810 as being impolitic and unjust. Maintains that as that law was neither a contract nor a treaty, the nation is under no obligation to France.

1523. Lloyd, James (Mass.). "Bank of the United States," *Annals of Congress.* 11th Cong., 3rd Sess. (12 Feb. 1811) pp. 155-172. Supports renewing the charter of the bank. Maintains that the bank has been beneficial, expedient and wisely managed. Addresses the constitutional objection. Discusses the injurious effects of not renewing the charter and presents testimony from two Philadelphia delegations in support of his conclusions.

1524. Pickering, Timothy (Mass.). "Bank of the United States," *Annals of Congress.* 11th Cong., 3rd Sess. (19 Feb. 1811) pp. 308-316. Supports renewing the charter of the United States Bank. Explains why he does not feel bound to the instructions of his constituents on this issue. Demonstrates why Congress has the constitutional authority to renew the charter. Addresses opponents' arguments and the consequences of the dissolution of the bank.

1525. Pickering, Timothy (Mass.). "Question of Order," *Annals of Congress.* 11th Cong., 3rd Sess. (2 Jan. 1811) pp. 75-78. Defends his disclosure of some previously confidential documents concerning the title to West Florida.

1526. Pickman, Benjamin, Jr. (Mass.). "Bank of the United States," *Annals of Congress.* 11th Cong., 3rd Sess. (19 Jan. 1811) pp. 663-668. Supports renewing the charter of the United States Bank. Maintains that its establishment was constitutional and that its actions do not interfere with states' rights. Discusses the benefits of a United States Bank over State banks and the problems caused by circulating paper exceeding specie.

1527. Quincy, Josiah (Mass.). "Amendment to the Constitution," *Annals of Congress.* 11th Cong., 3rd Sess. (30 Jan. 1811) pp. 843-852. Supports limiting the power to distribute offices by not allowing members of either House, or their close relatives, to accept a civil office during the time of their elected positions. Discusses "pecuniary influence" and executive influence, the constitutional authority, and the necessity of the amendment.

1528. Quincy, Josiah (Mass.). "Commercial Intercourse," *Annals of Congress.* 11th Cong., 3rd Sess. (25 Feb. 1811) pp. 1011-1025. Opposes the proposed amendments as continuing and enforcing the non-intercourse law. Discusses the injurious, non-coercive, and non-protective nature of a restrictive system. Maintains the non-intercourse system should be abandoned unless a national obligation exists and demonstrates that no such obligation exists.

1529. Quincy, Josiah (Mass.). "Territory of Orleans," *Annals of Congress.* 11th Cong., 3rd Sess. (14 Jan. 1811) pp. 524-525, 527-542. Opposes the bill to admit the Territory of Orleans. Maintains that passage of the bill is a violation of the Constitution that will result in the dissolution of the Union. Demonstrates that the Constitution intended to only admit new states that were created from within the original limits of the U.S., not by territorial annexations from without. Addresses opponents' arguments, the treaty-making power, and the moral and political consequences of passing the bill.

1530. Wheaton, Laban (Mass.). "Commercial Intercourse," *Annals of Congress.* 11th Cong., 3rd Sess. (2 Feb. 1811) pp. 887-889. Supports repealing the law restricting intercourse; discusses obligations to France.

1531. Wheaton, Laban (Mass.). "Territory of Orleans," *Annals of Congress.* 11th Cong., 3rd Sess. (4 Jan. 1811) pp. 493-495. Opposes admitting the Territory of Orleans into the Union as a state as unconstitutional and impolitic.

1532. "An Act to Erect a Lighthouse on Boon Island in the State of Massachusetts, to Place Buoys off Cape Fear River, and to Erect a Beacon at New Inlet, in the State of North Carolina, and to Place Buoys at the Entrance of the Harbor of Edgartown, and to Erect a Column of Stone on Cape Elizabeth, and to Complete the Beacons and Buoys at the Entrance of Beverly Harbor, in the State of Massachusetts," *Statutes at Large*, Vol. II (2 Mar. 1811) p. 659. Also printed in the *Annals of Congress* (11th Cong., 3rd Sess.) Appendix, p. 1347.

1533. "Application for a Revision of the Patent Laws," *American State Papers: Miscellaneous*, Vol. II (Doc. 291) pp. 149-151. (ASP 038). Memorial from the Massachusetts Association for the Encouragement of Useful Inventions deplores the patent laws as inadequate and insufficient to protect the inventor. Lists detailed suggestions for improvements.

1534. "Middlesex Canal," *American State Papers: Miscellaneous*, Vol. II (Doc. 285) pp. 142-144. (ASP 038). Also printed in the *Annals of Congress*, "Middlesex Canal," (11th Cong., 3rd Sess.) pp. 551-555 (entry **1521**). See entry **1521** for abstract.

1535. "Protection to Manufactures," *American State Papers: Finance*, Vol. II (Doc. 341) p. 471. (ASP 010). Petition from Charlestown requests protection for manufacturers of so-called morocco leather.

12TH CONGRESS, 1ST SESSION

1536. "Memorial of Boston Merchants," *Annals of Congress.* 12th Cong., 1st Sess. (6 May 1812) pp. 228-235. Debate on the memorial from Boston merchants petitioning to withdraw their property from Great Britain. Samuel Smith (Md.) offers objections, maintaining that the merchants should have been aware of the situation and that the U.S. has obligations to France. James Lloyd (Mass.) defends the petition, maintaining that these merchants' property was trapped by the ex post facto operation of the non-importation act.

1537. Bacon, Ezekiel (Mass.). "Louisiana Convention," *Annals of Congress.* 12th Cong., 1st Sess. (6 Apr. 1812) pp. 1252-1254. Remarks on the report of the committee to suspend the payment of certain bills until the French government provides the necessary documentation.

1538. Bacon, Ezekiel (Mass.). "War Taxes," *Annals of Congress.* 12th Cong., 1st Sess. (25 Feb. 1812) pp. 1093-1105. Reviews the financial considerations behind the proposed increased duties. Discusses the prospects of obtaining and paying loans to meet ordinary and extraordinary expenses. Reviews Britain's financial strengths. Supports the necessity of providing additional revenue; details objections to selected duties.

1539. Bigelow, Abijah (Mass.). "Additional Duties," *Annals of Congress.* 12th Cong., 1st Sess. (22 June 1812) pp. 1517-1519. Opposes the proposed additional duties on imported articles as unjust, unequal, and inadequate.

1540. Lloyd, James (Mass.). "Increase of the Navy," *Annals of Congress.* 12th Cong., 1st Sess. (27 Feb. 1812) pp. 131-147. Advocates increasing the navy by thirty new frigates. Maintains that if one is to enter into war, it is essential to have an efficient naval force. Compares expenses of measures adopted to those of a maritime force. Discusses how commerce has been abandoned. Reviews relations with France and Great Britain, concluding that France should be the first object of attack. Presents a memorial concerning the brig *Catharine*.

1541. Lloyd, James (Mass.). "Memorial of Boston Merchants," *Annals of Congress.* 12th Cong., 1st Sess. (6 May 1812) pp. 231-235. Reviews origin of the memorial and defends against objections. Maintains that the merchants have a just and equitable claim to suspend restrictions and that granting the petition would be expedient and in the best interests of the country.

1542. Quincy, Josiah (Mass.). "Naval Establishment," *Annals of Congress.* 12th Cong., 1st Sess. (25 Jan. 1812) pp. 949-968. Supports the protection of our maritime rights by maritime means. Demonstrates the relationship between the naval force and the safety and prosperity of the Union. Maintains that it is the duty of every nation to protect its essential interests. Discusses the geographic variations of the commercial interests, the financial and physical capabilities to provide a maritime defense, and the impact on relations with Great Britain.

1543. Quincy, Josiah (Mass.). "Rules and Orders," *Annals of Congress.* 12th Cong., 1st Sess. (23 Dec. 1811) pp. 572-576. Supports each legislative member's right to speak at least once upon the question. Maintains that the right of deliberation is inherent and a guaranteed civil liberty. Addresses opponents' arguments.

1544. Quincy, Josiah (Mass.). "Supplemental Journal - Embargo Bill," *Annals of Congress.* 12th Cong., 1st Sess. (3 Apr. 1812) pp. 1601-1606. Strongly opposes the proposed embargo; maintains that it is not preparation for war, but subterfuge from declaring war. Defends his advance release of information that an embargo would be proposed the following day.

1545. Taggart, Samuel (Mass.). "Supplemental Journal - Declaration of War," *Annals of Congress.* 12th Cong., 1st Sess. (4 June 1812) pp. 1638-1679. Lengthy speech opposes declaring war against Great Britain. Maintains that war would be unnecessary and contrary to the interests of the country, and that the country has no right to invade a country (Canada) that has done them no wrong. Discusses the principle causes of the war, the situation of the country, the objects to be obtained, the probability of success in obtaining those objects, and probable consequences. Reviews the history of attempts at negotiations. Addresses the military and financial preparedness of the country.

1546. Widgery, William (Mass.). "Additional Military Force," *Annals of Congress.* 12th Cong., 1st Sess. (31 Dec. 1811, 4 Jan. 1812) pp. 602-603; 658-659. Supports the militia and the army; defends the Nation's ability to war against Great Britain.

1547. Widgery, William (Mass.). "Naval Establishment," *Annals of Congress.* 12th Cong., 1st Sess. (27 Jan. 1812) pp. 995-999. Supports increasing the size of the navy; discusses the role of the navy in defense and the value of commerce to the country.

1548. Widgery, William (Mass.). "War Taxes," *Annals of Congress.* 12th Cong., 1st Sess. (3 Mar. 1812) pp. 1142-1144. Supports amending the proposed duties on imports, tonnage, salt and whiskey.

1549. "An Act to Alter the Time of Holding One of the Terms of the District Court in the District of Maine," *Statutes at Large*, Vol. II (12 Nov. 1811) p. 667. Also printed in the *Annals of Congress* (12th Cong., 1st Sess.) Appendix, p. 2225.

1550. "Opposition of Massachusetts to a War," *American State Papers: Miscellaneous*, Vol. II (Doc. 325) pp. 186-187. (ASP 038). Resolution and memorial oppose a war as impolitic, unnecessary, and ruinous.

12TH CONGRESS, 2ND SESSION

1551. "Refusal to Furnish Militia," *Annals of Congress.* 12th Cong., 2nd Sess. (6 Nov. 1812) Appendix, pp. 1295-1310. Correspondence between the Dept. of War and the Governors of Massachusetts and Connecticut. Massachusetts objects to the call for militia as unconstitutional; also maintains that the designated places for the detached militia already contain more militia than the portion to be assigned. Includes decision of the Justices of the Supreme Judicial Court of Massachusetts. Same as Mil.aff.115 (12-2) ASP 016 (entry **1570**).

1552. Bacon, Ezekiel (Mass.). "Regulation of Seamen," *Annals of Congress.* 12th Cong., 2nd Sess. (11 Feb. 1813) pp. 1023-1026. Supports excluding foreign seamen from American service. Maintains that the temporary shortage of seamen will raise wages, and that the proposal will provide a nursery of American seamen that are trained and always available for service.

1553. Bigelow, Abijah (Mass.). "Loan Bill," *Annals of Congress.* 12th Cong., 2nd Sess. (23 Jan. 1813) pp. 873-878. Opposes a loan to pay for the recently approved additional military forces. Maintains that funds should be established for paying the interest and discharging the principal, or else money will not be raised and revolution will follow. Defends his position by references to the Revolutionary War.

1554. Brigham, Elijah (Mass.). "Additional Military Force," *Annals of Congress.* 12th Cong., 2nd Sess. (4 Jan. 1813) pp. 512-515. Opposes the proposed additional troops; maintains that the war is wrong and unjustifiable, and is really a war of conquest to take possession of Canada and other British provinces in North America. Favors negotiation.

1555. Brigham, Elijah (Mass.). "Merchants' Bonds," *Annals of Congress.* 12th Cong., 2nd Sess. (14 Dec. 1812) pp. 379-381. Supports the merchants' rights to their property; maintains that they imported their goods with the promise that the non-importation law would no longer operate when the Orders in Council were revoked.

1556. Ely, William (Mass.). "Arming the Militia," *Annals of Congress.* 12th Cong., 2nd Sess. (28 Jan. 1813) pp. 926-928. Discusses the state of arms manufacture and the inability to produce additional arms of adequate quality.

1557. Quincy, Josiah (Mass.). "Additional Military Force," *Annals of Congress.* 12th Cong., 2nd Sess. (5 Jan. 1813) pp. 540-570. Lengthy speech opposes increasing the military by 20,000 men to invade Canada. Reviews and justifies his position that the invasion of Canada is intended to continue the war; maintains that the invasion will not result in an early and honorable peace, and that it is a means of advancing the ambitions of the members of the Cabinet.

1558. Quincy, Josiah (Mass.). "Arming the Militia," *Annals of Congress.* 12th Cong., 2nd Sess. (30 Jan. 1813) pp. 943-945. Opposes the proposed age classification system.

1559. Quincy, Josiah (Mass.). "Merchants' Bonds," *Annals of Congress.* 12th Cong., 2nd Sess. (14 Dec. 1812) pp. 382-393. Demonstrates that the Secretary of the Treasury does not have complete authority over fines, forfeitures, and penalties. Maintains that the restrictive system is meant to cause suffering to

Great Britain, not our own citizens. Questions the authority of Congress to pass the restrictive laws. Maintains that the merchants are legally free of guilt.

1560. Quincy, Josiah (Mass.). "Pay of the Army," *Annals of Congress.* 12th Cong., 2nd Sess. (21 Nov. 1812) pp. 167-173. Opposes the section of the bill concerning the enlistment of minors. Maintains that the bill attempts to seduce minors from the services of their guardians, masters, and parents, which is absurd, unequal and immoral. Discusses how the bill would unequally affect the North; maintains that the lack of manpower is due to lack of support of the war.

1561. Quincy, Josiah (Mass.). "Regulation of Seamen," *Annals of Congress.* 12th Cong., 2nd Sess. (12 Feb. 1813) pp. 1039-1046. Opposes the bill to exclude foreign seamen from American service with the condition that foreign governments reciprocate. Discusses the right of expatriation. Maintains that the provisions are unnatural and illusive and designed to continue the war.

1562. Richardson, William M. (Mass.). "Merchants' Bonds," *Annals of Congress.* 12th Cong., 2nd Sess. (7 Dec. 1812) pp. 286-298. Objects to enforcing payment of the bonds. Maintains that the merchants have suffered under the restrictive system. Addresses supporting arguments for the bill and its various modifications; reviews the history of events leading to legislation.

1563. Wheaton, Laban (Mass.). "Additional Military Force," *Annals of Congress.* 12th Cong., 2nd Sess. (8 Jan. 1813) pp. 649-659. Objects to raising the additional troops to be used to invade Canada. Discusses the constitutional authority of Congress to pass the act, the profit and costs of invasion, and the probability of coercing Britain into compliance. Maintains that invasion is morally unjustifiable and inexpedient.

1564. Wheaton, Laban (Mass.). "Pay of the Army," *Annals of Congress.* 12th Cong., 2nd Sess. (21 Nov. 1812) pp. 177-178. Objects to increasing the pay; also objects to releasing enlisting minors from their previous civil contracts.

1565. Widgery, William (Mass.). "Additional Military Force," *Annals of Congress.* 12th Cong., 2nd Sess. (6 Jan. 1813) pp. 582-588. Supports the additional twenty thousand troops. Addresses opponents' arguments, demonstrating that the war is justifiable. Maintains that the intent of the British aggressions was to destroy American commerce.

1566. Widgery, William (Mass.). "Increase of the Navy," *Annals of Congress.* 12th Cong., 2nd Sess. (17 Dec. 1812) pp. 417-419. Advocates building the smaller frigates and sloops of war rather than the larger seventy-fours.

1567. Widgery, William (Mass.). "Merchants' Bonds," *Annals of Congress.* 12th Cong., 2nd Sess. (8 Dec. 1812) pp. 310-314. Supports the merchants; maintains that as the declaration of war invalidated the non-importation act the goods are the property of the merchants, not of the government.

1568. "An Act Altering the Time for Holding the District Court in the District of Maine," *Statutes at Large*, Vol. II (3 Mar. 1813) p. 829. Also printed in the *Annals of Congress* (12th Cong., 2nd Sess.) Appendix, p. 1362.

1569. "An Act to Alter the Times of Holding the District Court in the Respective Districts of New York and Massachusetts," *Statutes at Large*, Vol. II (3 Mar. 1813) p. 815. Also printed in the *Annals of Congress* (12th Cong., 2nd Sess.) Appendix, p. 1345.

1570. "Refusal of the Governors of Massachusetts and Connecticut to Furnish Their Quotas of Militia," *American State Papers: Military Affairs*, Vol. I (Doc. 115) pp. 321-326. (ASP 016). First page numbered as 319. Also printed in the *Annals of Congress*, "Refusal to Furnish Militia," (12th Cong., 2nd Sess.) Appendix, pp. 1295-1310 (entry **1551**). See entry **1551** for abstract.

13TH CONGRESS, 1ST SESSION

1571. "Remonstrance of Massachusetts," *Annals of Congress*. 13th Cong., 1st Sess. (29 June 1813) pp. 333-351. Presentation and debate of the Massachusetts memorial against the war and the formation of new states from outside the original boundaries. Includes reprint of memorial and protest of the minority (Misc.346 (13-1) ASP 038 (entry **1575**)). Comments by Jonathan Fisk (N.Y.), Timothy Pickering (Mass.), Elijah Brigham (Mass.), and William Baylies (Mass.). The memorial was ordered to be printed.

1572. "Remonstrance of Massachusetts," *Annals of Congress*. 13th Cong., 1st Sess. (8 July 1813) pp. 403-405. The memorial was taken up to discuss further action.

1573. Brigham, Elijah (Mass.). "The Ways and Means," *Annals of Congress*. 13th Cong., 1st Sess. (8 July 1813) pp. 405-409. Opposes the proposed direct tax because it will be used to continue an unpopular and unnecessary war.

1574. Reed, John (Mass.). "The Ways and Means," *Annals of Congress*. 13th Cong., 1st Sess. (16 July 1813) pp. 449-453. Supports allowing drawbacks on imported salt that is used in exported dried fish and meat. Maintains that it is more equitable and beneficial to the nation. Reviews precedents.

1575. "Remonstrance of the Legislature of Massachusetts against the War, and the Formation of the New States from Lands Not within the Original Limits of the United States, and the Protest of the Minority of Said Legislature," *American State Papers: Miscellaneous*, Vol. II (Doc. 346) pp. 210-215. (ASP 038). Memorial opposes the war as improper, impolitic, and unjust; gives opinions and complaints, discusses the avowed causes of war, and concealed motive of conquest. Includes minority opinion.

13TH CONGRESS, 2ND SESSION

1576. Baylies, William (Mass.). "The Loan Bill," *Annals of Congress.* 13th Cong., 2nd Sess. (24 Feb. 1814) pp. 1652-1658. Opposes the bill; maintains that the money is requested to pursue an unnecessary and inexpedient war which has brought disaster. Discusses the causes of the war, particularly impressment; defends the Legislature of Massachusetts and its opposition to the embargo.

1577. Bigelow, Abijah (Mass.). "The Loan Bill," *Annals of Congress.* 13th Cong., 2nd Sess. (9 Feb. 1814) pp. 1274-1283. Opposes the loan; maintains that the money is be used to prosecute a war of invasion and conquest that is based on false pretenses. Reviews the European events that lead to the measures resulting in the war. Discusses the treaty of Monroe and Pinkney, the embargo, the Non-Intercourse Act of 1809, and the Berlin and Milan decrees.

1578. Brigham, Elijah (Mass.). "Extension of Enlistments," *Annals of Congress.* 13th Cong., 2nd Sess. (20 Jan. 1814) pp. 1060-1066. Objects to the inducements to enlistment; maintains that the increase in the army will increase executive patronage and prolong an unjustifiable war. Discusses his opposition to the war, the conquest of Canada, and the measures of the administration.

1579. Gore, Christopher (Mass.). "Executive Appointments," *Annals of Congress.* 13th Cong., 2nd Sess. (7 Mar., 12 Apr. 1814) pp. 651-657; 741-759. Speech and resolutions oppose the presidential appointments, made during the Senate recess, of Albert Gallatin, John Q. Adams, and James A. Bayard to be Envoys Extraordinary and Ministers Plenipotentiary. Resolutions are supported by a constitutional analysis of the power of appointment. Second speech defends the resolutions, addresses objections and presents further constitutional analysis.

1580. Gore, Christopher (Mass.). "Prohibition of Certain Imports," *Annals of Congress.* 13th Cong., 2nd Sess. (27 Jan. 1814) pp. 602-611. Opposes the proposed prohibitions, especially of wool and cotton articles. Reviews previous attempts made to pressure Great Britain by restrictions; maintains that such acts are ineffectual and produce misery and distress. Discusses the disastrous consequences of encouraging certain manufactures at the expense of others.

1581. King, Cyrus (Mass.). "Coasting Trade," *Annals of Congress.* 13th Cong., 2nd Sess. (14 Jan. 1814) pp. 936-938. Presents resolutions and supporting remarks to define the powers of Congress concerning the coasting trade.

1582. King, Cyrus (Mass.). "Extension of Enlistments," *Annals of Congress.* 13th Cong., 2nd Sess. (20 Jan. 1814) pp. 1071-1083. Objects to the requested aid. Questions the purpose of the war and the value of conquering Canada. Maintains that the war is the result of the policies and measures of the current

Administration; discusses the effect of commercial restriction on foreign nations and on the United States.

1583. King, Cyrus (Mass.). "Supplemental Journal - Embargo," *Annals of Congress.* 13th Cong., 2nd Sess. (17 Dec. 1813) pp. 2055-2058. Opposes the proposed embargo. Discusses the consequences to the citizens of Maine; lists the restrictive laws passed by Congress.

1584. Pickering, Timothy (Mass.). "The Loan Bill," *Annals of Congress.* 13th Cong., 2nd Sess. (28 Feb. 1814) pp. 1697-1767. Lengthy speech opposes the bill. Discusses in detail and with documentation, the alleged causes of war, relations with Great Britain and France, and attempts at reconciliation. Reviews the long established practice of impressment; demonstrates, using Massachusetts data, that the number of native American seamen impressed were grossly exaggerated. Also discusses the conquest of Canada, the navy, the Louisiana Purchase, and transactions in East Florida.

1585. Reed, John (Mass.). "Modification of the Embargo," *Annals of Congress.* 13th Cong., 2nd Sess. (22 Jan. 1814) pp. 1117-1121. Supports modifying the embargo to obtain relief for the citizens of Nantucket; describes their situation and the consequences of restricting trade between the island and the mainland.

1586. Reed, William (Mass.). "Repeal of the Embargo," *Annals of Congress.* 13th Cong., 2nd Sess. (6 Apr. 1814) pp. 1979-1983. Opposes the removal of the embargo as inexpedient. Maintains that he would rather endure the embargo a little longer than risk its removal. Discusses his objections.

1587. Ward, Artemus, Jr. (Mass.). "Military Establishment," *Annals of Congress.* 13th Cong., 2nd Sess. (4 Mar. 1814) pp. 1808-1830. Opposes the proposed appropriations to support the military establishment. Defends his position that the alleged causes of the war are false; contends that the real causes are a bias towards France and the intent of the administration to destroy the commerce of the country and change the form of government. Discusses the conquest of Canada and the rights of Britain to impress her subjects during times of war. Defends the patriotism of the citizens of Massachusetts and of the Federalists.

1588. Wheaton, Laban (Mass.). "Extension of Enlistments," *Annals of Congress.* 13th Cong., 2nd Sess. (21 Jan. 1814) pp. 1108-1113. Opposes the proposed measures to encourage enlistment. Reviews the steps leading to the war, and the probability of success if the war is continued. Defends the rights of Massachusetts' citizens to protest against the laws that have oppressed them.

1589. Wheaton, Laban (Mass.). "Supplemental Journal - Embargo," *Annals of Congress.* 13th Cong., 2nd Sess. (11 Dec. 1813) pp. 2046-2048. Opposes the proposed embargo; maintains it would be more harmful to the U.S. than to England.

1590. "An Act Authorizing the President of the United States to Grant Certain Permissions to the Inhabitants of the Island of Nantucket," *Statutes at Large*, Vol. III (25 Jan. 1814) p. 94. Also printed in the *Annals of Congress* (13th Cong., 2nd Sess.) Appendix, pp. 2788-2789.

1591. "Claim of the New England Mississippi Land Company," *American State Papers: Public Lands*, Vol. II (Doc. 222) pp. 877-880. (ASP 029). Lengthy petition for the speedy examination and settlement of their claim. Refutes arguments concerning Georgia's proof of title to the land. Objects to claims of having knowledge of the fraud. Discusses the proposition that the grants were originally void for fraud. Contends that the investors were not aware of objections to the grants and only trusted the sovereign government of Georgia.

1592. "Encouragement to Manufactures," *American State Papers: Finance*, Vol. II (Doc. 414) p. 832. (ASP 010). Petition from Worcester County requests a protective duty on scythes and mill saws.

13TH CONGRESS, 3RD SESSION

1593. "Relative Powers of the General and State Governments over the Militia," *Annals of Congress*. 13th Cong., 3rd Sess. (28 Feb. 1815) Appendix, pp. 1744-1795. Report of the Committee on Military Affairs supports the conduct of the Dept. of War relative to the powers of the general and state governments over the militia. Majority of the report is a response from the Sec. of the Dept. of War objecting to the resistance of Massachusetts, Connecticut, and Rhode Island to furnish their quota of the militia. Includes correspondence between the Dept. of War and the Governors of those states. Addresses the objections of the Governors. Same as Mil.aff.142 (13-3) ASP 016 (entry **1603**).

1594. Brigham, Elijah (Mass.). "Direct Tax," *Annals of Congress*. 13th Cong., 3rd Sess. (22 Dec. 1814) pp. 964-971. Objects to the tax that would enable the administration to continue the war and pursue the conquest of Canada. Maintains that the war is impolitic and wrong, and is the cause of the impoverishment and distress of the nation.

1595. Gore, Christopher (Mass.). "Direct Taxes," *Annals of Congress*. 13th Cong., 3rd Sess. (5 Jan. 1815) pp. 150-160. Opposes the tax; maintains that Massachusetts would not benefit. Discusses the responsibility of the government to provide for the common defense; indicates how Mass. is unprotected and defenseless. Justifies the refusal of the Gov. of Massachusetts in 1812 to honor an unconstitutional request to call forth the militia.

1596. Gore, Christopher (Mass.). "Militia of the United States," *Annals of Congress*. 13th Cong., 3rd Sess. (22 Nov. 1814) pp. 95-102. Objects to the proposal that would require the militia to serve for two years, class the men, and procure the requisite number by contract or compulsion. Demonstrates that these provisions are unconstitutional and a violation of states' rights and federal duty.

1597. King, Cyrus (Mass.). "Enlistments in the Army," *Annals of Congress.* 13th Cong., 3rd Sess. (3 Dec. 1814) pp. 720-732. Opposes the proposed methods of conscription to fill the ranks of the army as unconstitutional, destructive, immoral, and oppressive. Discusses previous military and revenue measures of the administration, and their ruinous results on the country. Accuses the Madison administration of high crimes and misdemeanors.

1598. King, Cyrus (Mass.). "Military Peace Establishment," *Annals of Congress.* 13th Cong., 3rd Sess. (27 Feb. 1815) pp. 1246-1249. Supports retaining a regular force of 6,000 men, nearly double the size of the former peace establishment. Includes comments on the return of peace.

1599. King, Cyrus (Mass.). "The Ways and Means," *Annals of Congress.* 13th Cong., 3rd Sess. (22 Oct. 1814) pp. 441-452. Opposes the taxes because 1) New England was not represented in the committee, 2) the citizens are already too impoverished, 3) none of the taxes are to be used to reimburse militia expenses incurred by the states, and 4) the administration is hostile to New England. Discusses the corrupt and ruinous measures of the Madison administration.

1600. Pickering, Timothy (Mass.). "Military Peace Establishment," *Annals of Congress.* 13th Cong., 3rd Sess. (27 Feb. 1815) pp. 1217-1220. Advocates reducing the military establishment.

1601. Varnum, Joseph B. (Mass.). "Militia of the United States," *Annals of Congress.* 13th Cong., 3rd Sess. (16 Nov. 1814) pp. 58-70. Objects to the bill to authorize the President to call on the states for their respective quotas of militia. Assesses each section of the bill for defects and possible remedies. Objects to the mode of drafting, classification, and enrollment, and to the two-year period of service. Maintains that the bill is contrary to correct military procedures.

1602. Ward, Artemus, Jr. (Mass.). "Militia Draughts," *Annals of Congress.* 13th Cong., 3rd Sess. (14 Dec. 1814) pp. 904-921. Opposes the bill to call upon the states for their respective quotas of militia as unconstitutional. Remarks against the administration and its leadership. Maintains that if the bill is unconstitutional, resistance is a duty. Defends the government and people of Massachusetts regarding the loss of her captured territory.

1603. "Relative Powers of the General and State Governments over the Militia," *American State Papers: Military Affairs*, Vol. I (Doc. 142) pp. 604-623. (ASP 016). Also printed in the *Annals of Congress*, (13-3), Appendix, pp. 1744-1795 (entry **1593**). See entry **1593** for abstract.

14TH CONGRESS, 1ST SESSION

1604. Bradbury, George (Mass.). "Commercial Restrictions," *Annals of Congress.* 14th Cong., 1st Sess. (7 Feb. 1816) pp. 918-920. Supports regulating, not restricting, commerce from places which exclude U.S. vessels.

1605. Conner, Samuel S. (Mass.). "Invalid Corps," *Annals of Congress.* 14th Cong., 1st Sess. (28 Dec. 1815) pp. 411-413. Supports hospitals for disabled veterans.

1606. Conner, Samuel S. (Mass.). "The Revenue," *Annals of Congress.* 14th Cong., 1st Sess. (24 Jan. 1816) pp. 758-762. Supports taxes to augment the navy and maintain the army for the possibility of hostilities. Discusses the merits of regular troops over the militia.

1607. Hulbert, John W. (Mass.). "Canadian Refugees," *Annals of Congress.* 14th Cong., 1st Sess. (16 Feb. 1816) pp. 999-1006. Opposes offering relief to Canadian refugees who entered American service; maintains that it would sanction and reward treason. Considers opponents' arguments, including the case of Colonel Wilcox (commander of the Canadian volunteers corps), retaliation, and General Hull's pledge.

1608. Hulbert, John W. (Mass.). "Military Academies," *Annals of Congress.* 14th Cong., 1st Sess. (2 Jan., 3 Jan. 1816) pp. 424-425; 443-446. Supports establishing more military academies to provide leadership against future hostilities. Addresses objections, including constitutionality, precedence, and appropriations.

1609. King, Cyrus (Mass.). "Commerce with Great Britain," *Annals of Congress.* 14th Cong., 1st Sess. (9 Jan. 1816) pp. 538-539. Supports the necessity of the House to sanction provisions of treaties that encroach upon its enumerated powers.

1610. King, Cyrus (Mass.). "Commercial Restrictions," *Annals of Congress.* 14th Cong., 1st Sess. (4 Feb. 1816) pp. 877-880, 880-881. Presents and defends a resolution to restrict trade from Great Britain's colonial ports which exclude United States' vessels.

1611. King, Cyrus (Mass.). "Military Academies," *Annals of Congress.* 14th Cong., 1st Sess. (3 Jan. 1816) pp. 438-443. Opposes the proposed military academies as unconstitutional and inexpedient; maintains that the real purpose of the bill is executive patronage.

1612. King, Cyrus (Mass.). "The Revenue," *Annals of Congress.* 14th Cong., 1st Sess. (30 Jan. 1816) pp. 804-817. Opposes the direct tax; maintains that it is unnecessary and his constituents are impoverished. Analyzes the report of the Secretary of the Treasury for other expenses to abolish. Compares the military peace establishment unfavorably to the militia. Discusses the Treaty of Peace,

Moose Island, and the gains of war. Reviews occasions when the interests of New England were sacrificed to those of the South and West.

1613. Mills, Elijah H. (Mass.). "Commerce with Great Britain," *Annals of Congress.* 14th Cong., 1st Sess. (9 Jan. 1816) pp. 539-542. Maintains that the House has no part of the treaty-making power.

1614. Parris, Albion K. (Mass.). "The Revenue," *Annals of Congress.* 14th Cong., 1st Sess. (29 Jan. 1816) pp. 772-776. Supports repealing the direct tax. Reviews the original intent of the tax. Maintains that it is unnecessary, expensive to assess and collect, and unequal in its operation.

1615. Pickering, Timothy (Mass.). "Commerce with Great Britain," *Annals of Congress.* 14th Cong., 1st Sess. (12 Jan. 1816) pp. 612-616. Maintains that the treaty-making power rests exclusively with the President and the Senate; contends that there is no need for the House to give its sanction.

1616. Reed, John (Mass.). "The Revenue," *Annals of Congress.* 14th Cong., 1st Sess. (23 Jan. 1816) pp. 739-743. Supports the salt duty as a fair tax. Considers other taxes. Defends the importance of fisheries as a nursery of seamen.

1617. Stearns, Asahel (Mass.). "The Revenue," *Annals of Congress.* 14th Cong., 1st Sess. (5 Feb. 1816) pp. 904-909. Questions the necessity of the proposed taxes. Discusses the previous budgeting of the government, the disposition of the money, and the accountability to constituents.

1618. "An Act to Authorize the Building of Three Light-houses, viz. One on Race Point, One on Point Gammon, and One on the Island of Petite Manon, in the State of Massachusetts," *Statutes at Large*, Vol. III (27 Apr. 1816) pp. 346-347. Also printed in the *Annals of Congress* (14th Cong., 1st Sess.) Appendix, p. 1879.

1619. "An Act to Increase the Compensation of the Superintendents of the Manufactories of Arms at Springfield and Harper's Ferry," *Statutes at Large*, Vol. III (29 Apr. 1816) p. 323. Also printed in the *Annals of Congress* (14th Cong., 1st Sess.) Appendix, p. 1888.

1620. "An Act for the Relief of Certain Owners of Goods, Entered at Hampden, in the District of Maine," *Annals of Congress.* 14th Cong., 1st Sess. (27 Apr. 1816) Appendix, p. 1876.

1621. "An Act for the Relief of the Baltimore and Massachusetts Bible Societies," *Annals of Congress.* 14th Cong., 1st Sess. (20 Apr. 1816) Appendix, pp. 1848-1849.

1622. "Amendments to the Constitution of the United States Proposed by Massachusetts and Connecticut, and Rejected by Ohio," *American State Papers: Miscellaneous*, Vol. II (Doc. 397) pp. 282-283. (ASP 038). Resolutions of Ohio oppose proposed amendments concerning taxes, admission of states into the Union, embargoes, commerce, declaration of war, eligibility to Congress or civil office, and the number of terms a President may serve.

1623. "Duty Bonds Captured by the British in 1814," *American State Papers: Finance*, Vol. III (Doc. 474) p. 102. (ASP 011). Supports petitioners' request for protection against the British courts of admiralty and against the loss of the bonds.

1624. "Remission of Duties," *American State Papers: Finance*, Vol. III (Doc. 471) p. 99. (ASP 011). Petition request to not pay a bond for securing duties on articles destroyed at the port of Castine is denied.

1625. "Remission of Forfeitures," *American State Papers: Finance*, Vol. III (Doc. 479) pp. 109-112. (ASP 011). Report responds to a petition from merchants of Massachusetts for relief of goods forfeited at Castine, Maine. Summarizes the facts; discusses the owner of the vessel employed, the owner of the goods imported, and the course of the importation and entry of the goods.

14TH CONGRESS, 2ND SESSION

1626. "Massachusetts Peace Society," *Annals of Congress.* 14th Cong., 2nd Sess. (31 Jan. 1817) pp. 93-96. Memorial represents the views of the Society on how to diminish the frequency of war and promote peace. The memorial requests the government to profess pacific principles and Congress to inquire how the pacific spirit could be incorporated into the governing of the country.

1627. Ashmun, Eli P. (Mass.). "Internal Improvements," *Annals of Congress.* 14th Cong., 2nd Sess. (26 Feb. 1817) pp. 179-180. Opposes appropriating money for internal improvements; concerned about the constitutionality and the consent of the states involved.

1628. Bradbury, George (Mass.). "Commercial Intercourse," *Annals of Congress.* 14th Cong., 2nd Sess. (31 Jan. 1817) pp. 806-810. Opposes the amendment, which would substitute discriminating duties in lieu of a total prohibition of trade. Maintains that navigation is in a state of dilapidation but the remedy is unclear. Discusses the effect of prohibition versus discriminating duties.

1629. Conner, Samuel S. (Mass.). "Compensation Law," *Annals of Congress.* 14th Cong., 2nd Sess. (15 Jan., 20 Jan. 1817) pp. 537-539; 652-653, 654-655. Various brief remarks support repealing the law, in compliance with the wishes of his constituents. Maintains that a Representative is obligated to comply with the instructions of his constituents.

1630. Conner, Samuel S. (Mass.). "Internal Duties," *Annals of Congress.* 14th Cong., 2nd Sess. (17 Feb. 1817) pp. 986-989. Opposes reducing the army as a means to repeal internal taxes. Defends the necessity of retaining at least 10,000 men; discusses the volatility of current foreign relations.

1631. Hulbert, John W. (Mass.). "Compensation Law," *Annals of Congress.* 14th Cong., 2nd Sess. (16 Jan. 1817) pp. 548-556. Objects to repealing the raise in compensation. Maintains that the original arguments in support of the law still hold. Addresses objections concerning the amount and mode of compensation, the voice of the people, and the right of state governments to interfere.

1632. King, Cyrus (Mass.). "Commercial Intercourse," *Annals of Congress.* 14th Cong., 2nd Sess. (20 Jan. 1817) pp. 772-783. Supports prohibiting trade with nations that won't reciprocate. Defends the power of Congress to regulate commerce; offers supporting opinions of distinguished statesmen. Addresses the principle features of the British navigation act and trade with British colonies. Discusses the status and importance of navigation in this country.

1633. King, Cyrus (Mass.). "Compensation Law," *Annals of Congress.* 14th Cong., 2nd Sess. (14 Jan. 1817) pp. 503-507. Advocates repealing the increased compensation law. Discusses the responsibility of legislators to their constituents; offers other considerations in opposition to the law.

1634. King, Cyrus (Mass.). "Internal Improvement," *Annals of Congress.* 14th Cong., 2nd Sess. (6 Feb. 1817) pp. 876-878, 912-914. Opposes appropriating money for internal improvements as inexpedient and unnecessary. Maintains that the people are already distressed and overburdened with taxes.

1635. Mills, Elijah H. (Mass.). "Compensation Law," *Annals of Congress.* 14th Cong., 2nd Sess. (20 Jan. 1817) pp. 658-665. Supports increased compensation for members of Congress. Addresses salaries of other officers of government, increased living expenses, temptation, and legislative candidates of moderate means. Maintains that public outcry is due to mode of payment - favors a daily allowance over an annual stipend. Addresses the responsibility of legislators to obey the instructions of their constituents.

1636. Parris, Albion K. (Mass.). "Compensation Law," *Annals of Congress.* 14th Cong., 2nd Sess. (16 Jan. 1817) pp. 541-546. Supports repealing the law which raised the pay of members of Congress and refunding extra compensation received last session; maintains that public opinion demands a repeal of the law and that Congress is obligated to obey.

1637. Pickering, Timothy (Mass.). "Compensation Law," *Annals of Congress.* 14th Cong., 2nd Sess. (16 Jan., 17 Jan. 1817) pp. 562-563; 592-594. Opposes repealing the compensation law and refunding the extra compensation received last session; considers inflation, the comparative value of the compensation in 1789, and his instructions from the Legislature of Massachusetts.

1638. Pickering, Timothy (Mass.). "Internal Improvement," *Annals of Congress.* 14th Cong., 2nd Sess. (4 Feb., 7 Feb. 1817) pp. 858-859; 916-918. Supports the constitutional authority of Congress to make roads and canals.

1639. "An Act for Erecting a Light-house on the West Chop of Holmes's Hole Harbour, in the State of Massachusetts," *Statutes at Large*, Vol. III (3 Mar. 1817) p. 360. Also printed in the *Annals of Congress* (14th Cong., 2nd Sess.) Appendix, pp. 1296-1297.

1640. "Agriculture," *American State Papers: Miscellaneous*, Vol. II (Doc. 433) pp. 442-443. (ASP 038). Petition supports the establishment of a national board of agriculture.

15TH CONGRESS, 1ST SESSION

1641. Holmes, John (Mass.). "Commutation of Soldiers' Pay," *Annals of Congress.* 15th Cong., 1st Sess. (16 Dec., 17 Dec. 1817) pp. 471-472; 482-483. Defends aid to disbanded officers; discusses the land bounty and the potential for speculation.

1642. Holmes, John (Mass.). "Ohio Contested Election," *Annals of Congress.* 15th Cong., 1st Sess. (5 Jan. 1818) pp. 558-562. Supports Mr. Herrick as a duly elected representative from Ohio. Maintains that the prohibition of Representatives holding office does not extend to the period of time for which one is elected. One is not a member until he has met with the others and taken the oath. Gives the rationale behind the restrictions; addresses arguments.

1643. Holmes, John (Mass.). "Spanish American Provinces," *Annals of Congress.* 15th Cong., 1st Sess. (27 Mar. 1818) pp. 1579-1585. Supports appropriating money to be applied to defray the expenses of a minister to Buenos Ayres if the investigating commissioners report that Buenos Ayres has an independent government the Executive wishes to recognize. Addresses objections, including the reactions of Spain and Great Britain.

1644. Holmes, John (Mass.). "Uniform Bankrupt Law," *Annals of Congress.* 15th Cong., 1st Sess. (17 Feb. 1818) pp. 913-918. Opposes the proposed relief of debtors. Maintains that it is a lure to speculation and fraud, promotes idleness, and is discriminatory in its support. Examines some of the reasons in support of the bill and projects some of its effects.

1645. Mason, Jonathan (Mass.). "Bankrupt Bill," *Annals of Congress.* 15th Cong., 1st Sess. (20 Feb. 1818) pp. 982-988. Supports a uniform system of bankruptcy that would administer equal justice in aid and protection of merchants. Justifies the need for the bill and addresses various objections.

1646. Mills, Elijah H. (Mass.). "Bankrupt Bill," *Annals of Congress.* 15th Cong., 1st Sess. (19 Feb. 1818) pp. 954-962. Supports establishing a uniform system of bankruptcy. Demonstrates the need for a system uniform in its operation throughout the U.S.; answers objections. Maintains the current bill would extend equal security to creditors and offer protection to honest debtors.

1647. Whitman, Ezekiel (Mass.). "Bankrupt Bill," *Annals of Congress.* 15th Cong., 1st Sess. (25 Feb. 1818) pp. 1014-1020. Supports a uniform bankruptcy system. Maintains that while it would primarily benefit merchants, it would not injure any other class of men. Discusses the relationship between agriculture and commerce. Reviews the need for the law; addresses objections.

1648. Whitman, Ezekiel (Mass.). "Case of Colonel Anderson," *Annals of Congress.* 15th Cong., 1st Sess. (14 Jan. 1818) pp. 740-742. Supports the authority of the House to proceed against Colonel John Anderson, accused of attempted bribery.

1649. "An Act Altering the Time for Holding a Session of the District Court in the District of Maine," *Statutes at Large*, Vol. III (3 Apr. 1818) p. 413. Also printed in the *Annals of Congress* (15th Cong., 1st Sess.) Appendix, p. 2522.

1650. "An Act Making the Port of Bath, in Massachusetts, a Port of Entry for Ships or Vessels Arriving from the Cape of Good Hope, and from Places Beyond the Same; and for Establishing a Collection District, whereof Belfast Shall Be the Port of Entry," *Statutes at Large*, Vol. III (20 Apr. 1818) pp. 464-465. Also printed in the *Annals of Congress* (15th Cong., 1st Sess.) Appendix, p. 2587.

1651. "An Act to Allow the Benefit of Drawback on Merchandise Transported by Land Conveyance from Bristol to Boston, and from Boston to Bristol, in Like Manner As if the Same Were Transported Coastwise," *Statutes at Large*, Vol. III (6 Feb. 1818) p. 405. Also printed in the *Annals of Congress* (15th Cong., 1st Sess.) Appendix, p. 2510.

1652. "Interest on Debenture Bonds," *American State Papers: Claims*, (Doc. 399) p. 582. (ASP 036). Report of the Committee of Claims against the request of inhabitants of Salem, Mass., and New York, for the interest on the earlier payment of debenture bonds.

1653. "Money Lost by a Deputy Collector in Massachusetts," *American State Papers: Claims*, (Doc. 376) pp. 541-543. (ASP 036). Report to grant relief to the petitioner, Gad Worthington, robbed of a sum of public money. Includes supporting documentation.

1654. "Ship Removed from Castine by the British in 1815, after the Treaty of Peace," *American State Papers: Claims*, (Doc. 388) p. 551. (ASP 036). Claim of petitioners for ship must await official interpretation of the first article of the treaty that stipulates the restitution of private property.

1655. U.S. House. *Letter from the Acting Secretary of War, Transmitting Information Relative to the Claims of the State of Massachusetts for Payment* *of the Expenses of the Militia, Ordered Out by the Executive Authority of the State, during the Late War.* 15th Cong., 1st Sess. (H.Doc.81). Washington: E. De Krafft, 1818. 59 pg. (Serial Set 8). Documents include the request by Massachusetts, giving circumstances and particulars of the claim, the response given by the War Dept., and the complete report of the Secretary of War to the Senate committee on military affairs in 1815.

1656. U.S. House. *Letter from the Secretary of War, on the Subject of a Call of the House of Representatives United States, for Information Relative to the Claim of Massachusetts for Expenses Incurred in Calling Out the Militia of That State during the Late War.* 15th Cong., 1st Sess. (H.Doc.80). Washington: E. De Krafft, 1818. 3 pg. (Serial Set 8). Very brief letter referring to earlier report for information on why the claims have not been allowed.

1657. U.S. House. *Report of the Committee to Whom Was Referred That Part of the President's Message, Which Relates to the Commercial Intercourse of the U. States with the British West India Islands and North American Colonies, and Also on the Petition of Sundry Inhabitants of Different Parts of the District of Maine, on the Same Subject.* 15th Cong., 1st Sess. (H.Doc.87/2). [Washington: E. De Krafft, 1818]. 25 pg. (Serial Set 8). Report recommends increased duties. Includes charts with amount and value of duties on various products traded with West Indies. An extensive document from the Dept. of State analyzes the effect of the latest treaty between Great Britain and the U.S.

1658. U.S. House. *Report of the Select Committee to Whom Was Referred a Resolution Relating to the Claim of Massachusetts, for Expenditures of Their Militia, for Services during the Late War.* 15th Cong., 1st Sess. (H.Doc.147). [Washington: E. De. Krafft, 1818]. 38 pg. (Serial Set 10). Report supports the claim; reviews the facts connected with the claim. Copies of relevant documents and correspondence included.

1659. U.S. Senate. *In Senate of the United States.* 15th Cong., 1st Sess. (S.Doc.147). [Washington: Edward De Krafft, Printer, 1818]. 1 pg. (Serial Set 3). Motion to survey the harbors of Boston, Newport, and New York to select sites for defense.

1660. U.S. Senate. [Resolution on Claims Due Massachusetts Militia]. 15th Cong., 1st Sess. (S.Doc.81). [Washington: Edward De Krafft, Printer, 1818]. 1 pg. (Serial Set 2).

15TH CONGRESS, 2ND SESSION

1661. "Massachusetts' Claim," *Annals of Congress.* 15th Cong., 2nd Sess. (18 Dec. 1818) pp. 419-421. Remarks on when to discuss the claim of Massachusetts for expenses incurred by her militia during the late war.

1662. Fuller, Timothy (Mass.). "Admission of Missouri," *Annals of Congress.* 15th Cong., 2nd Sess. (15 Feb. 1819) pp. 1179-1184. Supports the prohibition of slavery in Missouri. Maintains that Congress has the discretionary power to require any reasonable conditions to ensure that a new state has a republican form of government. Addresses objections of slave-holding states.

1663. Fuller, Timothy (Mass.). "Military Appropriation Bill," *Annals of Congress.* 15th Cong., 2nd Sess. (11 Jan. 1819) pp. 499-502. Supports appropriations for the construction of military and other roads; recommends using the army to assist with the necessary labor.

1664. Fuller, Timothy (Mass.). "Seminole War," *Annals of Congress.* 15th Cong., 2nd Sess. (2 Feb. 1819) pp. 985-1006. Discusses the conduct of General Jackson in Florida. Examines the origin of the war and determines that we have been the aggressors. Reviews the progress of the war and its conduct under General Jackson. Discusses the authority of Jackson to march into Florida and seize Spanish posts and garrisons. Maintains that General Jackson acted without authority for the purpose of conquest, not self-defense. Discusses the execution of prisoners, including Arbuthnot and Ambrister.

1665. Holmes, John (Mass.). "Seminole War," *Annals of Congress.* 15th Cong., 2nd Sess. (19 Jan. 1819) pp. 600-615. Defends the conduct of General Jackson. Maintains that the Seminoles were the aggressors and that the President was obligated to repel them. Supports General Jackson crossing into Florida and his actions towards the Spaniards. Details the acts of hostility of the Spanish officers.

1666. Lincoln, Enoch (Mass.). "Military Appropriation Bill," *Annals of Congress.* 15th Cong., 2nd Sess. (11 Jan. 1819) pp. 488-490. Discusses the definition of "military roads" and the authority of the President to construct them.

1667. Otis, Harrison Gray (Mass.). "Memorial of Matthew Lyon," *Annals of Congress.* 15th Cong., 2nd Sess. (8 Dec. 1818) pp. 52-54. Remarks on the sedition law and the circumstances under which it was passed. Maintains that the law, while inexpedient, was not unconstitutional.

1668. Whitman, Ezekiel (Mass.). "Arkansas Territory," *Annals of Congress.* 15th Cong., 2nd Sess. (19 Feb. 1819) pp. 1274-1279. Opposes restricting slavery from Arkansas. Supports admitting states with and without slavery restrictions on an alternating basis. Maintains that Congress has the power to require any stipulation as a condition of admission.

1669. "An Act to Authorize the Building, Erecting, and Placing, Lighthouses, Beacons, and Buoys, on Places Designated in Boston, Buzzard and Chesapeake Bays, Lakes Ontario and Erie, and for Other Purposes," *Statutes at Large*, Vol. III (3 Mar. 1819) pp. 534-536. Also printed in the *Annals of Congress.* (15th Cong., 2nd Sess.) Appendix, pp. 2546-2548.

1670. U.S. Senate. [Resolution to Establish a Circuit Court at Portland, Me.]. 15th Cong., 2nd Sess. (S.Doc.4). [Washington: E. De Krafft, 1818]. 1 pg. (Serial Set 14).

16ᵀᴴ CONGRESS, 1ˢᵀ SESSION

1671. "Duty on Molasses," *Annals of Congress.* 16th Cong., 1st Sess. (13 Apr. 1820) Appendix, pp. 2410-2411. Memorial from Boston opposes the proposed increase in duty on molasses. Same as Finance 588 (16-1) ASP 011 (entry **1690**).

1672. "Remonstrance against an Increase of Duties, &c.," *Annals of Congress.* 16th Cong., 1st Sess. (31 Jan. 1820) Appendix, pp. 2335-2348. Lengthy memorial from Salem opposes prohibiting foreign woolen and cotton goods, and abolishing drawbacks and credits upon duties for imported goods. Enumerates the benefits of commerce, contending that commerce should not be sacrificed to the interests of manufactures. Objects to fluctuations in the commercial policy as dangerous and inconvenient. Same as H.doc.59 (16-1) 35 (entry **1694**) and Finance 573 (16-1) ASP 011 (entry **1691**).

1673. Cushman, Joshua (Mass.). "The Missouri Bill," *Annals of Congress.* 16th Cong., 1st Sess. (14 Feb. 1820) pp. 1291-1309. Advocates restricting slavery in Missouri as a condition of statehood. Responds to Mr. Holmes' (Mass.) speech and defends Massachusetts and Maine. Supports the constitutional right of Congress to impose the restriction of slavery. Discusses the powers granted by the Constitution, sovereignty, states' rights, Louisiana treaty, self-government, slaves as property, and the evils and consequences of slavery.

1674. Cushman, Joshua (Mass.). "Revolutionary Pensions," *Annals of Congress.* 16th Cong., 1st Sess. (31 Mar. 1820) pp. 1707-1709. Defends the act granting pensions to the Revolutionary War soldiers. Discusses the consequences of rescinding the pensions, the soldiers' hardships, and Washington's words of support.

1675. Fuller, Timothy (Mass.). "The Missouri Bill," *Annals of Congress.* 16th Cong., 1st Sess. (24 Feb. 1820) pp. 1466-1489. Examines the powers of Congress to require the restriction of slavery as a condition of admission into the Union. Discusses the political equality of the new and original states, attributes of sovereignty, the implications of the treaty admitting Louisiana, implications of territorial legislatures, and the effects of excluding or continuing slavery.

1676. Fuller, Timothy (Mass.). "Settlement of Private Claims," *Annals of Congress.* 16th Cong., 1st Sess. (4 Apr. 1820) pp. 1740-1742. Supports his proposal to improve the method of settling private claims.

1677. Holmes, John (Mass.). "Admission of Missouri," *Annals of Congress.* 16th Cong., 1st Sess. (27 Jan. 1820) pp. 966-990. Opposes the proposition to abolish slavery in Missouri as a condition of her admission into the Union. Examines the powers of Congress to restrict a state in the establishment or abolishment of slavery. Maintains that a new state has all the rights and powers of the original states, including that of determining the status of slavery within its boundaries. Reviews reasons and precedents for imposing restrictions on Missouri.

1678. Holmes, John (Mass.). "Revision of the Tariff," *Annals of Congress.* 16th Cong., 1st Sess. (27 Apr. 1820) pp. 2080-2093. Opposes the proposed tariffs. Maintains that manufacturers in the U.S. are more protected than those of any other country. Discusses the proposed duty to exclude foreign fabrics and its consequences. Discusses the effects of applying heavy duties on the necessities of life and the fisheries. Maintains that protecting duties will result in a direct tax, and that the system will injure the manufacturers as well as the nation.

1679. Holmes, John (Mass.). "State of Maine," *Annals of Congress.* 16th Cong., 1st Sess. (30 Dec. 1819) pp. 833-834; 839-840. Supports the admission of Maine into the Union; discusses the representation of Maine in Congress.

1680. Mellen, Prentiss (Mass.). "Admission of Maine and Missouri," *Annals of Congress.* 16th Cong., 1st Sess. (13 Jan., 19 Jan. 1820) pp. 89-92; 175-187. Objects to connecting the admissions of Maine and Missouri. Opposes further extension of slavery; considers whether Congress has the right to impose the slavery restriction and if it is expedient to do so. Discusses the principles contained in the Constitution, the ordinance of 1787, and the Louisiana treaty.

1681. Mellen, Prentiss (Mass.). "The Bankrupt Bill," *Annals of Congress.* 16th Cong., 1st Sess. (16 Mar. 1820) pp. 511-516. Supports the bankrupt bill. Addresses arguments about the power of Congress to enact the law. Maintains that the bill would increase and protect the rights of creditors, provide relief to debtors, and strengthen the community.

1682. Otis, Harrison Gray (Mass.). "Admission of Maine and Missouri," *Annals of Congress.* 16th Cong., 1st Sess. (14 Jan. 1820) pp. 108-114. Objects to considering the admissions of Maine and Missouri in the same bill; maintains that they are two distinct subjects with no possible relation to each other. Considers precedents and geographical discrimination of interests. Defends the Congress as more than a ratifier of contracts and bargains.

1683. Otis, Harrison Gray (Mass.). "Maine and Missouri," *Annals of Congress.* 16th Cong., 1st Sess. (25 Jan. 1820) pp. 237-255. Supports restricting slavery as a condition for Missouri to be admitted as a state. Maintains that the government decided this question 33 years ago; reviews the ordinance of 1787 and its incorporation into the laws of the country. Examines the Louisiana treaty concerning the rights of sovereignty. Examines the Constitution and the articles on importation and migration of slaves, territories, and admission of new states. Addresses opponents' arguments.

1684. Otis, Harrison Gray (Mass.). "The Tariff," *Annals of Congress*. 16th Cong., 1st Sess. (4 May 1820) pp. 666-672. Opposes the bill protecting manufacturers; maintains that a bill that radically changes long established policies should be thoroughly investigated and deliberated. Recommends further investigation into the causes of the decline of manufacturing and the efficacy of the last protecting duties.

1685. Silsbee, Nathaniel (Mass.). "Revision of the Tariff," *Annals of Congress*. 16th Cong., 1st Sess. (24 Apr. 1820) pp. 1987-1997. Opposes the proposed new restrictions on commerce and navigation. Reviews the history and success of the present system of credits on revenue bonds and compares it to that of the commercial nations of Europe; examines the proposed system and its effects. Addresses arguments in support of the bill. Discusses the balance of trade.

1686. Whitman, Ezekiel (Mass.). "District of Columbia," *Annals of Congress*. 16th Cong., 1st Sess. (27 Dec. 1819) pp. 794-795, 797. Supports establishing a territorial government for the District of Columbia. Maintains that the affairs of the District are time consuming, expensive, and without representation.

1687. Whitman, Ezekiel (Mass.). "Revision of the Tariff," *Annals of Congress*. 16th Cong., 1st Sess. (25 Apr. 1820) pp. 1998-2008. Opposes the bill, whose intent is the encouragement of manufacturing. Maintains that manufacturing would be encouraged at the expense of commerce and agriculture, and that the high duties would eventually lead to land taxes and excises. Warns against manufacturers uniting; defends the merchants, commerce and the revenue it has produced for the country, and the India trade.

1688. Whitman, Ezekiel (Mass.). "State of Maine," *Annals of Congress*. 16th Cong., 1st Sess. (30 Dec. 1819) pp. 836-839. Supports the unconditional admission of Maine, decided independently from that of Missouri. Offers a solution to the problem of representation.

1689. "An Act for Apportioning the Representatives in the Seventeenth Congress, to Be Elected in the State of Massachusetts and Maine, and for Other Purposes," *Statutes at Large*, Vol. III (7 Apr. 1820) p. 555. Also printed in the *Annals of Congress* (16th Cong., 1st Sess.) Appendix, p. 2567.

1690. "Duty on Molasses," *American State Papers: Finance*, Vol. III (Doc. 588) p. 522. (ASP 011). Memorial from Boston opposes the proposed increase in duty on molasses. Also printed in the *Annals of Congress*, "Duty on Molasses," (16th Cong., 1st Sess.) Appendix, pp. 2410-2411 (entry **1671**).

1691. "Remonstrance against an Increase of Duties on Imports, and against a Change of the Revenue System in Relation to Credit and Drawback," *American*

State Papers: Finance, Vol. III (Doc. 573) pp. 463-468. (ASP 011). Same as H.doc.59 (16-1) 35 (entry **1694**). Also printed in the *Annals of Congress*, "Remonstrance Against an Increase of Duties, &c.," (16th Cong., 1st Sess.) Appendix, pp. 2335-2348 (entry **1672**). See entry **1672** for abstract.

1692. "Rent for a Wharf, &c. in Boston, Used As a Ship-Yard in the Revolution," *American State Papers: Claims*, (Doc. 521) pp. 704-706. (ASP 036). Report of the Committee on Pensions and Revolutionary Claims against the claim for rent and damages to a wharf owned by Benjamin Goodwine that was appropriated by the government. Concurs with earlier decision against the petition.

1693. "Uniform System of Bankruptcy," *American State Papers: Miscellaneous*, Vol. II (Doc. 472) pp. 548-550. (ASP 038). Memorial from Boston and other towns supports a uniform and permanent bankrupt law. Contends that the current law is unmerciful, unjust, and conducive to fraud.

1694. U.S. House. *Memorial of Sundry Merchants and Inhabitants of Salem, Massachusetts*. 16th Cong., 1st Sess. (H.Doc.59). Washington: Gales & Seaton, 1820. 15 pg. (Serial Set 35). Same as Finance 573 (16-1) ASP 011 (entry **1691**). Also printed in the *Annals of Congress*, "Remonstrance Against an Increase of Duties, &c.," (16th Cong., 1st Sess.) Appendix, pp. 2335-2348 (entry **1672**). See entry **1672** for abstract.

16TH CONGRESS, 2ND SESSION

1695. Cushman, Joshua (Mass.). "Admission of Missouri," *Annals of Congress*. 16th Cong., 2nd Sess. (2 Feb. 1821) pp. 1015-1022. Opposes slavery in the territories. Supports the entitlement of slaves to their constitutional rights as men. Maintains that slaves will not contribute to the growth or defense of the country and that the spread of slavery will upset the balance of power. Discusses the threats of resentment and redress by Missouri if her constitution is not accepted. Defends his letter.

1696. Eustis, William (Mass.). "Admission of Missouri," *Annals of Congress*. 16th Cong., 2nd Sess. (12 Dec. 1820) pp. 635-640. Opposes the resolution that would restrict blacks and mulattos from entering Missouri. Specifically addresses the argument that blacks and mulattos are not citizens as demonstrated by the condition of those in Massachusetts. Establishes that blacks in Massachusetts have the civil and political rights of free citizens.

1697. Fuller, Timothy (Mass.). "The Navy," *Annals of Congress*. 16th Cong., 2nd Sess. (8 Feb. 1821) pp. 1059-1061. Opposes reducing the size of the navy, including the number of officers. Maintains that it would be destructive, inexpedient and disgraceful.

1698. Otis, Harrison Gray (Mass.). "Admission of Missouri," *Annals of Congress.* 16th Cong., 2nd Sess. (9 Dec. 1820) pp. 89-98. Maintains that it is the right and duty of Congress to examine the constitution of Missouri for compliance. Reviews the circumstances of the admission of other states into the Union. Contends that people of color are citizens even though they are liable to certain disqualification; reviews other classes of citizens subjected to particular disqualification.

1699. Otis, Harrison Gray (Mass.). "Bankrupt Bill," *Annals of Congress.* 16th Cong., 2nd Sess. (7 Feb. 1821) pp. 290-306. Supports the bankruptcy bill. Explains some of the general and leading principles. Considers the circumstances, condition, and numbers of the debtors, creditors, and their families. Addresses objections, including the power of Congress to legislate over bankruptcy, the danger of frauds, and the experience of the nation under the former bankruptcy act.

1700. U.S. House. *Memorial of Sundry Inhabitants of the State of Massachusetts, on the Subject of Privateering.* 16th Cong., 2nd Sess. (H.Doc.76). Washington: Gales & Seaton, 1821. 32 pg. (Serial Set 52). Memorial deplores privateering and requests that it no longer be given legal sanction by the laws of maritime warfare; discusses its effects and the benefits of discontinuing the practice. Includes reprint of an article from *The North American Review*, July 1820, entitled "The Practice of Privateering Considered, in a Review."

1701. U.S. House. *Memorial of the Berkshire Agricultural Society of the Commonwealth of Massachusetts.* 16th Cong., 2nd Sess. (H.Doc.69). Washington: Gales & Seaton, 1821. 12 pg. (Serial Set 52). Memorial supports the proposed duties to encourage the manufacturing industry as ultimately benefiting agriculture. Discusses the relationship between commerce, manufacturing and agriculture; considers objections to the protective tariffs.

17TH CONGRESS, 1ST SESSION

1702. "Trade with the British West Indies," *Annals of Congress.* 17th Cong., 1st Sess. (15 Feb. 1822) Appendix, pp. 2221-2227. Same as Com.nav.250 (17-1) ASP 015 (entry **1709**) and H.doc.69 (17-1) 67 (entry **1712**). See entry **1709** for abstract.

1703. Baylies, Francis (Mass.). "Apportionment Bill," *Annals of Congress.* 17th Cong., 1st Sess. (30 Jan. 1822) pp. 840-843. Objects to a ratio of 1:45,000 as too large; maintains that it is particularly unfair to Rhode Island.

1704. Dwight, Henry W. (Mass.). "Military Appropriations," *Annals of Congress.* 17th Cong., 1st Sess. (9 Jan. 1822) pp. 680-682. Supports the appropriations promised to the Indian tribes.

1705. Eustis, William (Mass.). "Military Peace Establishment," *Annals of Congress.* 17th Cong., 1st Sess. (15 Apr. 1822) pp. 1587-1589. Supports the proposed reduction; answers objections.

1706. Eustis, William (Mass.). "Reconveyance of Land to New York," *Annals of Congress.* 17th Cong., 1st Sess. (31 Dec. 1821) pp. 603-604. Advocates maintaining Fort Clinton, in New York.

1707. Otis, Harrison Gray (Mass.). "Amendment to the Constitution," *Annals of Congress.* 17th Cong., 1st Sess. (14 Jan. 1822) pp. 92-94. Supports the conduct of Massachusetts and her militia during the late war.

1708. Reed, John (Mass.). "Apportionment Bill," *Annals of Congress.* 17th Cong., 1st Sess. (31 Jan. 1822) pp. 854-856, 860. Favors a ratio of approximately 1:40,000.

1709. "Trade with the British West Indies," *American State Papers: Commerce and Navigation,* Vol. II (Doc. 250) pp. 623-625. (ASP 015). Resolutions and memorial from Boston oppose the repeal of the navigation acts respecting trade with the British West Indies. Maintain that a repeal would destroy the carrying trade and would render the nation subservient to the policy of a foreign country. Same as H.doc.69 (17-1) 67 (entry **1712**). Also printed in the *Annals of Congress,* "Trade with the British West Indies," (17th Cong., 1st Sess.) Appendix, pp. 2221-2227 (entry **1702**).

1710. "Transfer of Three Per Cent. Stock Issued to the States," *American State Papers: Finance,* Vol. III (Doc. 628) p. 695. (ASP 011). Report supports the petition concerning the transferability of the certificates of the funded debt issued to the states. Same as S.doc.12 (17-1) 59 (entry **1713**).

1711. U.S. House. *Memorial of Merchants, Ship Owners, and Others, Inhabitants of Salem, Mass.* 17th Cong., 1st Sess. (H.Doc.86). Washington: Gales & Seaton, 1822. 4 pg. (Serial Set 67). Memorial supports current navigation laws and the policy of reciprocity, and equivalent restrictions.

1712. U.S. House. *Resolutions & Memorial of Sundry Merchants, Ship Owners, and Other Inhabitants of Boston, Relating to the Trade of the United States with Foreign Colonies.* 17th Cong., 1st Sess. (H.Doc.69). Washington: Gales & Seaton, 1822. 8 pg. (Serial Set 67). Same as Commerce 250 (17-1) ASP 015. See entry **1709**. Also printed in the *Annals of Congress,* "Trade with the British West Indies," (17th Cong., 1st Sess.) Appendix, pp. 2221-2227 (entry **1702**).

1713. U.S. Senate. *Report of the Secretary of the Treasury on the Petition of William Phillips and Gardner Greene.* 17th Cong., 1st Sess. (S.Doc.12). Washington: Gales & Seaton, 1822. 3 pg. (Serial Set 59). Same as Finance 628 (17-1) ASP 011. See entry **1710**.

17TH CONGRESS, 2ND SESSION

1714. "New England Mississippi Land Company," *Annals of Congress.* 17th Cong., 2nd Sess. (11 Feb. 1823) pp. 201-205. Same as S.doc.32 (17-2) 74 (entry **1727**) and Public Lands 377 (17-2) ASP 030 (entry **1724**). See entry **1724** for abstract.

1715. "The Revenue Laws," *Annals of Congress.* 17th Cong., 2nd Sess. (23 Dec. 1822) pp. 1280-1288. Boston memorial desires reform of the collection and revenue laws; discusses five categories of dissatisfaction, with reasons for complaint. Same as H.doc.11 (17-2) 76 (entry **1726**) and Finance 653 (17-2) ASP 012 (entry **1725**).

1716. Allen, Samuel C. (Mass.). "Military Appropriation Bill," *Annals of Congress.* 17th Cong., 2nd Sess. (22 Feb. 1823) pp. 1087-1089. Opposes appropriations to purchase the Indian titles to land in Georgia.

1717. Baylies, Francis (Mass.). "Columbia River," *Annals of Congress.* 17th Cong., 2nd Sess. (18 Dec. 1822) pp. 413-422. Supports a territorial settlement at the Columbia River. Discusses the relevance to the whale fishery industry. Answers objections concerning expense, expanded boundaries, encouraging war, and colonization. Discusses the importance of the northwest trade and commerce of the Pacific Ocean.

1718. Baylies, Francis (Mass.). "Columbia River," *Annals of Congress.* 17th Cong., 2nd Sess. (24 Jan. 1823) pp. 680-688. Answers further objections to the settlement at the Columbia River. Addresses the lack of petitions, distance from Washington D.C., the "natural" boundary at the Rocky Mountains, difficulties attending the entrance into the mouth of the Columbia River, the barrenness of the soil and the inclemency of the climate, trade in the Pacific, Russia's claims, and the objections of the natives.

1719. Baylies, Francis (Mass.). "New Tariff Bill," *Annals of Congress.* 17th Cong., 2nd Sess. (31 Jan. 1823) pp. 788-792. Opposes the proposed duties on coarse woolens and iron; maintains that those industries would benefit at the expense of agriculture and commerce.

1720. Dwight, Henry W. (Mass.). "Aid to the Greeks," *Annals of Congress.* 17th Cong., 2nd Sess. (24 Dec. 1822) pp. 457-458. Supports a petition requesting aid on behalf of the Greeks in their struggle for liberty against the Ottoman Empire.

1721. Eustis, William (Mass.). "New Tariff Bill," *Annals of Congress.* 17th Cong., 2nd Sess. (7 Feb. 1823) pp. 891-893. Advocates protecting duties to encourage the growth of particular industries. Addresses objections.

1722. Fuller, Timothy (Mass.). "Naval Fraternal Association," *Annals of Congress.* 17th Cong., 2nd Sess. (6 Jan. 1823) pp. 499-503. Supports a fund of contributions from officers to be used to assist their dependents upon death in service. Addresses objections; maintains that the act is constitutional and advantageous to the public.

1723. "Armory at Springfield," *American State Papers: Military Affairs*, Vol. II (Doc. 246) pp. 538-553. (ASP 017). Report describes the armory at Springfield and its location; includes statistics on arms and expenditures from 1795 through 1817. Detailed report of the investigation of the state of the armory.

1724. "Claim of the New England Mississippi Land Company," *American State Papers: Public Lands*, Vol. III (Doc. 377) pp. 620-622. (ASP 030). Report of the Committee on the Judiciary on the petition of the New England Mississippi Land Company. Reviews the settlement of the claim by the Board of Commissioners, the resulting suit of Brown vs. Gilman, and the erroneous award of the Commissioners. Regardless of the error, the Committee is of the opinion that the petition should not be granted. Same as S.doc.32 (17-2) 74 (entry **1727**). Also printed in the *Annals of Congress*, "New England Mississippi Land Company," (17th Cong., 2nd Sess.) pp. 201-205 (entry **1714**).

1725. "Revision of the Revenue Laws," *American State Papers: Finance*, Vol. IV (Doc. 653) pp. 3-5. (ASP 012). Boston memorial desires reform of the collection and revenue laws; discusses five categories of dissatisfaction, with reasons for complaint. Same as H.doc.11 (17-2) 76 (entry **1726**).

1726. U.S. House. *Memorial of Sundry Merchants of Boston, upon the Subject of the Revenue Laws.* 17th Cong., 2nd Sess. (H.Doc.11). Washington: Gales & Seaton, 1822. 9 pg. (Serial Set 76). Same as Finance 653 (17-2) ASP 012. See entry **1725**.

1727. U.S. Senate. [Claim of the New England Mississippi Land Company]. 17th Cong., 2nd Sess. (S.Doc.32). [Washington: Gales & Seaton, 1823]. 5 pg. (Serial Set 74). Same as Pub.land 377 (17-2) ASP 030. See entry **1724**. Also printed in the *Annals of Congress*, "New England Mississippi Land Company," (17-2) pp. 201-205 (entry **1714**).

18TH CONGRESS, 1ST SESSION

1728. "Claim of Massachusetts," *Annals of Congress.* 18th Cong., 1st Sess. (24 Feb. 1824) pp. 301-305. Message from the President supports the claim. Reviews the circumstances, including why Massachusetts refused to comply with the call for militia and the previous decision not to allow the claim. See S.doc.43 (18-1) 90 (entry **1767**), H.doc.83 (18-1) 97 (entry **1763**), or Mil.aff.275 (18-1) ASP 018 (entry **1756**) for same report plus appended relevant documents and correspondence.

1729. "Claim of Massachusetts," *Annals of Congress.* 18th Cong., 1st Sess. (3 May 1824) pp. 2510-2513. Report of the Committee on Military Affairs to authorize the settlement and payment of the claims of Massachusetts for services rendered by the militia during the War of 1812. Same as H.rp.120 (18-1) 106 (entry **1765**) and Mil.aff.278 (18-1) ASP 018 (entry **1755**).

1730. Contested Election, *Annals of Congress.* 18th Cong., 1st Sess. (20 Feb, 16 Mar., 17 Mar., 18 Mar. 1824) pp. 1594-1612; 1793-1807; 1809-1832; 1832-1856. Discussion and debate of the report of the Committee of Elections on the contested election of John Bailey of Massachusetts. Includes report, petition of citizens of Norfolk protesting the election, certificates in behalf of Mr. Bailey, and statement of Mr. Bailey. Speakers include John Bailey (Mass.), Timothy Fuller (Mass.), and Henry R. Storrs (N.Y.). Decision against Mr. Bailey.

1731. "Memorial of the Inhabitants of Boston, on the Subject of the Greeks," *Annals of Congress.* 18th Cong., 1st Sess. (5 Jan. 1824) Appendix, pp. 3107-3109. Memorial supports Greek independence from Turkish despotism. Same as For.rel.365 (18-1) ASP 05 (entry **1758**) and H.doc.21 (19-1) 94 (entry **1761**).

1732. "Mississippi Land Company," *Annals of Congress.* 18th Cong., 1st Sess. (10 Feb. 1824) pp. 234-236. Unfavorable report of the Committee on the Judiciary to the New England Mississippi Land Company. Reviews the actions on their claim; agree that the Commissioners made an erroneous decision, but maintain that their decision was legally final. Same as Pub.land 401 (18-1) ASP 030 (entry **1752**). Also included in S.doc.32 (18-1) 90 (entry **1766**).

1733. "Remonstrance of Sundry Merchants, Manufacturers, and Others, of the City of Boston and Its Vicinity, against the Bill to Amend the Several Acts Imposing Duties on Imports and Tonnage," *Annals of Congress.* 18th Cong., 1st Sess. (9 Feb. 1824) Appendix, pp. 3079-3092. Memorial, report and resolutions oppose the proposed increase of duties and protective tariffs in general. Report examines the proposed tariff, its consequences and principles. Same as H.doc.67 (18-1) 96 (entry **1764**) and Finance 695 (18-1) ASP 012 (entry **1757**).

1734. Bailey, John (Mass.). "Contested Election," *Annals of Congress.* 18th Cong., 1st Sess. (20 Feb. 1824) pp. 1603-1612. Defends his seat in the House. Discusses his claim of being an inhabitant of the Norfolk district, and his demonstrated intention of a temporary residence in Washington. Supports his position with the previous practice of Congress, the Executive, the courts, and public sentiment.

1735. Bailey, John (Mass.). "Mr. Bailey's Case," *Annals of Congress.* 18th Cong., 1st Sess. (16 Mar. 1824) pp. 1793-1807. Defends his seat in the House. Refers to the history of previous contested elections and examines the report of the Committee of Elections. Identifies errors and inconsistencies in the principle points and arguments contained.

1736. Baylies, Francis (Mass.). "The Greek Cause," *Annals of Congress.* 18th Cong., 1st Sess. (21 Jan. 1824) pp. 1139-1144. Supports sending an agent to

Greece for inquiry. Discusses the status of the insurrection against the Turks and the character of the Greek people; addresses objections to the resolution.

1737. Baylies, Francis (Mass.). "The Tariff Bill," *Annals of Congress.* 18th Cong., 1st Sess. (19 Mar. 1824) pp. 1859-1867. Supports an additional duty on imported tallow and tallow candles; demonstrates its advantages. Discusses the importance of the whaling industry to agriculture and defense.

1738. Dwight, Henry W. (Mass.). "The Greek Cause," *Annals of Congress.* 18th Cong., 1st Sess. (20 Jan. 1824) pp. 1116-1126. Supports sending an agent to Greece and opening new commercial relations. Reviews the character and condition of the Greeks, previous commercial policies, and the possible reactions of other European powers.

1739. Fuller, Timothy (Mass.). "The Greek Cause," *Annals of Congress.* 18th Cong., 1st Sess. (24 Jan. 1824) pp. 1197-1200. Opposes the resolution providing for the appointment of a commissioner for Greece; maintains that it would result in war and retaliation against Greece, and interfere with the duties of the President.

1740. Fuller, Timothy (Mass.). "Mr. Bailey's Case," *Annals of Congress.* 18th Cong., 1st Sess. (17 Mar. 1824) pp. 1809-1819. Supports the election of John Bailey to the House. Discusses the role of the House in determining the qualifications of its members and the definition and determination of an "inhabitant." Demonstrates that Bailey's intent to return allows him to retain his status as an inhabitant, just as the President and heads of executive departments retain citizenship status in their respective states.

1741. Fuller, Timothy (Mass.). "The Tariff Bill," *Annals of Congress.* 18th Cong., 1st Sess. (28 Feb. 1824) pp. 1705-1709. Opposes increasing the duty on iron and hemp. Discusses the effects of raising these duties on the shipping industry and trade with the Baltic. Also discusses the balance of trade and export of specie.

1742. Lloyd, James (Mass.). "Commerce with Portugal," *Annals of Congress.* 18th Cong., 1st Sess. (13 Apr. 1824) pp. 515-518. Supports his request for information on the status of commercial relations with Portugal. Reviews the history of trade with Portugal and the effect of the tariffs on that trade.

1743. Lloyd, James (Mass.). "Imprisonment for Debt," *Annals of Congress.* 18th Cong., 1st Sess. (16 Mar. 1824) pp. 346-350. Remarks on the bill to abolish imprisonment for debt. Submits official documents detailing the situation and number of persons in confinement for debt in the city of Boston.

1744. Lloyd, James (Mass.). "Navy Pension Fund," *Annals of Congress.* 18th Cong., 1st Sess. (9 Jan. 1824) pp. 104-107. Supports extending the term of the pensions already granted to widows and orphans. Reviews the origin of the fund, its present condition and future prospects.

1745. Mills, Elijah H. (Mass.). "Amendment to the Constitution," *Annals of Congress.* 18th Cong., 1st Sess. (29 Dec. 1823) pp. 59-65. Supports an amendment to reinstate the original method of electing the President and Vice President. Addresses objections; introduces resolution.

1746. Reed, John (Mass.). "The Tariff Bill," *Annals of Congress.* 18th Cong., 1st Sess. (23 Mar. 1824) pp. 1880-1888. Opposes the proposed two-cent/pound duty on hemp. Maintains that increasing the duty would be injurious to the navigating interests, including the navy. Discusses why the domestic hemp industry has not been successful and why cotton manufacturing was successful.

1747. Webster, Daniel (Mass.). "The Greek Cause," *Annals of Congress.* 18th Cong., 1st Sess. (19 Jan., 24 Jan. 1824) pp. 1084-1099; 1190-1197. Supports the Greek insurrection and the resolution to provide for sending an agent to Greece. Discusses the "Holy Alliance" and its implications concerning lawful resistance. Reviews the history of Turkish rule over Greece, the conduct of neighboring nations, and the late revolution. Second speech addresses various objections urged against the resolution.

1748. Webster, Daniel (Mass.). "The Tariff Bill," *Annals of Congress.* 18th Cong., 1st Sess. (2 Apr. 1824) pp. 2026-2068. Lengthy speech opposes the passage of the bill in its present shape. Discusses the appropriateness of the terms "American policy" and "foreign policy", the condition of the country, causes and remedies for depressed prices, the example of England concerning encouragement and protection, the balance of trade, the exportation of specie, and the rate of exchange. Objects to the doctrine of protection applied generally. Discusses the relief this bill would afford and the duty on woolens and cottons. Strenuously objects to the proposed increased duty on iron and hemp.

1749. "An Act to Allow a Salary to the Collectors of the Districts of Nantucket and Pensacola, and to Abolish the Office of Surveyor of the District of Pensacola," *Statutes at Large*, Vol. IV (26 May 1824) p. 43. Also printed in the *Annals of Congress* (18th Cong., 1st Sess.) Appendix., p. 3249.

1750. "An Act Making Appropriations for Deepening the Channel Leading into the Harbour of Presque Isle, and for Repairing Plymouth Beach," *Statutes at Large*, Vol. IV (26 May 1824) p. 38. Also printed in the *Annals of Congress* (18th Cong., 1st Sess.) Appendix, p. 3249.

1751. "Against Duty on Imported Tallow and for Drawback on Candles," *American State Papers: Finance*, Vol. IV (Doc. 685) pp. 390-392. (ASP 012). Boston memorial objects to the Nantucket and New Bedford petitions that requested an additional duty on imported tallow and tallow candles. Discusses the tallow industry; supports repealing existing duties. Includes supporting petition from New York City. Same as H.doc.105 (18-1) 98 (entry **1759**), but with additional New York petition.

1752. "Claim of the New England Mississippi Land Company," *American State Papers: Public Lands*, Vol. III (Doc. 401) p. 647. (ASP 030). Unfavorable report of the Committee on the Judiciary to the petition from the New England Mississippi Land Company. Reviews the actions on their claim; agree that the Commissioners made an erroneous decision, but maintain that their decision was legally final. Same as S.doc.32 (18-1) 90 (entry **1766**) without the documents from the Commissioners on the Yazoo Claims. Also printed in the *Annals of Congress*, "Mississippi Land Company," (18-1) pp. 234-236 (entry **1732**).

1753. "Duty on Imported Tallow," *American State Papers: Finance*, Vol. IV (Doc. 680) pp. 371-372. (ASP 012). Memorial from New Bedford requests additional duty on imported tallow. Same as H.doc.107 (18-1) 98 (entry **1760**).

1754. "Duty on Imported Tallow," *American State Papers: Finance*, Vol. IV (Doc. 681) pp. 372-373. (ASP 012). Petition from Nantucket requests an increase of duty on foreign tallow to assist the whaling industry. Same as H.doc.108 (18-1) 98 (entry **1762**).

1755. "On the Claim of Massachusetts for Services Rendered by the Militia of That State during the War of 1812-'15," *American State Papers: Military Affairs*, Vol. III (Doc. 278) p. 93. (ASP 018). Report of the Committee on Military Affairs in support of claims where the militia were called out in conformity with the request of the general government, or to repel real or perceived invasion. Same as H.rp.120 (18-1) 106 (entry **1765**).

1756. "On the Services of the Militia of Massachusetts during the War of 1812-'15 and Claim of That State for Pay Therefor," *American State Papers: Military Affairs*, Vol. III (Doc. 275) pp. 8-87. (ASP 018). Report supports the claim. Reviews the circumstances, including why Massachusetts refused to comply with the call for militia and the previous decision not to allow the claim. Relevant documents and correspondence appended. Same as H.doc.83 (18-1) 97 (entry **1763**) and S.doc.43 (18-1) 90 (entry **1767**).

1757. "Remonstrance against Increase of Duties on Imports," *American State Papers: Finance*, Vol. IV (Doc. 695) pp. 467-472. (ASP 012). Memorial, report and resolutions from Boston oppose the proposed increase of duties, and protective tariffs in general. Report examines the proposed tariff, its consequences and principles. Same as H.doc.67 (18-1) 96 (entry **1764**).

1758. "Sympathy for the Greeks," *American State Papers: Foreign Relations*, Vol. V (Doc. 365) pp. 261-262. (ASP 05). Memorial from Boston supports Greek independence from Turkish despotism. Same as H.doc.21 (18-1) 94 (entry **1761**).

1759. U.S. House. *Memorial of Edmund Winchester, et als. Tallow Chandlers and Soap Boilers, in Boston, Remonstrating against the Petition of the*

Nantucket and New Bedford Oil Merchants, and Praying for a Repeal of the Laws Laying Duties on Imported Tallow, and Allowing Drawbacks on Exported Foreign Candles. 18th Cong., 1st Sess. (H.Doc.105). Washington: Gales & Seaton, 1824. 6 pg. (Serial Set 98). Same as Finance 685 (18-1) ASP 012 (entry **1751**), without the supporting petition from New York City.

1760. U.S. House. *Memorial of the Citizens of New Bedford, in the State of Massachusetts; Praying an Increase of the Duty on Imported Tallow.* 18th Cong., 1st Sess. (H.Doc.107). Washington: Gales & Seaton, 1824. 5 pg. (Serial Set 98). Same as Finance 680 (18-1) ASP 012 (entry **1753**).

1761. U.S. House. *Memorial of the Inhabitants of Boston, on the Subject of the Greeks.* 18th Cong., 1st Sess. (H.Doc.21). Washington: Gales & Seaton, 1824. 5 pg. (Serial Set 94). Memorial in support of Greek independence from Turkish despotism. Same as For.rel.365 (18-1) ASP 05 (entry **1758**).

1762. U.S. House. *Memorial of the Inhabitants of Nantucket, Praying an Increase of Duty on Imported Tallow.* 18th Cong., 1st Sess. (H.Doc.108). Washington: Gales & Seaton, 1824. 5 pg. (Serial Set 98). Same as Finance 681 (18-1) ASP 012 (entry **1754**).

1763. U.S. House. *Message from the President of the United States, Transmitting Certain Documents Relating to the Claim of the State of Massachusetts, for Services Rendered by the Militia of That State, during the Late War with Great Britain.* 18th Cong., 1st Sess. (H.Doc.83). Washington: Gales & Seaton, 1824. 177 pg. (Serial Set 97). Same as S.doc.43 (18-1) 90 (entry **1767**) and Mil.aff.275 (18-1) ASP 018 (entry **1756**). See entry **1756** for abstract.

1764. U.S. House. *Remonstrance of Sundry Merchants, Manufacturers, and Others, of the City of Boston and its Vicinity, against the Bill to Amend the Several Acts Imposing Duties on Imports and Tonnage.* 18th Cong., 1st Sess. (H.Doc.67). Washington: Gales & Seaton, 1824. 18 pg. (Serial Set 96). Same as Finance 695 (18-1) ASP 012. See entry **1757**.

1765. U.S. House. *Report of the Committee on Military Affairs, upon the Subject of the Claim of the State of Massachusetts for Services Rendered by the Militia of Said State, during the Late War; with "a Bill Providing for the Settlement and Payment of Said Claim."* 18th Cong., 1st Sess. (H.Rpt.120). [Washington: 1824]. 3 pg. (Serial Set 106). Same as Mil.aff.278 (18-1) ASP 018. See entry **1755**.

1766. U.S. Senate. [Claim of the New England Mississippi Land Company]. 18th Cong., 1st Sess. (S.Doc.32). [Washington: Gales & Seaton, 1824]. 9 pg. (Serial Set 90). Same as Pub.land 401 (18-1) ASP 030 but with the additional Commissioners' documents. See entry **1752**. Committee's report also published in the *Annals of Congress*, "Mississippi Land Company," (18-1) pp. 234-236 (entry **1732**).

1767. U.S. Senate. *Message from the President of the United States, Transmitting Certain Documents in Relation to the Claim of the State of Massachusetts, for Services Rendered by the Militia of That State, during the Late War with Great Britain.* 18th Cong., 1st Sess. (S.Doc.43). Washington: Gales & Seaton, 1824. 177 pg. (Serial Set 90). Same as H.doc.83 (18-1) 97 (entry **1763**) and Mil.aff.275 (18-1) ASP 018 (entry **1756**). See entry **1756** for abstract.

18TH CONGRESS, 2ND SESSION

1768. "Massachusetts Claims," *Register of Debates.* 18th Cong., 2nd Sess. (22 Feb., 2 Mar. 1825) pp. 645-646; 735. Various short remarks support the claim of Massachusetts for militia services during the War of 1812.

1769. Dwight, Henry W. (Mass.). "Niagara Sufferers," *Register of Debates.* 18th Cong., 2nd Sess. (3 Jan. 1825) pp. 120-121. Advocates compensation to citizens whose property was destroyed during the government's occupation.

1770. Dwight, Henry W. (Mass.). "United States' Penal Code," *Register of Debates.* 18th Cong., 2nd Sess. (25 Jan. 1825) pp. 351-352. Supports capital punishment for arsonists.

1771. Lloyd, James (Mass.). "Suppression of Piracy," *Register of Debates.* 18th Cong., 2nd Sess. (31 Jan. 1825) pp. 379-383. Supports blockading the ports of islands harboring pirates. Gives historical review of the problem and proposed solutions, including examples of attacks. Maintains that blockading is the most efficient method proposed.

1772. Mills, Elijah H. (Mass.). "Suppression of Piracy," *Register of Debates.* 18th Cong., 2nd Sess. (31 Jan. 1825) pp. 375-379. Supports blockading the ports of Cuba to suppress piracy. Discusses the provision in relation to the other provisions of the bill; addresses objections to the measure.

1773. Webster, Daniel (Mass.). "Penal Laws of the United States," *Register of Debates.* 18th Cong., 2nd Sess. (10 Jan. 1825) pp. 166-168. Supports Congress legislating for the punishment of maritime crimes. Reviews the legislative and judicial power to punish crimes against the government.

1774. Webster, Daniel (Mass.). "Western National Road," *Register of Debates.* 18th Cong., 2nd Sess. (18 Jan. 1825) pp. 249-252, 254-255. Supports appropriations for the road as beneficial to the western states and the nation. Maintains that it would encourage settlement and increase the value of the public lands, and that Congress has an obligation to fulfill its promises of aid.

1775. "On the Audit of the Claim of Massachusetts for the Services of the Militia of That State during the War of 1812-'15," *American State Papers: Military Affairs*, Vol. III (Doc. 283) pp. 104-108. (ASP 018). Report of the auditor, as governed by the principles of the bill reported by the Military Committee of the last session, on the services of the militia commanded by Majors General King and Sewall. Same as H.doc.97 (18-2) 118 (entry **1777**).

1776. U.S. House. *Letter from the Secretary of War, Transmitting Copies of the Reports and Drawings of the Superintending Engineer, Relating to the Repair of Plymouth Beach.* 18th Cong., 2nd Sess. (H.Doc.27). Washington: Gales & Seaton, 1825. 11 pg. (Serial Set 114). Reports and estimates recommend repairs necessary to preserve Plymouth Beach.

1777. U.S. House. *Message from the President of the United States, Transmitting a Report of the Third Auditor of the Treasury, on So Much of the Claim of Massachusetts, As Has Been Fully Audited, for the Services of the Militia of Said State, Belonging to the Division Commanded by Major Generals King and Sewall.* 18th Cong., 2nd Sess. (H.Doc.97). Washington: Gales & Seaton, 1825. 13 pg. (Serial Set 118). Same as Mil.aff.283 (18-2) ASP 018 (entry **1775**).

1778. U.S. Senate. [Claim of the New England Mississippi Land Company]. 18th Cong., 2nd Sess. (S.Doc.14). [Washington: Gales & Seaton, 1825]. 7 pg. (Serial Set 109). Unfavorable report of the Committee on the Judiciary to the petition of the New England Mississippi Land Company. Reviews the actions on their claim. Includes copies of documents from the Commissioners on Yazoo Claims, Georgia Mississippi Company. Same as S.doc.32 (18-1) 90 (entry **1766**).

19ᵀᴴ CONGRESS, 1ˢᵀ SESSION

1779. Debate on the Massachusetts Militia Claims, *Register of Debates.* 19th Cong., 1st Sess. (25 Mar., 7 Apr., 8 Apr. 1826) pp. 1768-1796; 2099-2121; 2122-2133. Debate over the claims of Massachusetts for expenses incurred from the services of her militia during the War of 1812. Includes a review of the claims and previous action taken upon them, history of the events, arguments for and against the claims, and discussion of the constitutional issues involved. Major participants include Davis (Mass.), Houston (Tenn.), Dwight (Mass.), Sprague (Me.), Wright (Ohio), Stevenson (Pa.), and Whipple (N.H.).

1780. Baylies, Francis (Mass.). "Appropriations for Fortifications," *Register of Debates.* 19th Cong., 1st Sess. (27 Jan. 1826) pp. 1186-1188. Questions the value of the proposed fortifications.

1781. Davis, John (Mass.). "Massachusetts Militia Claims," *Register of Debates.* 19th Cong., 1st Sess. (25 Mar. 1826) pp. 1769-1782. Supports the claims. Reviews the claims, including the history of events, previous action taken, objections, and the constitutional issues involved.

1782. Dwight, Henry W. (Mass.). "Massachusetts Claims," *Register of Debates.* 19th Cong., 1st Sess. (7 Apr. 1826) pp. 2099-2110. Supports the claims of Massachusetts for expenses incurred from the services of her militia during the late war. Reviews and addresses the principles upon which the claims are sustained, the constitutional questions involved, the provisions of the bill, arguments of opponents, and the necessity for a legislative opinion.

1783. Dwight, Henry W. (Mass.). "Michigan Contested Election," *Register of Debates.* 19th Cong., 1st Sess. (20 Mar. 1826) pp. 1695-1698. Remarks on the contested election between Mr. Biddle and Mr. Wing; contends that Mr. Wing is entitled to the seat.

1784. Everett, Edward (Mass.). "Amendment of the Constitution," *Register of Debates.* 19th Cong., 1st Sess. (9 Mar. 1826) pp. 1570-1597. Responds to Mr. McDuffie's (S.C.) proposed amendments to the Constitution to modify the election of the President. Reviews the constitutional rights and power of amendment; addresses the general ticket versus the district system, the objections to the general ticket system, and the power of the Executive. Maintains that the current process has not failed.

1785. Everett, Edward (Mass.). "Mission to Panama," *Register of Debates.* 19th Cong., 1st Sess. (20 Apr. 1826) pp. 2427-2433. Opposes the amendments placing restrictions on the ministers to the Congress of Panama as uncalled for and unnecessary. Discusses the instructions to the ministers concerning religious liberty. Maintains that participation in the Congress is congruent with the foreign policy doctrines of Washington.

1786. Everett, Edward (Mass.). "Mission to Panama," *Register of Debates.* 19th Cong., 1st Sess. (20 Apr. 1826) pp. 2442-2443. Responds to Mr. Cambreleng (N.Y.) clarifying earlier comments on slavery.

1787. Everett, Edward (Mass.). "Revolutionary Officers," *Register of Debates.* 19th Cong., 1st Sess. (25 Apr. 1826) pp. 2566-2573. Supports the claims of the surviving Revolutionary officers for their due compensation; regrets that widows and children of those who are deceased cannot be included. Presents arguments for the bill; addresses objections.

1788. Lloyd, James (Mass.). "Discriminating Duties," *Register of Debates.* 19th Cong., 1st Sess. (25 Jan. 1826) pp. 70-76. Supports lifting discriminating duties from reciprocating nations. Reviews the evolution of U.S. commercial relations and the state of foreign trade. Addresses the beneficial effects of the proposed bill.

1789. Lloyd, James (Mass.). "Discriminating Duties," *Register of Debates.* 19th Cong., 1st Sess. (18 Apr. 1826) pp. 586-589. Opposes abolishing the discriminating duties on British Colonial vessels without any condition. Opposes conceding all inducements to fair trade while gaining nothing in return. Contends that the free port or warehousing system is disadvantageous.

1790. Reed, John (Mass.). "Mission to Panama," *Register of Debates.* 19th Cong., 1st Sess. (12 Apr. 1826) pp. 2215-2224. Supports appropriations to send ministers to the Congress at Panama; addresses objections. Maintains that the proposed conditional amendments are an unwarrantable assumption of power and interfere with the Executive's constitutional authority to instruct ministers and ambassadors.

1791. Webster, Daniel (Mass.). "Congress of Panama," *Register of Debates.* 19th Cong., 1st Sess. (3 Feb. 1826) pp. 1279-1282. Supports allowing executive discretion to judge the communication of the information requested concerning the Congress.

1792. Webster, Daniel (Mass.). "Judiciary System," *Register of Debates.* 19th Cong., 1st Sess. (4 Jan., 24 Jan., 25 Jan. 1826) pp. 872-880; 1111-1113; 1123-1124. Supports the proposed bill, which would increase the number of Supreme Court judges and retain these judges on the Circuits. Reviews the legislative history of the Judiciary. Maintains that the bill would address the pressing needs of the western states. Addresses various arguments against the bill and proposed amendments.

1793. Webster, Daniel (Mass.). "Judiciary System," *Register of Debates.* 19th Cong., 1st Sess. (25 Jan. 1826) pp. 1139-1148. Supports the proposed reforms. Reviews objections to the bill and alternative proposals. Maintains that the proposed bill is the best plan available.

1794. Webster, Daniel (Mass.). "Mission to Panama," *Register of Debates.* 19th Cong., 1st Sess. (14 Apr. 1826) pp. 2254-2277. Supports appropriations for the Congress and opposes the House interfering with the executive powers over foreign relations. Maintains that the House should not give instructions, advice or directions prescribing what the ministers may discuss. Lengthy review and discussion of the neutrality policy and its applicability to the Congress and South American independence.

1795. "Claim of the New England Mississippi Land Company," *American State Papers: Public Lands*, Vol. IV (Doc. 473) pp. 464-467. (ASP 031). Report from the Committee on the Judiciary to the petition from the New England Mississippi Land Company. Reviews the actions taken on their claim; agree that the Commissioners made an erroneous decision, but maintain that their decision was legally final. Supports the return of their money still in the Treasury. Includes copies of documents from the Commissioners on the Yazoo Claims, Georgia Mississippi Company, and the statement made by the petitioners to the Judiciary Committee. Reprints most of Pub.land 401 (18-1) ASP 030 (entry **1752**) and S.doc.32 (18-1) 90 (entry **1766**). Same as S.doc.17 (19-1) 125 (entry **1807**), but includes the additional statement by the petitioners.

1796. "On the Claims of Massachusetts on Account of the Services of the Militia of That State," *American State Papers: Military Affairs*, Vol. III (Doc. 288) pp. 159-161. (ASP 018). Report of the Committee on Military Affairs supports the claims; clarifies qualifications for compensation. Includes reprint of earlier report of that Committee (H.rp.120 (18-1) 106 (entry **1765**) or Mil.aff.278 (18-1) ASP 018 (entry **1755**)).

1797. "Rules for the Adjudication of Claims for Militia Services, and Report of Third Auditor on the Claim of Massachusetts," *American State Papers: Military Affairs*, Vol. III (Doc. 291) pp. 167-184. (ASP 018). Report and documents contain the rules used to adjust claims for the services of the militia. Includes reports relative to the claims for the Massachusetts militia during the late war while under the command of Major Generals Goodwin, Richardson, Hubbard, Cobb, Hovey, Whiton, Varnum, and Burbank. Same as H.doc.29 (19-1) 133 (entry **1802**).

1798. U.S. House. *Canal - Boston Harbor to Narraganset Bay*. 19th Cong., 1st Sess. (H.Rpt.214). [Washington: Gales & Seaton, 1826]. 9 pg. (Serial Set 142). Report supports a survey for a possible canal route from Taunton to Weymouth, Mass. to ascertain the practicality of uniting Boston Harbor with Narragansett Bay. Includes a supporting letter from Aaron Hobart, who offered the motion, and a relevant 1808 report ordered by the Massachusetts Legislature.

1799. U.S. House. *Letter for the Secretary of War, in Reply to a Resolution of the House of Representatives, of the 31st Ultimo, in Relation to the Survey for a Canal Route Between Buzzard's and Barnstable Bay*. 19th Cong., 1st Sess. (H.Doc.77). Washington: Gales & Seaton, 1826. 3 pg. (Serial Set 134). Brief note reports that the survey has been completed but has not yet been transmitted to the Department.

1800. U.S. House. *Letter from the Secretary of War, in Answer to the Resolution of the House of Representatives, of 31st Ultimo, in Relation to a Survey of the Harbor of Marblehead and Holmes' Hole*. 19th Cong., 1st Sess. (H.Doc.71). Washington: Gales & Seaton, 1826. 3 pg. (Serial Set 134). Letter indicates that the surveys have been completed and will be furnished to the House as soon as they are received.

1801. U.S. House. *Letter from the Secretary of War, Transmitting a Memoir on the Survey of the Route of a Canal, to Connect Buzzard and Barnstable Bays, in the State of Massachusetts, with Three Sheets of Drawings*. 19th Cong., 1st Sess. (H.Doc.174). Washington: Gales & Seaton, 1826. 15 pg., 2 maps. (Serial Set 140). Survey on the practicality of the canal. Includes a profile of the proposed route of the canal and maps entitled, "Survey across the Isthmus of Cape Cod, State of Massachusetts, and Town of Sandwich of a Proposed Canal between Buzzard's and Barnstable Bays," and "Survey of a Valley and Ponds Auxiliary to a Contemplated Canal Between Buzzard's & Barnstable Bays, State of Massachusetts and Town of Sandwich."

1802. U.S. House. *Letter from the Secretary of War, Transmitting the Information Required by a Resolution of the House of Representatives, of the 4th January, Instant, in Relation to the Rules Adopted in the Settlement of the Militia Claims of the Several States, and the Reports of the Third Auditor, on the Claim of the State of Massachusetts, for the Services of the Militia of That State.* 19th Cong., 1st Sess. (H.Doc.29). Washington: Gales & Seaton, 1826. 44 pg. (Serial Set 133). Same as Mil.aff.291 (19-1) ASP 018. See entry **1797**.

1803. U.S. House. *Letter from the Secretary of War, Transmitting the Information Required by a Resolution of the House of Representatives, of 30th Jan. Last, Respecting the Improvement of the Harbors of Marblehead & Holmes' Hole.* 19th Cong., 1st Sess. (H.Doc.172). Washington: Gales & Seaton, 1826. 10 pg. (Serial Set 140). Report on the contemplated improvement of the harbors by the erection of piers to protect shipping; includes copies of two drawings as well as an estimate of the expenses.

1804. U.S. House. *Massachusetts Militia Claims.* 19th Cong., 1st Sess. (H.Rpt.18). [Washington: 1826]. 191 pg. (Serial Set 141). Report of the Committee on Military Affairs supports the claims; clarifies qualifications for compensation. Includes reprints of the earlier report of the Committee (Mil.aff.278 (18-1) ASP 018 (entry **1755**) or H.rp.120 (18-1) 106 (entry **1765**)), President's message (Mil.aff.275 (18-1) ASP 018 (entry **1756**) or H.doc.83 (18-1) 97 (entry **1763**) or S.doc.43 (18-1) 90 (entry **1767**)), and auditor's report (Mil.aff.283 (18-2) ASP 018 (entry **1775**) or H.doc.97 (18-2) 118 (entry **1777**)).

1805. U.S. House. *Memorial of the Citizens of Newburyport, on the Subject of Depredations by France, Holland, Naples, and Denmark.* 19th Cong., 1st Sess. (H.Doc.45). Washington: Gales & Seaton, 1826. 4 pg. (Serial Set 133). Memorial for satisfaction of claims of spoliations on commerce committed in 1809 and 1810. Includes names of memorialists.

1806. U.S. House. *Message from the President of the United States, Transmitting the Information Required by a Resolution of the House of Representatives, of the 16th ult. in Relation to the Nett Revenue Derived from Imposts and Tonnage, from the 1st of January, 1790, from Ports within the Chesapeake and Delaware Bays, New York, and Boston, Also, the Expenditures at the Same Places, from the Same Period, to Aid Commerce, or for the Purposes of Defence.* 19th Cong., 1st Sess. (H.Doc.139). Washington: Gales & Seaton, 1826. 6 pg., 4 tables. (Serial Set 138).

1807. U.S. Senate. [Claim of the New England Mississippi Land Company]. 19th Cong., 1st Sess. (S.Doc.17). [Washington: Gales & Seaton, 1826]. 7 pg. (Serial Set 125). Report of the Committee on the Judiciary to the petition of the New England Mississippi Land Company. Reviews the actions on their claim; agrees that the Commissioners made an erroneous decision, but maintains that their decision was legally final. Supports the return of their money that is still in the Treasury. Includes copies of documents from the Commissioners on Yazoo Claims, Georgia Mississippi Company. Same as Pub.land 473 (19-1) ASP 031 (entry **1795**), but without the statement from the petitioners. Also reprinted as S.doc.6 (19-2) 145 (entry **1838**), S.doc.15 (20-1) 163 (entry **1870**), S.doc.21 (20-2) 181 (entry **1891**), Pub.land 701 (20-2) ASP 032 (entry **1886**), S.doc.52 (21-1) 193 (entry **1922**), and S.doc.29 (22-1) 212 (entry **1999**).

19TH CONGRESS, 2ND SESSION

1808. "Massachusetts Militia Claims," *Register of Debates.* 19th Cong., 2nd Sess. (14 Dec., 15 Dec. 1826) pp. 531-532; 532-537. Debate on the resolutions to refer the claim to the Secretary of War to report what items and classes of claims are within the same principles and rules that have been applied to the adjustment of claims of other states for militia services during the late war. Includes remarks by Ichabod Bartlett (N.H.) and Peleg Sprague (Maine).

1809. "The Yazoo Purchase," *Register of Debates.* 19th Cong., 2nd Sess. (3 Jan. 1827) pp. 30-35. Debate on the report to grant the claim of the Directors of the New England Mississippi Land Company.

1810. Davis, John (Mass.). "Duties on Wool and Woollens," *Register of Debates.* 19th Cong., 2nd Sess. (31 Jan. 1827) pp. 881-890. Supports the proposed modifications of the tariff of 1824 to alter the collection of duties upon woolens to provide the protection originally intended. Addresses the need for the bill, its provisions and their operation upon the revenue, and objections.

1811. Dwight, Henry W. (Mass.). "Accounts of Mr. Adams," *Register of Debates.* 19th Cong., 2nd Sess. (27 Feb. 1827) pp. 1447-1449. Defends Mr. Adams, late Minister to St. Petersburg, against accusations of charging for expenses for a journey not made.

1812. Dwight, Henry W. (Mass.). "Duties on Wool and Woollens," *Register of Debates.* 19th Cong., 2nd Sess. (23 Jan., 25 Jan. 1827) pp. 791-793; 825-827. Supports the bill to stop fraud and evasion of duties upon wool and woolens.

1813. Dwight, Henry W. (Mass.). "Internal Improvement," *Register of Debates.* 19th Cong., 2nd Sess. (20 Feb. 1827) pp. 1300-1310. Responds to previous speech of Mr. Rives (Va.). Maintains that the act of 1824, authorizing the President to institute surveys and estimates of roads and canals necessary for national military, commercial, or postal purposes, binds the House to approve appropriations for those purposes. Defends executive authority to execute the law. Maintains that the Treasury has the resources to meet the demands upon it as well as make payments towards the national debt.

1814. Dwight, Henry W. (Mass.). "Tacubaya Mission," *Register of Debates.* 19th Cong., 2nd Sess. (15 Feb. 1827) pp. 1208-1211. Supports appropriations for the minister to Tacubaya; reviews other cases where ministers transferred to another court were entitled to an additional outfit.

1815. Everett, Edward (Mass.). "Importation of Brandy in Small Casks," *Register of Debates.* 19th Cong., 2nd Sess. (3 Jan. 1827) pp. 593-596. Supports allowing the importation of brandy in small casks. Discusses objections concerning competition between agriculture and commerce, smuggling, and the manufacture of domestic spirits.

1816. Everett, Edward (Mass.). "Surviving Officers of the Revolution," *Register of Debates.* 19th Cong., 2nd Sess. (15 Jan. 1827) pp. 719-724. Objects to extending relief to the heirs and representatives of officers and soldiers of the Revolution that are deceased. Discusses objections.

1817. Silsbee, Nathaniel (Mass.). "The Colonial Trade Bill," *Register of Debates.* 19th Cong., 2nd Sess. (21 Feb. 1827) pp. 420-428. Supports closing United States ports to British trade unless Britain removes her prohibitions against colonial trade. Discusses the history of commercial relations with Britain, the comparative value of the export and import trade with the British colonies, the coasting trade, and the discriminating duties in the British colonies.

1818. Webster, Daniel (Mass.). "Accounts of Mr. Adams," *Register of Debates.* 19th Cong., 2nd Sess. (27 Feb. 1827) pp. 1449-1451. Supports charges against Mr. Adams for receiving improper compensation while a minister abroad.

1819. Webster, Daniel (Mass.). "British Colonial Trade," *Register of Debates.* 19th Cong., 2nd Sess. (2 Mar. 1827) pp. 1522-1527. Opposes the bill in its present form; supports an amendment whereby British vessels from the colonies would be excluded from U.S. ports if conditions are not met. Discusses the acts of 1818, 1820, and 1823, and the effect and operation of the proposed bill.

1820. Webster, Daniel (Mass.). "United States and Georgia," *Register of Debates.* 19th Cong., 2nd Sess. (9 Feb. 1837) pp. 1034-1036, 1046-1049. Remarks on the disputed Creek treaties, originally ceding land to the United States and later annulled. Reviews the circumstances; supports referring the issue to committee for consideration.

1821. "An Act Establishing a Port of Delivery at the Town of Marshfield, in the District of Plymouth, and a Port of Delivery at Rhinebeck Landing, in the

District of New York," *Statutes at Large*, Vol. IV (2 Mar. 1827) p. 237. Also printed in the *Register of Debates* (19th Cong., 2nd Sess.) Appendix, p. xx.

1822. "Duties on Imports of Woolen Goods," *American State Papers: Finance*, Vol. V (Doc. 784) p. 623. (ASP 013). Memorial from Boston opposes the proposed increase of duty on imported woolens. Same as H.doc.115 (19-2) 152 (entry **1831**), without the transmittal note, and S.doc.68 (19-2) 146 (entry **1839**).

1823. "Duty on Imported Salt," *American State Papers: Finance*, Vol. V (Doc. 774) p. 607. (ASP 013). Memorial from New Bedford, Dartmouth, Fairhaven, and adjacent towns, contends that investments in local salt manufacturing were based on a protective tariff and could not survive without the duty. Same as H.doc.80 (19-2) 152 (entry **1832**).

1824. "Duty on Imported Salt," *American State Papers: Finance*, Vol. V (Doc. 777) p. 613. (ASP 013). Memorial from Chatham against the repeal of the imported salt duty; contends that the local salt manufacturing could not survive without the duty. Same as H.doc.96 (19-2) 152 (entry **1835**).

1825. "Duty on Imported Salt," *American State Papers: Finance*, Vol. V (Doc. 776) p. 612. (ASP 013). Memorial from the inhabitants of Provincetown, Mass., opposes the repeal of the duty on salt; large investments in salt manufacturing were based on a protective duty. Same as H.Doc.95 (19-2) 152 (entry **1836**).

1826. "Protection to Woolen Manufactures," *American State Papers: Finance*, Vol. V (Doc. 771) pp. 599-600. (ASP 013). Report from the Massachusetts House of Representatives supports protection from foreign competition; includes statement from the Wolcott Woolen Manufacturing Company. Same as H.doc.70 (19-2) 151 (entry **1837**).

1827. "Revolutionary Bounty Land Claims," *American State Papers: Public Lands*, Vol. IV (Doc. 540) p. 861. (ASP 031). Report advises against the claim of James Raven, of Massachusetts, for his bounty land claim due as a Revolutionary soldier.

1828. U.S. House. *Letter from the Secretary of War, in Reply to a Resolution of the House of Representatives of the 2d of Jan. Last Requiring an Estimate of the Expense of Making a Canal Between Barnstable and Buzzard's Bays.* 19th Cong., 2nd Sess. (H.Doc.97). Washington: Gales & Seaton, 1827. 3 pg. (Serial Set 152). Brief note that an estimate of expenses has not yet been made.

1829. U.S. House. *Letter from the Secretary of War, in Reply to a Resolution of the House of Representatives, of 31st Ultimo, in Relation to a Survey of the Island of Nantucket, &t.* 19th Cong., 1st Sess. (H.Doc.72). Washington: Gales & Seaton, 1826. 3 pg. (Serial Set 134). Letter reports that the surveys are in progress and expected to be finished shortly.

1830. U.S. House. *Letter from the Secretary of War, Transmitting Reports of a Survey on the Flats on the Northwest Side of the Harbor of Edgartown; a Survey of the Mouth of Merrimack River; Also, a Survey of the Harbor of Hyannis, in the Vineyard Sound, with a Map of Each: Rendered in Obedience to a Resolution of the House of Representatives, of the Fourth of Last Month.* 19th Cong., 2nd Sess. (H.Doc.140). Washington: Gales & Seaton, 1827. 16 pg. (Serial Set 154). Reports and survey advise on the feasibility of building a lighthouse and deepening the channel at Edgartown Harbor and improving the safety at Newburyport, at the mouth of the Merrimack River.

1831. U.S. House. *Memorial of Citizens of Boston and Its Vicinity, against the Contemplated Increase of Duty on Certain Woollen Goods Imported.* 19th Cong., 2nd Sess. (H.Doc.115). Washington: Gales & Seaton, 1827. 4 pg. (Serial Set 152). Same as S.doc.68 (19-2) 146 (entry **1839**) and Finance 784 (19-2) ASP 013 (entry **1822**), but with additional transmittal note.

1832. U.S. House. *Memorial of Inhabitants of New Bedford, Dartmouth, &c. against Reducing the Duty on Salt.* 19th Cong., 2nd Sess. (H.Doc.80). Washington: Gales & Seaton, 1827. 4 pg. (Serial Set 152). Same as Finance 774 (19-2) ASP 013. See entry **1823**.

1833. U.S. House. *Memorial of Sundry Inhabitants of Massachusetts, Praying that the Duty on Imported Salt May Not Be Repealed.* 19th Cong., 2nd Sess. (H.Doc.91). Washington: Gales & Seaton, 1827. 4 pg. (Serial Set 152). Memorial maintains that salt manufacturing has increased and that the imported salt is not necessary.

1834. U.S. House. *Message from the President of the United States, Transmitting a Report of an Examination and Survey Which Has Been Made of a Site for a Dry Dock at Portsmouth, N.H., Charlestown, Mass., Brooklyn, N.Y., and Gosport, Va.* 19th Cong., 2nd Sess. (H.Doc.125). Washington: Gales & Seaton, 1827. 46 pg. (Serial Set 153). Report recommends construction of three dry docks in the following order of importance: Charlestown, Gosport, and Brooklyn. Report gives general topographical and soil information and indicates the most eligible site in each, with the corresponding expenses and advantages.

1835. U.S. House. *Remonstrance of Inhabitants of Chatham, in the State of Massachusetts, against a Repeal of the Law Imposing a Duty on Salt Imported.* 19th Cong., 2nd Sess. (H.Doc.96). Washington: Gales & Seaton, 1827. 3 pg. (Serial Set 152). Same as Finance 777 (19-2) ASP 013. See entry **1824**.

1836. U.S. House. *Remonstrance of Inhabitants of Provincetown, in the State of Massachusetts, against a Repeal of the Law Imposing a Duty on Salt Imported.* 19th Cong., 2nd Sess. (H.Doc.95). Washington: Gales & Seaton, 1827. 4 pg. (Serial Set 152). Same as Finance 776 (19-2) ASP 013. See entry **1825**.

1837. U.S. House. *Report of a Committee of the House of Representatives of the State of Massachusetts, on the Subject of Woollen Manufactures, &c.* 19th Cong., 2nd Sess. (H.Doc.70). Washington: Gales & Seaton, 1827. 5 pg. (Serial Set 151). Same as Finance 771 (19-2) ASP 013. See entry **1826**.

1838. U.S. Senate. [Claim of the New England Mississippi Land Company]. 19th Cong., 2nd Sess. (S.Doc.6). [Washington: Gales & Seaton, 1827]. 8 pg. (Serial Set 145). Same as S.doc.17 (19-1) 125 (entry **1807**), S.doc.15 (20-1) 163 (entry **1870**), S.doc.21 (20-2) 181 (entry **1891**), Pub.land 701 (20-2) ASP 032 (entry **1886**), S.doc.52 (21-1) 193 (entry **1922**), and S.doc.29 (22-1) 212 (entry **1999**). See entry **1807** for abstract.

1839. U.S. Senate. *Memorial of Inhabitants of Boston, and Its Vicinity, Adverse to an Increase of Duty on Imported Woollen Goods.* 19th Cong., 2nd Sess. (S.Doc.68). Washington: Gales & Seaton, 1827. 3 pg. (Serial Set 146). Same as H.doc.115 (19-2) 152 (entry **1831**), without the transmittal note, and Finance 784 (19-2) ASP 013 (entry **1822**).

20TH CONGRESS, 1ST SESSION

1840. Allen, Samuel C. (Mass.). "Case of Marigny D'Auterive," *Register of Debates.* 20th Cong., 1st Sess. (18 Jan. 1828) pp. 1060-1061. Opposes the claim for the injury of a slave that was impressed into service; considers rights of property as applies to slaves.

1841. Bates, Isaac C. (Mass.). "Case of Marigny D'Auterive," *Register of Debates.* 20th Cong., 1st Sess. (7 Feb. 1828) pp. 1484-1486. Opposes the claim for the injury of a slave that was impressed into service.

1842. Davis, John (Mass.). "Land Claims in Tennessee," *Register of Debates.* 20th Cong., 1st Sess. (30 Apr. 1828) pp. 2542-2548. Objects to the bill granting the remaining public lands in Tennessee to that state for the use of schools. Principle objections grow out of the terms of the cession of Tennessee from North Carolina, including the provisions for outstanding military claims. Maintains that the United States has no obligation to support the claim.

1843. Davis, John (Mass.). "Tariff Bill," *Register of Debates.* 20th Cong., 1st Sess. (13 Mar. 1828) pp. 1878-1899. Advocates amending the proposed bill to afford more protection for wool and woolens. Addresses the needs of wool-growers and manufacturers for aid and the arguments against protection. Discusses the effects of the proposed bill, its major objections and advantages.

1844. Dwight, Henry W. (Mass.). "Mr. Meade's Claim," *Register of Debates.* 20th Cong., 1st Sess. (22 Mar. 1828) pp. 1960-1962. Supports the claim as an obligation incurred by the 1819 treaty with Spain (Florida Treaty).

1845. Everett, Edward (Mass.). "Case of Marigny D'Auterive," *Register of Debates.* 20th Cong., 1st Sess. (18 Jan. 1828) pp. 1057-1060. Supports the claim of Marigny D'Auterive for an injury to a slave impressed into service.

1846. Everett, Edward (Mass.). "Claim of Mr. Meade," *Register of Debates.* 20th Cong., 1st Sess. (23 Feb. 1828) pp. 1594-1600. Supports the claims of Richard W. Meade that were assumed by the U.S. from Spain under the Florida Treaty. Reviews the case and presents arguments on its merits.

1847. Everett, Edward (Mass.). "Retrenchment," *Register of Debates.* 20th Cong., 1st Sess. (1 Feb. 1828) pp. 1300-1315. Defends President Adams against various charges concerning his compensation and allowances as a foreign minister. Discusses the circumstances and charges; compares to Monroe. Reviews the history of legislation governing funds for foreign service; addresses other charges of extravagant expenditures by the administration.

1848. Gorham, Benjamin (Mass.). "Internal Improvements," *Register of Debates.* 20th Cong., 1st Sess. (29 Feb. 1828) pp. 1690-1692. Objects to the government funding a system of internal improvements as impracticable and subject to great abuse; supports appropriations for surveys.

1849. Gorham, Benjamin (Mass.). "United States' Bank Stock," *Register of Debates.* 20th Cong., 1st Sess. (21 Dec. 1827) pp. 842-848. Supports the bank and opposes the sale of the bank stock. Considers the financial effect of the bank's expiring charter upon the stock; maintains that the proposed bill is based upon political considerations and opposition to the bank.

1850. Reed, John (Mass.). "Tariff Bill," *Register of Debates.* 20th Cong., 1st Sess. (3 Apr. 1828) pp. 2135-2156. Opposes the proposed bill. Discusses navigation, the foreign trade, the coasting trade, and the West Indies trade, and the reasons for their success. Addresses in detail the proposed increased duties on hemp and molasses.

1851. Webster, Daniel (Mass.). "Tariff Bill," *Register of Debates.* 20th Cong., 1st Sess. (9 May 1828) pp. 750-762. Denies that the proposed tariff bill is a New England measure. Reviews the history of New England toward protective policies; discusses the harmful effect of the proposed duties on wool, molasses and hemp. Opposes the bill as measure that would be felt by the whole nation.

1852. "Against Increase of Duties on Imports," *American State Papers: Finance,* Vol. V (Doc. 790) pp. 671-676. (ASP 013). Memorial from Boston opposes an increase of duties on woolen manufactured goods; maintains that the majority of public opinion is opposed to increased duties. Addresses the fallacies behind protective policies. Same as S.doc.6 (20-1) 163 (entry **1872**).

1853. "Against Increase of Duties on Imports," *American State Papers: Finance,* Vol. V (Doc. 823) pp. 735-736. (ASP 013). Memorial from Plymouth and Kingston, Mass. opposes increasing duties on woolen goods as impolitic and unjust. Same as S.doc.46 (20-1) 164 (entry **1874**), but without the memorialists names.

1854. "Against Increase of Duties on Imports," *American State Papers: Finance*, Vol. V (Doc. 834) pp. 757-759. (ASP 013). Memorial and transmittal letter from Westborough, Mass. against an increase of duties, particularly on woolens. Same as H.doc.95 (20-1) 171 (entry **1869**), but without the transmittal letter, and S.doc.64 (20-1) 164 (entry **1875**).

1855. "Claim of Massachusetts on Account of Militia Services during the War of 1812, 1815, Classified, Arranged, and Exemplified by Documentary Evidence," *American State Papers: Military Affairs*, Vol. III (Doc. 389) pp. 835-928. (ASP 018). Transfer of consideration of the claim from the House to the Secretary of War. Detailed examination of the claim, classed according to items allowed and not allowed by the governing principles of adjustment, the circumstances of each call of the militia into service, and the authority under which the call was made. Includes relevant documents. Same as H.doc.3 (20-2) 184 (entry **1887**).

1856. "For Specific Duty on Imported Umbrellas," *American State Papers: Finance*, Vol. V (Doc. 874) pp. 897-898. (ASP 013). Memorial requests a specific duty on imported cotton umbrellas, and a drawback on exported silk umbrellas. Same as H.doc.176 (20-1) 173 (entry **1866**).

1857. "In Favor of Duties on Salt," *American State Papers: Finance*, Vol. V (Doc. 880) p. 939. (ASP 013). Memorial from Barnstable, Mass. favors continuing the present duty on imported salt. Same as S.doc.131 (20-1) 166 (entry **1877**).

1858. "In Favor of Increase of Duties on Imports," *American State Papers: Finance*, Vol. V (Doc. 822) pp. 732-735. (ASP 013). Memorial from Boston maintains that a large majority of Boston citizens support protection for wool and woolens; discusses the most economical and effectual degree of encouragement needed. Same as S.doc.45 (20-1) 164 (entry **1873**), but without the memorialists names, and H.doc.84 (20-1) 171 (entry **1862**).

1859. "In Favor of Increase of Duties on Imports," *American State Papers: Finance*, Vol. V (Doc. 797) pp. 687-688. (ASP 013). Memorial and resolutions from Berkshire County, Mass. request increased duties and protection of the wool and woolens industries. Same as H.doc.29 (20-1) 170 (entry **1867**).

1860. "In Favor of Increase of Duties on Ready-Made Clothing," *American State Papers: Finance*, Vol. V (Doc. 918) pp. 1040-1041. (ASP 013). Memorial from Boston supports additional duties. Same as S.doc.190 (20-1) 167 (entry **1871**).

1861. U.S. House. *Letter from the Secretary of War, Transmitting a Report and Plan of the Survey of the Island of Nantucket.* 20th Cong., 1st Sess.

(H.Doc.77). Washington: Gales & Seaton, 1828. 18 pg. (Serial Set 171). Report of the hydrographic and land surveys of the north end of the island; accompanied by a plan, with estimates, for the improved harbor to be erected for the whaling vessels. Same as S.doc.44 (20-1) 164 (entry **1878**), slightly rearranged.

1862. U.S. House. *Memorial of Citizens of Boston, &c. in Favor of Further Protection to Manufactures.* 20th Cong., 1st Sess. (H.Doc.84). Washington: Gales & Seaton, 1828. 9 pg. (Serial Set 171). Same as S.doc.45 (20-1) 164 (entry **1873**), but without the memorialists names, and Finance 822 (20-1) ASP 013 (entry **1858**). See entry **1858** for abstract.

1863. U.S. House. *Memorial of Citizens of Duxbury, in the State of Massachusetts.* 20th Cong., 1st Sess. (H.Doc.96). Washington: Gales & Seaton, 1828. 4 pg. (Serial Set 171). Memorial opposes protective duties.

1864. U.S. House. *Memorial of Inhabitants of Nantucket, in the State of Massachusetts, Praying that an Expedition May Be Fitted Out, under the Sanction of Government, to Survey and Explore the Islands and Coasts of the Pacific.* 20th Cong., 1st Sess. (H.Doc.179). Washington: Gales & Seaton, 1828. 3 pg. (Serial Set 173).

1865. U.S. House. *Memorial of Inhabitants of Scituate, Pembroke, Hancock, &c. in the State of Massachusetts, Praying for the Improvement of North River Channel.* 20th Cong., 1st Sess. (H.Doc.266). Washington: Gales & Seaton, 1828. 4 pg. (Serial Set 174). Memorial requests a survey to determine the practicality, expediency, and expenses of improving the North River channel.

1866. U.S. House. *Memorial of the Proprietors of the Hingham Umbrella Manufactory.* 20th Cong., 1st Sess. (H.Doc.176). Washington: Gales & Seaton, 1828. 3 pg. (Serial Set 173). Same as Finance 874 (20-1) ASP 013. See entry **1856**.

1867. U.S. House. *Memorial of the Wool Growers and Manufacturers of Berkshire, State of Massachusetts.* 20th Cong., 1st Sess. (H.Doc.29). Washington: Gales & Seaton, 1828. 5 pg. (Serial Set 170). Same as Finance 797 (20-1) ASP 013. See entry **1859**.

1868. U.S. House. *Petition of Citizens of New Bedford, Praying that a Naval Expedition May Be Undertaken, for the Exploration of the North and South Pacific Ocean, and Other Seas, Visited by Whale Ships and Others.* 20th Cong., 1st Sess. (H.Doc.201). Washington: Gales & Seaton, 1828. 3 pg. (Serial Set 173).

1869. U.S. House. *Petition of Sundry Farmers and Landholders, of the Town of Westborough, County of Wooster, Commonwealth of Massachusetts, against a Further Increase of Duties on Imported Manufactures.* 20th Cong., 1st Sess. (H.Doc.95). Washington: Gales & Seaton, 1828. 5 pg. (Serial Set 171). Same as Finance 834 (20-1) ASP 013 (entry **1854**) and S.doc.64 (20-1) 164 (entry **1875**), but without the transmittal letter.

1870. U.S. Senate. [Claim of the New England Mississippi Land Company]. 20th Cong., 1st Sess. (S.Doc.15). [Washington: Duff Green, 1828]. 8 pg. (Serial Set 163). Same as Pub.land 701 (20-2) ASP 032 (entry **1886**), S.doc.21 (20-2) 181 (entry **1891**), S.doc.6 (19-2) 145 (entry **1838**), S.doc.17 (19-1) 125 (entry **1807**), S.doc.52 (21-2) 193 (entry **1922**), and S.doc.29 (22-1) 212 (entry **1999**). Same as Pub.land 473 (19-1) ASP 031 (entry **1800**) without the statement made by the petitioners to the Judiciary Committee. See entry **1807** for abstract.

1871. U.S. Senate. *Memorial of Certain Merchant Tailors of Boston, Praying that Additional Duty Be Imposed on Ready Made Clothing, When Imported into the United States.* 20th Cong., 1st Sess. (S.Doc.190). Washington: Duff Green, 1828. 5 pg. (Serial Set 167). Same as Finance 918 (20-1) ASP 013 (entry **1860**).

1872. U.S. Senate. *Memorial of Inhabitants of Boston, and Its Vicinity, Adverse to an Increase of Duty on Imported Woollen Goods.* 20th Cong., 1st Sess. (S.Doc.6). Washington: Duff Green, 1827. 15 pg. (Serial Set 163). Same as Finance 790 (20-1) ASP013. See entry **1852**.

1873. U.S. Senate. *Memorial of the Citizens of Boston, and Its Vicinity, in Favor of the Increase of Duty on Woollen Goods, as Contemplated by the Woollens Bill.* 20th Cong., 1st Sess. (S.Doc.45). Washington: Duff Green, 1828. 59 pg. (Serial Set 164). Includes 50 pages of memorialists' names. Same as H.doc.84 (20-1) 171 (entry **1862**) and Finance 822 (20-1) ASP 013 (entry **1858**) but also includes memorialists names. See entry **1858** for abstract.

1874. U.S. Senate. *Memorial of the Citizens of Plymouth and Kingston, Mass. Adverse to an Increase of Duty on Woollen Goods, as Contemplated by the Woollens Bill.* 20th Cong., 1st Sess. (S.Doc.46). Washington: Duff Green, 1828. 8 pg. (Serial Set 164). Memorial opposes an increase as impolitic and unjust. Same as Finance 823 (20-1) ASP 013 (entry **1853**), but additionally includes memorialists names.

1875. U.S. Senate. *Memorial of the Citizens of Westborough, Massachusetts, Protesting against Any Increase of Duties on Imports, and Especially on Woollen Goods.* 20th Cong., 1st Sess. (S.Doc.64). Washington: Duff Green, 1828. 7 pg. (Serial Set 164). Includes memorial and transmittal letter. Same as H.doc.95 (20-1) 171 (entry **1869**), but with the transmittal letter, and Finance 834 (20-1) ASP 013 (entry **1854**).

1876. U.S. Senate. *Memorial of the Inhabitants of Thomaston, and Its Vicinity, Adverse to a Further Increase of Duties on Imports, for the Protection of*

Domestic Manufactures. 20th Cong., 1st Sess. (S.Doc.79). Washington: Duff Green, 1828. 5 pg. (Serial Set 165).

1877. U.S. Senate. *Memorial of the Manufacturers of Salt, of Barnstable, Massachusetts, Praying that the Duty on Imported Salt May Not Be Repealed.* 20th Cong., 1st Sess. (S.Doc.131). Washington: Duff Green, 1828. 3 pg. (Serial Set 166). Same as Finance 880 (20-1) ASP 013 (entry **1857**).

1878. U.S. Senate. *Report from the Secretary of War, with Report and Plan of the Survey of the Island of Nantucket.* 20th Cong., 1st Sess. (S.Doc.44). Washington: Duff Green, 1828. 20 pg. (Serial Set 164). Same as H.doc.77 (20-1) 171, slightly rearranged. See entry **1861**.

1879. U.S. Senate. [Report on the Erection of a Breakwater at Nantucket]. 20th Cong., 1st Sess. (S.Doc.199). [Washington: Duff Green, 1828]. 2 pg. (Serial Set 167). Favorable report of the Committee on Commerce for annual appropriations to erect the breakwater at Nantucket; reviews benefits of it.

20TH CONGRESS, 2ND SESSION

1880. Everett, Edward (Mass.). "Occupancy of the Oregon River," *Register of Debates.* 20th Cong., 2nd Sess. (29 Dec. 1828, 6 Jan. 1829) pp. 132-134; 171-173. Advocates occupying the Oregon River and territory. Maintains that the proposed military post and establishment of a civil jurisdiction are necessary to vindicate the title and protect the rights of U.S. citizens in the territory. Later remarks describe the territory using excerpts from travelers' accounts.

1881. Gorham, Benjamin (Mass.). "Occupancy of the Oregon River," *Register of Debates.* 20th Cong., 2nd Sess. (30 Dec. 1828) pp. 137-138. Opposes establishing a military post in the Oregon territory and altering the relation with Britain established by the 1818 convention.

1882. Gorham, Benjamin (Mass.). "Tonnage Duty," *Register of Debates.* 20th Cong., 2nd Sess. (5 Feb. 1829) pp. 318-319. Supports repealing the tonnage duties in an effort to save and restore the navigating interest of the country.

1883. Reed, John (Mass.). "Tonnage Duty," *Register of Debates.* 20th Cong., 2nd Sess. (4 Feb. 1829) pp. 317-318. Supports repealing the tonnage duty; maintains that the duty is oppressive to the navigating interest and unequal in operation.

1884. Richardson, Joseph (Mass.). "Occupancy of the Oregon River," *Register of Debates.* 20th Cong., 2nd Sess. (30 Dec. 1828) pp. 138-141. Supports the U.S. claim to occupy the Oregon River and territory against the claim of Great Britain. Discusses the validity of the claim and the benefits of the acquisition. Describes Oregon through excerpts from travel accounts.

1885. Webster, Daniel (Mass.). "Instructions to Panama Ministers," *Register of Debates.* 20th Cong., 2nd Sess. (28 Feb. 1829) pp. 66-67. Supports the request to communicate the instructions to the ministers at Panama according to the discretion of the President.

1886. "Claim of Thomas L. Winthrop and Others of the New England Mississippi Land Company," *American State Papers: Public Lands,* Vol. V (Doc. 701) pp. 597-600. (ASP 032). Same as S.doc.15 (20-1) 163 (entry **1870**), S.doc.17 (19-1) 125 (entry **1807**), S.doc.6 (19-2) 145 (entry **1838**), S.doc.21 (20-2) 181 (entry **1891**), S.doc.52 (21-1) 193 (entry **1922**), and S.doc.29 (22-1) 212 (entry **1999**). See entry **1807** for abstract.

1887. U.S. House. *Letter from the Secretary of War, Transmitting, in Pursuance of a Resolution of the House of Representatives of the 15th of Dec. 1826, a Report upon the Subject of the Claims of the State of Massachusetts for Certain Services Rendered during the Late War.* 20th Cong., 2nd Sess. (H.Doc.3). [Washington]: Gales & Seaton, 1828. 181 pg. (Serial Set 184). Same as Mil.aff.389 (20-1) ASP 018. See entry **1855**.

1888. U.S. House. *Memorial of Inhabitants of Boston, Massachusetts, against the Tariff Law of 1828.* 20th Cong., 2nd Sess. (H.Doc.100). [Washington: Gales & Seaton, 1829]. 6 pg. (Serial Set 186). Memorial and transmittal letter oppose the protective system as impolitic and unjust. Same as S.doc.56 (20-2) 181 (entry **1892**), but includes the transmittal letter.

1889. U.S. House. *Memorial of Merchants of Boston, Praying to Be Allowed to Pay Duties on Goods, &c. Imported under the Old Tariff.* 20th Cong., 2nd Sess. (H.Doc.64). [Washington]: Gales & Seaton, [1829]. 5 pg. (Serial Set 185). Memorial discusses the effects of the tariff of 1828 on goods purchased or ordered prior to the passage of the law; requests an exemption from the new duties for such merchandise. Names of memorialists included. Same as S.doc.38 (20-2) 181 (entry **1893**), except includes names.

1890. U.S. House. *Survey of the Harbor of Nantucket.* 20th Cong., 2nd Sess. (H.Doc.97). [Washington: Gales & Seaton, 1829]. 6 pg. (Serial Set 186). Survey and recommendations as to the expediency and expense of making Nantucket harbor permanently free from obstructions; reviews advantages.

1891. U.S. Senate. [Claim of the New England Mississippi Land Company]. 20th Cong., 2nd Sess. (S.doc.21). [Washington: Duff Green, 1829]. 7 pg. (Serial Set 181). Same as S.doc.17 (19-1) 125 (entry **1807**), S.doc.6 (19-2) 145 (entry **1838**), S.doc.15 (20-1) 163 (entry **1870**), Pub.land 701 (20-2) ASP 032 (entry **1886**), S.doc.52 (21-1) 193 (entry **1922**), and S.doc.29 (22-1) 212 (entry **1999**). See entry **1807** for abstract.

1892. U.S. Senate. *Memorial of Sundry Citizens of Boston, Complaining of the Injurious Effects of the Tariff Law of the Last Session, and Praying for a*

Revision of the Present Tariff System. 20th Cong., 2nd Sess. (S.Doc.56). [Washington: Duff Green, 1829]. 6 pg. (Serial Set 181). Same as H.doc.100 (20-2) 186, but without the transmittal letter. See entry **1888**.

1893. U.S. Senate. *Memorial of Sundry Importing Merchants of Boston, Praying that the Collector of the Customs Be Directed to Settle Their Accounts for Duties on Goods Imported under the Former Tariff Laws, in Order that the Late Tariff Should Not Have a Retrospective and an Injurious Operation against Them, &c.* 20th Cong., 2nd Sess. (S.Doc.38). [Washington: Duff Green, 1829]. 4 pg. (Serial Set 181). Same as H.doc.64 (20-2) 185, but without the memorialists names. See entry **1889**.

1894. U.S. Senate. *Memorial of the Merchants of Boston, Representing Their Views in Relation to the System of Credit Duties on Imports.* 20th Cong., 2nd Sess. (S.Doc.12). [Washington: Duff Green, 1828]. 3 pg. (Serial Set 181). Memorial maintains that it would be injurious to establish a system of cash payment of duties, that a modification of the warehousing system could be used in the principal seaports, and that the carrying trade should not be restricted beyond protecting the revenue.

21ST CONGRESS, 1ST SESSION

1895. "Massachusetts Claim," *Register of Debates.* 21st Cong., 1st Sess. (5 Jan., 20 Apr. 1830) pp. 9-10; 357-359. Remarks on the claims of Massachusetts for expenses incurred from the services of her militia during the War of 1812. Brief justification and history of previous action taken on the claims by Benton (Mo.) as chairman of the Military Committee, and Silsbee (Mass.).

1896. Bates, Isaac C. (Mass.). "Pensions," *Register of Debates.* 21st Cong., 1st Sess. (3 Apr. 1830) pp. 735-736. Supports the resolution to extend benefits to all soldiers of the Revolution and to invalids of the War of 1812.

1897. Bates, Isaac C. (Mass.). "Removal of the Indians," *Register of Debates.* 21st Cong., 1st Sess. (19 May 1830) pp. 1049-1058. Maintains that the Indians are sovereign and entitled to the protection and enjoyment of their rights as guaranteed by treaty. Objects to approving of appropriations for removal as implicitly agreeing that the Indians are subject to the jurisdiction of Georgia. Provides a detailed history of the acts, laws, and treaties of Georgia with the Indians that established their sovereignty.

1898. Davis, John (Mass.). "The Tariff Laws," *Register of Debates.* 21st Cong., 1st Sess. (4 May 1830) pp. 873-884. Supports the protecting system and replies to Mr. McDuffie (S.C.). Maintains that the proposed bill would suppress the frauds being perpetrated on existing laws. Discusses the frauds being perpetrated. Examines the principle arguments of McDuffie in support of his amendment to appeal the laws of 1828 and 1824 and to reduce the duties.

1899. Everett, Edward (Mass.). "Removal of the Indians," *Register of Debates.* 21st Cong., 1st Sess. (19 May 1830) pp. 1058-1079. Opposes appropriating money to cooperate with Georgia, Alabama, and Mississippi in the compulsory removal of the Indians within their limits. Maintains that it is an unconstitutional and illegal extension of state laws over the Indians. Reviews the circumstances behind the proposal, the history of the policy of removal, and the details, cost and effects of the proposed plan.

1900. Everett, Edward (Mass.). "The Tariff," *Register of Debates.* 21st Cong., 1st Sess. (8 May 1830) pp. 902-912. Lengthy speech opposes withdrawing the protection of the tariff laws of 1828 and 1824. Majority of speech responds to Mr. McDuffie's (S.C.) claims that the southern states have born an unfair burden of the taxes while the northern states have received an unfair share of the revenue.

1901. Gorham, Benjamin (Mass.). "Navigation and Impost Law," *Register of Debates.* 21st Cong., 1st Sess. (30 Apr. 1830) pp. 865-866. Opposes the proposed bill; demonstrates its effect on the sugar trade.

1902. Richardson, Joseph (Mass.). "Buffalo and New Orleans Road," *Register of Debates.* 21st Cong., 1st Sess. (30 Mar. 1830) pp. 711-716. Supports the road and its extension from Buffalo to Lake Champlain, and then to Boston. Expounds on the benefits of internal improvements to the nation, and the inequitable distribution of improvements to all parts of the country. Addresses objections to the road.

1903. Richardson, Joseph (Mass.). "Committee on Education," *Register of Debates.* 21st Cong., 1st Sess. (16 Dec. 1829) p. 476. Supports forming a standing Committee on Education.

1904. Silsbee, Nathaniel (Mass.). "Massachusetts Claim," *Register of Debates.* 21st Cong., 1st Sess. (5 Jan., 20 Apr. 1830) pp. 9-10; 358-359. Supports the claim for reimbursement of expenses incurred by the Massachusetts militia during the War of 1812; provides a brief history and justification of the expenses.

1905. Webster, Daniel (Mass.). "Mr. Foot's Resolution," *Register of Debates.* 21st Cong., 1st Sess. (20 Jan. 1830) pp. 35-41. Answers Robert Hayne's (S.C.) assertion that the northeastern states are attempting to restrict settlement of the West. Defends the policy of the government towards the public lands and the new states of the West. Reviews the conditions of the original land cessions that were to be disposed of for the common benefit of the United States. Defends the policy of consolidation of the government and the Union.

1906. Webster, Daniel (Mass.). "Mr. Foot's Resolution," *Register of Debates.* 21st Cong., 1st Sess. (26 Jan, 27 Jan. 1830) pp. 58-82. Denies the constitutional doctrines advanced by Hayne; expounds on the nature of the Union. The states are sovereign only so far as their power is not qualified by the

Constitution; but only the Constitution and the national government are sovereign over the people. In the event of disagreement the settlement rests with the agencies provided for that purpose in the Constitution: the courts, the amending power, and regular elections.

1907. Webster, Daniel (Mass.). "Mr. Foot's Resolution," *Register of Debates.* 21st Cong., 1st Sess. (27 Jan. 1830) pp. 92-93. Further refutes Hayne's (S.C.) statements. Objects to Hayne's theory of the Constitution as a compact between the states where the general government does not possess authority that is binding upon the states.

1908. "An Act for the Relief of the Mercantile Insurance Company, in Salem, Massachusetts," *Register of Debates.* 21st Cong., 1st Sess. (15 Apr. 1830) Appendix, p. xvi.

1909. "An Act to Authorize the Payment of the Claim of the State of Massachusetts, for Certain Services of Her Militia during the Late War," *Statutes at Large*, Vol. IV (31 May 1830) p. 428. Also printed in the *Register of Debates* (21st Cong., 1st Sess.) Appendix, p. xxxiii.

1910. "Application of Massachusetts for the Settlement and Payment of the Claims of That State for Militia Services in the War of 1812-'15," *American State Papers: Military Affairs*, Vol. IV (Doc. 439) pp. 292-295. (ASP 019). Report and resolutions protest the delay in settlement and request a final adjustment of the claims; review past decisions and reports. Same as H.rp.223 (21-1) 200 (entry **1915**), but with the transmittal letter, and S.doc.60 (21-1) 193 (entry **1925**).

1911. "Surveys for a Naval Depot in Narraganset Bay and Newport Harbor," *American State Papers: Naval Affairs*, Vol. III (Doc. 401) pp. 463-468. (ASP 025). Report of the survey to select a site for a naval depot and navy yard. Lists the advantages and disadvantages of New York harbor, Narragansett Bay and Boston harbor as rendezvous and naval stations; examines the conditions necessary for naval depot sites; compares various sites. Recommends that a naval depot be formed at Charlestown, and that Hampton Roads, Boston, and Narragansett Bay be fortified and organized as naval and military rendezvous. Same as H.doc.21 (21-1) 195 (entry **1921**).

1912. U.S. House. *Canal - Boston Harbor to Narragansett Bay.* 21st Cong., 1st Sess. (H.Doc.62). [Washington: 1830]. 1 pg. (Serial Set 197). Letter reports that the requested survey is not completed.

1913. U.S. House. *Farmington and Hampshire Canal Company.* 21st Cong., 1st Sess. (H.Rpt.341). [Washington: 1830]. 2 pg. (Serial Set 201). Statement of the Connecticut River Company opposes the Farmington and Hampshire and Hampden canals as the best mode of transportation for the Connecticut Valley; maintains that the river route would be best. Reviews the improvements to the navigation of the Connecticut River and objections to the canals.

1914. U.S. House. *Lobster Fishery.* 21st Cong., 1st Sess. (H.Rpt.79). [Washington: 1830]. 1 pg. (Serial Set 199). Report responds to the memorial from Massachusetts lobster fishermen concerning the right of Massachusetts to regulate the fisheries along its coasts and one mile into the ocean; report maintains that it is a judicial, not legislative, question.

1915. U.S. House. *Massachusetts Claim.* 21st Cong., 1st Sess. (H.Rpt.223). [Washington: 1830]. 5 pg. (Serial Set 200). Same as S.doc.60 (21-1) 193 (entry **1925**) and Mil.aff.439 (21-1) ASP 019 (entry **1910**), but without the transmittal letter. See entry **1910** for abstract.

1916. U.S. House. *Memorial of Inhabitants of Hampshire County, Massachusetts, in Relation to the Indian Tribes.* 21st Cong., 1st Sess. (H.Rpt.310). [Washington: 1830]. 2 pg. (Serial Set 201). Memorial supports the rights of the Indians to property and self-government; quotes Thomas Jefferson.

1917. U.S. House. *Memorial of Inhabitants of the State of Massachusetts, in Relation to the Cherokee and Other Indian Tribes.* 21st Cong., 1st Sess. (H.Rpt.245). [Washington: 1830]. 7 pg. (Serial Set 200). Memorial supports the title of the Indians to their land, and their rights of continued occupancy and self-government; provides a history of past negotiations recognizing the sovereignty of the Indian nations.

1918. U.S. House. *Message from the President of the United States, Transmitting a Report of a Survey of Sandy Bay, in the State of Massachusetts.* 21st Cong., 1st Sess. (H.Doc.95). [Washington: Duff Green, 1830]. 5 pg. (Serial Set 198). Report includes a description of Sandy Bay, estimate of the cost of a harbor and a breakwater, and a comparative table of estimated costs for improvements to accommodate different classes of vessels. Map not included.

1919. U.S. House. *Report and Estimate on the Buzzard and Barnstable Bay Canal, Massachusetts.* 21st Cong., 1st Sess. (H.Doc.54). [Washington: 1830]. 17 pg. (Serial Set 197). Report discusses the planned route of the canal, location of the bottom of the canal, and locks; presents various estimates of the project. Map referred to not included.

1920. U.S. House. *Statement of the Petition of the Farmington, and Hampshire and Hampden, Canals.* 21st Cong., 1st Sess. (H.Rpt.221). [Washington: 1830]. [10 pg.]. (Serial Set 200). Petition requests aid to complete the canal to Northampton, Massachusetts. Reviews the current status of the canals and the benefits of completing them. Discusses the support of the other New England states who want to extend the canal through the valley of the Connecticut River to Canada. Includes supporting statement of the Agent of the Companies on their petition and "Answer to the Remonstrance of the Agent of the Connecticut River Company."

1921. U.S. House. Survey - *Narraganset Bay, &c. &c.* 21st Cong., 1st Sess. (H.Doc.21). [Washington: 1830]. 11 pg. (Serial Set 195). Same as Nav.aff.401 (21-1) ASP 025. See entry **1911**.

1922. U.S. Senate. [Claim of the New England Mississippi Land Company]. 21st Cong., 1st Sess. (S.doc.52). [Washington: 1830]. 7 pg. (Serial Set 193). Same as S.doc.17 (19-1) 125 (entry **1807**), S.doc.6 (19-2) 145 (entry **1838**), S.doc.15 (20-1) 163 (entry **1870**), Pub.land 701 (20-2) ASP 032 (entry **1886**), S.doc.21 (20-2) 181 (entry **1891**), and S.doc.29 (22-1) 212 (entry **1999**). See entry **1807** for abstract.

1923. U.S. Senate. *Memorial of Sundry Inhabitants of Boston, Massachusetts, that So Much of the Post Office Laws As Require the Mail to Be Transported on the Sabbath Day, May Be Repealed.* 21st Cong., 1st Sess. (S.Doc.124). [Washington: 1830]. 4 pg. (Serial Set 193). Memorial maintains that the laws referred to are unconstitutional, an invasion of states' rights, a violation of religious obligations, and a destructive influence on morality.

1924. U.S. Senate. *Memorial of Sundry Inhabitants of Salem, Massachusetts, Praying that Duty on Imported Molasses May Be Reduced to Five Cents Per Gallon, and that a Drawback to the Same Amount May Be Allowed on the Exportation of Spirits Distilled Therefrom.* 21st Cong., 1st Sess. (S.Doc.93). [Washington: 1830]. 5 pg. (Serial Set 193). Includes discussion of the West Indies trade.

1925. U.S. Senate. *Report and Resolves of the Legislature of Massachusetts, Relative to the Claims of That State for Militia Services during the Late War.* 21st Cong., 1st Sess. (S.Doc.60). [Washington: 1830]. 6 pg. (Serial Set 193). Same as H.rp.223 (21-1) 200 (entry **1915**), but with transmittal letter, and Mil.aff.439 (21-1) ASP 019 (entry **1910**). See entry **1910** for abstract.

21ST CONGRESS, 2ND SESSION

1926. Bates, Isaac C. (Mass.). "Indian Affairs," *Register of Debates.* 21st Cong., 2nd Sess. (28 Feb. 1831) pp. 822-827. Strongly objects to an executive order directing the payment of Indian annuities to individuals rather than to the nation's Treasury. Demonstrates that the order would be impossible to execute, violates the practice of the past forty years, is unjustifiable and unwanted, and would be prejudicial and harmful to the Indian nations.

1927. Bates, Isaac C. (Mass.). "Minister to Russia," *Register of Debates.* 21st Cong., 2nd Sess. (8 Feb. 1831) pp. 656-658. Objects to the conduct of the Executive in relation to the mission and the appointment of the minister.

1928. Davis, John (Mass.). "Claim of James Monroe," *Register of Debates.* 21st Cong., 2nd Sess. (31 Jan. 1831) pp. 547-549. Supports the claim of James

Monroe for unexpected expenses incurred while a minister to France during the French revolution.

1929. Davis, John (Mass.). "Reprinting Old Documents," *Register of Debates.* 21st Cong., 2nd Sess. (26 Feb. 1831) pp. 818-819. Favors reprinting selected older documents for the convenience of Congress and the public good.

1930. Davis, John (Mass.). "Revolutionary Soldiers," *Register of Debates.* 21st Cong., 2nd Sess. (16 Feb. 1831) pp. 727-728. Supports compensating the officers and soldiers of the militia; defends the militia of the North.

1931. Everett, Edward (Mass.). "Indian Affairs," *Register of Debates.* 21st Cong., 2nd Sess. (14 Feb. 1831) pp. 685-717. Lengthy speech pleads for Congress to address the welfare of the Indians. Reviews past governmental policy with the Indians, including that of removal. Discusses Georgia's legislation extending her jurisdiction over the Cherokees in contravention of the treaties and laws of the U.S.; demonstrates the injurious and destructive nature of subsequent laws.

1932. Webster, Daniel (Mass.). "Insolvent Debtors of the United States," *Register of Debates.* 21st Cong., 2nd Sess. (1 Mar. 1831) pp. 323-325. Supports a bill for the relief of certain insolvent debtors of the United States.

1933. "Application of the Officers of the Militia of Massachusetts that an Efficient and Uniform System Be Adopted for the Regulation and Government of the Militia of the United States," *American State Papers: Military Affairs,* Vol. IV (Doc. 482) pp. 701-705. (ASP 019). Memorial requests Congress to revise the militia laws. Suggestions include a reduction of the force, no longer requiring privates to arm themselves, an organization that more closely parallels that of the army, and improved training opportunities. Same as S.doc.62 (21-2) 204 (entry **1941**).

1934. U.S. House. *Documents to Accompany Bill H.R. No.622, Authorizing the Construction of Naval Hospitals at Charlestown, Massachusetts, Brooklyn, New York, and at Pensacola.* 21st Cong., 2nd Sess. (H.Doc.93). Washington: Duff Green, 1831. 8 pg. (Serial Set 208). Letters of transmittal and estimates of expenses to build the naval hospitals. Plans referred to are not included. Same as H.doc.16 (22-1) 216 (entry **1983**).

1935. U.S. House. *Memorial of the Citizens of Berkshire, Massachusetts, Adopted at a County Convention, Relative to the Indian Nations.* 21st Cong., 2nd Sess. (H.Doc.106). Washington: Duff Green, 1831. 5 pg. (Serial Set 209-1). Memorial supports the title of the Indians to their lands, discusses the situation of the Cherokees in Georgia, and reviews past treaties recognizing Indian titles and sovereignty.

1936. U.S. House. *Memorial of the Trustees of the New England Asylum for the Blind.* 21st Cong., 2nd Sess. (H.Doc.20). Washington: Duff Green, 1831. 4

pg. (Serial Set 206). Memorial requests aid to establish an institution for the education of the blind. Describes the advantages of these institutions and their great success in Europe; promises to aid other states desiring to establish similar institutions.

1937. U.S. House. *New England Asylum for the Blind.* 21st Cong., 2nd Sess. (H.Rpt.66). Washington: Duff Green, 1831. 2 pg. (Serial Set 210). Favorable report on the petition for the New England Asylum for the Blind. Describes the benefits of the proposed institution; supports government patronage.

1938. U.S. House. *Petition of the Inhabitants of Sheffield, Berkshire County, Massachusetts, Relative to Indian Affairs.* 21st Cong., 2nd Sess. (H.Doc.105). Washington: Duff Green, 1831. 1 pg. (Serial Set 209-1). Petition supports the rights of the Indians to territory and self-government as guaranteed by previous treaties.

1939. U.S. House. *Report on the Survey of North River, Massachusetts.* 21st Cong., 2nd Sess. (H.Doc.16). Washington: Duff Green, 1831. 3 pg. (Serial Set 206). Survey with recommendations and estimates for improvements; map referred to not included in this report.

1940. U.S. Senate. *Memorial of Inhabitants of Andover, Essex Co., Massachusetts, that the Indians Be Protected in Their Rights, &c.* 21st Cong., 2nd Sess. (S.Doc.34). Washington: Duff Green, 1831. 3 pg. (Serial Set 203). Specifically addresses the Cherokee and Choctaw nations.

1941. U.S. Senate. *Memorial of Officers of the Massachusetts Militia, Praying that an Efficient and Uniform System Be Adopted for the Regulation and Government of the Militia of the United States.* 21st Cong., 2nd Sess. (S.Doc.62). Washington: Duff Green, 1831. 9 pg. (Serial Set 204). Same as Mil.aff.482 (21-2) ASP 019. See entry **1933**.

1942. U.S. Senate. *Memorial of the Prudential Committee of the American Board of Commissioners for Foreign Missions of Massachusetts, Praying that All Treaty Stipulations with the Indians within the United States May Be Faithfully Observed, &c.* 21st Cong., 2nd Sess. (S.Doc.50). Washington: Duff Green, 1831. 10 pg. (Serial Set 204). Detailed report of the Board on the effects of the proposed removal of the Indians from the southeastern states. Discusses the missionary work of the Board with the Indians. Maintains that the removal is opposed by the Indians, would cause great distress and anarchy, and would disrupt civilizing and educational efforts.

22ND CONGRESS, 1ST SESSION

1943. Adams, John Quincy (Mass.). "Apportionment Bill," *Register of Debates.* 22nd Cong., 1st Sess. (1 Feb., 8 Feb. 1832) pp. 1723-1724; 1766-1775. Remarks and speech oppose the proposed ratio of forty-eight thousand.

Demonstrates that the large ratio proposed reverses the principle used at the adoption of the constitution to make the representative body numerous and the constituent numbers small. Favors the ratio of forty-four thousand.

1944. Adams, John Quincy (Mass.). "French Spoliations Prior to 1800," *Register of Debates.* 22nd Cong., 1st Sess. (13 Dec. 1831) pp. 1434-1435. Supports the claims.

1945. Adams, John Quincy (Mass.). "Mission to France," *Register of Debates.* 22nd Cong., 1st Sess. (28 Apr. 1832) pp. 2641-2647. Supports an appropriation to outfit a minister appointed by the President. Maintains that the Senate has stricken out the appropriation previously approved by the House in an attempt to control the President in his exercise of the power given to him by the constitution. Discusses the secret-service and diplomatic fund.

1946. Adams, John Quincy (Mass.). "Public Fast Day," *Register of Debates.* 22nd Cong., 1st Sess. (9 July 1832) pp. 3867-3869, 3870-3871. Maintains that it was a breach of order to read in the House a private letter of the President on the proposed Public Fast Day; contends that the President may not be permitted to influence the House in an indirect manner.

1947. Adams, John Quincy (Mass.). "South Carolina Claims," *Register of Debates.* 22nd Cong., 1st Sess. (5 Jan. 1832) pp. 1484-1485, 1498-1499. Supports the claims and advocates referring them to the Committee of Claims; discusses the role and duties of the Committee.

1948. Adams, John Quincy (Mass.). "The Tariff," *Register of Debates.* 22nd Cong., 1st Sess. (6 June, 26 June, 27 June 1832) pp. 3290-3293; 3795-3796; 3801-3802. Various remarks on proposed amendments concerning the tariff on woolen manufactures.

1949. Adams, John Quincy (Mass.). "Turkish Mission," *Register of Debates.* 22nd Cong., 1st Sess. (16 Mar. 1832) pp. 2194-2196. Supports appropriations for presents; reviews the custom of giving presents in foreign countries.

1950. Appleton, Nathan (Mass.). "Insolvent Debtors," *Register of Debates.* 22nd Cong., 1st Sess. (20 Mar. 1832) pp. 2229-2231. Supports a bill offering relief to insolvent debtors of the government.

1951. Appleton, Nathan (Mass.). "Minimum Duties," *Register of Debates.* 22nd Cong., 1st Sess. (21 Jan. 1832) pp. 1600-1606. Supports minimum duties. Discusses the origin of the system of minimum duties, and the role of South Carolina in establishing that system for the protection of cotton manufacturing.

1952. Appleton, Nathan (Mass.). "The Tariff," *Register of Debates.* 22nd Cong., 1st Sess. (30 May 1832) pp. 3189-3209. Lengthy speech rebuts South Carolina's charge that the tariff operates unequally upon different sections of the country, and that the impost duty is equivalent to a tax upon exports. Maintains that impost duties are taxes upon the consumption of the country, acting equally upon all consumers. Addresses the assertions in the report of the Committee of Ways and Means, and the effect of the tariff regarding free and slave labor. Reminds South Carolina that the tariff of 1816 was introduced and advocated by South Carolina, and opposed by Massachusetts.

1953. Briggs, George N. (Mass.). "Apportionment Bill," *Register of Debates.* 22nd Cong., 1st Sess. (19 Jan. 1832) pp. 1589-1593. Supports an apportionment ratio of forty-four thousand, which would allow each of the states their current number of representatives. Addresses arguments of those favoring a larger ratio.

1954. Choate, Rufus (Mass.). "Revolutionary Pensions," *Register of Debates.* 22nd Cong., 1st Sess. (9 Apr. 1832) pp. 2446-2458. Supports changing the pension system to not require proof of indigence, and to include the militia. Addresses the alternative proposal; refutes the leading objections to the bill.

1955. Choate, Rufus (Mass.). "The Tariff Bill," *Register of Debates.* 22nd Cong., 1st Sess. (13 June 1832) pp. 3511-3526. Opposes abolishing or substantially altering the existing protective policy. Maintains that the government has a responsibility to those it has encouraged to commit to manufacturing, that the protective tariffs do not unequally oppress the states of the South, that its benefits exceed its injuries, and that it has been proven successful. Addresses the opposition from South Carolina and her threat to secede from the Union. Recommends addressing specific sectional grievances.

1956. Davis, John (Mass.). "Apportionment Bill," *Register of Debates.* 22nd Cong., 1st Sess. (17 May 1832) pp. 3052-3057. Favors the minority proposition to allow for a more equitable distribution of representatives; rounds up or down on the remainder after the divisor is employed.

1957. Davis, John (Mass.). "Duties on Imports," *Register of Debates.* 22nd Cong., 1st Sess. (16 Jan. 1832) pp. 1549-1553. Discusses the proposed inquiry into minimum duties paid on certain goods, in particular, the percentage upon woolens. Defends the minimums in the woolens bill; advocates a broader inquiry, to include frauds and the statute value of the English pound sterling.

1958. Davis, John (Mass.). "Georgia and the United States," *Register of Debates.* 22nd Cong., 1st Sess. (5 Mar. 1832) pp. 2024-2025. Remarks on a petition concerning two missionaries detained in a penitentiary in Georgia under Georgian legislation that extended her jurisdiction over the Cherokee Indians.

1959. Davis, John (Mass.). "Revolutionary Pensions," *Register of Debates.* 22nd Cong., 1st Sess. (1 May 1832) pp. 2677-2679. Supports the pension bill for the enlisted troops and the militia serving in the Revolutionary War.

1960. Davis, John (Mass.). "The Tariff," *Register of Debates.* 22nd Cong., 1st Sess. (6 June 1832) pp. 3298-3318. Supports the protective policy. Reviews the origin of protective legislation. Discusses the doctrine that protectionism results in a sectional burden; demonstrates that no sectional oppression exists, and that the South has prospered under its policy. Discusses the effects of abandoning the protective system on wages, laborers, agriculture and manufacturing. Deplores the political nature of the bill in an election year.

1961. Dearborn, Henry A. S. (Mass.). "The Tariff," *Register of Debates.* 22nd Cong., 1st Sess. (20 June 1832) pp. 3684-3686. Supports increasing duty on cordage. Discusses the effect of the tariff on the hemp and cordage industries.

1962. Dearborn, Henry A. S. (Mass.). "Turkish Mission," *Register of Debates.* 22nd Cong., 1st Sess. (16 Mar. 1832) pp. 2189-2191. Supports appropriations for presents for the conclusion of the Turkish treaty; discusses the tradition of presents in foreign countries, and the advantages to be derived from the treaty.

1963. Everett, Edward (Mass.). "Apportionment Bill," *Register of Debates.* 22nd Cong., 1st Sess. (17 May 1832) pp. 3039-3052. Opposes the proposed apportionment bill, which leaves a large number of the people without representation. Supports an amendment that would allow for the representation of fractions. Addresses objections to the amendment, the connection between representation and taxation, and the history of previous decisions governing apportionment.

1964. Everett, Edward (Mass.). "Bank of the United States," *Register of Debates.* 22nd Cong., 1st Sess. (12 Mar. 1832) pp. 2101-2104. Supports the objectivity of a select committee to investigate the conduct of the bank.

1965. Everett, Edward (Mass.). "Chickasaw Treaty," *Register of Debates.* 22nd Cong., 1st Sess. (31 Jan. 1832) pp. 1676-1682. Requests a copy of the article of an unratified treaty negotiated with the Chickasaw tribe concerning the lease of some choice land in Tennessee originally granted under an 1818 treaty. Contends that private bargains were negotiated under the guise of public treaties. Provides a history of the circumstances.

1966. Everett, Edward (Mass.). "French Spoliations prior to 1800," *Register of Debates.* 22nd Cong., 1st Sess. (13 Dec. 1831) pp. 1435-1437. Favors honoring the claims.

1967. Everett, Edward (Mass.). "Mission to France," *Register of Debates.* 22nd Cong., 1st Sess. (28 Apr. 1832) pp. 2638-2639. Maintains that a minister's outfit should be paid out of the contingent fund rather than appropriated in advance.

1968. Everett, Edward (Mass.). "South Carolina Claims," *Register of Debates.* 22nd Cong., 1st Sess. (5 Jan. 1832) pp. 1488-1491. Supports fully paying the claims of South Carolina for services rendered by her militia in the War of 1812.

1969. Everett, Edward (Mass.). "The Tariff," *Register of Debates.* 22nd Cong., 1st Sess. (25 June 1832) pp. 3737-3771. Lengthy speech advocates compromise. Argues against South Carolina's proposition that the producer of exports pays the duties on imports and that the present system is responsible for the southern states' distress. Demonstrates that the South is in a prosperous condition, and that any pockets of distress do not proceed from the tariff. Maintains that slavery is an economic evil, causing the problems ascribed to the tariff. Discusses South Carolina's threat of nullification, and implores her not to nullify the law and leave the Union.

1970. Everett, Edward (Mass.). "Washington's Remains," *Register of Debates.* 22nd Cong., 1st Sess. (13 Feb. 1832) pp. 1786-1788. Supports removing Washington's remains from Mount Vernon to the capital.

1971. Grennell, George, Jr. (Mass.). "Apportionment Bill," *Register of Debates.* 22nd Cong., 1st Sess. (18 Jan. 1832) pp. 1572-1575. Supports an apportionment ratio of 44,000, which would allow each of the states their present number of representatives.

1972. Reed, John (Mass.). "The Tariff," *Register of Debates.* 22nd Cong., 1st Sess. (20 June 1832) pp. 3691-3694. Supports a protective duty on salt in order to be independent from foreign markets for a necessity of life; a table demonstrates how much the various states import and use.

1973. Silsbee, Nathaniel (Mass.). "Apportionment Bill," *Register of Debates.* 22nd Cong., 1st Sess. (9 Mar. 1832) pp. 518-520. Objects to the inequalities of the bill and its distribution of the underrepresented fractions. Maintains that it would unnecessarily reduce the representation of some of the parent states.

1974. Webster, Daniel (Mass.). "Apportionment Bill," *Register of Debates.* 22nd Cong., 1st Sess. (1 Mar. 1832) pp. 487-490. Supports forty-seven thousand as the apportionment ratio and advocates representation for fractional numbers over twenty-five thousand.

1975. Webster, Daniel (Mass.). "Bank of the United States," *Register of Debates.* 22nd Cong., 1st Sess. (25 May 1832) pp. 954-964. Supports renewing the charter. Briefly reviews the history of the bill creating the present bank. Addresses the influence of the bank in establishing a sound and uniform currency, in the collection and disbursement of the public revenue, in foreign and domestic exchanges, and in the agriculture and commerce of the West.

1976. Webster, Daniel (Mass.). "Bank of the United States," *Register of Debates.* 22nd Cong., 1st Sess. (28 May 1832) pp. 981-985. Opposes amendments that would allow the states to expel the bank from their limits, and give them the power to tax the circulation of the bank. Maintains that the bank is protected by the Constitution as an agency created by Congress, and that the states cannot tax and interfere with the currency of the country.

1977. Webster, Daniel (Mass.). "The Bank Veto," *Register of Debates.* 22nd Cong., 1st Sess. (11 July 1832) pp. 1221-1240. Supports renewing the charter of the Bank of the United States. Addresses the President's objections to the bank as unconstitutional, inexpedient and unnecessary for the public good. Warns of the effects of this veto upon the country. Focus of speech establishes the constitutionality of the bank.

1978. Webster, Daniel (Mass.). "Executive Proceedings," *Register of Debates.* 22nd Cong., 1st Sess. (24 Jan, 25 Jan. 1832) pp. 1329-1333; 1365-1367. Opposes Van Buren's nomination as minister to England. Reviews past actions that demonstrate that he would be a representative of his party rather than his country, thus making him an improper representative of the United States.

1979. "An Act Authorizing the Construction of Naval Hospitals at the Navy Yards at Charlestown, Massachusetts, Brooklyn, New York, and Pensacola," *Statutes at Large*, Vol. IV (10 July 1832) p. 570. Also printed in the *Register of Debates* (22nd Cong., 1st Sess.) Appendix, p. xxxiv.

1980. "An Act Authorizing the Entry of Vessels and Merchandise Arriving from the Cape of Good Hope, or beyond the Same, at the Port of Edgartown, in Massachusetts," *Statutes at Large*, Vol. IV (13 July 1832) p. 577. Also printed in the *Register of Debates* (22nd Cong., 1st Sess.) Appendix, p. xxxvii.

1981. "Application of Massachusetts for a More Perfect Organization of the Militia of the United States," *American State Papers: Military Affairs*, Vol. IV (Doc. 486) p. 768. (ASP 019).

1982. "On the Claim for the Use and Value of Certain Lands Included in the Navy Yard at Charlestown, Massachusetts," *American State Papers: Naval Affairs*, Vol. IV (Doc. 484) p. 149. (ASP 026). Report contends that the courts should decide the claim.

1983. U.S. House. *Documents to Accompany Bill H.R. No. 57, Authorizing the Construction of Naval Hospitals at Charlestown, Massachusetts, Brooklyn, New York, and at Pensacola.* 22nd Cong., 1st Sess. (H.Doc.16). Washington: Duff Green, 1831. 8 pg. (Serial Set 216). Letters of transmittal and estimates of expenses to build the naval hospitals. Plans referred to are not included. Same as H.doc.93 (21-2) 208 (entry **1934**).

1984. U.S. House. *Letter from the Secretary of State, Transmitting the Information Required by a Resolution of the House of Representatives, of the 26th of January, Instant, in Relation to Slaves Returned in the 5th Census, in Maine, Massachusetts, and Ohio.* 22nd Cong., 1st Sess. (H.Doc.84). Washington: Duff Green, 1832. 2 pg. (Serial Set 218). Letter gives the name of official returning the slave, name and county of family to which slave belongs, and sex and approximate age of slave.

1985. U.S. House. *Letter from the Secretary of the Treasury, Transmitting the Information Required by a Resolution of the House of Representatives, of the 15th Ultimo, of the Number of Persons Employed in the Custom-House Service in Boston, New York, Philadelphia, Baltimore, and Charleston, &c. &c.* 22nd Cong., 1st Sess. (H.Doc.202). Washington: Duff Green, 1832. 12 pg. (Serial Set 220). Consists of a list of persons employed in each customhouse, the service they perform, and the annual pay and extra pay received by each.

1986. U.S. House. *Letter from the Secretary of War, Transmitting a Report on the Examination of the Hampshire and Hampden and Farmington Canal.* 22nd Cong., 1st Sess. (H.Doc.113). Washington: Duff Green, 1832. 7 pg. (Serial Set 219). Favorable report on the examination of the route of the canals. Describes the routes and the status of the construction; provides estimates of necessary expenses. Discusses the benefits that would derive from the proposed improvements.

1987. U.S. House. *Memorial of Citizens of Boston, in Favor of Re-chartering the Bank of the United States.* 22nd Cong., 1st Sess. (H.Doc.92). Washington: Duff Green, 1832. 2 pg. (Serial Set 218). Same as S.doc.48 (22-1) 212 (entry **2002**).

1988. U.S. House. *Memorial of Citizens of Boston, Massachusetts, Praying for a Reduction of Postage on Newspapers, and Other Periodical Works.* 22nd Cong., 1st Sess. (H.Doc.106). Washington: Duff Green, 1832. 6 pg. (Serial Set 219). Includes statistics concerning periodicals and newspapers sent by mail from Boston. Same as S.doc.59 (22-1) 213 (entry **2003**).

1989. U.S. House. *Memorial of Citizens of Edgartown, upon the Subject of Slavery, Particularly in the District of Columbia.* 22nd Cong., 1st Sess. (H.Doc.96). Washington: Duff Green, 1832. 2 pg. (Serial Set 218). Memorial opposes the institution of slavery, particularly within the District.

1990. U.S. House. *Memorial of Citizens of Massachusetts for a Banking Privilege.* 22nd Cong., 1st Sess. (H.Doc.95). Washington: Duff Green, 1832. 4 pg. (Serial Set 218). Memorial opposes renewing the charter of the Bank of the United States, maintaining that its privileges benefit mostly foreigners and wealthy individuals; requests privileges for a similar bank. Same as S.doc.40 (22-1) 212 (entry **2000**) and H.doc.109 (22-1) 219 (entry **1996**), with different names of memorialists.

1991. U.S. House. *Memorial of Farmers, Mechanics, and Manufacturers, of Essex County, Massachusetts.* 22nd Cong., 1st Sess. (H.Doc.261). Washington: Duff Green, 1832. 3 pg. (Serial Set 221). Memorial supports protective tariffs, particularly for woolens and leather.

1992. U.S. House. *Memorial of Inhabitants of Lynn, Engaged in the Manufacture of Shoes.* 22nd Cong., 1st Sess. (H.Doc.257). Washington: Duff

Green, 1832. 2 pg. (Serial Set 221). Memorial supports the protective tariff; includes statistics of the shoe industry in Lynn, Massachusetts.

1993. U.S. House. *Memorial of the Association of Mechanics, Farmers, and other Working Men, of the Towns of Amesbury and Salisbury, in the State of Massachusetts.* 22nd Cong., 1st Sess. (H.Doc.258). Washington: Duff Green, 1832. 2 pg. (Serial Set 221). Memorial opposes reducing the protective tariff on wool and woolens.

1994. U.S. House. *Memorial of the Citizens of New Bedford, Praying that the Duty on Foreign Tallow, Olive, and Palm Oil, &c. May Not Be Repealed.* 22nd Cong., 1st Sess. (H.Doc.123). Washington: Duff Green, 1832. 3 pg. (Serial Set 219).

1995. U.S. House. *Memorial of Three Banks, and Sundry Citizens, of Middlesex County, Massachusetts, in Favor of the Renewal of the Charter of the Bank of the United States.* 22nd Cong., 1st Sess. (H.Doc.284). Washington: Duff Green, 1832. 3 pg. (Serial Set 221). Includes names and occupations of memorialists.

1996. U.S. House. *Petition of Citizens of Massachusetts, for a Banking Privilege.* 22nd Cong., 1st Sess. (H.Doc.109). Washington: Duff Green, 1832. 6 pg. (Serial Set 219). Petition against renewing the charter of the Bank of the United States, maintaining that its privileges benefit mostly foreigners and wealthy individuals; requests privileges for a similar bank. Petition same as S.doc.40 (22-1) 212 (entry **2000**) and H.doc.95 (22-1) 218 (entry **1990**), with different names of petitioners.

1997. U.S. House. *Remonstrance of Inhabitants of Nantucket, against the Repeal of the Duty on Foreign Tallow, and on Palm and Olive Oils.* 22nd Cong., 1st Sess. (H.Doc.235). Washington: Duff Green, 1832. 3 pg. (Serial Set 221). Memorial supports the protective system; reviews the injurious effects of the proposed repeal of duties on foreign oils.

1998. U.S. House. *Resolutions of the Wool Growers and Manufacturers of the County of Berkshire, Massachusetts.* 22nd Cong., 1st Sess. (H.Doc.269). Washington: Duff Green, 1832. 6 pg. (Serial Set 221). Report and resolutions oppose the proposed modifications of the tariff of 1828; favor continuing the protective policies, particularly for wool and woolens.

1999. U.S. Senate. [Claim of the New England Mississippi Land Company]. 22nd Cong., 1st Sess. (S.doc.29). Washington: Duff Green, 1832. 7 pg. (Serial Set 212). Same as S.doc.17 (19-1) 125 (entry **1807**), S.doc.6 (19-2) 145 (entry **1838**), S.doc.15 (20-1) 163 (entry **1870**), Pub.land 701 (20-2) ASP 032 (entry **1886**), S.doc.21 (20-2) 181 (entry **1891**), and S.doc.52 (21-1) 193 (entry **1922**). See entry **1807** for abstract.

2000. U.S. Senate. *Memorial of Certain Citizens of Salem, Massachusetts, Praying to Be Allowed a Charter for a Banking Institution, to Take Effect at the Expiration of the Present Charter of the Bank of the United States.* 22nd Cong., 1st Sess. (S.Doc.40). Washington: Duff Green, 1832. 3 pg. (Serial Set 212). Memorial opposes renewing the bank's charter, maintaining that its privileges benefit mostly foreigners and wealthy individuals; requests privileges for a similar bank. Memorial same as H.doc.109 (22-1) 219 (entry **1996**) and H.doc.95 (22-1) 218 (entry **1990**), with different names of memorialists.

2001. U.S. Senate. *Memorial of Merchants and Ship Owners, of Salem, Mass. that Certain Advantages Be Given to the Shipping Interest in the Arrangement of the Tariff.* 22nd Cong., 1st Sess. (S.Doc.181). Washington: Duff Green, 1832. 1 pg. (Serial Set 214).

2002. U.S. Senate. *Memorial of Sundry Citizens of Boston, Massachusetts, in Favor of Rechartering the Bank of the United States.* 22nd Cong., 1st Sess. (S.Doc.48). Washington: Duff Green, 1832. 2 pg. (Serial Set 212). Same as H.doc.92 (22-1) 218 (entry **1987**).

2003. U.S. Senate. *Memorial of Sundry Inhabitants of Boston, Praying that the Postage on Newspapers, &c. May Be Reduced, &c.* 22nd Cong., 1st Sess. (S.Doc.59). Washington: Duff Green, 1832. 6 pg. (Serial Set 213). Same as H.doc.106 (22-1) 219. See entry **1988**.

22ND CONGRESS, 2ND SESSION

2004. "Massachusetts Resolutions," *Register of Debates.* 22nd Cong., 2nd Sess. (31 Jan., 1 Feb. 1833) pp. 1522-1529; 1564-1572, 1576-1578. Debate on the Massachusetts resolutions concerning the tariff. Includes speeches by John Q. Adams (Mass.), John Davis (Mass.), and Edward Everett (Mass.). Also includes brief discussion and reprint of resolutions concerning the Maine boundary controversy.

2005. Adams, John Quincy (Mass.). "Massachusetts Resolutions," *Register of Debates.* 22nd Cong., 2nd Sess. (31 Jan., 1 Feb. 1833) pp. 1527-1529; 1564-1568. Objects to the motion to reconsider the vote concerning certain resolutions of the Legislature of Massachusetts; maintains that it would be an insult to Massachusetts and that the language was not unusually strong. Addresses the resolutions' claim that the proposed tariff would increase, rather than diminish, the revenue.

2006. Adams, John Quincy (Mass.). "The Tariff Bill," *Register of Debates.* 22nd Cong., 2nd Sess. (4 Feb., 7 Feb. 1833) pp. 1609-1616; 1640-1651. Addresses South Carolina's threat of nullification. Maintains that the proposed protection would protect the interests of some states at the expense of others, but that the rights of the injured states are equally protected in different ways.

Second speech responds to reactions to first speech and expands on argument against the theory that the Union is nothing more than a confederation of sovereign states.

2007. Appleton, Nathan (Mass.). "Estimated Revenue," *Register of Debates.* 22nd Cong., 2nd Sess. (29 Jan. 1833) pp. 1431-1433. Questions the figures of the Secretary of the Treasury.

2008. Appleton, Nathan (Mass.). "The Tariff Bill," *Register of Debates.* 22nd Cong., 2nd Sess. (22 Jan. 1833) pp. 1194-1225. Addresses the need for a tariff bill and whether this bill meets that need. Demonstrates that there will be no surplus revenue to reduce. Addresses South Carolina's threat of nullification; discusses the operation of the protective tariff on the southern states and the influence of slavery on manufacturing. Maintains that the proposed bill would be destructive to cotton and wool manufacturing and would not satisfy South Carolina.

2009. Bates, Isaac C. (Mass.). "The Tariff Bill," *Register of Debates.* 22nd Cong., 2nd Sess. (30 Jan. 1833) pp. 1478-1492. Opposes the bill; contends that government policy has always supported the protective policy. Demonstrates the detrimental effects this bill would have to the woolens and cottons manufactures. Maintains that the bill is unnecessary as there is no surplus revenue to reduce. Discusses the protective principle and nullification.

2010. Briggs, George N. (Mass.). "The Tariff Bill," *Register of Debates.* 22nd Cong., 2nd Sess. (14 Jan. 1833) pp. 1034-1044. Opposes the proposed bill as uprooting the foundations of the protective system and disastrous in its effects upon the country. Maintains that the bill would operate unjustly upon the New England states. Reviews the history of the protective policy since the constitution, and its support from leading statesmen and politicians of the South.

2011. Choate, Rufus (Mass.). "The Tariff," *Register of Debates.* 22nd Cong., 2nd Sess. (15 Jan. 1833) pp. 1064-1078. Opposes the proposed bill as rash, partial, unnecessary and originating from South Carolina's nullification of the past tariff. Supports a tariff bill that would base the revenue on imposts, yet incorporate the principle of protection without injustice to the South. Maintains that the public lands should not be considered a continuing source of revenue; contends that the tariff has not fallen disproportionately on the South.

2012. Davis, John (Mass.). "Massachusetts Resolutions," *Register of Debates.* 22nd Cong., 2nd Sess. (31 Jan., 2 Feb. 1833) pp. 1522-1524; 1576-1577. Defends the memorial from the Legislature of Massachusetts on the bill to alter the tariff; maintains that the language was not improper.

2013. Davis, John (Mass.). "The Tariff Bill," *Register of Debates.* 22nd Cong., 2nd Sess. (12 Feb., 19 Feb. 1833) pp. 1702-1704; 1740-1741. Opposes the equalization of duties as abandoning the right to protect American labor;

maintains that the policy is false and unsound, and would not reduce the revenue.

2014. Davis, John (Mass.). "The Tariff Bill," *Register of Debates.* 22nd Cong., 2nd Sess. (25 Feb. 1833) pp. 1773-1778. Opposes the bill introduced as a compromise on the tariff issues. Maintains that the legislation is hasty and abandons protectionism by equalizing duties. Briefly discusses the discontent of South Carolina.

2015. Davis, John (Mass.). "The Tariff Law of 1832," *Register of Debates.* 22nd Cong., 2nd Sess. (12 Feb. 1833) pp. 1688-1692. Clarifies the 18th section of the tariff law of 1832 protecting merchants who had imported goods subject to the old rate of duties; maintains that the intent is clear but that the language is ambiguous.

2016. Dearborn, Henry A. S. (Mass.). "The Naval Service," *Register of Debates.* 22nd Cong., 2nd Sess. (9 Feb. 1833) pp. 1669-1671. Supports the character of midshipmen; requests further information before deciding to diminish the number of officers.

2017. Dearborn, Henry A. S. (Mass.). "The Tariff," *Register of Debates.* 22nd Cong., 2nd Sess. (14 Jan. 1833) pp. 1044-1054. Supports protectionism. Favors graduating the revenue to the "wants" of the government, but differs as to what the "wants" of the government includes. Maintains that the North has more cause to complain about the collection of the revenue than the South. Discusses nullification and the differences between the North and South.

2018. Everett, Edward (Mass.). "Massachusetts Resolutions," *Register of Debates.* 22nd Cong., 2nd Sess. (31 Jan. 1833) pp. 1524-1526. Defends the Massachusetts resolutions on the tariff; compares them to previous resolutions by the Georgia Legislature.

2019. Everett, Edward (Mass.). "Reduction of Postage," *Register of Debates.* 22nd Cong., 2nd Sess. (28 Dec. 1832, 2 Jan. 1833) pp. 927-929; 934-937. Supports reducing the postage rates; maintains that the Post Office is partly for the service of the public, and as such the public should share the cost of unproductive post roads and the transportation of postage-free government letters and documents. Addresses objections.

2020. Everett, Edward (Mass.). "The Tariff Bill," *Register of Debates.* 22nd Cong., 2nd Sess. (19 Feb. 1833) pp. 1735-1738. Opposes reducing the duty on imported cotton; reviews the history of the protective duty on cotton.

2021. Reed, John (Mass.). "Tariff Bill," *Register of Debates.* 22nd Cong., 2nd Sess. (22 Jan. 1833) pp. 1176-1194. Opposes the proposed tariff bill, which would supersede the protective tariff of 1832. Addresses the general principles of the tariff and protectionism and the history of previous tariff bills. Discusses the proposed bill and its claims and provisions. Objects to the demands and threats of South Carolina.

2022. Webster, Daniel (Mass.). "Mr. Calhoun's Resolutions," *Register of Debates.* 22nd Cong., 2nd Sess. (26 Feb. 1833) pp. 774-777. Objects to Mr. Calhoun's interpretation of the Constitution as a compact between sovereign states rather than the union of the states under a popular government.

2023. Webster, Daniel (Mass.). "Revenue Collection Bill," *Register of Debates.* 22nd Cong., 2nd Sess. (8 Feb. 1833) pp. 409-411. Supports the bill and the President as its originator.

2024. Webster, Daniel (Mass.). "Revenue Collection Bill," *Register of Debates.* 22nd Cong., 2nd Sess. (16 Feb. 1833) pp. 553-587. Responds to Mr. Calhoun. Maintains that the Constitution is not a compact of the sovereign states, but rather the union of the states under a popular government. Discusses the Constitution, its formation, powers and provisions, in support of his position. Addresses the effects of nullification on the Union and the nature of sovereignty. Examines the ordinance and laws of South Carolina that nullify the U.S. laws to lay and collect duties.

2025. Webster, Daniel (Mass.). "The Tariff," *Register of Debates.* 22nd Cong., 2nd Sess. (25 Feb. 1833) pp. 727-729. Opposes the bill as perpetuating an uncertain and continually fluctuating protection policy. Gives objections; discusses effects. Maintains that the obstacles are insurmountable.

2026. "An Act Establishing a Port of Entry and Delivery at the Village of Fall River in Massachusetts, and Discontinuing the Office at Dighton," *Statutes at Large,* Vol. IV (2 Mar. 1833) p. 651. Also printed in the *Register of Debates* (22nd Cong., 2nd Sess.) Appendix, p. 21.

2027. U.S. House. *Custom-House - Newburyport.* 22nd Cong., 2nd Sess. (H.Rpt.67). Washington: Duff Green, 1833. 1 pg. (Serial Set 236). Report supports the memorialists' application for a new customhouse at Newburyport.

2028. U.S. House. *Memorial from Citizens of Middlesex Co., Massachusetts, in Favor of Protecting the Industry of the Farmer, Mechanic, and Manufacturer.* 22nd Cong., 2nd Sess. (H.Doc.85). Washington: Duff Green, 1832. 2 pg. (Serial Set 234). Memorial and resolutions support the protective tariff and disapprove of the nullification theory of South Carolina.

2029. U.S. House. *Memorial of Merchants and Others, of the District of Plymouth, Massachusetts.* 22nd Cong., 2nd Sess. (H.Doc.52). Washington: Duff Green, 1832. 1 pg. (Serial Set 234). Memorial requests appropriations to erect a building for the customhouse, post office, and storage of public goods.

2030. U.S. House. *Memorial of Merchants of Boston.* 22nd Cong., 2nd Sess. (H.Doc.56). Washington: Duff Green, 1832. 2 pg. (Serial Set 234). Memorial requests a repeal, or substantial reduction, of the duty on hemp.

2031. U.S. House. *Memorial of the Merrimack Manufacturing Company.* 22nd Cong., 2nd Sess. (H.Doc.71). Washington: Duff Green, 1832. 3 pg. (Serial Set 234). Memorial protests the reduction of duties on printed cotton goods. Reviews unrequited expenditures made under the policy of protectionism and the ruinous effect of the proposed measure upon the printing business.

2032. U.S. House. *Resolutions of the Legislature of Massachusetts, upon the Subject of a Reduction of the Duties on Imports, &c. &c.* 22nd Cong., 2nd Sess. (H.Doc.81). Washington: Duff Green, 1832. 7 pg. (Serial Set 234). Report and resolutions oppose a reduction of protective tariffs and a change in the economical policy of the government; disapprove of any action based on the threats of South Carolina. Same as S.doc.60 (22-2) 230 (entry **2034**).

2033. U.S. House. *Tariff - Resolutions of Citizens of Boston.* 22nd Cong., 2nd Sess. (H.Doc.110). Washington: Duff Green, 1832. 2 pg. (Serial Set 235). Resolutions support continuing the protective tariff.

2034. U.S. Senate. *Resolutions and Report of a Committee Adopted by the Legislature of Massachusetts Relative to the Measures of South Carolina, and Adverse to the Tariff Bill Now before the House of Representatives.* 22nd Cong., 2nd Sess. (S.Doc.60). Washington: Duff Green, 1832. 7 pg. (Serial Set 230). Same as H.doc.81 (22-2) 234. See entry **2032**.

23ᴿᴰ CONGRESS, 1ˢᵀ SESSION

2035. "Massachusetts Resolutions," *Register of Debates.* 23rd Cong., 1st Sess. (10 Mar. 1834) pp. 836-855. Debates on the resolutions from the Legislature of Massachusetts complaining of the state of the currency and asking to restore the deposits and re-charter the Bank of the United States. Includes remarks by Nathaniel Silsbee (Mass.), Daniel Webster (Mass.), John P. King (Ga.), John Forsyth (Ga.), and Ezekiel Chambers (Md.).

2036. "Massachusetts Resolutions," *Register of Debates.* 23rd Cong., 1st Sess. (17 Mar. 1834) pp. 3009-3014. Debate on the Massachusetts resolutions asking to restore the deposits and to either re-charter the Bank of the United States or establish a new national bank. Includes remarks by John Q. Adams (Mass.).

2037. "Memorial from Boston," *Register of Debates.* 23rd Cong., 1st Sess. (8 May 1834) pp. 1712-1716. Remarks from Thomas H. Benton (Mo.) and Thomas Ewing (Ohio) on the memorial from Boston against re-chartering the Bank of the United States and against the restoration of the deposits. Discuss winding up the affairs of the bank, and the exportation and importation of specie. Remarks of Benton also printed in the *Congressional Globe*, "Petitions," pp. 371-372.

2038. "New Bedford Memorial," *Register of Debates.* 23rd Cong., 1st Sess. (3 May 1834) pp. 1607-1612. Memorial from New Bedford, remonstrating against the removal of the public deposits, was presented. Debate on the cause of the distress of New Bedford includes brief remarks from Nathaniel Silsbee (Mass.), Daniel Webster (Mass.), and Peleg Sprague (Maine).

2039. Remarks on the Faneuil Hall Resolutions, *Congressional Globe.* 23rd Cong., 1st Sess. (3 Apr. 1834) pp. 285-287. Remarks from Thomas H. Benton (Mo.) and George M. Bibb (Ky.) on the 28 resolutions adopted at Faneuil Hall in support of the actions of the Executive and opposing the United States Bank. Discusses the political character of the bank. Slightly different version of these remarks printed in the *Register of Debates*, "Faneuil Hall Resolutions," pp. 1244-1250.

2040. Adams, John Quincy (Mass.). "Adjournment of Congress," *Register of Debates.* 23rd Cong., 1st Sess. (29 May 1834) pp. 4331-4332. Favors the 30th for the adjournment of Congress. Remarks on the bank committee's report; opposes the right of the House to send for the bank directors to punish them.

2041. Adams, John Quincy (Mass.). "Deposite Bank Charters, &c.," *Register of Debates.* 23rd Cong., 1st Sess. (29 Mar. 1834) pp. 3303-3304. Supports his resolution to inquire into the charters, debts, and affairs of the deposit banks; maintains that it is only fair that the scrutiny endured by the United States Bank and its branches be allowed for the deposit banks.

2042. Adams, John Quincy (Mass.). "Extension of the Pension Laws," *Register of Debates.* 23rd Cong., 1st Sess. (4 Feb. 1834) pp. 2614-2615. Supports including the men who fought the Indian wars on the pension rolls; maintains that the wars were public wars, not private.

2043. Adams, John Quincy (Mass.). "General Appropriation Bill," *Register of Debates.* 23rd Cong., 1st Sess. (8 Apr., 9 Apr. 1834) pp. 3543-3544, 3546-3547; 3575-3580. Opposes the appropriation for a clerk to arrange the archives of the State Department. Maintains that the appropriation is a wedge for a permanent additional position, that an appropriation bill should only provide money for expenses already sanctioned by law, and that there is no proper evidence that the expense is necessary.

2044. Adams, John Quincy (Mass.). "General Appropriation Bill," *Register of Debates.* 23rd Cong., 1st Sess. (23 Apr. 1834) pp. 3758-3763. Corrects the proceedings of the House reported in the *Journal*; clarifies the rules of the House when a quorum is not present. Requests that the House be permitted either to adjourn or to compel the attendance of its members when a quorum is not present and an important bill is under debate.

2045. Adams, John Quincy (Mass.). "General Appropriation Bill," *Register of Debates.* 23rd Cong., 1st Sess. (30 Apr., 1 May 1834) pp. 3871-3874; 3883-3888. Objects to the appropriations for ministers at Russia and England. Questions the use of former appropriations and the current expensive practice whereby ministers abroad return after a few weeks or months. Discusses the need for ministers at various foreign courts, the adequacy of their allowances, and the misuse of the right of appointment during the recess of Congress.

2046. Adams, John Quincy (Mass.). "General Appropriation Bill," *Register of Debates.* 23rd Cong., 1st Sess. (2 May 1834) pp. 3913-3915, 3926-3932. Requests the chairman of the Committee on Foreign Relations to justify the need for the requested ministers for Belgium and South America. Maintains that the government should only establish and maintain missions in countries where there is a necessity. He is not satisfied with the Executive's explanation concerning the situation in Buenos Ayres.

2047. Adams, John Quincy (Mass.). "Massachusetts Resolutions," *Register of Debates.* 23rd Cong., 1st Sess. (17 Mar. 1834) pp. 3009-3012. Presents and supports resolutions from the Legislature of Massachusetts asking to restore the public deposits and to either re-charter the Bank of the United States or establish a new national bank. Discusses the occasion and character of the resolutions.

2048. Adams, John Quincy (Mass.). "The Public Deposites," *Register of Debates.* 23rd Cong., 1st Sess. (13 June 1834) pp. 4459-4461. Favors an inquiry into the state, condition, and management, of the state deposit banks.

2049. Adams, John Quincy (Mass.). "The Public Deposites," *Register of Debates.* 23rd Cong., 1st Sess. (4 Apr. 1834) pp. 3477-3516. Speech, with notes, supports the resolutions of the Legislature of Massachusetts concerning the reasons assigned by the Secretary of the Treasury for the removal of the public moneys from the Bank of the United States. Maintains that the reasons were not sufficient to justify the measure and that the removal was unlawful, unjust and unauthorized. Reviews alleged precedents and annexed documents used to justify the removal. Discusses the alleged corruption and misconduct of the bank. Examines the role of the President of the United States and his efforts to destroy the bank.

2050. Adams, John Quincy (Mass.). Remarks on the Death of Mr. Wirt, *Register of Debates.* 23rd Cong., 1st Sess. (21 Feb. 1834) pp. 2758-2759. Remarks in memory of William Wirt, Attorney General of the United States.

2051. Adams, John Quincy (Mass.). "Report of Committee of Ways and Means," *Register of Debates.* 23rd Cong., 1st Sess. (12 Mar. 1834) pp. 2971-2976. Objects to allowing debate on the report of the Committee of Ways and Means on the removal of the deposits to take precedence over the other business of the House. Maintains that further debate will serve no useful purpose as no measure of relief is to be expected from the House. Discusses problems encountered when presenting minority petitions.

2052. Adams, John Quincy (Mass.). "Western (Indian) Territory," *Register of Debates.* 23rd Cong., 1st Sess. (25 June 1834) pp. 4768-4772. Opposes the bill to establish the Western Territory for the Indians. Objects that the territory created by the bill is intended to become a state of the Union, that it is unconstitutional, and that it transfers the power of legislation of the Indian tribes from Congress to the discretion of a governor and the Executive.

2053. Bates, Isaac C. (Mass.). "Springfield (Mass.) Memorial," *Register of Debates.* 23rd Cong., 1st Sess. (14 Apr. 1834) pp. 3637-3638. Presents resolutions and memorial against the removal of the deposits and in favor of the Bank of the United States.

2054. Baylies, William (Mass.). "Commutation Bill," *Register of Debates.* 23rd Cong., 1st Sess. (4 Apr. 1834) pp. 3439-3443. Supports transferring the examination and decision of claims for commutation pay from Congress to the Secretary of the Treasury. Offers reasons for support; answers objections concerning executive patronage, fraud, statute of limitations, lapse of time, and presumptions of evidence. Maintains that the proposed bill secures faster and more correct decisions.

2055. Choate, Rufus (Mass.). "The Deposites and United States Bank," *Congressional Globe.* 23rd Cong., 1st Sess. (28 Mar. 1834) pp. 272-273. Supports restoring the deposits as a temporary measure for public relief, to enable the banks to wind up affairs, and to prepare for a gradual transition. Discusses the necessity for the restoration and the lack of cause for the removal. Much longer version of this speech printed in the *Register of Debates*, "The Deposites and the United States Bank," pp. 3272-3296.

2056. Davis, John (Mass.). Remarks on the Petition of Noah Fletcher, *Congressional Globe.* 23rd Cong., 1st Sess. (31 Dec. 1833, 13 Jan. 1834) pp. 72; 98. Supports the petition of Noah Fletcher, a clerk in the House who was removed from his position. Petition included. Same remarks also printed in the *Register of Debates*, "Case of Noah Fletcher," pp. 2290-2292, 2368-2370.

2057. Everett, Edward (Mass.). "Bank Reports," *Register of Debates.* 23rd Cong., 1st Sess. (27 May 1834) pp. 4268-4269. Defends the printers and the report of the minority.

2058. Everett, Edward (Mass.). "Compensation for Property Lost, &c.," *Register of Debates.* 23rd Cong., 1st Sess. (12 Apr. 1834) pp. 3632-3635. Supports including Revolutionary War claimants on an equal basis to those of the last war seeking compensation for the destruction of their property. Addresses various objections.

2059. Everett, Edward (Mass.). "Salem (Mass.) Memorial," *Register of Debates.* 23rd Cong., 1st Sess. (14 Apr. 1834) pp. 3645-3648. Presents memorials from Salem, Mass. and Medford, Mass. praying for the restoration of the deposits. Supports the character of the memorialists; describes the hardships faced by the Medford shipping industry.

2060. Gorham, Benjamin (Mass.). "Fortification Bill," *Register of Debates.* 23rd Cong., 1st Sess. (19 June 1834) pp. 4581-4582. Supports appropriations for a fort on George's Island in Boston harbor; maintains that it has been recommended as one of the first rank, that the harbor is vulnerable to attack, and George's Island is an important point of defense.

2061. Gorham, Benjamin (Mass.). "Gold Coins," *Register of Debates.* 23rd Cong., 1st Sess. (21 June 1834) pp. 4650-4652. Addresses the necessity of fixing a proper standard and true ratio of gold and silver. Discusses the dangers of establishing an improper standard.

2062. Gorham, Benjamin (Mass.). "Memorial of Merchants, &c. of New York," *Register of Debates.* 23rd Cong., 1st Sess. (3 Feb. 1834) pp. 2597-2599. Discusses the derangement of the currency and commercial exchanges, specie payments and return to metallic currency, and loss of credit. Maintains that the remedy to the current economic distress is the renewal of the bank charter or the establishment of another national bank.

2063. Gorham, Benjamin (Mass.). "Removal of the Deposites," *Register of Debates.* 23rd Cong., 1st Sess. (16 Dec. 1833) pp. 2191-2193. Maintains that the House should come to a prompt decision on the subject of the report of the Secretary of the Treasury as the public confidence needs to be restored. Discusses the question of the currency and the public distress.

2064. Grennell, George, Jr. (Mass.). "Fortification Bill," *Register of Debates.* 23rd Cong., 1st Sess. (19 June 1834) pp. 4584-4585. Supports appropriations for the fort on George's Island in Boston harbor; discusses the importance of the site and its vulnerability without proper defense.

2065. Grennell, George, Jr. (Mass.). "Franklin County (Mass.) Memorial," *Register of Debates.* 23rd Cong., 1st Sess. (26 May 1834) pp. 4258-4263. Presents and supports the memorial asking that the deposits be restored and either the Bank of the United States be re-chartered or another national bank be established. Describes the character of the memorialists; detailed review of the memorial with excerpts included.

2066. Lincoln, Levi (Mass.). "The Appropriation Bill," *Congressional Globe.* 23rd Cong., 1st Sess. (25 Apr. 1834) p. 347. Objects to the Postmaster General employing clerks without authority of law; questions how they are being paid. Much longer version of these remarks, printed in the *Register of Debates*, "The General Appropriation Bill," pp. 3784-3794, reviews the financial condition of the Post Office Department.

2067. Lincoln, Levi (Mass.). "The General Appropriation Bill," *Register of Debates.* 23rd Cong., 1st Sess. (9 Apr. 1834) pp. 3554-3559. Objects to appropriations for an additional clerk in the Department of State. Offended that the additional clerkship was urged upon grounds of negligence of previous Secretaries of State. Maintains that such a charge should have an inquiry to determine the facts. Also contends that the public finances and the poverty of the people dictate that this is no time for unnecessary expenditures.

2068. Lincoln, Levi (Mass.). "Worcester (Mass.) Memorial," *Register of Debates*. 23rd Cong., 1st Sess. (17 Mar. 1834) pp. 3017-3021. Presents and supports a memorial and resolutions asking for a restoration of the public deposits. Describes Worcester County and the character and situation of the meeting and the memorialists.

2069. Osgood, Gayton P. (Mass.). Remarks on the Report and Resolutions of Lowell, Mass. on the National Currency, *Congressional Globe*. 23rd Cong., 1st Sess. (14 Apr. 1834) p. 308. Supports the report and resolutions that oppose re-chartering the Bank of the United States in favor of establishing a new Bank of the United States. Description of Lowell, Massachusetts. Same remarks printed in the *Register of Debates*, "Lowell (Mass.) Memorial," pp. 3638-3640.

2070. Osgood, Gayton P. (Mass.). Speech on the Memorial of the Third District of Mass. Which Supports the Restoration of the Deposites to the Bank of the United States, *Congressional Globe*. 23rd Cong., 1st Sess. (5 May 1834) pp. 363-366. Objects to the memorial. Elected in known opposition to re-chartering the bank, he cannot support the restoration of the deposits. Discusses his obligations to follow the instructions of his constituents. Almost exactly the same speech printed in the *Register of Debates*, "3rd Congressional District of Massachusetts Memorial," pp. 3934-3943.

2071. Reed, John (Mass.). "Fortification Bill," *Register of Debates*. 23rd Cong., 1st Sess. (19 June 1834) pp. 4597-4599. Supports appropriations for George's Island in Boston harbor; maintains that the fort is important for the defense of a valuable harbor.

2072. Reed, John (Mass.). "The General Appropriation Bill," *Register of Debates*. 23rd Cong., 1st Sess. (17 Apr. 1834) pp. 3655-3656. Requests that the system of salaries of collectors be corrected.

2073. Reed, John (Mass.). "The General Appropriation Bill," *Register of Debates*. 23rd Cong., 1st Sess. (1 May 1834) pp. 3903-3904. Opposes appropriations for a minister to Great Britain.

2074. Reed, John (Mass.). "Memorial from Bangor, Maine," *Register of Debates*. 23rd Cong., 1st Sess. (24 Feb. 1834) pp. 2765-2767. Defends the memorialists from Bangor, and all other memorialists petitioning to re-charter the Bank of the United States. Maintains that the distress of the country is real and that their requests are not politically motivated.

2075. Reed, John (Mass.). "New Bedford Memorial," *Register of Debates*. 23rd Cong., 1st Sess. (5 Mar. 1834) pp. 2897-2900. Presents and supports resolutions from the collection district of New Bedford protesting the removal of the public deposits and in favor of re-chartering the Bank of the United

States. Describes the character of New Bedford and the importance of the whaling industry to the national interest.

2076. Reed, John (Mass.). "New Bedford Resolutions," *Register of Debates.* 23rd Cong., 1st Sess. (27 Jan. 1834) pp. 2538-2539. Presents and supports resolutions from New Bedford, Mass., praying for the restoration of the public deposits.

2077. Silsbee, Nathaniel (Mass.). "General Appropriation Bill," *Register of Debates.* 23rd Cong., 1st Sess. (18 June 1834) pp. 2031-2035. Advocates revising the pay of the officers of the revenue. Reports on the existing situation, including relevant legislative acts and statistics. Maintains that as the business of many districts has changed since rates of pay were initially established, these rates are now unequal and unjust.

2078. Silsbee, Nathaniel (Mass.). "Massachusetts Resolutions," *Register of Debates.* 23rd Cong., 1st Sess. (10 Mar. 1834) pp. 836-838. Introduces and supports the resolutions from the Legislature of Massachusetts complaining of the state of the currency and asking to restore the deposits and re-charter the Bank of the United States.

2079. Silsbee, Nathaniel (Mass.). "Salem (Mass.) Memorial," *Register of Debates.* 23rd Cong., 1st Sess. (7 Apr. 1834) pp. 1258-1259. Supports the character of the memorialists and their position that the deranged state of the currency is due to the removal of the public deposits from the Bank of the United States.

2080. Webster, Daniel (Mass.). "Adams (Mass.) Memorial," *Register of Debates.* 23rd Cong., 1st Sess. (22 Apr. 1834) pp. 1424-1425. Supports the memorial asking to restore the public deposits.

2081. Webster, Daniel (Mass.). "Albany Memorial," *Register of Debates.* 23rd Cong., 1st Sess. (28 Mar. 1834) pp. 1177-1184. Supports the Albany memorial that asks to restore the deposits and renew the charter of the Bank of the United States. Describes Albany and its financial distress. Discusses the constitutional power of Congress to establish national banks.

2082. Webster, Daniel (Mass.). "Albany Memorial," *Register of Debates.* 23rd Cong., 1st Sess. (22 Apr. 1834) pp. 1423-1424. Explains and rectifies the problem of the missing names regarding the Albany memorial he presented earlier.

2083. Webster, Daniel (Mass.). "Boston Memorial," *Register of Debates.* 23rd Cong., 1st Sess. (18 Mar. 1834) pp. 978-982. Presents a memorial protesting against the actions of the Executive against the Bank of the United States. Defends the character of the memorialists; reviews the chief points of the memorial.

2084. Webster, Daniel (Mass.). "Columbia (Pa.) Proceedings," *Register of Debates.* 23rd Cong., 1st Sess. (20 May 1834) pp. 1761-1767. Supports Columbia, Pa., resolutions opposed to the removal of the deposits and in favor of re-chartering the Bank of the United States. Discusses the economic condition of the country and his earlier proposal to re-charter the bank for a short period. Maintains that a national bank is constitutional and indispensable.

2085. Webster, Daniel (Mass.). "Explanatory Message," *Register of Debates.* 23rd Cong., 1st Sess. (21 Apr. 1834) pp. 1397-1398. Objects to the President's assertion that the Houses of Congress do not have the right to express their opinions on the public conduct of executive officers.

2086. Webster, Daniel (Mass.). "Lancaster County (Pa.) Memorial," *Register of Debates.* 23rd Cong., 1st Sess. (7 Mar. 1834) pp. 825-826. Supports the memorialists and their memorial praying for the restoration of the public deposits.

2087. Webster, Daniel (Mass.). "Lynn (Mass.) Memorial," *Register of Debates.* 23rd Cong., 1st Sess. (24 Mar. 1834) pp. 1113-1115. Presents memorial from Lynn, Mass., requesting a restoration of the deposits. Describes the town of Lynn, its past prosperity, and current distress.

2088. Webster, Daniel (Mass.). "Memorials from Pennsylvania and New York," *Register of Debates.* 23rd Cong., 1st Sess. (21 May 1834) pp. 1788, 1790-1792. Remarks upon the President's practice of making appointments without the concurrence of the Senate. Responds to remarks about the Bank of the United States.

2089. Webster, Daniel (Mass.). "New York Memorial," *Register of Debates.* 23rd Cong., 1st Sess. (4 Feb. 1834) pp. 464-466. Supports the memorialists and their memorial on the financial distress of the country and the need for a national bank.

2090. Webster, Daniel (Mass.). "New York Resolutions," *Register of Debates.* 23rd Cong., 1st Sess. (30 Jan., 31 Jan. 1834) pp. 405-410; 435-442. Discusses the financial condition of the country and the Executive's solution to the distress; maintains that the remedy will be ineffective. Addresses charges that the distress is due to the conduct of the Bank of the U.S. and party motives rather than the removal of the deposits. Discusses the constitutional power to create a national bank versus the power to use a State bank. Addresses the issue of the restoration of the deposits as separate from re-chartering the bank; admonishes against claims that it is a question between the poor and the rich.

2091. Webster, Daniel (Mass.). "New York, Pennsylvania, and Michigan Memorials," *Register of Debates.* 23rd Cong., 1st Sess. (12 May 1834) pp. 1722-1724. Presents and supports memorials from Rochester, New York, Mifflin county, Pennsylvania, and Detroit, Michigan Territory, all requesting that the public deposits be restored.

2092. Webster, Daniel (Mass.). "North Carolina Resolutions," *Register of Debates.* 23rd Cong., 1st Sess. (14 Feb. 1834) pp. 540-543, 556-559. Defends the motives of the petitioners who disapprove of the removal of the deposits. Answers charges against the Bank of the United States that it has unnecessarily curtailed its discounts, broken up the internal exchanges, tried to break down the State banks, and purposefully not used power it possesses to relieve the country.

2093. Webster, Daniel (Mass.). "Ontario County (N.Y.) Memorial," *Register of Debates.* 23rd Cong., 1st Sess. (25 Apr. 1834) pp. 1475-1477. Supports the memorial remonstrating against the actions of the Executive towards the Bank of the United States; describes Ontario County and its people.

2094. Webster, Daniel (Mass.). "Petitions from Maine," *Register of Debates.* 23rd Cong., 1st Sess. (22 Feb. 1834) pp. 639-646, 648-651. Discusses the government's experiment to return to an exclusive specie currency by dispensing with all banks. Questions what object is to be accomplished; maintains that an exclusive specie currency is not desirable and that the country requires a mixed system of specie and bank paper. Recommends re-chartering the bank for a specified time and with necessary modifications to remove objections. Responds to remarks of Sen. Forsyth (Ga.) on the bank bill of 1816.

2095. Webster, Daniel (Mass.). "Philadelphia Mechanics' Memorial," *Register of Debates.* 23rd Cong., 1st Sess. (7 Mar. 1834) pp. 826-829. Supports the memorialists and their memorial and resolutions in favor of restoring the public deposits and re-chartering the Bank of the United States. Discusses the building business and the distress of the country.

2096. Webster, Daniel (Mass.). "Post Office Resolutions," *Register of Debates.* 23rd Cong., 1st Sess. (27 June 1834) pp. 2118-2120. Remarks on the resolutions charging the Post Office with gross misconduct and corrupt patronage. Recommends that the Post Office Department be immediately and thoroughly reformed.

2097. Webster, Daniel (Mass.). "President's Protest," *Register of Debates.* 23rd Cong., 1st Sess. (6 May, 7 May 1834) pp. 1660-1661; 1663-1690. Discusses the President's protest of the Senate resolution claiming that the President's removal of the public deposits was unconstitutional. Considers the circumstances behind the protest and examines the principles which it attempts to establish. Disproves the President's claim that the Senate has no right to express an opinion on the conduct of the President. Discusses why the removal of the deposits was an illegal, indefensible, and dangerous assumption of power. Discusses the need for constitutional restraints and the separation of the powers of government, the powers of appointment and removal, and the President's powers as executive.

2098. Webster, Daniel (Mass.). "Public Distress," *Register of Debates.* 23rd Cong., 1st Sess. (20 Jan. 1834) pp. 291-297. Supports the 14 resolutions from Boston concerning the state of the currency and finances of the country. Agrees that the removal of the deposits was the cause of the current distress. Reviews measures suggested to relieve the distress; favors the establishment of a new bank created by Congress as proper, necessary, and a practicable remedy.

2099. Webster, Daniel (Mass.). "Public Distress," *Register of Debates.* 23rd Cong., 1st Sess. (24 Jan. 1834) p. 338. Presents the proceedings of a public meeting held in New Bedford asking for the deposits to be restored and the Bank of the United States re-chartered. Describes New Bedford's distress.

2100. Webster, Daniel (Mass.). "Public Distress," *Register of Debates.* 23rd Cong., 1st Sess. (11 Feb. 1834) p. 528. Supports the memorial from Philadelphia asking for the restoration of the public deposits. Maintains that prompt action is demanded and that it is the duty of Congress to adopt some measures of relief.

2101. Webster, Daniel (Mass.). "Public Distress," *Register of Debates.* 23rd Cong., 1st Sess. (22 Mar. 1834) pp. 1107-1108. Supports a memorial from Chambersburg, Pa., which opposes the course of the Executive concerning the Bank of the United States.

2102. Webster, Daniel (Mass.). "Raleigh (N.C.) Memorial," *Register of Debates.* 23rd Cong., 1st Sess. (20 May 1834) pp. 1769-1771. Defends the Bank of the United States against charges.

2103. Webster, Daniel (Mass.). "Re-chartering Bank United States," *Register of Debates.* 23rd Cong., 1st Sess. (20 Mar. 1834) pp. 1036-1041. Defends the Bank of the United States and its supporters. Addresses the allegations made against the bank in the report of the Secretary of the Treasury. Maintains that a national bank is necessary to regulate the currency of the country.

2104. Webster, Daniel (Mass.). Remarks on His Resolution concerning Steamboat Accidents, *Congressional Globe.* 23rd Cong., 1st Sess. (23 Dec. 1833) p. 49. Advocates preventing accidents by regulating steam boilers. Different version of these remarks printed in the *Register of Debates*, "Steamboat Accidents," pp. 54-56.

2105. Webster, Daniel (Mass.). Remarks on Re-chartering the Bank, *Congressional Globe.* 23rd Cong., 1st Sess. (18 Mar. 1834) pp. 248-249. Introduces bill to re-charter the bank for six more years. Discusses the distress of the country and the pressing need for Congress to act. Maintains that his bill would provide prompt and efficient relief. Longer version of speech printed in the *Register of Debates*, "Re-Chartering Bank United States," pp. 984-996.

2106. Webster, Daniel (Mass.). Remarks on the Massachusetts Resolutions, *Congressional Globe.* 23rd Cong., 1st Sess. (10 Mar. 1834) p. 225. Supports the resolutions complaining of the state of the currency, and recommending restoration of the public deposits and re-chartering the Bank of the United States. Previews a bill he will be introducing to re-charter the bank for a limited time. Longer version of these remarks printed in the *Register of Debates*, "Massachusetts Resolutions," pp. 838-841, 842-844.

2107. Webster, Daniel (Mass.). Remarks on the Pennsylvania Memorial Pertaining to the Bank, *Congressional Globe*. 23rd Cong., 1st Sess. (3 Jun. 1834) pp. 421-422, 423. Advocates the authenticity of the memorial and the need for the requested relief. Longer version of these remarks printed in the *Register of Debates*, "Harrisburg (Pa.) Memorial," pp. 1860-1866, 1870.

2108. Webster, Daniel (Mass.). "Removal of the Deposites," *Register of Debates*. 23rd Cong., 1st Sess. (5 Feb. 1834) pp. 474-475. Remarks on the Secretary of the Treasury's report and the duty of Congress to examine the reasons that he has given for the removal of the deposits.

2109. Webster, Daniel (Mass.). "Reports on the Post Office," *Register of Debates*. 23rd Cong., 1st Sess. (10 June, 11 June 1834) pp. 1951-1953; 1958-1959. Advocates printing sufficient copies of the minority and majority reports on the administration of the Post Office. Requests the truth concerning the various charges against the Post Office.

2110. Webster, Daniel (Mass.). "Revenue Bonds," *Register of Debates*. 23rd Cong., 1st Sess. (7 Feb. 1834) pp. 520-522. Remarks on the proposed remedy to the country's economic distress; believes that the relief offered will only benefit importing merchants. Responds to remarks of Sen. King (Ga.) regarding the price of cotton.

2111. Webster, Daniel (Mass.). "Union County (Pa.) Memorial," *Register of Debates*. 23rd Cong., 1st Sess. (24 Apr. 1834) pp. 1453-1454. Supports the memorialists and their memorial protesting against the removal of the deposits and the executive experiment.

2112. Webster, Daniel (Mass.). "Utica (N.Y.) Memorial," *Register of Debates*. 23rd Cong., 1st Sess. (28 Apr. 1834) pp. 1527-1529. Presents and supports the memorial remonstrating against the removal of the public deposits. Describes the character of the memorialists and their county.

2113. "Application of Georgia in Relation to a Proper Disposition of the Public Lands," *American State Papers: Public Lands*, Vol. VI (Doc. 1202) p. 951. (ASP 033). Response of Georgia to the Massachusetts resolutions of March 1833 on the subject of the public lands; objects to distributing the proceeds of the sale of the public lands among the several states.

2114. "On Claim for Pay for Extra Services by an Officer of the Army in Inspecting Arms Made by Contract, while Superintendent of the Armory at

Springfield, Massachusetts," *American State Papers: Military Affairs*, Vol. V (Doc. 569) p. 269. (ASP 020). Report to allow the claim.

2115. "On Claim to Certain Lands in Massachusetts," *American State Papers: Public Lands*, Vol. VII (Doc. 1250) p. 172. (ASP 034). Report of the Committee on the Judiciary against the claim of the heirs of Silence Elliot to lands in Massachusetts. Maintains that the request is unreasonable.

2116. "On Claim to Land in Mississippi," *American State Papers: Public Lands*, Vol. VI (Doc. 1216) pp. 959-961. (ASP 033). Report of the Committee on the Judiciary on the petition of the New England Mississippi Land Company in favor of awarding them that portion of their money that is still in the Treasury. Reviews the facts and history of the claim. Same as S.doc.205 (23-1) 240 (entry **2141**), omitting the documents from the Commissioners on Yazoo Claims, Georgia Mississippi Claims.

2117. "On Making Provision for Naval Schools for Midshipmen, and for Increasing the Pay of Chaplains and Schoolmasters of the Navy," *American State Papers: Naval Affairs*, Vol. IV (Doc. 526) pp. 484-486. (ASP 026). Report on the condition of the naval schools at Boston, New York, and Norfolk. Submits a bill to improve instruction and the pay of various junior officers.

2118. "Plans and Estimates for the Reconstruction of Fort Independence, on Castle Island, Boston Harbor, Massachusetts, and the Construction of Fort Schuyler, Throg's Point, East River, New York," *American State Papers: Military Affairs*, Vol. V (Doc. 573) pp. 296-302. (ASP 020). Report with estimates from the Board of Engineers on each fort. The drawings are not included. Same as H.doc.237 (23-1) 257 (entry **2120**).

2119. U.S. House. *Failure of the Mail.* 23rd Cong., 1st Sess. (H.Rpt.265). [Washington: Gales & Seaton, 1834]. 2 pg. (Serial Set 261). Committee report on the number of failures of the mail between Washington and Boston, and the fines exacted for these failures.

2120. U.S. House. *Letter from the Secretary of War, Transmitting the Information Required by a Resolution of the House of Representatives of the 19th Instant, in Relation to the Fortifications Proposed to Be Built on Castle Island and Throg's Point.* 23rd Cong., 1st Sess. (H.Doc.237). [Washington: Gales & Seaton, Print., 1834]. 15 pg. (Serial Set 257). Same as Mil.aff.573 (23-1) ASP 020. See entry **2118**.

2121. U.S. House. *Memorial of Citizens of Berkshire County, Massachusetts, Asking the Restoration of the Public Deposites.* 23rd Cong., 1st Sess. (H.Doc.251). [Washington: Gales & Seaton, Print., 1834]. 5 pg. (Serial Set 257). Includes three pages of names of memorialists.

2122. U.S. House. *Memorial of Citizens of Boston, against Recharter of the Bank; Also, against a Restoration of the Deposites.* 23rd Cong., 1st Sess.

(H.Doc.382). [Washington: Gales & Seaton, 1834]. 21 pg. (Serial Set 258). Includes 20 pages of names of memorialists.

2123. U.S. House. *Memorial of Citizens of Boston, in Relation to the Existing State of Trade, Occasioned by the Deranged State of the Money Market.* 23rd Cong., 1st Sess. (H.Doc.54). [Washington: Gales & Seaton, Print., 1834]. 3 pg. (Serial Set 255). Resolutions to aid in re-establishing the credit; attribute present economic state to speculation, overtrading, and the removal of the public deposits from the Bank of the United States.

2124. U.S. House. *Memorial of Citizens of Boston, Massachusetts, in Relation to the Currency.* 23rd Cong., 1st Sess. (H.Doc.175). [Washington: Gales & Seaton, Print., 1834]. 57 pg. (Serial Set 256). Memorial supports the Bank of the United States. Includes 56 pages of names and occupations of memorialists.

2125. U.S. House. *Memorial of Citizens of Bristol County, in Relation to the Restoring of the Deposites and Extension of the Charter of the Bank of the United States.* 23rd Cong., 1st Sess. (H.Doc.253). [Washington: Gales & Seaton, Print., 1834]. 21 pg. (Serial Set 257). Memorial supports restoring the deposits and re-chartering the bank. Includes 19 pages of names and occupations of memorialists.

2126. U.S. House. *Memorial of Citizens of Medford, Engaged in Shipbuilding and Navigation, in Relation to the Currency.* 23rd Cong., 1st Sess. (H.Doc.325). [Washington: Gales & Seaton, Print., 1834]. 2 pg. (Serial Set 257). Memorial supports the Bank of the United States. Same as S.doc.258 (23-1) 240 (entry **2146**).

2127. U.S. House. *Memorial of Citizens of Salem, Massachusetts, in Relation to the Currency.* 23rd Cong., 1st Sess. (H.Doc.327). [Washington: Gales & Seaton, Print., 1834]. 12 pg. (Serial Set 257). Memorial supports the Bank of the United States and the restoration of the deposits; includes eight pages of names and occupations of memorialists. Same as S.doc.255 (23-1) 240 (entry **2144**).

2128. U.S. House. *Memorial of Inhabitants of New Bedford, Massachusetts, in Favor of the Recharter of the Bank of the United States.* 23rd Cong., 1st Sess. (H.Doc.153). [Washington: Gales & Seaton, Print., 1834]. 3 pg. (Serial Set 256). Memorial opposes the removal of the public deposits and favors re-chartering the bank. Same as S.doc.339 (23-1) 241 (entry **2147**), without the names of the memorialists.

2129. U.S. House. *Memorial of Inhabitants of the Town of Lynn, in the State of Massachusetts, in Favor of Restoring the Public Deposites to the Bank of the United States.* 23rd Cong., 1st Sess. (H.Doc.254). [Washington: Gales & Seaton, Print., 1834]. 7 pg. (Serial Set 257). Memorial supports restoring the deposits and re-chartering the bank. Includes six pages of names of memorialists. Same as S.doc.213 (23-1) 240 (entry **2149**).

2130. U.S. House. *Memorial of Merchants and Others, in New Bedford, Massachusetts, and Resolutions Adopted at a Public Meeting, upon the Subject of the Embarrassed State of the Currency.* 23rd Cong., 1st Sess. (H.Doc.66). [Washington: Gales & Seaton, Print., 1834]. 3 pg. (Serial Set 255). Resolutions contend that the removal of the deposits and changes of the Bank of the United States caused the currency problems. Same as S.doc.56 (23-1) 239 (entry **2151**), without transmittal notes.

2131. U.S. House. *Memorial of the Citizens of Charlestown, Mass., Praying Compensation for Their Property Destroyed on the 17th June, 1775.* 23rd Cong., 1st Sess. (H.Doc.55). [Washington: Gales & Seaton, Print., 1834]. 13 pg. (Serial Set 255). Claim presented for the burning of Charlestown during the battle of Bunker Hill. Includes earlier petition of 1776, response of Congress in 1777, copy of the letter from the delegates of Connecticut to Congress in 1777, and actions of the town meetings in 1776 and 1777.

2132. U.S. House. *Proceedings and Memorial of a Meeting of the Third Congressional District in the State of Massachusetts, Asking a Restoration of the Public Deposites to the Bank of the United States.* 23rd Cong., 1st Sess. (H.Doc.376). [Washington: Gales & Seaton, 1834]. 34 pg. (Serial Set 258). Proceedings and memorial support re-chartering the Bank of the United States and restoring the public deposits. Includes 31 pages of names and occupations of memorialists classed by town. Text of memorial also printed as S.doc.358 (23-1) 241 (entry **2148**).

2133. U.S. House. *Proceedings and Resolutions of a Meeting of Citizens of Salem, Massachusetts, against Rechartering the Bank of the United States, and Also against Restoring the Public Deposites.* 23rd Cong., 1st Sess. (H.Doc.331). [Washington: Gales & Seaton, Print., 1834]. 2 pg. (Serial Set 257). Same as S.doc.280 (23-1) 241 (entry **2153**).

2134. U.S. House. *Proceedings of a Meeting of Inhabitants of Franklin County, in Favor of a National Bank.* 23rd Cong., 1st Sess. (H.Doc.480). [Washington: Gales & Seaton, Print., 1834]. 12 pg. (Serial Set 259). Proceedings and memorial support a national bank and the restoration of the deposits.

2135. U.S. House. *Proceedings of Citizens of the County of Worcester, Massachusetts, in Relation to the Currency.* 23rd Cong., 1st Sess. (H.Doc.176). [Washington: Gales & Seaton, Print., 1834]. 43 pg. (Serial Set 256). Resolutions and memorial support restoring the public deposits and re-chartering the Bank of the United States. Same as S.doc.219 (23-1) 240 (entry **2142**), with an additional 40 pages of names of memorialists.

2136. U.S. House. *Proceedings, &c. of a Meeting of Citizens of Lowell, Massachusetts, Opposed to the Rechartering of the Bank of the United States.* 23rd Cong., 1st Sess. (H.Doc.338). [Washington: Gales & Seaton, Print.,

1834]. 4 pg. (Serial Set 257). Report and resolutions oppose re-chartering the present bank and favor establishing a new Bank of the United States.

2137. U.S. House. *Resolutions Adopted at a Meeting of Citizens Assembled at Fanneuil Hall, Boston; against the Bank of the United States.* 23rd Cong., 1st Sess. (H.Doc.255). [Washington: Gales & Seaton, Print., 1834]. 5 pg. (Serial Set 257).

2138. U.S. House. *Resolutions of Citizens of Springfield, Massachusetts, in Relation to the Currency.* 23rd Cong., 1st Sess. (H.Doc.324). [Washington: Gales & Seaton, Print., 1834]. 8 pg. (Serial Set 257). Resolutions and memorial against the removal of the deposits and in support of the Bank of the United States. Memorial includes six pages of names of memorialists with occupations. Resolutions also printed as S.doc.508 (23-1) 243 (entry **2152**).

2139. U.S. House. *Resolutions of the Legislature of Massachusetts, in Relation to the Currency, and the Removal of the Public Deposites.* 23rd Cong., 1st Sess. (H.Doc.174). [Washington: Gales & Seaton, Print., 1834]. 4 pg. (Serial Set 256). Resolutions support restoring the deposits and re-chartering the Bank of the United States. Same as S.doc.158 (23-1) 240 (entry **2154**).

2140. U.S. House. *Springfield Manufacturing Company.* 23rd Cong., 1st Sess. (H.Rpt.535). [Washington: Gales & Seaton, 1834]. 3 pg. (Serial Set 263). Report of the Committee of Claims on the petition of the Springfield Manufacturing Company against the Springfield armory. Reviews the circumstances; refers the matter to the Secretary of War for his decision. Also printed as part of H.rp.40 (24-1) 293 (entry **2257**).

2141. U.S. Senate. [Claim of the New England Mississippi Land Company]. 23rd Cong., 1st Sess. (S.doc.205). Washington: Duff Green, 1834. 9 pg. (Serial Set 240). Same as Pub.land 1216 (23-1) ASP 033 (entry **2116**), but also includes the documents from the Commissioners on Yazoo Claims, Georgia Mississippi Company. See entry **2116**.

2142. U.S. Senate. *Memorial and Resolutions of the Citizens of Worcester, Massachusetts, for Rechartering the Bank of the United States.* 23rd Cong., 1st Sess. (S.Doc.219). Washington: Duff Green, 1834. 3 pg. (Serial Set 240). Same as H.doc.176 (23-1) 256 (entry **2135**), but without the names of memorialists.

2143. U.S. Senate. *Memorial of Certain Citizens of Boston, in Relation to the Anti-Bank Memorial from That Place.* 23rd Cong., 1st Sess. (S.Doc.509). Washington: Duff Green, 1834. 1 pg. (Serial Set 243). Memorial reports that a comparison with the legal list of voters evinced that the majority of memorialists on the anti-bank memorial were not qualified voters.

2144. U.S. Senate. *Memorial of Inhabitants of Salem, Massachusetts, in Favor of the Bank of the United States.* 23rd Cong., 1st Sess. (S.Doc.255). Washington: Duff Green, 1834. 29 pg. (Serial Set 240). Memorial supports the bank and the restoration of the deposits; includes 25 pages of names and occupations of memorialists. Same as H.doc.327 (23-1) 257 (entry **2127**).

2145. U.S. Senate. *Memorial of Sundry Citizens of Massachusetts, Praying an Academy Be Instituted for the Instruction of Mariners, &c.* 23rd Cong., 1st Sess. (S.Doc.403). Washington: Duff Green, 1834. 7 pg. (Serial Set 242). Memorial includes six pages of names of memorialists classed by occupation.

2146. U.S. Senate. *Memorial of the Inhabitants of Medford, Massachusetts, in Favor of the Bank of the United States.* 23rd Cong., 1st Sess. (S.Doc.258). Washington: Duff Green, 1834. 2 pg. (Serial Set 240). Same as H.doc.325 (23-1) 257 (entry **2126**).

2147. U.S. Senate. *Memorial of the Inhabitants of the Collection District of New Bedford, Mass., Opposed to the Removal of the Deposites, and in Favor of the Recharter of the Bank of the United States.* 23rd Cong., 1st Sess. (S.Doc.339). Washington: Duff Green, 1834. 22 pg. (Serial Set 241). Same as H.doc.153 (23-1) 256 (entry **2128**), with additional 22 pages of names of memorialists.

2148. U.S. Senate. *Memorial of the Legal Voters of the Third Congressional District of Massachusetts, against the Removal of the Deposites, and in Favor of the Recharter of the Bank of the United States.* 23rd Cong., 1st Sess. (S.Doc.358). Washington: Duff Green, 1834. 1 pg. (Serial Set 241). Included as part of H.doc.376 (23-1) 258 (entry **2132**).

2149. U.S. Senate. *Memorial of the People of Lynn, Massachusetts, in Favor of the Bank of the United States.* 23rd Cong., 1st Sess. (S.Doc.213). Washington: Duff Green, 1834. 10 pg. (Serial Set 240). Memorial supports restoring the deposits and re-chartering the bank. Includes nine pages of names of memorialists. Same as H.doc.254 (23-1) 257 (entry **2129**).

2150. U.S. Senate. *Memorial of the Presidents and Directors of the Several Banking Institutions of New Bedford, Complaining of the Pecuniary Distresses of the Community, and Praying that Relief May Be Speedily Granted, &c.* 23rd Cong., 1st Sess. (S.Doc.127). Washington: Duff Green, 1834. 4 pg. (Serial Set 239).

2151. U.S. Senate. *Resolutions Adopted at a Meeting of the Citizens of New Bedford, Relative to the Embarrassments in the Moneyed Operations of the Country, &c.* 23rd Cong., 1st Sess. (S.Doc.56). Washington: Duff Green, 1834. 3 pg. (Serial Set 239). Same as H.doc.66 (23-1) 255, with additional transmittal notes. See entry **2130**.

2152. U.S. Senate. *Resolutions of a Meeting of the Citizens of Springfield, Mass., against the Removal of the Deposites, and in Favor of the Bank of the United States.* 23rd Cong., 1st Sess. (S.Doc.508). Washington: Duff Green,

1834. 1 pg. (Serial Set 243). Same as H.doc.324 (23-1) 257 (entry **2138**), without memorial.

2153. U.S. Senate. *Resolutions of Sundry Citizens of Salem, Mass., against Restoring the Deposites to the Bank of the United States.* 23rd Cong., 1st Sess. (S.Doc.280). Washington: Duff Green, 1834. 2 pg. (Serial Set 241). Resolutions against re-chartering the bank and restoring the deposits. Same as H.doc.331 (23-1) 257 (entry **2133**).

2154. U.S. Senate. *Resolutions of the Legislature of the State of Massachusetts, in Favor of the Restoration of the Deposites, and of Re-chartering the United States Bank.* 23rd Cong., 1st Sess. (S.Doc.158). Washington: Duff Green, 1834. 4 pg. (Serial Set 240). Same as H.doc.174 (23-1) 256 (entry **2139**).

23RD CONGRESS, 2ND SESSION

2155. "Relations with France," *Register of Debates.* 23rd Cong., 2nd Sess. (21 Feb. 1835) pp. 571-576. Presentation and debate on the printing of memorials from Massachusetts that recommend restrictive measures on trade with France.

2156. Adams, John Quincy (Mass.). "Chairman of Committee on Foreign Affairs," *Congressional Globe.* 23rd Cong., 2nd Sess. (21 Jan. 1835) pp. 146, 146-147, 150. Remarks on the election of the Chairman of the Committee on Foreign Affairs; requests that the election be made a matter of record in the journals of the House. Different version of these remarks printed in the *Register of Debates,* "Committee on Foreign Relations," pp. 1025-1026, 1035-1037.

2157. Adams, John Quincy (Mass.). "Relations with France," *Congressional Globe.* 23rd Cong., 2nd Sess. (7 Feb., 17 Feb., 28 Feb., 2 Mar. 1835) pp. 213-214; 302-303; 309-310; 322. Various remarks on the House's response to the President's message on relations with France. Discusses the need for the House to act, party politics, and the intended connection with the Bank of the United States. Offers objections to the resolution of the Committee on Foreign Relations. Introduces own resolution. Different versions of these remarks printed in the *Register of Debates,* "Relations with France," pp. 1233; 1517, 1518-1519; 1532-1537; 1622-1630.

2158. Adams, John Quincy (Mass.). Remarks on Relations with France, *Congressional Globe.* 23rd Cong., 2nd Sess. (14 Feb. 1835) pp. 243-244. Clarifies earlier remarks referring to the state of affairs with France. Different version of these remarks printed in the *Register of Debates,* pp. 1359-1360.

2159. Adams, John Quincy (Mass.). "Territorial Government of Wisconsin," *Register of Debates.* 23rd Cong., 2nd Sess. (9 Feb. 1835) pp. 1254-1257. Upholds the original compact establishing the boundary between Ohio and

Michigan as stated in the constitution of the Northwestern Territory. Suggests other documents on the subject which present the arguments of both parties.

2160. Briggs, George N. (Mass.). "Viva Voce Mode of Voting," *Congressional Globe.* 23rd Cong., 2nd Sess. (24 Jan. 1835) p. 161. Maintains that the Constitution stipulates election by ballot. Longer version of these remarks printed in the *Register of Debates*, "Viva Voce Elections," pp. 1063-1067.

2161. Everett, Edward (Mass.). "Chairman of Committee on Foreign Affairs," *Congressional Globe.* 23rd Cong., 2nd Sess. (21 Jan. 1835) p. 147. Clarifies the circumstances whereby he was removed from the position of Chairman of the Committee on Foreign Affairs. Different version of these remarks printed in the *Register of Debates*, "Committee on Foreign Relations," pp. 1027-1028.

2162. Everett, Edward (Mass.). "Relations with France," *Congressional Globe.* 23rd Cong., 2nd Sess. (7 Feb., 2 Mar. 1835) pp. 218-219; 318. Discusses the action the House should take to encourage France to execute the treaty of indemnity of July 4, 1831. Supports negotiations while insisting upon the stipulations of the treaty; opposes acts of reprisal. Speech of Feb. 7th printed in the *Register of Debates*, "Relations with France," pp. 1238-1242; longer version of speech of March 2nd printed in *Register of Debates*, "Relations with France," pp. 1571-1577.

2163. Everett, Edward (Mass.). "Removal of the Indians," *Congressional Globe.* 23rd Cong., 2nd Sess. (19 Jan. 1835) pp. 138-139. Presents and supports a memorial from the Cherokee Indians requesting Congress to facilitate their removal by compensating them for their sacrifices and by passing legislation ensuring their civil and political rights in the future.

2164. Jackson, William (Mass.). "Remission of Duties," *Register of Debates.* 23rd Cong., 2nd Sess. (18 Dec. 1834) pp. 819-821. Explains his vote on duties for locomotive engines; maintains that manufacturers of American engines do not need a protective tariff. Briefly discusses the locomotive industry.

2165. Jackson, William (Mass.). "Slavery in the District of Columbia," *Register of Debates.* 23rd Cong., 2nd Sess. (23 Feb. 1835) pp. 1464-1465. Supports the petitions and petitioners protesting the slave trade in the District.

2166. Lincoln, Levi (Mass.). "General Appropriation Bill," *Register of Debates.* 23rd Cong., 2nd Sess. (28 Jan. 1835) pp. 1121-1123. Objects to appropriations for the extra clerk hire in the Post Office Department; maintains that clerks had been employed without legal authority and that the Postmaster General had overridden his authority.

2167. Lincoln, Levi (Mass.). "Northeastern Boundary," *Register of Debates.* 23rd Cong., 2nd Sess. (24 Dec. 1834) pp. 851-854, 862-866. Supports his resolution requesting the President to disclose any communication between the government and Great Britain since the rejection of the advisory opinion of the

King of the Netherlands. Briefly reviews the reasons for a speedy settlement. Defends the resolution against the objections presented by Mr. Parks (Maine).

2168. Phillips, Stephen C. (Mass.). "Abolition of Slavery," *Register of Debates.* 23rd Cong., 2nd Sess. (16 Feb. 1835) pp. 1392-1393. Supports the memorial and memorialists favoring the abolition of slavery in the District.

2169. Reed, John (Mass.). "Marine Hospitals," *Register of Debates.* 23rd Cong., 2nd Sess. (24 Feb. 1835) pp. 1479-1480. Recommends a comprehensive review to determine where best to erect the marine hospitals. Discusses contributions made to the fund by his district and their need for relief.

2170. Reed, John (Mass.). "Pay of Navy Officers," *Register of Debates.* 23rd Cong., 2nd Sess. (7 Jan. 1835) pp. 944-952. Supports revising the law fixing the compensation of the officers of the navy to allow for proper compensation for their service. Addresses objections concerning comparisons with officers in the army. Maintains that the navy needs high ranks for its officers comparable to generals and major generals. Compares compensations and ranks to Great Britain. Explains some of the provisions of the bill. Reviews hardships endured by navy officers. Much shorter version of remarks in the *Congressional Globe*, "Pay of Naval Officers," p. 104.

2171. Silsbee, Nathaniel (Mass.). "Custom-house Officers," *Register of Debates.* 23rd Cong., 2nd Sess. (10 Feb. 1835) pp. 393-396. Supports the bill to fix the number and salaries of customhouse officers and to prevent inequities in compensation between officers of the same grade in different geographical locations. Examines background data; discusses the bill's provisions.

2172. Webster, Daniel (Mass.). "Cumberland Road," *Register of Debates.* 23rd Cong., 2nd Sess. (11 Feb. 1835) pp. 407-409. Supports completing and repairing the road so that it can acceptably be transferred to the states.

2173. Webster, Daniel (Mass.). "The Four Years Law," *Congressional Globe.* 23rd Cong., 2nd Sess. (16 Feb. 1835) p. 251. Opposes limiting the term of the Executive and public officers to four years. Advocates making the tenure of certain public officers conditional upon performance. Discusses the power of removal and appointment. Much longer version of these remarks printed in the *Register of Debates*, "Executive Patronage," pp. 458-470.

2174. Webster, Daniel (Mass.). "French Spoliations," *Congressional Globe.* 23rd Cong., 2nd Sess. (17 Dec. 1834) p. 44. Outlines the grounds of the claims for compensation for French aggressions against American commerce prior to 1800. Longer version of remarks printed in the *Register of Debates*, "French Spoliations prior to 1800," pp. 15-19.

2175. Webster, Daniel (Mass.). "French Spoliations," *Register of Debates.* 23rd Cong., 2nd Sess. (12 Jan. 1835) pp. 162-178. Supports the claims for compensation for French aggressions against American commerce prior to

1800. Provides a general history and description of the claims. Establishes that the claims existed prior to the treaty of Sept. 1800, that they were surrendered by that treaty for political and national considerations, and that the amount of indemnity proposed is reasonable.

2176. Webster, Daniel (Mass.). "The Public Deposites," *Congressional Globe.* 23rd Cong., 2nd Sess. (26 Feb. 1835) pp. 296-297. Advocates requiring drafts of the Bank of the United States to be paid in gold or silver in order to withdraw its paper currency from circulation. Discusses the status of the Bank of the United States and its operations. Slightly longer version of remarks printed in the *Register of Debates,* "Public Deposites," pp. 623-627.

2177. "Application of Massachusetts for the Rebuilding or Repairing of Fort Independence, on Castle Island, in Boston Harbor," *American State Papers: Military Affairs,* Vol. V (Doc. 603) p. 515. (ASP 020). Same as H.doc.160 (23-2) 274 (entry **2185**).

2178. "On the Expediency of Providing Immediately for the Reconstruction of Fort Independence, on Castle Island, Boston Harbor, Massachusetts," *American State Papers: Military Affairs,* Vol. V (Doc. 596) pp. 500-501. (ASP 020). Report from the Committee on Military Affairs confirms that the reconstruction of Fort Independence is critical and should begin immediately. Includes letter from the mayor of Boston. Same as H.rp.81 (23-2) 276 (entry **2180**).

2179. "On the Expediency of Repairing the Fortifications in the Harbor of Boston, Massachusetts," *American State Papers: Military Affairs,* Vol. V (Doc. 593) p. 474. (ASP 020). Report of the Chief Engineer on Fort Independence. Refers to earlier publications (H.doc.237 (23-1) 257 (entry **2120**) or Mil.aff.573 (23-1) ASP 020) (entry **2118**) for detailed report and estimates. Also printed as part of H.doc.86 (23-2) 273 (entry **2183**).

2180. U.S. House. *Fortifications on Castle Island.* 23rd Cong., 2nd Sess. (H.Rpt.81). [Washington: Gales & Seaton, Print., 1835]. 4 pg. (Serial Set 276). Same as Mil.aff.596 (23-2) ASP 020. See entry **2178**.

2181. U.S. House. *Letter from the Secretary of the Treasury, Communicating Information of the Amount Paid to the Custom-house Officers of Boston, New York, Philadelphia, and Baltimore, under the Provisions of the Second Section of the Act Making Appropriations for the Civil and Diplomatic Expenses of Government for the Year Eighteen Hundred and Thirty-four.* 23rd Cong., 2nd Sess. (H.Doc.104). [Washington: Gales & Seaton, 1835]. 2 pg. (Serial Set 273). Reports that no payments have yet been made.

2182. U.S. House. *Letter from the Secretary of the Treasury, Transmitting Information Relative to Sites Purchased for a Warehouse and Custom-houses, and the Sale of Public Grounds.* 23rd Cong., 2nd Sess. (H.Doc.24). [Washington]: Gales & Seaton, [1834]. 1 pg. (Serial Set 272). Provides for building customhouses at Newburyport, New Bedford, New London,

Middletown, and New York; for selling land purchased at Mobile; for selling timber on land at Sandy Hood; and for a warehouse at Baltimore.

2183. U.S. House. *Letter from the Secretary of War, Enclosing the Report of the Chief Engineer Relative to the Fortifications in Boston Harbor.* 23rd Cong., 2nd Sess. (H.Doc.86). [Washington: Gales & Seaton, Print., 1835]. 8 pg. (Serial Set 273). Report of the Chief Engineer and earlier report of the Board (included in H.doc.237 (23-1) 257 (entry **2120**) and Mil.aff.573 (23-1) ASP 020 (entry **2118**)) on Fort Independence. Transmittal letter and report of the Chief Engineer also published as Mil.aff.593 (23-2) ASP 020 (entry **2179**).

2184. U.S. House. *Petition of Jonathan H. Cobb, of Dedham, Mass., for Encouragement in the Production and Manufacture of Silk.* 23rd Cong., 2nd Sess. (H.Doc.106). [Washington: Gales & Seaton, 1835]. 2 pg. (Serial Set 273).

2185. U.S. House. *Resolutions of the Legislature of Massachusetts, in Relation to the Fortifications at Castle Island, Boston Harbor.* 23rd Cong., 2nd Sess. (H.Doc.160). [Washington: Gales & Seaton, Print., 1835]. 2 pg. (Serial Set 274). Resolutions support the need to rebuild or repair Fort Independence. Same as Mil.aff.603 (23-2) ASP 020 (entry **2177**).

2186. U.S. House. *Springfield Manufacturing Company.* 23rd Cong., 2nd Sess. (H.Rpt.21). [Washington]: Gales & Seaton, [1835]. 4 pg. (Serial Set 276). Favorable report on the claim of the Springfield Manufacturing Company against the Springfield armory for non-payment. Reviews the facts of the claim; maintains that the claimants fully and punctually fulfilled the contract and are entitled to receive the sum stipulated plus interest. This report was adopted by subsequent Congresses and printed again as H.rp.372 (25-2) 334 (entry **2381**), H.rp.305 (26-1) 371 (entry **2447**), and H.rp.6 (27-2) 407 (entry **2528**), and in H.rp.40 (24-1) 293 (entry **2257**).

2187. U.S. Senate. *Memorial of Sundry Citizens of Boston, Praying for a Drawback on Imported Hemp When Manufactured into Cordage.* 23rd Cong., 2nd Sess. (S.Doc.26). Washington: Duff Green, 1834. 2 pg. (Serial Set 267).

2188. U.S. Senate. *Memorial of Sundry Inhabitants of Beverly, Massachusetts, Suggesting the Propriety of a Non-Intercourse with France.* 23rd Cong., 2nd Sess. (S.Doc.131). Washington: Duff Green, 1834. 2 pg. (Serial Set 268).

2189. U.S. Senate. *Memorial of the East India Marine Society of Salem, Mass.; Praying that an Expedition Be Fitted Out by the Government to Make a Voyage of Discovery and Survey to the South Seas.* 23rd Cong., 2nd Sess. (S.Doc.75). Washington: Duff Green, 1834. 3 pg. (Serial Set 268). Memorial concurs with Rhode Island's resolution supporting a voyage to the South Seas to benefit shipping and commercial interests. Members of the Society are listed.

2190. U.S. Senate. [On the Petition of Christopher Bailey of Boston]. 23rd Cong., 2nd Sess. (S.Doc.46). Washington: Duff Green, 1834. 2 pg. (Serial Set 268). Favorable report for claim for funds spent on sick seamen.

2191. U.S. Senate. [Report on a Memorial from Boston Requesting a Drawback of the Duty on Imported Hemp When Manufactured into Cordage]. 23rd Cong., 2nd Sess. (S.Doc.127). Washington: Duff Green, 1834. 2 pg. (Serial Set 268). Supports a drawback on cordage manufactured from foreign hemp.

24TH CONGRESS, 1ST SESSION

2192. Adams, John Quincy (Mass.). "Abolition of Slavery in the District," *Congressional Globe.* 24th Cong., 1st Sess. (21 Dec. 1835, 25 Jan. 1836) pp. 39-40; 137-138. Remarks on the reception and disposition of abolition petitions. Supports the right of petition; advocates accepting the petition, referring it to a committee, and adopting their report without comment. Different version of these remarks printed in *Register of Debates*, "Slavery in the District of Columbia," pp. 2000-2002; 2316-2317, 2321.

2193. Adams, John Quincy (Mass.). "Admission of Arkansas," *Register of Debates.* 24th Cong., 1st Sess. (10 June 1836) pp. 4680-4682, 4682-4686. Discusses memorials he presented objecting to the admission of Arkansas into the Union as a slave state; maintains that while he personally disapproves of slavery, Arkansas is entitled to admission as a slave state under the conditions of the Louisiana Purchase.

2194. Adams, John Quincy (Mass.). "Banks in the District of Columbia," *Register of Debates.* 24th Cong., 1st Sess. (31 Dec. 1835) pp. 2116-2118. Opposes the committee to inquire into the bank; objects to them examining and exposing the private transactions of members of Congress.

2195. Adams, John Quincy (Mass.). "Defense of the Western Frontier," *Congressional Globe.* 24th Cong., 1st Sess. (7 May 1836) pp. 433, 434. Requests more information from the Executive regarding relations with Mexico and the conference with the Mexican minister. Shorter version of these remarks printed in *Register of Debates*, "Defence of the Western Frontier," pp. 3519-3520, 3521-3522.

2196. Adams, John Quincy (Mass.). "Indian Hostilities," *Congressional Globe, Appendix.* 24th Cong., 1st Sess. (25 May 1836) pp. 447-451. Advocates granting relief to sufferers of Indian hostilities in Alabama and Georgia as allowed by the war powers. Examines the war powers; maintains that the war powers also give Congress the authority to interfere with the institution of slavery in the states. Discusses relations with Mexico, the potential for war, and the annexation of Texas. Considers the causes of the present Indian war. Same speech also printed in *Register of Debates*, "Relation to Inhabitants of Alabama," pp. 4036-4049.

2197. Adams, John Quincy (Mass.). "Northern Boundary of Ohio," *Congressional Globe*. 24th Cong., 1st Sess. (28 Dec. 1835) pp. 53-54. Supports referring the northern Ohio boundary question to a select committee; briefly reviews prior proceedings. Different version of these remarks printed in *Register of Debates*, "Constitution of Michigan," pp. 2093-2095.

2198. Adams, John Quincy (Mass.). Remarks on Relations with Mexico, *Congressional Globe*. 24th Cong., 1st Sess. (10 May, 12 May, 13 May 1836) pp. 442; 451; 455-456. Defends his statement that the President, while a general, had reviewed and approved the southwestern boundary limits stipulated in the Florida treaty of 1819. Corrects and explains some misrepresentations of his words and opinions as reported in the daily newspapers. Almost exactly the same speech printed in the *Register of Debates*, "Public Lands," pp. 3579-3580; 3701-3705.

2199. Adams, John Quincy (Mass.). "Rules of the House," *Congressional Globe*. 24th Cong., 1st Sess. (10 Dec. 1835) p. 20. Various remarks support requiring general appropriation bills to be reported within thirty days. Different version of these remarks printed in *Register of Debates*, "Rules and Orders of the House," pp. 1949-1954.

2200. Adams, John Quincy (Mass.). "Seminole Hostilities," *Register of Debates*. 24th Cong., 1st Sess. (6 Jan. 1836) pp. 2139-2140. Supports appropriations; attempts to more clearly define under whose direction the money is to be expended.

2201. Adams, John Quincy (Mass.). Speech on the Fortification Bill of the Last Session, *Congressional Globe*. 24th Cong., 1st Sess. (22 Jan. 1836) pp. 128-132. Advocates a committee to inquire and report as to the true causes and circumstances relating to the loss of the three million appropriation bill. Maintains that the inquiry will vindicate the honor of the House and restore harmony between the House and the Senate. Defends the appropriation request; reviews the circumstances and the purposes of the appropriation. Different version of same speech printed in *Register of Debates*, "Fortification Bill of Last Session," pp. 2264-2279.

2202. Briggs, George N. (Mass.). "Northern Boundary of Ohio," *Congressional Globe, Appendix*. 24th Cong., 1st Sess. (15 June 1836) p. 585. Opposes the northern boundary claimed by Ohio. Maintains that the ordinance of 1787 fixed a permanent boundary that cannot be altered without the common consent. Same remarks printed in the *Register of Debates*, "Michigan and Arkansas," pp. 4310-4312.

2203. Briggs, George N. (Mass.). "Proceeds of the Public Lands," *Congressional Globe, Appendix*. 24th Cong., 1st Sess. (11 May 1836) pp. 676-

677. Supports committing the bill to distribute the proceeds of the sales of the Public Lands to the Committee of the Whole, where it may be considered with a kindred bill. Discusses proposed uses of the surplus revenue; maintains that the money should be restored to the people. Same speech printed in the *Register of Debates*, "Fortification Bill," pp. 3627-3630.

2204. Briggs, George N. (Mass.). "Slavery in Arkansas," *Congressional Globe, Appendix*. 24th Cong., 1st Sess. (8 June 1836) pp. 467-468. Remarks on the question of the admission of Arkansas into the Union as a slave state. Maintains that the proposed amendment does not impair the rights of the state yet protests the implied assent of Congress to the provision on slavery. Same remarks printed in the *Register of Debates*, "Michigan and Arkansas," (9 June 1836) pp. 4274-4277.

2205. Calhoun, William B. (Mass.). "The Deposit Banks," *Congressional Globe*. 24th Cong., 1st Sess. (23 Apr. 1836) pp. 393-394. Supports and proposes an amendment requesting an inquiry into the use and security of the public moneys in the deposit banks. Same remarks also printed in *Register of Debates*, "Deposite Banks," pp. 3355-3357.

2206. Cushing, Caleb (Mass.). "Michigan and Arkansas," *Register of Debates*. 24th Cong., 1st Sess. (9 June 1836) pp. 4260-4267. Opposes the clause in the constitution of Arkansas that would perpetuate slavery in Arkansas. Discusses obligations under the Missouri compromise and concludes that it is a totally different situation than was shown and decided in the case of Missouri.

2207. Cushing, Caleb (Mass.). "Michigan and Arkansas," *Register of Debates*. 24th Cong., 1st Sess. (14 June 1836) pp. 4301-4304. Opposes the Arkansas proposition that adjacent Indian lands revert to Arkansas whenever the Indian title is extinguished. Maintains that the proposition is inadmissible, premature, conflicts with the statue of 1830, and implies an intent to break the contract guaranteeing those lands to the Indians.

2208. Cushing, Caleb (Mass.). "Naval Appropriation Bill," *Register of Debates*. 24th Cong., 1st Sess. (11 Feb. 1836) pp. 2519-2524. Responds to Mr. Pearce (R.I.); defends the navy yard at Charlestown. Discusses the selection considerations of a navy yard; addresses charges of political influence.

2209. Cushing, Caleb (Mass.). "Public Lands," *Register of Debates*. 24th Cong., 1st Sess. (23 May 1836) pp. 3820-3855. Supports distributing the proceeds of the public lands among the states. Examines the practicality of this measure as a question of finance. Discusses whether there is in fact a surplus revenue; reviews the state of the Treasury. Discusses the system of public defense and anticipated military needs, including appropriations for the army and navy, foreign relations with other countries, the situation with Texas, and Indian hostilities. Addresses the accusation that the North has received more than its fair share of the advantages of the Union.

2210. Cushing, Caleb (Mass.). "Rations to Inhabitants of Alabama," *Register of Debates.* 24th Cong., 1st Sess. (25 May 1836) pp. 4035-4036. Supports providing relief to the inhabitants of Alabama and Georgia who were driven from their homes by the Creeks.

2211. Cushing, Caleb (Mass.). "Slavery in the District of Columbia," *Congressional Globe, Appendix.* 24th Cong., 1st Sess. (25 Jan. 1836) pp. 97-101. Presents petitions from the citizens of Haverhill and Amesbury, Mass., advocating the abolition of slavery and the slave trade in the District of Columbia. Examines the constitutional right of petition; reviews precedence and historical context. Discusses the potential of the subject matter for agitation. Maintains that the House is bound by the Constitution to receive the petitions under debate. Same speech printed in the *Register of Debates,* "Slavery in the District of Columbia," pp. 2322-2334.

2212. Cushing, Caleb (Mass.). "Treaty with Mexico," *Congressional Globe, Appendix.* 24th Cong., 1st Sess. (1 May 1836) pp. 620-621. Briefly reviews treaties and legislation on the boundary between the United States and the Mexican Republic. Maintains that the boundary established by the Florida Treaty should be honored and executed.

2213. Cushing, Caleb (Mass.). "United States and Mexico," *Register of Debates.* 24th Cong., 1st Sess. (16 May 1836) pp. 3724-3727. Supports the boundaries established under the authority of the Florida Treaty.

2214. Davis, John (Mass.). "Admission of Michigan," *Congressional Globe, Appendix.* 24th Cong., 1st Sess. (30 Mar. 1836) p. 558. Remarks on the admission of Michigan into the Union and the need for the inhabitants involved to consent to the new proposed boundaries. Same remarks printed in the *Register of Debates,* "Admission of Michigan," pp. 1019-1021.

2215. Davis, John (Mass.). "Foreign Paupers," *Congressional Globe.* 24th Cong., 1st Sess. (2 May 1836) p. 414. Supports the memorial and resolutions of the Massachusetts Legislature to prevent the emigration of foreign paupers into the United States.

2216. Davis, John (Mass.). "Foreign Paupers," *Register of Debates.* 24th Cong., 1st Sess. (2 May 1836) pp. 1378-1381. Supports the Massachusetts' resolution to prevent foreign paupers from entering this country. Maintains that Britain is persuading her most corrupt and indolent paupers to emigrate; discusses the burden they create and the effect of scaling allowances to benefit those who are married and have children.

2217. Davis, John (Mass.). "Fortification Bill," *Congressional Globe, Appendix.* 24th Cong., 1st Sess. (24 May 1836) pp. 616-619. Opposes the proposed fortifications for Massachusetts and any appropriations that would erect works leading towards an increase of the standing army. Supports the navy and the militia as the first available means of defense. Advocates returning the surplus to the people; discusses the value of internal improvements. Same remarks printed in the *Register of Debates*, "Fortification Bill," pp. 1552-1559.

2218. Davis, John (Mass.). "Incendiary Publications," *Congressional Globe*. 24th Cong., 1st Sess. (7 Apr., 12 Apr. 1836) pp. 331-332; 348. Opposes prohibiting incendiary publications on slavery from circulating through the mails. Maintains that it would be inexpedient and a violation of the liberty of the press. Different version of these remarks in the *Register of Debates*, "Incendiary Publications," pp. 1103-1108; 1148-1153.

2219. Davis, John (Mass.). "Incendiary Publications," *Register of Debates*. 24th Cong., 1st Sess. (8 June 1836) pp. 1726-1727. Opposes restricting the type of materials the Post Office can carry as unconstitutional and a violation of freedom of the press.

2220. Davis, John (Mass.). "Maine Boundary," *Register of Debates*. 24th Cong., 1st Sess. (23 Mar. 1836) pp. 958-961. Supports the Massachusetts' resolutions requesting a settlement of the boundary question and aid to enforce the rights of the states; discusses the need to protect the valuable timberland.

2221. Davis, John (Mass.). "Massachusetts Claims," *Register of Debates*. 24th Cong., 1st Sess. (11 Feb. 1836) pp. 464-465. Clarifies a resolution concerning outstanding claims from the War of 1812.

2222. Davis, John (Mass.). "Post Office," *Register of Debates*. 24th Cong., 1st Sess. (14 June 1836) pp. 1771-1775. Supports his amendment which would create a table of allowable charges for Post Office boxes; objects to the current system which operates unfairly at the postmaster's discretion.

2223. Davis, John (Mass.). "Slavery in the District of Columbia," *Register of Debates*. 24th Cong., 1st Sess. (11 Mar. 1836) pp. 806-809. Requests that the petition from the Friends, which advocates abolishing slavery in the District, receive proper consideration.

2224. Davis, John (Mass.). "Western Boatmen, &c.," *Register of Debates*. 24th Cong., 1st Sess. (8 Mar. 1836) pp. 748-751. Various remarks on the fund to support sick and disabled seamen; maintains that western mariners have not been contributing to the fund and are therefore not entitled to its benefits.

2225. Grennell, George, Jr. (Mass.). "Contested Election," *Register of Debates*. 24th Cong., 1st Sess. (8 Mar., 10 Mar. 1836) pp. 2700-2703; 2718-2719. Objects to allowing David Newland leave to appear and address the House by counsel in his prosecution of the contested election against James Graham (N.C.). Slightly different version of these remarks printed in the *Congressional Globe*, "North Carolina Contested Election," pp. 236, 242.

2226. Grennell, George, Jr. (Mass.). "Increase of the Navy," *Register of Debates*. 24th Cong., 1st Sess. (11 Jan. 1836) pp. 2166-2167. Objects to increasing the navy without a specific request from the Executive or departments. Explains the failure of the fortification bill of the last session.

2227. Hoar, Samuel (Mass.). "Abolition of Slavery in the District," *Congressional Globe, Appendix.* 24th Cong., 1st Sess. (21 Jan. 1836) pp. 204-207. Addresses the power of the Government to legislate upon slavery. Maintains that Congress does not have the power to legislate upon slavery in the states, but it does have the power to legislate upon slavery in the District. Addresses opponents' arguments, including the potential for insurrection and the violation of property rights. Same speech printed in *Register of Debates*, "Slavery in the District of Columbia," pp. 2253-2263. Summary of speech in *Congressional Globe*, p.128.

2228. Jackson, William (Mass.). "Cumberland Road," *Register of Debates*. 24th Cong., 1st Sess. (25 June 1836) pp. 4495-4498. Advocates substituting a railroad for that portion of the road not yet completed. Reviews motivation for original funding; compares costs; maintains that the railroad would be more economical and better meet the needs of the country.

2229. Lincoln, Levi (Mass.). "Proceeds of the Public Lands," *Congressional Globe, Appendix.* 24th Cong., 1st Sess. (10 May 1836) pp. 621-623. Maintains that a bill discussing an appropriation must go into the Committee of the Whole for discussion. The bill is inappropriate for the Committee on Public Lands and the Committee of Ways and Means has prejudged it. Discusses the disposition of the surplus revenues; maintains that they should go back to the states to be used for the general welfare. Same speech printed in *Register of Debates*, "Public Lands," pp. 3587-3592.

2230. Phillips, Stephen C. (Mass.). "Naval Service Bill," *Register of Debates*. 24th Cong., 1st Sess. (9 May 1836) pp. 3577-3578. Supports an expedition to the Southern Ocean.

2231. Phillips, Stephen C. (Mass.). "Sufferers by New York Fire," *Congressional Globe, Appendix.* 24th Cong., 1st Sess. (16 Feb. 1836) pp. 210-214. Supports relief of the debtors of New York City. Advocates an extension of credit, without interest, to the importers. Discusses the relationship between the government and the importer, the want and advantages of the warehousing system, and the circumstances surrounding the fire. States reasons in support; addresses objections. Same speech printed in *Register of Debates*, "Sufferers by Fire in New York," pp. 2542-2556.

2232. Reed, John (Mass.). "Defense of the Western Frontier," *Congressional Globe, Appendix.* 24th Cong., 1st Sess. (13 May 1836) pp. 610-611. Opposes involving the U.S. in the war between Texas and Mexico. Discusses the issue of boundaries and the political motivations of the Texans. Same speech printed in *Register of Debates*, "Defence of the Western Frontier," (7 May 1836) pp. 3526-3529.

2233. Reed, John (Mass.). "Exploring the Pacific," *Congressional Globe, Appendix.* 24th Cong., 1st Sess. (9 May 1836) pp. 569-573. Supports appropriations to survey and explore the Pacific Ocean and South Seas. Presents arguments in support; describes benefits to commerce and the navy. Reviews the value of American interests in the Pacific Ocean and earlier petitions. Addresses objections. Same speech printed in *Register of Debates,* "Naval Service Bill," pp. 3564-3576.

2234. Reed, John (Mass.). "Failure of Fortification Bill," *Congressional Globe, Appendix.* 24th Cong., 1st Sess. (27 Jan. 1836) pp. 553-558. Details the legislative history of the fortification bill of the last session and the surprise request for a three million dollar appropriation. Remarks on Representative Adams' (Mass.) justification of the war appropriation and relations with France. Supported appropriations for defense but believed the three million amendment unconstitutional and an unsafe precedent. Same speech printed in the *Register of Debates,* "Fortification Bill of Last Session," pp. 2372-2387. Summary of speech in Globe, pp.146-147.

2235. Webster, Daniel (Mass.). "Fortification Bill," *Congressional Globe.* 24th Cong., 1st Sess. (26 May 1836) pp. 504-505. Supports appropriations for fortifications; maintains that fortifications are useful defenses against sudden attack. Same remarks printed in the *Register of Debates,* "Fortification Bill," pp. 1591-1592.

2236. Webster, Daniel (Mass.). "Gold and Silver for Public Lands," *Congressional Globe.* 24th Cong., 1st Sess. (23 Apr. 1836) pp. 389-390, 391. Supports the Bank of the United States and the land bill, and opposes the removal of the public deposits and the proposal to return to a specie basis. Advocates distribution of the surplus revenue. Remarks on the currency resolution of 1816 and executive power. Almost identical speech printed in the *Register of Debates,* "Specie Payments," pp. 1259-1263, 1267-1268, 1269.

2237. Webster, Daniel (Mass.). "Incendiary Publications," *Congressional Globe, Appendix.* 24th Cong., 1st Sess. (8 June 1836) pp. 453-454, 456. Opposes the bill prohibiting the Post Office from distributing publications concerning slavery; maintains that the bill is unconstitutional and vague. Addresses opponents' arguments. Same remarks printed in the *Register of Debates,* "Incendiary Publications," pp. 1721-1722, 1731-1732.

2238. Webster, Daniel (Mass.). "Loss of the Fortification Bill," *Congressional Globe, Appendix.* 24th Cong., 1st Sess. (14 Jan. 1836) pp. 769-774. Remarks on the three million appropriation and the causes of the failure of the fortification bill at the previous session of Congress. Analyzes the history and progress of the bill; defends the conduct of the Senate. Discusses the responsibility of the President to inform Congress and make recommendations deemed necessary and expedient. Summary in the *Congressional Globe,* p. 107.

Same speech printed in the *Register of Debates*, "National Defence," pp. 148-163.

2239. Webster, Daniel (Mass.). "Louisville and Portland Canal," *Register of Debates*. 24th Cong., 1st Sess. (25 May 1836) pp. 1572-1575. Supports the canal as important, constitutional, expedient and desirable.

2240. Webster, Daniel (Mass.). Remarks on the Abolition of Slavery, *Congressional Globe*. 24th Cong., 1st Sess. (16 Mar. 1836) p. 257. Presents several petitions and makes remarks supporting the abolition of slavery and the slave trade within the District of Columbia. Different version of these remarks printed in *Register of Debates*, "Abolition Petitions," pp. 833-835.

2241. Webster, Daniel (Mass.). Remarks on the Condition of the Deposit Banks, *Congressional Globe*. 24th Cong., 1st Sess. (17 Mar. 1836) pp. 261-262. Questions the ability of the deposit banks to meet their liabilities; advocates the distribution of the surplus revenue. Different version of these remarks printed in *Register of Debates*, "The Deposite Banks," pp. 839-840.

2242. Webster, Daniel (Mass.). "Surplus Revenue," *Congressional Globe, Appendix*. 24th Cong., 1st Sess. (31 May 1836) pp. 526-529. Discusses the bill to regulate the deposits of the public moneys and distribute the surplus revenue. Advocates increasing the number of deposit banks, requiring banks to pay interest on public money in their custody, regulating the amount of specie banks must retain, and restraining transfers of public money. Examines the causes of the surplus revenue; recommends its distribution among the states. Same speech printed in the *Register of Debates*, "Public Deposites," pp. 1649-1657. Summary in the *Congressional Globe*, pp. 513-514.

2243. "An Act to Authorize the Construction of a Rail-road, through Lands of the United States in Springfield, Massachusetts," *Statutes at Large*, Vol. V (29 Apr. 1836) p. 17. Also printed in the *Register of Debates* (24th Cong., 1st Sess.) Appendix, pp. v-vi.

2244. "Application of Massachusetts for the Distribution of the Proceeds of the Sales of the Public Lands," *American State Papers: Public Lands*, Vol. VIII (Doc. 1519) p. 668. (ASP 035). Same as H.doc.240 (24-1) 291 (entry **2251**).

2245. "Application of Massachusetts that an Appropriation Be Made for the Works of Defence of Boston Harbor," *American State Papers: Military Affairs*, Vol. VI (Doc. 676) p. 410. (ASP 021). Same as H.doc.241 (24-1) 291 (entry **2250**).

2246. "On a Claim of the Superintendent of the Armory at Springfield, Massachusetts, for Extra Pay for Inspecting Arms Made by Contract," *American State Papers: Military Affairs*, Vol. VI (Doc. 662) pp. 169-173. (ASP 021). Report of the Committee of Claims for the petitioner; includes relevant correspondence and documentation of the claim.

2247. U.S. House. *Charlestown, Mass. - Revolutionary Claim.* 24th Cong., 1st Sess. (H.Rpt.582). [Washington]: Blair & Rives, Printers, [1836]. 3 pg. (Serial Set 295). Report of the Committee on Revolutionary Claims against the claim for compensation of losses sustained by fire in the battle of Bunker Hill.

2248. U.S. House. *Custom-House - Boston.* 24th Cong., 1st Sess. (H.Rpt.448). [Washington]: Blair & Rives, Printers, [1836]. 3 pg. (Serial Set 294). Report and statistics support increased appropriations for a customhouse at Boston.

2249. U.S. House. *Massachusetts - Merchants of Boston - for an Appropriation for the Erection of a Custom-house.* 24th Cong., 1st Sess. (H.Doc.65). [Washington: Blair & Rives, 1836]. 2 pg. (Serial Set 288). Memorial requests increased appropriations for the customhouse; includes names of memorialists.

2250. U.S. House. *Massachusetts Legislature - Fortifications.* 24th Cong., 1st Sess. (H.Doc.241). [Washington]: Blair & Rives, Printers, [1836]. 1 pg. (Serial Set 291). Resolutions support appropriations for the defense of Boston harbor. Same as Mil.aff.676 (24-1) ASP 021 (entry **2245**).

2251. U.S. House. *Massachusetts Legislature - Public Lands.* 24th Cong., 1st Sess. (H.Doc.240). [Washington]: Blair & Rives, Printers, [1836]. 1 pg. (Serial Set 291). Resolutions support the distribution of the proceeds of the public lands. Same as Pub.land 1519 (24-1) ASP 035 (entry **2244**).

2252. U.S. House. *Memorial of Citizens of Salem, Massachusetts, in Favor of the Remission of Duties upon Imported Goods, Burned in the Fire at New York.* 24th Cong., 1st Sess. (H.Doc.160). [Washington]: Blair & Rives, Printers, [1836]. 3 pg. (Serial Set 289). Includes names of memorialists.

2253. U.S. House. *Memorial of the Merchants of Boston, in Relation to an Increase of the Officers of the Customs, &c. and Enlarging the Public Stores.* 24th Cong., 1st Sess. (H.Rpt.527). [Washington]: Blair & Rives, Printers, [1836]. 2 pg. (Serial Set 294).

2254. U.S. House. *Plymouth Beach, Mass.* 24th Cong., 1st Sess. (H.Doc.142). [Washington]: Blair & Rives, Printers, [1836]. 2 pg. (Serial Set 289). Recommends an additional appropriation to repair a breach at Plymouth Beach.

2255. U.S. House. *Report of a Committee and a Resolution of the House of Representatives of the State of Massachusetts, upon the Subject of the Introduction into the United States of Paupers from Foreign Countries.* 24th Cong., 1st Sess. (H.Doc.219). [Washington]: Blair & Rives, Printers, [1836]. 3 pg. (Serial Set 291). Report and resolution oppose the introduction of foreign paupers into the United States.

2256. U.S. House. *Resolutions of the Legislature of the State of Massachusetts upon the Subject of the Northeastern Territory of the United States, the Title to Which Is Still Claimed by Great Britain.* 24th Cong., 1st Sess. (H.Doc.199).

[Washington]: Blair & Rives, Printers, [1836]. 2 pg. (Serial Set 290). Resolutions support a speedy decision of the disputed boundary. Same as S.doc.267 (24-1) 281 (entry **2259**), but also includes transmittal note.

2257. U.S. House. *Springfield Manufacturing Company.* 24th Cong., 1st Sess. (H.Rpt.40). [Washington: Blair & Rives, Printers, 1835]. 7 pg. (Serial Set 293). Committee of Claims concurs with the report of 1835 in favor of the claim of the Springfield Manufacturing Company. Reprints earlier report - H.rp.21 (23-2) 276 (entry **2186**). Also reprints report and resolution of the Committee of Claims of 1834, (originally printed as H.rp.535 (23-1) 263 (entry **2140**)), which referred the matter to the Secretary of War for his decision.

2258. U.S. Senate. *Resolution of the Legislature of Massachusetts, to Obtain the Passage of a Law to Prevent the Introduction of Paupers into the United States.* 24th Cong., 1st Sess. (S.Doc.342). Washington: Duff Green, 1836. 1 pg. (Serial Set 283).

2259. U.S. Senate. *Resolutions of the Legislature of Massachusetts, Relative to a Part of Land in Maine, Belonging to that State, Now in Dispute Between the United States and Great Britain, and Desiring a Speedy Decision upon the Subject, or Authority to That State to Appoint an Agent to Take Care of the Interest of That State.* 24th Cong., 1st Sess. (S.Doc.267). Washington: Gales & Seaton, 1836. 2 pg. (Serial Set 281). Same as H.doc.199 (24-1) 290 (entry **2256**), but without the transmittal note.

24TH CONGRESS, 2ND SESSION

2260. "Censure of Mr. Adams," *Register of Debates.* 24th Cong., 2nd Sess. (7 Feb. 1837) pp. 1610-1655. Debate over the resolutions to censure John Q. Adams (Mass.) for his alleged attempt to introduce a petition from slaves. Adams recounts his remarks of the previous day and discusses the right to petition. Includes speeches from John Robertson (Va.), Julius Alford (Ga.), Hopkins Holsey (Ga.), Levi Lincoln (Mass.), William Graves (Ky.), Waddy Thompson (S.C.), John Calhoon (Ky.), and Caleb Cushing (Mass.).

2261. "Censure of Mr. Adams," *Register of Debates.* 24th Cong., 2nd Sess. (9 Feb. 1837) pp. 1658-1685. Final day of the debate on the resolutions to censure John Q. Adams. Includes speech by Richard French (Ky.), and Adams' speech in his defense.

2262. Debate on Abolition Petitions and Censure of John Q. Adams, *Congressional Globe.* 24th Cong., 2nd Sess. (6 Feb. 1837) pp. 162-163. Debate over alleged attempt by John Q. Adams (Mass.) to present a petition from slaves; resolutions introduced for his censure. Longer version of this debate, including remarks by Adams and a speech of Henry Pinckney (S.C.), printed in *Register of Debates*, "Abolition of Slavery," pp. 1587-1609.

2263. Debate on the Censure of John Q. Adams, *Congressional Globe.* 24th Cong., 2nd Sess. (7 Feb. 1837) pp. 164-166. Debate on the resolutions to censure John Q. Adams (Mass.) for his conduct concerning the petition from slaves. Adams recounts his remarks of the previous day and discusses the right to petition.

2264. Adams, John Quincy (Mass.). "Abolition of Slavery," *Register of Debates.* 24th Cong., 2nd Sess. (9 Jan., 23 Jan., 6 Feb. 1837) pp. 1314-1315; 1424-1427; 1594-1596. Various remarks defend his actions and the right of all petitions to be received by the House.

2265. Adams, John Quincy (Mass.). "Bank Investigating Committee," *Congressional Globe, Appendix.* 24th Cong., 2nd Sess. (2 Mar. 1837) pp. 322-323. Defends the unanimous decision of the committee investigating the Bank of the United States in 1832 that acquitted the president of the bank of any wrongdoing. Same speech printed in the *Register of Debates*, "Civil and Diplomatic Appropriation Bill," pp. 2121-2126.

2266. Adams, John Quincy (Mass.). "Censure of Mr. Adams," *Register of Debates.* 24th Cong., 2nd Sess. (7 Feb. 1837) pp. 1610-1611. Recounts his remarks of the previous day and discusses the right to petition.

2267. Adams, John Quincy (Mass.). "The President's Message," *Register of Debates.* 24th Cong., 2nd Sess. (14 Dec. 1836) pp. 1068-1071. Remarks on his motion that the part of the message that relates to the protective duties be referred to the Committee on Manufactures.

2268. Adams, John Quincy (Mass.). "Protection of Seamen," *Register of Debates.* 24th Cong., 2nd Sess. (27 Dec. 1836) pp. 1166-1168. Supports continuing some form of document of nationality to protect American seamen.

2269. Adams, John Quincy (Mass.). "The Right of Slaves to Petition," *Congressional Globe, Appendix.* 24th Cong., 2nd Sess. (9 Feb. 1837) pp. 261-265. Defends himself from resolutions to censure him for putting the question of the petition from slaves before the Chair. Requests a vote on his original question as to whether the House will receive a petition from slaves. Examines the right of petition; maintains that it is not based on the character and condition of the petitioner. Addresses each resolution. Slightly different version of speech printed in *Register of Debates*, "Censure of Mr. Adams," pp. 1673-1683.

2270. Alford, Julius (Ga.). "Censure of Mr. Adams," *Register of Debates.* 24th Cong., 2nd Sess. (7 Feb. 1837) pp. 1617-1619. Opposes the abolition petitions and supports the censure.

2271. Bynum, Jesse A. (N.C.). "Abolition Petitions," *Congressional Globe, Appendix.* 24th Cong., 2nd Sess. (9 Jan. 1837) pp. 163-166. Opposes the reception of abolition petitions; maintains that the right to petition does not imply a right of reception. Discusses the petition from Massachusetts to abolish slavery in the District; denigrates the character of the petitioners as women, fanatics, and priests who are interfering with other people's business. Addresses opponents' arguments and the detrimental effect of the petitions.

2272. Calhoun, John (Ky.). "Censure of J.Q. Adams," *Congressional Globe, Appendix.* 24th Cong., 2nd Sess. (7 Feb. 1837) p. 316. Supports the censure of John Q. Adams (Mass.) for his extraordinary conduct concerning slavery. Addresses previous conduct of Mr. Adams; discusses the power of Congress to abolish slavery. Remarks also printed in the *Register of Debates*, "Censure of Mr. Adams," pp. 1639-1641.

2273. Cushing, Caleb (Mass.). "Appropriations for the Indian Department," *Congressional Globe, Appendix.* 24th Cong., 2nd Sess. (1 Feb. 1837) pp. 303-305. Supports the Indians and advocates fulfilling treaty obligations. Examines governmental policy towards the Indians, their treatment and rights. Reviews applicable laws and documents. Discusses duties and obligations towards their welfare. Speech also printed in the *Register of Debates*, "Indian Appropriation Bill," pp. 1525-1537.

2274. Cushing, Caleb (Mass.). "Censure of Mr. Adams," *Register of Debates.* 24th Cong., 2nd Sess. (7 Feb. 1837) pp. 1641-1654. Discusses the resolution to censure Mr. Adams for his inquiry regarding the right of slaves to petition. Maintains that the censure would be subversive to the freedoms of opinion, press and speech and would not check the anti-slavery agitation. Defends the right of petition. Responds to Mr. Thompson (S.C.); defends the character and honor of Massachusetts.

2275. Cushing, Caleb (Mass.). "Protection of Seamen," *Register of Debates.* 24th Cong., 2nd Sess. (27 Dec. 1836) pp. 1168-1169. Supports a document for seamen, similar to a passport, for proof of citizenship.

2276. Cushing, Caleb (Mass.). Remarks on Trade with Denmark, *Congressional Globe.* 24th Cong., 2nd Sess. (23 Jan. 1837) p. 118. Supports the memorial to re-negotiate trade conditions with Denmark. Remarks also printed in the *Register of Debates*, "Quarantine at Elsineur," pp. 1427-1429.

2277. Davis, John (Mass.). "Admission of Michigan," *Register of Debates.* 24th Cong., 2nd Sess. (5 Jan. 1837) pp. 317-321. Opposes the admission of Michigan into the Union. Maintains that Congress has not settled the boundaries or decided whether there should be one or two states in the territory; also maintains that the ordinance of 1787 did not give her the power to erect herself into a state.

2278. Davis, John (Mass.). "Distribution Question," *Register of Debates.* 24th Cong., 2nd Sess. (3 Mar. 1837) pp. 1032-1034. Advocates placing the surplus revenue in the custody of the states rather than the deposit banks.

2279. Davis, John (Mass.). "The Public Lands," *Congressional Globe, Appendix.* 24th Cong., 2nd Sess. (9 Feb. 1837) pp. 309-312. Opposes the bill to limit the sales of public lands to actual settlers as partial and unjust, encouraging speculation and fraud. Maintains that the title of the United States is unquestionable and should be used to benefit all the states. Reviews legislation concerning preemption rights; addresses opponents' arguments. Compares this bill unfavorably to the land bill. Speech also printed in the *Register of Debates*, "Public Lands," pp. 760-774.

2280. Davis, John (Mass.). "Reduction of the Revenue," *Congressional Globe, Appendix.* 24th Cong., 2nd Sess. (23 Feb., 24 Feb. 1837) pp. 284-286. Supports reducing the revenue but opposes removing the salt duty. Reviews the history of salt protection, the magnitude of the salt industry, the connection to the cod fishery industry, and salt manufacturing in New York. Second day's comments review the history of the politics behind the tariff of 1828 and 1832. Speech and comments also printed in the *Register of Debates*, "Reduction of the Tariff," pp. 894-902 and pp. 2191-2194.

2281. Davis, John (Mass.). "Reduction of the Tariff," *Congressional Globe, Appendix.* 24th Cong., 2nd Sess. (24 Feb. 1837) pp. 301-302. General remarks on the history of tariffs; maintains that they have operated against the New England states and the woolens interest. Also reported in the *Register of Debates*, "Reduction of the Tariff," pp. 936-938.

2282. Davis, John (Mass.). "Unexpended Balances of Appropriations," *Congressional Globe, Appendix.* 24th Cong., 2nd Sess. (28 Dec. 1836) pp. 41-42. Remarks on the unexpended appropriations; maintains that the revenues have not been shown to be inadequate to meet the needs. Also printed in *Register of Debates*, "Unexpended Appropriations," pp. 157-159.

2283. French, Richard (Ky.). "Abolition Petitions," *Congressional Globe, Appendix.* 24th Cong., 2nd Sess. (9 Feb. 1837) pp. 191-193. Supports the censure of John Q. Adams (Mass.) for his contempt of the House and questionable conduct. Maintains that Congress has no right to interfere with slavery in the states. Discusses for whom the right of petition belongs and the reception of abolition petitions. Speech also printed in *Register of Debates*, "Censure of Mr. Adams," pp. 1659-1663.

2284. Graves, William J. (Ky.). "Censure of Mr. Adams," *Register of Debates.* 24th Cong., 2nd Sess. (7 Feb. 1837) pp. 1627-1631. Opposes censuring Mr. Adams; maintains that it would set bad precedent and restrict freedom of speech. Discusses the slavery petitions.

2285. Grennell, George, Jr. (Mass.). "Appropriations for the Indian Department," *Congressional Globe, Appendix.* 24th Cong., 2nd Sess. (1 Feb. 1837) p. 308. Opposes the proposed mode of removal of the Indians as too liable to abuse; proposes to use officers of the army rather than contractors.

Considers governmental obligations; discusses the circumstances of the Creeks and the Creek War. Remarks also printed in the *Register of Debates*, "Indian Appropriation Bill," pp. 1557-1560.

2286. Hoar, Samuel (Mass.). "Civil and Diplomatic Appropriation Bill," *Register of Debates*. 24th Cong., 2nd Sess. (27 Feb. 1837) pp. 2024-2027. Opposes sending a diplomatic agent to Texas in recognition of its independence. Maintains that Texas needs to prove that it has sufficient citizens and exists independently from the United States.

2287. Holsey, Hopkins (Ga.). "Abolition Petitions," *Congressional Globe, Appendix*. 24th Cong., 2nd Sess. (6 Feb. 1837) p. 162. Supports the proposed censure of John Q. Adams (Mass.) for attempting to introduce into the House a petition from slaves. Maintains that Mr. Adams is constantly circumventing the rule forbidding debate upon abolition memorials and defying the rights of the slave-holding states. Speech also printed in the *Register of Debates*, "Censure of Mr. Adams," (7 Feb. 1837) pp. 1619-1621.

2288. Lawrence, Abbott (Mass.). "Surplus Revenue," *Congressional Globe.* 24th Cong., 2nd Sess. (11 Jan. 1837) pp. 87-88, 90. Various remarks adamantly oppose the bill to reduce the revenue by decreasing duties on imported articles. Discusses the principles contained in the bill; appeals to the cotton interest and supporters of the protective system. Remarks also printed in the *Register of Debates*, "Surplus Revenue," pp. 1347-1350, 1355-1358.

2289. Lincoln, Levi (Mass.). "Banking Institutions," *Congressional Globe, Appendix*. 24th Cong., 2nd Sess. (29 Dec. 1836) pp. 46-47. Addresses the Pennsylvania memorialists' complaints concerning state governments creating banking institutions; maintains that Congress has no power in this area. Argues against the proposed constitutional amendment to restrict states. Speech also printed in the *Register of Debates*, "National Currency," pp. 1184-1188.

2290. Lincoln, Levi (Mass.). "Censure of John Q. Adams," *Congressional Globe, Appendix*. 24th Cong., 2nd Sess. (7 Feb. 1837) pp. 320-321. Supports John Q. Adams. Maintains that exception was taken to the character of the petition rather than the manner of presenting it. Recounts the circumstances and conduct of Mr. Adams; addresses charges of mischievousness and contempt. Offers his views on abolitionists and their petitions; defends the citizens and petitioners of the North. Speech also printed in the *Register of Debates*, "Censure of Mr. Adams," pp. 1621-1627.

2291. Milligan, John J. (Del.). "Censure of Mr. Adams," *Register of Debates*. 24th Cong., 2nd Sess. (9 Feb. 1837) pp. 1663-1665. Opposes the resolutions of censure; maintains that they are unlikely to do any practical good and Congress has other matters to legislate upon.

2292. Pinckney, Henry L. (S.C.). "Abolition Petitions," *Congressional Globe, Appendix*. 24th Cong., 2nd Sess. (6 Feb. 1837) pp. 171-173. Supports the proposed censure of John Q. Adams (Mass.) for his reprehensible conduct regarding the abolition memorial from slaves. Maintains that the memorial is a hoax. Discusses the right of petition and the resolutions restricting the reception and discussion of slavery petitions.

2293. Reed, John (Mass.). "Abolition Petitions," *Congressional Globe, Appendix.* 24th Cong., 2nd Sess. (9 Jan. 1837) p. 309. Responds to Mr. Underwood (Ky.) and supports receiving petitions for the abolition of slavery within the District of Columbia. Addresses the right of petition.

2294. Reed, John (Mass.). "Naval Appropriation Bill," *Register of Debates.* 24th Cong., 2nd Sess. (23 Feb. 1837) pp. 1902-1904. Opposes appropriations to launch the ship Pennsylvania; prefers appropriations for a smaller class of vessels.

2295. Robertson, John (Va.). "Censure of John Q. Adams," *Congressional Globe, Appendix.* 24th Cong., 2nd Sess. (7 Feb. 1837) pp. 321-322. Supports the right of John Q. Adams to inquire about his petition; contends that he followed parliamentary procedure and was protected under the right of freedom of discussion. Disapproves of Adams' conduct concerning the abolition petitions. Discusses the right of petition; justifies his support of the resolution requiring abolition memorials to be laid upon the table. Same speech printed in the *Register of Debates*, "Censure of Mr. Adams," pp. 1613-1617.

2296. Thompson, Waddy Jr. (S.C.). "Right of Slaves to Petition," *Congressional Globe, Appendix.* 24th Cong., 2nd Sess. (7 Feb. 1837) pp. 265-267. Supports the censure of John Q. Adams. Maintains that he was disrespectful to the House and violated the rights of a portion of its members. Responds to Mr. Lincoln's (Mass.) speech. Defends the sentiments of the South. Responds to inquiries of Mr. Adams. Speech also printed in the *Register of Debates*, "Censure of Mr. Adams," pp. 1632-1639.

2297. Underwood, Joseph R. (Ky.). "Abolition Petitions," *Congressional Globe, Appendix.* 24th Cong., 2nd Sess. (9 Jan. 1837) pp. 308-309. Objects to receiving the Mass. petitions for the abolition of slavery within the District of Columbia. Maintains that the people of Massachusetts have no right to petition against laws and regulations that do not operate upon them or their territory.

2298. Webster, Daniel (Mass.). "Cession of the Public Lands," *Register of Debates.* 24th Cong., 2nd Sess. (11 Feb. 1837) pp. 784-786. Objects to ceding the lands with the proposed restrictions concerning settlers as unconstitutional and inexpedient; supports a slow and reasonable graduation.

2299. Webster, Daniel (Mass.). "The Expunging Resolution," *Congressional Globe, Appendix.* 24th Cong., 2nd Sess. (16 Jan. 1837) pp. 276-277. Protest against the expunging resolution and the manner of the proceedings. Maintains that it would be unconstitutional to expunge any votes given in the Senate and that the Constitution specifically declares that each House should keep a record of its proceedings. Speech also printed in the *Register of Debates*, "Expunging Resolution," pp. 499-502.

2300. Webster, Daniel (Mass.). "National Bank," *Register of Debates.* 24th Cong., 2nd Sess. (8 Feb. 1837) pp. 737-738. Presents a petition from New York City for the establishment of a national bank; briefly remarks in support.

2301. Webster, Daniel (Mass.). "Papers of Mr. Madison," *Congressional Globe, Appendix.* 24th Cong., 2nd Sess. (20 Feb. 1837) pp. 252-253. Supports purchasing the manuscript papers of Pres. Madison relative to the Constitutional Convention; maintains that these papers are immediately and intimately relevant. Remarks also printed in the *Register of Debates*, "Papers of Mr. Madison," pp. 861-862.

2302. Webster, Daniel (Mass.). "Public Lands," *Congressional Globe, Appendix.* 24th Cong., 2nd Sess. (11 Feb. 1837) p. 157. Opposes the land bill; maintains that the bill transcends the power of Congress and benefits the few at the expense of the many.

2303. Webster, Daniel (Mass.). "Recission of the Treasury Order," *Congressional Globe, Appendix.* 24th Cong., 2nd Sess. (21 Dec. 1836) pp. 53-57. Supports rescinding the Treasury order of July 11, 1836, which allows only gold and silver to be received in payment for public lands. Discusses its justification, "legal money," the authority of Congress to direct the medium of payment, the power of the Secretary of the Treasury, and the importance of the currency and its existing condition. Speech also printed in the *Register of Debates*, "Treasury Circular," pp. 89-104.

2304. Webster, Daniel (Mass.). "Reduction of the Tariff," *Register of Debates.* 24th Cong., 2nd Sess. (24 Feb. 1837) pp. 954-956, 958-961. Supports continuing a protective duty on imported coal. Protests against continual proposals to alter long-established and settled policy as injurious to American industry and enterprise. Responds to remarks of Sen. Niles (Conn.).

2305. Webster, Daniel (Mass.). "Treasury Circular," *Register of Debates.* 24th Cong., 2nd Sess. (30 Jan. 1837) pp. 643-644. Supports rescinding the Treasury order but objects to provisions of the proposed bill.

2306. "An Act to Change the Name of the Collection District of Dighton, in the State of Massachusetts, to Fall River, and for Other Purposes," *Statutes at Large,* Vol. V (13 Feb. 1837) pp. 146-147. Also printed in the *Register of Debates* (24th Cong., 2nd Sess.) Appendix, p. 7.

2307. "Claim of the New England Mississippi Land Company," *American State Papers: Public Lands,* Vol. VIII (Doc. 1594) pp. 985-986. (ASP 035). Petition to the Massachusetts delegates in Congress explains the claim and requests an equitable decision. Same as S.doc.212 (24-2) 298 (entry **2314**).

2308. U.S. House. *Letter from the Secretary of War, in Reply to the Resolutions of the House of Representatives of the 21st of March and 11th of April Last, Requiring Charts of the Harbors of Provincetown, Nantucket, Great Point, and Holmes's Hole.* 24th Cong., 2nd Sess. (H.Doc.165). [Washington]: Blair & Rives, Printers, [1837]. 2 pg. (Serial Set 304). Letter explains why the charts have not been completed.

2309. U.S. House. *Memorial of Inhabitants of Newburyport, in the State of Massachusetts, Praying that Their Claims for French Spoliations, Prior to the Year 1800, May Be Immediately Paid; the Government of the United States Having Virtually Assumed the Payment Thereof, under a Treaty with the Government of France.* 24th Cong., 2nd Sess. (H.Doc.42). [Washington]: Blair & Rives, Printers, [1836]. 2 pg. (Serial Set 302).

2310. U.S. House. *Memorial of Perez Morton and Others, Citizens of Massachusetts, to Be Remunerated for Property Seized by France, Previous to the Year 1800; Which Property Was Afterwards Converted to the Use of the United States, by Treaty Stipulations, Bearing Date the 30th of September, 1800.* 24th Cong., 2nd Sess. (H.Doc.40). [Washington]: Blair & Rives, Printers, [1836]. 3 pg. (Serial Set 302).

2311. U.S. House. *Remonstrance of Citizens of the County of Berkshire against the Passage of the Bill Reported by the Committee of Ways and Means, (No. 829) "To Reduce the Revenue of the United States to the Wants of the Government."* 24th Cong., 2nd Sess. (H.Doc.135). [Washington]: Blair & Rives, Printers, [1837]. 3 pg. (Serial Set 303). Resolutions oppose the repeal of the Compromise Act of 1833.

2312. U.S. House. *Remonstrance of the Legislature of Massachusetts, against the Passage of the Bill (H.R. No. 829), to Reduce the Revenue of the United States to the Wants of the Government.* 24th Cong., 2nd Sess. (H.Doc.170). [Washington]: Blair & Rives, Printers, [1837]. 3 pg. (Serial Set 304). Resolutions against reducing the tariff. Same as S.doc.202 (24-2) 298 (entry **2315**).

2313. U.S. Senate. [Claim of the New England Mississippi Land Company]. 24th Cong., 2nd Sess. (S.Doc.197). Washington: Gales & Seaton, 1837. 10 pg. (Serial Set 298). Favorable report of the Committee on the Judiciary on the petition of the New England Mississippi Land Company; adopts and concurs with the last report made in their favor. Reprints S.doc.205 (23-1) 240 (entry **2141**) and Pub.land 1216 (23-1) ASP 033 (entry **2116**).

2314. U.S. Senate. *Letter from Thomas L. Winthrop and Others, to the Delegation in Congress from the State of Massachusetts, in Relation to the Claim of the New England Mississippi Land Company.* 24th Cong., 2nd Sess. (S.Doc.212). Washington: Gales & Seaton, 1837. 2 pg. (Serial Set 298). Same as Pub.land 1594 (24-2) ASP 035. See entry **2307**.

2315. U.S. Senate. *Memorial of the Legislature of Massachusetts, Opposed to a Reduction of the Tariff.* 24th Cong., 2nd Sess. (S.Doc.202). Washington: Gales and Seaton, 1837. 3 pg. (Serial Set 298). Same as H.doc.170 (24-2) 304 (entry **2312**).

2316. U.S. Senate. [Report on Memorials Praying for a Repeal of the Duty on Foreign Coal]. 24th Cong., 2nd Sess. (S.Doc.102). Washington: Gales and Seaton, 1837. 12 pg. (Serial Set 298). Report responds to and supports memorials from Boston, Mass. and Norwich, Conn.; reviews historical duties on coal and objections to the duty; maintains that it is not wanted for revenue nor retained as a protection of the domestic coal trade.

25ᵀᴴ CONGRESS, 1ˢᵀ SESSION

2317. Adams, John Quincy (Mass.). "Adjournment of Congress," *Register of Debates.* 25th Cong., 1st Sess. (2 Oct. 1837) pp. 1168-1171. Opposes the special short session of Congress and favors extending it into the regular session; mentions various important bills needing consideration.

2318. Adams, John Quincy (Mass.). "Deposite Banks," *Congressional Globe.* 25th Cong., 1st Sess. (16 Oct. 1837) pp. 144-145. Strongly opposes an amendment of the bill granting relief to the deposit banks; maintains that it is a disgrace, has no operation, and gives undue power to the Secretary of the Treasury. Comments on the politics behind the history of the amendments. Same remarks printed in the *Register of Debates*, "Deposite Bank Adjustment Bill," pp. 1720-1723.

2319. Adams, John Quincy (Mass.). "Mississippi Election," *Register of Debates.* 25th Cong., 1st Sess. (3 Oct. 1837) pp. 1211-1215. Claims the election to fill the vacancies of the special session was null and void; however, as they were elected by such a large majority, accepts that Messrs. Claiborne and Gholson hold their seats until the November election so that Mississippi may be represented.

2320. Adams, John Quincy (Mass.). "Postponement of Fourth Instalment," *Congressional Globe, Appendix.* 25th Cong., 1st Sess. (29 Sept. 1837) pp. 338-340. Opposes the bill to postpone the fourth installment of the surplus revenue to the states. Maintains that its true intent is to repeal the installment act and to raise revenue. Requests a fixed payment date and an assurance of no more postponements. Discusses the ambiguous report of the Secretary of the Treasury. Examines the inequality of the deposits among the states and the flow of money from the North.

2321. Adams, John Quincy (Mass.). Remarks on the Annexation of Texas, *Congressional Globe.* 25th Cong., 1st Sess. (13 Sept., 9 Oct. 1837) pp. 24; 118. Presents and defends resolutions inquiring as to whether a proposition had been made by or to the government concerning the annexation of Texas. Maintains that such a proposition would be unconstitutional, unlike previous cessions, and should not be considered. Requests all relevant documents be printed. Different version of these remarks printed in the *Register of Debates*, "United States, Mexico, and Texas," pp. 606-608; pp. 1358-1359.

2322. Adams, John Quincy (Mass.). "Upon Nouns, Pronouns, Verbs, and Adverbs," *Congressional Globe, Appendix*. 25th Cong., 1st Sess. (14 Oct. 1837) pp. 265-270. Opposes the act to adjust the remaining claims upon the late deposit banks. Maintains that the unclear phraseology does not distinguish delinquent from nondelinquent banks. Discusses the bill for the postponement of the fourth installment of the surplus revenue to the states. Detailed comparative review of each state's entitlement and transactions; demonstrates how money has flowed from the northern states to benefit the southmost and western states. Same speech printed in the *Register of Debates*, "Accounts of the Deposite Banks," pp. 1687-1711.

2323. Briggs, George N. (Mass.). "Fourth Instalment Bill," *Register of Debates*. 25th Cong., 1st Sess. (21 Sept. 1837) pp. 733-737. Opposes postponing the payment of the fourth installment due to the states under the deposit law; maintains that withholding the money would create serious inconvenience and injury. Addresses opponents' objections.

2324. Calhoun, William B. (Mass.). "Making Public Officers Depositories," *Congressional Globe, Appendix*. 25th Cong., 1st Sess. (12 Oct. 1837) pp. 298-303. Opposes the Sub-Treasury scheme and the imposition of additional duties, as depositories, on public officers. Discusses the financial condition of the country and the causes of its distress, including over-trading and over-speculation. Argues against the postponement of the fourth installment, Treasury notes, and the Sub-Treasury. Defends the people and institutions of the North. Same speech printed in the *Register of Debates*, "Sub-Treasury Bill," pp. 1456-1471.

2325. Cushing, Caleb (Mass.). "Inquiry in Relation to the Florida War," *Congressional Globe*. 25th Cong., 1st Sess. (20 Sept. 1837) p. 46. Remarks on the war in Florida as disgraceful to the people and Government of the United States. Same remarks printed in the *Register of Debates*, "The Florida War," pp. 666-667.

2326. Cushing, Caleb (Mass.). "President's Message," *Congressional Globe, Appendix*. 25th Cong., 1st Sess. (25 Sept. 1837) pp. 249-256. Rebuts each part of the Message of the President on the difficulties concerning payment of the fourth installment. Mr. Cushing maintains that the Message focuses on the relief of executive difficulties; nothing is proposed for the relief of the people. Discusses the public distress, the national bank, State banks, and public finances. Same speech printed in the *Register of Debates*, "Fourth Instalment Bill," pp. 861-890.

2327. Fletcher, Richard (Mass.). "Treasury Notes," *Register of Debates.* 25th Cong., 1st Sess. (5 Oct. 1837) pp. 1259-1263. Opposes the proposed issue of Treasury notes. Maintains that the government does not need the loan; recommends selling bonds and issuing drafts upon the funds in the deposit banks. Also objects to the measure on constitutional grounds and because the rate of interest is not specified.

2328. Parmenter, William (Mass.). "Issue of Treasury Notes," *Congressional Globe, Appendix.* 25th Cong., 1st Sess. (4 Oct. 1837) pp. 86-87. Supports the bill to issue Treasury notes and explains the best method to raise the money. Defends the report of the Secretary of the Treasury; discusses the finances of the country. Presents objections to alternative measures to raise money; addresses objections to Treasury notes. Same speech printed in the *Register of Debates*, "Treasury Notes," (5 Oct. 1837), pp. 1263-1267.

2329. Phillips, Stephen C. (Mass.). "Fourth Instalment Bill," *Register of Debates.* 25th Cong., 1st Sess. (29 Sept. 1837) pp. 1136-1141. Discusses the proposed postponement of the fourth installment to be paid to the states. Maintains that the postponement acknowledges the obligation of the government to make the payment. As the Treasury is unable to provide for the payment, proposes that the government issue Treasury notes to the states as a pledge of public faith. Compares the effects to the states of postponing payment versus issuing Treasury notes.

2330. Webster, Daniel (Mass.). "Making Public Officers Depositories," *Congressional Globe, Appendix.* 25th Cong., 1st Sess. (28 Sept. 1837) pp. 167-174. Discusses the duties of Congress regarding the currency of the country. Reviews the history of the events leading to the derangement of the currency and exchange and the administration's denial of duty or power to regulate the currency. Maintains that it is the constitutional duty of government to provide a sound, safe, and uniform currency; details a history of nearly 50 years of exercising that power. Discusses the national bank. Same speech printed in the *Register of Debates*, "Sub-Treasury Bill," pp. 311-331.

2331. Webster, Daniel (Mass.). "Postponement of the Fourth Instalment," *Congressional Globe, Appendix.* 25th Cong., 1st Sess. (14 Sept. 1837) pp. 9-11, 13. Speech and remarks oppose postponing the fourth installment of the surplus revenue as ineffectual, inconvenient, and unnecessary. Maintains that the proposed measures offer nothing to the people and that government does have the power to regulate trade and commerce between the states as well as the necessary currency. Discusses the proposed Treasury notes; considers them paper money. Same speech and remarks printed in the *Register of Debates*, "Fourth Instalment," pp. 15-20, 25-26, 28-29.

2332. Webster, Daniel (Mass.). "Sub-Treasury Bill," *Register of Debates.* 25th Cong., 1st Sess. (3 Oct. 1837) pp. 485-492. Proclaims the constitutional power and duty of Congress to regulate the currency; maintains that this power has been admitted, acknowledged, and exercised. Discusses the Bank of England, paper circulation, private banking, and the current dual system of currency.

2333. U.S. House. *Remonstrance of Sarah Chapman and 3,028 Other Women, of Boston, in the State of Massachusetts, against the Annexation of Texas to the United States, As a Slave-holding Territory.* 25th Cong., 1st Sess. (H.Doc.45). Washington: Thomas Allen, 1837. 1 pg. (Serial Set 311).

2334. U.S. House. *Resolutions of the Legislature of the State of Massachusetts, upon the Subject of Slavery in the District of Columbia, and the Right of Petition.* 25th Cong., 1st Sess. (H.Doc.21). Washington: Thomas Allen, 1837. 2 pg. (Serial Set 311). Resolutions support abolishing slavery in the District and support the right of petition.

25TH CONGRESS, 2ND SESSION

2335. "Commonwealth Bank of Boston," *Congressional Globe.* 25th Cong., 2nd Sess. (17 Jan. 1838) pp. 113-118. Debate on Sen. Webster's request for an official inquiry into the payment of pensions and fishing bounties with bills of the Commonwealth Bank of Boston. Includes speeches by Daniel Webster (Mass.) and Henry Hubbard (N.H.).

2336. Debate on the Commonwealth Bank of Boston, *Congressional Globe.* 25th Cong., 2nd Sess. (6 Feb. 1838) pp. 164-166. Debate on the report of the Secretary of the Treasury responding to an inquiry into the Commonwealth Bank at Boston. Includes remarks made by Daniel Webster (Mass.) and John Niles (Conn.) on the use of bank notes to pay for pensions and bounties.

2337. Adams, John Quincy (Mass.). "Mississippi Election," *Congressional Globe.* 25th Cong., 2nd Sess. (6 Feb. 1838) pp. 162-163. Supports retrospective compensation for the Mississippi congressmen who were originally denied their seats.

2338. Adams, John Quincy (Mass.). "Northern Frontier," *Congressional Globe.* 25th Cong., 2nd Sess. (5 Jan. 1838) p. 77. Supports his resolution requesting information from the President as to differences existing between the U.S. and Mexico and the U.S. and Great Britain.

2339. Adams, John Quincy (Mass.). "Relations with Mexico," *Congressional Globe.* 25th Cong., 2nd Sess. (11 Jan. 1838) pp. 93-94. Supports the release of the name of the foreign minister that gave a copy of the pamphlet printed by the ex-minister from Mexico to the Secretary of State. Reviews the facts and their possible misrepresentation for political purposes.

2340. Cushing, Caleb (Mass.). "Cumberland Road," *Congressional Globe, Appendix.* 25th Cong., 2nd Sess. (19 Apr. 1838) pp. 523-525. Supports the Cumberland road. Addresses opponents' arguments, including the alleged inequality in the distribution of public money. Reviews the history of the road and obligations. Discusses federal policy towards the Mississippi states and the merits of the bill and its constitutionality.

2341. Cushing, Caleb (Mass.). "Oregon Territory," *Congressional Globe, Appendix.* 25th Cong., 2nd Sess. (17 May, 22 May 1838) pp. 565-570. Supports the title of the U.S. to the Oregon territory through both rights of discovery and treaty. Reviews the history of the exploration of the territory and the clear title of the United States. States reasons to occupy the territory and reaffirm sovereignty. Discusses the Hudson Bay Co. and its divisive influence. Addresses the divisive influence and power of Great Britain on Indian relations. Beginning of speech summarized in *Congressional Globe*, pp. 380-381.

2342. Cushing, Caleb (Mass.). "Pre-Emption to Settlers," *Congressional Globe, Appendix.* 25th Cong., 2nd Sess. (13 June 1838) pp. 492-494. Supports granting preemption rights to the settlers. Reviews the history of settlers' rights in Massachusetts and Maine, including the "betterment" laws. Discusses the "right" of the U.S. to these lands; reviews the history of preemption. Considers the alternatives if the bill fails; defends the settlers.

2343. Cushing, Caleb (Mass.). "President's Message," *Congressional Globe, Appendix.* 25th Cong., 2nd Sess. (19 Dec. 1837) pp. 574-577. Examines each of the powers of the Executive as defined by the Constitution, and compared with those of Congress. Demonstrates that the President has considerably more power over Congress than visa versa. Maintains that the executive powers have increased and have been abused. Advocates diminishing the power and influence of the Executive.

2344. Cushing, Caleb (Mass.). "Relations with Mexico," *Congressional Globe.* 25th Cong., 2nd Sess. (18 Jan. 1838) p. 119. Defends Mr. Fox, the British minister, concerning the release of the pamphlet by the ex-minister from Mexico.

2345. Davis, John (Mass.). "Bank of Washington, D.C.," *Congressional Globe, Appendix.* 25th Cong., 2nd Sess. (17 May 1838) pp. 335-336. Supports re-chartering the district banks. Clarifies previous comments about the Bank of Washington; defends the action and character of the bank.

2346. Davis, John (Mass.). "Independent Treasury," *Congressional Globe, Appendix.* 25th Cong., 2nd Sess. (8 Mar. 1838) p. 518. Opposes receiving the bills of non-specie-paying banks; maintains that it legalizes irredeemable paper. Examines the practicality of the proposal; discusses the law requiring public creditors to be paid in specie. Contends that public confidence and a uniform currency are necessary to resume specie payments.

2347. Davis, John (Mass.). "Mr. Calhoun's Resolutions," *Congressional Globe, Appendix.* 25th Cong., 2nd Sess. (6 Jan. 1838) pp. 36-38. Opposes Mr.

Calhoun's resolutions; maintains that they are political and favorable to the slave interest. Discusses the treatment of abolition petitions in the Senate; examines their alleged threat to the Union. Maintains that the first resolution is one of nullification and the second intended to abridge the rights of the states.

2348. Davis, John (Mass.). "Northeastern Boundary," *Congressional Globe, Appendix.* 25th Cong., 2nd Sess. (18 June 1838) pp. 538-540. Supports surveying the northeastern boundary line of the U.S. according to the treaty of 1783. Examines the treaty; demonstrates, with official acts and statements of Great Britain, that the treaty leaves no doubt of the boundaries and that the old lines and the treaty lines are identical. Addresses arguments against the survey.

2349. Davis, John (Mass.). "Slavery in the District," *Congressional Globe.* 25th Cong., 2nd Sess. (18 Dec. 1837) p. 35. Supports receiving the petitions to abolish slavery in the District of Columbia. Maintains that the current course is essentially rejection, violates the right of petition, and increases the agitation.

2350. Fletcher, Richard (Mass.). Remarks on the Relationship Between the Comm. of Ways and Means and the Executive, *Congressional Globe.* 25th Cong., 2nd Sess. (13 Dec. 1837) pp. 21-23. Denies and defends portions of a printed speech accusing the Committee of Ways and Means and the Executive of an improper relationship. Reprint of the alleged speech and rebuttal of the Committee included.

2351. Lincoln, Levi (Mass.). "Removal of the Treasury Building," *Congressional Globe, Appendix.* 25th Cong., 2nd Sess. (17 Apr. 1838) pp. 336-341. Explains the considerations behind the recommendation to take down the partially constructed Treasury building. Presents the circumstances under which the site and plan of the building was authorized and the architect appointed. Considers objections to the building, including plan, location, and strength of structure; supports recommendation with authoritative reports from other architects. Maintains that a new Treasury building would save money.

2352. Webster, Daniel (Mass.). "Banks and Bank Notes," *Congressional Globe.* 25th Cong., 2nd Sess. (12 June 1838) p. 447. Presents and supports petitions to repeal the prohibition against small bank notes.

2353. Webster, Daniel (Mass.). "Collection of the Revenue," *Congressional Globe, Appendix.* 25th Cong., 2nd Sess. (29 May 1838) pp. 572-574. Supports making it unlawful to discriminate as to medium of payment for debts due the government. Maintains that the Treasury circular of July 1836 was unequal, unjust, and ruinous. Reviews the object, history, and character of the resolution of 1816. Defends banking institutions.

2354. Webster, Daniel (Mass.). "Commonwealth Bank of Boston," *Congressional Globe.* 25th Cong., 2nd Sess. (17 Jan. 1838) pp. 113-114. Requests an official inquiry into the payment of pensions and fishing bounties with bills of the Commonwealth Bank of Boston. Questions by what authority the public officers acted. Generally remarks on the need for a uniform currency.

2355. Webster, Daniel (Mass.). "Independent Treasury," *Congressional Globe, Appendix.* 25th Cong., 2nd Sess. (31 Jan. 1838) pp. 606-608. Opposes the Sub-Treasury bill. Advocates one currency for both the people and the government; maintains that the government has a constitutional power and duty to provide a good national currency. Warns against irredeemable paper. Discusses the will of the people, a national bank, and the resumption of State banks.

2356. Webster, Daniel (Mass.). "Independent Treasury," *Congressional Globe, Appendix.* 25th Cong., 2nd Sess. (12 Mar. 1838) pp. 632-641. Opposes the Sub-Treasury bill. Reviews the functions and history of government respecting commerce and revenue. Outlines the system of currency and credit. Discusses the general condition of the country, using Mass. as an example, and the state of the currency. Considers the operation and effect of the bill. Discusses the constitutional obligations of Congress to regulate the currency. Addresses views of Sen. Calhoun (S.C.), including states' rights and nullification.

2357. Webster, Daniel (Mass.). "Mr. Calhoun's Resolutions," *Congressional Globe, Appendix.* 25th Cong., 2nd Sess. (10 Jan. 1838) pp. 64-65. Opposes the requested "plighted faith" restricting the authority of Congress over slavery. Refers to the original acts of cession by the states; maintains that the states fully intended to relinquish all jurisdiction.

2358. Webster, Daniel (Mass.). "Pre-emption to Actual Settlers," *Congressional Globe, Appendix.* 25th Cong., 2nd Sess. (29 Jan. 1838) pp. 135-136. Supports granting preemption rights to the actual settlers on public lands as necessary, just, and in the best interests of the country. Discusses the settlers' expectations, speculators' influence, and proposed amendments.

2359. Webster, Daniel (Mass.). Remarks on the Commonwealth Bank at Boston, *Congressional Globe.* 25th Cong., 2nd Sess. (6 Feb. 1838) pp. 164-165. Remarks on the report respecting the deposits in the Commonwealth Bank, at Boston. Establishes that, contrary to the law, depreciated bank notes have been offered and received as payment. Remarks on the need to reform the payment of pensions; refutes charges that he is a debtor to the Commonwealth Bank.

2360. Webster, Daniel (Mass.). Remarks on Treasury Notes, *Congressional Globe.* 25th Cong., 2nd Sess. (18 May 1838) pp. 384-385, 386-387, 388. Various remarks against issuing more Treasury notes. Maintains that there is no justification and that the government would be using depreciated paper for payment. Responds to remarks of Sen. Calhoun (S.C.) regarding Treasury notes and the currency.

2361. "Statement of the Balance Due on the Claims of Massachusetts for Militia Services and Expenditures during the War of 1812," *American State*

Papers: Military Affairs, Vol. VII (Doc. 750) p. 775. (ASP 022). Same as H.doc.45 (25-2) 322 (entry **2363**).

2362. U.S. House. *Letter from the Secretary of War, Accompanied with a Chart of the Harbor of Provincetown, &c.* 25th Cong., 2nd Sess. (H.Doc.121). [Washington]: Thomas Allen, Print., [1838]. 101 pg. (Serial Set 325). Report which accompanied the map (not included) on the extremity of Cape Cod, Massachusetts. Includes description and interpretation of the map. Majority of report consists of 81 pg. of tables detailing the time and height of the high and low tides, with remarks upon the weather, from July 1833 to July 1835.

2363. U.S. House. *Letter from the Secretary of War, in Reply to a Resolution of the House of Representatives, of March 1836, upon the Subject of the Claims of the State of Massachusetts for Militia Services and Expenditures during the Late War with Great Britain.* 25th Cong., 2nd Sess. (H.Doc.45). [Washington: Thomas Allen, Print., 1837]. 1 pg. (Serial Set 322). Same as Mil.aff.750 (25-2) ASP 022 (entry **2361**).

2364. U.S. House. *Letter from the Secretary of War, Transmitting Report of the Survey of the Harbor of Lynn, in the State of Massachusetts.* 25th Cong., 2nd Sess. (H.Doc.226). [Washington: Thomas Allen, Print., 1838]. 8 pg., 1 map. (Serial Set 328). Report includes a description of the harbor and beach, with proposal and cost estimates for improvements. Includes a map entitled "Plan of Lynn Harbor and Beach."

2365. U.S. House. *Memorial of 282 Citizens of Sutton and 325 Citizens of Millbury, in the State of Massachusetts, against Foreign Emigration.* 25th Cong., 2nd Sess. (H.Doc.70). [Washington]: Thomas Allen, Print., [1838]. 1 pg. (Serial Set 322).

2366. U.S. House. *Memorial of Citizens of New Bedford, against the Repeal of Duty on Foreign Tallow and Olive Oil.* 25th Cong., 2nd Sess. (H.Doc.232). [Washington]: Thomas Allen, Print., [1838]. 8 pg. (Serial Set 328). Memorial of those interested in whale fishery respond to a Boston memorial requesting a repeal of duties on foreign tallow and olive oil; identifies mistakes and fallacies of the Boston petitioners and presents arguments against the repeal of duties.

2367. U.S. House. *Memorial of Inhabitants of the State of Massachusetts: 1st. Upon the Subject of the Claims of the United States upon the Mexican Government; 2d. Praying that the Government of the United States Do Invite the Governments of the Christian World to a Congress of Peace.* 25th Cong., 2nd Sess. (H.Doc.68). [Washington]: Thomas Allen, Print., [1838]. 3 pg. (Serial Set 322). Includes names of memorialists.

2368. U.S. House. *Memorial of Professors and Students of the Theological Institution in Cambridge, Praying that This Government Will Adopt Measures for the Adjustment of International Disputes, Which May Avoid the Necessity* *of a Resort to War.* 25th Cong., 2nd Sess. (H.Doc.290). [Washington]: Thomas Allen, Print., [1838]. 2 pg. (Serial Set 328).

2369. U.S. House. *Memorial of Professors, Students of Theology and of Law, &c. of Cambridge, Massachusetts, on the Subject of Duelling.* 25th Cong., 2nd Sess. (H Doc.221). [Washington]: Thomas Allen, Print., [1838]. 2 pg. (Serial Set 328). Memorial opposes dueling as a bad practice and an insult to God.

2370. U.S. House. *Memorial of the Book-Sellers of Boston, Massachusetts, against the Passage of the International Copy-right Law.* 25th Cong., 2nd Sess. (H.Doc.340). [Washington]: Thomas Allen, Print., [1838]. 2 pg. (Serial Set 330).

2371. U.S. House. *Petition of Inhabitants of Massachusetts, Praying that a Law May Be Passed Explanatory of the Pension Act of July 4, 1836.* 25th Cong., 2nd Sess. (H.Doc.243). [Washington]: Thomas Allen, Print., [1838]. 1 pg. (Serial Set 328).

2372. U.S. House. *Petition of Thomas Thompson, Jr. and Members of the Legislature from 119 Towns, in the State of Massachusetts, upon the Subject of the Settlement of the Claims of the United States upon the Government of Mexico, &c.* 25th Cong., 2nd Sess. (H.Doc.291). [Washington]: Thomas Allen, Print., [1838]. 10 pg. (Serial Set 328). Petition favors settling the claims and using a disinterested party to arbitrate those claims that cannot be agreed upon. Majority of petition argues in support of establishing an international arbitration board or Congress of Nations to settle international disputes. Names and towns of residence of petitioners included.

2373. U.S. House. *Remonstrance of Inhabitants of Massachusetts, against the Passage of an International Copyright Law.* 25th Cong., 2nd Sess. (H.Doc.416). [Washington]: Thomas Allen, Print., [1838]. 3 pg. (Serial Set 330). Memorial opposes the law as unjust, impolitic, and hostile to the dissemination of literature.

2374. U.S. House. *Resolution of the Legislature of Massachusetts, against Duelling.* 25th Cong., 2nd Sess. (H.Doc.382). [Washington: Thomas Allen, Print., 1838]. 1 pg. (Serial Set 330).

2375. U.S. House. *Resolutions of the Legislature of Massachusetts against the Annexation of Texas to the United States.* 25th Cong., 2nd Sess. (H.Doc.373). [Washington]: Thomas Allen, Print., [1838]. 2 pg. (Serial Set 330). Same as S.doc.432 (25-2) 318 (entry **2390**).

2376. U.S. House. *Resolutions of the Legislature of Massachusetts, Relating to the Sub-Treasury.* 25th Cong., 2nd Sess. (H.Doc.405). [Washington: Thomas Allen, Print., 1838]. 1 pg. (Serial Set 330). Resolutions oppose the Sub-Treasury bill.

2377. U.S. House. *Resolutions of the Legislature of Massachusetts, in Relation to the Indians, and against the Cherokee Treaty.* 25th Cong., 2nd Sess. (H.Doc.404). [Washington]: Thomas Allen, Print., [1838]. 2 pg. (Serial Set 330). Resolutions oppose the war against the Indian tribes and the treaty that was forced upon them.

2378. U.S. House. *Resolutions of the Legislature of Massachusetts, Relating to the Militia.* 25th Cong., 2nd Sess. (H.Doc.390). [Washington]: Thomas Allen, Print., [1838]. 2 pg. (Serial Set 330). Resolutions on uniformity, age restrictions, and distribution of arms and supplies.

2379. U.S. House. *Resolutions of the Legislature of Massachusetts, concerning the Northeastern Boundary.* 25th Cong., 2nd Sess. (H.Doc.403). [Washington]: Thomas Allen, Print., [1838]. 2 pg. (Serial Set 330). Resolutions support Maine's claims and support establishing the treaty line of 1783. Same as S.doc.434 (25-2) 318 (entry **2391**).

2380. U.S. House. *Resolutions on the Commonwealth of Massachusetts, on the Right of Petition.* 25th Cong., 2nd Sess. (H.Doc.408). [Washington]: Thomas Allen, Print., [1838]. 2 pg. (Serial Set 330). Resolutions oppose the resolution of the House of Representatives that denies action to slavery petitions; maintains that the House resolution violates the right of petition.

2381. U.S. House. *Springfield Manufacturing Company.* 25th Cong., 2nd Sess. (H.Rpt.372). [Washington]: Thomas Allen, Print., [1838]. 4 pg. (Serial Set 334). Committee of Claims concurs with the report of 1835 in favor of the claim of the Springfield Manufacturing Company. Reprints the earlier report - H.rp.21 (23-2) 276 (entry **2186**). Report of 1835 also printed as H.rp.305 (26-1) 371 (entry **2447**) and H.rp.6 (27-2) 407 (entry **2528**), and as part of H.rp.40 (24-1) 293 (entry **2257**).

2382. U.S. House. *Thomas L. Winthrop et al.* 25th Cong., 2nd Sess. (H.Rpt.956). [Washington]: Thomas Allen, Print., [1838]. 9 pg. (Serial Set 336). Favorable report of the Committee on the Judiciary on the petition of the New England Land Company concurring with an earlier report of the Senate. Reprints S.doc.205 (23-1) 240 (entry **2141**), Pub.land 1216 (23-1) ASP 033 (entry **2116**), and most of S.doc.197 (24-2) 298 (entry **2313**).

2383. U.S. Senate. [Claim of the New England Mississippi Land Company]. 25th Cong., 2nd Sess. (S.Doc.42). Washington: Blair & Rives, Printers, 1838. 7 pg. (Serial Set 314). Report of the Committee on the Judiciary on the petition of the New England Mississippi Land Company in favor of awarding them that portion of their money that is still in the Treasury. Reviews the facts of the case, relying upon the earlier reports made to the Senate.

2384. U.S. Senate. *Document in Relation to the Payment of Pensions in the Bills of the Commonwealth Bank of Boston.* 25th Cong., 2nd Sess. (S.Doc.149). Washington: Blair and Rives, 1838. 1 pg. (Serial Set 316).

2385. U.S. Senate. *Memorial of a Number of Citizens of Boston, Praying the Passage of an International Copyright Law.* 25th Cong., 2nd Sess. (S.Doc.398). Washington: Blair and Rives, 1838. 4 pg. (Serial Set 318). Includes names of memorialists.

2386. U.S. Senate. *Memorial of a Number of Merchants of Boston, Praying an Alteration of the Laws Regulating the Admiralty Courts of the United States in Relation to Salvages on Wrecked Property.* 25th Cong., 2nd Sess. (S.Doc.429). Washington: Blair and Rives, 1838. 5 pg. (Serial Set 318). Memorial with supporting letters.

2387. U.S. Senate. *Report and Resolutions from a Committee of the Legislature of Massachusetts, in Relation to the Northeastern Boundary.* 25th Cong., 2nd Sess. (S.Doc.431). Washington: Blair and Rives, 1838. 37 pg., 2 maps. (Serial Set 318). Report and resolutions support the boundary line of 1783 and request speedy exploration and establishment of the line. Provides a detailed background of the boundaries; includes Mitchell's map, "Extract from a Map of the British and French Dominions in North America," and the "Map of the Northern Part of Maine and of the Adjacent British Provinces, Shewing the Portion of that State to which Great Britain Lays Claim."

2388. U.S. Senate. *Report from the Secretary of the Treasury, in Compliance with a Resolution of the Senate of the 17th Instant, in Relation to the Payment of Pensions and Fishing Bounties in Bills of the Commonwealth Bank of Boston.* 25th Cong., 2nd Sess. (S.Doc.148). Washington: Blair and Rives, 1838. 14 pg. (Serial Set 316). Report of the inquiry into the payment of pensions and bounties with bills of the Commonwealth Bank, including statistics and correspondence with the War Dept., the Navy Dept., and the collector at Boston. Discusses the authority to pay the pensions and bounties in these notes, and the financial status of the deposit banks in Massachusetts.

2389. U.S. Senate. *Resolutions of the Board of Commissioners of the Associated Banks in Boston, to Obtain the Repeal of the Law Which Prevents Collectors and Receivers from Taking in Payment the Bills of Such Banks As Have Issued Notes of a Less Denomination than Five Dollars, since the 4th July, 1836.* 25th Cong., 2nd Sess. (S.Doc.480). Washington: Blair and Rives, 1838. 1 pg. (Serial Set 319).

2390. U.S. Senate. *Resolutions of the Legislature of Massachusetts, against the Annexation of Texas to the United States.* 25th Cong., 2nd Sess. (S.Doc.432). Washington: Blair and Rives, 1838. 2 pg. (Serial Set 318). Same as H.doc.373 (25-2) 330 (entry **2375**).

2391. U.S. Senate. *Resolutions of the Legislature of Massachusetts, in Relation to the Northeastern Boundary.* 25th Cong., 2nd Sess. (S.Doc.434). Washington: Blair and Rives, 1838. 2 pg. (Serial Set 318). Resolutions support

Maine's claims and support establishing the treaty line of 1783. Same as H.doc.403 (25-2) 330 (entry **2379**).

25TH CONGRESS, 3RD SESSION

2392. Adams, John Quincy (Mass.). "Maine Boundary Question," *Congressional Globe, Appendix.* 25th Cong., 3rd Sess. (26 Feb. 1839) pp. 228-229. Concerned that the President has recommended that Maine negotiate directly with New Brunswick.

2393. Adams, John Quincy (Mass.). "Maine Boundary Question," *Congressional Globe, Appendix.* 25th Cong., 3rd Sess. (2 Mar. 1839) pp. 283-285. Supports the bill for the defense of the U.S. after the British aggressions against Maine. Maintains that the British government will recede and disavow the act. Supports Maine in her stand to defend her territory. Discusses alternative resolutions.

2394. Briggs, George N. (Mass.). "State of the Finances," *Congressional Globe, Appendix.* 25th Cong., 3rd Sess. (2 Feb., 9 Feb. 1839) pp. 316-318. Responds to Mr. Rhett and Mr. Pickens, from South Carolina; defends protective tariffs and internal improvements. Contends that the tariff was not of northern origin; supports his view with documented opinions of prominent southerners that favored a protective tariff and internal improvements. Offers other documentation on the history of support of protectionism.

2395. Cushing, Caleb (Mass.). "Defalcation of Samuel Swartwout," *Congressional Globe, Appendix.* 25th Cong., 3rd Sess. (8 Jan. 1839) pp. 32-33. Supports a non-partisan investigation of corruption beyond that of Samuel Swartwout; discusses the party implications and the protective attitude of the administration.

2396. Cushing, Caleb (Mass.). "Maine Boundary Question," *Congressional Globe, Appendix.* 25th Cong., 3rd Sess. (26 Feb. 1839) pp. 230-231. Discusses Great Britain and the contested Aroostook region. Maintains that Britain does not have right of exclusive jurisdiction over that region and that her claim of right is founded on a false pretension. Defends Maine's right to repel invasion.

2397. Cushing, Caleb (Mass.). "Maine Boundary Question," *Congressional Globe, Appendix.* 25th Cong., 3rd Sess. (3 Mar. 1839) pp. 269-272. Supports the positions taken by Maine and the Government of the United States. Discusses the seriousness of the situation, the unjust claims of Britain, Sir. John Harvey, the rights of jurisdiction and possession, and the history of U.S. sovereignty in the Aroostook. Reviews the merits of the bill; addresses objections. Reprints the resolutions of the Legislature of Massachusetts on the northern boundary. Opposes further delays in the resolution of the situation.

2398. Cushing, Caleb (Mass.). Memorial on the Right to Petition, *Congressional Globe.* 25th Cong., 3rd Sess. (7 Jan. 1839) p. 99. Presents a memorial from citizens of Reading, Mass., opposed to the House resolution that restricts debate on certain petitions; maintains that it is a violation of states' rights, the right to petition, and the privilege of speech. Text of memorial included.

2399. Cushing, Caleb (Mass.). "Wisconsin Contested Election," *Congressional Globe, Appendix.* 25th Cong., 3rd Sess. (3 Jan. 1839) pp. 319-321. Reviews the circumstances of the contested Wisconsin election between George W. Jones and James D. Doty.

2400. Davis, John (Mass.). "Maine Boundary Question," *Congressional Globe, Appendix.* 25th Cong., 3rd Sess. (26 Feb., 27 Feb., 1 Mar. 1839) pp. 212; 257-258; 311-312, 314. Various remarks on the disputed Aroostook region. Maintains that the right of Maine and the U.S. is clear. Discusses Sir. John Harvey's alleged agreement to exclusive jurisdiction. Briefly reviews the diplomatic history of the negotiations. Advocates a speedy settlement. Maintains that Maine has the right to repel invasion and that the government has a constitutional duty to aid in repelling the invasion.

2401. Lincoln, Levi (Mass.). "Maine Boundary Question," *Congressional Globe, Appendix.* 25th Cong., 3rd Sess. (26 Feb. 1839) pp. 229-230. Supports conciliation and forbearance on the part of Maine concerning the disputed Aroostook region. Offers documentation of previous confusion concerning jurisdiction of the territory.

2402. Parmenter, William (Mass.). "Board of Navy Commissioners," *Congressional Globe, Appendix.* 25th Cong., 3rd Sess. (15 Feb. 1839) pp. 217-219. Advocates deferring action on the Navy Board until Congress can modify the law defining its duties and authority. Maintains that the current law gives too much power to the commissioners. Discusses the duties regarding procurement, construction and armament of vessels, and employment of vessels during war. Requests more written reports.

2403. Reed, John (Mass.). "Public Defaulters," *Congressional Globe.* 25th Cong., 3rd Sess. (28 Dec. 1838) p. 69. Advocates opening the books of the Treasury. Maintains that the defaulters are the responsibility of the administration and should have been audited properly.

2404. Saltonstall, Leverett (Mass.). "Maine Boundary Question," *Congressional Globe, Appendix.* 25th Cong., 3rd Sess. (2 Mar. 1839) pp. 272-274, 277-278. Supports protecting Maine but opposes taking any steps as a result of Maine's indiscreet actions which could induce war. Reviews the controversy concerning the disputed boundary; offers documentary evidence that it is a long-standing claim. Advocates reconciliation. Maintains that Sir

John Harvey has mistaken or misunderstood his instructions. Later remarks clarify the intent of earlier speech.

2405. Webster, Daniel (Mass.). "Maine Boundary Question," *Congressional Globe, Appendix.* 25th Cong., 3rd Sess. (26 Feb., 27 Feb., 1 Mar. 1839) pp. 212; 258-259; 314, 315. Various brief remarks on the disputed Aroostook boundary. Maintains that the U.S. has undisputed title over the territory; questions why there has been no progress towards negotiation. Argues for a speedy settlement of the dispute. Contends that Maine is entitled to repel an invasion and that the country must support her; if Maine takes hostile action against her peaceable neighbors, it must be prevented and suppressed. Only the government can decide when there will be peace and war.

2406. "An Act to Authorize the Secretary of the Navy to Purchase a Tract of Land Belonging to the Heirs of John Harris, Deceased, Being within the Limits of the Navy Yard in Charlestown, Massachusetts," *Statutes at Large,* Vol. V (3 Mar. 1839) pp. 329-330.

2407. U.S. House. *Letter from the Secretary of the Treasury, in Reply to a Resolution of the House of Representatives of the 14th Instant, in Relation to Debts Due to the United States (if Any) by the Commonwealth, Franklin, and Lafayette Banks, of Massachusetts.* 25th Cong., 3rd Sess. (H.Doc.120). [Washington: Thomas Allen, Print., 1839]. 8 pg. (Serial Set 346). Report details the financial status of the Commonwealth Bank of Boston. Brief report on the Franklin Bank; nothing on the Lafayette Bank.

2408. U.S. House. *Letter from the Secretary of the Treasury, Transmitting the Information Required by a Resolution of the House of Representatives of the 28th Instant, Respecting the Official Bonds of the Collectors and Naval Officers of the Ports of Philadelphia, New York, and Boston, &c.* 25th Cong., 3rd Sess. (H.Doc.130). [Washington: Thomas Allen, Print., 1839]. 2 pg. (Serial Set 347). Information on the dates, amounts of, and sureties on, the official bonds.

2409. U.S. House. *Massachusetts - Inhabitants of Springfield.* 25th Cong., 3rd Sess. (H.Rpt.296). [Washington]: Thomas Allen, Print., [1839]. 1 pg. (Serial Set 352). Report against the petition of the inhabitants of Springfield requesting Congress to surrender their exclusive jurisdiction over some land purchased to erect an armory and other necessary buildings.

2410. U.S. House. *R.T. Paine - Latitude and Longitude of Light-Houses in Massachusetts.* 25th Cong., 3rd Sess. (H.Doc.187). [Washington]: Thomas Allen, Print., [1839]. 5 pg. (Serial Set 347). Paine's report gives the latitude and longitude of Massachusetts's lighthouses, and the distances at which the lights can be seen.

2411. U.S. House. *Resolutions of the Legislature of Massachusetts, in Relation to the Duty on Salt and Bounty to Fishermen.* 25th Cong., 3rd Sess.

(H.Doc.226). [Washington: Thomas Allen, Print., 1839]. 1 pg. (Serial Set 348). Resolutions oppose a repeal of the duty on salt or the bounty on fishing vessels.

2412. U.S. Senate. "Letter from the Secretary of War to the Chairman of the Committee on Indian Affairs, with Two Communications from the Governor of Massachusetts, and other Documents, Showing Objections, by the New York Indians, to the Treaty Made for Them, As Amended by the Senate, &c.," *U.S. Senate Executive Documents and Reports* [Washington]: Blair & Rives, Printers. [1839]. (CIS microfiche 25-3-16). Confidential. Includes communications from the Gov. of Massachusetts and the Superintendent of Mass. concerning the negotiations with the Seneca Indians and their opposition to the treaty and the procedures used to obtain their assent to the treaty.

26TH CONGRESS, 1ST SESSION

2413. Adams, John Quincy (Mass.). "Abolition Petitions," *Congressional Globe, Appendix.* 26th Cong., 1st Sess. (22 Jan. 1840) pp. 761-764. Objects to the resolution concerning the reception of abolition petitions. Maintains that the proposal will not allay agitation; advocates open discussion. Examines the character of the proposition and compares it to the proposition of last year. Discusses the right of petition, which includes reception and consideration. Considers Parliamentary precedents and the right of petition in the British House of Commons. Argues in support of his own proposition. Summary of speech in *Congressional Globe*, pp. 133-134.

2414. Adams, John Quincy (Mass.). "New Jersey Contested Election," *Congressional Globe, Appendix.* 26th Cong., 1st Sess. (20 Dec. 1839) pp. 151-155. Discusses the contested New Jersey seat, and the powers of the House over the returns, elections, and qualifications of its members. Maintains that it would be unconstitutional not to recognize the members with the governor's certificates; discusses proof of record. Establishes that Blackstone and Parliament provide that the gentlemen with certificates should have their seats until the returns should be proved illegal. Summary of speech in the *Congressional Globe*, p. 65.

2415. Adams, John Quincy (Mass.). Remarks on National Defenses, *Congressional Globe.* 26th Cong., 1st Sess. (9 Apr. 1840) pp. 311-312. Brief remarks on relations with Great Britain; maintains that there is no immediate danger of war, particularly from Maine.

2416. Adams, John Quincy (Mass.). Remarks on Organizing the House, *Congressional Globe.* 26th Cong., 1st Sess. (5 Dec. 1839) pp. 18-20. Various remarks request the uncontested members of the House to organize the House and the Clerk to proceed with the call of the members.

2417. Cushing, Caleb (Mass.). "Independent Treasury," *Congressional Globe, Appendix.* 26th Cong., 1st Sess. (20 May, 21 May 1840) pp. 764-775. Opposes the Independent Treasury bill. Examines the merits and objectives of the measure. Discusses its probable effect, expense and comparative convenience. Reviews the history of the measure and the experience of other nations. Demonstrates that bank depositories are safer and superior; discusses the question of an independent government currency and the powers of the government relative to banks and the currency.

2418. Cushing, Caleb (Mass.). Remarks on Organizing the House, *Congressional Globe.* 26th Cong., 1st Sess. (3 Dec. 1839) pp. 7-8. Requests the Clerk to explain why he did not recognize the members from New Jersey.

2419. Cushing, Caleb (Mass.). Remarks on the Civil and Diplomatic Bill, *Congressional Globe.* 26th Cong., 1st Sess. (9 Apr. 1840) p. 315. Supports the additional appropriations for public defenses.

2420. Cushing, Caleb (Mass.). Remarks on Viva-Voce Voting, *Congressional Globe.* 26th Cong., 1st Sess. (21 Dec. 1839) pp. 73-74. Advocates public voting; maintains that constituents should be able to see how their Representatives vote. Addresses opponents' arguments and the practice in England and France.

2421. Cushing, Caleb (Mass.). "Treasury Note Bill," *Congressional Globe.* 26th Cong., 1st Sess. (12 Mar., 17 Mar. 1840) pp. 266-267; 278. Opposes issuing Treasury notes; maintains that it would unconstitutional and oppressive.

2422. Davis, John (Mass.). "Assumption of State Debts," *Congressional Globe, Appendix.* 26th Cong., 1st Sess. (3 Mar., 6 Mar. 1840) pp. 232-234; 248-250. Replies to Mr. Buchanan's (Pa.) response to an earlier speech, also made in reply to Mr. Buchanan (Jan. 23rd). Maintains that the Senator was present and no objection or correction was made at the time of the speech. Reviews and defends the contested paragraphs and sentiments.

2423. Davis, John (Mass.). "The Independent Treasury," *Congressional Globe, Appendix.* 26th Cong., 1st Sess. (23 Jan. 1840) pp. 157-161. Opposes the Independent Treasury and responds to remarks of Senators Walker (Miss.) and Buchanan (Pa.). Demonstrates that the banks alone are not responsible for the distress of the country; maintains that it began in 1833 with Pres. Jackson's State bank deposit system. Reviews the history of reform and the effects of banks and bank paper in European countries. Discusses the effects of the bill upon public policy, including credit and speculation, and labor.

2424. Lincoln, Levi (Mass.). Remarks on Matthew Lyon's Fine, *Congressional Globe.* 26th Cong., 1st Sess. (23 May 1840) pp. 412-413. Objects to refunding a fine imposed on Matthew Lyon under the sedition law of Adams.

2425. Lincoln, Levi (Mass.). "Repairs to President's House," *Congressional Globe, Appendix.* 26th Cong., 1st Sess. (16 Apr. 1840) pp. 703-706. Supports appropriations for repairs and furnishings for the President's house. Reviews the necessary repairs and present state of the dwelling. Maintains that, regardless of political affiliations, the President should have a dwelling worthy of the Office and adequate to represent the Nation. Summary of speech in *Congressional Globe*, pp. 333-335.

2426. Parmenter, William (Mass.). "General Appropriation Bill," *Congressional Globe, Appendix.* 26th Cong., 1st Sess. (20 Apr. 1840) pp. 446-453. Defends the President and his administration; addresses the charges of the Whig party. Discusses public finances. Examines the various political parties and the history of the Whig party. Discusses the Hartford Convention, its principles and political similarities. Summary of speech in *Congressional Globe*, pp. 340-341.

2427. Saltonstall, Leverett (Mass.). "New Jersey Contested Election," *Congressional Globe, Appendix.* 26th Cong., 1st Sess. (13 Dec. 1839) pp. 36-39. Supports the authority and constitutional right of the returned members from New Jersey to their seats in the House. Examines the constitutional and legal rights of the members; reviews New Jersey election law. Addresses opponents' arguments.

2428. Saltonstall, Leverett (Mass.). "Policy of the Administration," *Congressional Globe, Appendix.* 26th Cong., 1st Sess. (21 Apr. 1840) pp. 729-733. Responds to Mr. Parmenter's (Mass.) (April 20th) attack on the old and disbanded Federal party. Defends the Federal party; reviews its history, principles and actions. Maintains that the old Federal party and the Opposition party are not the same. Defends Massachusetts. Reviews the Hartford Convention. Opposes the principles and conduct of the administration.

2429. Saltonstall, Leverett (Mass.). "Rules of the House," *Congressional Globe, Appendix.* 26th Cong., 1st Sess. (21 Dec. 1839) pp. 186-187. Opposes the viva voce mode of voting; maintains that it does not secure free elections and that there is no reason to change existing practice.

2430. Webster, Daniel (Mass.). "Assumption of State Debts," *Congressional Globe, Appendix.* 26th Cong., 1st Sess. (3 Mar. 1840) pp. 211-213. Responds to Sen. Calhoun (S.C.). Discusses protecting duties. Maintains that the burden falls upon different parts of the country in proportion to their consumption; demonstrates that the South does not bear an unequal and unjust portion. Discusses the relationship between production, currency, and labor.

2431. Webster, Daniel (Mass.). "Bankrupt Act," *Congressional Globe, Appendix.* 26th Cong., 1st Sess. (18 May 1840, 5 June 1840) pp. 822-826; 844-846. Supports the bankrupt bill and its necessity. Discusses the power of Congress over the subject of bankruptcies, including whether the bill should be limited to traders and voluntary cases. Advocates a uniform system. Opposes including the State banks in the bill. Second speech focuses on the rights and benefits of the creditors if the bill does not contain the compulsory clause.

2432. Webster, Daniel (Mass.). "Cumberland Road," *Congressional Globe, Appendix.* 26th Cong., 1st Sess. (1 Apr. 1840) p. 367. Advocates continuing work on the Cumberland road. Reviews reasons for his support.

2433. Webster, Daniel (Mass.). "Treasury Note Bill," *Congressional Globe, Appendix.* 26th Cong., 1st Sess. (30 Mar. 1840) pp. 304-308. Speech on the bill authorizing the issue of Treasury notes. Discusses the state of the Treasury, and its recent history of revenue and expenditures. Addresses objections to the bill. Discusses the objects of the bill. Maintains that existing provisions for revenue are inadequate to meets the needs of the country.

2434. Williams, Henry (Mass.). "Independent Treasury Bill," *Congressional Globe, Appendix.* 26th Cong., 1st Sess. (4 June 1840) pp. 533-540. Supports the bill that would place the revenue under the control of government rather than the banks. Reviews the bill's principal features; contrasts it with the alternative proposal. Addresses objections. Addresses charges against the administration concerning the distress of the country. Discusses the interests of labor and the condition of the laboring classes abroad. Discusses the deleterious effects of the paper system. Reviews the beneficial effects of the bill. Speech summarized in *Congressional Globe,* pp. 442-443.

2435. U.S. House. *Communication from Thomas H. Perkins, and a Great Number of Other Merchants, of Boston and Salem, Mass., Interested in the China Trade, Containing a Statement of Intelligence Recently Received from Undoubted Sources in China, Which Has Not Before Been Made Publicly Known.* 26th Cong., 1st Sess. (H.Doc.170). [Washington]: Blair & Rives, Printers, [1840]. 4 pg. (Serial Set 366). Petition advocates sending forces to China to protect American commerce from the hostilities between England and China. Includes an extract from a letter supporting the need.

2436. U.S. House. *Letter from the Postmaster General, in Reply to a Resolution of the House of Representatives of the 6th Instant, Respecting Irregularities in the Mail Between New York and Boston.* 26th Cong., 1st Sess. (H.Doc.203). [Washington]: Blair & Rives, Printers, [1840]. 3 pg. (Serial Set 366). Report on the causes of delays and irregularities along the various routes.

2437. U.S. House. *Letter from the Secretary of the Navy, Transmitting Information in Relation to Certain Lots Situated within the Limits of the Navy Yard at Charlestown, Massachusetts, &c.* 26th Cong., 1st Sess. (H.Doc.81). [Washington]: Blair & Rives, Printers, [1840]. 41 pg. (Serial Set 365). Report of the appraisers' valuation of the land situated in the navy yard at Charlestown, claimed by the heirs of John Harris, for possible purchase by the government. Includes court decisions, statements, and other relevant documents.

2438. U.S. House. *Letter from the Secretary of War, Transmitting a Copy of the Correspondence Between the Delegation from the State of Massachusetts and the War Department, upon the Subject of the Claim of the Said State for Militia Services during the Last War with Great Britain.* 26th Cong., 1st Sess. (H.Doc.160). [Washington]: Blair & Rives, Printers, [1840]. 4 pg. (Serial Set 366). Correspondence on the status of the claim.

2439. U.S. House. *Massachusetts Legislature - Claim of the State.* 26th Cong., 1st Sess. (H.Doc.181). [Washington]: Blair & Rives, Printers, [1840]. 1 pg. (Serial Set 366). Resolutions oppose the actions of Congress concerning the Massachusetts claims for expenses incurred in the War of 1812.

2440. U.S. House. *Memorial of Amana Walker and 445 Others, Citizens of Boston and Its Vicinity, in Favor of Granting Land in Aid of the Continuous Line of Railroads from Boston to the Mississippi River.* 26th Cong., 1st Sess. (H.Doc.213). [Washington: Blair & Rives, Printers, 1840]. 2 pg. (Serial Set 368).

2441. U.S. House. *Memorial of Inhabitants of Southbridge, Massachusetts, for a Revision of the Laws for the Collection of Duties, &c.* 26th Cong., 1st Sess. (H.Doc.42). [Washington]: Blair & Rives, Printers, [1840]. 3 pg. (Serial Set 364). Includes names of memorialists.

2442. U.S. House. *Petition of Parks, Wright, and Compay, and Others, in Relation to Frauds upon the Revenue.* 26th Cong., 1st Sess. (H.Doc.67). [Washington]: Blair & Rives, Printers, [1840]. 17 pg. (Serial Set 365). Same memorial as H.doc.42 (26-1) 364 (entry **2441**), requesting a revision of the laws for the collection of duties to prevent frauds. Includes report of U.S. vs. Samuel R. Wood (N.Y. District Court) as an example of a case of fraud.

2443. U.S. House. *Resolutions of the Legislature of Massachusetts, on the Subject of the Public Lands.* 26th Cong., 1st Sess. (H.Doc.41). [Washington]: Blair & Rives, Printers, [1840]. 2 pg. (Serial Set 364).

2444. U.S. House. *Resolutions of the Legislature of Massachusetts, in Relation to Steamboats.* 26th Cong., 1st Sess. (H.Doc.208). [Washington]: Blair & Rives, Printers, [1840]. 1 pg. (Serial Set 368). Resolutions support measures to protect passengers on steamboats.

2445. U.S. House. *Resolutions of the Legislature of the State of Massachusetts, concerning Claim for Services, Disbursements, and Expenditures, during the Late War.* 26th Cong., 1st Sess. (H.Doc.64). [Washington]: Blair & Rives, Printers, [1840]. 1 pg. (Serial Set 365).

2446. U.S. House. *Resolves of the Legislature of Massachusetts, concerning the Duty on Salt, and the Bounty to Fishing Vessels.* 26th Cong., 1st Sess.

(H.Doc.207). [Washington]: Blair and Rives, Printers, [1840]. 1 pg. (Serial Set 368). Resolutions opposed repealing the duty on salt and the bounty to fishing vessels.

2447. U.S. House. *Springfield Manufacturing Company.* 26th Cong., 1st Sess. (H.Rpt.305). [Washington: Blair & Rives, Printers, 1840]. 4 pg. (Serial Set 371). Committee of Claims concurs with the report of 1835 in favor of the claim of the Springfield Manufacturing Company. Reprints the earlier report - H.rp.21 (23-2) 276 (entry **2186**). Report of 1835 also printed as H.rp.372 (25-2) 334 (entry **2381**) and H.rp.6 (27-2) 407 (entry **2528**), and as part of H.rp.40 (24-1) 293 (entry **2257**).

2448. U.S. Senate. [Claim of the New England Mississippi Land Company]. 26th Cong., 1st Sess. (S.doc.470). Washington: Blair & Rives, Printers, 1840. 2 pg. (Serial Set 360). Favorable report of the Committee on the Judiciary on the petition of the New England Mississippi Land Company. Briefly reviews the facts.

2449. U.S. Senate. "Message from the President of the United States, Transmitting a Letter from the Governor of Massachusetts, with a Communication on Behalf of the Chiefs of the Seneca Tribe of Indians, Opposed to the Treaty of Buffalo," *U.S. Senate Executive Documents and Reports.* [Washington]: Blair & Rives, Printers. [1840]. (CIS microfiche 26-1-4). Confidential. Letter describes the circumstances of the alleged assent to the Treaty of Buffalo. Clarifies who and what are the officers of their nation; maintains that the chiefs of the Seneca nation did not give their consent to the sale and removal.

2450. U.S. Senate. [Report on the Steamers Between Boston and Nova Scotia]. 26th Cong., 1st Sess. (S.Doc.390). Washington: Blair and Rives, 1840. 1 pg. (Serial Set 359). Report opposes restricting the number of passengers permitted on board the steamers.

26TH CONGRESS, 2ND SESSION

2451. "Resignation of Mr. Webster," *Congressional Globe, Appendix.* 26th Cong., 2nd Sess. (22 Feb., 1 Mar. 1841) pp. 328-332. Debate following the resignation of Senator Webster as to the Senator's opinions concerning the transfer of slaves from one state or territory to another.

2452. Adams, John Quincy (Mass.). "Treasury Note Bill," *Congressional Globe, Appendix.* 26th Cong., 2nd Sess. (4 Feb. 1841) pp. 319-324. Supports issuing the Treasury notes; advocates that the bill provide the means of discharging the obligation. Discusses the incoming Harrison administration, the dueling law, slave petitions, internal improvements and the assumption of the state debts, and his opposition to Mr. Wise (Va.) assuming the position of leader of the House.

2453. Saltonstall, Leverett (Mass.). "Naval Appropriation Bill," *Congressional Globe, Appendix.* 26th Cong., 2nd Sess. (25 Feb. 1841) p. 186. Supports greater appropriations for the navy. Discusses the need for more money, the importance of the navy, and means to obtain the money.

2454. Webster, Daniel (Mass.). "Finances of the Country," *Congressional Globe.* 26th Cong., 2nd Sess. (16 Dec., 17 Dec. 1840) pp. 26-28; 35. Speeches discuss the message of the President relating to the finances of the country. Reviews the national debt and future liabilities. Maintains that the message gives an erroneous impression. Responds to remarks by Sen. Wright (N.Y.).

2455. U.S. House. *F.C. Sanford, for the Owners of the Ship Lexington, of Nantucket.* 26th Cong., 2nd Sess. (H.Rpt.98). [Washington: 1841]. 1 pg. (Serial Set 388). Favorable report of the Committee on Commerce for the relief of the owners.

2456. U.S. Senate. *Memorial of a Number of Citizens of Newburyport, Mass., Praying the Modification or Repeal of the Act of May 29, 1830, "To Amend the Acts Regulating the Commercial Intercourse Between the United States and Certain Colonies of Great Britain."* 26th Cong., 2nd Sess. (S.Doc.31). Washington: Blair and Rives, 1841. 2 pg. (Serial Set 376). Includes names of memorialists.

2457. U.S. Senate. *Petition of a Number of Citizens of Massachusetts, Praying that Jurisdiction over Offences Committed within the Admiralty and Maritime Jurisdiction of the United States May Be Extended to the District Courts of the United States.* 26th Cong., 2nd Sess. (S.Doc.62). Washington: Blair and Rives, 1841. 3 pg. (Serial Set 377).

2458. U.S. Senate. *Report of a Committee of the Boston Chamber of Commerce, in Relation to the Present Commercial Arrangements with Great Britain.* 26th Cong., 2nd Sess. (S.Doc.234). Washington: Blair and Rives, 1841. 5 pg. (Serial Set 378). Report deplores current commercial arrangements with Great Britain concerning the colonies. Maintains that British shipping is favored; gives specific examples and supporting statistics.

2459. U.S. Senate. *Resolutions of the Legislature of Massachusetts, in Relation to the Claims for French Spoliations Committed Prior to the 31st Day of July, 1801.* 26th Cong., 2nd Sess. (S.Doc.218). Washington: Blair and Rives, 1841. 6 pg. (Serial Set 378). Resolutions favor satisfying the claims. Includes committee report justifying position.

27TH CONGRESS, 1ST SESSION

2460. Adams, John Quincy (Mass.). "Case of McLeod," *Congressional Globe, Appendix.* 27th Cong., 1st Sess. (4 Sept. 1841) pp. 432-434. Addresses the resolution of inquiry; maintains that the resolution is a party measure, that Great Britain is better prepared for war, and that the U.S. was in the wrong in an act of aggression and hostility. Discusses the relationship between the government and New York.

2461. Adams, John Quincy (Mass.). Remarks on Adopting the Rules of the Last House, *Congressional Globe.* 27th Cong., 1st Sess. (1 June 1841) p. 9. Remarks on the political aspects of the passage of the 21st rule concerning abolitionist petitions.

2462. Adams, John Quincy (Mass.). Remarks on Foreign Ministers, *Congressional Globe.* 27th Cong., 1st Sess. (27 Aug. 1841) p. 394. Remarks on the powers concerning appointment of foreign ministers.

2463. Bates, Isaac C. (Mass.). "Fiscal Bank," *Congressional Globe, Appendix.* 27th Cong., 1st Sess. (6 July 1841) p. 361. Supports a national bank, as necessary to administer finances, expedite the return of specie payments, equalize the exchanges, and give a uniform currency to the people.

2464. Briggs, George N. (Mass.). "Family of the Late President," *Congressional Globe.* 27th Cong., 1st Sess. (17 June 1841) p. 69. Supports appropriations for the relief of President Harrison's widow and descendants.

2465. Choate, Rufus (Mass.). "Case of McLeod," *Congressional Globe, Appendix.* 27th Cong., 1st Sess. (11 June 1841) pp. 417-419. Supports the letter and course of action of the Secretary of State. Maintains that McLeod is entitled to personal immunity under international law while acting under the command of his government. Discusses any special circumstances that would apply, the principles of immunity of soldiers of war, and the rights of New York State.

2466. Choate, Rufus (Mass.). "Fiscal Bank," *Congressional Globe, Appendix.* 27th Cong., 1st Sess. (2 July 1841) pp. 355-357. Supports the amendment to establish branches only with the assent of the states. Maintains that although Congress has the power to establish branches over all the states, this amendment will enable the act to pass and a national bank to be established far sooner than otherwise. It would also preserve the harmony.

2467. Cushing, Caleb (Mass.). "Case of McLeod," *Congressional Globe, Appendix.* 27th Cong., 1st Sess. (24 June, 15 June 1841) pp. 419-422. Responds in detail to Mr. Ingersoll's (Pa.) speech that found fault with the foreign policy of the government and the letter of the Secretary of State. Reviews foreign policy of Mr. Van Buren in relation to Great Britain; discusses the party consequences of the controversy. Maintains that the true issue is the attack on the Caroline, which was unjustifiable and an indisputable claim for redress. Defends Mr. Webster's letter to Mr. Fox.

2468. Cushing, Caleb (Mass.). "Convention with Mexico," *Congressional Globe.* 27th Cong., 1st Sess. (28 Aug. 1841) p. 401. Brief remarks on the request to reconsider the vote concerning the convention between the United States and the Mexican Republic.

2469. Cushing, Caleb (Mass.). "Fortification Bill," *Congressional Globe.* 27th Cong., 1st Sess. (17 July 1841) pp. 225-226. Supports appropriations for fortifications. Recommends reading the relevant War Department documents; deplores the delays; addresses objections.

2470. Cushing, Caleb (Mass.). "Post Office Appropriation Bill," *Congressional Globe, Appendix.* 27th Cong., 1st Sess. (25 Aug. 1841) pp. 452-456. Supports paying the debts contracted to deliver the mail. Addresses objections. Recommends that the federal government should pay for delivery of newspapers and all government matter and that printed matter should be charged by weight. Defends the conduct of President Tyler, particularly regarding the bank bills. Reviews the rise of the Whig party and its actions during the present session.

2471. Cushing, Caleb (Mass.). Remarks on the Survey of the Coast, *Congressional Globe.* 27th Cong., 1st Sess. (24 June 1841) p. 111. Requests an accounting of the expenditures and the progress of the survey; questions the character of Mr. Hassler.

2472. Parmenter, William (Mass.). "Distribution and Pre-Emption Bill," *Congressional Globe.* 27th Cong., 1st Sess. (3 July 1841) pp. 146-147. Opposes distributing the proceeds of the public lands as unconstitutional and establishing bad precedent; advocates delaying consideration of the bill. Quotes President Jackson in support; reviews the resolutions of Massachusetts concerning the public lands.

2473. Winthrop, Robert C. (Mass.). "Revenue Bill," *Congressional Globe, Appendix.* 27th Cong., 1st Sess. (28 July 1841) pp. 487-489. Opposes the bill. Admits to the necessity of generating increased revenues. Maintains that this bill is so complicated and extensive that it should not be hastily adopted. Discusses the proposed bill's effect on wool, type metal, indigo, flaxseed, refined sugar, and distilled spirits. Supports the substitute amendment presented by Mr. Kennedy (Md.). Discusses the injustices of the Compromise Act of 1833 and the need for its modification.

2474. U.S. House. *Memorial of Josiah Stickney and Others, of Massachusetts, on the Subject of the Drawback on Rum.* 27th Cong., 1st Sess. (H.Doc.36). [Washington: Gales and Seaton, 1841]. 2 pg. (Serial Set 392). Memorial supports graduating the drawback according to the strength of the liquor.

2475. U.S. House. *Resolves of the Legislature of Massachusetts, concerning the North Eastern Boundary.* 27th Cong., 1st Sess. (H.Doc.18). Washington: Gales & Seaton, 1841. 2 pg. (Serial Set 392). Resolutions support the immediate execution of the terms of the treaty of 1783 and the end of the controversy regarding the northeastern boundary.

2476. U.S. Senate. *Memorial of a Number of Citizens of Boston, Praying the Modification of the Bill (H.R. 12) "Relating to Duties and Drawbacks."* 27th Cong., 1st Sess. (S.Doc.107). [Washington]: Thomas Allen, Print., 1841. 2 pg. (Serial Set 390). Memorial requests that previous rates of duty apply to goods that cleared from foreign ports before the bill was passed.

2477. U.S. Senate. *Resolutions of the Legislature of Massachusetts, in Favor of the Distribution of the Proceeds of the Sales of the Public Lands Among the Several States.* 27th Cong., 1st Sess. (S.Doc.15). [Washington]: Thomas Allen, Print., [1841]. 2 pg. (Serial Set 390).

2478. U.S. Senate. *Resolutions of the Legislature of Massachusetts, Relative to the Re-eligibility of the President of the United States, and to the Limitation of the Office to a Single Term.* 27th Cong., 1st Sess. (S.Doc.29). [Washington]: Thomas Allen, Print., [1841]. 1 pg. (Serial Set 390).

27TH CONGRESS, 2ND SESSION

2479. Adams, John Quincy (Mass.). "The Apportionment Bill," *Congressional Globe.* 27th Cong., 2nd Sess. (13 June 1842) pp. 620-621. Opposes the Senate's recommendation to increase the apportionment ratio from fifty to seventy thousand; maintains that it would diminish representation. Supports fractional representation.

2480. Adams, John Quincy (Mass.). "Debate on Censuring Mr. Adams," *Congressional Globe, Appendix.* 27th Cong., 2nd Sess. (4 Feb., 5 Feb. 1842) pp. 975-980; 980-983. Continues his defense. Maintains that there is a conspiracy against himself, the right of petition, freedom of the press and the confidence of the Post Office. Justifies any acrimony against his accusers. Discusses the bias of the reports in the press. Presents documentary evidence of the Post Office censoring incendiary publications. Discusses the resolutions of the Secretary of the Navy recommending dissolution of the Union.

2481. Adams, John Quincy (Mass.). "The District of Columbia," *Congressional Globe.* 27th Cong., 2nd Sess. (9 June 1842) pp. 569-570. Opposes restricting the right of suffrage in the town of Alexandria to free white males. Maintains that universal suffrage applies to men of all color; discusses the rights of colored men in Massachusetts.

2482. Adams, John Quincy (Mass.). "General Appropriation Bill," *Congressional Globe.* 27th Cong., 2nd Sess. (14 Apr., 15 Apr. 1842) pp. 423-

425; 426-429. Responds to Mr. Ingersoll's (Pa.) and Mr. Wise's (Va.) remarks concerning relations with Great Britain and Mexico. Challenges arguments concerning the right of search; maintains that there is no exemption from the right of search on the high seas. Discusses the possibility of war with Great Britain and Mexico and the perpetuation of slavery and the slave trade. Opposes annexation of Texas into the Union.

2483. Adams, John Quincy (Mass.). "The Navy Appropriation Bill," *Congressional Globe.* 27th Cong., 2nd Sess. (22 July 1842) pp. 777-778. Defends the number of Massachusetts' citizens in the navy; also maintains that his administration was not responsible for the present number of captains and commanders.

2484. Adams, John Quincy (Mass.). "Question of Privilege," *Congressional Globe.* 27th Cong., 2nd Sess. (25 Jan., 26 Jan., 28 Jan., 2 Feb., 3 Feb., 4 Feb. 1842) pp. 170; 176-177; 192-194; 202; 207-210; 211-212. Various remarks and speeches in his defense against accusations of perjury and high treason. Maintains that his petitioners had the right to petition to dissolve the Union. Also maintains that the House has no authority to try or punish him; contends that slaveholders are not the impartial jurors guaranteed by the Constitution. Complains about the *Intelligencer*'s reporting of his case.

2485. Adams, John Quincy (Mass.). Remarks on Army Reductions, *Congressional Globe.* 27th Cong., 2nd Sess. (6 June 1842) pp. 585-586. Supports reducing the size of the standing army. Reviews the history of reductions and increases; makes recommendations for retrenchment.

2486. Adams, John Quincy (Mass.). Remarks on Requesting Documents from the President, *Congressional Globe.* 27th Cong., 2nd Sess. (4 June 1842) pp. 580-581. Maintains that the House has the power to request documents from heads of departments, with the exception of papers concerning foreign negotiations. Bases arguments upon the power of impeachment and an examination of Jefferson's memoirs.

2487. Adams, John Quincy (Mass.). Remarks on the Death of William S. Hastings, *Congressional Globe.* 27th Cong., 2nd Sess. (27 June 1842) pp. 689-690. Announcement and remarks upon the death of William S. Hastings, a Representative from Massachusetts.

2488. Adams, John Quincy (Mass.). Remarks on the Executive and Legislative Differences, *Congressional Globe.* 27th Cong., 2nd Sess. (10 Aug. 1842) pp. 871-873. Remarks on differences of opinion of the Legislative branches and the Executive branch over the bankrupt act, the establishment of a national bank, retrenchment, the apportionment bill, distribution of the public lands, and the tariff.

2489. Adams, John Quincy (Mass.). Remarks on the Provisional Tariff, *Congressional Globe.* 27th Cong., 2nd Sess. (19 Aug. 1842) p. 915. Remarks on the legality and authority of the President to levy duties; maintains that the bill is an *ex post facto* criminal law.

2490. Adams, John Quincy (Mass.). Remarks on the Report of the New York Custom-house, *Congressional Globe.* 27th Cong., 2nd Sess. (30 Apr. 1842) pp. 460-461. Defends the manufacturers of Lowell; questions the relationship between Governor Poindexter, the New York customhouse, and the tariff.

2491. Appleton, Nathan (Mass.). "Tariff and Compromise Act," *Congressional Globe, Appendix.* 27th Cong., 2nd Sess. (5 July 1842) pp. 798-799. Supports protective tariffs to raise the necessary revenue. Discusses the Compromise Act of 1833, its history and foundation; maintains that the act is inconvenient, unsafe, abandons discrimination, and is not a binding compact. Presents arguments in support of discrimination and the protective policy; discusses some specific duties. Same speech reprinted in *Congressional Globe, Appendix,* "The Tariff Bill," pp. 575-577 (entry **2492**).

2492. Appleton, Nathan (Mass.). "The Tariff Bill," *Congressional Globe, Appendix.* 27th Cong., 2nd Sess. (5 July 1842) pp. 575-577. Same speech reprinted in *Congressional Globe, Appendix,* "Tariff and Compromise Act," pp. 798-799. See entry **2491** for abstract.

2493. Bates, Isaac C. (Mass.). "The Apportionment Bill," *Congressional Globe, Appendix.* 27th Cong., 2nd Sess. (6 June 1842) pp. 792-794. Supports making the district system the uniform mode of electing Representatives. Argues that Congress has the constitutional power to make this rule and that the states are bound to conform their legislation to it. Maintains that the states should do the actual districting. Reviews the advantages of the district system over the general-ticket system in providing a more constitutional and fairer representation. Summary of speech in *Congressional Globe,* pp. 583-584.

2494. Bates, Isaac C. (Mass.). "Navy Pension Fund," *Congressional Globe.* 27th Cong., 2nd Sess. (9 Aug. 1842) p. 863. Opposes amending the pension act of 1837 to reduce benefits; maintains that the government should honor the original contract.

2495. Bates, Isaac C. (Mass.). Remarks on the Armory Superintendents, *Congressional Globe.* 27th Cong., 2nd Sess. (25 June, 29 June 1842) pp. 683-684; 691-692. Various remarks support civil superintendents for the Springfield and Harper's Ferry armories. Discusses the advantages of civil over military appointment and the unhappiness of the armorers under military discipline.

2496. Bates, Isaac C. (Mass.). Remarks on the Exchequer Bank, *Congressional Globe.* 27th Cong., 2nd Sess. (4 Jan. 1842) p. 88. Supports referring the plan for an Exchequer Bank to a select committee; maintains that the committee would offer an impartial and respectful consideration of the report.

2497. Briggs, George N. (Mass.). "Veto of the Provisional Tariff Bill," *Congressional Globe, Appendix.* 27th Cong., 2nd Sess. (30 June 1842) pp. 765-767. Defends the provisional tariff bill. Analyzes the objections of the President and the claim that it abrogates and suspends existing laws. Discusses the origins and history of the compromise act and the distribution act and their effects upon the country. Objects to giving the proceeds of the public lands to the U.S. treasury. Discusses the veto power.

2498. Calhoun, William B. (Mass.). "The Reorganization of the Army," *Congressional Globe.* 27th Cong., 2nd Sess. (2 Aug. 1842) pp. 831-832. Objects to putting a military superintendent in charge of the armories. Gives an example of the oppression practiced upon the armorers at Springfield.

2499. Campbell, John (S.C.). "Appropriation Bill," *Congressional Globe, Appendix.* 27th Cong., 2nd Sess. (15 Apr. 1842) pp. 333-338. General remarks support the resolutions against John Quincy Adams for presenting a petition advocating the dissolution of the Union. Defends slavery. In response to remarks of Mr. Adams, discusses the right of petition, the 21st rule, the progress of the South, the history of African slavery, emancipation, the Anti-slavery Society, and abolition petitions.

2500. Choate, Rufus (Mass.). "The Bankrupt Law," *Congressional Globe.* 27th Cong., 2nd Sess. (27 Jan. 1842) p. 179. Supports the bankrupt law, particularly the retrospective part of the law. Maintains that it would benefit creditors as well as debtors, and that it is a humane measure.

2501. Choate, Rufus (Mass.). "Courts of the United States," *Congressional Globe, Appendix.* 27th Cong., 2nd Sess. (10 May 1842) pp. 536-542. Supports giving the district courts qualified jurisdiction in disputes arising upon the laws of nations, and affecting the subjects of foreign governments domiciled abroad. Justifies the constitutional history and authority for the bill; answers opponents' objections. Summary of speech in *Congressional Globe,* p. 485.

2502. Choate, Rufus (Mass.). "The Naval Appropriation Bill," *Congressional Globe.* 27th Cong., 2nd Sess. (15 June 1842) pp. 630-631. Objects to prohibiting new appointments in the navy.

2503. Choate, Rufus (Mass.). "Retrenchment and Reform," *Congressional Globe.* 27th Cong., 2nd Sess. (14 Mar. 1842) p. 316. Advocates increasing the tariff above the maximum of the Compromise Act of 1833. Maintains that government has the constitutional power to protect and encourage American industry.

2504. Cushing, Caleb (Mass.). "Army Bill," *Congressional Globe, Appendix.* 27th Cong., 2nd Sess. (26 May 1842) pp. 778-781. Opposes the proposed reduction of the army; maintains that the proposition was not supported by any executive departments or the Committee on Naval and Military Affairs. Discusses the wisdom of reducing defenses considering the negotiations with

Mexico and Great Britain. Discusses reductions in naval appropriations. Addresses opponents' arguments; indicates political implications. Summary of speech in *Congressional Globe*, pp. 542-543.

2505. Cushing, Caleb (Mass.). "Navy Appropriation Bill," *Congressional Globe, Appendix.* 27th Cong., 2nd Sess. (17 May, 20 May, 21 May 1842) pp. 922-928. Various speeches and remarks support permanent appropriations for the navy. Recommends a permanent judge advocate to reduce court-martial expenses. Reviews the numbers of naval stations, ships, and officers, and defends expenditures on construction, equipment, provisioning, and sailing; suggests means of economy. Compares the pay of British and American naval officers and seamen. Summary of speeches in *Congressional Globe*, pp. 508-509 and 521-522.

2506. Cushing, Caleb (Mass.). "New York Custom House Reports," *Congressional Globe.* 27th Cong., 2nd Sess. (4 May, 9 May 1842) pp. 478-479; 481-482. Various remarks assert that the Committee on Expenditures acted improperly when it brought the report before Congress; maintains that the report should have reached the House through the executive department. Addresses opponents' arguments. Demonstrates that the President has the constitutional power to appoint offices to investigate abuses and procure information; presents historical precedents.

2507. Cushing, Caleb (Mass.). "Reduction of the Navy," *Congressional Globe, Appendix.* 27th Cong., 2nd Sess. (21 July, 3 Aug. 1842) pp. 828-830. Defends the appropriations to meet the needs of the navy. Maintains that it is up to Congress to legislate to provide and limit a naval peace establishment. Second speech opposes the reorganization, or reduction, of the army. Discusses standing armies, public finances, and the Indian frontier.

2508. Cushing, Caleb (Mass.). Remarks on Obligations to Communicate Requested Papers, *Congressional Globe.* 27th Cong., 2nd Sess. (4 June 1842) p. 580. Maintains that the President has the right to refuse to communicate papers according to his discretion and considerations of state.

2509. Cushing, Caleb (Mass.). Remarks on the Frauds at the New York Customhouse, *Congressional Globe.* 27th Cong., 2nd Sess. (8 June 1842) pp. 599-600. Remarks on the report from the commissioners appointed to investigate the affairs of the New York customhouse. Discusses the authority of the government to investigate, the alleged injustices, frauds committed upon the revenue at the New York customhouse, and the allegations against the eastern manufacturers.

2510. Cushing, Caleb (Mass.). Remarks on the Provisional Tariff, *Congressional Globe.* 27th Cong., 2nd Sess. (19 Aug. 1842) pp. 915-916. Supports the President following the advice of the Attorney General to continue to collect duties; maintains that present revenue laws are sufficient to collect duties. Discusses objections and intentions of Mr. Adams (Mass.).

2511. Cushing, Caleb (Mass.). "The Tariff Bill," *Congressional Globe, Appendix.* 27th Cong., 2nd Sess. (22 June 1842) pp. 919-922. Supports the expediency and necessity of a tariff bill. Argues for giving protective advantages to various industries. Discusses proposed tariffs on carpeting, wool and woolens, blankets, cotton, silk, flax, iron, copper, and leather. Discusses the distribution of the proceeds of the public lands. Maintains that the conditions of the distribution act should not be tied to the tariff legislation.

2512. Cushing, Caleb (Mass.). "The Tariff Bill," *Congressional Globe.* 27th Cong., 2nd Sess. (27 Aug. 1842) p. 953. Supports the tariff bill to provide relief to the government and country and to reassure the Whigs. Defends the need to postpone distribution for later consideration.

2513. Cushing, Caleb (Mass.). "The Tariff," *Congressional Globe.* 27th Cong., 2nd Sess. (10 June 1842) p. 616. Advocates extending the current tariff laws another month to enable further debate on a permanent tariff.

2514. Cushing, Caleb (Mass.). "Veto of the Provisional Tariff Bill," *Congressional Globe, Appendix.* 27th Cong., 2nd Sess. (29 June, 6 July, 9 Aug., 11 Aug. 1842) pp. 891-894. Various remarks discuss the veto of the provisional tariff bill. Addresses colleagues objections; discusses the veto power. Examines the relationship of the bill to the distribution of the land fund and the assumption of the state debts. Later remarks (partially summarized in *Congressional Globe,* pp. 724-725) defend the right of the President to communicate his reasons for signing a bill; maintains that signing a bill is a legislative function according to the Constitution and Federalist papers No. 47-51, by Mr. Madison.

2515. Hudson, Charles (Mass.). "Reference of the President's Message," *Congressional Globe.* 27th Cong., 2nd Sess. (27 Dec., 28 Dec. 1841) pp. 60-62; 64-65. Responds to Mr. Rhett (S.C.); supports the power of Congress to regulate commerce absolutely and unconditionally. Maintains that Congress has the authority for protecting manufactures that were recommended in the Executive message. Discusses the value of protection to agriculture and the general prosperity of the country; addresses opponents' objections.

2516. Hudson, Charles (Mass.). "The Tariff Bill," *Congressional Globe, Appendix.* 27th Cong., 2nd Sess. (8 July 1842) pp. 928-932. Supports protectionism and the tariff bill. Reviews the reasons for different rates of duty. Defends the proposed rates of duties; compares with duties under the administrations of Jackson and Van Buren. Discusses competition with Europe, the condition of her laborers, and the need for discriminating and countervailing duties. Maintains that protecting manufactures would benefit agriculture and the various geographical sections of the country.

2517. Marshall, Thomas F. (Ky.). "Censure of Mr. Adams," *Congressional Globe, Appendix.* 27th Cong., 2nd Sess. (25 Jan., 26 Jan., 28 Jan. 1842) pp. 983-989. Proposes and justifies resolutions for the censure of John Quincy Adams for presenting a petition for the dissolution of the Union. Maintains that he is not charging Mr. Adams with perjury and high treason, but rather with contempt. Reviews earlier comments from Mr. Wise (Va.); maintains that the objects of the resolutions are not sectional and have nothing to do with Great Britain. Discusses slavery petitions, and the concept of a peaceable dissolution of the Union. Addresses Mr. Adams' defense.

2518. Parmenter, William (Mass.). Remarks on Appropriations for the Navy, *Congressional Globe.* 27th Cong., 2nd Sess. (21 May 1842) pp. 522-523. Opposes the proposed appropriations as extravagant and unpopular. Maintains that much of the opposition to the navy is due to its organization and the creation of the Board of Navy Commissioners.

2519. Saltonstall, Leverett (Mass.). "The Loan Bill," *Congressional Globe.* 27th Cong., 2nd Sess. (17 Mar. 1842) p. 331. Addresses the progress of the Committee on Manufactures on the tariff bill. Blames the past administration for the country's financial distress.

2520. Saltonstall, Leverett (Mass.). Remarks on the President's Veto of the Tariff Bill, *Congressional Globe.* 27th Cong., 2nd Sess. (29 June 1842) p. 696. Objects to the President's use of the veto power.

2521. Underwood, Joseph R. (Ky.). "Mr. Marshall's Resolution," *Congressional Globe, Appendix.* 27th Cong., 2nd Sess. (27 Jan. 1842) pp. 234-240. Opposes the resolutions to censure John Quincy Adams for presenting a petition praying for the dissolution of the Union. Discusses previous attempts to censure members of the House; maintains that the House does not have jurisdiction or authority in this case. Examines constitutional privilege and the *ex post facto* nature of the resolutions. Discusses the right of petition, and Adams' commitment to this right. Denounces "gag-laws" and the 21st rule. Discusses the deleterious effects of the dissolution of the Union upon slavery.

2522. Winthrop, Robert C. (Mass.). "Protective Tariff," *Congressional Globe, Appendix.* 27th Cong., 2nd Sess. (30 Dec. 1841) pp. 91-97. Supports referring the issue of the protective tariff to the Committee on Manufactures. Reviews arguments for and against protectionism, including constitutionality, necessity and propriety. Considers the compromise act; maintains that the tariff question is not a controversy between New England and the other parts of the Union. Discusses the effects of the foreign markets, particularly on cotton. Summary in *Congressional Globe,* pp. 79-80.

2523. "An Act to Annex a Part of the Town of Tiverton in the State of Rhode Island, to the Collection District of Fall River in the State of Massachusetts," *Statutes at Large,* Vol. V (9 Aug. 1842) p. 504.

2524. U.S. House. *Armories - Springfield and Harper's Ferry.* 27th Cong., 2nd Sess. (H.Doc.289). [Washington]: 1842. 3 pg. (Serial Set 405). Reply to the House's resolution inquiring into the discharge of the workmen at the Springfield and Harper's Ferry armories and the closing of those shops.

2525. U.S. House. *Report of the Board Convened at Springfield, (Mass.) August 30, 1841, to Examine into the Condition and Management of Springfield Armory.* 27th Cong., 2nd Sess. (H.Doc.207). [Washington: 1842]. 46 pg. (Serial Set 404). Detailed report describes the armory and its operations, and makes recommendations for improvements. Includes documentation, testimony of the inspectors, and detailed tables of payrolls, labor costs, and other expenses.

2526. U.S. House. *Resolution of the Legislature of Massachusetts, upon the Subject of the Apportionment of Representatives under the Sixth Census.* 27th Cong., 2nd Sess. (H.Doc.69). [Washington: 1842]. 1 pg. (Serial Set 402).

2527. U.S. House. *Resolutions of the Legislature of Massachusetts, respecting the Claim of Massachusetts upon the United States for Military Services.* 27th Cong., 2nd Sess. (H.Doc.97). [Washington: 1842]. 1 pg. (Serial Set 402). Resolutions support the claim.

2528. U.S. House. *Springfield Manufacturing Company.* 27th Cong., 2nd Sess. (H.Rpt.6). [Washington: 1841]. 4 pg. (Serial Set 407). Committee of Claims concurs with the report of 1835 in favor of the claim of the Springfield Manufacturing Company. Reprints the earlier report - H.rp.21 (23-2) 276 (entry **2186**). Report of 1835 also printed as H.rp.372 (25-2) 334 (entry **2381**), and H.rp.305 (26-1) 371 (**2447**) and as part of H.rp.40 (24-1) 293 (entry **2257**).

2529. U.S. Senate. *Memorial of a Number of Distillers of Spirit in Boston, Mass., Praying that the Drawback on Domestic Spirit Manufactured from Foreign Molasses May Not Be Abolished.* 27th Cong., 2nd Sess. (S.Doc.379). [Washington]: Thomas Allen, Print., [1842]. 5 pg. (Serial Set 399).

2530. U.S. Senate. *Report from the Secretary of War, in Compliance with a Resolution of the Senate in Relation to the Removal of the Superintendents of the Public Armories at Springfield and Harper's Ferry.* 27th Cong., 2nd Sess. (S.Doc.345). [Washington]: Thomas Allen, Print., [1842]. 1 pg. (Serial Set 399). Reports that the Superintendents have been removed; no successors have been appointed.

2531. U.S. Senate. [Report on the Relief of the Owners of the Ship Lexington of Nantucket]. 27th Cong., 2nd Sess. (S.Doc.326). [Washington]: Thomas Allen, Print., [1842]. 2 pg. (Serial Set 398). Unfavorable report of the Committee on Commerce for the relief of the owners of the ship Lexington; reviews the circumstances and the law in question.

27TH CONGRESS, 3RD SESSION

2532. Adams, John Quincy (Mass.). "Assumption of State Debts," *Congressional Globe.* 27th Cong., 3rd Sess. (10 Feb. 1843) pp. 269-270. Requests that the proposition be fully and impartially considered. Maintains that the debts incurred by the states should be paid on the basis of morality, sound policy, and expediency. Discusses the alternative consequence of incurring war.

2533. Adams, John Quincy (Mass.). "General Jackson's Fine," *Congressional Globe.* 27th Cong., 3rd Sess. (5 Jan., 6 Jan. 1843) pp. 123; 128-129. Remarks on the bill to refund the fine imposed on General Jackson at the battle of New Orleans. Maintains that the bill is a party bill, which should not reproach the judicial tribunal that imposed the fine. Discusses implications of passage and the recommendations of the President.

2534. Adams, John Quincy (Mass.). "Presentation of Washington's Sword and Franklin's Staff," *Congressional Globe.* 27th Cong., 3rd Sess. (8 Feb. 1843) pp. 254-255. Remarks and resolutions express appreciation and acceptance to Samuel T. Washington for the present of the battle sword used by George Washington and the cane used by Benjamin Franklin. Documents authenticity of ownership.

2535. Burnell, Barker (Mass.). "The General Appropriation Bill," *Congressional Globe.* 27th Cong., 3rd Sess. (22 Dec. 1842) pp. 75-76. Supports continuing funding for the coastal survey. Reviews advantages pertaining to discoveries, avoiding lost and damaged property, and the preservation of commerce; maintains that it is wise economy.

2536. Choate, Rufus (Mass.). Defense of Remarks on the Oregon Bill, *Congressional Globe.* 27th Cong., 3rd Sess. (6 Feb. 1843) pp. 243-244. Corrects an editorial in the *Globe* concerning his statements on Mitchell's map and the northwest boundary.

2537. Choate, Rufus (Mass.). "The Oregon Bill," *Congressional Globe, Appendix.* 27th Cong., 3rd Sess. (3 Feb. 1843) pp. 222-229. Details his objections to that portion of the bill which grants lands to future settlers of the Oregon territory; maintains that it infringes upon the existing convention with Great Britain. Disregards the claim that England has already infringed upon the convention. Responds to remarks and accusations of Mr. Benton (Mo.) concerning the withholding of relevant communications and the treaty of 1842. Discusses the general character and merits of the treaty as a treaty of boundary; addresses objections.

2538. Choate, Rufus (Mass.). "The Oregon Territory," *Congressional Globe.* 27th Cong., 3rd Sess. (18 Jan. 1843) pp. 171-172. Opposes the proposed grant of lands to settlers; maintains that it would violate the treaty with Great Britain.

Discusses relations with Great Britain pertaining to the Oregon territory and the northeastern boundary line.

2539. Cushing, Caleb (Mass.). "The Bankrupt Law," *Congressional Globe.* 27th Cong., 3rd Sess. (27 Dec. 1842) pp. 87-88. Opposes the repeal of the bankrupt law. Responds to remarks made by Mr. Arnold (Tenn.); discusses the political aspects of the proposal.

2540. Cushing, Caleb (Mass.). "The British Treaty," *Congressional Globe, Appendix.* 27th Cong., 3rd Sess. (28 Feb. 1843) pp. 214-220. Analyzes the provisions of the Ashburton treaty that call for legislation by Congress. Reviews the history of negotiations concerning 1) the boundaries between the northern United States and Great Britain and 2) the suppression of the African slave trade and the right of search on the high seas. Includes the treaty and annexation of the treaty between Great Britain, Austria, France, Prussia, and Russia, for the suppression of the African slave trade.

2541. Cushing, Caleb (Mass.). "Comet and Encomium," *Congressional Globe.* 27th Cong., 3rd Sess. (13 Feb. 1843) pp. 276-277. Supports paying the entitled claimants indemnities received from the British government for the loss of slaves from the Comet and Encomium at Nassau. Addresses objections.

2542. Cushing, Caleb (Mass.). "The Exchequer Bill," *Congressional Globe.* 27th Cong., 3rd Sess. (24 Jan. 1843) pp. 197-198. Supports the exchequer plan recommended by the President; maintains that with the demise of the United States Bank, the country demands legislation on the currency and the safekeeping and disbursement of the public money. Addresses objections.

2543. Cushing, Caleb (Mass.). "General Jackson's Fine," *Congressional Globe.* 27th Cong., 3rd Sess. (5 Jan. 1843) pp. 122-123. Supports marking the anniversary of the victory of New Orleans by restoring Andrew Jackson's fine.

2544. Cushing, Caleb (Mass.). "Plan of the Exchequer," *Congressional Globe.* 27th Cong., 3rd Sess. (9 Jan. 1843) p. 135. Requests that the bill be refereed to the Committee of the Whole to take up the resolution for practical legislation.

2545. Cushing, Caleb (Mass.). Remarks on the British Treaty, *Congressional Globe.* 27th Cong., 3rd Sess. (19 Jan. 1843) pp. 176-177. Briefly remarks on House rules governing appropriations for carrying out the treaty.

2546. Cushing, Caleb (Mass.). "Repeal of the Bankrupt Law," *Congressional Globe.* 27th Cong., 3rd Sess. (19 Jan. 1843) pp. 178-180. Responds to opponents' charges. Addresses the dissension among the Whig party; defends and supports the Tyler administration. Maintains that the people oppose a United States Bank.

2547. Cushing, Caleb (Mass.). "Treasury Notes and Loans," *Congressional Globe.* 27th Cong., 3rd Sess. (20 Feb. 1843) p. 319. Supports the exchequer bill. Presents his objections to the alternate proposition before the House on the currency and deposits.

2548. Cushing, Caleb (Mass.). "Treaty of Washington," *Congressional Globe.* 27th Cong., 3rd Sess. (8 Mar. 1843) p. 369. Remarks on the provisions of the Treaty of Washington concerning the right to search. Maintains that no government has the right to visit or search U.S. ships.

2549. Saltonstall, Leverett (Mass.). "The Bankrupt Law," *Congressional Globe.* 27th Cong., 3rd Sess. (27 Dec. 1842) p. 86. Opposes the repeal of the bankrupt law; maintains that it is popular and operating favorably.

2550. Winthrop, Robert C. (Mass.). "The Bankrupt Law," *Congressional Globe.* 27th Cong., 3rd Sess. (20 Dec. 1842) pp. 66-67. Opposes the unconditional repeal of the bankrupt law; maintains that Congress has a duty to establish a uniform system of bankruptcy.

2551. Winthrop, Robert C. (Mass.). "The Exchequer," *Congressional Globe, Appendix.* 27th Cong., 3rd Sess. (25 Jan. 1843) pp. 112-117. Opposes the report of the Committee of Ways and Means concerning the exchequer bill. Maintains that Congress has an obligation to make provision for the collection, custody and disbursement of the public moneys. Reviews objectionable features of the exchequer plan; discusses the Committee report. Defends Daniel Webster against political misconstructions, particularly concerning the Whigs of Massachusetts. Summary of speech in *Congressional Globe*, pp. 203-204.

2552. U.S. House. *Nantucket Marine Camel Company.* 27th Cong., 3rd Sess. (H.Rpt.213). [Washington: 1843]. 3 pg. (Serial Set 427). Report of the Committee on Commerce supports appropriations for the production of "camels," which can assist in the navigation of obstructed harbors and rivers.

2553. U.S. Senate. [Claim of the New England Mississippi Land Company]. 27th Cong., 3rd Sess. (S.Doc.18). [Washington]: Thomas Allen, Print., [1843]. 10 pg. (Serial Set 414). Favorable report of the Committee on the Judiciary on the petition of the New England Mississippi Land Company; adopts and concurs with an earlier Senate report, S.doc.197 (24-2) 298. Reprints S.doc.197 (24-2) 298 (entry **2313**), S.doc.205 (23-1) 240 (entry **2141**), and Pub.land 1216 (23-1) ASP 033 (entry **2116**).

28TH CONGRESS, 1ST SESSION

2554. "Slave Representation," *Congressional Globe.* 28th Cong., 1st Sess. (23 Jan., 8 Feb. 1844) pp. 180; 249. Brief debate on the Massachusetts' resolutions to base apportionment on only the number of free persons, thereby abrogating slave representation.

2555. Adams, John Quincy (Mass.). "Amendment of the Constitution," *Congressional Globe.* 28th Cong., 1st Sess. (22 Dec. 1843) pp. 66-68. Supports receiving the resolutions from the Massachusetts Legislature requesting an amendment to the Constitution whereby apportionment and taxation would be based on the number of free persons. Discusses the right of petition and threats of dissolution of the Union.

2556. Adams, John Quincy (Mass.). "Death of Hon. B. Burnell," *Congressional Globe.* 28th Cong., 1st Sess. (14 Dec. 1843) pp. 36-37. Announcement, remarks, and resolutions on the death of Barker Burnell, a Representative from Massachusetts.

2557. Adams, John Quincy (Mass.). "Eastern Harbors Bill," *Congressional Globe.* 28th Cong., 1st Sess. (13 June 1844) p. 723. Briefly remarks to appeal the decision against reconsidering the vote on the eastern harbors bill; maintains that reconsideration of the bill with the President's objections is required by the Constitution.

2558. Adams, John Quincy (Mass.). "Petition of a Runaway Negro," *Congressional Globe.* 28th Cong., 1st Sess. (29 Dec. 1843) pp. 88-89. Defends the freeman confined to jail and advertised to be sold to pay for his jail fees; advocates abolishing this mode of imprisonment.

2559. Adams, John Quincy (Mass.). "Petitions," *Congressional Globe.* 28th Cong., 1st Sess. (21 Dec. 1843) pp. 61-62. Remarks on petitions opposed to the transmission of the mails upon the Sabbath; maintains that they should be received, read and referred.

2560. Bates, Isaac C. (Mass.). "Protective System," *Congressional Globe, Appendix.* 28th Cong., 1st Sess. (21 Feb. 1844) pp. 294-298. Strongly supports the protective system. Reviews the history of the system, including its original support by South Carolina and rejection by Massachusetts. Discusses the advantages of protectionism to labor, the stability of business, and the general public benefit. Defends manufacturers. Addresses objections by Mr. Woodbury (N.H.) concerning commercial and navigating interests. Summary of speech in *Congressional Globe*, pp. 308-310.

2561. Bates, Isaac C. (Mass.). Remarks on the Death of Barker Burnell, *Congressional Globe.* 28th Cong., 1st Sess. (14 Dec. 1843) p. 36. Announcement, remarks and resolutions on the death of the Hon. Barker Burnell, a Representative from Massachusetts.

2562. Black, Edward J. (Ga.). "Report of the Committee of Elections," *Congressional Globe, Appendix.* 28th Cong., 1st Sess. (12 Feb. 1844) pp. 204-206. Supports the discussion of the consequences of sustaining the districting act by reviewing the history of censure and expulsion in Congress, including the cases of Matthew Lyon (Vt.) and John Quincy Adams (Mass.). Reviews Adams' role in the 1807 case of John Smith.

2563. Choate, Rufus (Mass.). "The Oregon Question," *Congressional Globe.* 28th Cong., 1st Sess. (22 Feb. 1844) pp. 314-315. Supports continuing the existing convention concerning the settlement of the Oregon territory. Maintains that abrogating the convention is unnecessary, imprudent, and could lead to war; favors negotiation.

2564. Choate, Rufus (Mass.). "Oregon Territory," *Congressional Globe, Appendix.* 28th Cong., 1st Sess. (21 Mar. 1844) pp. 583-588. Opposes annulling the convention for the common occupation of the Oregon territory. Majority of speech replies to Mr. Buchanan (Pa.). Maintains that there is no immediate necessity, that annulment would have injurious effects upon negotiations, and that a treaty may not be produced; discusses consequences. Reviews historical support and success of the convention. Discusses the occupation of agricultural land in Oregon; maintains that the Hudson Bay Company is not an obstacle. Partial summary of speech in *Congressional Globe*, pp. 415-416.

2565. Choate, Rufus (Mass.). "The Tariff," *Congressional Globe, Appendix.* 28th Cong., 1st Sess. (12 Apr., 15 Apr. 1844) pp. 641-650. Supports protectionism. Presents a detailed history of the origin and debate of the law of 1789 in which the principle of protection was established and maintained. Reviews extent and causes of the growth of the manufacturing interests from 1789 to 1816. Addresses the adequacy of the duties of 1789 to 1842 and the fluctuations of imports and revenue during those years. Advocates stability and permanency. Defends Massachusetts against charges. Partial summary of speech in *Congressional Globe*, pp. 530-531, 536-537.

2566. Choate, Rufus (Mass.). "The Tariff," *Congressional Globe, Appendix.* 28th Cong., 1st Sess. (31 May 1844) pp. 753-757. Responds to Mr. McDuffie's (S.C.) comments on Mr. Choate's earlier speech. Defends the views presented in his earlier speech, in particular his contention that the law of 1789 was a protective measure. Defends choice of speeches of Mr. Fitzsimmons (Pa.) as representative of that debate.

2567. Hudson, Charles (Mass.). "Report on the Rules," *Congressional Globe.* 28th Cong., 1st Sess. (18 Jan. 1844) p. 166. Supports the fundamental right to petition and have that petition considered; opposes the 21st rule.

2568. Winthrop, Robert C. (Mass.). "Abolition Petitions," *Congressional Globe, Appendix.* 28th Cong., 1st Sess. (23 Jan., 24 Jan. 1844) pp. 290-294. Opposes the 21st rule limiting the reception or consideration of abolitionist petitions; maintains that the rule is inconsistent, unwarranted, subversive, unconstitutional, and sets bad precedence. Contends that the right of petition includes the obligation of consideration. Argues that the framers of the Constitution intended the right of petition as a constitutional right. Illustrates that English history also recognized it as an inherent right. Partial summary of speech in *Congressional Globe*, pp. 183-184.

2569. Winthrop, Robert C. (Mass.). "Oregon Territory," *Congressional Globe, Appendix.* 28th Cong., 1st Sess. (18 Mar. 1844) pp. 318-322. Opposes terminating the convention on joint occupancy; maintains that it is ill timed in view of the domestic condition and relations with the British government. Refutes claims that Oregon is only a western interest; discusses the territorial title; advocates negotiation. Defends the Treaty of Washington; maintains that the British government acted fairly and the treaty had the support of the people. Remarks on the annexation of Texas.

2570. Winthrop, Robert C. (Mass.). "Reference of President's Message," *Congressional Globe.* 28th Cong., 1st Sess. (19 Dec. 1843) p. 53. Remarks on the appropriate committee for the internal improvements bill; discusses northern support for the western legislation.

2571. U.S. House. *Custom-House and Post Office at Fall River.* 28th Cong., 1st Sess. (H.Rpt.570). [Washington]: Blair & Rives, Print., [1844]. 1 pg. (Serial Set 447). Report of the Committee on Commerce supports appropriations to obtain the site for the customhouse and post office.

2572. U.S. House. *Massachusetts Resolutions.* 28th Cong., 1st Sess. (H.Rpt.404). [Washington]: Blair & Rives, Printers, [1844]. 121 pg. (Serial Set 446). Report on the Massachusetts resolutions concerning apportionment and taxation according to the number of free persons. Debate over whether slave representation is against the principles of popular representation as specified in the Declaration of Independence and the Constitution. Contains reports representing the views of various members of the Select Committee on the Massachusetts Resolutions as well as the *Journal of the Select Committee on the Massachusetts Resolutions.*

2573. U.S. House. *Resolutions of the Legislature of Massachusetts, concerning the Annexation of Texas.* 28th Cong., 1st Sess. (H.Doc.238). [Washington]: Blair & Rives, Print., [1844]. 1 pg. (Serial Set 443). Resolutions oppose the annexation. Same as S.doc.219 (28-1) 434 (entry **2580**).

2574. U.S. House. *Resolutions of the Legislature of Massachusetts, against the Annexation of Texas to the United States.* 28th Cong., 1st Sess. (H.Doc.21). [Washington]: Blair & Rives, Printers, [1843]. 1 pg. (Serial Set 441). Same as S.doc.61 (28-1) 432 (entry **2581**).

2575. U.S. House. *Resolutions of the Legislature of Massachusetts, Recommending an Amendment of the Constitution.* 28th Cong., 1st Sess. (H.Doc.27). [Washington]: Blair & Rives, Printers, [1843]. 1 pg. (Serial Set 441). Resolutions recommend that apportionment and taxation be based on the number of free persons.

2576. U.S. House. *Resolutions of the Legislature of the State of Georgia, in Response to Resolves of the Commonwealth of Massachusetts, Proposing an Amendment of the Constitution.* 28th Cong., 1st Sess. (H.Doc.239).

[Washington]: Blair & Rives, Print., [1844]. 2 pg. (Serial Set 443). Resolutions oppose apportionment and taxation based on the number of free persons. Same as S.doc.106 (28-1) 433 (entry **2582**).

2577. U.S. House. *Sale of Land Attached to the Naval Hospital in Chelsea, Massachusetts.* 28th Cong., 1st Sess. (H.Rpt.480). [Washington]: Blair and Rives, Print., [1844]. 1 pg. (Serial Set 446). Report recommends that it is inexpedient to sell the land until it is decided whether and where a national foundry shall be established.

2578. U.S. Senate. *Memorial of a Number of Distillers in Massachusetts, Praying that the Drawback on Spirits Distilled from Foreign Molasses May Not Be Reduced below the Duty on Molasses.* 28th Cong., 1st Sess. (S.Doc.73). Washington: Gales and Seaton, 1844. 8 pg. (Serial Set 432). Includes a legislative history of the duty on molasses and drawbacks on spirits, statistics, and a memorial of Boston merchants engaged in trade with the West Indies.

2579. U.S. Senate. *Memorial of a Number of Merchants of Boston, Massachusetts, Praying that the Drawback on Spirits Distilled from Foreign Molasses May not Be Reduced.* 28th Cong., 1st Sess. (S.Doc.74). Washington: Gales and Seaton, 1844. 2 pg. (Serial Set 432).

2580. U.S. Senate. *Resolutions of the General Assembly of Massachusetts, Adverse to the Annexation of Texas.* 28th Cong., 1st Sess. (S.Doc.219). Washington: Gales and Seaton, 1844. 1 pg. (Serial Set 434). Same as H.doc.238 (28-1) 443 (entry **2573**).

2581. U.S. Senate. *Resolutions of the General Assembly of Massachusetts, Adverse to the Annexation of Texas to the United States.* 28th Cong., 1st Sess. (S.Doc.61). Washington: Gales and Seaton, 1844. 1 pg. (Serial Set 432). Same as H.doc.21 (28-1) 441 (entry **2574**).

2582. U.S. Senate. *Resolutions of the General Assembly of Georgia, Adverse to Any Amendment to the Constitution of the United States Affecting Representation and Direct Taxation.* 28th Cong., 1st Sess. (S.Doc.106). Washington: Gales and Seaton, 1844. 1 pg. (Serial Set 433). Same as H.doc.239 (28-1) 443 (entry **2576**).

2583. U.S. Senate. *Resolutions of the General Assembly of Massachusetts, in Favor of Making Indemnification for French Depredations on the Commerce of the United States Prior to 1800.* 28th Cong., 1st Sess. (S.Doc.60). Washington: Gales and Seaton, 1844. 1 pg. (Serial Set 432).

2584. U.S. Senate. *Resolutions of the Legislature of Massachusetts, in Relation to French Spoliations Prior to 1800.* 28th Cong., 1st Sess. (S.Doc.158). Washington: Gales & Seaton, 1844. 1 pg. (Serial Set 433). Resolutions support speedy satisfaction of the claims.

2585. U.S. Senate. *Resolutions of the Legislature of Massachusetts, in Favor of the Establishment of a Congress of Nations, for the Adjustment of International Disputes.* 28th Cong., 1st Sess. (S.Doc.159). Washington: Gales and Seaton, 1844. 1 pg. (Serial Set 433).

28TH CONGRESS, 2ND SESSION

2586. Adams, John Quincy (Mass.). "Annexation of Texas," *Congressional Globe.* 28th Cong., 2nd Sess. (24 Jan. 1845) pp. 188-189. Summary of speech opposing the annexation of Texas. Addresses opponents' arguments. Maintains that the Louisiana treaty did not cede Texas. Contends he would still be in favor of the acquisition provided it could be obtained with the laws of freedom and with the consent of the owners.

2587. Adams, John Quincy (Mass.). "Oregon Bill," *Congressional Globe.* 28th Cong., 2nd Sess. (31 Jan. 1845) pp. 227-228. Favors giving the twelve month's notice to terminate the joint occupancy. Maintains that this would bring the negotiation to a close and that Great Britain would concede a great deal to avoid war. Advocates postponing further action.

2588. Adams, John Quincy (Mass.). "Territorial Government for Oregon," *Congressional Globe.* 28th Cong., 2nd Sess. (27 Jan. 1845) p. 202. Recommends waiting for Greenhow's book on the history of the territory in dispute and for more information on the state of negotiation before discussing the boundary line. Supports termination of the joint occupancy.

2589. Choate, Rufus (Mass.). "Annexation of Texas," *Congressional Globe.* 28th Cong., 2nd Sess. (18 Feb. 1845) pp. 303-305. Advocates that Congress has no constitutional power to pass a resolution for the admission of Texas into the Union. Discusses points of constitutional law at issue; maintains that the congressional power to admit new states into the Union does not include the power to annex an entire foreign nation.

2590. Choate, Rufus (Mass.). "The New States of Iowa and Florida," *Congressional Globe.* 28th Cong., 2nd Sess. (1 Mar. 1845) p. 379. Opposes the joint bill for the admission of Iowa and Florida; maintains that they should be considered separately. Alludes to the joint resolutions for the annexation of Texas. Objects to two provisions in the constitution of Florida; maintains that there is no constitutional obligation to admit new states into the Union.

2591. Choate, Rufus (Mass.). "Smithsonian Institute," *Congressional Globe, Appendix.* 28th Cong., 2nd Sess. (8 Jan. 1845) pp. 62-65. Opposes the proposal to use the bequest to establish a college; maintains that it is unnecessary and contrary to the previous proceedings of Congress. Supports provisions for experiments in seeds and plants and a corps of lecturers. Proposes that the funds be used to establish a great national library of the history of man and of nature. Presents arguments demonstrating the need, benefits and importance. Summary of speech in *Congressional Globe*, pp. 105-106.

2592. Choate, Rufus (Mass.). "Smithsonian Institution," *Congressional Globe*. 28th Cong., 2nd Sess. (21 Jan. 1845) p. 163. Supports the Library Committee's recommendations for the structure of the board of managers to administer the bequest. Reviews deliberations and former propositions.

2593. Hudson, Charles (Mass.). "Annexation of Texas," *Congressional Globe, Appendix*. 28th Cong., 2nd Sess. (20 Jan. 1845) pp. 333-338. Opposes the annexation of Texas. Defends Massachusetts against charges of hostility to the Union; accuses of the South of the same. Addresses the purported commercial, agricultural and military advantages of the annexation. Objects to the annexation as violating the national faith, treaty stipulations and the Constitution. Maintains that annexation would lead to war and saddle the country with a large debt. Contends that the purpose of the annexation is to extend and strengthen the institution of slavery. Summary of speech in *Congressional Globe*, pp. 159-160.

2594. Williams, Henry (Mass.). "Rhode Island Controversy," *Congressional Globe, Appendix*. 28th Cong., 2nd Sess. (28 Feb. 1845) pp. 277-283. Defends the right of the people of Rhode Island to self-government, including the legal authority to frame and amend their constitution. Supports his position using the Declaration of Independence, quotes from patriots and statesmen, and precedence. Discusses the charter government and its claims of exclusive jurisdiction. Supports the right of free suffrage to all adult males. Discusses consequences of the opposition's doctrine; addresses objections.

2595. Winthrop, Robert C. (Mass.). "Annexation of Texas," *Congressional Globe, Appendix*. 28th Cong., 2nd Sess. (6 Jan. 1845) pp. 394-397. Opposes the annexation of Texas as unconstitutional and contrary to the law of nations; also maintains that it would extend slavery and precipitate a dishonorable war. Addresses constitutional objections to admitting a foreign nation into U.S. boundaries; discusses arguments of Louisiana and Florida precedents. Discusses the power to admit new states and the treaty-making power; maintains that the House has no authority to make treaty compacts with foreign powers. Summary of speech in *Congressional Globe*, pp. 94-95.

2596. Winthrop, Robert C. (Mass.). "Oregon Territory," *Congressional Globe, Appendix*. 28th Cong., 2nd Sess. (1 Feb. 1845) pp. 292-295. Opposes any action concerning the Oregon territory as unwise, ill timed, and impolitic as long as negotiations are pending between the two countries for the settlement of the disputed boundary. Defends the necessity and value of negotiations. Discusses the settlement in the Treaty of Washington. Defends Great Britain against accusations of aggression and encroachment. Remarks upon specific provisions of the bill. Summary of speech in *Congressional Globe*, p. 230.

2597. U.S. House. *Henry Gardner, and Others.* 28th Cong., 2nd Sess. (H.Rpt.164). [Washington]: Blair & Rives, Printers, [1845]. 1 pg. (Serial Set 468). Favorable report of the Committee on the Judiciary to the petition of the New England Mississippi Land Company; adopts and concurs with the 1842-43 report of the Senate (S.doc.18 (27-3) 414) (entry **2553**).

2598. U.S. House. *Letter from the Secretary of the Treasury, Transmitting Statements Showing the Number of Officers, and the Amount of Revenue Collected, at Boston, New York, Philadelphia, and New Orleans, &c.* 28th Cong., 2nd Sess. (H.Doc.97). [Washington: Blair & Rives, Printer, 1845]. 10 pg. (Serial Set 465). Report documents the need for additional inspectors; statistics included.

2599. U.S. House. *Massachusetts Militia.* 28th Cong., 2nd Sess. (H.Rpt.122). [Washington]: Blair & Rives, Print., [1845]. 9 pg. (Serial Set 468). Report of the Committee on Military Affairs on an act to refund the balance due to Massachusetts on claims for services of her militia during the War of 1812. Reviews the origin and previous actions on the claim; maintains that no further balance is due.

2600. U.S. House. *Resolutions of the Legislature of Alabama, Relative to the Proposed Amendment of the Constitution of the United States, by Massachusetts, &c., &c.* 28th Cong., 2nd Sess. (H.Doc.128). [Washington]: Blair & Rives, Print., [1845]. 4 pg. (Serial Set 465). Resolutions against the Massachusetts resolutions to amend the Constitution to limit representation and taxation to free persons.

2601. U.S. House. *Resolutions of the Legislature of Massachusetts, Relative to the Annexation of Texas.* 28th Cong., 2nd Sess. (H.Doc.160). [Washington]: Blair & Rives, Print., [1845]. 11 pg. (Serial Set 466). Report of a joint committee and resolutions of the Legislature oppose the annexation of Texas. Same as S.doc.141 (28-2) 457 (entry **2602**).

2602. U.S. Senate. *Report of a Joint Committee and Resolutions of the General Assembly of Massachusetts Adverse to the Annexation of Texas.* 28th Cong., 2nd Sess. (S.Doc.141). Washington: Gales and Seaton, 1845. 12 pg. (Serial Set 457). Same as H.doc.160 (28-2) 466 (entry **2601**).

29TH CONGRESS, 1ST SESSION

2603. Debate on Sen. Webster's Activities as Secretary of State, *Congressional Globe.* 29th Cong., 1st Sess. (9 Apr., 11 Apr., 13 Apr., 27 Apr. 1946) pp. 636-643; 656-657; 708-710; 729-735. Introduction of resolutions and debate concerning Senator Webster's use of the secret-service fund when he was serving as Secretary of State. The resolutions request Sen. Webster to furnish an account of all payments made from the fund since March 4, 1841. Remarks in support of Sen. Webster by Robert C. Winthrop (Mass.), John Quincy Adams (Mass.), and George Ashmun (Mass.); brief defense by Senator Webster also included.

2604. Adams, John Quincy (Mass.). "American Settlers in Oregon," *Congressional Globe.* 29th Cong., 1st Sess. (13 Apr. 1846) pp. 662-664. Proposes that the boundary line be settled at 54 degrees, 40 minutes. Briefly reviews commissions and treaties affecting title to lands west of the Mississippi, including the Nootka Sound convention of 1790 and Meares' rights of discovery. Maintains that Great Britain forfeited any rights of settlement under the conventions of 1818 and 1827 by omitting to provide for that right.

2605. Adams, John Quincy (Mass.). "Message - Foreign Intercourse," *Congressional Globe.* 29th Cong., 1st Sess. (8 Aug. 1846) pp. 1215-1216. Supports appropriations to negotiate peace with Mexico.

2606. Adams, John Quincy (Mass.). "Oregon," *Congressional Globe.* 29th Cong., 1st Sess. (2 Jan., 9 Feb. 1846) pp. 126-128; 340-342. Discusses the bill to raise two regiments of riflemen. Maintains that measures to protect citizens in Oregon should only be considered after notice is given to Great Britain to terminate the convention of 1827. Advocates termination of the convention; reviews the foundation and question of title and eminent domain. Maintains that actual possession is the best claim to title. Contends that the convention was not a treaty of joint occupancy but rather of free navigation and free commercial intercourse.

2607. Adams, John Quincy (Mass.). "Oregon," *Congressional Globe.* 29th Cong., 1st Sess. (6 Aug. 1846) pp. 1200-1201. Briefly remarks on the bill establishing the territorial government of Oregon; questions why the boundaries were not defined. Also remarks on the treaty and rights of navigation of the Columbia River.

2608. Adams, John Quincy (Mass.). "Personal and Historical," *Congressional Globe.* 29th Cong., 1st Sess. (7 Jan. 1846) pp. 156-157. Defends himself from charges made by Mr. Rhett (S.C.); defends his support of the War of 1812 and reviews the circumstances of his involvement concerning the negotiations and the restoration of slaves taken by the British.

2609. Adams, John Quincy (Mass.). "Question of Privilege," *Congressional Globe.* 29th Cong., 1st Sess. (6 May 1846) p. 769. Remarks on the privilege exempting members of the House from arrest.

2610. Adams, John Quincy (Mass.). Remarks on Revolutionary War Pensions, *Congressional Globe.* 29th Cong., 1st Sess. (17 Feb. 1846) pp. 384-385. Supports amendments designed to facilitate widows obtaining their pensions by eliminating the requirement for unnecessary evidence and the limitation upon the time of marriage.

2611. Adams, John Quincy (Mass.). "Senator Webster," *Congressional Globe.* 29th Cong., 1st Sess. (9 Apr. 1846) pp. 640-642. Details objections against the resolution; advocates that it be pared down to a request for documents from the Department of State. Discusses the benefits of the secret-service fund; explains how the President alone has the power and authority to expend the fund, that the Secretary of State (Webster) could only abuse the fund by order of the President. Discusses impeachment.

2612. Ashmun, George (Mass.). "The Mexican War," *Congressional Globe, Appendix.* 29th Cong., 1st Sess. (27 July 1846) pp. 809-812. Opposes the war with Mexico as a war of conquest and colonization. Reviews the history of the passage of the war bill, the causes leading to the war, the character of the war, and the lack of consultation with Congress. Maintains that the war was caused by the unauthorized and unnecessary movement of troops to the Rio Grande and the march upon Matamoros.

2613. Ashmun, George (Mass.). "Personal Explanation," *Congressional Globe.* 29th Cong., 1st Sess. (13 Apr. 1846) p. 661. Responds to Mr. Yancey's (Ala.) allusions to him; defends Mr. Webster against charges of being a pensioned agent of the manufacturing interest.

2614. Ashmun, George (Mass.). "The Secret-Service Fund," *Congressional Globe.* 29th Cong., 1st Sess. (27 Apr. 1846) pp. 730-733. Defends Mr. Webster against charges of the misuse of the secret-service fund. Discusses the character of the accuser (C.J. Ingersoll, Pa.) and his acquisition of confidential information. Reviews Ingersoll's earlier removal from public office for abuses connected with public moneys.

2615. Davis, John (Mass.). "Duty on Salt," *Congressional Globe.* 29th Cong., 1st Sess. (24 Mar. 1846) pp. 538-539. Supports the memorial from Marblehead that opposes the repeal of the duty upon imported dry fish and the bounties to vessels engaged in cod fishery. Briefly reviews protective policy towards this industry and the need to protect the industry as a nursery of seamen.

2616. Davis, John (Mass.). "Negotiation with Mexico," *Congressional Globe.* 29th Cong., 1st Sess. (10 Aug. 1846) pp. 1220-1221. Questions the need for the two million dollar appropriation to negotiate with Mexico; maintains that the money's true purpose is to acquire additional territory. Supports the clause forbidding slavery in any territory newly acquired from Mexico.

2617. Davis, John (Mass.). "The Tariff," *Congressional Globe, Appendix.* 29th Cong., 1st Sess. (16 July, 17 July 1846) pp. 1107-1115. Opposes reducing the duties on imports. Objects to the bill because revenue is a secondary concern, it would discourage American labor and enterprise while encouraging that of foreign countries, and because it would be devastating to the laborer. Considers the general features of the bill and responds to the positions of the Secretary of the Treasury. Discusses free trade, the European market, competition, the doctrine of twofold taxation, and the need for protectionism. Partial summary of speech in *Congressional Globe*, pp. 1105-1106.

2618. Grinnell, Joseph (Mass.). "Bounty to Fishing Vessels," *Congressional Globe*. 29th Cong., 1st Sess. (25 Apr. 1846) pp. 726-727. Favors allowing the bounty of the owner and crew of the schooner Success, lost at sea. Describes the cod fishery industry; reviews the merits of granting fishing bounties. Reprints most of the memorial from citizens of Marblehead remonstrating against a proposed repeal of the fishing bounty (S.Doc.247 (29-1) 474 (entry **2654**)).

2619. Hudson, Charles (Mass.). "Map of Oregon and Public Printing," *Congressional Globe*. 29th Cong., 1st Sess. (7 Jan. 1846) p. 155. Objects to printing a map of the territory of Oregon to accompany the President's Message if it would further delay supplying the message. Proposes an inquiry into the delay and the public printers.

2620. Hudson, Charles (Mass.). "The Mexican War," *Congressional Globe, Appendix*. 29th Cong., 1st Sess. (14 May 1846) pp. 912-916. Opposes the appropriations to rescue General Taylor's army. Maintains that the funds are not to supply the army, but to prosecute an unnecessary war and to invade Mexico. Reviews how the declaration of war was passed, events leading to the declaration, and the question of boundary. Responds to Mr. Douglass (Ill.) concerning title and alleged acts of aggression. Responds to Mr. Thurman's (Ohio) comments on the Federal party. Brief remarks opposed to slavery. Summary of speech in *Congressional Globe*, p. 824.

2621. Hudson, Charles (Mass.). "A Question of Privilege," *Congressional Globe*. 29th Cong., 1st Sess. (10 Jan. 1846) pp. 176-177. Replies to an article in the *Union*. Responds to accusations regarding his earlier comments about public printing delays.

2622. Hudson, Charles (Mass.). "The Tariff," *Congressional Globe, Appendix*. 29th Cong., 1st Sess. (29 June 1846) pp. 997-1001. Objects to reducing duties; maintains that it would be injurious to manufacturers, impair commerce and navigation, turn the balance of trade, derange the currency, and reduce rather than increase the revenue. Discusses the "revenue standard" policy; offers objections and illustrations of its operation. Examines the features of the bill submitted, the report of the Secretary of the Treasury, the Sub-Treasury bill, and projected imports. Defends protectionism and the importance of the coasting trade and internal commerce.

2623. Hudson, Charles (Mass.). "Wheat Trade," *Congressional Globe, Appendix*. 29th Cong., 1st Sess. (26 Feb., 5 Mar. 1846) pp. 459-464. Opposes the repeal of the English corn laws. Discusses the effect of the repeal or modification of these laws on commerce. Reviews the wheat and flour trade of the United States, its relative importance here and abroad, and the available markets and capacity. Maintains that America would lose in direct and indirect trade; discusses the colonial trade monopoly and free trade. Contends that Great Britain is looking after her own prosperity. Summary of later part of speech in *Congressional Globe*, p. 462.

2624. Rockwell, Julius (Mass.). "Admission of Texas," *Congressional Globe, Appendix.* 29th Cong., 1st Sess. (16 Dec. 1845) pp. 50-54. Opposes admitting Texas as a state with its present constitutional provisions on slavery. Maintains that Congress has the authority to give consent or not. Discusses the constitutional power of Congress to annex Texas as foreign state. Examines the slavery question pertaining to Texas and its annexation, and compares it to colonial slavery in provincial Massachusetts. Presents arguments against the extension of slavery. Summary of speech in *Congressional Globe*, pp. 62-64.

2625. Webster, Daniel (Mass.). "Admission of Texas," *Congressional Globe.* 29th Cong., 1st Sess. (22 Dec. 1845) p. 88. Opposes the annexation of Texas to the Union, particularly as a slave state; reviews objections.

2626. Webster, Daniel (Mass.). "The Army - Increase of Generals," *Congressional Globe.* 29th Cong., 1st Sess. (26 May 1846) pp. 866-867. Briefly remarks on the bill to create a provisional army; recommends that all military forces be employed, paid, and officered by the U.S. Government.

2627. Webster, Daniel (Mass.). "Call for Troops by General Gaines," *Congressional Globe.* 29th Cong., 1st Sess. (5 June 1846) pp. 928-929. Questions the authority by which General Gaines raised regiments for the service of the United States at the Rio Grande.

2628. Webster, Daniel (Mass.). "The Constitutional Treasury Bill," *Congressional Globe.* 29th Cong., 1st Sess. (1 Aug. 1846) pp. 1174-1176. Opposes the Sub-Treasury bill as a new means of disbursing the public money that will embarrass the Treasury, is of no advantage and of no necessity. Maintains that the public moneys are safe. Addresses the consequences of the bill on the operation of the government, particularly regarding specie payments and treasury notes.

2629. Webster, Daniel (Mass.). "Diplomatic Correspondence," *Congressional Globe.* 29th Cong., 1st Sess. (30 Mar. 1846) pp. 567-568, 569. Various remarks on the joint occupation of the Oregon territory; maintains that we should stand by the offer made in 1825 and that the line of 49 degrees should be a general basis of agreement.

2630. Webster, Daniel (Mass.). "National Defence," *Congressional Globe.* 29th Cong., 1st Sess. (16 Dec. 1845) pp. 56-57. Remarks on the Oregon territory convention; questions whether the proposed resolutions might create unnecessary alarm.

2631. Webster, Daniel (Mass.). "Paymasters in the Army," *Congressional Globe.* 29th Cong., 1st Sess. (14 May 1846) pp. 819, 820-821. Various remarks on the bill to repeal the law by which paymasters are appointed for four years; discusses the power of the President to remove officers.

2632. Webster, Daniel (Mass.). Remarks on Duties to Be Assessed, *Congressional Globe.* 29th Cong., 1st Sess. (6 Aug. 1846) pp. 1197-1198. Clarifies that the duties to be assessed are to be collected on the foreign, not home, valuation.

2633. Webster, Daniel (Mass.). Remarks on the Tariff, *Congressional Globe.* 29th Cong., 1st Sess. (14 July, 16 July 1846) pp. 1089-190; 1102-1103. Presents a petition from dry goods importing firms of the city of Boston against the bill to reduce the duties on imports. Maintains that the bill is unexpected, dangerous, rash, extreme, uncertain and untried. Opposes a universal system of *ad valorem* duties. Discusses the amount of revenue the bill will produce. Maintains that the measure, if passed, will not meet the revenue wants of government.

2634. Webster, Daniel (Mass.). "Secret-Service Fund," *Congressional Globe.* 29th Cong., 1st Sess. (22 Apr. 1846) pp. 708-709. Defends the expenditures made by President Tyler and himself from the fund for contingent expenses.

2635. Webster, Daniel (Mass.). "Special Order," *Congressional Globe.* 29th Cong., 1st Sess. (26 Feb. 1846) pp. 430-432. Various remarks request the opinion of the Executive on the proposed notice to annul the Oregon territory convention of 1818; questions whether negotiations or preparations for war are expected.

2636. Webster, Daniel (Mass.). "Special Order," *Congressional Globe.* 29th Cong., 1st Sess. (1 June 1846) pp. 896-897. Objects to establishing a temporary northern boundary line and provisional government in Oregon; supports the establishment of an actual territorial government over Oregon.

2637. Webster, Daniel (Mass.). Speech on Supporting and Conducting the Mexican War, *Congressional Globe.* 29th Cong., 1st Sess. (24 June 1846) pp. 1014-1016. Discusses the proposals to raise revenue to support the war. Supports a tax upon tea and coffee and the issue of Treasury notes as efficient and certain. Reduction of duties, the warehouse system, and the graduation bill are too uncertain and risky. Maintains that without a substantial taxation public debt will be incurred. Discusses the objects and purposes of conducting the war further. Contends that Mexico must listen to terms of peace.

2638. Webster, Daniel (Mass.). "The Tariff Bill," *Congressional Globe.* 29th Cong., 1st Sess. (28 July 1846) pp. 1152-1153; 1154-55; 1157-1158. Various remarks oppose the bill to reduce duties. Maintains that the bill is not a Democratic measure in favor of the people; it taxes the poor man and the laborer and takes away men's employment by raising the duty on raw materials. Discusses Massachusetts' and his own opposition to protectionism as stated in the resolutions of 1821. Defends the right to change his mind. Predicts a bill next session to repeal this law.

2639. Webster, Daniel (Mass.). "The Tariff," *Congressional Globe, Appendix.* 29th Cong., 1st Sess. (25 July, 27 July 1846) pp. 1139-1152. Opposes the bill to reduce the duties on imports. Examines the principles and details of the bill; discusses *ad valorem* duties and the effect of the bill upon currently and formerly protected articles such as iron and coal. Maintains that the *ad valorem* system is open to innumerable frauds and will not meet revenue needs, and that the bill benefits foreign manufacturers and laborers at the expense of domestic. Discusses the effect of the bill upon commerce and navigation, and its effect on employment, labor and industry.

2640. Webster, Daniel (Mass.). "The Tariff," *Congressional Globe.* 29th Cong., 1st Sess. (18 July 1846) pp. 1112-1113. Remarks on England's interest in the tariff legislation.

2641. Webster, Daniel (Mass.). "Treaty of Washington," *Congressional Globe, Appendix.* 29th Cong., 1st Sess. (6 Apr., 7 April 1846) pp. 524-537. Defends the Treaty of Washington of 1842. Reviews the history and diplomacy concerning the question of the northeastern boundary of the United States; maintains that it was a favorable arrangement that gave up no important military point. Also reviews the negotiations and events surrounding the destruction of the steamboat Caroline and the subsequent capture of McLeod, and the provisions for extradition, the right of search, and impressment. Summary of speech in *Congressional Globe*, pp. 609-612, 616-621.

2642. Winthrop, Robert C. (Mass.). "Harbors and Rivers," *Congressional Globe, Appendix.* 29th Cong., 1st Sess. (12 Mar. 1846) pp. 483-487. Supports appropriations for the improvement of certain rivers and harbors. Addresses opponents' objections. Discusses constitutionality, the power to regulate commerce, and the origin of the internal improvements policy. Uses Boston harbor as an example to illustrate the national character of local improvements. Supports regular appropriations for internal improvements.

2643. Winthrop, Robert C. (Mass.). "Message - Foreign Intercourse," *Congressional Globe.* 29th Cong., 1st Sess. (8 Aug. 1846) p. 1214. Opposes appropriating two million dollars for the President to use for emergencies concerning intercourse with foreign nations. Concerned the money would be used to purchase more territory and extend slavery rather than to secure peace.

2644. Winthrop, Robert C. (Mass.). "The Oregon Question," *Congressional Globe, Appendix.* 29th Cong., 1st Sess. (3 Jan. 1846) pp. 98-101. Opposes terminating the convention of joint occupancy; maintains that termination would result in an unnecessary and destructive war. Strongly supports negotiation and compromise, and, if necessary, arbitration. Discusses the character of the title to the Oregon territory, the concept of manifest destiny, and previous admissions and attempts at negotiation. Almost entirely reprinted in *Congressional Globe*, pp. 132-135.

2645. Winthrop, Robert C. (Mass.). Remarks on the Naturalization Laws, *Congressional Globe*. 29th Cong., 1st Sess. (17 Dec. 1845) p. 69. Remarks on the resolutions of the Legislature of Massachusetts requesting a revision of the naturalization laws.

2646. Winthrop, Robert C. (Mass.). "Senator Webster," *Congressional Globe*. 29th Cong., 1st Sess. (9 Apr., 11 Apr. 1846) pp. 639-640; 656-657. Various remarks on the charges against Daniel Webster when he held the office of Secretary of State. Advocates reviewing all the papers on the secret-service fund. Clarifies and defends remarks incorrectly reported on Mr. Webster's investments in manufacturing companies and the annuity raised by his friends.

2647. Winthrop, Robert C. (Mass.). "The Tariff," *Congressional Globe, Appendix*. 29th Cong., 1st Sess. (25 June 1846) pp. 969-974. Opposes the bill to reduce duties on imports; maintains that it will not produce the necessary revenue. Contends that the tariff of 1842 proved itself as a revenue tariff, benefiting labor and the Treasury. Recommends issuing Treasury notes and imposing a specific duty upon tea and coffee. Remarks on Oregon, the causes of the Mexican War, *ad valorem* duties, domestic trade, protectionism, and the proposal to increase imports.

2648. U.S. House. *Fortifications at New Bedford.* 29th Cong., 1st Sess. (H.Rpt.327). [Washington]: Ritchie & Heiss, Printers, [1846]. 4 pg. (Serial Set 489). Report of the Committee on Military Affairs supports the memorial requesting military defenses at New Bedford harbor; includes correspondence on estimates of expenses.

2649. U.S. House. *Naturalization Laws.* 29th Cong., 1st Sess. (H.Rpt.231). [Washington]: Ritchie & Heiss, Print., [1846]. 5 pg. (Serial Set 489). Report of the Committee on the Judiciary against the resolutions of the Legislature of Massachusetts demanding a revision of the naturalization laws.

2650. U.S. House. *Resolutions of the Legislature of Georgia, Relative to the Controversy Between the State of Massachusetts and the States of South Carolina and Louisiana.* 29th Cong., 1st Sess. (H.Doc.87). [Washington]: Ritchie & Heiss, Print., [1846]. 3 pg. (Serial Set 483). Resolutions support South Carolina and Louisiana in their opposition to Massachusetts's resolutions considering free Negroes as citizens. Same as S.doc.100 (29-1) 473 (entry **2662**).

2651. U.S. House. *Resolutions of the Legislature of Massachusetts, Relative to the Admission of Texas into the Union.* 29th Cong., 1st Sess. (H.Doc.35). [Washington]: Ritchie & Heiss, Print., [1845]. 2 pg. (Serial Set 482). Resolutions oppose the admission of slave-holding Texas.

2652. U.S. House. *Resolutions of the Legislature of Massachusetts, in Relation to Louisiana and South Carolina.* 29th Cong., 1st Sess. (H.Doc.34). [Washington]: Ritchie & Heiss, Printers, [1845]. 4 pg. (Serial Set 482). Report and resolutions support the rights of citizenship for individuals of all origins, races and colors. Maintains that the rights of Massachusetts' citizens Samuel Hoar and Hon. Henry Hubbard were violated in South Carolina and Louisiana, respectively.

2653. U.S. Senate. [Claim of the New England Mississippi Land Company]. 29th Cong., 1st Sess. (S.Doc.88). Washington: Ritchie & Heiss, 1846. 16 pg. (Serial Set 473). Favorable report of the Committee on the Judiciary to the petition of the New England Mississippi Land Company. Adopts the 1842 report, S.doc.18 (27-3) 414. Reprints S.doc.18 (27-3) 414 (entry **2553**), S.doc.205 (23-1) 240 (entry **2141**), and Pub.land 1216 (23-1) ASP 033 (entry **2116**). Also includes a detailed historical synopsis of the case.

2654. U.S. Senate. *Memorial of Citizens of Marblehead, Mass., against the Repeal of the Fishing Bounty, &c.* 29th Cong., 1st Sess. (S.Doc.247). Washington: Ritchie & Heiss, 1846. 7 pg. (Serial Set 474). Includes three pages of names of memorialists.

2655. U.S. Senate. *Memorial of Importing Merchants of Boston, Praying that, in All Cases Where Practicable, the Principle of Specific Duties May Be Adhered to in the Bill Now under Consideration for Reducing the Duties on Imports.* 29th Cong., 1st Sess. (S.Doc.431). Washington: Ritchie & Heiss, 1846. 2 pg. (Serial Set 477). Includes names of memorialists.

2656. U.S. Senate. *Memorial of Merchants of Boston, against the Imposition of Ad Valorem Duties on Wines and Liquors.* 29th Cong., 1st Sess. (S.Doc.419). Washington: Ritchie & Heiss, 1846. 2 pg. (Serial Set 477).

2657. U.S. Senate. *Petition of Citizens of Barnstable County, Mass., Remonstrating against the Repeal of the Act Allowing Bounty to Vessels Engaged in the Codfishery.* 29th Cong., 1st Sess. (S.Doc.168). Washington: Ritchie & Heiss, 1846. 1 pg. (Serial Set 473).

2658. U.S. Senate. *Petition of Citizens of Barnstable County, Mass., Praying an Increase of the Duty on Foreign Salt.* 29th Cong., 1st Sess. (S.Doc.169). Washington: Ritchie & Heiss, 1846. 1 pg. (Serial Set 473).

2659. U.S. Senate. *Petition of Citizens of Barnstable County, Mass., Praying an Increase of the Duty on Imported Epsom Salts.* 29th Cong., 1st Sess. (S.Doc.170). Washington: Ritchie & Heiss, 1846. 1 pg. (Serial Set 473).

2660. U.S. Senate. *Petition of the Publishers of Boston, against and Ad Valorem Duty on Books.* 29th Cong., 1st Sess. (S.Doc.458). Washington: Ritchie & Heiss, 1846. 1 pg. (Serial Set 478).

2661. U.S. Senate. *Report of the Secretary of War, Communicating, in Compliance with a Resolution of the Senate, Copies of the Proceedings of the Court of Inquiry in the Case of Major J.W. Ripley, Superintendent of the Armory at Springfield.* 29th Cong., 1st Sess. (S.Doc.344). Washington: Ritchie & Heiss, 1846. 326 pg. (Serial Set 476). Proceedings of the Court of Inquiry, including a copy of the memorial listing the charges against Major Ripley, testimony of witnesses, statistics on the expenditures and production of the armory, names of workmen with age and years employed, inspection reports, and other supporting documentation. Favorable verdict received and Major Ripley acquitted.

2662. U.S. Senate. *Resolutions of the Legislature of Georgia, in Relation to the Difficulties Between the Authorities of the States of South Carolina and Louisiana and Those of the State of Massachusetts.* 29th Cong., 1st Sess. (S.Doc.100). Washington: Ritchie & Heiss, 1846. 3 pg. (Serial Set 473). Same as H.doc.87 (29-1) 483. See entry **2650**.

2663. U.S. Senate. *Resolutions of the Legislature of Georgia, in Opposition to the Principles of Certain Resolves of the Legislature of Massachusetts in Relation to an Amendment of the Constitution on the Subject of Federal Representation.* 29th Cong., 1st Sess. (S.Doc.101). Washington: Ritchie & Heiss, 1846. 2 pg. (Serial Set 473).

29TH CONGRESS, 2ND SESSION

2664. Adams, John Quincy (Mass.). "The Amistad," *Congressional Globe, Appendix.* 29th Cong., 2nd Sess. (2 Mar. 1847) pp. 437-438. Opposes the claim of the Spanish Government for reimbursement for the Negroes on board the Amistad, a Spanish slave ship. Reviews the facts of the case.

2665. Ashmun, George (Mass.). "The Mexican War," *Congressional Globe, Appendix.* 29th Cong., 2nd Sess. (4 Feb. 1847) pp. 289-293. Maintains that the Mexican War is a direct consequence of the annexation of Texas, and that the purpose of the war is to acquire foreign territory for the extension of slavery. Reviews the causes of the war, the question of boundary between Texas and Mexico, and evidence supporting his contention that it is a war of conquest. Discusses the political implications of the extension of slavery.

2666. Ashmun, George (Mass.). "Military Appropriation Bill," *Congressional Globe, Appendix.* 29th Cong., 2nd Sess. (3 Mar. 1847) pp. 446-448. Opposes the passage of a bill that has already been defeated three times by the House. Discusses the effects of executive patronage and the defeat of the Wilmot proviso. Briefly discusses Mr. C.J. Ingersoll's (Pa.) views on slavery and earlier inconsistencies regarding the Texas border.

2667. Ashmun, George (Mass.). Remarks on Amending the Washington City Charter, *Congressional Globe.* 29th Cong., 2nd Sess. (21 Jan. 1847) p. 224. Supports the right of the freemen of the city of Washington to vote for their rulers.

2668. Ashmun, George (Mass.). Speech on the Resolution concerning General Taylor, *Congressional Globe.* 29th Cong., 2nd Sess. (30 Jan. 1847) pp. 296-298. Defends General Taylor. Maintains that the administration intends to sacrifice General Taylor in order to have a Democratic general at the head of the army. Discusses the politics of the Mexican War and the resolution prohibiting officers from publishing their correspondence during a war. Amends the resolution requesting General Taylor's correspondence to also request information on the return of Santa Ana to Mexico and on the instructions given to Mr. Slidell. Discusses the suspicious circumstances of Santa Ana's return and the two million dollars.

2669. Davis, John (Mass.). "Army Bill," *Congressional Globe.* 29th Cong., 2nd Sess. (20 Jan. 1847) p. 214. Advocates not restricting the transfer of title of bounties granted to enlisted soldiers.

2670. Davis, John (Mass.). "Memorial of the Society of Friends," *Congressional Globe.* 29th Cong., 2nd Sess. (23 Dec. 1846) pp. 69-70. Supports printing the memorial of the Society of Friends for New England asking to terminate the Mexican War.

2671. Davis, John (Mass.). "The Three Million Bill," *Congressional Globe, Appendix.* 29th Cong., 2nd Sess. (25 Feb. 1847) pp. 416-420. Opposes appropriating the money for ending the Mexican War. Discusses the causes and circumstances of the war, particularly the annexation of Texas. Maintains that the President mediated hostilities calculated to promote war. Questions what "extraordinary expenses" require the proposed appropriation. Supports provisions restraining slavery in acquired territories to eliminate the motive for wars of acquisition. Summary of speech in *Congressional Globe*, pp. 506-509.

2672. Davis, John (Mass.). "War Steamers," *Congressional Globe.* 29th Cong., 2nd Sess. (15 Feb. 1847) pp. 422-423. Supports increasing the number of steamers in the navy; reviews advantages.

2673. Hudson, Charles (Mass.). "The President's Message," *Congressional Globe.* 29th Cong., 2nd Sess. (16 Dec. 1846) pp. 48-52. Repudiates the President's declaration that the war with Mexico was provoked by Mexico and that all honorable means were resorted to prevent it. Addresses the President's arguments in support of his position, discussing spoliations upon our commerce and refusal to make reparation, Mexico's refusal to see Mr. Slidell, and the charge that Mexico invaded U.S. territory. Examines arguments concerning the Texas boundary; establishes with documents submitted by the President himself that the valley of the Rio Grande never belonged to Texas. Maintains that the

Mexican War was commenced by the Executive to acquire territory to extend slavery.

2674. Hudson, Charles (Mass.). "The Three Million Bill," *Congressional Globe, Appendix.* 29th Cong., 2nd Sess. (13 Feb. 1847) pp. 366-371. Opposes the appropriation. Briefly reviews the causes of the Mexican War. Demonstrates that the Mexican War is aggressive, commenced by the Executive without the consent of Congress, for the purpose of acquiring territory to extend slavery. Maintains that Congress has the constitutional power to withhold supplies; discusses executive patronage and power in times of war. Considers the losses incurred by waging the war, the prospects for success, and the divisiveness of the slavery question should the war be won. Brief summary of speech in *Congressional Globe,* p. 418.

2675. King, Daniel P. (Mass.). "General Appropriation Bill," *Congressional Globe, Appendix.* 29th Cong., 2nd Sess. (4 Feb. 1847) pp. 293-296. Remarks on several topics. Introduces and supports an amendment to provide for sick and disabled seamen. Discusses the Mexican War; maintains that it is unconstitutional, unnecessary and unjust. Reviews his record of votes opposing the war. Maintains that the war is one of conquest, with no definite prospect of termination, to acquire territory for slavery. Discusses the origin of the 1787 ordinance excluding slavery from the Northwestern Territory.

2676. King, Daniel P. (Mass.). Remarks on the Memorial of the Society of Friends, *Congressional Globe.* 29th Cong., 2nd Sess. (29 Dec. 1846) p. 96. Supports printing the memorial of the Society of Friends for New England asking for the termination of the Mexican War.

2677. Rockwell, Julius (Mass.). Remarks on the Territorial Government in Oregon, *Congressional Globe.* 29th Cong., 2nd Sess. (12 Jan. 1847) pp. 168-169. Objects to the proposed limitations on people entitled to vote. Advocates the precedents of the Territories of Wisconsin and Iowa who extended suffrage to persons who declared upon oath their intention to become citizens.

2678. Webster, Daniel (Mass.). "Army Bill," *Congressional Globe.* 29th Cong., 2nd Sess. (20 Jan. 1847) p. 214. Further remarks support a land bounty to entice soldiers to enlist; reviews the bounty offered in the War of 1812.

2679. Webster, Daniel (Mass.). "Harvard College," *Congressional Globe.* 29th Cong., 2nd Sess. (9 Dec. 1846) p. 12. Remarks on a memorial from Harvard College concerning the effects of the new tariff law on an order for a refracting telescope.

2680. Webster, Daniel (Mass.). "Military Bill and Bounty Lands," *Congressional Globe.* 29th Cong., 2nd Sess. (19 Jan. 1847) p. 207. Supports a land bounty to induce soldiers to speedily enlist in the army and the volunteer corps.

2681. Webster, Daniel (Mass.). "Mr. Barry's Case," *Congressional Globe*. 29th Cong., 2nd Sess. (17 Feb. 1847) pp. 434-435. Various remarks support the propriety of receiving petitions from citizens of a foreign country to whom the country might be under an obligation. Discusses precedents.

2682. Webster, Daniel (Mass.). Remarks on the President Pro Tem. of the Senate, *Congressional Globe*. 29th Cong., 2nd Sess. (11 Jan. 1847) pp. 163-164. Remarks on the election of a President pro tem. of the Senate; discusses the importance of the office in case of the death of President and Vice President.

2683. Webster, Daniel (Mass.). Remarks on the Resolution concerning General Taylor, *Congressional Globe*. 29th Cong., 2nd Sess. (3 Feb. 1847) pp. 318-319. Remarks support a clear and simple resolution expressing the appreciation of Congress to General Taylor; contends that no other issues should be included.

2684. Webster, Daniel (Mass.). "Three Million Bill," *Congressional Globe*. 29th Cong., 2nd Sess. (1 Mar. 1847) pp. 555-556. Objects to the prosecution of the Mexican War for the acquisition of territory and the subsequent extension of slavery. Reads and discusses the resolutions of the Massachusetts Legislature (S.doc.219 (29-2) 495 (entry **2692**)) and the actions of the "Northern Democracy" in support of annexing Texas and further extending the territory.

2685. Winthrop, Robert C. (Mass.). "Admission of Iowa into the Union," *Congressional Globe*. 29th Cong., 2nd Sess. (21 Dec. 1846) pp. 58-59. Briefly remarks on the Mexican War.

2686. Winthrop, Robert C. (Mass.). "The Army Bill," *Congressional Globe, Appendix*. 29th Cong., 2nd Sess. (22 Feb. 1847) pp. 406-409. Opposes the appropriations bill that is without limitations or conditions; proposes several restrictions. Recommends waiting for the new Congress. Reviews the recent encroachments of the Executive upon the Legislative authority. Discusses the propriety of withholding all supplies. Defends his vote on the three million bill; supports the Wilmot proviso and excluding slavery from territories. Objects to the new tariff and proposed taxes.

2687. Winthrop, Robert C. (Mass.). "Increase of the Army," *Congressional Globe*. 29th Cong., 2nd Sess. (8 Jan. 1847) pp. 143-147. Explains his objections to the Mexican War and an increase of the army to pursue a war of conquest. Supports the right to openly question the policy of the administration. Discusses the reasons behind his vote to give the Executive the war power. Contends that although Mexico's conduct has not been without fault, it was not grounds for making war upon her. Maintains that the primary objective of the war is the annexation of territory to extend the institution of slavery. Declares New England's opposition to the extension of slavery. Maintains that the current bill has no relation to the immediate support of the army in Mexico but would only apply to a protracted war.

2688. Winthrop, Robert C. (Mass.). "The Mexican War," *Congressional Globe, Appendix.* 29th Cong., 2nd Sess. (21 Dec. 1846) p. 90. Responds to Seaborn Jones (Ga.).

2689. Winthrop, Robert C. (Mass.). "The Relief of Ireland," *Congressional Globe, Appendix.* 29th Cong., 2nd Sess. (3 Mar. 1847) pp. 440-441. Advocates employing the ships Jamestown and Macedonian to carry contributions to the suffering people of Ireland; addresses objections.

2690. Winthrop, Robert C. (Mass.). Remarks on the President's Message, *Congressional Globe.* 29th Cong., 2nd Sess. (9 Dec. 1846) pp. 17-18. Remarks on the President's Message, particularly the request for appropriations to fortify California. Questions whether the establishment of this "permanent" government over the California territory implies eventual annexation to the Union. Supports an inquiry into the President's instructions regarding the establishment of new governments in the conquered provinces.

2691. U.S. House. *Fire-Proof Building at Nantucket.* 29th Cong., 2nd Sess. (H.Rpt.68). [Washington]: Richie & Heiss, Printers, [1847]. 1 pg. (Serial Set 501). Favorable report for appropriations to erect a fireproof building for customs.

2692. U.S. Senate. *Resolves of the Legislature of Massachusetts, concerning Slavery.* 29th Cong., 2nd Sess. (S.Doc.219). Washington: Ritchie and Heiss, 1847. 1 pg. (Serial Set 495).

30TH CONGRESS, 1ST SESSION

2693. "Death of Hon. J.Q. Adams," *Congressional Globe.* 30th Cong., 1st Sess. (24 Feb. 1848) pp. 388-389. Testimonials and resolutions in honor of John Quincy Adams by John Davis (Mass.) and Thomas H. Benton (Mo.).

2694. Debate on Claims of Massachusetts and Maine, *Congressional Globe.* 30th Cong., 1st Sess. (15 July 1848) pp. 940-941. Debate on proposed appropriations to pay Massachusetts and Maine the balance due for services of their militia during the late war with Britain. Concludes that as law did not authorize an appropriation, the presentment of the claim is premature.

2695. "Illness of John Quincy Adams," *Congressional Globe.* 30th Cong., 1st Sess. (21 Feb., 22 Feb. 1848) p. 383. Requests by Sen. Benton (Mo.) and Sen. Davis (Mass.) to adjourn in consequence of the collapse of John Quincy Adams.

2696. Remarks on the Death of John Quincy Adams, *Congressional Globe.* 30th Cong., 1st Sess. (24 Feb. 1848) pp. 384-387. Testimonials and resolutions on the life of John Quincy Adams presented by Robert C. Winthrop (Mass.), Charles Hudson (Mass.), Isaac E. Holmes (S.C.), Samuel F. Vinton (Ohio), and Frederick A. Tallmadge (N.Y.).

2697. Adams, John Quincy (Mass.). "Return of Santa Anna to Mexico," *Congressional Globe.* 30th Cong., 1st Sess. (13 Jan. 1848) p. 167. Supports the right of the House to insist upon the information for which they have called.

2698. Adams, John Quincy (Mass.). "Whig of '76," *Congressional Globe, Appendix.* 30th Cong., 1st Sess. (25 Jul. 1848) pp. 62-63. Various quotes from his "Novanglus" letters on the powers of the British Parliament. Located in the Appendix to the *Congressional Globe* of the 30th Congress, 2nd Session.

2699. Ashmun, George (Mass.). "Revolution in France," *Congressional Globe, Appendix.* 30th Cong., 1st Sess. (10 Apr., 11 Apr. 1848) pp. 477-482. Discusses resolutions to congratulate France upon achieving a republican government. Maintains that the resolutions are premature, that France has not yet achieved republican liberty and needs a charter and constitution. Responds to attacks on his previous proposal to congratulate France on emancipating the slaves in her colonies. Remarks on the obligations of states to assist in the capture of fugitive slaves. Summary of speech in *Congressional Globe*, pp. 599-601, 613-615.

2700. Davis, John (Mass.). "Death of Hon. J.Q. Adams," *Congressional Globe.* 30th Cong., 1st Sess. (24 Feb. 1848) p. 388. Eulogy recalling the life of John Quincy Adams.

2701. Davis, John (Mass.). "Deficiency Bill," *Congressional Globe.* 30th Cong., 1st Sess. (20 March 1848) p. 510. Requests an explanation of the deficiencies, particularly regarding the foreign missions.

2702. Davis, John (Mass.). "The Pilot Laws," *Congressional Globe.* 30th Cong., 1st Sess. (13 Apr. 1848) pp. 626-627. Objects to repealing the law that authorizes pilots of New Jersey, as well as those of New York, to bring vessels into the harbor. Briefly reviews the case; addresses opponents' arguments and states' rights.

2703. Davis, John (Mass.). "Protection of Property in the District of Columbia," *Congressional Globe, Appendix.* 30th Cong., 1st Sess. (20 Apr. 1848) pp. 507-508. Supports allowing the reception of the bill; maintains that the bill relates to nothing but the protection of property against a mob.

2704. Davis, John (Mass.). "Temporary Occupation of Yucatan," *Congressional Globe, Appendix.* 30th Cong., 1st Sess. (11 May 1848) pp. 620-625. Opposes a temporary military occupation of Yucatan. Reviews the request and arguments in support of the occupation. Maintains that Yucatan looks to annexation with the United States. Discusses parallels between this situation and the annexation of Texas, the possibilities of English interference and/or war, the Monroe doctrine and the Panama mission, and the effects of occupation on the treaty currently pending with Mexico. Summary of speech in *Congressional Globe*, pp. 761-762.

2705. Davis, John (Mass.). "Territorial Government of Oregon," *Congressional Globe, Appendix.* 30th Cong., 1st Sess. (8 July 1848) pp. 894-897. Discusses the issue of slavery in Oregon; maintains that Congress has the constitutional power to regulate slavery in the territories. Reviews the sentiments of the framers of the Constitution, the ordinance of 1787, the issue of slaves as property, representation between slave and free states, the consequences of the annexation of Texas, and the public temperament. Summery of speech in *Congressional Globe,* pp. 909-910.

2706. Hudson, Charles (Mass.). "Boundary of Texas," *Congressional Globe, Appendix.* 30th Cong., 1st Sess. (8 Aug. 1848) pp. 924-928. Refutes the claim that the Texan boundary extended to the Rio Grande. Maintains that the western boundary of revolutionary Texas extended to the Nueces; contends that only her possessions and civil jurisdiction at the time of annexation are relevant. Addresses the President's claims that the boundary extended to the Rio Grande; uses excerpts of documents submitted with his annual message and his war message in May, 1846, to refute his claim. Addresses the principal arguments in support of the Rio Grande boundary claims.

2707. Hudson, Charles (Mass.). "The Loan Bill and the War," *Congressional Globe.* 30th Cong., 1st Sess. (15 Feb. 1848) pp. 355-359. Opposes the loan bill; maintains that the amount requested is inadequate. Briefly reviews the causes and objectives of the war; discusses its financial burdens. Reviews the report of the Secretary of the Treasury concerning expenditures and revenue from imports, exports, and the public land; maintains that the report is intentionally obscure and unreliable to keep appropriations small until after the election. Discusses the failure of the tariff of 1846; advocates a direct tax and modification of the tariff to meet revenue needs.

2708. Hudson, Charles (Mass.). "The Public Revenue," *Congressional Globe.* 30th Cong., 1st Sess. (16 Mar. 1848) pp. 475-476. Supports the amendment requiring the Sec. of the Treasury to make his report more detailed and clearer.

2709. Hudson, Charles (Mass.). Remarks on the Death of John Quincy Adams, *Congressional Globe.* 30th Cong., 1st Sess. (24 Feb. 1848) p. 385. Eulogy recalls the life of John Quincy Adams. Presents resolutions of respect.

2710. Hudson, Charles (Mass.). "Slavery in the Territories," *Congressional Globe, Appendix.* 30th Cong., 1st Sess. (20 June 1848) pp. 663-667. Details his views against slavery. Discusses the annexation of Texas and the Mexican War as a means to perpetuate domestic slavery. Demonstrates that Congress has jurisdiction over slavery in the territories. Fortifies his position with writers on elementary law, the Constitution, interpretations by the Supreme Court, and acts of legislation. Discusses slavery as a political and moral evil; maintains that the North will not allow its extension into New Mexico and California.

2711. King, Daniel P. (Mass.). "Peace Memorial from the Quakers," *Congressional Globe.* 30th Cong., 1st Sess. (10 Feb. 1848) p. 329. Presents memorial from the Society of Friends for New England requesting the speedy termination of the Mexican War. Supports the memorialists and their request.

2712. Mann, Horace (Mass.). "Slavery and the Territories," *Congressional Globe, Appendix.* 30th Cong., 1st Sess. (30 June 1848) pp. 832-841. Advocates excluding slavery from the territories. Addresses whether Congress has the power to legislate on the subject of slavery in the territories and whether it is expedient to exclude slavery from them. Argues that the Constitution, precedence, the uniform practice of legislation, and judicial decisions all show the power of Congress to legislate on the subject. Considers the balance of power between the South and the North, and the economical, educational, and moral aspects of slavery.

2713. Palfrey, John G. (Mass.). "Peace Memorial from the Quakers," *Congressional Globe.* 30th Cong., 1st Sess. (10 Feb. 1848) p. 330. Various remarks support printing the memorial from the Society of Friends for New England.

2714. Palfrey, John G. (Mass.). Remarks on the French Revolution and Colored Persons in Massachusetts, *Congressional Globe.* 30th Cong., 1st Sess. (11 Apr. 1848) pp. 609-610. Remarks to reconsider the resolution of the Senate on the French Revolution. Addresses the status of colored persons in Massachusetts regarding participation in the judicial, legislative, and educational system. Also remarks on Virginia's response to John Quincy Adams' death.

2715. Palfrey, John G. (Mass.). Remarks on the Loan Bill, *Congressional Globe.* 30th Cong., 1st Sess. (17 Feb. 1848) p. 370. Supports a direct tax.

2716. Palfrey, John G. (Mass.). "The Slave Question," *Congressional Globe, Appendix.* 30th Cong., 1st Sess. (26 Jan. 1848) pp. 133-137. Addresses the political aspect of the slave question. Discusses the relative power of the free and slave states on the floor of the House and in public offices, including the original apportionment of power. Looks at the rights of petition, speech and the press, the annexation of Texas and the Mexican War. Responds to various statements made by Mr. Clingman (N.C.) on slavery and abolitionist classifications. Summary of speech in *Congressional Globe*, pp. 245-246.

2717. Rockwell, Julius (Mass.). "Territorial Government of Oregon," *Congressional Globe, Appendix.* 30th Cong., 1st Sess. (27 June 1848) pp. 789-794. Supports the organization of a territorial government for Oregon. Maintains that Congress has power over the territorial possessions according to universal law, authority of the Constitution, and precedent. Addresses opponents' objections. Supports the exclusion of domestic slavery from the territories; addresses counter opinions. Discusses the possibilities of dissolution of the Union and further expansion. Defends his support of the Whig ticket in the approaching presidential election.

2718. Webster, Daniel (Mass.). "The Loan Bill," *Congressional Globe.* 30th Cong., 1st Sess. (23 Mar. 1848) pp. 530-535. Opposes appropriating moneys for continuing the war against Mexico. Questions the value of the treaty ratified and the necessity of the additional regiments. Contends that the additional regiments will only increase executive patronage. Opposes the acquisition of new territory to form new states. Maintains that peace without the territory would be safer, more enduring and more honorable. Describes New Mexico; discusses the political implications of admitting new states.

2719. Webster, Daniel (Mass.). "Oregon," *Congressional Globe.* 30th Cong., 1st Sess. (12 Aug. 1848) p. 1077. Opposes extending slavery to the territories and increasing the slave representation in Congress.

2720. Webster, Daniel (Mass.). "The Ten-Regiment Bill," *Congressional Globe.* 30th Cong., 1st Sess. (17 Mar. 1848) pp. 484-485, 495. Opposes the further prosecution of the Mexican War. Maintains that the attempts of the Executive to levy and collect taxes in Mexico is unconstitutional, illegal and in opposition to the law of nations.

2721. Winthrop, Robert C. (Mass.). Acceptance Speech as Speaker of the House, *Congressional Globe.* 30th Cong., 1st Sess. (6 Dec. 1847) pp. 2-3.

2722. Winthrop, Robert C. (Mass.). Remarks on the Death of John Quincy Adams, *Congressional Globe,* 30th Cong., 1st Sess. (24 Feb. 1848) pp. 384-385.

2723. "An Act to Annex the Town of Essex, in the State of Massachusetts, to the Collection District of Gloucester," *Statutes at Large*, Vol. IX (7 Aug. 1848) p. 275.

2724. U.S. House. *New England Mississippi Land Company.* 30th Cong., 1st Sess. (H.Rpt.765). [Washington: 1848]. 11 pg. (Serial Set 527). Favorable report of the Committee on the Judiciary on the petition of the New England Mississippi Land Company; adopts 1834 Senate report, S.doc.205 (23-1) 240. Reprints S.doc.205 (23-1) 240 (entry **2141**) and Pub.land 1216 (23-1) ASP 033 (entry **2116**).

2725. U.S. House. *Resolutions of the Legislature of Massachusetts, Tendering the Thanks of the Government and People of That Commonwealth to the House of Representatives of the United States, and the Committee of Escort Appointed Thereby, for Their Proceedings upon the Occasion of the Death of the Late John Quincy Adams.* 30th Cong., 1st Sess. (H.Misc.Doc.67). Washington: Tippin & Streeper, 1848. 2 pg. (Serial Set 523).

2726. U.S. Senate. *Memorial and Resolutions of the Legislature of Massachusetts, in Favor of a Reduction of the Rates of Postage.* 30th Cong.,

1st Sess. (S.Misc.Doc.140). Washington: Tippin & Streeper, 1848. 7 pg. (Serial Set 511). Memorial and resolutions support reducing the postage to raise only that amount of revenue necessary to enable the Post Office Dept. to meet its expenses. Discusses the effects of high postage rates; submits a proposal.

2727. U.S. Senate. *Petition of Citizens of Maine and Massachusetts, Praying that Lumber Manufactured in New Brunswick, from Timber Grown in Maine, May Be Admitted into the United States Free of Duty.* 30th Cong., 1st Sess. (S.Misc.Doc.90). Washington: Tippin & Streeper, 1848. 2 pg. (Serial Set 511). Petition supports eliminating the duty since lumber from Maine must be transported to New Brunswick via the Aroostook and Saint John Rivers in rough logs and timber for processing and shipment out of Saint John.

2728. U.S. Senate. *Petition of Importing Merchants of Boston, Praying for an Amendment of the Proviso of the Eighth Section of the Tariff Act of July 30, 1846.* 30th Cong., 1st Sess. (S.Misc.Doc.34). Washington: Tippin & Streeper, 1848. 2 pg. (Serial Set 511). Petition requests revision of the proviso requiring that duty be paid on the amount of goods declared on the invoice, rather than the amount received by the importer.

30ᵀᴴ CONGRESS, 2ᴺᴰ SESSION

2729. Ashmun, George (Mass.). "Bust of Mr. Adams," *Congressional Globe.* 30th Cong., 2nd Sess. (3 Mar. 1849) p. 692. Resolution presented and adopted to place a bust of John Quincy Adams in the Speaker's room to mark the spot and commemorate the circumstances of his death.

2730. Davis, John (Mass.). "Civil and Diplomatic Bill," *Congressional Globe.* 30th Cong., 2nd Sess. (13 Feb. 1849) p. 527. Supports appropriations to provide for a light-boat or lighthouse for traffic between Boston and New York.

2731. Davis, John (Mass.). "The Coast Survey," *Congressional Globe, Appendix.* 30th Cong., 2nd Sess. (19 Feb. 1849) pp. 209-210. Supports the coast survey and defends Mr. Hassler, former Superintendent of the Coast Survey. Maintains that triangulation is the most accurate, permanent and useful method of surveying and that the survey is indispensable to the safety of navigation.

2732. Davis, John (Mass.). "Government Land Purchases," *Congressional Globe.* 30th Cong., 2nd Sess. (27 Dec. 1848) p. 103. Remarks on land speculation for government purchases; maintains that the proposed value of the tract of land on which a lighthouse stands is too high.

2733. Davis, John (Mass.). "Naturalist to a Naval Expedition," *Congressional Globe.* 30th Cong., 2nd Sess. (18 Jan., 25 Jan. 1849) pp. 291-292; 362. Supports the claim of Captain John Percival for charges incurred by appointing a naturalist to accompany him to the East Indies and China. Reviews the circumstances.

2734. Davis, John (Mass.). "Territory of Minesota [sic]," *Congressional Globe*. 30th Cong., 2nd Sess. (1 Mar. 1849) pp. 636-637. Clarifies the short delay in date of execution of the law establishing a territorial government in Minnesota; discusses executive patronage.

2735. Mann, Horace (Mass.). "Slavery and the Slave Trade in the District of Columbia," *Congressional Globe, Appendix*. 30th Cong., 2nd Sess. (23 Feb. 1849) pp. 318-326. Supports abolishing the slave trade and slavery in the District of Columbia. States reasons why it should be discontinued by law; addresses opponents' arguments. Defends Massachusetts. Maintains that Congress has exclusive jurisdiction over the District; reviews the prohibitions of the Constitutions and the conditions of the original cession of land from Maryland. Maintains that slavery in the District exists only by the force of precedent and example. Summary of speech in *Congressional Globe*, p. 590.

2736. Palfrey, John G. (Mass.). "American Archives," *Congressional Globe*. 30th Cong., 2nd Sess. (13 Feb. 1849) p. 531. Resolution and remarks support distributing copies of the *American Archives* to literary institutions.

2737. Palfrey, John G. (Mass.). "The Census of 1850," *Congressional Globe*. 30th Cong., 2nd Sess. (1 Mar. 1849) pp. 638-639. Resolution and remarks to make arrangements for taking the seventh Census.

2738. Palfrey, John G. (Mass.). "The Territorial Governments," *Congressional Globe, Appendix*. 30th Cong., 2nd Sess. (26 Feb. 1849) pp. 313-317. Opposes the introduction of slavery into California and New Mexico. Addresses opponents' arguments; reviews schemes that tried to introduce slavery into territories; declares the need for a legal prohibition of slavery. Discusses slavery as a local institution, political precedence, the sectional issue, and dissolution of the Union. Reviews the consequences of introducing slavery into these provinces. Responds to remarks against Massachusetts concerning her treatment of witches, Indians, Quakers, and Catholics.

2739. Palfrey, John G. (Mass.). "The Unfinished Business," *Congressional Globe*. 30th Cong., 2nd Sess. (12 Jan. 1849) pp. 240-241. Opposes the claim of Antonio Pacheco for the loss of a slave conscripted into the Florida war; maintains that neither the Constitution nor the U.S. courts recognize slaves as property.

2740. Webster, Daniel (Mass.). "Call for Instructions," *Congressional Globe, Appendix*. 30th Cong., 2nd Sess. (12 Mar. 1849) p. 332. Requests information to ascertain if the minister in England has been authorized to further extend the navigation laws towards reciprocity and equality.

2741. Webster, Daniel (Mass.). "Civil and Diplomatic Appropriations," *Congressional Globe.* 30th Cong., 2nd Sess. (3 Mar. 1849) pp. 687-688. Recalls his original objections to including amendments concerning California in the annual appropriation bill. Maintains that the amendment simply reaffirms the law of nations by saying that the laws existing in conquered territories continue to be in force until the conquering power withdraws them.

2742. Webster, Daniel (Mass.). "John P. Baldwin," *Congressional Globe.* 30th Cong., 2nd Sess. (2 Jan. 1849) p. 135. Supports the claim of John P. Baldwin for the destruction of his property by commissioned officers of the United States. Maintains that the lead was not in eminent danger of being seized by the enemy and that the government is responsible.

2743. Webster, Daniel (Mass.). "New Mexico and California," *Congressional Globe, Appendix.* 30th Cong., 2nd Sess. (23 Feb., 24 Feb. 1849) pp. 259-260; 272-274. Remarks support providing a temporary, substantially military, government for the territories of New Mexico and California for the purposes of peace and security. Opposes the proposal to "extend the Constitution of the United States to the Territories." Maintains that Congress and the judicature on the subject support his position; addresses opponents' objections.

2744. Webster, Daniel (Mass.). "The Panama Railroad," *Congressional Globe.* 30th Cong., 2nd Sess. (6 Feb. 1849) pp. 462-463. Supports the Panama Railroad. Maintains that it is necessary and expedient and that the proposed terms are reasonable. Discusses the treaty with New Granada, and the advantages to defense, trade and commerce.

2745. Webster, Daniel (Mass.). "Railroad Across Isthmus of Panama," *Congressional Globe.* 30th Cong., 2nd Sess. (31 Jan. 1849) p. 413. Supports the railroad to connect the Atlantic to the Pacific; contends that it is necessary, practical, and can be attained at a reasonable expense.

2746. Webster, Daniel (Mass.). Remarks on Salaries of Foreign Ministers, *Congressional Globe.* 30th Cong., 2nd Sess. (26 Feb. 1849) pp. 596-597. Supports increasing the salaries of American ministers abroad.

2747. U.S. House. *Citizens of Essex County, Massachusetts.* 30th Cong., 2nd Sess. (H.Rpt.33). [Washington: 1849]. 1 pg. (Serial Set 545). Report against the petition from Essex County on extending pension benefits to widows.

2748. U.S. House. *Resolutions of the Legislature of Massachusetts, Relative to Slavery and the Slave Trade.* 30th Cong., 2nd Sess. (H.Misc.Doc.62). Washington: Tippin & Streeper, 1849. 2 pg. (Serial Set 544). Resolutions oppose slavery in the territories and slavery and the slave trade in the District of Columbia.

2749. U.S. Senate. *Opinions of the Judges of the Supreme Court of the United States, in the Case of "Smith vs. Turner," and "Norris vs. the City of Boston."*

30th Cong., 2nd Sess. (S.Misc.Doc.60). Washington: Tippin & Streeper, 1849. 149 pg. (Serial Set 533). Opinions on the two related cases concerning the restrictions and payment required in order for alien passengers to land in the ports of New York and Boston. Discusses the constitutional authority of Congress over commerce as opposed to the power of a state to protect itself from foreign paupers who would become a public charge.

2750. U.S. Senate. [Relief of Asa Andrews, of Ipswich, Massachusetts]. 30th Cong., 2nd Sess. (S.Rpt.271). Washington: [Tippin & Streeper], 1849. 5 pg. (Serial Set 535). Report of the Committee of Claims recommends not paying Asa Andrews the money judged to be due to him by the district court for Massachusetts. Reviews the circumstances of the case; includes supporting documentation from the Treasury Department.

NEW HAMPSHIRE

1ST CONGRESS, 1ST SESSION

2751. Livermore, Samuel (N.H.). "Department of Foreign Affairs," *Annals of Congress.* 1st Cong., 1st Sess. (16 June, 18 June 1789) pp. 477-479; 543, 544. Remarks on the power of appointment and removal of ambassadors and other public ministers. Maintains that if the advice and consent of the Senate is necessary to appoint these officers, it is likewise necessary for their removal.

2752. Livermore, Samuel (N.H.). "Duties on Tonnage," *Annals of Congress.* 1st Cong., 1st Sess. (6 May 1789) pp. 271-274. Opposes lowering the duty on foreign tonnage; maintains that the current duty is too low, rather than too high, to encourage navigation. Establishes that the duty is a tax upon foreigners only, and that it is no heavier on the southern states than the northern states.

2753. Livermore, Samuel (N.H.). "The Judiciary," *Annals of Congress.* 1st Cong., 1st Sess. (24 Aug., 29 Aug., 31 Aug. 1789) pp. 783-785; 796-797; 820-821, 831. Opposes establishing a federal district court system; maintains that it is unnecessary, inconvenient, expensive, and would establish two jurisdictions in the same place. Proposes that Congress establish a Supreme Court for appeals and State Courts of Admiralty for deciding cases of a maritime nature.

2754. Livermore, Samuel (N.H.). "Treasury Department," *Annals of Congress.* 1st Cong., 1st Sess. (25 June 1789) pp. 597-598. Brief remarks on the powers of the Secretary of the Treasury.

1ST CONGRESS, 2ND SESSION

2755. Livermore, Samuel (N.H.). "Public Credit," *Annals of Congress.* 1st Cong., 2nd Sess. (9 Feb. 1790) pp. 1145-1147, 1155-1156. Distinguishes between foreign and domestic creditors. Opposes paying domestic creditors the full interest and principal of the amount that appears on the face of the certificates. Maintains that as the domestic debt was contracted in depreciated notes, justice requires that less interest should be paid upon it.

2756. Livermore, Samuel (N.H.). "Public Credit," *Annals of Congress.* 1st Cong., 2nd Sess. (25 Feb. 1790) pp. 1352-1354, 1362-1363. Opposes the assumption of state debts until the accounts are settled and the proportion of the debt exceeding each state's just requisition is known.

1ST CONGRESS, 3RD SESSION

[no references]

2ND CONGRESS, 1ST SESSION

2757. Gilman, Nicholas (N.H.). "Post Office Bill," *Annals of Congress.* 2nd Cong., 1st Sess. (2 Feb. 1792) pp. 356-358. Defends the establishment of a postal route through Exeter, N.H. Discusses the importance of the town and competition between Portsmouth and Exeter.

2758. Smith, Jeremiah (N.H.). "The Public Debt," *Annals of Congress.* 2nd Cong., 1st Sess. (30 Mar. 1792) pp. 513-516. Opposes the assumption of state debts; if assumption prevails, would like debts to be calculated according to the number of each state's respective inhabitants.

2ND CONGRESS, 2ND SESSION

[no references]

3RD CONGRESS, 1ST SESSION

2759. Remonstrance of New Hampshire against a Decree of the Circuit Court of the United States, *Annals of Congress.* 3rd Cong., 1st Sess. (5 May 1794) pp. 92-93. Reiterates N.H.'s right to try, condemn, and distribute any prizes captured from the common enemy.

2760. "An Act Transferring, for a Limited Time, the Jurisdiction of Suits and Offences from the District to the Circuit Court of New Hampshire, and Assigning Certain Duties in Respect to Invalid Pensioners, to the Attorney of the Said District," *Statutes at Large*, Vol. I (3 Apr. 1794) pp. 352-353. Also printed in the *Annals of Congress* (3rd Cong., 1st Sess.) Appendix, p. 1429.

2761. "Remonstrance of the Legislature of New Hampshire against Certain Powers Exercised by the Judiciary of the United States," *American State Papers: Miscellaneous*, Vol. I (Doc. 51) p. 81. (ASP 037). Statement opposes interference by the Judiciary of the United States in the decision of the brig Susanna, tried for privateering by New Hampshire.

2762. "Remonstrance of the Legislature of New Hampshire against Certain Powers Exercised by the Judiciary of the United States," *American State Papers: Miscellaneous*, Vol. I (Doc. 48) p. 79. (ASP 037). Statement opposes interference of the judiciary of the United States, or Congress, with the rights of the states; Congress is an advisory body only.

3RD CONGRESS, 2ND SESSION

2763. "Claims for an Increase of Compensation to the Commissioner on Loans for New Hampshire; for Expenses Incurred and Advances Made on Public Account, and Additional Pay As a Aid-de-Camp; and for Money Lost," *American State Papers: Claims*, (Doc. 62) pp. 147-148. (ASP 036). Reports on the petitions of William Gardner, Moses White, and Thomas Coit.

2764. "Remonstrance of New Hampshire against the Exercise of Certain Powers by the Judiciary of the United States," *American State Papers: Miscellaneous*, Vol. I (Doc. 65) pp. 123-124. (ASP 037). Memorial supports the judicial power of the state court and opposes encroachment by the Judiciary of the United States; particularly refers to the case of the capture of the Susannah.

4TH CONGRESS, 1ST SESSION

2765. Smith, Jeremiah (N.H.). "Treaty with Great Britain," *Annals of Congress*. 4th Cong., 1st Sess. (7 Mar. 1796) pp. 593-601. Discusses the House's request for documentation from the President on instructions, etc. related to the treaty with Great Britain. Maintains that the power of making treaties is exclusively vested in the President and the Senate, not in the House, and that therefore such a request was inappropriate.

4TH CONGRESS, 2ND SESSION

[no references]

5ᵀᴴ CONGRESS, 1ˢᵀ SESSION

2766. Freeman, Jonathan (N.H.). "Answer to the President's Speech," *Annals of Congress*. 5th Cong., 1st Sess. (23 May 1797) pp. 88-93. Responds to the Directory of France and their rejection of Charles Pinckney, Minister to France.

5ᵀᴴ CONGRESS, 2ᴺᴰ SESSION

2767. Gordon, William (N.H.). "Alien Enemies," *Annals of Congress*. 5th Cong., 2nd Sess. (19 June 1798) pp. 1983-1986. Supports a bill to expel aliens guilty of treasonable or seditious practices.

2768. Gordon, William (N.H.). "Case of Griswold and Lyon," *Annals of Congress*. 5th Cong., 2nd Sess. (16 Feb. 1798) pp. 1054-1055. Testimony of events occurring in the assault.

2769. Sprague, Peleg (N.H.). "Case of Griswold and Lyon," *Annals of Congress*. 5th Cong., 2nd Sess. (20 Feb. 1798) pp. 1049-1050. Testimony of events occurring in the assault.

5ᵀᴴ CONGRESS, 3ᴿᴰ SESSION

2770. Gordon, William (N.H.). "Impeachment of William Blount," *Annals of Congress*. 5th Cong., 3rd Sess. (21 Dec. 1798) pp. 2479-2482. Remarks on the ability and necessity of the House to command his personal appearance.

2771. Gordon, William (N.H.). "Uniform Bankruptcy," *Annals of Congress*. 5th Cong., 3rd Sess. (15 Jan. 1799) pp. 2664-2668. Opposes a uniform bankruptcy act, particularly in the eastern states where it would undermine state laws.

6ᵀᴴ CONGRESS, 1ˢᵀ SESSION

[no references]

6ᵀᴴ CONGRESS, 2ᴺᴰ SESSION

2772. "An Act to Establish the District of Bristol, and to Annex the Towns of Kittery and Berwick to the District of Portsmouth," *Statutes at Large*, Vol. II Vol. II (25 Feb. 1801) pp. 101-102. Also printed in the *Annals of Congress* (6th Cong., 2nd Sess.) Appendix, p. 1550.

7TH CONGRESS, 1ST SESSION

[no references]

7TH CONGRESS, 2ND SESSION

2773. "An Act for the Relief of the Sufferers by Fire, in the Town of Portsmouth," *Statutes at Large*, Vol. II (19 Feb. 1803) p. 201.

2774. "Extension of Duty Bonds," *American State Papers: Finance*, Vol. II (Doc. 192) p. 21. (ASP 010). Report to suspend collection of bonds due from merchants who suffered from the Dec. 1802 fire at Portsmouth, N.H.

8TH CONGRESS, 1ST SESSION

2775. Plumer, William, Jr. (N.H.). "Amendment to the Constitution," *Annals of Congress.* 8th Cong., 1st Sess. (2 Dec. 1803) pp. 153-156. Opposes the amendment revising the process for election of President and Vice President; comments on the process of constitutional amendments.

8TH CONGRESS, 2ND SESSION

[no references]

9TH CONGRESS, 1ST SESSION

[no references]

9TH CONGRESS, 2 ND SESSION

2776. "Fees of Officers of State Courts," *Annals of Congress.* 9th Cong., 2nd Sess. (24 Oct. 1806) Appendix, pp. 1147-1149. List of fees allowed to officers of the court and others in New Hampshire for performing various services.

2777. "Norfolk and Portsmouth Memorial," *Annals of Congress.* 9th Cong., 2nd Sess. (12 Feb. 1806) Appendix, pp. 910-912. Memorial and resolutions address the aggressions of Great Britain against the U.S.; maintain that it is expedient to adopt measures to maintain the rights of the country and to redress injuries.

2778. "An Act for the Relief of the Suffers by Fire, in the Town of Portsmouth, New Hampshire," *Annals of Congress.* 9th Cong., 2nd Sess. (10 Feb. 1807) Appendix, p. 1252.

10TH CONGRESS, 1ST SESSION

2779. Durell, Daniel M. (N.H.). "Additional Army," *Annals of Congress*. 10th Cong., 1st Sess. (30 Mar. 1808) pp. 1877-1879. Supports appropriations to increase the size of the military force.

2780. Durell, Daniel M. (N.H.). "Fortifications and Gunboats," *Annals of Congress*. 10th Cong., 1st Sess. (9 Dec. 1807) pp. 1084-1086. Remarks to amend the bill appropriating more money for gunboats; contends that gunboats would be ineffective in northern ports and money would be better spent on forty-four gun frigates.

2781. Durell, Daniel M. (N.H.). "Yazoo Claims," *Annals of Congress*. 10th Cong., 1st Sess. (12 Feb. 1808) pp. 1606-1607. Supports hearing the claim at the bar of the House to determine the merits of the case.

2782. Gardner, Francis (N.H.). "Fortifications and Gunboats," *Annals of Congress*. 10th Cong., 1st Sess. (9 Dec. 1807) pp. 1086-1087. Prefers frigates to defend the northern and eastern ports; willing to test the utility of gunboats with a smaller number than proposed.

10TH CONGRESS, 2ND SESSION

2783. Durell, Daniel M. (N.H.). "Repeal of the Embargo," *Annals of Congress*. 10th Cong., 2nd Sess. (2 Feb. 1809) pp. 1311-1318. Supports repealing the embargo; discusses the ramifications for war.

11TH CONGRESS, 1ST SESSION

[no references]

11TH CONGRESS, 2ND SESSION

[no references]

11TH CONGRESS, 3RD SESSION

2784. Blaisdell, Daniel (N.H.). "Commercial Intercourse," *Annals of Congress*. 11th Cong., 3rd Sess. (26 Feb. 1811) pp. 1039-1056. Opposes the renewal of the Non-Intercourse Act of 1809. Provides a history of the effects of the act; discusses foreign policy obligations with the revocation of the French decrees.

2785. "An Act to Establish the Districts of Mumphreymagog, of Oswegatchie, and of the White Mountains," *Statutes at Large*, Vol. II (2 Mar. 1811) pp. 655-

656. Also printed in the *Annals of Congress* (11th Cong., 3rd Sess.) Appendix, pp. 1343-1344.

2786. "Extension of Patent Rights," *American State Papers: Miscellaneous*, Vol. II (Doc. 288) p. 146. (ASP 038). Favorable report on the petition of Benjamin and John Tyler for Benjamin's invention for the construction of flour and other mills. Committee also recommends that future provision be made to better provide for the renewal of letters patents.

12TH CONGRESS, 1ST SESSION

2787. Harper, John A. (N.H.). "Assistant Secretaries of War," *Annals of Congress*. 12th Cong., 1st Sess. (30 Apr. 1812) pp. 1362-1364. Defends the Secretary of War and his prompt action.

2788. "Protection to Manufactures," *American State Papers: Finance*, Vol. II (Doc. 364) p. 528. (ASP 010). Petition from the N.H. Iron Factory Company requests encouragement and protection to American manufactures by imposing duties on imported iron ware.

12TH CONGRESS, 2ND SESSION

2789. Harper, John A. (N.H.). "Yazoo Claims," *Annals of Congress*. 12th Cong., 2nd Sess. (15 Feb. 1813) pp. 1066-1073. Opposes amendments to the bill relative to the compromise of the Yazoo purchases. Provides a history of the claims; supports the rights of the innocent sub-purchasers.

13TH CONGRESS, 1ST SESSION

2790. Webster, Daniel (N.H.). "French Decrees," *Annals of Congress*. 13th Cong., 1st Sess. (10 June 1813) pp. 149-151. Reads resolutions requesting information on the repeal of the French Decrees as they relate to the present war.

13TH CONGRESS, 2ND SESSION

2791. Mason, Jeremiah (N.H.). "The Embargo," *Annals of Congress*. 13th Cong., 2nd Sess. (16 Dec. 1813) pp. 554-561. Opposes the embargo act, prohibiting all exports, as arbitrary and oppressive and an unconstitutional use of Presidential power.

2792. Webster, Daniel (N.H.). "Encouragement of Enlistments," *Annals of Congress*. 13th Cong., 2nd Sess. (14 Jan. 1814) pp. 940-951. Discusses the bill to encourage enlistments with bounty of money and land. Questions the purpose of increased enlistments; supports defense of our borders, but not continued invasion of Canada. Discusses the embargo.

2793. Webster, Daniel (N.H.). "Foreign Relations," *Annals of Congress.* 13th Cong., 2nd Sess. (3 Jan. 1814) pp. 824-825. Reopens the inquiry into the repeal of the French Decrees to shed light on the original commencement of the war and to determine if it was necessary and unavoidable.

2794. Webster, Daniel (N.H.). "Punishment of Treason," *Annals of Congress.* 13th Cong., 2nd Sess. (10 Jan. 1814) pp. 885-886. Opposes the resolution to try accusations of treason before military instead of civil tribunals.

2795. Webster, Daniel (N.H.). "Relations with France," *Annals of Congress.* 13th Cong., 2nd Sess. (12 Jan. 1814) pp. 904-906. Remarks on the resolution to obtain information about a purported letter from the French minister to the Secretary of State that was withdrawn from the possession of the Dept. of State.

2796. Webster, Daniel (N.H.). "Repeal of the Embargo," *Annals of Congress.* 13th Cong., 2nd Sess. (6 Apr. 1814) pp. 1965-1973. Supports the repeal of the embargo. Discusses the history of the embargo, intended impact and faults, and protective legislation.

13ᵀᴴ CONGRESS, 3ᴿᴰ SESSION

2797. Mason, Jeremiah (N.H.). "Militia of the United States," *Annals of Congress.* 13th Cong., 3rd Sess. (16 Nov. 1814) pp. 77-91. Discusses the proposed plan of military conscription; addresses the constitutionality of enforced enlistment, conflict with states' rights, enlistment of minors, and the current status of the military force.

2798. Webster, Daniel (N.H.). "Bank of the United States," *Annals of Congress.* 13th Cong., 3rd Sess. (2 Jan. 1815) pp. 1014-1023. Opposes the bill for a second Bank of the United States. Discusses the effects on State banks; compares the results to those of national banks in England and Europe.

2799. Webster, Daniel (N.H.). "The Ways and Means," *Annals of Congress.* 13th Cong., 3rd Sess. (24 Oct. 1814) pp. 459-465. Blames the need for a tax increase on those who made the taxes necessary by the declaration of war. Discusses the public credit, the war and the embargo.

14ᵀᴴ CONGRESS, 1ˢᵀ SESSION

2800. Atherton, Charles H. (N.H.). "The Revenue," *Annals of Congress.* 14th Cong., 1st Sess. (5 Feb. 1816) pp. 900-904. Opposes a direct tax as unequal, burdensome to collect, and inappropriate at a time when the country should be retrenching.

2801. Mason, Jeremiah (N.H.). "Amendment to the Constitution," *Annals of Congress.* 14th Cong., 1st Sess. (20 Mar. 1816) pp. 214-215. Opposes the election of Representatives by district but favors the election of electors by district.

2802. Mason, Jeremiah (N.H.). "Bank of the United States," *Annals of Congress.* 14th Cong., 1st Sess. (25 Mar. 1816) pp. 236-237; 244-246. Presents a proposal to increase the proportion of specie to be paid in at the time of subscription; defends his proposal.

2803. Webster, Daniel (N.H.). "Collection of the Revenue," *Annals of Congress.* 14th Cong., 1st Sess. (26 Apr. 1816) pp. 1440-1449. Presents and defends resolutions asserting that only the legal money of the U.S., or Treasury notes, are acceptable payment for duties and taxes. Objects to the acceptance of depressed paper as unequal, unjust, unconstitutional, and dangerous. Discusses the consequences to the public revenue of continuing to accept these notes. Addresses objections to his resolutions.

2804. Webster, Daniel (N.H.). "National Bank," *Annals of Congress.* 14th Cong., 1st Sess. (28 Feb. 1816) pp. 1091-1094. Opposes the establishment of a national bank; supports a specie bank and the resumption of specie payments as a remedy to the depreciated paper currency.

2805. "Extension of a Patent Right," *American State Papers: Miscellaneous,* Vol. II (Doc. 393) p. 278. (ASP 038). Favorable report on the petition of Benjamin and John Tyler to grant their request for exclusive rights to Benjamin's invention to improve the construction of flour and other mills.

14TH CONGRESS, 2ND SESSION

2806. Atherton, Charles H. (N.H.). "Vaccination," *Annals of Congress.* 14th Cong., 2nd Sess. (11 Jan. 1817) pp. 468-470. Supports vaccination of army personnel by army medical staff. Objects to Congress distributing vaccine upon request to the general public; questions constitutionality, expense, expertise needed, and conflict with existing state legislation.

2807. Mason, Jeremiah (N.H.). "Military Peace Establishment," *Annals of Congress.* 14th Cong., 2nd Sess. (17 Feb. 1817) pp. 124-130; 162-164. Resolution and speech support reducing the Military Peace Establishment. Contends that standing armies in free governments, maintained in times of peace, are dangerous to the rights and liberties of the people and are a great expense. Briefly reviews past legislation and expenses incurred.

15TH CONGRESS, 1ST SESSION

2808. Clagett, Clifton (N.H.). "Case of John Anderson," *Annals of Congress.* 15th Cong., 1st Sess. (14 Jan. 1818) pp. 738-740. Supports the propriety of the House continuing proceedings against John Anderson.

2809. Clagett, Clifton (N.H.). "Fugitives from Justice," *Annals of Congress.* 15th Cong., 1st Sess. (28 Jan. 1818) pp. 825-827. Maintains that the proposed bill is unnecessary.

2810. Clagett, Clifton (N.H.). "Internal Improvements," *Annals of Congress.* 15th Cong., 1st Sess. (6 Mar. 1818) pp. 1132-1135. Maintains that Congress does not have the constitutional power to construct roads and canals.

2811. Livermore, Arthur (N.H.). "Case of Colonel Anderson," *Annals of Congress.* 15th Cong., 1st Sess. (8 Jan. 1818) pp. 594-595; 599-601. Favors discharging John Anderson due to the irregularity of the proceedings and the fact that no statute of the U.S. declares bribery an offense.

2812. Morril, David L. (N.H.). "African Slave Trade," *Annals of Congress.* 15th Cong., 1st Sess. (12 Jan. 1818) pp. 102-105. Political and moral remarks support the abolition of slavery and the slave trade; defends position with passages from the Treaty of Ghent and the Constitution.

2813. Morril, David L. (N.H.). "Fugitive Slaves," *Annals of Congress.* 15th Cong., 1st Sess. (9 Mar. 1818) pp. 242-255. Disagrees with sections of the fugitive slave bill that unconstitutionally authorize an officer, under a state government, to perform duties under the criminal laws of Congress and that give unwarranted validity to certificates granted in the fugitives states. Gives legal precedence.

2814. Morril, David L. (N.H.). "Surviving Officers of the Revolution," *Annals of Congress.* 15th Cong., 1st Sess. (29 Jan. 1818) pp. 150-152. Supports providing relief to surviving officers and soldiers of the Revolution who are now in indigent circumstances.

2815. U.S. Senate. [Report on Memorial from Portsmouth, New Hampshire, etc. concerning Claims against France]. 15th Cong., 1st Sess. (S.Doc.124). [Washington: Edward De Krafft, Printer, 1818]. 4 pg. (Serial Set 2). Report against the claims of the memorialists for losses incurred from French aggressions during the late European wars. Maintains that the government fulfilled its duty; reviews relevant articles of the conventions of 1800 and 1803.

15TH CONGRESS, 2ND SESSION

2816. Livermore, Arthur (N.H.). "Admission of Missouri," *Annals of Congress.* 15th Cong., 2nd Sess. (15 Feb. 1819) pp. 1191-1193. Opposes slavery, particularly its expansion.

2817. Morril, Daniel L. (N.H.). "Duelling," *Annals of Congress.* 15th Cong., 2nd Sess. (9 Feb. 1819) pp. 218-219, 221-223. Remarks and resolution opposing dueling.

2818. Morril, Daniel L. (N.H.). "Memorial of Matthew Lyon," *Annals of Congress.* 15th Cong., 2nd Sess. (9 Dec. 1818) p. 60. Opposed to the petition of Matthew Lyon; maintains that the sedition law was constitutional and just.

16TH CONGRESS, 1ST SESSION

2819. Butler, Josiah (N.H.). "Military Appropriations," *Annals of Congress.* 16th Cong., 1st Sess. (14 Mar. 1820) pp. 1636-1637. Opposes the requested appropriations for fortifications of the coast; maintains that the government must economize and retrench.

2820. Clagett, Clifton (N.H.). "Admission of Missouri," *Annals of Congress.* 16th Cong., 1st Sess. (1 Feb. 1820) pp. 1033-1042. Opposes slavery in Missouri; addresses the states' rights issues, the treaty of 1803, the Constitution and the ordinance of 1787.

2821. Clagett, Clifton (N.H.). "Revolutionary Pensions," *Annals of Congress.* 16th Cong., 1st Sess. (1 Apr. 1820) pp. 1712-1715. Opposes reducing the pension due officers and soldiers of the Revolutionary War.

2822. Morril, David L. (N.H.). "Admission of Maine and Missouri," *Annals of Congress.* 16th Cong., 1st Sess. (17 Jan., 28 Jan. 1820) pp. 135-156; 294-299. Opposes the spread of slavery; demonstrates that Congress has the constitutional right and power to prohibit slavery in its territories and in states formed from those territories. Reviews the admissions of previous states, relevance of states' rights, and the evils of slavery; responds to comments.

2823. Morril, David L. (N.H.). "Duelling," *Annals of Congress.* 16th Cong., 1st Sess. (24 Apr. 1820) pp. 631-636. Resolution and remarks against dueling, in reaction to the duel between Commodores Decatur and Barron.

2824. Plumer, William, Jr. (N.H.). "Missouri Bill," *Annals of Congress.* 16th Cong., 1st Sess. (21 Feb. 1820) pp. 1412-1440. Opposes slavery in Missouri; addresses the powers of Congress in admitting new states, the admission of previous states, the treaty of 1803, moral, political and economic arguments against the institution of slavery, and the threat of dissolution of the Union.

2825. "An Act to Authorize the Erection of a Lighthouse on One of the Isles of Shoals, Near Portsmouth, in New Hampshire, and for Other Purposes," *Statutes at Large,* Vol. III (15 May 1820) pp. 598-600. Also printed in the *Annals of Congress* (16th Cong., 1st Sess.) Appendix, pp. 2622-2623.

2826. U.S. Senate. *Memorial of Thomas Sheafe, and Others, Citizens of Portsmouth, N.H.* 16th Cong., 1st Sess. (S.Doc.122). Washington: Gales &

Seaton, 1820. 5 pg. (Serial Set 27). Memorial opposes the unfair advantages of foreign nations in trade, particularly France; gives examples.

16TH CONGRESS, 2ND SESSION

2827. Butler, Josiah (N.H.). "Missouri," *Annals of Congress.* 16th Cong., 2nd Sess. (30 Jan. 1821) pp. 986-989. Opposes the admission of Missouri into the Union until her constitution conforms to the Constitution of the United States. Maintains that every citizen has the right, regardless of color, to emigrate and become a citizen of another state.

2828. Morril, David L. (N.H.). "Admission of Missouri," *Annals of Congress.* 16th Cong., 2nd Sess. (11 Dec. 1820) pp. 102-115. Speech on the Missouri resolution, particularly addressing the constitution of Missouri, and that section which denies free citizens of some states the privilege of settling in Missouri because of their color.

2829. "Extension of a Patent Right," *American State Papers: Miscellaneous,* Vol. II (Doc. 495) pp. 627-628. (ASP 038). Favorable report on the petition of Benjamin and John Tyler to grant their request for exclusive rights to Benjamin's invention to improve the construction of mills. Same as H.rpt.13 (16-2) 57 (entry **2830**).

2830. U.S. House. *Report of the Select Committee, to Which Was Referred the Petition of Benjamin Tyler and John Tyler, Accompanied with a Bill for Their Relief.* 16th Cong., 2nd Sess. (H.Rpt.13). [Washington: Gales & Seaton, 1820]. 2 pg. (Serial Set 57). Same as Misc.495 (16-2) ASP 038. See entry **2829**.

17TH CONGRESS, 1ST SESSION

2831. "Trade with the British West Indies," *Annals of Congress.* 17th Cong., 1st Sess. (15 Mar. 1822) Appendix, pp. 2227-2228. Same as Com.nav.254 (17-1) ASP 015 (entry **2837**) and S.doc.64 (17-1) 60 (entry **2838**). See entry **2837** for abstract.

2832. Butler, Josiah (N.H.). "Compensation Bill," *Annals of Congress.* 17th Cong., 1st Sess. (27 Apr. 1822) pp. 1718-1719. Supports reducing compensation to members of the House and other public officers.

2833. Whipple, Thomas, Jr. (N.H.). "Compensation Bill," *Annals of Congress.* 17th Cong., 1st Sess. (30 Apr. 1822) pp. 1764-1766. Defends the Committee of Retrenchment; addresses accusations concerning the necessity and public demand for retrenchment.

2834. "An Act to Amend the Act, Entitled "An Act to Establish the District of Bristol, and to Annex the Towns of Kittery and Berwick to the District of

Portsmouth," Passed February Twenty-fifth, Eighteen Hundred and One," *Statutes at Large*, Vol. III (17 Apr. 1822) p. 662. Also printed in the *Annals of Congress* (17th Cong., 1st Sess) Appendix, p. 2588.

2835. "Application of New Hampshire for a Grant of Land for the Purpose of Education," *American State Papers: Public Lands*, Vol. III (Doc. 338) pp. 499-500. (ASP 030). Resolutions from New Hampshire support a just appropriation of public land to each state for the purposes of education.

2836. "Light-Houses, &c.," *American State Papers: Commerce and Navigation*, Vol. II (Doc. 239) pp. 505-506. (ASP 015). Correspondence, report, and estimate of expenses support building a seawall between Smutty Nose Island and Cedar Island, part of the Isles of Shoals.

2837. "Trade with the British West Indies," *American State Papers: Commerce and Navigation*, Vol. II (Doc. 254) pp. 629-630. (ASP 015). Memorial from Portsmouth supports the existing system of navigation laws until foreign nations will consent to a mutual relaxation of the prohibitory laws; opposes a repeal of these acts as injurious to the commerce of the country. Same as S.doc.64 (17-1) 60 (entry **2838**). Also printed in *Annals of Congress*, "Trade with the British West Indies," Appendix, pp. 2227-2228 (entry **2831**).

2838. U.S. Senate. *Memorial and Resolutions of the Merchants and Others, of the Town of Portsmouth, N.H. in Relation to the Acts Restricting the West India Trade.* 17th Cong., 1st Sess. (S.Doc.64). Washington: Gales & Seaton, 1822. 4 pg. (Serial Set 60). Same as Com.nav.254 (17-1) ASP 015. See entry **2837**. Also printed as *Annals of Congress*, "Trade with the British West Indies," Appendix, pp. 2227-2228 (entry **2831**).

17TH CONGRESS, 2ND SESSION

2839. Morril, David L. (N.H.). "Revolutionary Pensions," *Annals of Congress.* 17th Cong., 2nd Sess. (28 Feb. 1823) pp. 308-313. Supports the bill to review cases erroneously decided under the 1820 Revolutionary pensions bill. Provides a brief history of Revolutionary pension bills and their problems.

2840. "An Act Altering the Time of Holding the Circuit Court in the Districts of Maine (a) and New Hampshire (b)," *Statutes at Large*, Vol. III (3 Mar. 1823) pp. 773-774. Also printed in the *Annals of Congress* (17th Cong., 2nd Sess.) Appendix, p. 1400.

18TH CONGRESS, 1ST SESSION

2841. Bartlett, Ichabod (N.H.). "Address of Ninian Edwards," *Annals of Congress.* 18th Cong., 1st Sess. (22 Apr. 1824) pp. 2478-2479. Brief remarks on the proper course of action concerning the recall of Ninian Edwards as minister to Mexico.

2842. Bartlett, Ichabod (N.H.). "The Greek Cause," *Annals of Congress.* 18th Cong., 1st Sess. (24 Jan. 1824) pp. 1200-1201. Brief remarks on the resolution to appoint a commissioner to Greece.

2843. Livermore, Arthur (N.H.). "The Tariff Bill," *Annals of Congress.* 18th Cong., 1st Sess. (4 Mar. 1824) pp. 1743-1745. Remarks on the tariff bill as it affects the New England farmer; particularly addresses the duty on wool.

2844. U.S. House. *Memorial of the Merchants, Ship Owners, and Mechanics, of Portsmouth, in the State of New Hampshire.* 18th Cong., 1st Sess. (H.Doc.87). Washington: Gales & Seaton, 1824. 5 pg. (Serial Set 97). Memorial supports the present tariffs and opposes the proposed increase of duties on articles imported for the construction and equipment of ships.

18TH CONGRESS, 2ND SESSION

2845. Bartlett, Ichabod (N.H.). "Suppression of Piracy," *Register of Debates.* 18th Cong., 2nd Sess. (1 Mar. 1825) pp. 720-726. Discusses piracy; opposes the bill to increase naval power, permit merchant vessels to arm, and reward captors of pirates as ineffectual. Recommends furnishing merchant vessels with armament, and authorizing reprisals upon the inhabitants of Cuba.

19TH CONGRESS, 1ST SESSION

2846. Bartlett, Ichabod (N.H.). "Amendment of the Constitution," *Register of Debates.* 19th Cong., 1st Sess. (30 Mar. 1826) pp. 1914-1930. Opposes the proposed electoral amendments to the Constitution; particularly objects to election by districts.

2847. Bartlett, Ichabod (N.H.). "Judiciary System," *Register of Debates.* 19th Cong., 1st Sess. (24 Jan. 1826) pp. 1106-1109. Recommends that rather than increase the number of Supreme Court judges and compromise their impartiality, that District judges take some work of the Circuit Courts judges.

2848. Bartlett, Ichabod (N.H.). "Mission to Panama," *Register of Debates.* 19th Cong., 1st Sess. (20 Apr. 1826) pp. 2415-2419. Debates the propriety of the House offering opinions in relation to foreign policy and the instruction of foreign ministers; supports U.S. representation at the Panama Congress.

2849. Whipple, Thomas, Jr. (N.H.). "Amendment of the Constitution," *Register of Debates.* 19th Cong., 1st Sess. (28 Mar. 1826) pp. 1821-1839. After stating reluctance and safeguards to making constitutional amendments, addresses the proposed change for states to district for the election of members to the House, as well as for the choice of a President and Vice President.

2850. Whipple, Thomas, Jr. (N.H.). "Massachusetts Claims," *Register of Debates*. 19th Cong., 1st Sess. (8 Apr. 1826) pp. 2125-2128. Supports the claims of Massachusetts for militia services rendered for the purpose of repelling invasion. Discusses the refusal of Massachusetts to obey the call for militia during the late war.

2851. Woodbury, Levi (N.H.). "The Judicial System," *Register of Debates*. 19th Cong., 1st Sess. (11 Apr., 12 Apr. 1826) pp. 463-483; 508-509. Lengthy speech against increasing the number of Supreme Court judges; reviews arguments for and against proposition.

2852. Woodbury, Levi (N.H.). "On the Panama Mission," *Register of Debates*. 19th Cong., 1st Sess. (14 Mar. 1826) pp. 184-198. Opposes involvement in the Panama Congress; maintains that the Congress is permanent and many of its objects are belligerent. Contends that it would be difficult to maintain neutrality.

19TH CONGRESS, 2ND SESSION

2853. Woodbury, Levi (N.H.). "The Bankrupt Bill," *Register of Debates*. 19th Cong., 2nd Sess. (24 Jan., 27 Jan. 1827) pp. 89-91; 145-151. Contends that previous bankruptcy legislation had been limited essentially to persons engaged in trade; opposes the inclusion of farmers in this bill and the violation of the right of states to enact insolvent systems for persons not traders. Provides a history of bankruptcy legislation as a foundation for the current system.

2854. Woodbury, Levi (N.H.). "The Colonial Trade Bill," *Register of Debates*. 19th Cong., 2nd Sess. (24 Feb. 1827) pp. 468-469. Offers amendment, arguments, and deadline for Great Britain to remove her prohibition to trade with her colonies and to reduce duties to no higher than her own.

2855. Woodbury, Levi (N.H.). "Duty on Salt," *Register of Debates*. 19th Cong., 2nd Sess. (2 Feb. 1827) pp. 232-243, 250-252. Supports a repeal of the duty on salt as a war-tax that is unequal and exorbitant. Discusses the salt tax in England and France; compares it to duties on other commodities.

2856. Woodbury, Levi (N.H.). "Gradual Improvement of the Navy," *Register of Debates*. 19th Cong., 2nd Sess. (15 Feb. 1827) pp. 367-370. Supports building a dry dock at Portsmouth New Hampshire.

2857. "Application of the Citizens of Portsmouth, New Hampshire, for the Construction of a Dry Dock at That Place," *American State Papers: Naval Affairs*, Vol. III (Doc. 337) pp. 46-47. (ASP 025). Memorial requests the construction of a dry dock at Portsmouth; gives the historical role and environmental and defense advantages. Same as S.doc.57 (19-2) 146 (entry **2861**) and H.doc.92 (19-2) 152 (entry **2858**).

2858. U.S. House. *Memorial of the Citizens of Portsmouth, N.H. respecting the Construction of a Dry Dock, at the Navy Yard at That Place.* 19th Cong., 2nd Sess. (H.Doc.92). Washington: Gales & Seaton, 1827. 5 pg. (Serial Set 152). Same as S.doc.57 (19-2) 146 (entry **2861**) and Nav.aff.337 (19-2) ASP 025 (entry **2857**).

2859. U.S. House. *Message from the President of the United States, Transmitting a Report of an Examination and Survey Which Has Been Made of a Site for a Dry Dock at Portsmouth, N.H., Charlestown, Mass., Brooklyn, N.Y., and Gosport, Va.* 19th Cong., 2nd Sess. (H.Doc.125). Washington: Gales & Seaton, 1827. 46 pg. (Serial Set 153). Report recommends construction of three dry docks in the following order of importance: Charlestown, Gosport, and Brooklyn. Report gives topographical and soils information and indicates the most eligible site, with the corresponding expenses and advantages.

2860. U.S. Senate. *Memorial of Sundry Citizens of Portsmouth, N.H. on the Subject of Their Claims against France, for Injuries Sustained since A.D. 1806.* 19th Cong., 2nd Sess. (S.Doc.51). Washington: Gales & Seaton, 1827. 4 pg. (Serial Set 146). Memorial seeks claims for injuries caused by seizure, destruction and capture of American vessels by the French government.

2861. U.S. Senate. *Memorial of the Citizens of Portsmouth, N.H. respecting the Construction of a Dry Dock, at the Navy Yard at That Place.* 19th Cong., 2nd Sess. (S.Doc.57). Washington: Gales & Seaton, 1827. 5 pg. (Serial Set 146). Same as Nav.aff.337 (19-2) ASP 025 (entry **2857**) and H.doc.92 (19-2) 152 (entry **2858**). See entry **2857** for abstract.

2862. U.S. Senate. [Report on Memorials of Merchants of Portsmouth, New Hampshire, New York, Philadelphia, and Baltimore on the Subject of Their Claims against France]. 19th Cong., 2nd Sess. (S.Doc.52). [Washington: Gales & Seaton, 1827]. 1 pg. (Serial Set 146). Supports the claims; does not recommend legislative action as negotiation belongs to the Executive branch.

20TH CONGRESS, 1ST SESSION

2863. Bartlett, Ichabod (N.H.). "Accounting Officers of the Treasury," *Register of Debates.* 20th Cong., 1st Sess. (24 Mar. 1828) pp. 1963-1965. Supports the discretionary power of the President over the contingent expenses of the government.

2864. Bartlett, Ichabod (N.H.). "Historical Paintings," *Register of Debates.* 20th Cong., 1st Sess. (9 Jan. 1828) pp. 942-944. Remarks on appropriate subjects for historical paintings proposed for the Rotunda.

2865. Bartlett, Ichabod (N.H.). "Retrenchment," *Register of Debates.* 20th Cong., 1st Sess. (6 Feb. 1828) pp. 1401-1417. Supports investigation of finances as it will vindicate charges upon the Executive; reviews the finances of the country; addresses each charge of misconduct.

2866. Bell, Samuel (N.H.). "Imprisonment for Debt," *Register of Debates.* 20th Cong., 1st Sess. (18 Jan. 1828) pp. 85-87. Opposes the bill to abolish imprisonment for debt.

2867. Bell, Samuel (N.H.). "Powers of the Vice President," *Register of Debates.* 20th Cong., 1st Sess. (12 Feb. 1828) pp. 306-308. Discusses the power of the Vice President, as presiding officer of the Senate, to preserve order in the Senate; maintains that the power is incident to the office.

2868. Bell, Samuel (N.H.). "Revolutionary Officers," *Register of Debates.* 20th Cong., 1st Sess. (12 Mar. 1828) pp. 436-440. Contends that when officers voluntarily accepted the commutation of five years full pay in return for the promised half pay for life, the responsibility of the government for further compensation was negated.

2869. Brown, Titus (N.H.). "Land Claims in Tennessee," *Register of Debates.* 20th Cong., 1st Sess. (29 Apr. 1828) pp. 2520-2523. Opposes the land claims of Tennessee. Reviews the basis of her claim. Maintains that Tennessee should provide full evidence of her claim that the lands are of no value to the U.S.

2870. Whipple, Thomas, Jr. (N.H.). "Internal Improvements," *Register of Debates.* 20th Cong., 1st Sess. (28 Feb. 1828) pp. 1669-1672. Supports the professionalism, accuracy, and importance of the surveys completed for considered roads, canals, and other works of internal improvement.

2871. Whipple, Thomas, Jr. (N.H.). "Retrenchment," *Register of Debates.* 20th Cong., 1st Sess. (26 Jan. 1828) pp. 1198-1200. Defends the recommendation of the Committee on Public Lands to print a revised compilation of the public land laws under the direction of an officer of the House instead of by contract.

2872. Whipple, Thomas, Jr. (N.H.). "Retrenchment," *Register of Debates.* 20th Cong., 1st Sess. (5 Feb. 1828) pp. 1396-1398. Supports an inquiry into the expenditures of the present administration compared to those of former ones.

2873. Woodbury, Levi (N.H.). "Discriminating Duties," *Register of Debates.* 20th Cong., 1st Sess. (6 Feb. 1828) pp. 237-243. Addresses the history and condition of the discriminating duties, the changes that will be effected by the proposed bill, and the reasons in favor of those changes.

2874. Woodbury, Levi (N.H.). "French Colonial Trade," *Register of Debates.* 20th Cong., 1st Sess. (31 Mar. 1828) pp. 553-554. Supporting remarks on the bill to regulate trade with the islands of Martinique and Guadeloupe.

2875. Woodbury, Levi (N.H.). "Imprisonment for Debt," *Register of Debates.* 20th Cong., 1st Sess. (18 Jan. 1828) pp. 89-90. Compares the treatment of debtors in New Hampshire to that proposed under this legislation.

2876. Woodbury, Levi (N.H.). "Powers of the Vice President," *Register of Debates.* 20th Cong., 1st Sess. (12 Feb. 1828) pp. 323-324. Briefly remarks on the power of the Vice President to call the Senate to order.

2877. Woodbury, Levi (N.H.). "Revolutionary Officers," *Register of Debates.* 20th Cong., 1st Sess. (12 Mar. 1828) pp. 440-448. Addresses arguments presented opposing the pension for Revolutionary officers.

2878. Woodbury, Levi (N.H.). "Surviving Officers of the Revolution," *Register of Debates.* 20th Cong., 1st Sess. (24 Jan. 1828) pp. 128-137, 137-138. Supports paying the pension; provides a history of promises and legislation.

2879. "In Favor of Increase of Duties on Imports," *American State Papers: Finance,* Vol. V (Doc. 828) pp. 748-749. (ASP 013). Inhabitants of New Hampshire plea for protection of wool-growing and manufacturing industries by increasing duties on imports. Same as H.doc.80 (20-1) 171 (entry **2882**) and H.doc.81 (20-1) 171 (entry **2873**).

2880. "On the Construction of Dry Docks at Brooklyn, New York, and Portsmouth, New Hampshire," *American State Papers: Naval Affairs,* Vol. III (Doc. 350) pp. 137-139. (ASP 025). Report supports the construction of dry docks at the navy yards at Brooklyn and Portsmouth, in addition to those authorized at Charlestown and Gosport, as essential to the navy in time of war.

2881. U.S. House. *Letter from the Secretary of War, Transmitting a Report of the Surveys of the Kennebec River, and of Contemplated Routes for Canals, Connected with the Waters of the Said Rivers.* 20th Cong., 1st Sess. (H.Doc.173). Washington: Gales & Seaton, 1828. 57 pg. (Serial Set 173). Reports of the various surveys in the States of Maine, N.H., and Vermont. Surveys include: the Kennebec River, from its mouth up to Augusta; the Brunswick Canal, to join the waters of Merrymeeting and Casco Bays (reviews three possible routes); Cobbisecontee Canal, to connect the waters of the Kennebec at Gardner, with those of the Androscoggin at Leeds; Ammonoosuck Canal, to unite the waters of the Connecticut with those of the Androscogign; Oliverian Canal, to connect the waters of the Connecticut with those of the Pemigawasset or Merrimac; Sunapee Canal, to connect the Connecticut River with the Merrimac; Pasumpsic Canal, to unite the waters of the Connecticut with those of Lake Memphremagog; Montpelier Canal, to connect the waters of Lake Champlain with those of Connecticut River; Rutland Canal, to connect the town of Rutland, Vt. with the northern canal at Whitehall, N.Y.; and La Moille Canal, to connect Lake Memphremagog with Lake Champlain.

2882. U.S. House. *Memorial of Citizens of New Hampshire, in Favor of Further Protection to Domestic Manufactures.* 20th Cong., 1st Sess.

(H.Doc.80). Washington: Gales & Seaton, 1828. 5 pg. (Serial Set 171). Same as Finance 828 (20-1) ASP 013 (entry **2879**) and H.doc.81 (20-1) 171 (entry **2883**). See entry **2879** for abstract.

2883. U.S. House. *Petition of Farmers in New Hampshire, Praying Protection for the Interests of Agriculture and Manufactures.* 20th Cong., 1st Sess. (H.Doc.81). Washington: Gales & Seaton, 1828. 5 pg. (Serial Set 171). Same as H.doc.80 (20-1) 171 (entry **2882**) and Finance 828 (20-1) ASP 013 (entry **2879**). See entry **2879** for abstract.

2884. U.S. House. *Subscribe Stock Tenth Turnpike Road Company, N.H.* 20th Cong., 1st Sess. (H.Rpt.233). [Washington: 1828]. 8 pg. (Serial Set 179). Report supports the petition to Congress for aid in repairing and completing the road through the White Mountains, N.H., and for extending that road to the Vermont border in one direction, and to the Maine border in another.

20TH CONGRESS, 2ND SESSION

2885. U.S. House. *Dry Docks.* 20th Cong., 2nd Sess. (H.Rpt.8). [Washington: Gales & Seaton, 1828. 8 pg. (Serial Set 190). Includes reprint of Nav.aff.350 (20-1) ASP 025 (entry **2880**) in support of constructing dry docks at Portsmouth and Brooklyn; also includes report on the value of dry docks.

21ST CONGRESS, 1ST SESSION

2886. Bell, Samuel (N.H.). "Graduation Bill," *Register of Debates.* 21st Cong., 1st Sess. (5 May 1830) pp. 416-417. Opposes the bill; particularly objects to special prices for settlers.

2887. Hubbard, Henry (N.H.). "Buffalo and New Orleans Road Bill," *Register of Debates.* 21st Cong., 1st Sess. (12 Apr. 1830) pp. 760-768. Opposes such roads as objects of local and internal improvement designed for the few at the expense the many. Responds to Mr. Richardson's (Mass.) plans for extending the road into New England; maintains that N.H. would not support such a waste of the public funds. Contends that the proposed road is unnecessary, and that it is unconstitutional, unequal and unjust. Addresses opponents' arguments. Discusses the current incomes and expenses of the government.

2888. Hubbard, Henry (N.H.). "Indian Affairs," *Register of Debates.* 21st Cong., 1st Sess. (1 Mar. 1830) pp. 590, 591-592. Objects to printing the memorial at this time; maintains that it offers no new arguments or views of the subject which have not been considered by the Committee on Indian Affairs. Defends himself against disparaging remarks by Mr. Burges (R.I.).

2889. Hubbard, Henry (N.H.). "Revolutionary Pensioners," *Register of Debates.* 21st Cong., 1st Sess. (18 Mar. 1830) pp. 627-628. Opposes the present pension system as partial and unjust because it is based upon need rather than actual services rendered. Supports extending the benefits of the pension system to include every individual who performed the requisite term of service.

2890. Woodbury, Levi (N.H.). "The Graduation Bill," *Register of Debates.* 21st Cong., 1st Sess. (5 May, 7 May 1830) pp. 413-414; 424. Supports the bill to graduate the price of public lands that failed to sell at public auction.

2891. Woodbury, Levi (N.H.). "Mr. Foot's Resolution," *Register of Debates.* 21st Cong., 1st Sess. (19 Jan., 24 Feb. 1830) pp. 29-30; 179-196. Proposes an amendment of the resolution to have all public lands surveyed speedily and then sold on such terms as proper. Discusses the resolution in the context of politics, sectionism, economics and the previous war.

21ST CONGRESS, 2ND SESSION

2892. Woodbury, Levi (N.H.). "Post Office Department," *Register of Debates.* 21st Cong., 2nd Sess. (4 Feb., 10 Feb. 1831) pp. 93-96; 182-193. Defends his Committee's report of their examination of Post Office expenditures and supports the resolution to examine witnesses as to the causes of removals in the Post Office Department.

2893. Woodbury, Levi (N.H.). "Turkish Commission," *Register of Debates.* 21st Cong., 2nd Sess. (22 Feb. 1831) pp. 239-241. Supports the power of the President to appoint diplomatic agents, including the ones sent to Constantinople, without the advice of the Senate, to be paid out of the President's contingent fund or by an appropriation.

22ND CONGRESS, 1ST SESSION

2894. Hill, Isaac (N.H.). "Apportionment Bill," *Register of Debates.* 22nd Cong., 1st Sess. (25 Apr. 1832) pp. 863-865. Opposes an apportionment based on the arbitrary and unequal principle presented, even though it would result in increased representation for New Hampshire.

2895. Hill, Isaac (N.H.). "Bank of the United States," *Register of Debates.* 22nd Cong., 1st Sess. (8 June 1832) pp. 1056-1068. Objects to renewing the charter of the Bank of the United States. Contends that it has created an unsound currency, illicitly influenced elections and public opinion, and extorted memorials supporting the renewal of the charter. Maintains that the Senate should wait until the charter expires in four years before considering its renewal. Gives examples of New Hampshire bank experiences.

2896. Hill, Isaac (N.H.). "Newspaper Postage," *Register of Debates.* 22nd Cong., 1st Sess. (9 May 1832) pp. 907-918. Opposes abolishing postage on newspapers for the following reasons: current postage already doesn't cover their expenses, it would impose a financial burden on the Post Office to transport them free of charge, it would be harmful to small newspaper establishments, and it would be an unequal tax.

2897. Hill, Isaac (N.H.). "The Tariff," *Register of Debates.* 22nd Cong., 1st Sess. (1 Feb., 7 Feb. 1832) pp. 227-253; 298-302. Opposes the proposed tariff modification. Devotes majority of speech to demonstrating that the tariff of 1824 and 1828 did not benefit manufactures; describes manufacturing in New Hampshire, compared with Vermont, and demonstrates through examples of iron, woolens, and hemp tariffs. Maintains that the North and South have common tariff interests, and that extensive evasion of duties occurs.

2898. Hubbard, Henry (N.H.). "Apportionment Bill," *Register of Debates.* 22nd Cong., 1st Sess. (1 Feb. 1832) pp. 1709-1716. Opposes the proposed 48,000 apportionment ratio as detrimental to N.H., Vt., and Massachusetts.

2899. Hubbard, Henry (N.H.). "Revolutionary Pensions," *Register of Debates.* 22nd Cong., 1st Sess. (29 Feb., 24 May 1832) pp. 1919-1943; 3098-3099. Speech and brief remarks support the pension bill; arguments detail the deficiencies of past legislation, including number of terms of enlistments, and whether the enlistments are in regiments raised by the Continental Congress, or by the authority of the states, militia of the country, or by voluntary association of individuals. Provides a sectional analysis of remedies presented in the proposed bill.

2900. U.S. House. *Memorial of Inhabitants of Cheshire County, New Hampshire.* 22nd Cong., 1st Sess. (H.Doc.277). Washington: Duff Green, 1832. 2 pg. (Serial Set 221). Memorial supports the tariff of 1828 and opposes proposed changes.

2901. U.S. House. *Memorial of the Farmers' Bank in Amherst, N.H., Praying for the Renewal of the Charter of the Bank of the United States.* 22nd Cong., 1st Sess. (H.Doc.110). Washington: Duff Green, 1832. 5 pg. (Serial Set 219).

2902. U.S. House. *Proceedings of a Public Meeting at Claremont, New Hampshire, Relative to the Protection of American Industry.* 22nd Cong., 1st Sess. (H.Doc.288). Washington: Duff Green, 1832. 2 pg. (Serial Set 221). Statement supports tariffs enacted from 1788 to 1828; objects to weakening their protection.

22ND CONGRESS, 2ND SESSION

2903. Bell, Samuel (N.H.). "The Tariff," *Register of Debates.* 22nd Cong., 2nd Sess. (25 Feb. 1833) pp. 742-745. Supports the proposed protective tariff bill; maintains that it would give adequate protection to all and restore peace and harmony to agitated sections of the country. Discusses the provisions of the proposed bill and gives reasons for his support.

2904. Hill, Isaac (N.H.). "Public Lands," *Register of Debates.* 22nd Cong., 2nd Sess. (23 Jan. 1833) pp. 193-203. Opposes distributing the proceeds from the public lands to the states. Examines the effect on N.H., claiming the expense of collection and the greater portion of duties paid by consumers on the seaboard make it uneconomical for them; discusses connection with the tariff.

2905. Hill, Isaac (N.H.). "The Tariff," *Register of Debates.* 22nd Cong., 2nd Sess. (25 Feb. 1833) pp. 703-704. Supports the protective system.

2906. U.S. House. *Proceedings of a Meeting of the Democratic Republican Citizens of Portsmouth, New Hampshire, on the Subject of the Tariff, Nullification, and the Public Lands.* 22nd Cong., 2nd Sess. (H.Doc.99). Washington: Duff Green, 1832. 4 pg. (Serial Set 234). Meeting held to discuss the relations between the federal government and South Carolina. Resolutions support the actions of President Jackson regarding South Carolina and the proposed reduction of tariffs; miscellaneous resolutions passed oppose distribution of the proceeds of the sales of public lands, appropriations for the Maysville road, and the renewal of the charter of the United States Bank.

2907. U.S. Senate. *Report of a Select Committee of the Legislature of New Hampshire, on the Subject of Internal Improvements, Tariff, Public Lands, Revenue, &c.* 22nd Cong., 2nd Sess. (S.Doc.53). Washington: Duff Green, 1832. 9 pg. (Serial Set 230). Report of the Committee states that Congress does not have the constitutional right to adopt and execute, at national expense, a system of internal improvements; also opposes an amendment to the Constitution giving Congress the power to make roads, bridges, and canals.

23RD CONGRESS, 1ST SESSION

2908. "Portsmouth (N.H.) Memorial," *Register of Debates.* 23rd Cong., 1st Sess. (17 Feb. 1834) pp. 566-569. Debate on memorial from Portsmouth praying for the restoration of the public deposits. Remarks by Samuel Bell (N.H.) and Isaac Hill (N.H.).

2909. Bell, Samuel (N.H.). "New Hampshire Memorials," *Register of Debates.* 23rd Cong., 1st Sess. (29 Apr. 1834) pp. 1538-1541. Supports the memorials and memorialists from Dover and Somersworth requesting the restoration of the deposits and the currency. Remarks on the financial distress in New England.

2910. Bell, Samuel (N.H.). "Portsmouth (N.H.) Memorial," *Register of Debates.* 23rd Cong., 1st Sess. (17 Feb. 1834) pp. 566, 568-569. Presents memorial requesting the restoration of the public deposits; defends the character of the memorialists.

2911. Harper, Joseph M. (N.H.). Remark on New Hampshire Resolutions," *Congressional Globe.* 23rd Cong., 1st Sess. (17 Feb. 1834) p. 181. Presents a memorial from Portsmouth requesting a restoration of the deposits to the Bank of the United States, the removal of which they blame for the current distress of the country. Mr. Harper disagrees with the stated reasons for the distress and presents opposing resolutions passed at district meetings which he contends more accurately represent public opinion. Same remarks printed in the *Register of Debates*, "Memorial from Portsmouth, N.H.," pp. 2715-2717.

2912. Hill, Isaac (N.H.). "General Appropriation Bill," *Register of Debates.* 23rd Cong., 1st Sess. (21 June 1834) pp. 2046-2050. Opposes appropriations to print books for members of Congress, particularly Clarke and Force's *Documentary History of the American Revolution.* Maintains that the printers are realizing huge profits at the public's expense.

2913. Hill, Isaac (N.H.). "Interest to States for Advances," *Register of Debates.* 23rd Cong., 1st Sess. (14 June 1834) pp. 2003-2006. Objects to paying interest on the claims of several states for services rendered during the War of 1812. Considers the effects of setting the precedence; estimates the amount of money required. Discusses the Massachusetts' claims.

2914. Hill, Isaac (N.H.). "New Hampshire Resolutions," *Register of Debates.* 23rd Cong., 1st Sess. (23 June 1834) pp. 2057-2062. Supports resolutions from the Legislature of N.H. approving the actions of the President against the Bank of the United States. Discusses the Executive's treatment of the petitioners; discounts petitions supporting the bank. Text of resolutions included.

2915. Hill, Isaac (N.H.). "New Hampshire Resolutions," *Register of Debates.* 23rd Cong., 1st Sess. (24 June 1834) pp. 2066-2069. Defends the writers of the resolutions. Reprint of remarks printed in *Congressional Globe* that he was unable to make concerning the reception of the resolutions.

2916. Hill, Isaac (N.H.). Remarks on State Claims on Advances Made during the Last War, *Congressional Globe.* 23rd Cong., 1st Sess. (14 June 1834) pp. 450-451. Objects to paying any interest on state claims; contends that the Treasury cannot support it, the books would need to be reopened. Particularly objects to the claim of Massachusetts, recollecting her refusal to call out her militia during the late war.

2917. Hill, Isaac (N.H.). Remarks on the Bank of the United States, *Congressional Globe.* 23rd Cong., 1st Sess. (17 Feb. 1834) pp. 178-179. Remarks on the removal of the deposits and the conduct of the United States Branch Bank at Portsmouth, N.H. Questions the validity of memorials and petitions supporting the bank. Same remarks also printed in the *Register of Debates*, "Portsmouth (N.H.) Memorial," pp. 566-568.

2918. Hill, Isaac (N.H.). "Removal of the Deposits," *Register of Debates.* 23rd Cong., 1st Sess. (3 Mar., 4 Mar. 1834) pp. 756-802. Supports the removal of the deposits and the demise of the Bank of the U.S. Examines the report of the Committee on Finance; maintains that the distress is being manufactured to produce a panic and that the bank is the cause of existing evils. Demonstrates that financial distress is not confined to the U.S. Discusses the currency and the role of the bank. Discredits the petitions in favor of the bank.

2919. Hill, Isaac (N.H.). "Reports on the Post Office," *Register of Debates.* 23rd Cong., 1st Sess. (11 June 1834) pp. 1961-1969. Defends the Post Office and its attempt to pay its own way. Maintains that the administration's political opponents are deliberately trying to embarrass the department. Addresses charges of borrowing money and expending large sums to effect the presidential election. Discusses the "newspaper privilege," the amount paid to contractors for carrying the mails in New Hampshire, and the appointment of postmasters. Disproves alleged claims of political favoritism.

2920. Hubbard, Henry (N.H.). "Extension of the Pension Laws," *Register of Debates.* 23rd Cong., 1st Sess. (31 Jan. 1834) pp. 2561-2569. Opposes extending the pension system to those called into the military service since the Revolutionary War; distinguishes between compensation of those soldiers and those who fought later wars. Defends the pension act of 1832 against charges of operating unequally upon the North and South.

2921. Hubbard, Henry (N.H.). "Kentucky Contested Election," *Congressional Globe.* 23rd Cong., 1st Sess. (3 June 1834) pp. 425-426. Supports the Committee of Election's decision to reject the votes given by the persons who had no legal residence in Anderson County. Same speech printed in the *Register of Debates*, "Kentucky Election," pp. 4375-4378.

2922. Hubbard, Henry (N.H.). "Kentucky Election," *Register of Debates.* 23rd Cong., 1st Sess. (5 Dec. 1833) pp. 2151-2154. Supports receiving the qualification presented by T. P. Moore (Ky.) and accepting him as a member of the House; subsequent investigation or dispute should be referred to the Committee of Elections.

2923. Hubbard, Henry (N.H.). "Military Appropriation Bill," *Register of Debates.* 23rd Cong., 1st Sess. (13 Mar. 1834) pp. 2982-2989. Various remarks support appropriations for Fort Gibson; concurs with the recommendations of the Secretary of War. Responds to criticism.

2924. Hubbard, Henry (N.H.). Remarks on the New York Memorial, *Congressional Globe.* 23rd Cong., 1st Sess. (3 Feb. 1834) pp. 150-151. Maintains that the memorial should be referred to the Committee of Ways and Means, along with all the other memorials on the removal of the public deposits from the Bank of the United States. Same speech printed in the *Register of Debates*, "Memorial of Merchants, &c. of New York," pp. 2603-2605.

2925. Hubbard, Henry (N.H.). "Susan Decatur," *Register of Debates.* 23rd Cong., 1st Sess. (19 Apr. 1834) pp. 3684-3715. Supports the bill to compensate the captors of the frigate Philadelphia. Recounts the story of Captain Decatur's capture of the frigate; reviews the circumstances surrounding the capture. Establishes rights according to the "prize act." Presents decisions, precedents and various acts of Congress in relation to the subject, to show that the claimants are entitled to her value. Considers and answers various objections.

2926. Pierce, Franklin (N.H.). "Revolutionary Claims," *Congressional Globe.* 23rd Cong., 1st Sess. (27 Feb. 1834) pp. 206-208. Remarks against the bill. Concerned about proof of service and commutation rights. Same remarks printed in the *Register of Debates*, "Revolutionary Claims," pp. 2819-2825.

2927. "Application of New Hampshire for a More Perfect and Uniform Organization of the Militia of the United States," *American State Papers: Military Affairs*, Vol. V (Doc. 553) p. 238. (ASP 020).

2928. U.S. House. *Memorial of Citizens of the Town of Dover, in Relation to the Currency.* 23rd Cong., 1st Sess. (H.Doc.326). [Washington: Gales & Seaton, 1834]. 5 pg. (Serial Set 257). Request to restore the currency and the Bank of the United States to its previous situation. Four pages of names of memorialists.

2929. U.S. House. *Memorial of Inhabitants of Somersworth, New Hampshire, in Favor of Restoring the Public Deposites, &c.* 23rd Cong., 1st Sess. (H.Doc.252). [Washington: Gales & Seaton, 1834]. 5 pg. (Serial Set 257). Includes three pages of names of the memorialists.

2930. U.S. House. *Memorial of Merchants and Others, of Portsmouth, N.H. in Relation to the Public Deposites.* 23rd Cong., 1st Sess. (H.Doc.102). [Washington: Gales & Seaton, 1834]. 4 pg. (Serial Set 256). Memorial supports the restoration of the deposits. Names of memorialists included.

2931. U.S. House. *Resolution of the Legislature of New Hampshire, in Relation to the More Perfect Organization of the Militia of the United States.* 23rd Cong., 1st Sess. (H.Doc.10). [Washington: Gales & Seaton, 1833]. 1 pg. (Serial Set 254). Same as S.doc.11 (23-1) 238 (entry **2933**).

2932. U.S. House. *Resolutions of the Legislature of New Hampshire, against the Bank of the United States.* 23rd Cong., 1st Sess. (H.Doc.520). [Washington: Gales & Seaton, 1834]. 2 pg. (Serial Set 259). Miscellaneous resolutions support the actions of the President against the Bank of the United States, request a resolution of the Senate declaring those actions unconstitutional be expunged, and request N.H. Senator Samuel Bell to resign his seat.

2933. U.S. Senate. *Resolution of the Legislature of New Hampshire, Recommending Provision for an Efficient and Uniform Militia throughout the*

United States. 23rd Cong., 1st Sess. (S.Doc.11). Washington: Duff Green, 1834. 1 pg. (Serial Set 238). Same as H.doc.10 (23-1) 254 (entry **2931**).

23RD CONGRESS, 2ND SESSION

2934. Hill, Isaac (N.H.). "Branch Mints," *Congressional Globe.* 23rd Cong., 2nd Sess. (24 Feb. 1835) pp. 284-285. Opposes the bill to establish branches of the Mint of the United States in North Carolina, Georgia, and New Orleans as expensive and unnecessary. Same speech printed in the *Register of Debates,* "Branches of the Mint," pp. 596-599.

2935. Hill, Isaac (N.H.). "The Four Years' Law," *Congressional Globe.* 23rd Cong., 2nd Sess. (20 Feb. 1835) pp. 271-273. Supports rotation in office as administrations change; gives history of political patronage under earlier administrations. Same speech printed in the *Register of Debates,* "Executive Patronage," pp. 563-570.

2936. Hill, Isaac (N.H.). "French Spoliation Bill," *Congressional Globe.* 23rd Cong., 2nd Sess. (23 Dec. 1834) pp. 62-67. Opposes claims for French spoliations committed prior to 1800. Gives the history of unfavorable reports from both Houses and the rational to the claims. Contends that the war ended the obligations of prior treaties and that the money would only go to the underwriters and insurers, not to those who sacrificed. Same speech printed in the *Register of Debates,* "French Spoliations," pp. 47-67.

2937. Hill, Isaac (N.H.). "The History of Congress," *Congressional Globe.* 23rd Cong., 2nd Sess. (12 Feb. 1835) pp. 234-235. Remarks on printing costs and obligations of Congress; proposes that printing books, etc. for private use of members of Congress cease.

2938. Hill, Isaac (N.H.). "Lucy Bond," *Register of Debates.* 23rd Cong., 2nd Sess. (3 Feb. 1835) pp. 285-287. Objects to paying interest on the claim allowed to the heirs of Lucy Bond; maintains that it would establish bad precedence.

2939. Hill, Isaac (N.H.). Remarks on the Pay of the Officers of the Navy, *Congressional Globe.* 23rd Cong., 2nd Sess. (2 Mar. 1835) pp. 315-317. Opposes raising the salaries of officers in the navy. Compares the pay of American officers to that of comparable French and British officers and demonstrates that American pay is much better. Same speech printed in the *Register of Debates,* "Pay of the Navy," pp. 716-720.

2940. U.S. House. *Memorial of Inhabitants of the State of New Hampshire, in Relation to Appeals in Cases Arising under the Patent Laws of the United States.* 23rd Cong., 2nd Sess. (H.Doc.101). [Washington: Gales & Seaton, 1835]. 2 pg. (Serial Set 273). Advocates a law extending the right to a writ of error or an appeal to the Supreme Court in patent cases where the matter in dispute, or the sum involved exceeds five hundred dollars.

24TH CONGRESS, 1ST SESSION

2941. Cushman, Samuel (N.H.). "Navy Appropriation Bill," *Congressional Globe, Appendix.* 24th Cong., 1st Sess. (7 Apr. 1836) pp. 273-275. Advocates the navy yard at Portsmouth, N.H. as the best site for a national naval depot. Reasons include economics, depth of water, geographic location, and its accessibility. Same speech printed in the *Register of Debates,* "Naval Service Bill," pp. 3209-3218.

2942. Cushman, Samuel (N.H.). "Sufferers by New York Fire," *Congressional Globe, Appendix.* 24th Cong., 1st Sess. (17 Feb. 1836) pp. 101-102. Opposes a portion of the bill that sets precedence by extending credit upon bonds owed to the government in times of disaster. Same remarks printed in the *Register of Debates,* "Sufferers by Fire in New York," pp. 2568-2570.

2943. Hill, Isaac (N.H.). "Expurgation of the Journal," *Congressional Globe, Appendix.* 24th Cong., 1st Sess. (27 May 1836) pp. 406-417. Argues in support of the resolution to expunge from the journal of the Senate certain resolutions censuring the President; chronicles abuse of the Bank of the United States, including the Portsmouth branch. Beginning of speech printed in the *Register of Debates,* "Expunging Resolution," pp. 1593-1598.

2944. Hill, Isaac (N.H.). "The Land Bill - Surplus Revenue," *Congressional Globe, Appendix.* 24th Cong., 1st Sess. (17 Mar. 1836) pp. 172-181. Details opposition to distributing the proceeds from the sales of public lands among the several states. Offers alternatives for use of the money, particularly demonstrating the benefits of a further reduction of tariffs. Same speech printed in the *Register of Debates,* "Land Bill," pp. 848-877.

2945. Hill, Isaac (N.H.). "National Defense," *Congressional Globe, Appendix.* 24th Cong., 1st Sess. (28 Jan. 1836) pp. 45-47. Discusses the failure of the last defense appropriation bill to pass through the Senate. Same speech printed in the *Register of Debates,* "National Defence," pp. 315-322.

2946. Hill, Isaac (N.H.). Remarks on the Printing Costs and Practices of Congress, *Congressional Globe.* 24th Cong., 1st Sess. (5 May 1836) pp. 421-422. Opposes excessive appropriations for publications, as well as the political patronage of the public press. Same speech printed in the *Register of Debates,* "General Appropriation Bill," pp. 1404-1407.

2947. Hill, Isaac (N.H.). "Resignation of Mr. Hill," *Congressional Globe.* 24th Cong., 1st Sess. (28 May 1836) p. 509. Brief letter of resignation.

2948. Hill, Isaac (N.H.). "Slavery in the District of Columbia," *Congressional Globe, Appendix.* 24th Cong., 1st Sess. (12 Feb. 1836) pp. 89-93. Defends the northern states and their desire not to interfere with the abolition of slavery in the District. Contends that the abolitionists are "a few misguided fanatics" without the support of the northern citizens. Documents anti-abolitionist sentiment in New Hampshire; responds to article in the *Herald of Freedom,* published at Concord, which disagrees with his views. Same speech printed in the *Register of Debates,* "Slavery Memorials," pp. 484-495.

2949. Hill, Isaac (N.H.). "Widows of Colonels Bond and Douglass," *Congressional Globe.* 24th Cong., 1st Sess. (22 Apr. 1836) pp. 383-384. Remarks on Revolutionary War commutation claims and their abuse; opposes claims for interest on a former allowance to the heirs of Bond and Douglass. Same remarks printed in the *Register of Debates,* "Colonels Bond and Douglass," pp. 1250-1252.

2950. Hubbard, Henry (N.H.). "Bank Notes," *Congressional Globe.* 24th Cong., 1st Sess. (6 May 1836) pp. 427-428. Supports distribution of the Secretary of the Treasury's report written in response to a Senate inquiry on bank notes received from the land offices by the deposit banks and the general transfer of the public money.

2951. Hubbard, Henry (N.H.). "Banking in Florida," *Congressional Globe.* 24th Cong., 1st Sess. (14 May 1836) pp. 457-458. Introduces and supports a resolution to inquire into whether the business of the Territory of Florida warrants the recent increase of moneyed institutions. Also printed in the *Register of Debates,* "Florida Banks," pp. 1447-1448.

2952. Hubbard, Henry (N.H.). "Fortification Bill," *Congressional Globe, Appendix.* 24th Cong., 1st Sess. (24 May 1836) pp. 417-420. Supports fortifications at Portsmouth, N.H.; gives a history of previous recommendations and actions. Same speech printed in the *Register of Debates,* "Fortification Bill," pp. 1538-1550.

2953. Hubbard, Henry (N.H.). "General Eleazer W. Ripley," *Congressional Globe.* 24th Cong., 1st Sess. (3 June 1836) pp. 524-527. Introduces and supports a bill for the relief of General Eleazer W. Ripley, injured in the War of 1812. Same speech also printed in the *Register of Debates,* "General Ripley," pp. 1676-1686.

2954. Hubbard, Henry (N.H.). "National Defense," *Congressional Globe, Appendix.* 24th Cong., 1st Sess. (19 Jan., 20 Jan. 1836) pp. 30-39. Supports the appropriations and legislation for the general defense of the country. Majority of speech discusses the fate of previous appropriation measures for national defense. Same speech printed in the *Register of Debates,* "National Defence," (20 Jan. 1836) pp. 217-249.

2955. Hubbard, Henry (N.H.). Remarks on the Petition of David Melville, *Congressional Globe*. 24th Cong., 1st Sess. (15 Apr. 1836) pp. 362-363. Various remarks oppose the petition of David Melville, a customs officer removed from office; defends the Sec. of the Treasury. Same remarks printed in the *Register of Debates*, "Removal of David Melville," pp. 1182-1185.

2956. Hubbard, Henry (N.H.). "Slavery in the District," *Congressional Globe, Appendix*. 24th Cong., 1st Sess. (7 Mar. 1836) pp. 167-170. Contends that to abolish slavery in the District would be unjust, impolitic, inexpedient, and impracticable, but the right to petition for it is an inalienable right. Same speech printed in the *Register of Debates*, "Slavery in the District of Columbia," pp. 738-748.

2957. Hubbard, Henry (N.H.). "Transfers of Public Money," *Congressional Globe, Appendix*. 24th Cong., 1st Sess. (19 May 1836) pp. 371-373. Defends the reports of the Secretary of the Treasury that were written in response to requests of the Senate for information on the transfer of funds from various deposit banks. Contends that the information requested has been supplied. Same remarks printed in the *Register of Debates*, "Transfers of Public Money," pp. 1471-1476.

2958. Pierce, Franklin (N.H.). "The Military Academy," *Congressional Globe, Appendix*. 24th Cong., 1st Sess. (30 June 1836) pp. 513-515. Opposes appropriations for the military academy until an investigation is made into its principles and operations. Considers the academy gratuitous and exclusive, fruitless and extravagant. Same speech printed in the *Register of Debates*, "West Point Academy," pp. 4569-4576.

2959. Pierce, Franklin (N.H.). Remarks on Abolition Petitions, *Congressional Globe*. 24th Cong., 1st Sess. (15 Feb. 1836) pp. 185-186. Replies to a newspaper article published at Concord, N.H. that contends that he is incorrect when he states that New Hampshire inhabitants are opposed to petitions for abolition. Reprints article. Same remarks and reprint printed in the *Register of Debates*, "Abolitionism in N.H.," pp. 2528-2532.

2960. Pierce, Franklin (N.H.). Remarks on the Mode of Selecting Deposit Banks, *Congressional Globe*. 24th Cong., 1st Sess. (28 Apr. 1836) pp. 408-410. Opposes the resolution calling on the Treasury Dept. for information regarding the deposit of the public moneys in banks. Same remarks printed in the *Register of Debates*, "Deposite Banks," pp. 3423-3427.

2961. U.S. Senate. *Memorial of Samuel Sheafe and Others, Merchants, Portsmouth, New Hampshire, Praying Indemnity for Spoliations by France Prior to 1800.* 24th Cong., 1st Sess. (S.Doc.82). Washington: Gales & Seaton, 1836. 3 pg. (Serial Set 280). Same as H.doc.58 (24-2) 302 (entry **2969**).

2962. U.S. Senate. *Resolution of the Legislature of New Hampshire, in Favor of Expunging a Certain Resolution from the Journal of the Senate.* 24th Cong.,

1st Sess. (S.Doc.294). Washington: Gales & Seaton, 1836. 1 pg. (Serial Set 282). Resolution to expunge resolution that the President has acted unconstitutionally in his proceedings relating to the public revenue. Also printed in the *Register of Debates*, p. 1109.

24TH CONGRESS, 2ND SESSION

2963. "Petitions, Memorials, Etc.", *Congressional Globe*. 24th Cong., 2nd Sess. (30 Jan. 1837) p. 139. Resolutions from New Hampshire oppose the revenue from tariffs exceeding the needs of the government; also oppose using excess revenue for internal improvements or distributing it to the states. Reprints H.doc.112 (24-2) 303 (entry **2970**).

2964. Cushman, Samuel (N.H.). "On the Bill Reducing the Revenue," *Congressional Globe, Appendix*. 24th Cong., 2nd Sess. (12 Jan. 1837) pp. 118-120. Supports reducing the revenue to meet the needs of an economical government; desires a modification of the tariff and a limitation of the sale of the public lands. Speech also printed in *Register of Debates*, "Surplus Revenue," pp. 1375-1382.

2965. Hubbard, Henry (N.H.). "Cession of the Public Lands," *Congressional Globe, Appendix*. 24th Cong., 2nd Sess. (11 Feb. 1837) pp. 166-167. Opposes the bill to cede the public lands to the respective states in which the lands lie. Maintains that he is a friend of the new states, but that this bill would defeat final passage of the bill now before the Senate, and has been introduced too late in session for extended discussion. Contends that the public lands belong to all the states. Speech also printed in *Register of Debates*, "Cession of the Public Lands," pp. 780-784.

2966. Hubbard, Henry (N.H.). "Public Lands," *Congressional Globe, Appendix*. 24th Cong., 2nd Sess. (9 Feb. 1837) pp. 156-157. Opposes consideration of the bill ceding public lands to the respective states where the lands are located. Remarks also printed in *Register of Debates*, "Public Lands," pp. 752-753.

2967. Hubbard, Henry (N.H.). "Recission of the Treasury Order," *Congressional Globe, Appendix*. 24th Cong., 2nd Sess. (27 Dec. 1836) pp. 57-64. Opposes rescinding the Treasury order of 11 July 1838, known as "the specie circular." Maintains that Congress cannot repeal orders of the Executive branch. Establishes the executive authority to issue the order, and its necessity. Defends the Secretary of the Treasury and his execution of the deposit bill. Speech also printed in the *Register of Debates*, "Treasury Circular," pp. 128-150.

2968. Hubbard, Henry (N.H.). "Unexpended Balances of Appropriations," *Congressional Globe, Appendix*. 24th Cong., 2nd Sess. (28 Dec. 1836) pp. 40,

43-44. Advocates distributing a document concerning the deposit fund to the Senate, but not to the state legislatures. Remarks also printed in the *Register of Debates*, "Unexpended Appropriations," pp. 152-153, 165-166.

2969. U.S. House. *French Spoliations Prior to 1800.* 24th Cong., 2nd Sess. (H.Doc.58). [Washington]: Blair & Rives, Printers, [1836]. 2 pg. (Serial Set 302). Same as S.Doc.82 (24-1) 280 (entry **2961**).

2970. U.S. House. *Joint Resolutions of the Legislature of New Hampshire, upon the Subject of the Tariff &c.* 24th Cong., 2nd Sess. (H.Doc.112). [Washington]: Blair & Rives, Printers, [1837]. 2 pg. (Serial Set 303). Resolutions against allowing the revenue from tariffs to exceed the needs of the government; also opposes using excess revenue for internal improvements or distributing it to the states. Reprinted in *Congressional Globe*, p. 139 (entry **2963**).

2971. U.S. House. *Letter from the President of the United States, Transmitting Resolutions of the Legislature of New Hampshire in Relation to the Claim of That State for Expenses Incurred in Maintaining Jurisdiction over That Portion of Their Territory North of 45° North Latitude.* 24th Cong., 2nd Sess. (H.Doc.155). [Washington]: Blair & Rives, Printers, [1837]. 4 pg. (Serial Set 304). Claim for reimbursement of expenses caused by dispute with the Province of Lower Canada over Indian Stream, in the county of Coos, N.H.

25TH CONGRESS, 1ST SESSION

2972. Atherton, Charles G. (N.H.). "Postponement of Deposite," *Congressional Globe, Appendix.* 25th Cong., 1st Sess. (21 Sept. 1837) pp. 23-25. Supports postponing payment of the fourth installment, particularly when there is no agreement as to the condition of the Treasury. Defends the Secretary of the Treasury and his report. Addresses arguments of the opposition and the financial condition of the country. Same speech printed in the *Register of Debates*, "Fourth Instalment Bill," pp. 725-730.

2973. Cushman, Samuel (N.H.). "Postponement of Fourth Instalment," *Congressional Globe, Appendix.* 25th Cong., 1st Sess. (22 Sept. 1837) pp. 76-77. Opposes the payment of the fourth installment; maintains that the deposit law was not a contract, and that the government is not bound to make the deposit. Summary of speech in *Congressional Globe*, p. 57. Same speech printed in the *Register of Debates*, "Fourth Instalment Bill," pp. 749-751.

2974. Hubbard, Henry (N.H.). "District Banks," *Congressional Globe, Appendix.* 25th Cong., 1st Sess. (11 Oct. 1837) pp. 127-128. Advocates requiring the banks in the District of Columbia to resume specie payments within four months; maintains that resuming payments would induce a corresponding action in other states. Same speech printed in the *Register of Debates*, "District Banks," pp. 531-532.

2975. Hubbard, Henry (N.H.). "Making Public Officers Depositories," *Congressional Globe, Appendix.* 25th Cong., 1st Sess. (28 Sept. 1837) pp. 55-61. Supports the proposed bill to separate the public funds from the banks. Examines the causes of the country's financial distress and the condition of the deposit banks. Defends the Secretary of the Treasury and his execution of the deposit law. Addresses objections to the bill; supports postponement of the fourth deposit. Same speech printed in the *Register of Debates*, "Sub-Treasury Bill," pp. 331-351.

2976. U.S. Senate. *Resolutions of the Legislature of New Hampshire against the Incorporation of a National Bank.* 25th Cong., 1st Sess. (S.Doc.19). Washington: Blair & Rives, 1837. 1 pg. (Serial Set 309).

25ᵀᴴ CONGRESS, 2ᴺᴰ SESSSION

2977. Atherton, Charles G. (N.H.). "Cumberland Road," *Congressional Globe, Appendix.* 25th Cong., 2nd Sess. (June 1838) pp. 452-453. Opposes appropriations for the continuance of the Cumberland road. Maintains that the internal improvements system is intimately connected with a high protecting tariff, and is unconstitutional and inexpedient.

2978. Atherton, Charles G. (N.H.). Remarks on His Defense, *Congressional Globe.* 25th Cong., 2nd Sess. (13 Dec. 1837) p. 23. Briefly responds to a published speech of Mr. Fletcher (Mass.) which cast aspersions upon Mr. Atherton and the Committee of Ways and Means.

2979. Cushman, Samuel (N.H.). "Branch Bank of the U.S., Portsmouth, N.H.," *Congressional Globe, Appendix.* 25th Cong., 2nd Sess. (15 May 1838) p. 335. Defends the memorialists requesting a removal of the head of that branch.

2980. Hubbard, Henry (N.H.). "Banks and Bank Notes," *Congressional Globe.* 25th Cong., 2nd Sess. (12 June 1838) pp. 447-448. Objects to repealing the part of the deposit act of 1836 which prohibits the government from receiving notes from banks that have issued notes of a denomination of less than five dollars.

2981. Hubbard, Henry (N.H.). "Commonwealth Bank of Boston," *Congressional Globe.* 25th Cong., 2nd Sess. (17 Jan. 1838) pp. 114-116. Supports the call for information in relation to Boston Commonwealth Bank.

2982. Hubbard, Henry (N.H.). "Independent Treasury Bill," *Congressional Globe.* 25th Cong., 2nd Sess. (31 Jan. 1838) p. 152. Advocates immediate action upon this bill; addresses reasons given for the postponement of its consideration.

2983. Hubbard, Henry (N.H.). "Making Public Officers Depositaries," *Congressional Globe, Appendix.* 25th Cong., 2nd Sess. (7 Feb., 8 Feb. 1838) pp. 97-108. Supports making public officers depositaries; also supports the regulation, safekeeping, transfer, and disbursement, of the public money, thus dissolving the financial connection between the government and the banks of the states. Provides a sectional analysis of objections to bill.

2984. Hubbard, Henry (N.H.). "Mr. Calhoun's Resolutions," *Congressional Globe, Appendix.* 25th Cong., 2nd Sess. (4 Jan. 1838) pp. 22-23, 26-27. Remarks support a resolution that any interference on the part of any section of the Union with domestic slavery as it exists in the southern states, with a view to its alteration or subversion, would be considered unconstitutional.

2985. Hubbard, Henry (N.H.). "Mr. Clay's Resolution," *Congressional Globe, Appendix.* 25th Cong., 2nd Sess. (25 May 1838) pp. 343-345. Opposes Mr. Clay's resolution prohibiting any discrimination as regards the currency or medium of payment in the several branches of the public revenue.

2986. Hubbard, Henry (N.H.). "Pre-emption to Actual Settlers," *Congressional Globe, Appendix.* 25th Cong., 2nd Sess. (29 Jan. 1838) pp. 140-142. Supports preemption rights; contends that they would result in an increase of power, wealth and population of the country. Gives a history of the rise, progress, and effect of previous preemption legislation.

2987. Hubbard, Henry (N.H.). "Slavery in the District," *Congressional Globe.* 25th Cong., 2nd Sess. (18 Dec. 1837) pp. 36-37. Maintains that the citizens of New Hampshire consider slavery a sectional, local, issue that is sanctioned by the Constitution and the land. Advocates the right of petition.

2988. Pierce, Franklin (N.H.). "Increase of the Army," *Congressional Globe, Appendix.* 25th Cong., 2nd Sess. (4 July 1838) pp. 488-489, 491-492. Supports increasing the army but opposes provisions discriminating against line officers for promotions and restricting visitation rights to Washington.

2989. Pierce, Franklin (N.H.). "Mr. Calhoun's Resolutions," *Congressional Globe, Appendix.* 25th Cong., 2nd Sess. (9 Jan. 1838) pp. 54-55. Opposes abolishing slavery in the District of Columbia; describes the growing strength of abolitionists in New Hampshire and New England.

2990. Pierce, Franklin (N.H.). Remarks on Duelling, *Congressional Globe.* 25th Cong., 2nd Sess. (5 Apr. 1838) p. 284. Supports a bill to suppress dueling; defends the bravery of the people of New England.

2991. U.S. House. *Memorial of a Convention Held at Claremont, New Hampshire, upon the Subject of the Importation of Foreign Spirits, and the Use of Spirituous Liquors in the Navy of the United States.* 25th Cong., 2nd Sess. (H.Doc.436). [Washington]: Thomas Allen, Print., [1838]. 2 pg. (Serial Set

331). Memorial objects to importing liquor and furnishing it as rations to navy or army personnel.

25TH CONGRESS, 3RD SESSION

2992. Atherton, Charles G. (N.H.). "Rights of the South," *Congressional Globe.* 25th Cong., 3rd Sess. (11 Dec. 1838) pp. 21-22. Presents and supports resolutions declaring that petitions for the abolition of slavery in the District and the territories of the United States are outside the jurisdiction of Congress and destructive of the Union, and, as such, these petitions should be laid upon the table without debate, printing, or referral.

2993. Cushman, Samuel (N.H.). "Reference of the President's Message," *Congressional Globe, Appendix.* 25th Cong., 3rd Sess. (2 Jan. 1839) pp. 69-72. Supports Mr. Woodbury, the Secretary of the Treasury, and the Jackson and Van Buren administrations. Defends Mr. Woodbury against charges of negligence and fraud; reviews the cases offered in evidence. Defends the Executive of the U.S. and the Democratic Party against charges of extravagance and profligacy. Compares the expenses of the Adams, Monroe, and Jackson administrations. Discusses the right to appoint and remove public officers.

2994. Hubbard, Henry (N.H.). "Punishment of Defaulters," *Congressional Globe, Appendix.* 25th Cong., 3rd Sess. (21 Feb. 1839) pp. 192-195. Supports the need for further legislation to protect the public moneys from fraud and to punish public defaulters. Defends the Secretary of the Treasury from charges of neglect; maintains that the discharges of his appropriate duties could not enable him to detect frauds practiced by collectors and receivers. Reviews the existing laws concerning the duties of the Secretary of the Treasury and of the accounting officers of the department; concludes that existing laws do not afford sufficient checks and guards.

2995. Hubbard, Henry (N.H.). Remarks on Revolutionary War Pensions, *Congressional Globe.* 25th Cong., 3rd Sess. (18 Dec. 1838) pp. 40, 41. Supports appropriations to continue the payments for Revolutionary pensions as provided for by the pension law. Briefly reviews pension legislation.

2996. Pierce, Franklin (N.H.). Remarks on Revolutionary War Pensions, *Congressional Globe.* 25th Cong., 3rd Sess. (18 Dec. 1838) p. 43. Describes some of the frauds perpetrated under the pension law.

2997. Pierce, Franklin (N.H.). Remarks on the Memorial for the Abolition of Slavery in the District, *Congressional Globe.* 25th Cong., 3rd Sess. (21 Feb. 1839) pp. 196-197. Regretfully presents a memorial from Antrim, N.H., praying for the abolition of slavery in the District. Remarks on the disposition of slavery petitions.

2998. U.S. House. *Claim of New Hampshire.* 25th Cong., 3rd Sess. (H.Rpt.176). [Washington]: Thomas Allen, Print., [1839]. 12 pg., 1 map. (Serial Set 351). Report of the Committee on Foreign Affairs on New Hampshire's claim for reimbursement of expenses incurred in maintaining jurisdiction over that portion of its territory north of the 45th degree of latitude, known by the name of Indian Stream settlement. History of the boundary dispute, relevant correspondence and map entitled "Plan of the Sources of Connecticut River" accompany report.

2999. U.S. Senate. *Memorial of a Number of Citizens of New Castle, New Hampshire, against the Repeal of the Law Allowing a Bounty to Vessels Engaged in the Cod Fisheries.* 25th Cong., 3rd Sess. (S.Doc.220). Washington: Blair and Rives, 1839. 2 pg. (Serial Set 340).

3000. U.S. Senate. *Report from the Secretary of the Treasury, with a Resolution of the Senate, in Relation to the Allowances to the Marshals of the Several Districts for Distributing the Venires, and the Fees Now Allowed to the Marshal of New Hampshire for That Service.* 25th Cong., 3rd Sess. (S.Doc.265). Washington: Blair and Rives, 1839. 9 pg. (Serial Set 341). Audit of Pearson Cogswell, marshal for the district of New Hampshire.

3001. U.S. Senate. *Resolutions of the General Assembly of New Hampshire, to Obtain the Adjustment of Claims for Spoliations Committed by France, Prior to 1800.* 25th Cong., 3rd Sess. (S.Doc.293). Washington: Blair and Rives, 1839. 1 pg. (Serial Set 342).

26TH CONGRESS, 1ST SESSION

3002. Atherton, Charles G. (N.H.). "Appropriation Bill," *Congressional Globe, Appendix.* 26th Cong., 1st Sess. (23 Apr., 24 Apr. 1840) pp. 405-412. Remarks stress the connection of the principles distinguishing the political parties to their views of expenditures; addresses the charge of extravagant expenditures of the administration. Partial summary of speech in *Congressional Globe*, p. 356.

3003. Atherton, Charles G. (N.H.). "Independent Treasury," *Congressional Globe, Appendix.* 26th Cong., 1st Sess. (27 May 1840) pp. 580-588. Supports the bill. Addresses merits and objections, including constitutionality, expense, and the currency feature; gives examples from other nations. Synopsis of remarks in the *Congressional Globe*, pp. 427-428.

3004. Burke, Edmund (N.H.). "Independent Treasury," *Congressional Globe, Appendix.* 26th Cong., 1st Sess. (13 June 1840) pp. 570-579. Addresses the effects of the bill on farmers and laboring men. Expounds upon the causes of fluctuations in property prices, wages, and the derangement of the exchanges.

3005. Eastman, Ira A. (N.H.). "Independent Treasury Bill," *Congressional Globe.* 26th Cong., 1st Sess. (2 June 1840) pp. 435-439. Supports the bill. Examines the officers to be appointed, the impact on the Post Office Dept., the transfer of the public moneys, the transfer of funds under the United States Bank, and the expense of the bill.

3006. Hubbard, Henry (N.H.). "Assumption of State Debts," *Congressional Globe, Appendix.* 26th Cong., 1st Sess. (31 Jan., 18 Feb. 1840) pp. 111-114; 195-203. Comments in defense of the committee's report and resolutions on the assumption of state debts. Supports resolutions that it would not be just, expedient, or constitutional for the Government to assume the debts of the states, or to set apart the proceeds of the public lands for that purpose.

3007. Hubbard, Henry (N.H.). "Bankrupt Law," *Congressional Globe, Appendix.* 26th Cong., 1st Sess. (25 May 1840) pp. 482-488. Opposes the bill as unconstitutional and inexpedient. Analyzes the bill and its potential negative effects on the debtor, the community and the nation.

3008. Hubbard, Henry (N.H.). "Commissioner of Pensions," *Congressional Globe.* 26th Cong., 1st Sess. (4 Mar. 1840) p. 234. Advocates the immediate passage of the bill.

3009. Hubbard, Henry (N.H.). "Losses by Indian Wars," *Congressional Globe, Appendix.* 26th Cong., 1st Sess. (12 Mar. 1840) pp. 301-302. Supports the payment of damages sustained by individuals in the wars with Indian tribes since 1830.

3010. Hubbard, Henry (N.H.). "Public Expenditures," *Congressional Globe, Appendix.* 26th Cong., 1st Sess. (7 May 1840) pp. 438-440. Defends the expenditures of the administration.

3011. Hubbard, Henry (N.H.). Remarks on Congressional Printing Appropriations, *Congressional Globe.* 26th Cong., 1st Sess. (4 May 1840) pp. 375-376. Opposes appropriations to print Clarke and Force's *Documentary History of the American Revolution.* Gives a brief history of relevant congressional legislation.

3012. Hubbard, Henry (N.H.). Remarks on the Howard Institution of Washington, D.C., *Congressional Globe.* 26th Cong., 1st Sess. (27 May 1840) pp. 421-423. Various remarks object to donating government property in Washington, D.C. to the Howard Institution; contends that the government cannot be a charitable institution.

3013. Hubbard, Henry (N.H.). Remarks on the Right to Petition, *Congressional Globe.* 26th Cong., 1st Sess. (13 Feb. 1840) pp. 193-197. Discusses the right to petition; contends that the abolitionists have the right to petition, but that the Senate doesn't have to take any action.

3014. Hubbard, Henry (N.H.). "Treasury Note Bill," *Congressional Globe, Appendix.* 26th Cong., 1st Sess. (30 Mar. 1840) pp. 323-329. Supports the authorization of the issue of Treasury notes. Distinguishes it from a similar act of 1837; gives the state of the Treasury and financial implications.

3015. Pierce, Franklin (N.H.). "Armed Occupation of Florida," *Congressional Globe, Appendix.* 26th Cong., 1st Sess. (9 Jan. 1840) pp. 82-84. Supports the actions of the Sec. of War in the armed occupation and settlement of Florida.

3016. Pierce, Franklin (N.H.). "Claims of Capt. Williams and Others," *Congressional Globe, Appendix.* 26th Cong., 1st Sess. (1 May 1840) pp. 465-469. Opposes their claims. Provides a history of claims legislation.

3017. Pierce, Franklin (N.H.). "Commissioner of Pensions," *Congressional Globe.* 26th Cong., 1st Sess. (4 Mar. 1840) pp. 233-234. Supports the Commissioner of Pensions and opposes the bill that would reduce his salary.

3018. Pierce, Franklin (N.H.). "General Bankrupt Law," *Congressional Globe.* 26th Cong., 1st Sess. (5 June 1840) pp. 445-446. Remarks on the seriousness of his forthcoming vote on the bill for a uniform system of bankruptcy.

3019. U.S. House. *Resolutions of the Legislature of New Hampshire, against the Distribution of the Proceeds of Sales of the Public Lands.* 26th Cong., 1st Sess. (H.Doc.174). [Washington]: Blair & Rives, Printers, [1840]. 1 pg. (Serial Set 366). Same as S.doc.27 (26-1) 355 (entry **3022**).

3020. U.S. House. *Resolutions of the Legislature of New Hampshire, in Relation to the Collection, Safekeeping and Disbursement, of the Public Revenue.* 26th Cong., 1st Sess. (H.Doc.176). [Washington]: Blair & Rives, Printers, [1840]. 1 pg. (Serial Set 366). Resolutions support an Independent Treasury. Same as S.Doc.28 (26-1) 355 (entry **3023**).

3021. U.S. Senate. *Memorial of a Number of Citizens of Portsmouth, N.H., Praying the Establishment of a Congress of Nations for the Adjustment of International Difficulties.* 26th Cong., 1st Sess. (S.Doc.184). Washington: Blair and Rives, 1840. 3 pg. (Serial Set 357).

3022. U.S. Senate. *Resolutions of the Legislature of New Hampshire, Opposed to Any Measure to Divide the Proceeds of the Sales of the Public Lands Among the Several States.* 26th Cong., 1st Sess. (S.Doc.27). Washington: Blair and Rives, 1840. 1 pg. (Serial Set 355). Same as H.doc.174 (26-1) 366 (entry **3019**).

3023. U.S. Senate. *Resolutions of the Legislature of New Hampshire, in Favor of a Metallic Currency and the Adoption of the Independent Treasury System.* 26th Cong., 1st Sess. (S.Doc.28). Washington: Blair and Rives, 1840. 1 pg. (Serial Set 355). Same as H.doc.176 (26-1) 366 (entry **3020**).

26TH CONGRESS, 2ND SESSION

3024. Debate on Compensation to New Hampshire for Services of Her Militia, *Congressional Globe.* 26th Cong., 2nd Sess. (5 Jan. 1841) pp. 82-83. Debate over New Hampshire's claim for expenses incurred maintaining jurisdiction at Indian Stream area. Includes remarks by Senators Pierce and Hubbard.

3025. Hubbard, Henry (N.H.). "Election of Printer," *Congressional Globe.* 26th Cong., 2nd Sess. (19 Feb. 1841) pp. 188-190. Advocates the immediate election of a Public Printer; gives a brief legislative background.

3026. Hubbard, Henry (N.H.). "Pre-emption Law," *Congressional Globe, Appendix.* 26th Cong., 2nd Sess. (7 Jan. 1841) pp. 38-41. Supports a prospective preemption bill; contends that this bill differs from previous legislation by encouraging emigration to induce the improvement and settlement of the public lands. Gives a history of preemptive policy.

3027. Hubbard, Henry (N.H.). "Pre-emption Law," *Congressional Globe, Appendix.* 26th Cong., 2nd Sess. (2 Feb. 1841) pp. 209-217. Opposes the motion to distribute the proceeds of the sales of the public lands among the states or to cede the lands to the states within which they lie. Contends that it is unconstitutional and that the condition of the Treasury is such that it is not expedient. Demonstrates that the suggested tax on luxuries is unworkable.

3028. Pierce, Franklin (N.H.). "Newspaper Postage," *Congressional Globe, Appendix.* 26th Cong., 2nd Sess. (28 Jan. 1841) pp. 191-193. Advocates reducing postage rates on newspapers sent less than thirty miles from their place of publication. Comments on the general legislative obstacles faced in Congress.

3029. Pierce, Franklin (N.H.). "Pre-emption Law," *Congressional Globe, Appendix.* 26th Cong., 2nd Sess. (2 Feb. 1841) p. 217. Opposes distributing the proceeds from public land sales to the states; supports the proposition that some of the proceeds should be applied to the general defense of the country.

3030. U.S. Senate. *Memorial of a Number of Citizens of New Hampshire, Remonstrating against the Passage of a Bankrupt Law.* 26th Cong., 2nd Sess. (S.Doc.224). Washington: Blair and Rives, 1841. 1 pg. (Serial Set 378). Names of memorialists included.

3031. U.S. Senate. *Resolutions of the General Assembly of New Hampshire, on the Subject of Appointing the Same Day throughout the Union for the Choice of Presidential Electors.* 26th Cong., 2nd Sess. (S.Doc.217). Washington: Blair and Rives, 1841. 1 pg. (Serial Set 378).

27ᵀᴴ CONGRESS, 1ˢᵀ SESSION

3032. Atherton, Charles G. (N.H.). "Duties and Drawbacks," *Congressional Globe, Appendix.* 27th Cong., 1st Sess. (26 July 1841) pp. 231-234. Criticizes the estimates of expenditures and revenues presented; opposes direct and indirect taxation, such as duties, as a burden on the people that will not be tolerated. Summary of speech in the *Congressional Globe*, p. 252.

3033. Atherton, Charles G. (N.H.). "Loan Bill," *Congressional Globe, Appendix.* 27th Cong., 1st Sess. (12 July 1841) pp. 202-205. Opposes the bill authorizing the loan of $12,000,000 to the government. Critical of the report of the Secretary of Treasury on the state of the national debt; claims that it is a proposition to borrow money for the purpose of giving it to the states.

3034. Eastman, Ira A. (N.H.). "Fortification Bill," *Congressional Globe.* 27th Cong., 1st Sess. (19 Aug. 1841) pp. 353-354. Opposes additional appropriations for fortifications while funds already approved have not yet been spent.

3035. Eastman, Ira A. (N.H.). "Loan Bill," *Congressional Globe, Appendix.* 27th Cong., 1st Sess. (9 July 1841) pp. 136-140. Opposes the bill; reviews expenditures and revenues of Van Buren's administration and analyses the figures by which the loan is attempted to be justified.

3036. Pierce, Franklin (N.H.). Remarks on the Fiscal Bank Bill, *Congressional Globe.* 27th Cong., 1st Sess. (26 July 1841) pp. 249-250. Opposes the fiscal bank bill without the amendments adopted in the Committee; discusses its corrupting influence and the corruptibility of members of Congress.

3037. Pierce, Franklin (N.H.). "Appropriation to the Widow of General Harrison," *Congressional Globe.* 27th Cong., 1st Sess. (25 June 1841) pp. 116-118. Objects to appropriating money for the late President's widow on the grounds that it would set dangerous precedent for other civil officers.

3038. Pierce, Franklin (N.H.). "Removals from Office," *Congressional Globe, Appendix.* 27th Cong., 1st Sess. (1 July, 2 July 1841) pp. 155-159. Supports requesting the President to furnish the names of persons removed from office and those appointed. Opposes removals from office for political reasons; claims that New Hampshire officers have been replaced with abolitionists.

3039. Woodbury, Levi (N.H.). "Fiscal Bank," *Congressional Globe, Appendix.* 27th Cong., 1st Sess. (10 July 1841) pp. 177-187. Discusses his motion to eliminate the capital from the bill, so as to affect only the public deposits. The government would retain supervision of the capital. Discusses the virtues and failings of a national bank.

3040. Woodbury, Levi (N.H.). "Loan Bill," *Congressional Globe, Appendix.* 27th Cong., 1st Sess. (19 July 1841) pp. 127-129. Supports using Treasury notes for a temporary loan until the tariff can be revised to increase duties.

3041. Woodbury, Levi (N.H.). "Naval Appropriation Bill," *Congressional Globe.* 27th Cong., 1st Sess. (2 Aug. 1841) pp. 280-281. Supports appropriations for fortifications at the mouth of Portsmouth harbor.

3042. Woodbury, Levi (N.H.). "The Navy Pension Bill," *Congressional Globe.* 27th Cong., 1st Sess. (29 July, 5 Aug. 1841) pp. 262; 297-298. Supports the bill and supports limiting it to those for whom the fund was originally designed.

3043. Woodbury, Levi (N.H.). "Public Lands," *Congressional Globe, Appendix.* 27th Cong., 1st Sess. (25 Aug. 1841) pp. 245-251. Opposes the bill for the distribution of the proceeds of the public lands to the states. Contends that no surplus exists, or is likely to exist, revenues are down, and the bill is unequal and unjust. Addresses arguments of supporters and the tariff implications. Earlier remarks are printed in the *Congressional Globe*, pp. 315-316, 342-343, 365-366, 405.

3044. Woodbury, Levi (N.H.). Remarks on the Bill for the Relief of Mrs. Harrison, *Congressional Globe.* 27th Cong., 1st Sess. (24 June 1841) p.108. Opposes relief on the grounds that it would set precedence for other civil officers and that the widow is not in poverty.

3045. Woodbury, Levi (N.H.). Remarks on the Mails, *Congressional Globe.* 27th Cong., 1st Sess. (31 Aug. 1841) p. 410. Supports increasing postage to cover Post Office expenses.

3046. Woodbury, Levi (N.H.). Remarks on the Revenue Bill, *Congressional Globe.* 27th Cong., 1st Sess. (4 Sept. 1841) pp. 424-427. Addresses the revenue bill and the state of the nation's finances.

3047. Woodbury, Levi (N.H.). "Repeal of Independent Treasury," *Congressional Globe, Appendix.* 27th Cong., 1st Sess. (9 June 1841) pp. 18-21. Opposes the repeal of the Sub-Treasury on the grounds that it is successful, constitutional, independent, enforceable, economical, safe, and free from executive influence. The proponents of the bill provide no substitute measures to succeed this system.

3048. Woodbury, Levi (N.H.). "Report of the Secretary of the Treasury," *Congressional Globe, Appendix.* 27th Cong., 1st Sess. (16 June, 18 June 1841) pp. 33-42; 50-51. Criticizes the report and the many errors and the discrepancies; validates the inflated reporting of the public debt. Summary of remarks in the *Congressional Globe*, pp. 71-72.

3049. Woodbury, Levi (N.H.). "Tariff Bill," *Congressional Globe, Appendix.* 27th Cong., 1st Sess. (31 Aug. 1841) pp. 251-252. Discusses the motion to eliminate duties on tea and coffee. Voices concerns on the necessity of duties tied in with the distribution of the proceeds of the public lands.

3050. U.S. House. *Resolutions of the Legislature of the State of New Hampshire, Relating to the Constitutionality and Expediency of a National*

Bank; to a Connexion between the United States Treasury and Banks; to the Creation of a National Debt; to a Distribution of the Public Revenue, whether from Public Lands or Other Sources, and to a Protective Tariff. 27th Cong., 1st Sess. (H.Doc.25). Washington: Gales & Seaton, 1841. 2 pg. (Serial Set 392). Resolutions against the establishment of a national bank, the distribution of the proceeds of the public lands, and a protective tariff. Same as S.doc.56 (27-1) 390 (entry **3051**), but omits a resolution concerning French spoliations.

3051. U.S. Senate. *Resolutions of the Legislature of New Hampshire, Adverse to the Establishment of a National Bank, the Distribution of the Proceeds of the Public Lands, and a Protective Tariff.* 27th Cong., 1st Sess. (S.Doc.56). [Washington]: Thomas Allen, Print., [1841]. 2 pg. (Serial Set 390). Also includes resolution to repeal resolutions relative to French spoliations. Same as H.doc.25 (27-1) 392 (entry **3050**), except for the French spoliations resolution.

27TH CONGRESS, 2ND SESSION

3052. Atherton, Charles G. (N.H.). "Apportionment Bill," *Congressional Globe, Appendix.* 27th Cong., 2nd Sess. (25 Apr. 1842) pp. 350-51. Addresses the number of Representatives entitled to each state. Recommends a different ratio than that proposed; opposes limiting the size of the House.

3053. Atherton, Charles G. (N.H.). "Apportionment Bill," *Congressional Globe, Appendix.* 27th Cong., 2nd Sess. (3 May 1842) pp. 397-400. Concedes that Congress has the power to district the states, but not the power to regulate their elections. Refers to the ratification of the Constitution at the various state conventions; addresses the arguments of his colleagues. Synopsis of speech in *Congressional Globe*, pp. 470-471.

3054. Atherton, Charles G. (N.H.). "Loan Bill," *Congressional Globe, Appendix.* 27th Cong., 2nd Sess. (30 Mar. 1842) pp. 261-265. Supports the proposal to procure the loan and use the proceeds from the public land sales to secure the payment of this loan. Argues against those who want to distribute proceeds to the states. Summary of speech in *Congressional Globe*, p. 374.

3055. Atherton, Charles G. (N.H.). "Protective Tariff," *Congressional Globe, Appendix.* 27th Cong., 2nd Sess. (23 Dec. 1841) pp. 35-37. Supports a tariff for revenue, not for protection; remarks on the operation of the protective system and the views of N.H. Summary of speech in *Congressional Globe*, pp. 52-53.

3056. Burke, Edmund (N.H.). Remarks on the Character of New Hampshire, *Congressional Globe*. 27th Cong., 2nd Sess. (28 Dec. 1841) pp. 66-68. Defends the moral, natural, and social condition of New Hampshire. Describes New Hampshire and contrasts its geography, agriculture, manufacturing, and education with that of Tennessee.

3057. Burke, Edmund (N.H.). "The Tariff Bill," *Congressional Globe, Appendix.* 27th Cong., 2nd Sess. (8 July 1842) pp. 563-568. Supports a tariff for revenue, rather than protection. Maintains that protective tariffs benefit manufacturers at the expense of the agriculturists, and that tariffs are indirect taxes that operate upon consumption, and are therefore an unfair per capita tax. Calculates effects of protective tariffs on a family of ten and on the economy; addresses arguments of friends of protectionism.

3058. Eastman, Ira A. (N.H.). "Protective Tariff," *Congressional Globe, Appendix.* 27th Cong., 2nd Sess. (28 Dec., 29 Dec. 1841) pp. 46-52. Debate arises from assigning the bill to the correct committee, according to whether it is a tariff for revenue or protection. Discusses tariffs and the principle of protection. Remarks on the large expenditures of the present administration and the Whig party. Summary of remarks in *Congressional Globe*, pp. 68, 72, 72-73.

3059. Wilcox, Leonard (N.H.). "Apportionment Bill," *Congressional Globe, Appendix.* 27th Cong., 2nd Sess. (1 June 1842) pp. 422-424. Remarks against the apportionment bill and interference with state regulations on elections. Maintains that the general election works better for New Hampshire than the district system; addresses the pros and cons of each.

3060. Woodbury, Levi (N.H.). "The Apportionment Bill," *Congressional Globe.* 27th Cong., 2nd Sess. (1 June 1842) p. 562. Brief remarks opposed to the district system as an unnecessary violation of states' rights.

3061. Woodbury, Levi (N.H.). "Cotton Bagging," *Congressional Globe, Appendix.* 27th Cong., 2nd Sess. (22 July 1842) pp. 661-662. Remarks supporting reducing the duty on cotton bagging.

3062. Woodbury, Levi (N.H.). "Debate on the Fine on General Jackson," *Congressional Globe, Appendix.* 27th Cong., 2nd Sess. (12 May 1842) pp. 364-365. Remarks in support of General Jackson's actions and for refunding the fine.

3063. Woodbury, Levi (N.H.). "Exchequer Board," *Congressional Globe, Appendix.* 27th Cong., 2nd Sess. (6 Jan. 1842) pp. 52-59. Speech in opposition to the proposal. Argues against each of the features: to keep the public money (from banks), transact private exchanges, furnish a public paper currency, and borrow money. Advances alternative means of achieving each of the goals. Summary of speech in *Congressional Globe*, pp. 96-99.

3064. Woodbury, Levi (N.H.). "Freights and Tonnage," *Congressional Globe, Appendix.* 27th Cong., 2nd Sess. (14 Apr. 1842) pp. 307-312. Speech on the state of our tonnage, freights, and commerce with foreign nations. Presents an historical sketch of the treaties existing with England and other powers of Europe, describes current situation, and provides a statistical profile of status. Summary of remarks in *Congressional Globe*, p. 420.

3065. Woodbury, Levi (N.H.). "The General Appropriation Bill," *Congressional Globe.* 27th Cong., 2nd Sess. (3 May 1842) pp. 467-468. Remarks on the proper mode of making appropriations for publishing and distributing historical and political books such as Madison's papers; maintains that such purchases are not a proper contingent or a proper incidental to a general appropriation bill.

3066. Woodbury, Levi (N.H.). "The Little Tariff," *Congressional Globe.* 27th Cong., 2nd Sess. (23 June 1842) p. 669. Remarks on provisions of the proposed bill, home valuation, and the distribution of the proceeds of the public lands.

3067. Woodbury, Levi (N.H.). "Loan Bill," *Congressional Globe, Appendix.* 27th Cong., 2nd Sess. (9 Apr. 1842) pp. 298-304. Speech in support of the proposition of the loan bill to pledge the land fund for the redemption of the public debt. Discusses the necessity of the bill, the fact that the resources are currently available, that it will aid in discharging the principle as well as the interest of the loan, and the implications on the tariff. Partial summary of speech in *Congressional Globe*, pp. 403-404, 405.

3068. Woodbury, Levi (N.H.). "The Mandamus to the States," *Congressional Globe.* 27th Cong., 2nd Sess. (23 Aug. 1842) p. 928. Remarks opposed to requiring the states to make single districts as unconstitutional and inexpedient.

3069. Woodbury, Levi (N.H.). "Naval Schools," *Congressional Globe.* 27th Cong., 2nd Sess. (9 Aug. 1842) p. 864. Remarks on educating naval officers.

3070. Woodbury, Levi (N.H.). "The Navy Appropriation Bill," *Congressional Globe.* 27th Cong., 2nd Sess. (15 June 1842) pp. 632-633. Remarks in favor of reducing navy appropriations to a peace establishment level. Tables provided on expenses, number of officers and seamen, and number of guns afloat.

3071. Woodbury, Levi (N.H.). "Pursers in the Navy," *Congressional Globe.* 27th Cong., 2nd Sess. (9 Aug. 1842) p. 865. Remarks in support of improving naval rations; discusses the implications of increasing the pay of pursers.

3072. Woodbury, Levi (N.H.). Remarks on Navy Appropriations, *Congressional Globe.* 27th Cong., 2nd Sess. (16 June 1842) p. 641. Remarks opposed to additional funding for a navy depot at Pensacola; maintains that it is unnecessary and that there are great physical difficulties.

3073. Woodbury, Levi (N.H.). Remarks on Previous Vote, *Congressional Globe.* 27th Cong., 2nd Sess. (14 Feb. 1842) p. 232. Remarks in response to misstatements by Sen. Clay (Ky.); defends his votes respecting the last tariff bill, the proceeds of the public lands, and the Treasury note bill.

3074. Woodbury, Levi (N.H.). Remarks on Raising Revenue, *Congressional Globe.* 27th Cong., 2nd Sess. (30 Mar. 1842) p. 372. Remarks in support of recalling the proceeds of the public lands and reducing expenses; maintains that the tariff can never raise enough revenue to meet current demands.

3075. Woodbury, Levi (N.H.). "Report upon the Fiscal Agent," *Congressional Globe.* 27th Cong., 2nd Sess. (21 Dec. 1841) pp. 43-44. Remarks in support of the repeal of the distribution act and the subsequent restoration of public land revenues to the Treasury. Recommends establishing a select committee for the bill's consideration.

3076. Woodbury, Levi (N.H.). "Revenue and Home Valuation," *Congressional Globe.* 27th Cong., 2nd Sess. (1 July 1842) pp. 703-704. Introduces and defends bills to extend the tariff laws to retain the duties of the Compromise Act of 1832 and to provide for a system of home valuation on goods imported into the United States.

3077. Woodbury, Levi (N.H.). "Revenues and Expenditures," *Congressional Globe, Appendix.* 27th Cong., 2nd Sess. (10 Mar. 1842) pp. 199-205. Advocates waiting for official reports before considering some of the proposals. Supports retrenchment; analyzes previous administrations expenditures and revenues. Details of the rise and progress of the Treasury note system; reviews the consequences of distribution and the propriety of restoring the land fund. Briefly discusses the tariff. Summary of speech in *Congressional Globe*, pp. 304-306.

3078. Woodbury, Levi (N.H.). "The Tariff Bill," *Congressional Globe, Appendix.* 27th Cong., 2nd Sess. (20 July 1842) pp. 688-694. Opposes the bill on two accounts: the amount of the tax imposed (unnecessarily large), and the manner of imposing it (unequal and oppressive). Discusses various tariffs and their effects. Summary of remarks in *Congressional Globe*, pp. 790-791.

3079. Woodbury, Levi (N.H.). "The Tariff Bill," *Congressional Globe.* 27th Cong., 2nd Sess. (27 Aug. 1842) pp. 955-957. Remarks and responses oppose the bill as incompetent and illegitimate.

3080. Woodbury, Levi (N.H.). "The Tariff Bill," *Congressional Globe.* 27th Cong., 2nd Sess. (2 Aug., 3 Aug., 4 Aug., 5 Aug. 1842) pp. 828-829; 835-836; 841-842; 851. Various remarks on the tariff bill. Opposes the proposed repeal of a proviso of the distribution act of the last Congress; maintains that there is no surplus in the Treasury and that the proceeds are needed. Proposes several amendments to promote commerce and navigation. Discusses the duty on salt. Responds to remarks of Sen. Evans (Maine).

3081. Woodbury, Levi (N.H.). "Treasury Note Bill," *Congressional Globe.* 27th Cong., 2nd Sess. (20 Jan., 21 Jan. 1842) pp. 148-149; 155-156. Remarks on a proviso of the bill and the general public finances. Recommends pledging the public lands as credit for the redemption of the Treasury notes.

3082. Woodbury, Levi (N.H.). "The Veto Power," *Congressional Globe, Appendix.* 27th Cong., 2nd Sess. (23 Feb. 1842) pp. 157-164. Supports the veto power and opposes the proposed amendment to the Constitution. Demonstrates the necessity of the veto power and its role as a check on the legislative branch;

gives examples of how it is used differently by monarchs. Summary of speech in *Congressional Globe*, pp. 259-260.

3083. U.S. House. *Resolution of the Legislature of New Hampshire, in Relation to French Spoliations Prior to 1800.* 27th Cong., 2nd Sess. (H.Doc.96). [Washington: 1842]. 1 pg. (Serial Set 402). Repeal of 1838 resolutions relative to French spoliations prior to 1800.

27TH CONGRESS, 3RD SESSION

3084. Atherton, Charles G. (N.H.). "Plan of an Exchequer," *Congressional Globe.* 27th Cong., 3rd Sess. (26 Jan. 1843) pp. 209-211. Supports an Independent Treasury; maintains that the objections to a government bank would also apply to a United States bank. Discusses possible abuses of a national bank.

3085. Woodbury, Levi (N.H.). "The British Treaty," *Congressional Globe, Appendix.* 27th Cong., 3rd Sess. (Aug. 1842) pp. 27-29. Discusses the northeastern boundary as represented on various maps; maintains that the Senate could not justify ratification except that Maine and Massachusetts, the two principles involved, had given their assent.

3086. Woodbury, Levi (N.H.). "On Funding Treasury Notes," *Congressional Globe, Appendix.* 27th Cong., 3rd Sess. (19 Feb. 1843) pp. 185-186. Supports funding the Treasury notes; reviews the state of the Treasury and contends that this is a temporary emergency requiring additional revenue.

3087. Woodbury, Levi (N.H.). "The Oregon Bill," *Congressional Globe, Appendix.* 27th Cong., 3rd Sess. (24 Jan. 1843) pp. 91-93. Supports the occupation and settlement of Oregon. Advocates the legality of the U.S. title; examines the treaty of 1818, and its renewal in 1827, to demonstrate that there would be no conflict with the treaty so long as British subjects have rights to trade and commerce. Contends that it is expedient to exercise American rights and our duty to protect U.S. citizens in the territory. Summary of speech in *Congressional Globe*, pp. 192-193.

3088. Woodbury, Levi (N.H.). "Right of Search - the Construction of the Ashburton Treaty," *Congressional Globe.* 27th Cong., 3rd Sess. (23 Feb. 1843) p. 336. Remarks that while he assented to the treaty as a whole, he was opposed to the part concerning the right of search.

3089. U.S. House. *Memorial of Fifty-Seven Members of the Legislature of the State of New Hampshire, Praying Congress to District the State for the Election of Members of Congress.* 27th Cong., 3rd Sess. (H.Doc.32). [Washington: 1842]. 2 pg. (Serial Set 420).

3090. U.S. House. *Preamble and Resolutions of the Legislature of New Hampshire, Declaring the Distribution Act, the Tariff Act, and the Bankrupt Act, to Be Inexpedient and Unconstitutional, and Instructing the Senators and Requesting the Representatives from That State to Use Their Best Exertions to Procure the Repeal of Said Acts.* 27th Cong., 3rd Sess. (H.Doc.63). [Washington: 1843]. 4 pg. (Serial Set 420). Same as S.doc.70 (27-3) 415 (entry **3095**).

3091. U.S. House. *Resolution of the Legislature of New Hampshire, concerning the Refunding of the Fine Paid by General Jackson in 1815.* 27th Cong., 3rd Sess. (H.Doc.47). [Washington: 1843]. 1 pg. (Serial Set 420). Resolution requests the refunding of the fine and interest paid by General Andrew Jackson for an alleged contempt of court relating to the defense of New Orleans.

3092. U.S. House. *Resolutions of the Legislature of New Hampshire, in Relation to the Franking Privilege and a Reduction of Letter Postage.* 27th Cong., 3rd Sess. (H.Doc.61). [Washington: 1843]. 2 pg. (Serial Set 420). Same as S.doc.68 (27-3) 415 (entry **3093**).

3093. U.S. Senate. *Resolutions of the Legislature of New Hampshire, in Favor of Restricting the Franking Privilege, and of Reducing the Rates of Letter Postage.* 27th Cong., 3rd Sess. (S.Doc.68). [Washington]: Thomas Allen, Print., [1843]. 2 pg. (Serial Set 415). Same as H.doc.61 (27-3) 420 (entry **3092**).

3094. U.S. Senate. *Resolutions of the Legislature of New Hampshire, Declining to Receive Its Portion of the Proceeds of the Sales of the Public Lands under the Distribution Law, and Requesting to Have the Same Applied "to the General Charge and Expenditure of the United States."* 27th Cong., 3rd Sess. (S.Doc.69). [Washington: Thomas Allen, Print., 1843]. 1 pg. (Serial Set 415). Maintains that the distribution of the proceeds is unconstitutional.

3095. U.S. Senate. *Resolutions of the Legislature of New Hampshire, in Favor of the Repeal of the Distribution and Bankrupt Laws, and of the Modification of the Tariff Act of 1842.* 27th Cong., 3rd Sess. (S.Doc.70). [Washington]: Thomas Allen, Print., [1843]. 4 pg. (Serial Set 415). Same as H.doc.63 (27-3) 420 (entry **3090**).

28TH CONGRESS, 1ST SESSION

3096. Atherton, Charles G. (N.H.). "The Tariff," *Congressional Globe, Appendix.* 28th Cong., 1st Sess. (25 May 1844) pp. 544-548. Opposes protectionism and the restrictive policy of the act of 1842. Gives an historical review of the tariff policy from 1789; ties in party politics, tariffs, and the national bank. Summary of speech in *Congressional Globe*, p. 663.

3097. Hale, John P. (N.H.). "The Amendment of the *Journal* - Protest of the Minority," *Congressional Globe.* 28th Cong., 1st Sess. (6 Dec. 1843) p. 15. Protests against the *Journal* report as incorrect and prejudged concerning the eligibility of gentlemen elected under the general-ticket system to their seats.

3098. Hale, John P. (N.H.). "Home Squadron," *Congressional Globe.* 28th Cong., 1st Sess. (28 Dec. 1843) pp. 81-82. Questions expenditures on the home squadron - when established, how long in operation, at what cost, and what services rendered.

3099. Hale, John P. (N.H.). "Naval Appropriations," *Congressional Globe.* 28th Cong., 1st Sess. (20 May 1844) p. 646. Remarks on the abuses and extravagances of the navy; opposes the proposed appropriations.

3100. Hale, John P. (N.H.). "Private Letter Expresses," *Congressional Globe.* 28th Cong., 1st Sess. (12 June 1844) pp. 717-718. Opposes higher postage rates. Maintains that if postage is lowered, the volume of business will increase.

3101. Norris, Moses (N.H.). "Report of the Committee of Elections," *Congressional Globe, Appendix.* 28th Cong., 1st Sess. (10 Feb. 1844) pp. 137-141. Opposes enforced district elections as unconstitutional and a violation of states' rights. Summary of remarks in *Congressional Globe*, pp. 261-262.

3102. Woodbury, Levi (N.H.). "Annexation of Texas," *Congressional Globe, Appendix.* 28th Cong., 1st Sess. (4 June 1844) pp. 760-775. Speech in secret session on the treaty for the annexation of Texas. Addresses the constitutionality of purchasing Texas and admitting her into the Union, whether the present government of Texas has the right to make such a cession of her territory, and whether the treaty should be ratified if the above answers are favorable.

3103. Woodbury, Levi (N.H.). "The Compromise Act," *Congressional Globe.* 28th Cong., 1st Sess. (18 Jan. 1844) p. 164. Remarks on the origination of Mr. McDuffie's tariff bill. Discusses the subject of Senate bills affecting revenue originating in the Senate; offers precedents on the subjects on imports, lands, and postage.

3104. Woodbury, Levi (N.H.). "Duties on Railroad Iron," *Congressional Globe.* 28th Cong., 1st Sess. (11 June 1844) p. 708. Opposes the bill.

3105. Woodbury, Levi (N.H.). "Naval Depot and Dock-Yard," *Congressional Globe.* 28th Cong., 1st Sess. (11 Apr. 1844) p. 527. Supports a survey of other potential sites.

3106. Woodbury, Levi (N.H.). Remarks on the Public Finances, *Congressional Globe.* 28th Cong., 1st Sess. (17 June 1844) p. 745. Brief remarks on the condition of the finances of the government.

3107. Woodbury, Levi (N.H.). "Revenue Bills," *Congressional Globe, Appendix.* 28th Cong., 1st Sess. (18 Jan. 1844) pp. 52-53. Remarks on the constitutionality of originating revenue bills in the Senate. Maintains that if it imposes no additional tax there is no violation of the spirit of the Constitution.

3108. Woodbury, Levi (N.H.). "The Tariff - The Compromise Act," *Congressional Globe.* 28th Cong., 1st Sess. (27 Mar., 27 May 1844) pp. 456; 667. Various remarks on particular objections to the proposed tariff table; compares his views on revenue sources with those of Senator Rives (Va.).

3109. Woodbury, Levi (N.H.). "The Tariff," *Congressional Globe, Appendix.* 28th Cong., 1st Sess. (7 Feb., 8 Feb. 1844) pp. 143-159. Advocates reducing the rates of duties under the present tariff to the standard of the Compromise Act. Opposes the protective tariff; gives facts and figures comparing past and present duties and their effects on the national economy; compares to England. Statistical tables referred to are appended. Summary of speech in *Congressional Globe*, pp. 244-246, 250-253.

3110. U.S. House. *Relative to the Right of Members to Their Seats in the House of Representatives.* 28th Cong., 1st Sess. (H.Rpt.60). [Washington]: Blair & Rives, Print., [1844]. [26 pg.]. (Serial Set 445). Report from the Committee of Elections on whether members returning to serve in the House have been elected in conformity with the Constitution and laws. Majority report supports elections of New Hampshire, Georgia, Mississippi, and Missouri, who elected Representatives by a general ticket rather than by districts. Minority report also given.

3111. U.S. House. *Resolutions of the Legislature of New Hampshire, Relative to General Jackson's Fine.* 28th Cong., 1st Sess. (H.Doc.19). [Washington]: Blair & Rives, Print., [1843]. 2 pg. (Serial Set 441). Same as S.doc.2 (28-1) 432 (entry **3115**).

3112. U.S. House. *Resolutions of the Legislature of New Hampshire, Relative to the West Point Academy.* 28th Cong., 1st Sess. (H.Doc.20). [Washington]: Blair & Rives, Print., [1843]. 3 pg. (Serial Set 441). Resolutions oppose further funding and favor the abolishment of the academy. Contends that it is a charity school for the aristocracy, resulting in "dandy" officers who resign when placed in danger. Same as S.doc.5 (28-1) 432 (entry **3116**).

3113. U.S. Senate. *Petition of Bela Young, of New Hampshire, for an Increase of Pension.* 28th Cong., 1st Sess. (S.Doc.232). Washington: Gales & Seaton, 1844. 8 pg. (Serial Set 434). Petition requests an increase of pension for the promotion he was entitled to but never received. Includes documentation of his disability and testimonials of support.

3114. U.S. Senate. [Petition of Bela Young, of New Hampshire]. 28th Cong., 1st Sess. (S.Doc.342). Washington: Gales & Seaton, 1844. 1 pg. (Serial Set

435). Committee on Pensions reports against granting the request of Bela Young for an increase of pension based upon an alleged promised promotion.

3115. U.S. Senate. *Resolutions of the Legislature of the State of New Hampshire, in Favor of Refunding the Fine Imposed on General Jackson in the Year 1815.* 28th Cong., 1st Sess. (S.Doc.2). Washington: Gales and Seaton, 1844. 2 pg. (Serial Set 432). Same as H.doc.19 (28-1) 441 (entry **3111**).

3116. U.S. Senate. *Resolutions of the Legislature of the State of New Hampshire, in Relation to the Military Academy at West Point.* 28th Cong., 1st Sess. (S.Doc.5). Washington: Gales and Seaton, 1844. 3 pg. (Serial Set 432). Same as H.doc.20 (28-1) 441. See entry **3112**.

28TH CONGRESS, 2ND SESSION

3117. Norris, Moses (N.H.). "Annexation of Texas," *Congressional Globe, Appendix.* 28th Cong., 2nd Sess. (24 Jan. 1845) pp. 184-193. Supports the annexation of Texas as a State. Addresses whether Congress has the constitutional power to admit a state from a foreign and contiguous territory. Answers various arguments opposed to admission, including the slavery issue; presents reasons in support of the measure.

3118. Woodbury, Levi (N.H.). "Annexation of Texas," *Congressional Globe, Appendix.* 28th Cong., 2nd Sess. (17 Feb. 1845) pp. 233-238. Contends that the annexation of Texas is both expedient and constitutional. Responds to charge that it is an attempt to appropriate lands without consent. Discusses the power of Congress to admit new states. Briefer version of speech in the *Congressional Globe*, pp. 296-300.

3119. Woodbury, Levi (N.H.). "Post Office Reform," *Congressional Globe.* 28th Cong., 2nd Sess. (6 Feb. 1845) p. 253. Concerned about government having a monopoly over carrying letters, newspapers and periodicals.

3120. Woodbury, Levi (N.H.). "Smithsonian Institution," *Congressional Globe.* 28th Cong., 2nd Sess. (21 Jan. 1845) pp. 161, 163. Various remarks and an amendment on the proposed members of the board of management, their mode of election and residence, their payment, and their fiscal responsibilities.

3121. U.S. House. *Letter from the Secretary of War, Transmitting a Copy of the Report of Major Graham upon His Survey of the "Oliverian Canal Route."* 28th Cong., 2nd Sess. (H.Doc.113). [Washington]: Blair & Rives, Printers, [1845]. 35 pg. (Serial Set 465). Report on a survey to determine the route for the Oliverian canal to connect the Connecticut River at Haverhill, and the Pemigewasset River at or near Plymouth, N.H. Includes topographic, water supply, and astronomical observations, and an inventory of the drawings that originally accompanied the report.

3122. U.S. House. *Resolutions of the Legislature of New Hampshire, Relative to the Re-Annexation of Texas, and the Assertion and Maintenance of Our Rights to the Territory of Oregon.* 28th Cong., 2nd Sess. (H.Doc.34). [Washington]: Blair & Rives, Print., [1845]. 2 pg. (Serial Set 464). Same as S.doc.22 (28-2) 450 (entry **3126**).

3123. U.S. House. *Resolutions of the Legislature of New Hampshire, in Favor of a Repeal or Modification of the Tariff Law of 1842.* 28th Cong., 2nd Sess. (H.Doc.53). [Washington: Blair & Rives, Print., 1845]. 1 pg. (Serial Set 464). Same as S.doc.24 (28-2) 450 (entry **3128**).

3124. U.S. House. *Resolutions of the Legislature of the State of New Hampshire, Relative to the Rates of Postage, and to the Franking Privilege.* 28th Cong., 2nd Sess. (H.Doc.18). [Washington]: Blair & Rives, Printers, [1844]. 2 pg. (Serial Set 463). Resolutions favor reducing the postage rates and restricting the franking privilege. Same as S.doc.8 (28-2) 449 (entry **3125**).

3125. U.S. Senate. *Resolutions of the General Assembly of New Hampshire, in Favor of a Reduction of the Rates of Postage, and a Restriction of the Franking Privilege.* 28th Cong., 2nd Sess. (S.Doc.8). Washington: Gales and Seaton, 1845. 2 pg. (Serial Set 449). Same as H.doc.18 (28-2) 463 (entry **3124**).

3126. U.S. Senate. *Resolutions of the General Assembly of New Hampshire, in Favor of the Annexation of Texas, and of Maintaining the Rights of the United States over the Territory of Oregon.* 28th Cong., 2nd Sess. (S.Doc.22). Washington: Gales and Seaton, 1845. 2 pg. (Serial Set 450). Same as H.doc.34 (28-2) 464 (entry **3122**).

3127. U.S. Senate. *Resolutions of the General Assembly of New Hampshire, Condemning, as a Violation of the Constitution, the Trial and Imprisonment of Thomas Wilson Dorr, by the Authorities of Rhode Island.* 28th Cong., 2nd Sess. (S.Doc.23). Washington: Gales and Seaton, 1845. 3 pg. (Serial Set 450).

3128. U.S. Senate. *Resolutions of the General Assembly of New Hampshire, in Favor of the Modification or Repeal of the Tariff Act of 1842.* 28th Cong., 2nd Sess. (S.Doc.24). Washington: Gales and Seaton, 1845. 1 pg. (Serial Set 450). Same as H.doc.53 (28-2) 464 (entry **3123**).

29ᵀᴴ CONGRESS, 1ˢᵀ SESSION

3129. Debate on Claims of New Hampshire against the United States, *Congressional Globe.* 29th Cong., 1st Sess. (7 Jan.; Jan. , 28 Jan., 28 Apr., 6 May 1846) pp. 153-154; 183-184; 262-263; 736-737; 766. Debate over New Hampshire's claim for expenses incurred maintaining jurisdiction at Indian Stream area. Includes remarks by Senators Atherton (N.H) and Phelps (Vt.).

3130. Atherton, Charles G. (N.H.). "Claims of New Hampshire...," *Congressional Globe.* 29th Cong., 1st Sess. (7 Jan., 12 Jan., 28 Jan., 28 Apr., 6 May 1846) pp. 154; 183-184; 262; 736-737; 766. Defends claims for expenses incurred while maintaining the jurisdiction of the Indian Stream territory in 1835-36; provides background information on the dispute over the boundary with Canada.

3131. Norris, Moses (N.H.). "The Naval Appropriation Bill," *Congressional Globe.* 29th Cong., 1st Sess. (13 June 1846) p. 968. Supports a dry-dock at Kittery, Maine, in the harbor of Portsmouth; details the advantages.

3132. Norris, Moses (N.H.). "The Tariff," *Congressional Globe, Appendix.* 29th Cong., 1st Sess. (2 July 1846) pp. 920-928. Discusses the tariff. Addresses the Whigs reversal of opinion regarding the tariff of 1842; compares provisions in the proposed bill with the existing law as affects duties on various items. Concludes that the tariff acts of 1828 and 1842 were oppressive and unjust, of no benefit to the manufacturer, farmer or mechanic.

3133. U.S. House. *New Hampshire Claims.* 29th Cong., 1st Sess. (H.Rpt.833). [Washington]: Ritchie & Heiss, Printers, [1846]. 4 pg. (Serial Set 491). Report of the Committee on Military Affairs supports reimbursement to New Hampshire for maintaining jurisdiction of the Indian River settlement in 1835-1836.

3134. U.S. House. *Report to the Legislature of New Hampshire, Relative to the Imprisonment of Thomas W. Dorr.* 29th Cong., 1st Sess. (H.Doc.41). [Washington]: Ritchie & Heiss, Printers, [1845]. 8 pg. (Serial Set 482). Report of the New Hampshire select committee details the reasons for their resolutions opposed to the unfair trial of R.I. Governor Thomas W. Dorr.

3135. U.S. House. *Resolutions of the Legislature of New Hampshire, Relative to the Tariff and Independent Treasury.* 29th Cong., 1st Sess. (H.Doc.20). [Washington]: Ritchie & Heiss, Printers, [1845]. 2 pg. (Serial Set 482). Resolutions support a protective tariff and an Independent Treasury.

3136. U.S. House. *Resolutions of the Legislature of New Hampshire, Relative to the Northeastern Boundary.* 29th Cong., 1st Sess. (H.Doc.33). [Washington]: Ritchie & Heiss, Print., [1845]. 2 pg. (Serial Set 482). Resolutions oppose the interference of Great Britain in both the Oregon territory and the annexation of Texas to the Union.

3137. U.S. House. *Resolutions of the Legislature of New Hampshire, in Relation to the Purchase and Distribution of the Reports of the Decisions of the Supreme Court to the Several States.* 29th Cong., 1st Sess. (H.Doc.40). [Washington]: Ritchie & Heiss, Print., [1845]. 2 pg. (Serial Set 482). Resolutions support distribution of the *Reports*, including at least one copy to each state library.

3138. U.S. House. *Resolutions of the Legislature of New Hampshire, Recommending a Modification of the Post Office Laws, &c.* 29th Cong., 1st Sess. (H.Doc.58). [Washington: Ritchie & Heiss, Printers, 1846]. 1 pg. (Serial Set 483). Same as S.doc.33 (29-1) 472 (entry **3140**).

3139. U.S. Senate. [Petition of Pearson Cogswell, Late Marshal for District of New Hampshire]. 29th Cong., 1st Sess. (S.Doc.393). Washington: Ritchie & Heiss, 1846. 1 pg. (Serial Set 477). Favorable report on Cogswell's petition for payment of a judgment rendered in his favor in a suit instituted against him by the United States. Subsequently printed in S.doc.117 (29-2) 495 (entry **3150**).

3140. U.S. Senate. *Resolutions of the Legislature of New Hampshire, for the Alteration of the Post Office Law, So As to Allow Newspapers to Pass through the Post Office Free of Postage in the State in Which They Are Published.* 29th Cong., 1st Sess. (S.Doc.33). Washington: Ritchie & Heiss, 1846. 1 pg. (Serial Set 472). Same as H.doc.58 (29-1) 483 (entry **3138**).

3141. U.S. Senate. *Resolutions of the Legislature of New Hampshire, in Favor of the Protective System.* 29th Cong., 1st Sess. (S.Doc.452). Washington: Ritchie & Heiss, 1846. 1 pg. (Serial Set 478).

29TH CONGRESS, 2ND SESSION

3142. Atherton, Charles G. (N.H.). "Memorial of the Society of Friends," *Congressional Globe.* 29th Cong., 2nd Sess. (23 Dec. 1846) pp. 69-70. Defends not printing the memorial of the Society of Friends for New England that asked for the termination of the Mexican War.

3143. Atherton, Charles G. (N.H.). "Printing of Memorials," *Congressional Globe.* 29th Cong., 2nd Sess. (7 Jan. 1847) p. 133. Justifies the Committee's decision to not print the memorial opposed to the tariffs.

3144. Atherton, Charles G. (N.H.). Remarks on a Dry-Dock in Portsmouth Harbor, *Congressional Globe.* 29th Cong., 2nd Sess. (1 Feb. 1847) pp. 299-300. Supports the memorial praying for a dry-dock at Kittery, Maine, in Portsmouth harbor.

3145. Cilley, Joseph (N.H.). "Withdrawal of Our Troops," *Congressional Globe.* 29th Cong., 2nd Sess. (27 Jan. 1847) p. 267. Supports temporarily withdrawing the army from Mexico for reinforcements properly appointed and trained; advocates pushing forward into Mexico when the army is strong.

3146. Norris, Moses (N.H.). "Appropriations for the Army," *Congressional Globe.* 29th Cong., 2nd Sess. (23 Feb. 1847) pp. 484-488. Supports the Mexican War as just and necessary; reviews the necessity and constitutionality of the war. Presents the sequence of events leading to the war; responds to charges and arguments of his opponents.

3147. U.S. House. *New Hampshire Claim.* 29th Cong., 2nd Sess. (H.Rpt.47). [Washington]: Ritchie & Heiss, Print., [1847]. 4 pg. (Serial Set 501). Reprint of earlier report (H.rp.833 (29-1) 491 (entry **3133**)) supporting claims of New Hampshire for reimbursement of expenses incurred while maintaining jurisdiction of Indian Stream settlement.

3148. U.S. House. *Resolutions of the Legislature of New Hampshire Relative to the Annexation of Texas, and the Encroachment of the Slave Power.* 29th Cong., 2nd Sess. (H.Doc.23). [Washington: Ritchie and Heiss, Printers, 1846]. 2 pg. (Serial Set 499). Same as S.doc.154 (29-2) 495 (entry **3151**).

3149. U.S. House. *Resolutions of the Legislature of New Hampshire, Relative to Slavery in the District of Columbia and Territories Belonging or Which May Hereafter Belong to the United States.* 29th Cong., 2nd Sess. (H.Doc.24). [Washington: Ritchie & Heiss, Printers, 1846. 1 pg. (Serial Set 499). Same as S.doc.155 (29-2) 495 (entry **3152**).

3150. U.S. Senate. [Petition of Pearson Cogswell, Late Marshal for District of New Hampshire]. 29th Cong., 2nd Sess. (S.Doc.117). Washington: Ritchie and Heiss, 1847. 2 pg. (Serial Set 495). Committee of Claims adopts earlier favorable report on Pearson Cogswell's petition for payment of a judgment rendered in his favor in a suit instituted against him by the United States. Reprints S.doc.393 (29-1) 477 (entry **3139**).

3151. U.S. Senate. *Resolutions of the Legislature of New Hampshire, in Relation to Slavery.* 29th Cong., 2nd Sess. (S.Doc.154). Washington: Ritchie and Heiss, 1847. 2 pg. (Serial Set 495). Resolutions oppose slavery and support its suppression and extermination. Same as H.doc.23 (29-2) 499 (entry **3148**).

3152. U.S. Senate. *Resolutions of the Legislature of New Hampshire, in Relation to Slavery and the Domestic Slave Trade.* 29th Cong., 2nd Sess. (S.Doc.155). Washington: Ritchie and Heiss, 1847. 1 pg. (Serial Set 495). Resolutions oppose slavery in D.C., Oregon and other territories, and advocate the suppression of the domestic slave trade. Same as H.doc.24 (29-2) 499 (entry **3149**).

30ᵀᴴ CONGRESS, 1ˢᵀ SESSION

3153. Atherton, Charles G. (N.H.). "The Loan Bill," *Congressional Globe, Appendix.* 30th Cong., 1st Sess. (22 Mar., 27 Mar. 1848) pp. 410-415; 476-477. Discusses the loan bill; explains its provisions and the necessity for its passage, and corrects some positions in relation to the Secretary's report on the finances of the country. Discusses the amount for which the bill provides, the nature of its provisions, and the war with Mexico. Examines the receipts and expenditures of the country and the report of the Secretary of the Treasury. Explains the operation of the Treasury note system. Remarks on the public debt and past actions of political opponents. Later speech responds to remarks of Mr. Niles (Conn.).

3154. Hale, John P. (N.H.). "The French Revolution," *Congressional Globe, Appendix.* 30th Cong., 1st Sess. (6 Apr. 1848) pp. 456-457. Supports the resolution of congratulation to the French people.

3155. Hale, John P. (N.H.). "Increase of the Army," *Congressional Globe, Appendix.* 30th Cong., 1st Sess. (6 Jan. 1848) pp. 53-57. Opposes increasing the size of the army in response to the Mexican War. Objects to the war and any appropriations for money or men. Maintains that the cause of the war is to extend slavery; repudiates the President's claims and actions. Almost exact reprint of speech in *Congressional Globe*, pp. 122-126.

3156. Hale, John P. (N.H.). "Increase of the Army," *Congressional Globe.* 30th Cong., 1st Sess. (30 Dec. 1847) pp. 80-81. Opposes further appropriations to continue the Mexican War until the President informs the country how much he wants, how long it will take, and how he proposes to effect his result.

3157. Hale, John P. (N.H.). "Protection of Property in the District of Columbia," *Congressional Globe, Appendix.* 30th Cong., 1st Sess. (20 Apr. 1848) pp. 500-504. Various remarks support the bill he introduced relating to protection of property from mobs and riots. Maintains that the bill is almost identical to a Maryland law and that it has no allusions to the subject of slavery. Defends himself from accusations that the bill is anti-slavery.

3158. Hale, John P. (N.H.). Remarks on Resolution of Thanks to Generals Scott and Taylor, *Congressional Globe.* 30th Cong., 1st Sess. (11 Feb., 16 Feb. 1848) pp. 341, 342; 364-365. Opposes the resolution as it would imply he approved of the war with Mexico. Gives British precedents.

3159. Hale, John P. (N.H.). "Temporary Occupation of Yucatan," *Congressional Globe, Appendix.* 30th Cong., 1st Sess. (4 May 1848) pp. 594-595. Asserts that the war with Mexico was an aggressive war intended to protect the institution of slavery; maintains that it would violate the treaty between the U.S. and Mexico to send uninvited forces to the Yucatan.

3160. Hale, John P. (N.H.). "Territorial Government of Oregon," *Congressional Globe, Appendix.* 30th Cong., 1st Sess. (31 May, 1 June 1848) pp. 688; 691-693. Opposes the spread of slavery in new territories. Discusses the concept of slaves as property and whether that concept is maintained upon leaving the local jurisdiction maintaining that definition.

3161. Tuck, Amos (N.H.). "Oregon," *Congressional Globe.* 30th Cong., 1st Sess. (1 Aug. 1848) p. 1022. Opposes the extension of slavery into the Oregon territory and supports the abolition of slavery in the District of Columbia.

3162. Tuck, Amos (N.H.). "The Slave Question," *Congressional Globe, Appendix.* 30th Cong., 1st Sess. (19 Jan. 1848) pp. 209-213. Examines the remote and immediate causes of the Mexican War and the connection with slavery. Maintains that the annexation of Texas and the Mexican War were both schemes for the maintenance and extension of slavery. Lengthy summary of speech in *Congressional Globe*, pp. 197-200.

3163. U.S. House. *New Hampshire Claims.* 30th Cong., 1st Sess. (H.Rpt.149). [Washington: 1848]. 4 pg. (Serial Set 524). Reprint of earlier report (H.rp.833 (29-1) 491 (entry **3133**)) which was also reprinted again in H.rp.47 (29-2) 501 (entry **3147**).

3164. U.S. House. *Resolutions of the General Assembly of New Hampshire, Voting Thanks to Generals Taylor and Scott, Approbatory of the Conduct of the Executive in Relation to the War with Mexico, &c.* 30th Cong., 1st Sess. (H.Misc.Doc.3). Washington: Tippin & Streeper, 1848. 1 pg. (Serial Set 523).

3165. U.S. Senate. *Resolutions of the Legislature of New Hampshire in Relation to the Franking Privilege, and the Postage on Newspapers.* 30th Cong., 1st Sess. (S.Misc.Doc.14). Washington: Tippin & Streeper, 1848. 1 pg. (Serial Set 511). Resolution requests repeal of earlier act that enlarged the franking privilege of members of Congress and increased postage on newspapers.

3166. U.S. Senate. *Resolutions of the Legislature of New Hampshire, in Favor of the Removal of the Terms of the United States Circuit and District Courts from Exeter to Concord.* 30th Cong., 1st Sess. (S.Misc.Doc.16). Washington: Tippin & Streeper, 1848. 1 pg. (Serial Set 511).

3167. U.S. Senate. *Resolutions of the Legislature of New Hampshire in Relation to Slavery.* 30th Cong., 1st Sess. (S.Misc.Doc.17). Washington: Tippin & Streeper, 1848. 2 pg. (Serial Set 511). Resolutions oppose slavery.

30TH CONGRESS, 2ND SESSION

3168. Atherton, Charles G. (N.H.). "Civil and Diplomatic Appropriations," *Congressional Globe*. 30th Cong., 2nd Sess. (12 Feb. 1849) pp. 505-506. Remarks on proposed amendments. Explains why the Finance Committee approved of various provisions concerning salaries, buildings, discipline in the navy, medical treatment of paupers, and payment to Mexico.

3169. Atherton, Charles G. (N.H.). "The Coast Survey," *Congressional Globe, Appendix.* 30th Cong., 2nd Sess. (19 Feb. 1849) pp. 203-204. Supports maintaining the Coast Survey in its present administrative structure. Provides a history of the organization of the Coast Survey.

3170. Atherton, Charles G. (N.H.). "Indian Appropriation Bill," *Congressional Globe*. 30th Cong., 2nd Sess. (29 Jan. 1849) pp. 384-385, 386-387. Various remarks on the bill to pay the Cherokees additional money due them under the treaty of 1846; discusses the discrepancy between report of the Commissioner of Indian Affairs and the Comptroller and Auditor's report.

3171. Atherton, Charles G. (N.H.). "The New Territories," *Congressional Globe.* 30th Cong., 2nd Sess. (20 Feb. 1849) p. 565. Maintains that it is improper to introduce the important subjects, such as the protection of the people of California and New Mexico, into an appropriation bill.

3172. Hale, John P. (N.H.). "Civil and Diplomatic Bill," *Congressional Globe.* 30th Cong., 2nd Sess. (27 Feb. 1849) pp. 602, 603. Supports an increase of the salaries of the foreign ministers to France, Great Britain, and Russia.

3173. Hale, John P. (N.H.). "Colonization of Colored Persons," *Congressional Globe.* 30th Cong., 2nd Sess. (10 Jan. 1849) pp. 207-208. Supports the right of petition and opposes slavery.

3174. Hale, John P. (N.H.). "Flogging in the Navy," *Congressional Globe.* 30th Cong., 2nd Sess. (9 Feb., 12 Feb. 1849) pp. 488-489; 506-510, 512. Various brief remarks support petitions to abolish flogging in the navy.

3175. Hale, John P. (N.H.). "John P. Baldwin," *Congressional Globe.* 30th Cong., 2nd Sess. (2 Jan. 1849) p. 132. Maintains that officers, not the government, should be held accountable for property they ordered destroyed unnecessarily.

3176. Hale, John P. (N.H.). "Law for California," *Congressional Globe.* 30th Cong., 2nd Sess. (1 Mar. 1849) pp. 632-633. Remarks on whether the Constitution extends the right of *habeas corpus* to the residents of the territory of California; addresses objections of Southerners.

3177. Hale, John P. (N.H.). "New Mexico and California," *Congressional Globe, Appendix.* 30th Cong., 2nd Sess. (24 Feb. 1849) pp. 269-270. Opposes slavery in the territories; debates the power to extend the Constitution over the recently acquired territories.

3178. Hale, John P. (N.H.). "New Mexico," *Congressional Globe.* 30th Cong., 2nd Sess. (13 Dec. 1848) p. 36. Brief remarks on the memorial from a convention in New Mexico.

3179. Hale, John P. (N.H.). "Railroad Across the Isthmus," *Congressional Globe.* 30th Cong., 2nd Sess. (18 Dec. 1848) p. 50. Objects to entering into the proposed contract with Messrs. William H. Aspinwall, John L. Stephens, and Chauncey; maintains that it would give them a monopoly over the benefits derived from the railroad.

3180. Hale, John P. (N.H.). Remarks on the Proposition to Finish the City Hall, Washington, *Congressional Globe.* 30th Cong., 2nd Sess. (13 Feb. 1849) p. 526. Supports an appropriation for the building.

3181. Tuck, Amos (N.H.). "Mileage of Members," *Congressional Globe*. 30th Cong., 2nd Sess. (9 Jan. 1849) pp. 200-201. Various remarks support reimbursing mileage according to the shortest mail route from their residences to the city of Washington.

3182. Wilson, James (N.H.). "Compensation for Slave," *Congressional Globe*. 30th Cong., 2nd Sess. (29 Dec. 1848) pp. 123-125. Opposes the bill to compensate Antonio Pancheco for the loss of a slave conscripted into the Florida war; cites earlier cases for similar claims. Contends that there is no right of persons to property in slaves.

3183. Wilson, James (N.H.). "A Privileged Question," *Congressional Globe*. 30th Cong., 2nd Sess. (4 Dec. 1848) p. 2. Defends Mr. Sibley (Wis.) as a rightful delegate from the Territory of Wisconsin.

3184. Wilson, James (N.H.). "Slavery in the Territories," *Congressional Globe, Appendix*. 30th Cong., 2nd Sess. (16 Feb. 1849) pp. 192-196. Discusses the political implications of slavery as they pertain to the extension of slavery into the territories. Addresses the introduction of slavery into the country and its effect on the acquisition of other territories. Maintains that there were no perpetualists among the fathers of the Constitution, and that Congress has the power to legislate for the territories.

3185. "An Act for the Settlement of the Claims of New Hampshire against the United States," *Statutes at Large*, Vol. IX (2 Mar. 1849) p. 353.

3186. U.S. House. *Resolution of the Legislature of New Hampshire, Relative to the Territory Acquired by the Mexican War and the Introduction of Slavery Therein*. 30th Cong., 2nd Sess. (H.Misc.Doc.9). Washington: Tippin & Streeper, 1849. 2 pg. (Serial Set 544). Resolutions support the Mexican War and oppose slavery in the newly acquired territory.

3187. U.S. House. *Resolutions of the Legislature of New Hampshire, Relative to the Introduction of Slavery into the Territories of New Mexico and California*. 30th Cong., 2nd Sess. (H.Misc.Doc.10). Washington: Tippin & Streeper, 1849. 1 pg. (Serial Set 544). Resolution to prohibit slavery in all new territories.

3188. U.S. House. *Resolutions of the Legislature of New Hampshire, Approving the Vote of the Representatives in Congress from that State on the Subject of the Slave Trade in the District of Columbia*. 30th Cong., 2nd Sess. (H.Misc.Doc.8). Washington: Tippin & Streeper, 1849. 1 pg. (Serial Set 544).

RHODE ISLAND

1ST CONGRESS, 1ST SESSION

3189. Resolution and Debate on the Admission of Rhode Island into the Union, *Annals of Congress.* 1st Cong., 1st Sess. (5 June 1789) pp. 420-424. Debate over a resolution to invite the people of Rhode Island to hold a convention to adopt the Constitution and join the confederacy.

3190. "Rhode Island Desires to Maintain Friendly Relations with the United States," *American State Papers: Miscellaneous*, Vol. I (Doc. 10) pp. 9-10. (ASP 037). Memorial from the Governor of Rhode Island assures the U.S. of Rhode Island's attachment and friendship to its sister states; explains why they have not yet adopted the Constitution for themselves.

1ST CONGRESS, 2ND SESSION

3191. Page, John (Va.). "Rhode Island," *Annals of Congress.* 1st Cong., 2nd Sess. (26 May 1790) pp. 1616-1619. Opposes the bill to induce Rhode Island to join the Union and to prevent smuggling. Maintains that the bill is inconsistent, improper, rash, cruel, violates her rights, and will not accomplish its purpose. Discusses the consequences if passed.

3192. "An Act Declaring the Assent of Congress to Certain Acts of the States of Maryland, Georgia, and Rhode Island and Providence Plantations," *Statutes at Large*, Vol. I (11 Aug. 1790) pp. 184-185. Certain acts related to the tonnage of vessels declared to be in operation for six months. Also printed in the *Annals of Congress* (1st Cong., 2nd Sess.) Appendix, p. 2302.

3193. "An Act for Giving Effect to an Act Intituled 'An Act to Establish the Judicial Courts of the United States,' within Rhode Island and Providence

Plantations," *Statutes at Large*, Vol. I (23 June 1790) p. 128. Judicial act of 1789 declared in force as to Rhode Island. Also printed in the *Annals of Congress* (1st Cong., 2nd Sess.) Appendix, p. 2232.

3194. "An Act for Giving Effect to an Act Intituled 'An Act Providing for the Enumeration of the Inhabitants of the United States,' in Respect to the State of Rhode Island and Providence Plantations," *Statutes at Large*, Vol. I (5 July 1790) p. 129. Also printed in the *Annals of Congress* (1st Cong., 2nd Sess.) Appendix, p. 2233.

3195. "An Act for Giving Effect to the Several Acts Therein Mentioned, in Respect to the State of Rhode Island and Providence Plantations," *Statutes at Large*, Vol. I (14 June 1790) pp. 126-128. Acts concerning imports and tonnage, the regulation of vessels and the coasting trade, and the establishment of collection districts in Rhode Island at Newport and Providence. Also printed in the *Annals of Congress* (1st Cong., 2nd Sess.) Appendix, pp. 2230-2232.

1ST CONGRESS, 3RD SESSION

3196. "An Act to Continue an Act Intituled 'An Act Declaring the Assent of Congress to Certain Acts of the States of Maryland, Georgia, and Rhode Island and Providence Plantations,' So Far As the Same Respects the States of Georgia and Rhode Island and Providence Plantations," *Statutes at Large*, Vol. I (10 Jan. 1791) p. 189. Also printed in the *Annals of Congress* (1st Cong., 3rd Sess.) Appendix, p. 2309.

2ND CONGRESS, 1ST SESSION

3197. "An Act Declaring the Consent of Congress to a Certain Act of the State of Maryland, and to Continue for a Longer Time, an Act Declaring the Assent of Congress to Certain Acts of the States of Maryland, Georgia, and Rhode Island and Providence Plantations, So Far as the Same Respects the States of Georgia, and Rhode Island and Providence Plantations," *Statutes at Large*, Vol. I (19 Mar. 1792) p. 243. Also printed in the *Annals of Congress* (2nd Cong., 1st Sess.) Appendix, p. 1346.

2ND CONGRESS, 2ND SESSION

3198. "Drawback on Cordage," *American State Papers: Finance*, Vol. I (Doc. 48) p. 202. (ASP 09). Report supports memorials from Philadelphia and Providence in favor of protecting domestic manufacturers of cordage.

3RD CONGRESS, 1ST SESSION

3199. "Slave Trade," *American State Papers: Miscellaneous*, Vol. I (Doc. 44) p. 76. (ASP 037). Report supports petitions from the Quakers, the Providence Society for Abolishing the Slave Trade, and other societies who requested a prohibition of the slave trade.

3RD CONGRESS, 2ND SESSION

3200. "An Act for Allowing an Additional Compensation to the Judges of the Districts of Rhode Island and Delaware," *Statutes at Large*, Vol. I (27 Feb. 1795) p. 423. Also printed in the *Annals of Congress* (3rd Cong., 2nd Sess.) Appendix, p. 1508.

3201. "An Act Relative to the Passing of Coasting Vessels Between Long Island and Rhode Island," *Statutes at Large*, Vol. I (2 Mar. 1795) p. 426. Also printed in the *Annals of Congress* (3rd Cong., 2nd Sess.) Appendix, p. 1511.

4TH CONGRESS, 1ST SESSION

3202. Bourne, Benjamin (R.I.). "Additional Revenue," *Annals of Congress*. 4th Cong., 1st Sess. (1 Apr. 1796) pp. 844-845. Supports a plan for direct taxation necessary in times of war when revenues from commerce are interrupted.

3203. Bourne, Benjamin (R.I.). "Execution of British Treaty," *Annals of Congress*. 4th Cong., 1st Sess. (20 Apr. 1796) pp. 1102-1106. Supports the treaty; addresses objections to constitutionality, relations with France, encroachment upon the Judiciary, and stipulations on trade. Maintains that the treaty is a national compact that the House is obligated to carry into effect.

3204. "An Act Altering the Sessions of the Circuit Courts in the Districts of Vermont and Rhode Island, and for Other Purposes," *Statutes at Large*, Vol. I (27 May 1796) pp. 475-476. Also printed in the *Annals of Congress* (4th Cong., 2nd Sess.) Appendix, p. 2917.

3205. "An Act Declaring the Consent of Congress to a Certain Act of the State of Maryland, and to Continue an Act Declaring the Assent of Congress to Certain Acts of the States of Maryland, Georgia, and Rhode Island and Providence Plantations, So Far As the Same Respects the States of Georgia, and Rhode Island and Providence Plantations," *Statutes at Large*, Vol. I (12 May 1796) pp. 463-464. Also printed in the *Annals of Congress* (4th Cong., 2nd Sess.) Appendix, pp. 2903-2904.

4TH CONGRESS, 2ND SESSION

[no references]

5TH CONGRESS, 1ST SESSION

[no references]

5TH CONGRESS, 2ND SESSION

3206. Champlin, Christopher G. (R.I.). "Breach of Privilege," *Annals of Congress.* 5th Cong., 2nd Sess. (8 Feb. 1798) pp. 974-976. Supports expelling Matthew Lyon (Vt.) for his assault upon Roger Griswold (Conn.).

3207. "Additional Duties on Imported Spirits," *American State Papers: Finance*, Vol. I (Doc. 131) p. 576. (ASP 09). Report against the petition from Providence, R.I., requesting additional duties on imported rum and rye.

5TH CONGRESS, 3RD SESSION

[no references]

6TH CONGRESS, 1ST SESSION

3208. "Rhode Island College," *Annals of Congress.* 6th Cong., 1st Sess. (19 Mar. 1800) pp. 634-635. Debate and summary of report support the petition for compensation to the college for occupation and injuries sustained while being used as a hospital for the army of the U.S. during the war.

3209. "An Act for the Relief of the Corporation of Rhode Island College," *Annals of Congress.* 6th Cong., 1st Sess. (16 Apr. 1800) Appendix, p. 1473.

3210. "Remission of Duties," *American State Papers: Finance*, Vol. I (Doc. 162) p. 698. (ASP 09). Report favors granting relief from duties to the petitioners from Providence, R.I., whose goods were destroyed by fire while under the care of the officers of the customs.

6TH CONGRESS, 2ND SESSION

3211. "An Act Authorizing the Remission of Duties on Certain Teas Destroyed by Fire, while under the Care of the Officers of the Customs, in Providence, Rhode Island," *Statutes at Large*, Vol. II (3 Mar. 1801) p. 117. Also printed in the *Annals of Congress* (6th Cong., 2nd Sess.) Appendix, p. 1565.

3212. "An Act for Erecting Lighthouses on New Point Comfort, and on Smith's Point, in the State of Virginia, and on Faulkner's Island in Long Island Sound, in the State of Connecticut, and for Placing Buoys in Naraganset Bay," *Statutes at Large*, Vol. II (3 Mar. 1801) p. 125. Also printed in the *Annals of Congress* (6th Cong., 2nd Sess.) Appendix, pp. 1576-1578.

3213. "An Act to Establish the District of Bristol, and to Annex the Towns of Kittery and Berwick to the District of Portsmouth," *Statutes at Large*, Vol. II (25 Feb. 1801) pp. 101-102. Also printed in the *Annals of Congress* (6th Cong., 2nd Sess.) Appendix, p. 1550.

7ᵀᴴ CONGRESS, 1ˢᵀ SESSION

[no references]

7ᵀᴴ CONGRESS, 2ᴺᴰ SESSION

3214. "An Act to Make Beaufort and Passamaquoddy, Ports of Entry and Delivery; to Make Easton and Tiverton, Ports of Delivery; and to Authorize the Establishment of a New Collection District on Lake Ontario," *Statutes at Large*, Vol. II (3 Mar. 1803) pp. 228-229. Also printed in the *Annals of Congress* (7th Cong., 2nd Sess.) Appendix, pp. 1592-1593.

8ᵀᴴ CONGRESS, 1ˢᵀ SESSION

3215. Stanton, Joseph, Jr. (R.I.). "Amendment to the Constitution," *Annals of Congress*. 8th Cong., 1st Sess. (8 Dec. 1803) pp. 762-764. Supports the proposed constitutional amendment of the electoral process.

3216. Stanton, Joseph, Jr. (R.I.). "Importation of Slaves," *Annals of Congress*. 8th Cong., 1st Sess. (15 Feb. 1804) pp. 1016-1018. Objects to the buying and selling of slaves; addresses the repeal of the non-importation act of South Carolina. Advocates taxing slaves to increase revenue and reduce importation.

3217. Stanton, Joseph, Jr. (R.I.). "State Balances," *Annals of Congress*. 8th Cong., 1st Sess. (17 Jan. 1804) pp. 903-904. Opposes eliminating the balances due from debtor states for debts incurred during the Revolutionary War; reviews Rhode Island's situation.

3218. "An Act Altering the Sessions of the District Courts of the United States for the Districts of Virginia, Rhode Island, and for the District of West Tennessee," *Statutes at Large*, Vol. I (23 Mar. 1804) pp. 273-374. Also printed in the *Annals of Congress* (8th Cong., 1st Sess.) Appendix, pp. 1281-1282.

3219. "Fishing Bounty," *American State Papers: Finance*, Vol. II (Doc. 204) p. 60. (ASP 010). Report against granting the petition from New Shorehand, R.I., that requested a bounty for dried fish caught in boats with a capacity of less than five tons.

8ᵀᴴ CONGRESS, 2ᴺᴰ SESSION

3220. Stanton, Joseph, Jr. (R.I.). "District of Columbia," *Annals of Congress.* 8th Cong., 2nd Sess. (10 Jan. 1805) pp. 961-962. Supports the District of Columbia as the seat of government and opposes the proposed retrocession.

3221. Stanton, Joseph, Jr. (R.I.). "Georgia Claims," *Annals of Congress.* 8th Cong., 2nd Sess. (2 Feb. 1805) pp. 1169-1171. Remarks on the settlement of the Yazoo claimants.

9ᵀᴴ CONGRESS, 1ˢᵀ SESSION

3222. Stanton, Joseph, (R.I.). "Non-Importation of Goods from Great Britain," *Annals of Congress.* 9th Cong., 1st Sess. (13 Mar. 1806) pp. 764-767. Supports non-intercourse with Great Britain as a necessary and constitutional measure to be used until Great Britain discontinues her piratical conduct and makes restoration.

9ᵀᴴ CONGRESS, 2ᴺᴰ SESSION

3223. "Collection Districts," *Annals of Congress.* 9th Cong., 2nd Sess. (4 Feb. 1807) p. 456. Reprint of the report opposed to granting the petitions to form a new collection district to include Stonington and Groton, in Connecticut, and Pawcatuck, in Rhode Island.

3224. "Fees of Officers of State Courts," *Annals of Congress.* 9th Cong., 2nd Sess. (29 Nov. 1806) Appendix, pp. 1153-1156. List of fees allowed to officers of the courts and others in Rhode Island for performing various services.

3225. Statement from the Newport Insurance Company on Losses Incurred, *Annals of Congress.* 9th Cong., 2nd Sess. (7 Dec., 11 Dec. 1805) Appendix, pp. 881-884; 884-889. Statement from the Newport Insurance Company detailing losses sustained from captures by pirates in the West Indies and by British armed vessels in the British Channel. Describes circumstances of each loss. Requests speedy compensation for the sufferers.

3226. "Collection Districts," *American State Papers: Finance*, Vol. II (Doc. 263) p. 226. (ASP 010). Report against granting the petitions to form a new collection district to include Stonington and Groton, in Connecticut, and Pawcatuck, in Rhode Island.

10ᵀᴴ CONGRESS, 1ˢᵀ SESSION

3227. "An Act to Erect a Lighthouse on Point Judith, in the State of Rhode Island," *Statutes at Large*, Vol. II (10 Feb. 1808) p. 462. Also printed in the *Annals of Congress* (10th Cong., 1st Sess.) Appendix, p. 2826.

3228. "Remission of Duties," *American State Papers: Finance*, Vol. II (Doc. 272) pp. 258-262. (ASP 010). Petition and supporting documents concerning whether duties should be charged on saltpeter. Includes the petition of Walter Channing, of Gibbs and Channing, Newport, R.I., protesting the charge of duties. Also includes opinions of counsel, and statements from collectors and from the Treasury Department.

10ᵀᴴ CONGRESS, 2ᴺᴰ SESSION

[no references]

11ᵀᴴ CONGRESS, 1ˢᵀ SESSION

3229. Announcement of the Death of Francis Malbone, *Annals of Congress.* 11th Cong., 1st Sess. (2 June 1809) p. 24.

11ᵀᴴ CONGRESS, 2ᴺᴰ SESSION

3230. Potter, Elisha R. (R.I.). "American Navigation Act," *Annals of Congress.* 11th Cong., 2nd Sess. (19 Jan. 1810) pp. 1241-1245. Supports the end of the embargo and the consequential death of the restrictive system. Reviews the operation of the restrictive system on the farmers; maintains that the system operates at the expense of farmers and common people. Recommends that the southern planter and eastern farmer unite for free and unrestrained commerce.

3231. Potter, Elisha R. (R.I.). "Conduct of the British Minister," *Annals of Congress.* 11th Cong., 2nd Sess. (19 Dec. 1809) pp. 756-762. Opposes the resolution approving the conduct of the Executive in refusing to hold further communication with Mr. Jackson, the British minister. Examines the development of the situation; concludes that Mr. Jackson offered no insult and that the resolution has party implications. Maintains that the non-intercourse act operates exclusively in Great Britain's favor. Offers several recommendations.

3232. Potter, Elisha R. (R.I.). "Detachment of Militia," *Annals of Congress.* 11th Cong., 2nd Sess. (20 Mar. 1810) pp. 1586-1597. Opposes raising a voluntary and involuntary army; objects to the necessity, expense, and inconvenience. Maintains that it would do much harm and no possible good.

Discusses the lack of necessity for this army and possible uses in New Orleans or against Canada. Addresses whether the soldiers are truly volunteers according to provisions of the bill. Opposes detaching men from the militia; discusses the consequences. Maintains that to add to the army you ought to enlist the men; if you want the militia to do their duty, arm them.

3233. "An Act to Allow the Benefit of Drawback on Merchandise Transported by Land Conveyance from Newport to Boston, and from Boston to Newport, in Like Manner As if the Same Were Transported Coastwise," *Statutes at Large*, Vol. II (25 Apr. 1810) p. 578. Also printed in the *Annals of Congress* (11th Cong., 2nd Sess.) Appendix, pp. 2541-2542.

11TH CONGRESS, 3RD SESSION

3234. Champlin, Christopher G. (R.I.). "Question of Order," *Annals of Congress.* 11th Cong., 3rd Sess. (2 Jan. 1811) pp. 78-79. Objects to censuring Timothy Pickering (Mass.) for disclosing some previously confidential documents concerning the title to West Florida.

3235. Potter, Elisha R. (R.I.). "Deposites in State Banks," *Annals of Congress.* 11th Cong., 3rd Sess. (6 Feb. 1811) pp. 908-909. Remarks and resolution provide that the deposits be made in those State banks that will pay the most for the privilege while offering the necessary security.

12TH CONGRESS, 1ST SESSION

3236. "Rhode Island Resolutions," *Annals of Congress.* 12th Cong., 1st Sess. (9 June 1812) pp. 252-254. Resolutions oppose direct taxes and war; indicate the defenseless situation of the state. Reprint of Misc.324 (12-1) ASP 038 (entry **3238**).

3237. Potter, Elisha R. (R.I.). "Additional Duties," *Annals of Congress.* 12th Cong., 1st Sess. (22 June 1812) pp. 1527-1530. Opposes the additional duties which would benefit Great Britain and harm the consumer; advocates a repeal or suspension of the non-importation act.

3238. "Opposition of Rhode Island to a War," *American State Papers: Miscellaneous*, Vol. II (Doc. 324) pp. 185-186. (ASP 038). Resolutions oppose direct taxes and war; indicate the defenseless situation of the state. Also printed in the *Annals of Congress* (12th Cong., 1st Sess.) pp. 252-254 (entry **3236**).

12TH CONGRESS, 2ND SESSION

3239. Potter, Elisha R. (R.I.). "Increase of the Navy," *Annals of Congress.* 12th Cong., 2nd Sess. (23 Dec. 1812) pp. 444-449. Opposes the proposed increase of the navy as too expensive to the nation. Discusses the willingness of the people to pay for the increase; objects to any loans or taxes necessary to carry on a war he opposes. Addresses the need to protect commerce, the desire of the people for the navy, and the necessity of a navy to carry on the war.

3240. Potter, Elisha R. (R.I.). "Suspension of Non-Importation," *Annals of Congress.* 12th Cong., 2nd Sess. (20 Feb. 1813) pp. 1091-1099. Opposes the bill to partially suspend the non-importation acts and to lay additional duties on foreign tonnage. Contends that the bill will raise revenue at the expense of the commercial and manufacturing interests of the U.S. and will act to Great Britain's advantage. Considers alternative sources of revenue. Reviews the restrictive actions by government; requests consistency in its measures.

3241. Potter, Elisha R. (R.I.). "Treasury Notes," *Annals of Congress.* 12th Cong., 2nd Sess. (27 Jan. 1813) pp. 908-912. Objects to issuing Treasury notes because it would extend the patronage of the Treasury Dept. to certain banks; advocates adding the sum needed to the loan bill where the government would derive an advantage from the money deposited. Addresses alternatives. Comments on the similarities of the current administration to Adams' administration.

13TH CONGRESS, 1ST SESSION

[no references]

13TH CONGRESS, 2ND SESSION

3242. Potter, Elisha R. (R.I.). "Extension of Enlistments," *Annals of Congress.* 13th Cong., 2nd Sess. (21 Jan. 1814) pp. 1099-1108. Objects to raising more men to carry on the war. Responds to charges of inconsistency by Mr. McKee (Ky.). Discusses the power of the minority in the administration, the popularity of the war, the objects of the war, and the conquest of Canada. Maintains that the war is being continued when its original causes have been removed.

3243. Potter, Elisha R. (R.I.). "Modification of the Embargo," *Annals of Congress.* 13th Cong., 2nd Sess. (8 Feb. 1814) pp. 1253-1255. Supports continuing the embargo in the interests of stability and consistency; maintains that it is better for the people to have steady laws. Reviews the situation in Rhode Island and Massachusetts.

3244. Potter, Elisha R. (R.I.). "Repeal of the Embargo," *Annals of Congress.* 13th Cong., 2nd Sess. (7 Apr. 1814) pp. 1992-2000. Opposes the repeal as inconsistent and premature. Maintains that the country's difficulties arise from the British blockade and the war, not the embargo. Objects to the repeal of the non-importation act that would give Great Britain all the advantages of commerce and remove any inducement to make peace. Discusses the consequences of a repeal; makes alternative recommendations for revenue.

13TH CONGRESS, 3RD SESSION

3245. "Relative Powers of the General and State Governments over the Militia," *Annals of Congress.* 13th Cong., 3rd Sess. (28 Feb. 1815) Appendix, pp. 1744-1795. Report of the Committee on Military Affairs supports the conduct of the Dept. of War relative to the powers of the general and state governments over the militia. Majority of the report is a response from the Sec. of the Dept. of War objecting to the resistance of Massachusetts, Connecticut, and Rhode Island to furnish their quota of the militia. Includes correspondence between the Dept. of War and the Governors of those states. Addresses the objections of the Governors. Same as Mil.aff.142 (13-3) ASP 016 (entry 3247).

3246. Potter, Elisha R. (R.I.). "Military Peace Establishment," *Annals of Congress.* 13th Cong., 3rd Sess. (25 Feb. 1815) pp. 1203-1204. Supports reducing the army in times of peace to only the two thousand men necessary to garrison the seaboard posts.

3247. "Relative Powers of the General and State Governments over the Militia," *American State Papers: Military Affairs,* Vol. I (Doc. 142) pp. 604-623. (ASP 016). Also printed in the *Annals of Congress* (13th Cong., 3rd Sess.) Appendix, pp. 1744-1795. See entry 3245 for abstract.

14TH CONGRESS, 1ST SESSION

3248. "Protection to Manufacturers," *American State Papers: Finance,* Vol. III (Doc. 458) pp. 52-54. (ASP 011). Petition from the cotton manufacturers of Providence supports extending protection to manufacturers; reviews the present ruinous situation, and the advantages of prohibiting the importation of cotton goods. Describes the extent of cotton manufacturing in Providence.

14TH CONGRESS, 2ND SESSION

[no references]

15TH CONGRESS, 1ST SESSION

3249. Burrill, James, Jr. (R.I.). "African Slave Trade," *Annals of Congress.* 15th Cong., 1st Sess. (12 Jan. 1818) pp. 95-97. Supports an inquiry into the expediency of negotiating with other nations to abolish the slave trade. Discusses obligations under the Treaty of Ghent.

3250. "An Act to Allow the Benefit of Drawback on Merchandise Transported by Land Conveyance from Bristol to Boston, and from Boston to Bristol, in Like Manner as if the Same Were Transported Coastwise," *Statutes at Large*, Vol. III (6 Feb. 1818) p. 405. Also printed in the *Annals of Congress* (15th Cong., 1st Sess.) Appendix, p. 2510.

15ᵀᴴ CONGRESS, 2ᴺᴰ SESSION

3251. Burrill, James, Jr. (R.I.). "Memorial of Matthew Lyon," *Annals of Congress*. 15th Cong., 2nd Sess. (8 Dec. 1818) pp. 48-49. Supports the unfavorable report on the petition of Matthew Lyon. Maintains that the petition offers no proof and that interference in this case would set bad precedence.

3252. "Remission of Duties," *American State Papers: Finance*, Vol. III (Doc. 3) Appendix, p. 836. (ASP 011). Report denies the request of memorialists from Providence who asked for relief from alleged excess duties paid on ivory and palm oil; principle reasons for refusal are outlined.

3253. "Remission of Duties," *American State Papers: Finance*, Vol. III (Doc. 3) Appendix, pp. 836-837. (ASP 011). Report against the memorial of Nicholas Brown and Thomas P. Ives, of Providence, R.I., requesting a remission of excess duties paid in barter for other commodities.

16ᵀᴴ CONGRESS, 1ˢᵀ SESSION

3254. "Prohibition of Slavery in Missouri," *Annals of Congress*. 16th Cong., 1st Sess. (18 Jan. 1820) Appendix, pp. 2457-2463. Memorial requests that Congress forbid the extension of slavery into Missouri. Reviews the circumstances of the introduction and legislation of the slave trade; discusses the temptations for illegal traffic in Missouri. Maintains that Congress has a right to impose conditions to sovereign states. Same as Misc.479 (16-1 ASP 038 (entry **3258**).

3255. Burrill, James, Jr. (R.I.). "Admission of Maine and Missouri," *Annals of Congress*. 16th Cong., 1st Sess. (13 Jan. 1820) pp. 94-97. Supports considering the subjects of Maine and Missouri separately. Maintains that Maine is an uncontested question of policy, of division of one of the original states, while Missouri is a complex question involving the erection of a state out of an acquired territory. Consideration of Missouri needs more information.

3256. Burrill, James, Jr. (R.I.). "Admission of Maine and Missouri," *Annals of Congress*. 16th Cong., 1st Sess. (20 Jan. 1820) pp. 209-219. Opposes extending slavery into the territories. Discusses the power of Congress to impose this restriction on new states. Reviews the ordinance of 1787, the principle of compromise, the intent of the Constitution, acts of cession and admission, and slave representation. Maintains that Congress has the power over the migration and importation of slaves. Addresses opponents' arguments.

3257. Burrill, James, Jr. (R.I.). "The Bankrupt Bill," *Annals of Congress.* 16th Cong., 1st Sess. (16 Mar. 1820) pp. 516-518. Supports the bill as an act to secure the rights of creditors and provide for an equal distribution of a bankrupt's estate among all his creditors.

3258. "Prohibition of Slavery in Missouri," *American State Papers: Miscellaneous,* Vol. II (Doc. 479) pp. 568-570. (ASP 038). Also printed in the *Annals of Congress* (16th Cong., 1st Sess.) pp. 2452-2457. See entry **3254** for abstract.

16ᵀᴴ CONGRESS, 2ᴺᴰ SESSION

3259. Burrill, James, Jr. (R.I.). "Admission of Missouri," *Annals of Congress.* 16th Cong., 2nd Sess. (7 Dec. 1820) pp. 45-50. Objects to accepting the Missouri constitution. Maintains that the consent of Congress is necessary to admit new states and that Congress has the authority to examine new states' constitutions to ascertain whether they conform to the Constitution of the United States. Objects to clause that would "prevent free negroes and mulattoes from coming to and settling in this State" as unconstitutional. Contends it would establish a bad precedence; discusses the consequences of not accepting Missouri's constitution.

3260. Knight, Nehemiah R. (R.I.). "Bankrupt Bill," *Annals of Congress.* 16th Cong., 2nd Sess. (14 Feb. 1821) pp. 344-345. Supports explicitly including manufacturers to be benefited by the provisions of the bill.

17ᵀᴴ CONGRESS, 1ˢᵀ SESSION

3261. De Wolf, James (R.I.). "Drawback on Cordage," *Annals of Congress.* 17th Cong., 1st Sess. (4 Apr. 1822) pp. 366-369. Supports the drawback on the exportation of domestic cordage manufactured from foreign hemp. Maintains that it would not harm the domestic production of hemp nor injure the revenue.

3262. Durfee, Job (R.I.). "Apportionment Bill," *Annals of Congress.* 17th Cong., 1st Sess. (17 Jan. 1822) pp. 737-743. Opposes the proposed increase of the ratio to 42,000. Addresses objections to increasing the number of members of the House; presents some considerations justifying an increase, including the character of the population, the geographical extent of the territory, the rights and sovereignty of the smaller states, and the control of executive influence.

3263. "An Act to Amend the Act, Entitled, "An Act to Establish the District of Bristol, and to Annex the Towns of Kittery and Berwick to the District of Portsmouth," Passed February Twenty-fifth, Eighteen Hundred and One,"

Statutes at Large, Vol. III (17 Apr. 1822) p. 662. Also printed in the *Annals of Congress* (17th Cong., 1st Sess.) Appendix, p. 2588.

3264. "Application of Rhode Island for a Grant of Land for the Purpose of Education," *American State Papers: Public Lands*, Vol. III (Doc. 339) p. 500. (ASP 030).

17TH CONGRESS, 2ND SESSION

3265. De Wolf, James (R.I.). "Drawback on Cordage," *Annals of Congress*. 17th Cong., 2nd Sess. (27 Dec. 1822) pp. 48-53. Supports a drawback on the exportation of domestic cordage manufactured from foreign hemp. Addresses opponents' objections. Maintains that the drawback would encourage labor, increase the exports of the country, and benefit the revenue.

3266. Durfee, Job (R.I.). "New Tariff Bill," *Annals of Congress*. 17th Cong., 2nd Sess. (4 Feb. 1823) pp. 813-824. Opposes the proposed tariff bill as unnecessary and inexpedient. Addresses arguments in support of the bill. Maintains that the bill does not promote existing manufactures, but proposes to create additional manufactures without necessary preparation. Discusses the effects of the bill.

18TH CONGRESS, 1ST SESSION

3267. De Wolf, James (R.I.). "Drawback on Cordage," *Annals of Congress*. 18th Cong., 1st Sess. (11 Feb. 1824) pp. 243-247. Supports a drawback on the exportation of domestic cordage manufactured from foreign hemp. Maintains that it would extend trade, give new employment to the shipping industry, and encourage domestic manufactures.

3268. "Remission of Interest of Duties," *American State Papers: Finance*, Vol. IV (Doc. 682) pp. 373-374. (ASP 012). Favorable report of the Committee of Ways and Means on a petition to grant a longer period to pay the bond for interest still due. Same as H.rp.3 (18-1) 105 (entry **3269**).

3269. U.S. House. *Report of the Committee of Ways and Means on the Petition of Jacob Babbitt, with a Bill for His Relief*. 18th Cong., 1st Sess. (H.Rpt.3). [Washington: 1823]. 3 pg. (Serial Set 105). Same as Finance 682 (18-1) ASP 012. See entry **3268**.

3270. U.S. Senate. [Report on the Memorial from the Merchants' Bank of Newport]. 18th Cong., 1st Sess. (S.Doc.18). [Washington: 1824]. 1 pg. (Serial Set 89). Request for a refund of money paid under the stamp law denied.

18TH CONGRESS, 2ND SESSION

3271. De Wolf, James (R.I.). "Drawback on Cordage," *Register of Debates.* 18th Cong., 2nd Sess. (11 Jan. 1825) p. 169. Supports the drawback on exports of domestic cordage manufactured from foreign hemp.

19TH CONGRESS, 1ST SESSION

3272. Burges, Tristam (R.I.). "Judiciary System," *Register of Debates.* 19th Cong., 1st Sess. (23 Jan. 1826) pp. 1081-1095. Opposes the proposed bill to extend the judicial system. Discusses objections to the bill, the alleged evils of the present system, and the need to accommodate the present and future wants of the nation. Maintains that the bill will not solve the problems of caseloads, equalize political representation, or equalize knowledge of state laws, if such an inequality exists. Supports the resolution for a system where the Supreme Court is a supervising tribunal, regulating and correcting inferior jurisdiction.

3273. Pearce, Dutee J. (R.I.). "Amendment of the Constitution," *Register of Debates.* 19th Cong., 1st Sess. (14 Mar. 1826) pp. 1653-1671. Opposes the amendment to establish a uniform mode of voting for the President and Vice President in districts; maintains that it is an invasion of the rights of the small states. Advocates leaving the method of choice to the state legislatures. Reviews the amendment of 1804 and different modes of appointing electors. Discusses the proposed removal of the election of the President from the House, the relative rights of the small states, and the relative loss and gain of power between the large and small states. Answers opponents' arguments.

3274. Pearce, Dutee J. (R.I.). "Appropriation for Fortifications," *Register of Debates.* 19th Cong., 1st Sess. (26 Jan. 1826) pp. 1160-1161. Supports appropriations to continue fortifications already begun; maintains that they benefit the whole Union rather than any particular section of the country.

3275. Pearce, Dutee J. (R.I.). "Case of Penelope Denney," *Register of Debates.* 19th Cong., 1st Sess. (10 Feb. 1826) pp. 1332-1334. Supports a pension for Penelope Denney whose son died protecting the commerce of the country.

3276. Pearce, Dutee J. (R.I.). "Judiciary System," *Register of Debates.* 19th Cong., 1st Sess. (18 Jan. 1826) pp. 1020-1029. Opposes the proposed extension of the judicial system. Maintains that the measure should not be sectional and benefit the western population only. Discusses the need for a permanent plan to address the needs of the future. Contends that the Constitution advocates two distinct Courts, and guarantees two distinct tribunals with separate judges. Addresses objections to this proposal, including the location of the Court, lack of local business knowledge, and similarities to the system of 1801.

3277. Robbins, Asher (R.I.). "The Judicial System," *Register of Debates.* 19th Cong., 1st Sess. (11 Apr. 1826) pp. 497-507. Opposes the proposed amendment that would continue the present system; maintains that this plan is a temporary expedient that will not suffice for the future growth of the country. Discusses the delay of justice and the expense and consequential losses caused by the delay. Recommends separating the duties of the two jurisdictions, the original and the appellate, to be exercised by different persons, as was intended by the Constitution. Addresses objections to this plan; discusses the advantages.

3278. Robbins, Asher (R.I.). "On the Panama Mission," *Register of Debates.* 19th Cong., 1st Sess. (14 Mar. 1826) pp. 175-184. Supports sending a minister to the Congress at Panama. Maintains that the Congress is not a confederate sovereignty, but rather a diplomatic council with no powers but to advise and consult. Contends that the mission will not compromise the country's neutral relations. Discusses the right to send a minister to an independent nation and the advantages to be gained.

3279. "Application of Rhode Island for Lands for Education," *American State Papers: Public Lands,* Vol. IV (Doc. 499) p. 552. (ASP 031). R.I. requests her proportion of the public lands for the establishment of an education fund.

3280. "On the Expediency of Establishing a Navy Yard and Station on the Narraganset Bay, in Rhode Island," *American State Papers: Naval Affairs,* Vol. II (Doc. 298) p. 637. (ASP 024). Committee on Naval Affairs reports that it is not expedient, at this time, to establish a navy yard at Narragansett Bay. Same as H.rp.93 (19-1) 141 (entry **3282**).

3281. U.S. House. *Letter from the Secretary of the Treasury, in Relation to the Erection of a Light House on Dutch Island, in Narraganset Bay, and a Beacon Light on Warwick Neck, in the State of Rhode Island.* 19th Cong., 1st Sess. (H.Doc.30). Washington: Gales & Seaton, 1826. 4 pg. (Serial Set 133). Letter reports that work has been postponed until sufficient appropriations are obtained for the purchase of the land and the erection of the necessary buildings.

3282. U.S. House. *Navy Yard - Narraganset Bay, R.I.* 19th Cong., 1st Sess. (H.Rpt.93). [Washington: 1826]. 1 pg. (Serial Set 141). Same as Nav.aff.298 (19-1) ASP 024. See entry **3280**.

3283. U.S. House. *Petition of Delegates from Rhode Island, New York, New Jersey, Pennsylvania and South Carolina, in Behalf of the Officers of the Revolutionary Army.* 19th Cong., 1st Sess. (H.Doc.4). Washington: Gales & Seaton, 1825. 4 pg. (Serial Set 131). Petition claims the rewards promised.

19TH CONGRESS, 2ND SESSION

3284. Burges, Tristam (R.I.). "Duties on Wool and Woollens," *Register of Debates.* 19th Cong., 2nd Sess. (22 Jan. 1827) p. 782. Supports protection for the manufacturers of woolen goods.

3285. Burges, Tristam (R.I.). "Seminary of Learning in Florida, &c.," *Register of Debates.* 19th Cong., 2nd Sess. (24 Jan. 1827) p. 813. Disapproves of extensive colleges for the instruction of the deaf and mute.

3286. Burges, Tristam (R.I.). "Surviving Officers of the Revolution," *Register of Debates.* 19th Cong., 2nd Sess. (4 Jan. 1827) pp. 603-621. Supports the pensions due the officers and soldiers of the Revolutionary War. Considers the character of the army, the nature of their service, and their compensation. Detailed discussion of the compensation arrangements, depreciation of the currency, and the promises of Congress. Addresses specific objections. Discusses the proposed provision, and the amount and manner of its payment.

3287. Burges, Tristam (R.I.). "Tacubaya Mission," *Register of Debates.* 19th Cong., 2nd Sess. (15 Feb. 1827) pp. 1191-1200. Supports $9,000 for the mission at Tacubaya. Mr. Poinsett, currently minister at Mexico, will perform additional duties as ambassador to the Congress of American Nations. Reviews the history of appropriations for diplomatic missions; addresses charges of Mr. Ingham (Pa.) concerning a history of Executive abuses and extravagant allowances in the diplomatic expenditures of Mr. Adams and Mr. Clay.

3288. Pearce, Dutee J. (R.I.). "British Colonial Trade," *Register of Debates.* 19th Cong., 2nd Sess. (17 Feb. 1827) pp. 1460-1464. Supports the proposed general restrictions on trade and commerce; maintains that the privations and sufferings are necessary and that the bill must operate on all parts of the country to achieve permanent benefits. Responds to Mr. Mallary (Vt.).

3289. Pearce, Dutee J. (R.I.). "Duties on Wool and Woolens," *Register of Debates.* 19th Cong., 2nd Sess. (30 Jan. 1827) pp. 857-870. Supports providing the aid and protection promised in the tariff act of 1824 to the wool and woolens manufacturers. Maintains that this protection will benefit the agricultural interest, extend commerce, increase the coasting trade, and benefit the poorer classes of the country. Shows that the bill would not affect the revenue. Discusses the benefits cotton manufacturers have received from protection. Describes conditions in the wool and woolens industry.

3290. Pearce, Dutee J. (R.I.). "Importation of Brandy in Small Casks," *Register of Debates.* 19th Cong., 2nd Sess. (3 Jan. 1827) pp. 597-599. Maintains that facilitating the trade of brandy would not injure the trade of whiskey as the two liquors are consumed by two different classes of people.

3291. Robbins, Asher (R.I.). "Gradual Improvement of the Navy," *Register of Debates.* 19th Cong., 2nd Sess. (15 Feb. 1827) pp. 360-363. Supports a naval academy. Discusses the need for an academy and its preparatory education; argues that the academy is expedient for the common defense of the country.

3292. U.S. House. *Memorial of Merchants and Others, of the State of Rhode Island, in Relation to Spoliations Committed on the Commerce of the United States, by the Vessels of War of France and Other European Nations.* 19th

Cong., 2nd Sess. (H.Doc.78). Washington: Gales & Seaton, 1827. 4 pg. (Serial Set 152). Memorial requests reparation for the wrongs done by France; also requests authorization of a special minister to obtain that remuneration.

20TH CONGRESS, 1ST SESSION

3293. Burges, Tristam (R.I.). "Case of Marigny D'Auterive," *Register of Debates*. 20th Cong., 1st Sess. (23 Jan. 1828) pp. 1093-1114. Opposes Marigny D'Auterive's claim for compensation for lost time and diminished value of his slave who was impressed into service in defense of New Orleans and consequently injured. Examines the principles of the claim; discusses slavery and slaves as property, and the right to impress. Rejects the claim as stale, not covered by the 1816 compensation law, unconstitutional, and against precedent.

3294. Burges, Tristam (R.I.). "Historical Paintings," *Register of Debates*. 20th Cong., 1st Sess. (9 Jan. 1828) pp. 938-939. Objects to paying to have the Battle of Orleans painted; also objects to painting the victory on Lake Erie as an addendum to that resolution. Compares both battles. Advocates addressing the petitions of the survivors before spending money on paintings.

3295. Burges, Tristam (R.I.). "Militia Courts Martial," *Register of Debates*. 20th Cong., 1st Sess. (11 Feb. 1828) pp. 1489-1490. Supports the immediate release of the requested papers relating to the court martial.

3296. Burges, Tristam (R.I.). "Mobile Court Martial," *Register of Debates*. 20th Cong., 1st Sess. (16 Jan. 1828) pp. 1046-1047. Supports the request for information on a court martial of certain Tennessee militiamen at Mobile.

3297. Burges, Tristam (R.I.). "Retrenchment," *Register of Debates*. 20th Cong., 1st Sess. (5 Feb. 1828) pp. 1399-1400. Supports requesting the history of expenditures from the discretionary fund in order to compare the current administration to those that have preceded it.

3298. Burges, Tristam (R.I.). "Tariff Bill," *Register of Debates*. 20th Cong., 1st Sess. (7 Apr. 1828) pp. 2210-2211, 2212-2214. Various remarks respond to charges by Mr. McDuffie (S.C.); maintains that the pamphlet abused by Mr. McDuffie is a speech he gave, and published, on the true principle of protection. Charges that Mr. McDuffie plagiarized his publication, "A Report on the State of the Finances," from a Boston report.

3299. Pearce, Dutee J. (R.I.). "Improvement of Harbors, &tc.," *Register of Debates*. 20th Cong., 1st Sess. (2 May 1828) pp. 2564-2570. Supports appropriations to build a pier in Warren for the improvement of the harbor. Reviews evidence in favor of the practicability and expediency of the appropriation; discusses the navigation and commerce of Warren and the advantages of an improved harbor. Compares the commercial importance of Warren to other places for which appropriations are recommended.

3300. Pearce, Dutee J. (R.I.). "Retrenchment," *Register of Debates.* 20th Cong., 1st Sess. (29 Jan. 1828) pp. 1230-1246. Supports the proposed inquiry into the expenditures of the administration; maintains that it will show no useless expenditures or abuse. Discusses the Nation's debt and argues against paying it immediately at the expense of other interests; addresses opponents' arguments. Discusses retrenchment, including the issues of compensation of members of the House, the Military School at West Point, the Panama Mission, and the contingent fund. Defends the Military School; describes its benefits.

3301. Robbins, Asher (R.I.). "Captors of the Philadelphia," *Register of Debates.* 20th Cong., 1st Sess. (7 Feb. 1828) pp. 256-259. Supports the claim for the capture and destruction of the frigate Philadelphia, in the harbor of Tripoli. Reviews the merits and circumstances of the case; maintains that as the frigate was a captured prize destroyed by order of the government, the government has a legal obligation to honor the claim of the captors.

3302. Robbins, Asher (R.I.). "Duty on Salt," *Register of Debates.* 20th Cong., 1st Sess. (7 Apr. 1828) pp. 596-601. Objects to reducing the duty on salt as an unnecessary experiment and inexpedient to the public interest. Describes the operation and consequences of this measure upon the salt industry; maintains that it would be ruinous. Contends that Great Britain has been successful in trade by following the protective principle steadily and unvaryingly; advocates that the U.S. should likewise permanently adhere to this principle.

3303. Robbins, Asher (R.I.). "Revolutionary Claims," *Register of Debates.* 20th Cong., 1st Sess. (11 Mar. 1828) pp. 423-427. Further remarks support the Revolutionary War claims. Discusses the special contract made with these petitioners, the commutation act, and the legal obligations of the government.

3304. Robbins, Asher (R.I.). "Surviving Officers of the Revolution," *Register of Debates.* 20th Cong., 1st Sess. (29 Jan. 1828) pp. 198-200. Supports honoring the claims of surviving officers of the Revolutionary War as a legal obligation. Describes the contractual nature of the agreement, and the evidence of compulsory assent for the commutation notes given in lieu of the half pay.

3305. "Against Increase of Duties on Imported Molasses," *American State Papers: Finance,* Vol. V (Doc. 863) pp. 877-878. (ASP 013). Memorial from Warren, R.I., opposes the proposed increase of duty on molasses and the abolishment of the drawback allowed on the exportation of spirits distilled from molasses. Maintains that they are entitled to equal protection and that the bill would destroy their businesses. Same as H.doc.160 (20-1) 172 (entry **3314**).

3306. "Against Increase of Duties on Imports," *American State Papers: Finance,* Vol. V (Doc. 875) pp. 898-899. (ASP 013). Memorial from Bristol, Rhode Island, opposes increasing duties on molasses and abolishing the drawback of duty on the exportation of rum. Maintains that additional duty would be impolitic and ruinous. Same as H.doc.177 (20-1) 173 (entry **3313**).

3307. "Against Increase of Duties on Imports," *American State Papers: Finance*, Vol. V (Doc. 872) pp. 894-895. (ASP 013). Memorial from Providence, R.I., against the increased duty on certain imports, particularly hemp, iron, and molasses; maintains that the bill is objectionable and harmful to navigation and foreign commerce. Includes table of value of exports to various locations. Same as H.doc.174 (20-1) 173 (entry **3317**).

3308. "In Favor of Increase of Duties on Imports," *American State Papers: Finance*, Vol. V (Doc. 833) p. 757. (ASP 013). Resolution from Rhode Island in support of increasing duties on selected imports to protect domestic manufactures. Same as H.doc.98 (20-1) 171 (entry **3318**) and S.doc.63 (20-1) 164 (entry **3319**).

3309. "In Favor of Increase of Duties on Imports," *American State Papers: Finance*, Vol. V (Doc. 853) p. 863. (ASP 013). Memorial from Providence, R.I., supports increasing the duties on fine and printed cottons; reviews the advantages of foreign manufacturers and the consequences of not protecting this branch of cotton manufacturing. Same as H.doc.133 (20-1) 172 (entry **3312**).

3310. "In Favor of Increase of Duties on Imports," *American State Papers: Finance*, Vol. V (Doc. 818) pp. 723-724. (ASP 013). Memorial from Kent county, Rhode Island, advocates extending further protection to the growers and manufacturers of wool. Same as H.doc.64 (20-1) 171 (entry **3315**).

3311. U.S. House. *Letter from the Secretary of War, Transmitting Reports of Surveys of Church's Cove Harbor; of the Shores North End of Goat Island, and of the River and Harbor of Warren, All in the State of Rhode Island.* 20th Cong., 1st Sess. (H.Doc.154). Washington: Gales & Seaton, 1828. 10 pg. (Serial Set 172). Surveys with recommendations on the expediency and expense of erecting piers and beacons, and building walls, to improve the navigation of these sites.

3312. U.S. House. *Memorial of a Committee in Behalf of Cotton Manufacturers, of Providence, in the State of Rhode Island.* 20th Cong., 1st Sess. (H.Doc.133). Washington: Gales & Seaton, 1828. 4 pg. (Serial Set 172). Same as Finance 853 (20-1) ASP 013. See entry **3309**.

3313. U.S. House. *Memorial of Citizens of Bristol, in the State of Rhode Island, against an Increase of Duty on Certain Imported Manufactures.* 20th Cong., 1st Sess. (H.Doc.177). Washington: Gales & Seaton, 1828. 4 pg. (Serial Set 173). Same as Finance 875 (20-1) ASP 013. See entry **3306**.

3314. U.S. House. *Memorial of Citizens of the Town of Warren, in the State of Rhode Island, against an Increase of Duty on Molasses Imported, &c.* 20th Cong., 1st Sess. (H.Doc.160). Washington: Gales & Seaton, 1828. 5 pg. (Serial Set 172). Same as Finance 863 (20-1) ASP 013. See entry **3305**.

3315. U.S. House. *Memorial of the Farmers and Manufacturers of the County of Kent, in the State of Rhode Island, Praying for Further Protection to Domestic Manufactures.* 20th Cong., 1st Sess. (H.Doc.64). Washington: Gales & Seaton, 1828. 4 pg. (Serial Set 171). Same as Finance 818 (20-1) ASP 013. See entry **3310**.

3316. U.S. House. *Petition of Inhabitants of Newport, R. Island, Distillers of Rum and Importers of Molasses, against an Increase of Duty on Molasses.* 20th Cong., 1st Sess. (H.Doc.118). Washington: Gales & Seaton, 1828. 3 pg. (Serial Set 171).

3317. U.S. House. *Representation of Sundry Citizens of Providence, in the State of Rhode Island, upon the Subject of an Increased Duty on Certain Imports.* 20th Cong., 1st Sess. (H.Doc.174). Washington: Gales & Seaton, 1828. 5 pg. (Serial Set 173). Same as Finance 872 (20-1) ASP 013. See entry **3307**.

3318. U.S. House. *Resolution of the General Assembly of Rhode Island, in Favor of Further Protection to Domestic Manufactures.* 20th Cong., 1st Sess. (H.Doc.98). Washington: Gales & Seaton, 1828. 3 pg. (Serial Set 171). Resolution supports increasing duties upon selected imports. Same as S.doc.63 (20-1) 164 (entry **3319**) and Finance 833 (201-) ASP 013 (entry **3308**).

3319. U.S. Senate. *Resolution of the State of Rhode Island & Providence Plantations, on the Subject of Protecting Duties, &c.* 20th Cong., 1st Sess. (S.Doc.63). Washington: Duff Green, 1828. 3 pg. (Serial Set 164). Resolution supports increasing duties upon selected imports. Same as H.doc.98 (20-1) 171 (entry **3318**) and Finance 833 (20-1) ASP 013 (entry **3308**).

20ᵀᴴ CONGRESS, 2ᴺᴰ SESSION

3320. Knight, Nehemiah R. (R.I.). "Congress Printing," *Register of Debates.* 20th Cong., 2nd Sess. (16 Dec., 17 Dec. 1828) pp. 3; 4. Various remarks support his amendment to advertise for the lowest bidder; maintains that it would promote competition and save money.

3321. U.S. House. *Memorial of Auctioneers of Providence.* 20th Cong., 2nd Sess. (H.Doc.81). [Washington: Gales & Seaton, 1829]. 2 pg. (Serial Set 185). Memorial objects to assessing duties upon sales at auction. Reviews the benefits of auctions for revenue and the operation of trade; maintains that the proposal operates unequally.

3322. U.S. Senate. [Report on Increasing Salaries of District Judges in Rhode Island, Maine, and South Carolina]. 20th Cong., 2nd Sess. (S.Doc.51). [Washington: Duff Green, 1829]. 1 pg. (Serial Set 181). Report against an increase in compensation in these particular cases, even though it is probably inadequate; contends that the whole subject needs a general revision.

21ST CONGRESS, 1ST SESSION

3323. Burges, Tristam (R.I.). "Indian Affairs," *Register of Debates.* 21st Cong., 1st Sess. (1 Mar. 1830) pp. 591, 593-594. Remarks on the printing of a memorial from the Friends of New England and the policy of the government towards the Cherokees.

3324. Burges, Tristam (R.I.). "The Tariff Laws," *Register of Debates.* 21st Cong., 1st Sess. (10 May 1830) pp. 923-942. Opposes Mr. McDuffie's (S.C.) amendment to the tariff bill. Detailed discussion of the intent and operation of protectionism; maintains that changing to free trade and the English system would place the U.S. in a condition of colonial dependence upon Great Britain. Responds in detail to allegations of South Carolina against the American system. Examines the cotton industry in relation to the allegations. Discusses the potential market of England. Reviews the consequences on the North and the South of implementing the English system. Comments on slavery.

3325. Knight, Nehemiah R. (R.I.). "Mr. Foot's Resolution," *Register of Debates.* 21st Cong., 1st Sess. (1 Mar. 1830) pp. 223-224. Defends Rhode Island against allegations of perpetuating slavery.

3326. Pearce, Dutee J. (R.I.). "Buffalo and New Orleans Road," *Register of Debates.* 21st Cong., 1st Sess. (12 Apr. 1830) pp. 768-774. Supports appropriations for the Buffalo and New Orleans road. Maintains that the road is needed and will strengthen the Union and improve intercourse. Addresses opponents' arguments concerning the ability of the states to combine to improve the system of internal improvements, the national debt, the best use of the money, the need for the road, and the unequal bearing of the appropriation.

3327. Pearce, Dutee J. (R.I.). "Penitentiary Punishment," *Register of Debates.* 21st Cong., 1st Sess. (27 Apr. 1830) pp. 824-826. Opposes limiting the operation of the bill to just free persons in the District; maintains that they should be legislating for the entire population, not a portion of them. Discusses the consequences of limiting the bill; addresses opponents' arguments.

3328. Robbins, Asher (R.I.). "Controversies Between States," *Register of Debates.* 21st Cong., 1st Sess. (3 May 1830) pp. 409-411. Supports the bill giving the Supreme Court the authority to decide controversies between two or more states. Addresses the lack of provisions for enforcement of the decision. Briefly reviews historic precedence. Maintains that it is a constitutional obligation to provide a means to settle these controversies.

3329. Robbins, Asher (R.I.). "The Indians," *Register of Debates.* 21st Cong., 1st Sess. (21 Apr. 1830) pp. 374-377. Opposes the proposed removal of the Indians west of the Mississippi. Discusses whether the Indian nations are competent to make treaties; contends that previous doctrine and practice has recognized them as competent and sovereign. Addresses opponents' arguments.

3330. Robbins, Asher (R.I.). "Mr. Foot's Resolution," *Register of Debates.* 21st Cong., 1st Sess. (20 May 1830) pp. 435-438. Discusses the rights of states under the Constitution. Maintains that the authority of the government is binding upon the states; otherwise it would be unconstitutional and dangerous to the Union. Reviews the relevant provisions in the Constitution and discusses various theories of states' rights. Addresses the value of the Union.

3331. "Surveys for a Naval Depot in Narraganset Bay and Newport Harbor," *American State Papers: Naval Affairs*, Vol. III (Doc. 401) pp. 463-468. (ASP 025). Report of the survey to select a site for a naval depot and navy yard. Lists the advantages and disadvantages of New York harbor, Narragansett Bay and Boston harbor; examines the relative value to each other and to the general defense. Reviews conditions necessary for naval depot sites; compares various sites. Recommends that a naval depot be formed at Charlestown, and that Hampton Roads, Boston, and Narragansett Bay be fortified and organized as naval and military rendezvous. Same as H.doc.21 (21-1) 195 (entry **3333**).

3332. U.S. House. *Letter from the Secretary of the Treasury, in Reply to a Resolution of the House of Representatives of the 6th Instant, in Relation to Providing for Sick and Disabled Seamen in Providence, Rhode Island, and Providing for the Erection of a Marine Hospital in Said District, &c. &c. &c.* 21st Cong., 1st Sess. (H.Doc.96). [Washington: Duff Green, 1830]. 20 pg. (Serial Set 198). Letter from Secretary suspends the application of funds towards the establishment of the marine hospital. Correspondence details the appropriations and transfer of land towards that purpose. Includes statistics on the receipts and expenditures under the fund for sick and disabled seamen and the number and manner of seamen cared for at Providence.

3333. U.S. House. *Survey - Narraganset Bay, &c. &c.* 21st Cong., 1st Sess. (H.Doc.21). [Washington: 1830]. 11 pg. (Serial Set 195). Same as Nav.aff.401 (21-1) ASP 025. See entry **3331**.

21ST CONGRESS, 2ND SESSION

3334. Burges, Tristam (R.I.). "Minister to Russia," *Register of Debates.* 21st Cong., 2nd Sess. (13 Jan. 1831) pp. 490-496. Opposes the appropriation as it is intended to support a mission formed to suit the talents, health and habits of John Randolph. Maintains that the situation in Russia requires that the minister be in residence and accountable.

3335. Burges, Tristam (R.I.). "Minister to Russia," *Register of Debates.* 21st Cong., 2nd Sess. (3 Feb. 1831) p. 575-608. Objects to approving an appropriation for John Randolph as the minister to Russia. Maintains that the mission is illegal. Reviews circumstances under which some payment might be due. Responds to opponents' arguments; reviews previous retrenchment efforts of Mr. Cambreleng (N.Y.). Maintains that the Senate did not consent to this non-resident appointment, that the power to accredit and receive ministers does not extend to non-resident ministers, and that the mission ended when he left Russia. Reviews the diplomatic history and character of John Randolph.

3336. Pearce, Dutee J. (R.I.). "Minister to Russia," *Register of Debates.* 21st Cong., 2nd Sess. (8 Feb. 1831) pp. 632-639. Objects to appropriations for John Randolph, minister to Russia. Reviews the official communications on the subject and the importance of the mission. Maintains that this discretionary exercise of privilege is unprecedented, irregular and illegal. Discusses the right of the House to withhold the appropriation and methods of payment. Reviews alleged precedents. Remarks on Mr. Randolph's character.

3337. "An Act to Provide for the Further Compensation of the Marshal of the District of Rhode Island," *Statutes at Large*, Vol. IV (2 Mar. 1831) p. 482. Also printed in the *Register of Debates* (21st Cong., 2nd Sess.) Appendix, pp. 60-61.

22ND CONGRESS, 1ST SESSION

3338. Burges, Tristam (R.I.). "Another Breach of Privilege," *Register of Debates.* 22nd Cong., 1st Sess. (14 May 1832) pp. 3032-3033. Remarks on the inquiry to investigate attacks upon members of the House.

3339. Burges, Tristam (R.I.). "Breach of Privilege," *Register of Debates.* 22nd Cong., 1st Sess. (14 Apr. 1832) pp. 2529-2531. Supports the power of the House to arrest an accused man when a breach of privilege was committed.

3340. Burges, Tristam (R.I.). "Case of Samuel Houston," *Register of Debates.* 22nd Cong., 1st Sess. (11 May 1832) pp. 2941-2976. Examines the case of Samuel Houston for contempt and breach of the privileges of the House. Reviews the circumstances of the assault against Mr. Stanberry (Ohio) for words spoken by him in the House regarding fraudulent contracts for Indian rations. Refutes the arguments for the defense, addressing other available remedies and the jurisdiction of the House over the case. Discusses the right to petition, the fraudulent contracts, the rights of freedom of speech and press for representatives, and the right of the House protect his members from violence.

3341. Burges, Tristam (R.I.). "The English Memorial," *Register of Debates.* 22nd Cong., 1st Sess. (2 Apr. 1832) pp. 2337-2338, 2343-2345, 2348-2349. Various remarks support reading the memorial from England on the foreign slave trade. Maintains that he cannot vote intelligently until he knows the contents. Defends himself from accusations of reproaching the South with the slavery issue; contends that it unconstitutional for the government to interfere with the slave issue. Defends the people of New England against accusations.

3342. Burges, Tristam (R.I.). "Georgia and the United States," *Register of Debates.* 22nd Cong., 1st Sess. (5 Mar. 1832) pp. 2031-2033. Maintains that Georgia would do her duty and not openly resist the laws of the Union; reviews the benefits Georgia has received from the government. Discusses the referral of the memorial concerning two missionaries detained in a penitentiary in Georgia as a result of her alleged jurisdiction over the Cherokee Indians.

3343. Burges, Tristam (R.I.). "Public Fast Day," *Register of Debates.* 22nd Cong., 1st Sess. (5 July 1832) pp. 3865-3866. Advocates a fast day to help against the "Asiatic Scourge."

3344. Burges, Tristam (R.I.). "South Carolina Claims," *Register of Debates.* 22nd Cong., 1st Sess. (5 Jan. 1832) pp. 1491-1493. Objects to recommitting the bill for the relief of South Carolina for blankets furnished to the militia during the late war; maintains that the facts are agreed upon, and that the claim is obviously valid and protected by common law.

3345. Burges, Tristam (R.I.). "The Tariff," *Register of Debates.* 22nd Cong., 1st Sess. (16 June 1832) pp. 3608-3652. Opposes reducing the tariff. Discusses the relationship between consumption and production. Reviews the operation of the current system and the effect of the proposal. Discusses the American system; addresses opponents' objections. Maintains that there is no evidence of oppression and unequal tax paying in the anti-protection states. Considers the declining navigation and its causes, labor and the distribution of profits, free trade, imposts paid by the states, and the payment of bounties and export duty.

3346. Burges, Tristam (R.I.). "Washington's Remains," *Register of Debates.* 22nd Cong., 1st Sess. (13 Feb. 1832) pp. 1800-1803. Supports removing Washington's remains from Mount Vernon and depositing them in the national cemetery provided under the foundation of the House. Discusses the wishes of the family and the nation; addresses opponents' objections.

3347. Knight, Nehemiah R. (R.I.). "The Tariff," *Register of Debates.* 22nd Cong., 1st Sess. (14 Feb. 1832) pp. 377-390. Supports the encouragement of the industry and manufacture of cotton. Discusses the benefits of the domestic manufacture of cotton goods. Reviews reasons for the decline of the navigating interest. Discusses some of the features of the tariff of 1824 and the need for a protective cotton tariff. Reviews the benefits of the American system over free trade. Addresses opponents' arguments.

3348. Pearce, Dutee J. (R.I.). "Mounted Troops," *Register of Debates.* 22nd Cong., 1st Sess. (9 June 1832) pp. 3392-3393. Objects to authorizing the President to organize a mounted corps and retain them at his discretion; proposes using the regular troops and teaching them to ride and care for horses.

3349. Pearce, Dutee J. (R.I.). "Ordnance Corps," *Register of Debates.* 22nd Cong., 1st Sess. (26 Mar. 1832) pp. 2247-2252. Opposes the proposed military bill. Examines the provisions of the bill; objects to increasing the size of the army, restricting the selection of men for the ordnance corps to the artillery corps, confusing rank, and increasing executive patronage. Maintains that it would benefit the entire army to disperse the knowledge gained by service in the ordnance corps to other branches of the military.

3350. Pearce, Dutee J. (R.I.). "The Tariff," *Register of Debates*. 22nd Cong., 1st Sess. (26 June 1832) pp. 3789-3794. Supports the protective policy. Reviews the effect of the additional duties of 1828 on molasses and iron and hemp production. Discusses the reasons for the differences in bounty between the registered and the enrolled vessels and the need for their protection.

3351. Pearce, Dutee J. (R.I.). "Wiscasset Collector," *Register of Debates*. 22nd Cong., 1st Sess. (4 Apr. 1832) pp. 2397-2428. Addresses the allegations against Thomas McCrate, the Wiscasset collector. Examines the complaint, the relationship of inspector to the collector, and the need to alter the mode of appointment. Maintains that a complete and impartial investigation can only be had in the House. Discusses the probable consequences of the investigation if managed by the Treasury Department. Responds to previous speakers. Discusses the possibility of further corruption in government, the right to petition, the Jackson administration and retrenchment, and President Jackson's popularity.

3352. Robbins, Asher (R.I.). "Colonel John Laurens," *Register of Debates*. 22nd Cong., 1st Sess. (22 May 1832) pp. 939-942. Supports the claim for the relief of the representatives of Colonel John Laurens. Addresses opponents' objections concerning the staleness of the claim and a previous adjustment.

3353. Robbins, Asher (R.I.). "The Tariff," *Register of Debates*. 22nd Cong., 1st Sess. (2 Mar. 1832) pp. 490-502. Addresses the expediency of continuing protecting duties. Discusses the successful exports of manufacturers under the policy, the demand for labor created by manufactures, and the resulting increase in the national wealth. Contends that manufacturers create a market for agriculture and that the protective policy augments foreign and domestic commerce. Advocates the steady pursuit of this policy. Denies that the policy is the cause of the distress in the South.

3354. "On the Expediency of Establishing a Naval Depot and Port of Expedition and Rendezvous in Narraganset Bay," *American State Papers: Naval Affairs*, Vol. IV (Doc. 469) p. 91. (ASP 026). Resolution with appropriations for a minute survey and examination of the most advantageous locations in the Bay.

3355. "Prices and Materials and Workmanship at Fort Hamilton, New York, and Fort Adams, at Newport, Rhode Island, in 1828-'29-'30," *American State Papers: Military Affairs*, Vol. V (Doc. 521) p. 5. (ASP 020). Report, with table, on prices paid for lumber, stone, lime, brick, and labor. Same as H.doc.179 (22-1) 219 (entry **3356**).

3356. U.S. House. *Letter from the Secretary of War, Transmitting the Information Required by a Resolution of the House of Representatives of 15th*

Instant, in Relation to Prices of Materials and Workmanship, at Fort Hamilton and Fort Adams. 22nd Cong., 1st Sess. (H.Doc.179). Washington: Duff Green, 1832. 2 pg. (Serial Set 219). Same as Mil.aff.521 (22-1) ASP 020. See entry **3355**.

3357. U.S. House. *Memorial of the Officers and Soldiers of the Late Rhode Island Brigade, Their Heirs and Representatives.* 22nd Cong., 1st Sess. (H.Doc.77). Washington: Duff Green, 1832. 5 pg. (Serial Set 217). Memorial requests payment of wages lost due to depreciated currency while serving during the Revolutionary War. Reviews the circumstances, acts of the state legislature, and confirmations by Congress, under which the Rhode Island Brigade was formed and financed.

3358. U.S. House. *Resolution of the Legislature of the State of Rhode Island, against Any Reduction of the Duties on Woollen Manufactures.* 22nd Cong., 1st Sess. (H.Doc.236). Washington: Duff Green, 1832. 1 pg. (Serial Set 221).

3359. U.S. House. *Soldiers of the Revolution - Rhode Island.* 22nd Cong., 1st Sess. (H.Doc.246). Washington: Duff Green, 1832. 8 pg. (Serial Set 221). Statement supports the claim of the Rhode Island Brigade for wages lost due to depreciation of the paper currency. Reviews the circumstances and the original contract; maintains that the raising of the Brigade was urged and insisted upon by Congress and that Congress should honor its original obligation. Same as H.doc.55 (22-2) 234 (entry **3372**).

3360. U.S. Senate. *Proceedings of a Meeting of the Citizens of Rhode Island in Favor of the Protection of American Manufactures, &c.* 22nd Cong., 1st Sess. (S.Doc.162). Washington: Duff Green, 1832. 2 pg. (Serial Set 214). Resolutions object to repealing or modifying past legislation. Maintain that the proposed bill is unjustifiable and would be disastrous.

22ND CONGRESS, 2ND SESSION

3361. Burges, Tristam (R.I.). "Appointments of Members of Congress," *Register of Debates.* 22nd Cong., 2nd Sess. (22 Dec. 1832) p. 905. Supports disclosing past Representatives that were appointed to salaried offices.

3362. Burges, Tristam (R.I.). "Matthew Lyon's Fine," *Register of Debates.* 22nd Cong., 2nd Sess. (12 Jan. 1833) pp. 1011-1012. Maintains that the House does not have the authority to reconsider a judicial decision of the Supreme Court concerning a fine charged to Matthew Lyon under the sedition law.

3363. Burges, Tristam (R.I.). "Remission of Duties," *Register of Debates.* 22nd Cong., 2nd Sess. (7 Jan. 1833) pp. 952-953. Supports the importers who lost money from the unexpected duties due under the act of May 19, 1828; maintains that the law did not give them enough time to sufficiently protect themselves.

3364. Burges, Tristam (R.I.). "The Tariff Bill," *Register of Debates*. 22nd Cong., 2nd Sess. (26 Jan. 1833) pp. 1358-1412. Opposes the proposed abandonment of the protective policy. Reviews the history of protectionism and the benefits of that policy. Discusses the effects of protectionism on production, labor, competition, agriculture, the fisheries, navigation, commerce, independence, and national defense. Examines the provisions and effects of the proposed bill. Discusses the power of Congress to coin money and regulate the currency and the value of the Bank of the United States. Objects that the bill provides for the wants of government, but makes no provision for the wants of the people. Examines the hostility of the South against the North and threats of nullification.

3365. Burges, Tristam (R.I.). "The Tariff," *Register of Debates*. 22nd Cong., 2nd Sess. (26 Feb. 1833) pp. 1780-1791. Opposes the proposed tariff bill. Protests against the provisions of the bill, denounces the intended purposes to be effected by its enactment, and reviews its origins. Reprints resolutions from the Legislature of Rhode Island protesting against the abandonment of protection (S.doc.43 (22-2) 230 (entry **3373**) and H.doc.57 (22-2) 234) (entry **3371**). Maintains that the bill will ruin the labor of the non-slave states and will establish a system of national taxation of the necessities. Contends that the bill will operate unequally and oppressively on New England.

3366. Pearce, Dutee J. (R.I.). "The Tariff Bill," *Register of Debates*. 22nd Cong., 2nd Sess. (30 Jan. 1833) pp. 1492-1521. Opposes the proposed tariff. Maintains that the bill has no advocates, promotes no interests, and is being considered under peculiar circumstances. Discusses the need for a settled policy. Demonstrates the unequal operation of the bill upon Rhode Island; discusses the consequences of the proposed duties on hemp, molasses, wool and woolens, and olive oil. Reviews the whaling and cottons industries and the effect of this bill upon them. Refutes the alleged profits of cotton manufacturers. Discusses the hostile attitude of South Carolina.

3367. Robbins, Asher (R.I.). "The Tariff," *Register of Debates*. 22nd Cong., 2nd Sess. (1 Mar. 1833) pp. 787-791. Opposes the proposed bill and the abolishment of protection. Discusses the importance of the protective policy to develop the resources of the country, the results of free trade, the advantages of a surplus in the treasury, and threats of the dissolution of the Union.

3368. "Report on the Survey of Narraganset Bay, and on the Expediency of Establishing a Naval Depot Therein," *American State Papers: Naval Affairs*, Vol. IV (Doc. 489) p. 224. (ASP 026). General description of the survey; indicates advantageous positions. Same as H.doc.19 (22-2) 233 (entry **3369**).

3369. U.S. House. *Letter from the Secretary of the Navy, Transmitting a Report and Survey of Narragansett Bay, &c.* 22nd Cong., 2nd Sess. (H.Doc.19). Washington: Duff Green, 1832. 3 pg. (Serial Set 233). General description of the survey which was undertaken to ascertain the practicability and expediency of establishing a naval depot at Narragansett Bay. Indicates two advantageous positions. Same as Nav.aff.489 (22-2) ASP 026 (entry **3368**).

3370. U.S. House. *Memorial of Citizens of Rhode Island, against Reducing the Duties on Goods, &c.* 22nd Cong., 2nd Sess. (H.Doc.101). Washington: Duff Green, [1833]. 5 pg. (Serial Set 234). Memorial opposes reducing the duties on cotton goods. Maintains that the bill operates unequally with disastrous consequences and will destroy the cotton manufacturers and the coasting trade.

3371. U.S. House. *Resolutions of the Legislature of the State of Rhode Island, on the Subject of Protection to Domestic Industry.* 22nd Cong., 2nd Sess. (H.Doc.57). Washington: Duff Green, [1833]. 3 pg. (Serial Set 234). Resolutions oppose abandoning the principle of protection to domestic industry; maintain that change is unnecessary, that protection is essential to the manufacturing industry, and that a vacillating and altering policy is destructive to the national industry. Same as S.doc.43 (22-2) 230 (entry **3373**).

3372. U.S. House. *Soldiers of the Revolution - Rhode Island.* 22nd Cong., 2nd Sess. (H.Doc.55). Washington: Duff Green, [1833]. 8 pg. (Serial Set 234). Same as H.doc.246 (22-1) 221. See entry **3359**.

3373. U.S. Senate. *Resolutions of the Legislature of Rhode Island, in Favor of Maintaining the Principle of Protecting Duties.* 22nd Cong., 2nd Sess. (S.Doc.43). Washington: Duff Green, [1833]. 3 pg. (Serial Set 230). Same as H.doc.57 (22-1) 234. See entry **3371**.

23RD CONGRESS, 1ST SESSION

3374. Communications on the Bank of the United States, *Congressional Globe*. 23rd Cong., 1st Sess. (7 Apr. 1834) p. 294. Reprint of two communications from Rhode Island constituents opposed to re-chartering the Bank of the United States.

3375. Debate on the Rhode Island Contested Election, *Register of Debates*. 23rd Cong., 1st Sess. (2 Dec., 4 Dec. 1833) pp. 2-11; 12-14. Debate over the proper Senate procedure concerning the contested election between Asher Robbins and Elisha Potter. Mr. Robbins' credentials were accepted; Mr. Potter's credentials were referred to the Committee on Elections. Shorter version of the first day's debate printed in the *Congressional Globe*, pp.1-2.

3376. "Providence (R.I.) Memorial," *Register of Debates*. 23rd Cong., 1st Sess. (17 Feb. 1834) pp. 569-573. Remarks by Nehemiah R. Knight (R.I.) and Asher Robbins (R.I.) on the memorial asking to restore the public deposits.

3377. "Rhode Island Contested Election," *Register of Debates*. 23rd Cong., 1st Sess. (10 June 1834) p. 1918. Motion to allow Elisha Potter compensation of mileage and per diem allowance during the time he was waiting for a decision.

3378. "Rhode Island Election," *Register of Debates.* 23rd Cong., 1st Sess. (1 Apr. 1834) pp. 1229-1230. Debate over the proper content and reception of a minority report on the election.

3379. "Rhode Island Memorials," *Register of Debates.* 23rd Cong., 1st Sess. (17 Feb. 1834) pp. 2717-2724. Debate on the memorial from Providence, in favor of restoring the deposits and re-chartering the Bank of the United States. Includes remarks by Tristam Burges (R.I.) and Dutee J. Pearce (R.I.).

3380. "Rhode Island Senator," *Register of Debates.* 23rd Cong., 1st Sess. (4 Mar. 1834) pp. 804-807. Majority report of the committee on the credentials of Asher Robbins and Elisha Potter is favorable to the right of Mr. Robbins to his seat in the Senate. Debates the propriety of allowing a minority report.

3381. "Rhode Island Senator," *Register of Debates.* 23rd Cong., 1st Sess. (4 Apr. 1834) pp. 1252-1257. Debate over the proper parliamentary procedure concerning the reception and printing of the minority report of the Committee.

3382. Burges, Tristam (R.I.). "Bank Reports," *Register of Debates.* 23rd Cong., 1st Sess. (27 May 1834) pp. 4271-4273. Supports printing the majority and minority reports of the bank committee attached together; discusses the party implications of presenting a partial view on this question.

3383. Burges, Tristam (R.I.). "The General Appropriation Bill," *Register of Debates.* 23rd Cong., 1st Sess. (10 Apr. 1834) pp. 3585-3586. Opposes reducing members' salaries.

3384. Burges, Tristam (R.I.). "The Pension Laws," *Congressional Globe.* 23rd Cong., 1st Sess. (17 Jan. 1834) p. 112. Objects to allowing pensions to the frontier settlers for their conflicts against the Indians; maintains that they acted to further their own interests and that it would establish bad precedent.

3385. Burges, Tristam (R.I.). "The Public Deposites," *Register of Debates.* 23rd Cong., 1st Sess. (26 Mar. 1834) pp. 3159-3236. Discusses the origin, history, and current circumstances of the Bank of the United States. Desires that the Secretary's reasons for his order to remove the public money be judged by the House. Discusses the causes and effects of the removal of the deposits. Maintains that the object of the removal was the extension of executive power. Discusses the growth of executive power, the purposes of the bank, attempts of the Executive to unite the money power with the political power, executive powers as defined by the Constitution, and the removal of Mr. Wm. Duane as Secretary of the Treasury.

3386. Burges, Tristam (R.I.). "Rhode Island Memorials," *Register of Debates.* 23rd Cong., 1st Sess. (17 Feb. 1834) pp. 2717-2718, 2720-2722, 2724. Supports the memorial and the memorialists and their request to restore the deposits and re-charter the Bank of the United States. Addresses attempts to discredit the memorialists and their memorial.

3387. Burges, Tristam (R.I.). "Rhode Island Resolutions," *Register of Debates.* 23rd Cong., 1st Sess. (23 June 1834) pp. 4676-4677. Defends the character of the House of Representatives of the Rhode Island Legislature and the resolutions they presented.

3388. Knight, Nehemiah R. (R.I.). "Kent County (R.I.) Memorial," *Register of Debates.* 23rd Cong., 1st Sess. (18 June 1834) pp. 2029-2030. Supports the memorial praying for the restoration of the deposits and other measures to sustain the currency. Explains why specie has not been exported.

3389. Knight, Nehemiah R. (R.I.). "Memorial from Rhode Island," *Register of Debates.* 23rd Cong., 1st Sess. (9 May 1834) pp. 1717-1718. Supports the memorial and memorialists praying for a restoration of the deposits and re-chartering of the bank.

3390. Knight, Nehemiah R. (R.I.). "Post Office Resolutions," *Register of Debates.* 23rd Cong., 1st Sess. (27 June 1834) pp. 2083-2086. Remarks on the accuracy of the memorial of F.P. Blair and the report of the Committee on the Post office regarding Post Office accounts and debts.

3391. Knight, Nehemiah R. (R.I.). "Providence (R.I.) Memorial," *Register of Debates.* 23rd Cong., 1st Sess. (17 Feb. 1834) pp. 569-570. Briefly presents a memorial for the restoration of the deposits.

3392. Pearce, Dutee J. (R.I.). "Providence (R.I.) Memorial," *Register of Debates.* 23rd Cong., 1st Sess. (14 Apr. 1834) pp. 3641-3642. Presents memorials from Providence and Bristol approving the course of the Executive relative to the Bank of the U.S.; supports the character of the memorialists.

3393. Pearce, Dutee J. (R.I.). "Rhode Island Memorials," *Register of Debates.* 23rd Cong., 1st Sess. (17 Feb. 1834) pp. 2718-2720, 2722-2724. Discredits the memorial from Providence that requested that the deposits be restored and the Bank of the United States be re-chartered.

3394. Pearce, Dutee J. (R.I.). "Rhode Island Resolutions," *Register of Debates.* 23rd Cong., 1st Sess. (23 June 1834) pp. 4674-4676, 4677-4678. Discredits the resolutions from the Legislature of Rhode Island asking for the restoration of the deposits and re-charter of the bank. Maintains that they were not resolutions of the popular branch of the legislature as Rhode Island does not have a truly representative popular branch due to her system of apportionment. States objections; claims the resolutions originated from broken-down politicians.

3395. Robbins, Asher (R.I.). "Kent County (R.I.) Proceedings," *Register of Debates.* 23rd Cong., 1st Sess. (24 June 1834) pp. 2069-2071. Supports the resolutions from Kent County disapproving of the actions of the Executive towards the Bank of the United States. Describes Kent County and its current distress. Responds to claims that the country is in a state of prosperity.

3396. Robbins, Asher (R.I.). "Providence (R.I.) Memorial," *Register of Debates.* 23rd Cong., 1st Sess. (17 Feb. 1834) pp. 570-573. Reviews the financial condition of the country and the current and future effect of the removal of the deposits on the leading resources of the country. Supports the memorial and restoring the public deposits.

3397. Robbins, Asher (R.I.). "Rhode Island Memorials," *Register of Debates.* 23rd Cong., 1st Sess. (24 Apr. 1834) pp. 1456-1462. Supports the character of the memorialists and their memorials from Bristol and Providence counties praying for a stable national currency, the restoration of the deposits, and a national bank. Maintains that a national bank is expedient and constitutional.

3398. Robbins, Asher (R.I.). "Rhode Island Memorials," *Register of Debates.* 23rd Cong., 1st Sess. (22 Mar. 1834) pp. 1108-1112. Presents memorials from Newport and from Smithfield and Cumberland, R.I., remonstrating against the removal of the deposits. Briefly describes the towns, their past prosperity, and current distress.

3399. Robbins, Asher (R.I.). "Rhode Island Resolutions," *Register of Debates.* 23rd Cong., 1st Sess. (9 June 1834) pp. 1910-1913. Supports the character of the people of Rhode Island and their disapproval of the Executive's actions concerning the Bank of the United States. Favors a restoration of the public deposits and renewal of the charter of the bank.

3400. U.S. House. *Memorial of Citizens of Bristol County, Praying a Restoration of the Deposites, and the Continuation of a National Bank.* 23rd Cong., 1st Sess. (H.Doc.262). [Washington: Gales & Seaton, 1834]. 6 pg. (Serial Set 257). Memorial supports relieving the present distress and continuing a sound currency by restoring the deposits and continuing the Bank of the United States. Includes names and occupations of memorialists. Text of memorial same as S.doc.301 (23-1) 241 (entry **3417**).

3401. U.S. House. *Memorial of Citizens of Bristol, Rhode Island, against Restoring the Public Deposites, and Also against Rechartering the Bank of the United States.* 23rd Cong., 1st Sess. (H.Doc.332). [Washington: Gales & Seaton, 1834]. 2 pg. (Serial Set 257). Maintains that restoring the deposits would increase the distress of the country and that the current problems are due to the uncertainty surrounding the bank and deposits. Includes names of memorialists.

3402. U.S. House. *Memorial of Citizens of Pawtucket, and Other Towns and Villages, against Restoring the Public Deposites, and Also against Rechartering the Bank of the United States.* 23rd Cong., 1st Sess. (H.Doc.383). [Washington: Gales & Seaton, 1834]. 3 pg. (Serial Set 258). Memorialists accuse the bank of deranging the currency and possessing power dangerous to the liberties of the people. Protest against prolonging the bank's existence. Text same as H.doc.333 (23-1) 257 (entry **3405**). Includes the names of the memorialists.

3403. U.S. House. *Memorial of Citizens of Providence County, Rhode Island, in Relation to the Currency.* 23rd Cong., 1st Sess. (H.Doc.256). [Washington: Gales & Seaton, 1834]. 9 pg. (Serial Set 257). Memorialists from Cumberland and Smithfield request measures of relief from the financial distress of the country. Includes nine pages of the names and occupations of the memorialists. Memorial, including names, same as S.doc.209 (23-1) 240 (entry **3414**).

3404. U.S. House. *Memorial of Citizens of Providence, Rhode Island, in Relation to the Money Market.* 23rd Cong., 1st Sess. (H.Doc.109). [Washington: Gales & Seaton, 1834]. 9 pg. (Serial Set 256). Memorial supports restoring governmental relations with the Bank of the U.S.; maintains that since the withdrawal of the deposits the currency has become deranged and the country in deep distress. Includes seven pages of names of the memorialists.

3405. U.S. House. *Memorial of Citizens of Providence, Rhode Island, against Rechartering Bank United States, and Approving of the Removal of the Public Deposites.* 23rd Cong., 1st Sess. (H.Doc.333). [Washington: Gales & Seaton, 1834]. 10 pg. (Serial Set 257). Includes nine pages of names of the memorialists. Text of memorial same as H.doc.383 (23-1) 258 (entry **3402**). See entry **3402** for abstract.

3406. U.S. House. *Memorial of Inhabitants of Newport, Rhode Island, in Relation to the Currency.* 23rd Cong., 1st Sess. (H.Doc.299). [Washington: Gales & Seaton, 1834]. 9 pg. (Serial Set 257). Memorial supports restoring the public deposits and renewing the charter of the Bank of the United States; maintains that these actions will stabilize the currency and relieve the current financial distress of the country. Includes names of memorialists both for and against the memorial. Almost the same as S.doc.210 (23-1) 240 (entry **3418**).

3407. U.S. House. *Memorial of Inhabitants of the County of Providence, R.I., In Relation to the Currency.* 23rd Cong., 1st Sess. (H.Doc.328). [Washington: Gales & Seaton, 1834]. 25 pg. (Serial Set 257). Memorial supports restoring the deposits and re-chartering the Bank of the United States; maintains that these recent "experiments" upon the national currency have been disastrous to the prosperity of the country. Includes 23 pages of names of the memorialists.

3408. U.S. House. *Resolutions Adopted at a Meeting Held at Pawtucket, North Providence, Rhode Island, against the Bank of the United States.* 23rd Cong., 1st Sess. (H.Doc.263). [Washington: Gales & Seaton, 1834]. 2 pg. (Serial Set 257). Resolutions support the course of the President and his veto of the bank charter. Maintains that the bank is unconstitutional, unnecessary unequal, unjust and responsible for the present deranged state of business.

3409. U.S. House. *Resolutions Adopted at a Meeting of the Citizens of Kent County, in Favor of a National Bank, and a Restoration of the Public*

Deposites. 23rd Cong., 1st Sess. (H.Doc.386). [Washington: Gales & Seaton, 1834]. 2 pg. (Serial Set 258). Resolutions from Kent County, Rhode Island, concerned with the current distress of the country; maintains that a national bank is essential to preserve a sound currency and to collect and disburse the public revenue. Same as S.doc.477 (23-1) 243 (entry **3419**).

3410. U.S. House. *Resolutions and Memorial of a Convention of Mechanics and Artisans, in Favor of the Restoration of the Deposites to, and the Recharter of, the Bank of the United States.* 23rd Cong., 1st Sess. (H.Doc.378). [Washington: Gales & Seaton, 1834]. 22 pg. (Serial Set 258). Resolutions maintain that the distress of the country is due to the interference of the Executive with the Bank of the United States. Reprints memorial S.doc.342 (23-1) 241 (entry **3416**), complaining of the distresses and praying for measures of relief. Includes 20 pages of the names and occupations of the memorialists.

3411. U.S. House. *Resolutions of Citizens of Providence, Rhode Island, in Relation to the Currency.* 23rd Cong., 1st Sess. (H.Doc.264). [Washington: Gales & Seaton, 1834]. 2 pg. (Serial Set 257). Resolutions oppose the Bank of the United States; they support the course of Andrew Jackson in vetoing the charter, removing the deposits, and exposing its corrupt practices. Contend that the bank and its supporters have subsidized the press and corrupted elections.

3412. U.S. House. *Resolutions of the Legislature of Rhode Island, in Relation to the Currency.* 23rd Cong., 1st Sess. (H.Doc.482). [Washington: Gales & Seaton, 1834]. 2 pg. (Serial Set 259). Resolutions oppose the removal of the deposits and support the Bank of the United States; maintain that the bank is necessary to maintain a sound and permanent national currency and to meet the needs of government, commerce and business.

3413. U.S. House. *Resolutions of the Working Men of Providence, Approving the Course of the Executive in Relation to the United States Bank.* 23rd Cong., 1st Sess. (H.Doc.265). [Washington: Gales & Seaton, 1834]. 2 pg. (Serial Set 257). Resolutions oppose the Bank of the U.S. and support the proceedings of the Executive. Other resolutions support free suffrage, encourage meetings for working men, and denounce the Providence Association of Mechanics and Artisans as not representing the interests of true working men.

3414. U.S. Senate. *Memorial and Resolutions of the People of Cumberland and Smithfield, R.I., Praying to be Relieved from the Pecuniary Distresses of the Community.* 23rd Cong., 1st Sess. (S.Doc.209). Washington: Duff Green, 1834. 11 pg. (Serial Set 240). Resolutions support chartering a national bank to provide relief from the financial distress of the country. Includes reprint of memorial, H.doc.256 (23-1) 257 (entry **3403**), with the 10 pages of the names of the memorialists.

3415. U.S. Senate. *Memorial of the Citizens of Kent County, Rhode Island, against the Removal of the Deposites, and in Favor of the United States Bank.*

23rd Cong., 1st Sess. (S.Doc.452). Washington: Duff Green, 1834. 2 pg. (Serial Set 243). Memorial maintains that the removal of the deposits shook the stability of the currency and the credit of the country. They advocate a restoration of the deposits and the re-chartering of the bank.

3416. U.S. Senate. *Memorial of the Mechanics and Artisans of Several of the Towns of Rhode Island, Complaining of the Distresses, and Praying for Measures of Relief, &c.* 23rd Cong., 1st Sess. (S.Doc.342). Washington: Duff Green, 1834. 2 pg. (Serial Set 241). Memorial highlights the problems with cotton, iron, and lumber; maintains that the derangement of the currency caused these problems. Text reprinted as H.doc.378 (23-1) 258 (entry **3410**); includes the names and occupations of the memorialists.

3417. U.S. Senate. *Memorial of the People of Bristol County, Rhode Island, for the Restoration of the Deposites, and Recharter of the Bank of the United States.* 23rd Cong., 1st Sess. (S.Doc.301). Washington: Duff Green, 1834. 3 pg. (Serial Set 241). Reprint of H.doc.262 (23-1) 257 (entry **3400**), without the names of the memorialists. See entry **3400** for abstract.

3418. U.S. Senate. *Memorial of the People of Newport, Rhode Island, in Favor of the Bank of the United States.* 23rd Cong., 1st Sess. (S.Doc.210). Washington: Duff Green, 1834. 5 pg. (Serial Set 240). Almost the same as H.doc.299 (23-1) 257. See entry **3406**.

3419. U.S. Senate. *Resolutions of Sundry Citizens of Kent County, Rhode island, for the Restoration of the Deposites, and Renewal of the Charter of the Bank of the United States.* 23rd Cong., 1st Sess. (S.Doc.477). Washington: Duff Green, 1834. 2 pg. (Serial Set 243). Same as H.doc.386 (23-1) 258. See entry **3409**.

23RD CONGRESS, 2ND SESSION

3420. Burges, Tristam (R.I.). "Louisville and Portland Canal," *Register of Debates.* 23rd Cong., 2nd Sess. (5 Feb. 1835) pp. 1198-1200. Opposes the government purchasing stock in the canal; maintains that it should be held by individual stockholders to enable the necessary tolls to be charged.

3421. Pearce, Dutee J. (R.I.). "Election of Officers of the House of Representatives," *Congressional Globe.* 23rd Cong., 2nd Sess. (26 Jan. 1835) pp. 166-167. Opposes the use of viva voce voting for officers of the House; supports the continued use of the balloting system. Same speech printed in the *Register of Debates*, "Viva Voce Elections," pp. 1080- 1082.

3422. Pearce, Dutee J. (R.I.). "Louisville and Portland Canal," *Register of Debates.* 23rd Cong., 2nd Sess. (5 Feb. 1835) pp. 1207-1208. Opposes the tolls at Louisville.

3423. Pearce, Dutee J. (R.I.). "Pay of the Army and Navy," *Congressional Globe.* 23rd Cong., 2nd Sess. (22 Dec. 1834) p. 58. Supports increasing the pay of officers of the navy and army to be more commensurate with that of other government officers. Same remarks printed in the *Register of Debates*, "Pay of Navy Officers," pp. 833-835.

3424. Robbins, Asher (R.I.). "French Spoliations," *Register of Debates.* 23rd Cong., 2nd Sess. (5 Jan. 1835) pp. 97-104. Supports the right of the claimants for spoliations prior to 1800. Reviews the circumstances of the claims and the release of these claims according to treaty. Maintains that the benefits to the country were incalculable and were obtained at the sole expense of these petitioners. Addresses objections.

3425. "Application of Rhode Island for a Distribution of the Proceeds of the Sales of the Public Lands Among the States," *American State Papers: Public Lands*, Vol. VII (Doc. 1314) pp. 626-627. (ASP 034). Resolutions support distributing the proceeds to the states, according to their representative population, to be applied towards public education and other purposes. Same as H.doc.169 (23-2) 274 (entry **3427**) and H.doc.137 (23-2) 274 (entry **3428**).

3426. U.S. House. *Letter from the Secretary of the Treasury, Transmitting Information in Relation to Marine Hospital Money Collected and Paid in the Rhode Island District.* 23rd Cong., 2nd Sess. (H.Doc.30). [Washington: Gales & Seaton, 1834]. 3 pg. (Serial Set 272). Report of the money collected and expended under various acts for the relief of sick and disabled seamen.

3427. U.S. House. *Resolutions of the Legislature of the State of Rhode Island, in Favor of a Distribution of the Proceeds of the Sales of the Public Lands Among the Several States, &c. &c.* 23rd Cong., 2nd Sess. (H.Doc.169). [Washington: Gales & Seaton, 1835]. 1 pg. (Serial Set 274). Same as Pub.land 1314 (23-2) ASP 034 (entry **3425**) and H.doc.137 (23-2) 274 (entry **3428**). See entry **3425** for abstract.

3428. U.S. House. *Resolutions of the Legislature of the State of Rhode Island, in Relation to the Disposition of the Proceeds of the Public Lands.* 23rd Cong., 2nd Sess. (H.Doc.137). [Washington: Gales & Seaton, 1835]. 1 pg. (Serial Set 274). Same as H.doc.169 (23-2) 274 (entry **3427**) and Pub.land 1314 (23-2) ASP 034 (entry **3425**). See entry **3425** for abstract.

3429. U.S. House. *Rhode Island Brigade.* 23rd Cong., 2nd Sess. (H.Rpt.128). [Washington: Gales & Seaton, 1835]. 40 pg. (Serial Set 276). Report supports the claim of the Rhode Island Brigade for wages lost due to the depreciation of the currency. Reviews in detail the circumstances, legislative recommendations respecting the depreciated currency and payment of the army, and payment of the claims of other state troops. Includes records of the proceedings of the Providence and Springfield conventions. Maintains that Congress expressly promised to pay the officers and soldiers of this Brigade what was due to them on account of depreciation and thus they should be paid their claim.

24ᵀᴴ CONGRESS, 1ˢᵀ SESSION

3430. Knight, Nehemiah R. (R.I.). "Joseph Grant," *Register of Debates.* 24th Cong., 1st Sess. (23 June 1836) pp. 1864-1866. Presents the case of Joseph Grant's application for a renewal of a patent for his invention of a machine that makes hat bodies.

3431. Pearce, Dutee J. (R.I.). Remarks on the Bank of the United States, *Congressional Globe.* 24th Cong., 1st Sess. (23 Mar. 1836) p. 281. Advocates an immediate decision of the question concerning the incorporation of the subscribers to the Bank of the United States. Same remarks printed in the *Register of Debates,* "United States Bank," pp. 2928-2931.

3432. Robbins, Asher (R.I.). "Captors of the Frigate Philadelphia," *Congressional Globe, Appendix.* 24th Cong., 1st Sess. (31 May 1836) pp. 558-559. Supports compensating the recaptors of the frigate Philadelphia after her capture by the barbarians of Tripoli. Recounts the events of the recapture and destruction; discusses the value of the achievement. Same speech printed in the *Register of Debates,* "Recaptors of the Frigate Philadelphia," pp. 1647-1649.

3433. Robbins, Asher (R.I.). "Defence of Narragansett Bay," *Register of Debates.* 24th Cong., 1st Sess. (17 June 1836) pp. 1787-1793. Presents and supports the resolutions from the Legislature of Rhode Island recommending provision for the defense of Narragansett Bay. Discusses the importance and advantages of the site for national defense. Reprints resolutions (H.doc.277 (24-1) 292 (entry **3438**), Mil.aff.692 (24-1) ASP021 (entry **3436**), and S.doc.408 (24-1) 284 (entry **3444**)).

3434. Robbins, Asher (R.I.). "Surplus Revenue to Fortifications," *Congressional Globe, Appendix.* 24th Cong., 1st Sess. (18 Feb. 1836) pp. 293-295. Justifies his vote against a $3,000,000 appropriation to be used at the President's discretion for the defense and armament of the country; maintains that the resolution was a violation of the Constitution. Reviews his objections; considers possible amendments and interpretations. Objects to transferring to the Executive the congressional authority to raise armies and provide navies. Responds to remarks of previous speakers. Same speech printed in the *Register of Debates,* "National Defence," pp. 566-571.

3435. "Application of Rhode Island for the Distribution of the Proceeds of the Sales of the Public Lands," *American State Papers: Public Lands,* Vol. VIII (Doc. 1448) p. 497-498. (ASP 035). Same as H.doc.137 (24-1) 289 (entry **3439**) and S.doc.195 (24-1) 281 (entry **3443**).

3436. "Application of Rhode Island that the Fortifications for the Defence of Narraganset Bay May Be Completed without Delay," *American State Papers: Military Affairs*, Vol. VI (Doc. 692) pp. 783-784. (ASP 021). Same as S.doc.408 (24-1) 284 (entry **3444**) and H.doc.277 (24-1) 292 (entry **3438**).

3437. "On a Claim for Bounty-Land Warrant," *American State Papers: Public Lands*, Vol. VIII (Doc. 1461) p. 531. (ASP 035). Favorable report on the claim of William C. Hazard asking for the bounty land and pay allowed as a child and heir of the soldier Ezekiel Hazard.

3438. U.S. House. *Fortify Narragansett Bay - Resolutions of the State of Rhode Island & Providence Plantations.* 24th Cong., 1st Sess. (H.Doc.277). [Washington: Blair & Rives, Printers, 1836]. 1 pg. (Serial Set 292). Resolutions support the fortification of Narragansett Bay. Same as S.doc.408 (24-1) 284 (entry **3444**) and Mil.aff.692 (24-1) ASP 021 (entry **3436**).

3439. U.S. House. *Resolution of the Legislature of the State of Rhode Island, in Relation to a Distribution of the Moneys Received from the Sale of the Public Lands.* 24th Cong., 1st Sess. (H.Doc.137). [Washington: Blair & Rives, Printers, 1836]. 1 pg. (Serial Set 289). Resolutions favor the distribution of the proceeds among the states. Same as S.doc.195 (24-1) 281 (entry **3443**) and Pub.land 1448 (24-1) ASP 035 (entry **3435**).

3440. U.S. House. *Rhode Island Brigade.* 24th Cong., 1st Sess. (H.Rpt.337). [Washington: Blair & Rives, Printers, 1836]. 42 pg. (Serial Set 293). Report supports the claim of the Rhode Island Brigade for wages lost due to depreciation. Reviews the circumstances, presents supporting correspondence and documents. Includes large excerpts from H.rp.128 (23-2) 276 (entry **3429**). Report includes reprint of the memorial of the Rhode Island Brigade for their claim, relevant correspondence between Governor Cook and General Washington, and proceedings of the conventions at Providence and Springfield.

3441. U.S. Senate. [Memorial of David Melvill of Newport, Rhode Island]. 24th Cong., 1st Sess. (S.Doc.430). Washington: Gales & Seaton, 1836. 31 pg. (Serial Set 284). Report on the memorial of David Melvill protesting against the discharge of officers, himself included, from the customhouse at Newport for political reasons. Includes lengthy correspondence between David Melvill and the Secretary of the Treasury discussing his removal from office.

3442. U.S. Senate. *Memorial of Nicholas Brown and Others, of Providence, Rhode Island, for Indemnity for Spoliations by France Prior to 1800.* 24th Cong., 1st Sess. (S.Doc.100). Washington: Gales & Seaton, 1836. 2 pg. (Serial Set 280).

3443. U.S. Senate. *Resolutions of the Legislature of Rhode Island, in Favor of the Distribution of the Proceeds of the Sales of the Public Lands Among the States.* 24th Cong., 1st Sess. (S.Doc.195). Washington: Gales & Seaton, 1836.

1 pg. (Serial Set 281). Same as H.doc.137 (24-1) 289 (entry **3439**) and Pub.land 1448 (24-1) ASP 035 (entry **3435**).

3444. U.S. Senate. *Resolutions of the Legislature of Rhode Island, Recommending Provision for the Defence of Narragansett Bay, in That State.* 24th Cong., 1st Sess. (S.Doc.408). Washington: Gales & Seaton, 1836. 1 pg. (Serial Set 284). Same as H.doc.277 (24-1) 292 (entry **3438**) and Mil.aff.692 (24-1) ASP 021 (entry **3436**).

24TH CONGRESS, 2ND SESSION

3445. Pearce, Dutee J. (R.I.). "Banking Institutions," *Congressional Globe, Appendix.* 24th Cong., 2nd Sess. (29 Dec. 1836) pp. 48-49. Discusses the appropriate action to take on the memorial from Pennsylvania complaining about the deposit banks. Questions whether the memorialists have done all they were able to do; discusses the power of Congress to restrain or restrict the issue of bank paper by local banks. Speech also printed in the *Register of Debates,* "National Currency," pp. 1192-1195.

3446. Pearce, Dutee J. (R.I.). "Deposite Banks," *Congressional Globe.* 24th Cong., 2nd Sess. (31 Dec. 1836) p. 66. Remarks on the limited authority of the House to investigate the deposit banks and ascertain whether Reuben M. Whitney was acting improperly as a deposit bank agent. Another report of these remarks is printed in the *Register of Debates,* "Deposite Banks," pp. 1214-1215.

3447. Pearce, Dutee J. (R.I.). Remarks on the Committee to Investigate the Executive Departments, *Congressional Globe.* 24th Cong., 2nd Sess. (15 Dec. 1836) p. 27. Opposes approving a committee to investigate whether the President spoke the truth when complimenting the executive departments. Maintains that there are other committees in the House to examine the condition and expenditures of the departments and that the resolution is without justification. Speech also printed in the *Register of Debates,* "The President's Message," pp. 1082-1084.

3448. Robbins, Asher (R.I.). "Purchase the Copy-right of Mr. Madison's Manuscript Works," *Congressional Globe, Appendix.* 24th Cong., 2nd Sess. (18 Feb. 1837) pp. 187-188. Supports purchasing the copyright for Mr. Madison's manuscripts as a valuable contribution to the study of the science of free government and an analysis of the steps leading to our government. Also contends that it would express the nation's gratitude to its benefactor. Speech also printed in the *Register of Debates,* "Papers of Mr. Madison," pp. 849-852.

3449. U.S. House. *Resolutions of the Legislature of Rhode Island, Instructing the Senators of That State to Vote for Expunging the Resolution of the Senate (from Its Journal) of 28th of March, 1834, in Relation to the President of the*

United States; and to Vote for R.M. Johnson, of Kentucky, for Vice President of the United States, &c., &c. 24th Cong., 2nd Sess. (H.Doc.157). [Washington: Blair & Rives, Printers, 1837]. 1 pg. (Serial Set 304). Resolutions to expunge the resolution censuring the President in regards to the public revenue, and to vote for R.M. Johnson if the election of Vice President devolves upon the Senate.

3450. U.S. Senate. *Report from the Secretary of the Navy, of an Examination of Narragansett Bay, with a View to the Establishment of a Naval Depot; in Obedience to a Resolution of the Senate of the 25th June, 1836.* 24th Cong., 2nd Sess. (S.Doc.56). Washington: Gales & Seaton, 1837. 2 pg. (Serial Set 297). Report supports the advantages of Narragansett Bay for a port of rendezvous as expedient and desirable; recommends further examinations.

3451. U.S. Senate. *Resolutions of the Legislature of Rhode Island, Opposed to Any Reduction of the Duties on Imports.* 24th Cong., 2nd Sess. (S.Doc.118). Washington: Gales & Seaton, 1837. 1 pg. (Serial Set 298). Resolutions support protection to national industry.

25TH CONGRESS, 1ST SESSION

[no references]

25TH CONGRESS, 2ND SESSION

3452. Robbins, Asher (R.I.). "Independent Treasury," *Congressional Globe, Appendix.* 25th Cong., 2nd Sess. (14 Mar. 1838) pp. 621-623. Opposes the Sub-Treasury bill and the use of specie to pay the public dues. Discusses the ruinous results of the exaction of public dues in specie; maintains that specie is now an article of merchandise and banished from circulation as a currency. Discusses the influence of the banking system, the advantages of the national bank and a national currency, and the importance of developing the physical resources of the country. Addresses opponents' arguments concerning the power of banks.

3453. Tillinghast, Joseph L. (R.I.). "Duel Reports," *Congressional Globe, Appendix.* 25th Cong., 2nd Sess. (24 Apr. 1838) pp. 550-551. Supports the importance of following the rules of the House while investigating the causes leading to the death of Mr. Cilley. Maintains that it is the option of the House to either pursue the investigation and trial in the House, or to give special authority to their committee for the inquiry.

3454. U.S. House. *Memorial of Robinson Potter and 361 Others, Citizens of Newport, Rhode Island, against the Passage of the Sub-Treasury Bill, and the Bill for a Surrender of the Public Domain to a Few New and Favored States.*

25th Cong., 2nd Sess. (H.Doc.229). [Washington: Thomas Allen, Print., 1838]. 2 pg. (Serial Set 328). Same as S.doc.265 (25-2) 317 (entry **3459**), without the names of the memorialists.

3455. U.S. House. *Resolutions of the Legislature of Rhode Island against the Annexation of Texas to the Union.* 25th Cong., 2nd Sess. (H.Doc.55). [Washington: Thomas Allen, Print., 1837]. 2 pg. (Serial Set 322). Resolutions strongly oppose the annexation; maintain that it is unconstitutional and would dissolve the Union; list various evils that would result. Same as S.doc.80 (25-2) 314 (entry **3461**).

3456. U.S. House. *Resolutions of the State of Rhode Island, Relative to Sub-Treasury, &c.* 25th Cong., 2nd Sess. (H.Doc.175). [Washington: Thomas Allen, Print., 1838]. 3 pg. (Serial Set 327). Resolutions oppose the Sub-Treasury scheme as unsafe, impolitic, injurious, unnecessary, odious, and dangerous. Same as S.doc.147 (25-2) 316 (entry **3460**).

3457. U.S. House. *Rhode Island Temperance Society - Against Use of Ardent Spirits - Navy Rations.* 25th Cong., 2nd Sess. (H.Doc.321). [Washington: Thomas Allen, Print., 1838]. 3 pg. (Serial Set 329). Memorial requests the repeal of the law allowing a daily ration of spirit to seamen in the navy; reviews various consequences of the existing law.

3458. U.S. Senate. *Memorial of a Number of Citizens of Providence, Rhode Island, Praying the Rejection of the "Sub-Treasury Bill."* 25th Cong., 2nd Sess. (S.Doc.211). Washington: Blair & Rives, Printers, 1838. 1 pg. (Serial Set 316). Memorial objects to the Sub-Treasury as odious and subversive.

3459. U.S. Senate. *Memorial of a Number of Merchants, and Others, Citizens of Newport, Rhode Island, against the Passage of the Bills for the Establishment of Sub-Treasuries and to Cede the Public Lands to the New States.* 25th Cong., 2nd Sess. (S.Doc.265). Washington: Blair & Rives, Printers, 1838. 5 pg. (Serial Set 317). Text of memorial same as H.doc.229 (25-2) 328 (entry **3454**); includes the names of the memorialists.

3460. U.S. Senate. *Resolutions of the House of Representative of Rhode Island, against the Passage of the Sub-Treasury Bill.* 25th Cong., 2nd Sess. (S.Doc.147). Washington: Blair & Rives, Printers, 1838. 3 pg. (Serial Set 316). Same as H.doc.175 (25-2) 327. See entry **3456**.

3461. U.S. Senate. *Resolutions of the Legislature of Rhode Island, against the Annexation of Texas to the United States.* 25th Cong., 2nd Sess. (S.Doc.80). Washington: Blair & Rives, Printers, 1838. 2 pg. (Serial Set 314). Same as H.doc.55 (25-2) 322. See entry **3455**.

25TH CONGRESS, 3RD SESSION

3462. Robbins, Asher (R.I.). "Smithsonian Bequest," *Congressional Globe, Appendix.* 25th Cong., 3rd Sess. (10 Jan. 1839) pp. 297-298. Recommends that Mr. Smithson's bequest be used for an institution and system of learning styled after that of ancient Athens. Discusses the importance of nurturing ability rather than knowledge in an educational system.

3463. Tillinghast, Joseph L. (R.I.). "Maine Boundary Question," *Congressional Globe, Appendix.* 25th Cong., 3rd Sess. (2 Mar. 1839) p. 286. Objects to conceding, as the proposed bill implies, that Great Britain has a claim to exclusive jurisdiction over the disputed territory of Maine.

3464. Tillinghast, Joseph L. (R.I.). "Public Defaulters," *Congressional Globe.* 25th Cong., 3rd Sess. (28 Dec. 1838) pp. 67-68. Supports printing the documents relating to the public defaulters; advocates printing documents of information and evidence and saving money by not printing documents of argument and opinion.

26TH CONGRESS, 1ST SESSION

3465. Dixon, Nathan F. (R.I.). "Bankrupt Act," *Congressional Globe, Appendix.* 26th Cong., 1st Sess. (20 May 1840) pp. 832-835. Supports the bankrupt bill and a uniform system of bankruptcy. Discusses the authority of Congress to legislate on the subject of bankruptcies. Addresses the bankrupt laws of England, local objections, preferences for state insolvent laws, and the bankrupt law of 1800. Maintains that the system is for voluntary bankruptcy only. Objects to the principle of compulsory bankruptcy and to extending the bill to embrace corporations and banks as impracticable, absurd and outside the power of Congress.

3466. Dixon, Nathan F. (R.I.). "System of Bankruptcy," *Congressional Globe.* 26th Cong., 1st Sess. (24 June 1840) pp. 482-483. Opposes limiting the operation of the bill to establish a uniform system of bankruptcy to two years. Maintains that the permanent national system would be considered temporary and not get a fair chance to prove itself.

3467. Knight, Nehemiah (R.I.). "Duty on Umbrellas, &c.," *Congressional Globe, Appendix.* 26th Cong., 1st Sess. (11 Mar. 1840) pp. 848-851. Opposes including umbrellas and parasols in the act to repeal duties. Responds to remarks by Sen. John Calhoun (S. C.), defending the American system and protective tariffs; discusses the tariff of 1816, protection of cotton manufacture, importation of gold and silver, the effect of reducing duties on imports and exports, and the effects of the protective system on exports.

3468. "An Act concerning Prisoners of the United States Committed to the Gaol in the County of Providence and State of Rhode Island," *Statutes at Large*, Vol. V (12 June 1840) p. 385.

3469. U.S. Senate. *Resolutions of the General Assembly of Rhode Island, Adverse to the Cession of the Public Lands to the States in Which They Are Located and in Favor of the Distribution of the Proceeds of the Sales of the Public Lands Among the Several States.* 26th Cong., 1st Sess. (S.Doc.190). Washington: Blair & Rives, Printers, 1840. 2 pg. (Serial Set 357). Resolutions oppose ceding more public lands to the new states; maintain that the new states have already received sufficient grants of land and that the old states' vested rights in the public domain should not be capriciously ceded.

26ᵀᴴ CONGRESS, 2ᴺᴰ SESSION

3470. U.S. House. *Resolutions of the Legislature of Rhode Island, on the Subject of So Amending the Constitution of the United States As to Provide That the Election of President and Vice President Be Holden on the Same Day throughout the United States.* 26th Cong., 2nd Sess. (H.Doc.99). [Washington: 1841]. 1 pg. (Serial Set 384).

3471. U.S. House. *Resolutions of the Legislature of Rhode Island, in Relation to the Distribution of the Proceeds of the Public Lands, the Repeal of the Sub-Treasury, and the Establishment of a National Bank.* 26th Cong., 2nd Sess. (H.Doc.106). [Washington: 1841]. 3 pg. (Serial Set 384). Resolutions request that each state receive its equitable proportion of the proceeds of the sale of the public lands, that the law establishing the Sub-Treasury be repealed, and that a national bank be established to secure the national currency.

27ᵀᴴ CONGRESS, 1ˢᵀ SESSION

3472. Simmons, James F. (R.I.). "Fiscal Bank," *Congressional Globe, Appendix.* 27th Cong., 1st Sess. (2 July 1841) pp. 357-358. Discusses the bill and amendment to establish a national bank. Addresses the constitutionality of establishing a national bank under state jurisdiction; maintains that the bank must be either local or national. Examines objections to the reported bill. Shows that Congress has always had the power to establish a national bank. Discusses the refusal to re-charter the banks and the authority of the Supreme Court to determine the question of the constitutionality of a national bank.

3473. U.S. House. *Resolutions of the Legislature of Rhode Island, Relative to the Presidential Term - Discriminating Duties.* 27th Cong., 1st Sess. (H.Doc.56). [Washington: Gales & Seaton, 1841]. 1 pg. (Serial Set 392). Resolutions support discriminating duties and a constitutional amendment to limit the term of President to one term.

27ᵀᴴ CONGRESS, 2ᴺᴰ SESSION

3474. "Affairs of Rhode Island," *Congressional Globe.* 27th Cong., 2nd Sess. (17 May 1842) pp. 506-507. Debate on the new republican system of government adopted in Rhode Island. Includes speech and resolutions by William Allen (Ohio), reviewing the circumstances and supporting the right of the people of Rhode Island to establish for themselves a constitutional republican form of state government without interference from the federal government. Also includes speech by James F. Simmons defending the old charter government system.

3475. The Death of Nathan F. Dixon, *Congressional Globe.* 27th Cong., 2nd Sess. (1 Feb. 1842) p. 199. Description of the funeral of Nathan F. Dixon, a Senator from Rhode Island.

3476. "The Difficulties in Rhode Island - Three Companies of United States Troops Marching into That State by Order of the President, to Put Down the Suffrage Party and Constitution," *Congressional Globe.* 27th Cong., 2nd Sess. (2 May 1842) pp. 462-463. William Allen (Ohio) attempts to report that the President has ordered troops to Rhode Island.

3477. "Difficulties in Rhode Island," *Congressional Globe.* 27th Cong., 2nd Sess. (22 Apr. 1842) p. 438. Resolutions and brief remarks by William Allen (Ohio) request information from the President concerning the controversy in Rhode Island over establishing a constitutional republican form of government for Rhode Island which would replace the land company charter granted by King Charles II of England under which that state has hitherto been governed.

3478. "The Rhode Island Difficulties," *Congressional Globe.* 27th Cong., 2nd Sess. (27 Apr., 23 May, 21 June 1842) pp. 446; 523; 659-660. Brief debates as to when Mr. Allen's resolutions requesting information from the President concerning the controversy over Rhode Island's form of government should be discussed in the Senate. Nathaniel Tallmadge (N.Y.) offers amended resolutions.

3479. Simmons, James F. (R.I.). "Affairs of Rhode Island," *Congressional Globe.* 27th Cong., 2nd Sess. (17 May 1842) p. 507. Defends the constitution and charter of Rhode Island; maintains that no other state or power has the right to interfere with its state constitution. Discusses suffrage requirements in Rhode Island and the results of the convention.

3480. Simmons, James F. (R.I.). "Proposed Board of Exchequer," *Congressional Globe.* 27th Cong., 2nd Sess. (5 Jan. 1842) p. 94. Offers alternatives regarding objections concerning an increase of executive power. Maintains that the proposed modifications would not endanger the success of the measure to provide an institution for currency and exchanges.

3481. Simmons, James F. (R.I.). Remarks on the Death of Nathan F. Dixon, *Congressional Globe.* 27th Cong., 2nd Sess. (31 Jan. 1842) pp. 196-197. Announces and remarks on the death of Nathan F. Dixon, Senator from Rhode Island; includes comments and resolution by William Woodbridge (Mich.).

3482. Simmons, James F. (R.I.). "Retrenchment and Reform," *Congressional Globe.* 27th Cong., 2nd Sess. (11 Mar. 1842) pp. 309-310. Summary of speech in support of increasing the tariff above the maximum of the Compromise Act. Discusses the most reliable revenue source for the government; maintains that the land fund is unreliable as it fluctuates with the economy. Discusses the expenditures of the Van Buren and Jackson administrations. Advocates a protective tariff and home valuation.

3483. Simmons, James F. (R.I.). "The Tariff Bill," *Congressional Globe.* 27th Cong., 2nd Sess. (27 July 1842) pp. 797-798. Supports increasing duties; contends that it would be a uniform system of revenue which would meet the needs of the government. Responds to remarks of Sen. Woodbury (N.H.). Discusses objections about the amount of revenue necessary, alternative means of raising revenue, and the effectiveness of the measure to increase the revenue, and the measure's effects upon the agricultural and laboring population.

3484. Tillinghast, Joseph L. (R.I.). "Operation of the Tariff Laws," *Congressional Globe.* 27th Cong., 2nd Sess. (6 Jan., Feb. 8 1842) pp. 101; 218. Favors allowing the Committee on Manufactures to collect information regarding the current operation of the tariff and probable results of proposed alterations. Addresses opponents' objections.

3485. Tillinghast, Joseph L. (R.I.). Remarks on the Death of Nathan F. Dixon, *Congressional Globe.* 27th Cong., 2nd Sess. (31 Jan. 1842) pp. 198-199. Resolution and eulogy of the life of Nathan F. Dixon, a Senator from Rhode Island.

3486. Tillinghast, Joseph L. (R.I.). "Veto of the Provisional Tariff Bill," *Congressional Globe, Appendix.* 27th Cong., 2nd Sess. (30 June 1842) pp. 886-890. Discusses the Presidential veto of the provisional tariff bill. Examines the distribution law concerning the distribution of the proceeds of the public lands and the implications if the bill is defeated. Addresses the Executive's desire to use the land fund as a source of revenue for the government. Maintains that each state is entitled to receive its respective proportion of the proceeds. Discusses the Presidential veto power, the sanctity of the Compromise Act, and the congressional power to alter and repeal existing laws.

3487. "An Act Making an Appropriation for the Repair of the Custom-house in Providence," *Statutes at Large,* Vol. V (27 July 1842) p. 496.

3488. "An Act to Annex a Part of the Town of Tiverton in the State of Rhode Island, to the Collection District of Fall River in the State of Massachusetts," *Statutes at Large,* (9 Aug. 1842) p. 504.

3489. U.S. House. *Repairs of Custom-House in Providence.* 27th Cong., 2nd Sess. (H.Rpt.65). [Washington: 1842]. 1 pg. (Serial Set 407). Report favors the repair of the customhouse at Providence.

3490. U.S. House. *Resolution of the Legislature of Rhode Island, Requesting a Suspension of the Bankrupt Law.* 27th Cong., 2nd Sess. (H.Doc.53). [Washington: 1842]. 1 pg. (Serial Set 402).

3491. U.S. House. *Resolutions of the Legislature of Rhode Island, on the Subject of the Tariff.* 27th Cong., 2nd Sess. (H.Doc.125). [Washington: Gales & Seaton, 1842]. 2 pg. (Serial Set 403). Resolutions favor a protective tariff to protect labor and to counter the legislation and restrictions of other nations. Same as S.doc.155 (27-2) 397 (entry **3498**).

3492. U.S. House. *Resolutions of the Legislature of Rhode Island, in Relation to the Embarrassed Condition of the Public Treasury and the Critical State of Our Foreign Relations.* 27th Cong., 2nd Sess. (H.Doc.185). [Washington: 1842]. 1 pg. (Serial Set 404).

3493. U.S. House. *Resolutions of the Legislature of the State of Rhode Island, Relative to the Election of President and Vice President.* 27th Cong., 2nd Sess. (H.Doc.126). [Washington: Gales & Seaton, 1842]. 1 pg. (Serial Set 403). Resolutions support a law designating the same day throughout the U.S. for the choice of electors of President and Vice President. Same as S.doc.164 (27-2) 397 (entry **3499**).

3494. U.S. Senate. *In Senate of the United States.* 27th Cong., 2nd Sess. (S.Doc.303). [Washington: Thomas Allen, Print., 1842]. 1 pg. (Serial Set 398). Resolution states that it is the right of the people of Rhode Island to establish, alter or modify a constitutional republic form of state government provided its form be left republican; role of the federal government also defined.

3495. U.S. Senate. *In Senate of the United States.* 27th Cong., 2nd Sess. (S.Doc.304). [Washington: Thomas Allen, Print., 1842]. 1 pg. (Serial Set 398). Resolutions on the rights of the people of Rhode Island to modify their state government and the powers and obligations of the general government to protect that state against invasion and domestic violence.

3496. U.S. Senate. [Petition of John S. Harris, Assistant Marshal for District of Rhode Island]. 27th Cong., 2nd Sess. (S.Doc.20). [Washington]: Thomas Allen, Print., [1841]. 1 pg. (Serial Set 396). Report of the Committee on Claims opposes the claim of the petitioner for additional compensation for his services in taking the 6th census.

3497. U.S. Senate. *Resolution Calling for Information As to the Proceedings of the Authorities and People of the State of Rhode Island in Relation to the Constitution of That State.* 27th Cong., 2nd Sess. (S.Doc.244). [Washington: Thomas Allen, Print., 1842]. 1 pg. (Serial Set 398). Request for any information concerning the possible establishment of a constitutional republic form of government for the people of Rhode Island in place of the land company charter under which that state has hitherto been governed.

3498. U.S. Senate. *Resolutions of the General Assembly of Rhode Island, in Favor of the Establishment of a Protective Tariff.* 27th Cong., 2nd Sess. (S.Doc.155). [Washington: Thomas Allen, Print., 1842]. 2 pg. (Serial Set 397). Same as H.doc.125 (27-2) 403. See entry **3491**.

3499. U.S. Senate. *Resolutions of the General Assembly of Rhode Island, in Favor of Designating the Same Day throughout the United States for the Choice of Electors of President and Vice President of the United States.* 27th Cong., 2nd Sess. (S.Doc.164). [Washington: Thomas Allen, Print., 1842]. 1 pg. (Serial Set 397). Same as H.doc.126 (27-2) 403 (entry **3493**).

27ᵀᴴ CONGRESS, 3ᴿᴰ SESSION

3500. U.S. House. *Resolution of the Legislature of Rhode Island for a Reduction of Postage, &c.* 27th Cong., 3rd Sess. (H.Doc.96). [Washington: 1843]. 1 pg. (Serial Set 420).

3501. U.S. House. *Resolutions of the Legislature of the State of Rhode Island, to Refund the Fine Imposed on General Andrew Jackson.* 27th Cong., 3rd Sess. (H.Doc.94). [Washington: 1843]. 1 pg. (Serial Set 420).

3502. U.S. Senate. [Memorial of Samuel Brown, of Providence]. 27th Cong., 3rd Sess. (S.Doc.48). [Washington]: Thomas Allen, Print., [1843]. 2 pg. (Serial Set 414). Report opposes the claim of Samuel Brown, who requested payment for extra services he performed while a naval officer at Providence.

28ᵀᴴ CONGRESS, 1ˢᵀ SESSION

3503. "Rhode Island," *Congressional Globe.* 28th Cong., 1st Sess. (8 Mar. 1844) p. 368. Debate on the Rhode Island memorial. Remarks by Henry Y. Cranston (R.I.) and George Rathbun (N.Y.).

3504. "Rhode Island Affairs," *Congressional Globe.* 28th Cong., 1st Sess. (7 Mar. 1844) pp. 364-365. Debate on the resolution to give the Select Committee reviewing the Rhode Island memorial the power to send for persons and papers. Includes brief remarks by Henry Y. Cranston (R.I.) on Dorr's constitution.

3505. "The Rhode Island Affairs," *Congressional Globe.* 28th Cong., 1st Sess. (16 Apr. 1844) pp. 543-545. Debate on the additional papers that were improperly printed with the resolutions from the Rhode Island Legislature protesting against the right of the House to inquire into Rhode Island affairs.

3506. "Rhode Island Memorial," *Congressional Globe.* 28th Cong., 1st Sess. (9 Mar., 14 Mar., 19 Mar., 20 Mar., 21 Mar. 1844) pp. 371-372; 392-393; 416-417; 424; 428. Summary of debate on the memorial concerning the new republican constitution and government. Includes summary of speeches by George Rathbun (N.Y.), Caleb B. Smith (Ind.), and John A. McClernand (Ill.) that are reported in full in the *Congressional Globe, Appendix.*

3507. "Rhode Island Revolution - Executive Interference," *Congressional Globe.* 28th Cong., 1st Sess. (10 Apr. 1844) pp. 522-523. Message from the President responds to the House's request for information on the alleged interference of the Executive during Rhode Island's struggle for a new constitution. Maintains that his only actions were to strengthen the garrison at Fort Adams.

3508. Cranston, Henry Y. (R.I.). "Rhode Island Memorial," *Congressional Globe.* 28th Cong., 1st Sess. (8 Mar. 1844) p. 368. Summary of speech opposed to the memorial supporting the new republican constitution and government; maintains that the memorial is false. Briefly reviews the "true" history of the Rhode Island question.

3509. Kennedy, Andrew (Ind.). "Rhode Island Memorial," *Congressional Globe, Appendix.* 28th Cong., 1st Sess. (13 Mar. 1844) pp. 262-264. Supports the new republican constitution and government of Rhode Island and the continued inquiry into the Rhode Island controversy. Maintains that Congress has jurisdiction in this matter. Discusses the right of petition, the unrepublican nature of the charter granted by King Charles II of England, the use of military force to suppress the people of Rhode Island, the right of suffrage, and the prescribed method to change government.

3510. McClernand, John A. (Ill.). "Rhode Island Memorial," *Congressional Globe, Appendix.* 28th Cong., 1st Sess. (19 Mar. 1844) pp. 327-331. Supports authorizing the committee on the Rhode Island controversy to send for persons and papers. Addresses objections concerning the authority of the House. Discusses the charges against the President of interfering in the domestic affairs of a state. Reviews the grievances set forth in the memorial; maintains that the charges are true. Reviews the history of the controversy and the proceedings against Thomas W. Dorr. Discusses the power of the people to change their form of government. Alludes to party politics.

3511. Potter, Elisha R. (R.I.). "Rhode Island Memorial," *Congressional Globe, Appendix.* 28th Cong., 1st Sess. (9 Mar., 12 Mar. 1844) pp. 267-272. Opposes the motions to inquire into the troubles in Rhode Island. Maintains that the present constitution is republican and represents popular opinion. Defends government under the charter of Charles II. Describes circumstances leading to the revolution. Demonstrates that the alleged majority of the Dorrites was obtained through fraud. Discusses extended suffrage. Considers claims of rejected petitions and invited investigations. Includes two Appendixes: 1)

Statistics of Population and Elections, and 2) Extracts from "Considerations on the Rhode Island Question."

3512. Rathbun, George (N.Y.). "Rhode Island Memorial," *Congressional Globe, Appendix.* 28th Cong., 1st Sess. (9 Mar. 1844) pp. 334-337. Supports the investigation of the facts concerning the Rhode Island memorial. Responds to Mr. Cranston's (R.I.) speech. Maintains that the people have the inherent right to alter their constitution or form of government at any time. Refers to the admission of Michigan and quotes from various statesmen to sustain his argument. Discusses the use of martial law and the allegations of the memorialists. Compares the peoples' constitution to the charter of Charles II.

3513. Simmons, James F. (R.I.). "The Tariff - The Compromise Act," *Congressional Globe.* 28th Cong., 1st Sess. (27 Mar., 28 Mar. 1844) pp. 455-456; 461-462. Summary of his speeches opposed to reducing the rates of duties to the standard of the Compromise Act. Defends the tariff of 1842. Responds to remarks from Sen. Benton (Mo.) comparing the respective amounts of revenue, imports and exports for the revenue period (1779-1816) and the protective period (1816 to present). Responds to Sen. Woodbury (N.H.) to show that the interests of agriculture and manufactures are interwoven. Responds to Sen. McDuffie (S.C.); discusses the advantages of encouraging the home market over the foreign market.

3514. Smith, Caleb B. (Ind.). "Rhode Island Memorial," *Congressional Globe, Appendix.* 28th Cong., 1st Sess. (14 Mar. 1844) pp. 462-466. Opposes the proposed investigation as not beneficial, dangerous to the public interest, and a waste of money and time. Objects to the implied principle that the majority can do whatever they desire, at all times, and under all circumstances. Reviews the history of the Rhode Island insurrection. Discusses the "natural right" of suffrage; questions its limits. Remarks on the anti-republican features of the New Hampshire constitution. Discusses the opinions and votes of Martin Van Buren upon the right of suffrage.

3515. Sprague, William (R.I.). "Resignation of Mr. Sprague," *Congressional Globe.* 28th Cong., 1st Sess. (23 Jan. 1844) p. 179. Letter of resignation from the Senate.

3516. Stetson, Lemuel (N.Y.). "Rhode Island Memorial," *Congressional Globe, Appendix.* 28th Cong., 1st Sess. (20 Mar. 1844) pp. 331-334. Defends Mr. Van Buren on the right of suffrage; presents extracts from debates and proceedings of the constitutional convention called in New York in 1821. Maintains that Mr. Van Buren wished to extend the elective franchise and eliminate the freehold qualifications, much as Rhode Island desires. Supports the sovereignty of the people and their right to determine their own constitution.

3517. U.S. House. *Memorial of the Democratic Members of Rhode Island Legislature, Protesting against the Course Pursued by the President during the Late Difficulties, and Requesting the House of Representatives to Make Certain Specified Inquiries in Relation Thereto.* 28th Cong., 1st Sess. (H.Doc.136). [Washington: Blair & Rives, Printers, 1844]. 4 pg. (Serial Set 442). Memorial protests the interference of the President into the affairs of Rhode Island and its new republican constitution and government. Reviews the need to modify the old charter system; questions the power of the President to interfere. Maintains that there was no "insurrection". Requests inquiries into the President's actions and into whether members of the House from Rhode Island are entitled to remain due to the circumstances of their election. Supports the constitution of 1841.

3518. U.S. House. *Message from the President of the United States, in Answer to a Resolution of the House of Representatives Relative to the Employment of United States Troops in Rhode Island, and Transmitting Documents in Relation to the Recent Difficulties in That State.* 28th Cong., 1st Sess. (H.Doc.225). [Washington: Blair & Rives, Printers, 1844]. 179 pg. (Serial Set 443). President justifies his actions relative to the Rhode Island constitutional difficulties. Maintains that the only orders issued by the Executive were to strengthen the garrison at Fort Adams. Discusses the executive responsibility to protect and defend states against domestic violence and obligation to furnish aid upon application. Appended supporting documents include copies of the 1841 and 1842 constitutions, charters and legislative documents, requests and applications for military support, and instructions and other relevant correspondence, papers and documents.

3519. U.S. House. *Protest of the Legislature of Rhode Island, against the Right of the Congress of the United States, or of Either House Thereof, to Decide or Inquire into the Question Whether the Constitution of the State, Legally, Peaceably, and Freely Adopted by the People Thereof, in November, 1842, Is or Is Not the Lawful Constitution of the State.* 28th Cong., 1st Sess. (H.Doc.232). [Washington: Blair & Rives, Printers, 1844]. 6 pg. (Serial Set 443). Reviews the history of the establishment of the federal government, the conditions under which the Constitution was ratified, and the provision that each state retains its sovereignty.

3520. U.S. House. *Protest of the Minority of the Members of the Legislature of the State of Rhode Island, against the Protest and Declaration of the Majority of the Same Legislature.* 28th Cong., 1st Sess. (H.Doc.233). [Washington: Blair & Rives, Printers, 1844]. 4 pg. (Serial Set 443). Memorial supports an inquiry by the House of Representatives to ascertain whether the state rights and sovereign power of the people of Rhode Island have been violated, whether there was an "insurrection", and whether the President had the authority to interfere.

3521. U.S. House. *Report and Resolutions of the General Assembly of Rhode Island, Relative to French Spoliations.* 28th Cong., 1st Sess. (H.Doc.152). [Washington: Blair & Rives, Printers, 1844]. 12 pg. (Serial Set 442). Resolutions and detailed report of the history of claims against France; discusses the obligations of France and the U.S., reviews various negotiations and the convention of 1800, addresses the current status of the claims. Same as S.doc.164 (28-1) 433 (entry **3524**).

3522. U.S. House. *Rhode Island - Interference of the Executive in the Affairs of.* 28th Cong., 1st Sess. (H.Rpt.546). [Washington: Blair & Rives, Printers, 1844]. 1070 pg. (Serial Set 447). Majority report of the Select Committee on the constitutional controversy in Rhode Island and the President's intervention. Discusses at length the issues surrounding the adoption of the new constitution and its subsequent suppression. Reviews the history of the origin of the charter government, its fundamental principles and causes for grievance, and efforts made to change the charter government. Also reviews the history of the people's constitution and subsequent actions; presents resolutions in support of the new constitution; maintains that the President was unauthorized to interfere. Includes various testimony and depositions, charters and legislative documents, and extracts from the message of the President.

3523. U.S. House. *Rhode Island Memorial.* 28th Cong., 1st Sess. (H.Rpt.581). [Washington: Blair & Rives, Printers, 1844]. 172 pg. (Serial Set 447). Minority report of the Select Committee on the constitutional controversy in Rhode Island and the President's subsequent intervention. Refutes the premises of the memorial of the Rhode Island Legislature and of the majority report. Reviews the charter history of Rhode Island, the Court of Commissions, the Dorr movement, and subsequent proceedings. Discusses the right of suffrage. Appended documents include relevant charters, legislative acts, and correspondence.

3524. U.S. Senate. *Resolutions of the General Assembly of Rhode Island, on the Subject of Making Indemnity for French Spoliations Prior to 1800.* 28th Cong., 1st Sess. (S.Doc.164). Washington: Gales & Seaton, 1844. 12 pg. (Serial Set 433). Same as H.doc.152 (28-1) 442. See entry **3521**.

28TH CONGRESS, 2ND SESSION

3525. Elmer, Lucius Q. C. (N.J.). "Rhode Island Controversy," *Congressional Globe, Appendix.* 28th Cong., 2nd Sess. (28 Feb. 1845) pp. 260-263. Objects to the resolutions supporting the Rhode Island memorial as erroneous and dangerous. Discusses the principles of political freedom. Reviews the circumstances of the insurrection. Maintains that the people have a right to make and alter their government, but that it should be exercised through constitutional and legal modes when provided. Discusses the sovereign power of each state to define and punish treason. Addresses the right of suffrage. Approves of the President's actions to suppress the domestic violence in Rhode Island. Summary of speech in *Congressional Globe*, p. 370.

3526. Simmons, James F. (R.I.). "Post Office Bill," *Congressional Globe, Appendix*. 28th Cong., 2nd Sess. (6 Feb. 1845) pp. 364-367. Supports reducing the postage to a uniform rate of five cents for a single letter, regardless of distance. Maintains that it would satisfy the public, regain the business from the private carriers, and increase the correspondence. Discusses the revenue to be expected from the recommended reduction, a partial reduction, and from different rates for longer distances. Refers to England as an example. Reviews the advantages and benefits of correspondence to society.

3527. Simmons, James F. (R.I.). "Post Office Reform," *Congressional Globe*. 28th Cong., 2nd Sess. (29 Jan. 1845) pp. 212-213. Supports reducing the postage; maintains that the reduction would increase the volume of correspondence, creating more revenue. If insufficient revenue is raised, the postage could be increased.

3528. Simmons, James F. (R.I.). "Postage Bill," *Congressional Globe*. 28th Cong., 2nd Sess. (8 Feb. 1845) pp. 263-264. Defends reducing the postage rates. Addresses claim that postage is a tax; reviews the benefits of a lower postage rate.

3529. Williams, Henry (Mass.). "Rhode Island Controversy," *Congressional Globe, Appendix*. 28th Cong., 2nd Sess. (28 Feb. 1845) pp. 277-283. Defends the right of the people of Rhode Island to self-government, including the legal authority to frame and amend their constitution. Supports his position using the Declaration of Independence, quotes from patriots and statesmen, and precedence. Discusses the charter government and its claims of exclusive jurisdiction. Supports the right of free suffrage to all adult males. Discusses the consequences of the opposition's doctrine; addresses objections.

29TH CONGRESS, 1ST SESSION

3530. Simmons, James F. (R.I.). "The Tariff," *Congressional Globe*. 29th Cong., 1st Sess. (24 July 1846) p. 1136. Summary of speech opposed to the proposed reduced duties. Discusses the revenue estimate of the Secretary of the Treasury, the revenue obtained from specific duties versus *ad valorem*, and the hostility towards mechanics and manufacturers.

3531. U.S. House. *Bristol and Warren Collection District*. 29th Cong., 1st Sess. (H.Rpt.651). [Washington: Ritchie & Heiss, Print., 1846]. 1 pg. (Serial Set 490). Report advocates that the collector's office for Bristol and Warren be moved from Bristol to Warren to be more convenient for the majority of merchants and shipmasters.

3532. U.S. House. *Resolutions of the General Assembly of Rhode Island, Responding to Certain Resolutions of the General Court of New Hampshire, Which Were Considered by the Legislature of Rhode Island As an Improper Interference, on the Part of New Hampshire, with the Domestic Affairs of Rhode Island.* 29th Cong., 1st Sess. (H.Doc.28). [Washington: Ritchie & Heiss, 1845]. 2 pg. (Serial Set 482). Rhode Island responds to New Hampshire resolutions on the trial and imprisonment of Thomas W. Dorr.

3533. U.S. House. *Resolutions of the Legislature of Rhode Island, Relative to General Taylor.* 29th Cong., 1st Sess. (H.Doc.220). [Washington: Ritchie & Heiss, 1846]. 2 pg. (Serial Set 486). Resolutions support General Zachary Taylor and the men serving under him for their valor in battle.

3534. U.S. House. *Resolutions of the Legislature of Rhode Island, Relative to the French Spoliations.* 29th Cong., 1st Sess. (H.Doc.203). [Washington: Ritchie & Heiss, 1846]. 2 pg. (Serial Set 485). Resolutions favor paying the claims, with interest. Same as S.doc.347 (29-1) 476 (entry **3538**).

3535. U.S. House. *Resolutions of the Legislature of Rhode Island, Relative to the Tariff Act of 1842, and the Law Reducing the Rates of Postage, Passed at the Last Session of Congress.* 29th Cong., 1st Sess. (H.Doc.123). [Washington: Ritchie & Heiss, 1846]. 2 pg. (Serial Set 483). Resolutions support the protective tariff of 1842 and support of the act reducing the rates of postage.

3536. U.S. Senate. *Memorial of Merchants and Shipmasters of Bristol, Rhode Island, Remonstrating against the Removal of the Custom-House at That Place.* 29th Cong., 1st Sess. (S.Doc.440). Washington: Ritchie & Heiss, 1846. 3 pg. (Serial Set 478). Memorial outlines the advantages of Bristol over Warren for the site of the customhouse; includes table of duties paid in the district of Bristol and Warren from 1831 to 1845. Includes the names of the memorialists.

3537. U.S. Senate. *Resolutions of the General Assembly of Rhode Island, in Relation to the Distribution, Among the States, of the Decisions of the Supreme Court of the United States.* 29th Cong., 1st Sess. (S.Doc.80). Washington: Ritchie & Heiss, 1846. 1 pg. (Serial Set 473). Resolutions favor purchasing and distributing the reports of the decisions of the Supreme Court to the states and territories.

3538. U.S. Senate. *Resolutions of the Legislature of Rhode Island, in Favor of the Payment of the Claims for French Spoliations Prior to 1800.* 29th Cong., 1st Sess. (S.Doc.347). Washington: Ritchie & Heiss, 1846. 2 pg. (Serial Set 476). Same as H.doc.203 (29-2) 485 (entry **3534**).

29TH CONGRESS, 2ND SESSION

3539. Simmons, James F. (R.I.). "Printing of Memorials," *Congressional Globe.* 29th Cong., 2nd Sess. (7 Jan. 1847) p. 132. Supports printing the memorial from Louisiana suggesting a modification of the tariff. Maintains that a duty on sugar is an appropriate means of raising revenue.

3540. Simmons, James F. (R.I.). "Three Million Bill," *Congressional Globe.* 29th Cong., 2nd Sess. (20 Feb. 1847) pp. 464-466. Opposes the proposed appropriations to bring the war with Mexico to a speedy and honorable conclusion. Discusses the character of the war, its origin and objects. Opposes taking territory from Mexico as indemnity for the expenses of the war as unfair and dishonorable. Also objects to the expansion of slavery into new territories.

3541. Simmons, James F. (R.I.). "Treasury Note and Loan Bill," *Congressional Globe.* 29th Cong., 2nd Sess. (26 Jan. 1847) pp. 260-261. Presents and justifies an amendment to pledge the sales of public land as security for the payment of interest, and the redemption or purchase of the proposed Treasury notes.

3542. U.S. House. *Resolutions of the General Assembly of Rhode Island Relative to the Tariff, Slavery, Mexican War, &c.* 29th Cong., 2nd Sess. (H.Doc.85). [Washington: Ritchie & Heiss, 1847]. 3 pg. (Serial Set 500). Resolutions support the protective tariff of 1842, and oppose the Sub-Treasury, slavery, the Mexican War, and the acquisition of territory for the purpose of establishing slave-holding states.

30TH CONGRESS, 1ST SESSION

3543. Clarke, John H. (R.I.). "California Claims," *Congressional Globe, Appendix.* 30th Cong., 1st Sess. (27 Apr. 1848) pp. 569-571. Addresses the validity of the claims. Reviews the sequence of events leading to the revolution in California and the role played by John C. Fremont; maintains that the government wholly authorized Fremont's actions. Establishes that the insurrection in California was directed by the government, originated with the executive department, and was consequent upon orders conveyed to Colonel Fremont. Contends that it was intention of the Executive to possess California.

3544. Clarke, John H. (R.I.). "The Ten-Regiment Bill," *Congressional Globe.* 30th Cong., 1st Sess. (25 Jan. 1848) pp. 242-244. Opposes the proposed additional military force to further prosecute the war against Mexico. Discusses the alleged objectives of the war, the necessity of the increased military force, and possible means to support them. Reviews the financial aspects of the situation. Discusses the financial situation of the country. Maintains that large loans will be required and that sacrifice and commercial distress would result from these loans.

3545. Clarke, John H. (R.I.). "Territorial Government of Oregon," *Congressional Globe, Appendix.* 30th Cong., 1st Sess. (24 July 1848) pp. 1148-1150. Objects to the proposed bill to establish territorial governments in

Oregon, California, and New Mexico. Opposes the introduction of slavery into a free state and the extension of slavery to any territory acquired by conquest. Maintains that the bill does not adequately safeguard against the extension of slavery; presents several resolutions to make the bill less objectionable. Establishes that under existing law, slavery had been abolished within all the States of Mexico. Summary of speech in *Congressional Globe*, p. 992.

3546. Greene, Albert C. (R.I.). "The Ten-Regiment Bill," *Congressional Globe, Appendix.* 30th Cong., 1st Sess. (18 Feb. 1848) pp. 341-344. Opposes the proposed increase in military force as unnecessary for any legitimate purpose. Documents how the character and objects of the war have changed to one of conquest. Traces the history of the departure from the intent and spirit of the Constitution to where it is now claimed that the government has the power to acquire and hold foreign territory by right of conquest. Discusses the expediency of the proposed annexation of Mexico in regard to the slavery question and representation of its citizens. Summary of speech in *Congressional Globe*, p. 379.

3547. U.S. House. *Resolutions of the Legislature of Rhode Island, Relative to the Abolition of Slavery in the District of Columbia.* 30th Cong., 1st Sess. (H.Misc.Doc.92). Washington: Tippin & Streeper, 1848. 1 pg. (Serial Set 523). Resolutions support the abolition of slavery in the District.

3548. U.S. Senate. *Message from the President of the United States, Communicating, in Compliance with a Resolution of the Senate, a Report of the Secretary of State, in Relation to the Claim of the Owners of the Ship Miles, of Warren, Rhode Island, against the Government of Portugal.* 30th Cong., 1st Sess. (S.Exec.Doc.64). Washington: Wendell and Van Benthuysen, [1848]. 20 pg. (Serial Set 509). Correspondence in relation to the claim of the owners of the ship Miles for the payment of a cargo of oil, taken by Portuguese officials. Reviews the circumstances; supports the claim according to principles of general average and the laws and usage of commercial nations relating to this subject.

3549. U.S. Senate. *Resolution of the Legislature of Rhode Island, against a Duty on Tea and Coffee.* 30th Cong., 1st Sess. (S.Misc.Doc.38). Washington: Tippin & Streeper, 1848. 1 pg. (Serial Set 511).

3550. U.S. Senate. *Resolutions of the Legislature of Rhode Island, in Favor of Whitney's Plan for a Railroad from Lake Michigan to the Pacific.* 30th Cong., 1st Sess. (S.Misc.Doc.4). Washington: Tippin & Streeper, 1848. 1 pg. (Serial Set 511). Resolutions support the plan that would unite the two coasts, thereby extending commerce, and advancing manufacturing.

3551. U.S. Senate. *Resolutions of the Legislature of Rhode Island, in Relation to the War with Mexico.* 30th Cong., 1st Sess. (S.Misc.Doc.61). Washington: Tippin & Streeper, 1848. 2 pg. (Serial Set 511). Resolutions oppose the war and any appropriations to assist the war; maintain that it is a war of conquest and occupation, a usurpation of the power of Congress, and a dangerous, subversive and unprecedented measure.

3552. U.S. Senate. *Response of the Legislature of Alabama, to the Legislature of Rhode Island, on the Subject of the Tariff, and the War with Mexico.* 30th Cong., 1st Sess. (S.Misc.Doc.86). Washington: Tippin & Streeper, 1848. 2 pg. (Serial Set 511). Resolutions support the repeal of the tariff of 1842 and support the Mexican War.

30TH CONGRESS, 2ND SESSION

3553. Clarke, John H. (R.I.). "Naval Appropriation Bill," *Congressional Globe.* 30th Cong., 2nd Sess. (2 Mar. 1849) pp. 653-654. Contends that the government has a political and moral obligation to provide for more direct communication between the Pacific and the Atlantic. Briefly reviews various proposals.

3554. Greene, Albert C. (R.I.). "Flogging in the Navy," *Congressional Globe.* 30th Cong., 2nd Sess. (1 Mar. 1849) pp. 624-625. Opposes abolishing this means of punishment without providing a substitute means; apprehensive that officers could then arbitrarily substitute equally cruel and degrading punishments.

3555. U.S. Senate. *Resolutions of the Legislature of Rhode Island, in Favor of the Prohibition of Corporeal Punishment and the Use of Ardent Spirits in the Navy.* 30th Cong., 2nd Sess. (S.Misc.Doc.63). Washington: Tippin & Streeper, 1849. 1 pg. (Serial Set 533).

3556. U.S. Senate. *Resolutions of the Legislature of Rhode Island, in Relation to Slavery.* 30th Cong., 2nd Sess. (S.Misc.Doc.62). Washington: Tippin & Streeper, 1849. 1 pg. (Serial Set 533). Resolutions support prohibiting the extension of slavery into the territories and oppose prisons and marts for the sale of slaves in the District of Columbia.

VERMONT

1ST CONGRESS, 1ST SESSION

[no references]

1ST CONGRESS, 2ND SESSION

[no references]

1ST CONGRESS, 3RD SESSION

3557. "An Act for the Admission of the State of Vermont into This Union," *Statutes at Large*, Vol. I (18 Feb. 1791) p. 191. Also printed in the *Annals of Congress* (1st Cong., 3rd Sess.) Appendix, p. 2311.

3558. "An Act Giving Effect to the Laws of the United States within the State of Vermont," *Statutes at Large*, Vol. I (2 Mar. 1791) pp. 197-198. Gives effect to laws establishing the judiciary system in Vermont and provides for the enumeration of inhabitants. Also printed in the *Annals of Congress* (1st Cong., 3rd Sess.) Appendix, pp. 2318-2320.

3559. "An Act Regulating the Number of Representatives to be Chosen by the States of Kentucky and Vermont," *Statutes at Large*, Vol. I (25 Feb. 1791) p. 191. Also printed in the *Annals of Congress* (1st Cong., 3rd Sess.) Appendix, pp. 2311-2312.

2ND CONGRESS, 1ST SESSION

[no references]

2ND CONGRESS, 2ND SESSION

[no references]

3RD CONGRESS, 1ST SESSION

[no references]

3RD CONGRESS, 2ND SESSION

[no references]

4TH CONGRESS, 1ST SESSION

3560. "Contested Election," *Annals of Congress.* 4th Cong., 1st Sess. (4 Feb., 11 Feb., 12 Feb., 15 Feb., 16 Feb., 31 May 1796) pp. 296-297; 315-320; 320-325; 326-328; 331-334; 1496-1498. Discussion and debate of the committee report on the contested election of Israel Smith of Vermont. Comments by Zephaniah Swift (Conn.), Israel Smith (Vt.), William Lyman (Mass.), Nathaniel Smith (Conn.), Ezekiel Gilbert (N.Y.), Uriah Tracy (Conn.), James Hillhouse (Conn.), and Theodore Sedgwick (Mass.).

3561. Buck, Daniel (Vt.). "Case of Randall and Whitney," *Annals of Congress.* 4th Cong., 1st Sess. (2 Jan. 1796) pp. 205-206. Deposition in the case of Robert Randall and Charles Whitney.

3562. Buck, Daniel (Vt.). "Treaty with Great Britain," *Annals of Congress.* 4th Cong., 1st Sess. (7 Mar., 24 Mar. 1796) pp. 430-435; 703-717. Opposes requesting the information concerning the treaty from the Executive. Discusses the status of the treaty, the potential benefits and consequences of the information, and the power of the House to make the request. Addresses opponents' arguments. Maintains that the House does not have the constitutional power to judge upon the merits or expediency of the treaty.

3563. "An Act Altering the Sessions of the Circuit Courts in the Districts of Vermont and Rhode Island, and for Other Purposes," *Statutes at Large*, Vol. I (27 May 1796) pp. 475-476. Also printed in the *Annals of Congress* (4th Cong., 1st Sess.) Appendix, p. 2917.

3564. "Contested Election of Israel Smith, a Representative from Vermont," *American State Papers: Miscellaneous*, Vol. I (Doc. 72) p. 139. (ASP 037). Petition of Matthew Lyon, contesting the election of Israel Smith, is denied. Committee of Elections finds the election irregular, but has insufficient evidence to alter the results.

3565. "Contested Election of Israel Smith, a Representative from Vermont," *American State Papers: Miscellaneous*, Vol. I (Doc. 88) p. 152. (ASP 037). Additional information about the election is supplied; election still upheld.

4TH CONGRESS, 2ND SESSION

3566. Buck, Daniel (Vt.). "Compensation to Public Officers," *Annals of Congress*. 4th Cong., 2nd Sess. (9 Feb. 1797) pp. 2100-2103. Favors permanently raising the salaries of the President and Vice President, and temporarily raising salaries of the members of the Legislature.

5TH CONGRESS, 1ST SESSION

[no references]

5TH CONGRESS, 2ND SESSION

3567. "Breach of Privilege," *Annals of Congress*. 5th Cong., 2nd Sess. (30 Jan., 1 Feb., 2 Feb., 6 Feb., 7 Feb., 8 Feb., 9 Feb., 12 Feb. 1798) pp. 955; 959; 961-962; 966-968; 969; 970-980; 981-1000; 1000-1029. Report of the attack of Matthew Lyon (Vt.) upon Roger Griswold (Conn.) and introduction of a resolution calling for Lyon's expulsion from the House. Letter from Matthew Lyon responds to the accusation; report of the Committee of Privileges details the course of events and supports the resolution. Includes brief statements by Samuel W. Dana (Conn.) and Nathaniel Chipman (S-Vt.), correction of printed account of Samuel W. Dana, Matthew Lyon's defense, brief remarks by Christopher G. Champlin (R.I.), William Shepard (Mass.), et. al., letter from Nathaniel Chipman (S-Vt.), debate on the impropriety of extending the power of expulsion (the vote for expulsion, which failed, two-thirds not concurring), and a complete transcript of the testimony taken at the trial (including testimony of David Brooks (N.Y.), Hezekiah L. Hosmer (N.Y.), Samuel W. Dana (Conn.), Joshua Coit (Conn.), Chauncey Goodrich (Conn.), Nathaniel Chipman (S-Vt.), Joseph B. Varnum (Mass.), and Matthew Lyon's defense statement).

3568. "Case of Griswold and Lyon," *Annals of Congress*. 5th Cong., 2nd Sess. (16 Feb., 23 Feb. 1798) pp. 1036-1040, 1040-1043; 1063-1068. Debate on the resolutions that Roger Griswold and Matthew Lyon be expelled for violent and disorderly behavior and that they promise not to commit any act of violence upon each other again.

3569. "Case of Griswold and Lyon," *Annals of Congress*. 5th Cong., 2nd Sess. (20 Feb. 1798) pp. 1048-1058. Evidence gathered on the resolution that Roger Griswold and Matthew Lyon be expelled for violent and disorderly behavior committed in the House. Includes testimony from Peleg Sprague (N.H.), William Shepard (Mass.), and William Gordon (N.H.).

3570. "Fracas in the House," *Annals of Congress.* 5th Cong., 2nd Sess. (15 Feb. 1798) p. 1034. Account of Roger Griswold's attack on Matthew Lyon.

3571. Chipman, Nathaniel (Vt.). "Breach of Privilege," *Annals of Congress.* 5th Cong., 2nd Sess. (9 Feb. 1798) pp. 999-1000. Letter in defense of Matthew Lyon.

3572. Chipman, Nathaniel (Vt.). "Breach of Privilege," *Annals of Congress.* 5th Cong., 2nd Sess. (12 Feb. 1798) pp. 1022-1024. Testimony in the case of Matthew Lyon assaulting Roger Griswold.

3573. Lyon, Matthew (Vt.). "Breach of Privilege," *Annals of Congress.* 5th Cong., 2nd Sess. (8 Feb. 1798) pp. 971-974. Matthew Lyon's testimony in his defense concerning the assault on Roger Griswold.

3574. "Breach of Privileges," *American State Papers: Miscellaneous*, Vol. I (Doc. 103) pp. 166-173. (ASP 037). Report of the Committee of Privileges details the assault upon Roger Griswold and supports the resolution calling for Lyon's expulsion from the House. Includes testimony taken at the trial from David Brooks (N.Y.), Hezekiah L. Hosmer (N.Y.), Samuel W. Dana (Conn.), Joshua Coit (Conn.), Chauncey Goodrich (Conn.), Nathaniel Chipman (Vt.), and Joseph B. Varnum (Mass.). Also printed in the *Annals of Congress* (5th Cong., 2nd Sess.), "Breach of Privilege," pp. 961-962, 1009-1025.

3575. "Breach of Privileges," *American State Papers: Miscellaneous*, Vol. I (Doc. 104) pp. 174-178. (ASP 037). Depositions taken on the assault upon Roger Griswold; includes those from Peleg Sprague (N.H.), William Shepard (Mass.), and William Gordon (N.H.). Also printed in the *Annals of Congress* (5th Cong., 2nd Sess.), "Case of Griswold and Lyon," pp. 1048-1058.

5TH CONGRESS, 3RD SESSION

3576. "On Expelling Matthew Lyon," *Annals of Congress.* 5th Cong., 3rd Sess. (22 Feb. 1799) pp. 2959-2973. Debate of the resolution presented earlier (20 Feb. 1799, p. 2954) to expel Matthew Lyon from the House for his violation of the sedition law. He had already been fined and imprisoned, yet re-elected to another term in the House. Includes brief comments by John Allen (Conn.) and Matthew Lyon (Vt.). Resolution fails, two-thirds not concurring.

3577. "An Act Altering the Time of Holding the District Court in Vermont," *Statutes at Large*, Vol. I (28 Feb. 1799) p. 627. Also printed in the *Annals of Congress* (5th Cong., 3rd Sess.) Appendix, pp. 3811-3812.

6TH CONGRESS, 1ST SESSION

[no references]

6TH CONGRESS, 2ND SESSION

3578. Lyon, Matthew (Vt.). "Sedition Act," *Annals of Congress.* 6th Cong., 2nd Sess. (23 Jan. 1801) pp. 973-975. Debate on the Sedition Act as personally experienced.

7TH CONGRESS, 1ST SESSION

3579. Resolutions of the Legislature of the State of Vermont Regarding the Electors of President and Vice President of the United States and of Representatives to Congress, *Annals of Congress.* 7th Cong., 1st Sess. (19 Feb. 1802) p. 190.

3580. Chipman, Nathaniel (Vt.). "Judiciary System," *Annals of Congress.* 7th Cong., 1st Sess. (19 Jan. 1802) pp. 122-132. Opposes repealing the present judiciary system and returning to the system of 1793. Discusses arguments concerning the expediency of repealing the law, the courts and judges in France and England, the need for knowledge of the local laws and customs, and the constitutional power of Congress to repeal the law. Reviews the failures of the system of 1793. Maintains that the Judiciary is independent of the Legislature.

7TH CONGRESS, 2ND SESSION

[no references]

8TH CONGRESS, 1ST SESSION

3581. Chittenden, Martin (Vt.). "Salaries of Certain Officers," *Annals of Congress.* 8th Cong., 1st Sess. (18 Nov. 1803) pp. 574-576. Opposes the proposed salaries for public officers.

3582. Elliot, James (Vt.). "Amendment to the Constitution," *Annals of Congress.* 8th Cong., 1st Sess. (7 Dec., 8 Dec. 1803) pp. 668-669, 685-686, 687-688, 698-699; 711-712, 765. Opposes the proposed constitutional amendment of the electoral process.

3583. Elliot, James (Vt.). "The Louisiana Treaty," *Annals of Congress.* 8th Cong., 1st Sess. (24 Oct., 25 Oct., 27 Oct. 1803) pp. 394-396, 412-413; 446-453; 507-508. Supports proceeding with the ratification of the Louisiana treaty and opposes the resolution requesting the President to transmit a copy of the

Oct. 1, 1800 secret treaty between the French Republic and Spain. Addresses the constitutionality and expediency of the treaty; opposes the temporary delegation of legislative power to the President.

3584. Elliot, James (Vt.). "Official Conduct of Judge Chase," *Annals of Congress.* 8th Cong., 1st Sess. (5 Jan. 1804) pp. 807, 814-815. Questions the authority of the House over the conduct of judges of the Supreme Court.

3585. Elliot, James (Vt.). "Official Conduct of Judge Chase," *Annals of Congress.* 8th Cong., 1st Sess. (12 Mar. 1804) pp. 1171-1177. Supports the resolution to impeach Judge Chase. Reviews evidence and finds justification in the trial of James Callender.

3586. Elliot, James (Vt.). "Salaries of Certain Officers," *Annals of Congress.* 8th Cong., 1st Sess. (21 Nov. 1803) pp. 591-592. Supports the proposed salaries; maintains that the amount has been established for some years and is sufficiently liberal so as not to require modification soon.

8TH CONGRESS, 2ND SESSION

3587. Elliot, James (Vt.). "Georgia Claims," *Annals of Congress.* 8th Cong., 2nd Sess. (30 Jan. 1805) pp. 1034-1042. Addresses the Georgia land claims; discusses the rights of Georgia to sell its lands to certain land companies, and whether the rights of the present claimants were protected.

3588. Elliot, James (Vt.). "Official Conduct of Judge Chase," *Annals of Congress.* 8th Cong., 2nd Sess. (3 Dec. 1804) pp. 744-745. Opposes the articles of impeachment reported against Judge Chase (a reversal of his earlier position).

3589. Elliot, James (Vt.). "Pennsylvania Contested Election," *Annals of Congress.* 8th Cong., 2nd Sess. (19 Dec. 1804) pp. 850-851. Supports the finding of the Committee of Elections that the election was conducted constitutionally.

3590. Elliot, James (Vt.). "Postmaster General," *Annals of Congress.* 8th Cong., 2nd Sess. (1 Feb. 1805) pp. 1112-1114, 1116-1117. Supports the Postmaster General's request for an inquiry to respond to charges against his character.

9TH CONGRESS, 1ST SESSION

3591. Elliot, James (Vt.). "General Eaton," *Annals of Congress.* 9th Cong., 1st Sess. (12 Dec. 1805) pp. 277-278. Favors honoring General William Eaton with a gold medal rather than a sword.

3592. Elliot, James (Vt.). "Importation of British Goods," *Annals of Congress.* 9th Cong., 1st Sess. (8 Mar. 1806) pp. 636-643. Supports the resolution to limit the importation of goods from Great Britain to retaliate for injuries received from impressing American seamen and interfering with commerce; gives statistics on imports and exports from Great Britain for the last three years and discusses the effects of limiting trade.

3593. Fisk, James (Vt.). "Spanish Affairs," *Annals of Congress.* 9th Cong., 1st Sess. (7 Apr. 1806) pp. 966-968. Opposes the motion to publish secret documents of negotiations with Spain. Maintains that the resulting animosity against Spain would be misdirected - Great Britain has done far more injury by aggression on commerce and impressing seamen.

3594. Smith, Israel (Vt.). "British Aggressions," *Annals of Congress.* 9th Cong., 1st Sess. (13 Feb. 1806) pp. 94-96. Objects to the resolution on the impressment of American seamen and the spoliations of American commerce by the British. Supports measures leading to no commerce with Great Britain, but feels this resolution is disrespectful to the Executive.

3595. "Great Britain - Ira Allen," *American State Papers: Foreign Relations,* Vol. II (Doc. 200) p. 800. (ASP 02). Support for and request from Ira Allen for restitution of losses incurred during his 1796 capture by the British government.

9TH CONGRESS, 2ND SESSION

3596. Elliot, James (Vt.). "National Defence," *Annals of Congress.* 9th Cong., 2nd Sess. (15 Dec. 1806) pp. 160-165. Deplores the state of the navy in particular and the national defenses in general. Recommends augmenting the navy and changing its organization and management to a new and more efficient system to establish the United States as a powerful armed neutrality.

3597. Elliot, James (Vt.). "Public Debt," *Annals of Congress.* 9th Cong., 2nd Sess. (8 Jan. 1807) pp. 267-269. Discusses a resolution asking the Secretary of the Treasury to give a summary of the public debt of the United States.

3598. Elliot, James (Vt.). "Suspension of the Writ of Habeas Corpus," *Annals of Congress.* 9th Cong., 2nd Sess. (26 Jan. 1807) pp. 406-409. Opposed to suspending the writ of habeas corpus. Gives brief review of the origins, history and constitutional interpretation of habeas corpus.

3599. Elliot, James (Vt.). "Writ of Habeas Corpus," *Annals of Congress.* 9th Cong., 2nd Sess. (18 Feb., 19 Feb. 1807) pp. 528-533; 577-579. Discusses the merits and propriety of a resolution to temporarily suspend the writ of habeas corpus; responds to comments of speech on 18 February.

3600. Fisk, James (Vt.). "National Defence," *Annals of Congress.* 9th Cong., 2nd Sess. (4 Feb., 5 Feb. 1807) pp. 448-449; 460-461; 465-466. Maintains that there is no need to increase defenses as there is no probability of war. Objects to more fortifications as unnecessary, expensive and inadequate. Favors gunboats as the preferable means of defense over fortifications and frigates.

3601. "An Act Regulating Fees," *Annals of Congress.* 9th Cong., 2nd Sess. (15 Oct. 1806) Appendix, pp. 1159-1163. List of fees allowed to officers of the courts and others in Vermont for performing various services.

10TH CONGRESS, 1ST SESSION

3602. Chittenden, Martin (Vt.). "Philadelphia Memorial," *Annals of Congress.* 10th Cong., 1st Sess. (15 Dec. 1807) pp. 1180-1181. Supports a proper consideration of the memorial from Philadelphia asking for a repeal of the non-importation act; discusses the right of petition.

3603. Elliot, James (Vt.). "Foreign Relations," *Annals of Congress.* 10th Cong., 1st Sess. (18 Feb. 1808) pp. 1641-1644. Favors requesting from the President a general view of the current foreign relations situation.

3604. Elliot, James (Vt.). "Fortifications and Gunboats," *Annals of Congress.* 10th Cong., 1st Sess. (10 Dec. 1807) pp. 1106-1121. Opposes a bill to appropriate money to build more gunboats. Addresses the effectiveness of gunboats as a system of national defense, the economical implications, and the supposed popularity of gunboats. Feels that the President is advancing gunboats to the exclusion of other systems of national defense.

3605. Elliot, James (Vt.). "General Wilkinson," *Annals of Congress.* 10th Cong., 1st Sess. (5 Jan., 13 Jan. 1808) pp. 1310-1314; 1441-1444. Presents arguments in support of the constitutionality of the resolution requesting the President to provide the House information on General Wilkinson. Further remarks contend that the House cannot institute inquiries into the conduct or character of this officer except for the purpose of acquiring information to enable the House to exercise its legislative functions.

3606. Elliot, James (Vt.). "Military Courts," *Annals of Congress.* 10th Cong., 1st Sess. (11 Mar. 1808) pp. 1772-1776. Strongly opposes a bill granting certain civilian judicial rights to the military judicial system. Specifically addresses the ability to coerce the attendance of civil witnesses before military tribunals.

3607. Elliot, James (Vt.). "Philadelphia Memorial," *Annals of Congress.* 10th Cong., 1st Sess. (27 Nov. 1807) p. 970. Remarks on the right of the petition to be referred to committee.

3608. Elliot, James (Vt.). "Yazoo Land Claims," *Annals of Congress.* 10th Cong., 1st Sess. (4 Jan. 1808) pp. 1283-1286. Supports the Massachusetts memorial on the Yazoo land claims.

3609. Fisk, James (Vt.). "Fortifications and Gunboats," *Annals of Congress.* 10th Cong., 1st Sess. (9 Dec. 1807) pp. 1102-1103. Supports gunboats over frigates as the preferred mode of defense.

3610. Fisk, James (Vt.). "General Wilkinson," *Annals of Congress.* 10th Cong., 1st Sess. (5 Jan., 12 Jan. 1808) pp. 1315-1317; 1413-1416. Defends the rights of the General to be tried in the courts without unconstitutional interference from the House.

3611. Fisk, James (Vt.). "Military Courts," *Annals of Congress.* 10th Cong., 1st Sess. (8 Mar. 1808) pp. 1748-1750. Supports court-martials or inquiries having the power to summon witnesses.

3612. Fisk, James (Vt.). "Suspension of the Embargo," *Annals of Congress.* 10th Cong., 1st Sess. (13 Apr. 1808) pp. 2110-2118. Strongly opposes repealing the embargo against Great Britain. Discusses the question of impressments; reviews negotiation attempts to remedy this problem. Considers the constitutionality of the embargo; addresses opponents' arguments.

3613. Witherell, James (Vt.). "Arming the Militia," *Annals of Congress.* 10th Cong., 1st Sess. (4 Dec. 1807) pp. 1046-1047. Supports arming the seaports as well as the militia.

10TH CONGRESS, 2ND SESSION

3614. Elliot, James (Vt.). "Execution and Evasions of the Embargo Laws," *Annals of Congress.* 10th Cong., 2nd Sess. (10 Nov. 1808) pp. 478, 479-480. Supports his resolution inquiring into the embargo law; maintains that the Constitution and laws have been violated in the execution of the law and wishes to ascertain whether these violations were authorized by the Executive.

3615. Elliot, James (Vt.). "Motion to Repeal the Embargo," *Annals of Congress.* 10th Cong., 2nd Sess. (10 Nov. 1808) pp. 476-477. Supports an inquiry into the embargo laws, including their constitutionality, propriety, and manner of execution.

11TH CONGRESS, 1ST SESSION

[no references]

11ᵀᴴ CONGRESS, 2ᴺᴰ SESSION

[no references]

11ᵀᴴ CONGRESS, 3ᴿᴰ SESSION

3616. "An Act to Establish the Districts of Mumphreymagog, of Oswegatchie, and of the White Mountains," *Statutes at Large*, Vol. II (2 Mar. 1811) pp. 655-656. Also printed in the *Annals of Congress* (11th Cong., 3rd Sess.) Appendix, pp. 1343-1344.

12ᵀᴴ CONGRESS, 1ˢᵀ SESSION

3617. "Prosecutions for Libel," *Annals of Congress.* 12th Cong., 1st Sess. (13 Nov. 1811) pp. 345-348. Debate on the proper committee referral and scope of Matthew Lyon's claim for the fine that he paid under the sedition law.

3618. Fisk, James (Vt.). "Apportionment of Representation," *Annals of Congress.* 12th Cong., 1st Sess. (5 Dec. 1811) pp. 408-409. Advocates the rights and interest of the small states in the apportionment issue.

3619. Fisk, James (Vt.). "British Intrigues," *Annals of Congress.* 12th Cong., 1st Sess. (9 Mar. 1812) pp. 1187-1189. Remarks on the credibility of Mr. Henry and the alleged policy of Great Britain to exacerbate party divisiveness in order to divide the Union.

3620. Fisk, James (Vt.). "Naval Establishment," *Annals of Congress.* 12th Cong., 1st Sess. (25 Jan. 1812) pp. 968-970. Objects to a proposed increase of the naval establishment to help protect and encourage commerce.

12ᵀᴴ CONGRESS, 2ᴺᴰ SESSION

3621. Fisk, James (Vt.). "Additional Military Force," *Annals of Congress.* 12th Cong., 2nd Sess. (2 Jan. 1813) pp. 490-492. Supports the war and a bill to quickly increase the size of the military force by allowing for a one-year enlistment period. Maintains that a speedy infusion of manpower is needed to take the Provinces.

3622. Fisk, James (Vt.). "Pay of the Army," *Annals of Congress.* 12th Cong., 2nd Sess. (21 Nov. 1812) pp. 173-175. Supports the bill and the War of 1812.

13TH CONGRESS, 1ST SESSION

3623. Bradley, William C. (Vt.). "Conduct of the War," *Annals of Congress.* 13th Cong., 1st Sess. (9 July 1813) pp. 413-415, 420. Supports his resolution to inquire into the causes of military failure during the past year of war.

3624. Butler, Ezra (Vt.). "French Decrees," *Annals of Congress.* 13th Cong., 1st Sess. (21 June 1813) pp. 303-308. Opposes requesting documents from the President. Maintains that Great Britain is the cause of the war, not the governments of France or the United States, and this resolution and its implied distrust serves only to weaken our own government.

13TH CONGRESS, 2ND SESSION

3625. "Governor Chittenden," *Annals of Congress.* 13th Cong., 2nd Sess. (6 Jan. 1814) pp. 859-861. Resolutions opposed to the proclamation of Vermont Governor Martin Chittenden to entice soldiers of that state to desert from their military positions on the frontier. References to Ethan Allen and the Green Mountain Boys. Remarks by James Fisk (Vt.) indicate that Governor Chittenden did not have the support of the Vermont delegation and that the proclamation was unjustifiable, but that the resolutions are objectionable on several counts. The resolutions were tabled.

3626. Fisk, James (Vt.). "Encouragement of Enlistments," *Annals of Congress.* 13th Cong., 2nd Sess. (13 Jan. 1814) pp. 934-935. Remarks on the difficulty of enlisting men; War of 1812 is compared to Revolutionary War.

13TH CONGRESS, 3RD SESSION

3627. Fisk, James (Vt.). "Bounty to Deserters," *Annals of Congress.* 13th Cong., 3rd Sess. (28 Sept. 1814) pp. 328-330. Supports giving each deserter from the British army 100 acres of public lands to help settle the frontier, thus enabling them to become useful citizens as opposed to burdens on society.

3628. Rich, Charles (Vt.). "Classification of Militia," *Annals of Congress.* 13th Cong., 3rd Sess. (6 Feb. 1815) pp. 1125-1128. Presents and explains a resolution to enlist men by subjecting classes of citizens to a direct tax for which they could substitute a man enlisting in the army in lieu of the tax.

3629. "Revenue Laws," *American State Papers: Finance*, Vol. II (Doc. 435) pp. 881-882. (ASP 010). Treasury Department responds to Vermont complaints of defects of the revenue laws regarding trade with the enemy.

14ᵀᴴ CONGRESS, 1ˢᵀ SESSION

3630. Lyon, Asa (Vt.). "Commerce with Great Britain," *Annals of Congress.* 14th Cong., 1st Sess. (4 Feb. 1816) pp. 884-897. Rules out treaties that might have set precedent, and clarifies the role of the House in the treaty-making process. Contends that the Constitution is clear that no right is given to the House to interfere with this process.

3631. "An Act to Alter the Times of Holding the Circuit and Districts Courts of the United States for the District of Vermont," *Statutes at Large*, Vol. III (22 Mar. 1816) p. 258. Also printed in the *Annals of Congress* (14th Cong., 1st Sess.) Appendix, pp. 1801-1802.

14ᵀᴴ CONGRESS, 2ᴺᴰ SESSION

[no references]

15ᵀᴴ CONGRESS, 1ˢᵀ SESSION

3632. Rich, Charles (Vt.). "Case of Colonel Anderson," *Annals of Congress.* 15th Cong., 1st Sess. (15 Jan. 1818) pp. 773-775. Remarks on the appropriateness of the House proceeding with the trial of Colonel John Anderson, accused of attempting to bribe one of its members.

15ᵀᴴ CONGRESS, 2ᴺᴰ SESSION

3633. "Memorial of Matthew Lyon," *Annals of Congress.* 15th Cong., 2nd Sess. (8 Dec., 9 Dec. 1818) pp. 47-58; 60-64. Debate and defeat of the motion to reverse the report of the Judiciary Committee unfavorable to the petition of Matthew Lyon. Debate focuses on the constitutionality of the sedition law.

16ᵀᴴ CONGRESS, 1ˢᵀ SESSION

3634. Memorial of Matthew Lyon Presented, *Annals of Congress.* 16th Cong., 1st Sess. (9 Dec. 1819) p. 710. Memorial presented for claims of losses suffered from prosecution for sedition.

3635. "Vermont Contested Election," *Annals of Congress.* 16th Cong., 1st Sess. (5 Jan., 12 Jan. 1820) pp. 860-876; 902-903. Report of the Committee of Elections supports the petition of Rollin C. Mallary, contesting the election of Orsamus C. Merrill. Background information on the contested results, statement by the petitioner and response by Merrill. Same as Misc. 476 (16-1) ASP 038 (entry **3637**) and H.rp.27 (16-1) 40 (entry **3638**). On 12 Jan., decision against Mr. Merrill taking a seat in this House.

3636. Rich, Charles (Vt.). "Admission of Missouri," *Annals of Congress.* 16th Cong., 1st Sess. (17 Feb. 1820) pp. 1394-1403. Opposes slavery; offers constitutional arguments. Indicates the need to maintain the current geographic balance.

3637. "Contested Election of Orsamus C. Merrill, a Representative from Vermont," *American State Papers: Miscellaneous,* Vol. II (Doc. 476) pp. 558-565. (ASP 038). Report of the Committee of Elections supports the petition of Rollin C. Mallary contesting the election of Orsamus C. Merrill. Background information on the contested results, statement by the petitioner and response by Merrill. Same as H.rp.27 (16-1) 40 (entry **3638**). Also printed in the *Annals of Congress* (16th Cong., 1st Sess.) pp. 860-876 (entry **3635**).

3638. U.S. House. *Report of the Committee of Elections, on the Petition of Rollin C. Mallary, Contesting the Election of Orsamus C. Merrill, and Praying to Be Admitted to a Seat in His Stead.* 16th Cong., 1st Sess. (H.Rpt.27). [Washington: 1820]. 19 pg. (Serial Set 40). Same as Misc.476 (16-1) ASP 038. See entry **3637**. Also printed in the *Annals of Congress* (16th Cong., 1st Sess.) pp. 860-876 (entry **3635**).

3639. U.S. Senate. [Relief of Matthew Lyon]. 16th Cong., 1st Sess. (S.Doc.109). [Washington: Gales & Seaton, 1820]. 1 pg. (Serial Set 27). Resolutions to refund fines collected under the Sedition Act, including those from Matthew Lyon.

3640. U.S. Senate. [Report of the Committee of Claims on the Petition of Matthew Lyon]. 16th Cong., 1st Sess. (S.Doc.106). [Washington: Gales & Seaton, 1820]. 2 pg. (Serial Set 27). The Committee reports a bill for the relief of the petitioner.

16TH CONGRESS, 2ND SESSION

3641. "Case of Matthew Lyon," *Annals of Congress.* 16th Cong., 2nd Sess. (4 Dec. 1820) pp. 478-486. The House select committee recommends reporting a bill to reimburse Matthew Lyon for fines paid for violation of the sedition law. Includes a copy of the record of proceedings from the Vermont District Court. Same as Claims 534 (16-2) ASP 036 (entry **3645**) and H.rp.8 (16-2) 57 (entry **3646**), without circuit court notes of certification.

3642. Dickerson, Mahlon (N.J.). "Matthew Lyon," *Annals of Congress.* 16th Cong., 2nd Sess. (19 Jan. 1821) pp. 191-210. Supports Matthew Lyon's claim for reimbursement of expenses incurred while being prosecuted under the sedition law. Maintains that the law was unconstitutional and that money collected under the sedition law should be restored. Addresses opponents' arguments; considers judicial opinions, cases, and precedents.

3643. Rich, Charles (Vt.). "Prohibition of Imports," *Annals of Congress.* 16th Cong., 2nd Sess. (2 Jan. 1821) pp. 704-709. Speaks on the necessity of temporarily prohibiting imports of commodities to enable the citizens and economy to strengthen themselves. Resolutions proposed.

3644. Talbot, Isham (Ky.). "On the Report of the Committee on the Petition of Matthew Lyon," *Annals of Congress.* 16th Cong., 2nd Sess. (17 Jan. 1821) pp. 418-430. Supports the favorable report on the petition of Matthew Lyon for redress of wrongs incurred under the Sedition Act. Discusses the unconstitutionality of the act, the politics behind it, and freedom of the press. Reviews the facts of the petition. Addresses objections concerning precedence, expediency, and legislative authority.

3645. "Penalties under the Sedition Law," *American State Papers: Claims*, (Doc. 534) pp. 737-741. (ASP 036). The House select committee recommends reporting a bill to reimburse Matthew Lyon for fines paid for violation of the sedition law. Includes a copy of the record of proceedings from the Vermont District Court. Same as H.rp.8 (16-2) 57 (entry **3646**), without circuit court notes of certification. Also printed in *Annals of Congress*, "Case of Matthew Lyon," (16th Cong., 2nd Sess.) pp. 478-486 (entry **3641**).

3646. U.S. House. *Report of the Committee to Whom Was Referred, on the 21st Ult. the Petition of Matthew Lyon.* 16th Cong., 2nd Sess. (H.Rpt.8). [Washington: Gales & Seaton, 1821]. 12 pg. (Serial Set 57). Same as Claims 534 (16-2) ASP 036, with additional circuit court notes of certification. See entry **3645**. Report also printed in the *Annals of Congress*, "Case of Matthew Lyon," (16th Cong., 2nd Sess.) pp. 478-486 (entry **3641**).

3647. U.S. Senate. [Report of the Committee Reviewing the Petition of Matthew Lyon]. 16th Cong., 2nd Sess. (S.Doc.11). [Washington: Gales & Seaton, 1820]. 4 pg. (Serial Set 42). The committee, supporting the petition of Matthew Lyon, submits resolutions that 1) the sedition law is unconstitutional, and 2) fines collected under the act should be restored.

17TH CONGRESS, 1ST SESSION

3648. Keyes, Elias (Vt.). "Revolutionary Pension Bill," *Annals of Congress.* 17th Cong., 1st Sess. (25 Mar. 1822) pp. 1362-1365. Supports providing a pension for Revolutionary War soldiers that are over the age of sixty-five and have property not exceeding one hundred dollars.

3649. Mallary, Rollin C. (Vt.). "Apportionment Bill," *Annals of Congress.* 17th Cong., 1st Sess. (5 Feb., 6 Feb. 1822) pp. 916-918; 924-925. Favors an apportionment ratio of 38,500, thus allowing Virginia, Connecticut and Vermont to preserve their present number of representatives. Chart shows difference between a 40,000 and a 38,500 ratio.

3650. Mallary, Rollin C. (Vt.). "Bankrupt Bill," *Annals of Congress.* 17th Cong., 1st Sess. (7 Feb. 1822) pp. 955-966. Opposes the proposed bill that would enable debtors to surrender their property to their creditors in return for exoneration from their debts. Discusses similar bills in other countries, causes of bankruptcy, and the implications of this bill. Contends that this bill would invite thousands to become bankrupt, and others to pursue risky activities.

3651. Mallary, Rollin C. (Vt.). "Military Appropriations," *Annals of Congress.* 17th Cong., 1st Sess. (7 Jan. 1822) pp. 657-659. Debates the wisdom of paying debts incurred by the War Department without prior congressional approval.

3652. Rich, Charles (Vt.). "Prohibitory Duties," *Annals of Congress.* 17th Cong., 1st Sess. (7 Jan. 1822) pp. 647-653. Modifies earlier speech and resolution on prohibiting imports (*Annals of Congress*, 2 Jan. 1821, pp. 704-709). To increase acceptability of the proposal, advocates increasing duties on imports, which would serve to aid industry and also to raise revenue.

3653. "Application of Vermont for a Grant of Land for the Purpose of Education," *American State Papers: Public Lands*, Vol. III (Doc. 349) pp. 514-515. (ASP 030). Resolutions from Vermont support a just appropriation of public land to each state for the purposes of education.

17TH CONGRESS, 2ND SESSION

3654. Keyes, Elias (Vt.). "Disciplining the Militia," *Annals of Congress.* 17th Cong., 2nd Sess. (9 Jan., 10 Jan. 1823) pp. 558-560; 575-576. Opposes spending money to unnecessarily discipline the militia. Supplies accounts of performance of militia in Revolutionary War and War of 1812.

3655. Keyes, Elias (Vt.). "General Appropriation Bill," *Annals of Congress.* 17th Cong., 2nd Sess. (14 Feb. 1823) pp. 1020-1023. Favors appropriations to repair the Cumberland road as a national road; opposes giving the road to the involved states for them to erect tollgates.

3656. Mallary, Rollin C. (Vt.). "Columbia River," *Annals of Congress.* 17th Cong., 2nd Sess. (13 Jan. 1823) pp. 589-590. Favors a military occupation of the Columbia River.

3657. Mallary, Rollin C. (Vt.). "New Tariff Bill," *Annals of Congress.* 17th Cong., 2nd Sess. (31 Jan. 1823) pp. 772-783. Favors increasing duties on foreign fabrics.

3658. White, Phineas (Vt.). "Education Fund," *Annals of Congress.* 17th Cong., 2nd Sess. (12 Feb. 1823) pp. 960-964. Presents and defends resolution to appropriate money from sales of public lands to be distributed for the promotion of education in the states. General remarks on the value of education to society and country.

3659. White, Phineas (Vt.). "General Appropriation Bill," *Annals of Congress.* 17th Cong., 2nd Sess. (14 Feb. 1823) pp. 1018-1020. Favors appropriations to repair the Cumberland road provided that the road be ceded to the involved states and that they pay for future repairs with tolls collected.

3660. "An Act to Alter the Times of Holding the District Court of the United States for the District of Vermont," *Statutes at Large*, Vol. III (3 Mar. 1823) p. 776. Also printed in the *Annals of Congress* (17th Cong., 2nd Sess.) Appendix, p. 1402.

18ᵀᴴ CONGRESS, 1ˢᵀ SESSION

3661. "Partridge's Military Academy," *Annals of Congress.* 18th Cong., 1st Sess. (24 Dec. 1823) pp. 877-878. Resolution to inquire into issuing ammunition to Captain Partridge's American Literary, Scientific, and Military Academy to teach the pupils in practical gunnery. Includes remarks in support of the Academy and Capt. Partridge by Daniel A.A. Buck (Vt.).

3662. "Partridge's Military Academy," *Annals of Congress.* 18th Cong., 1st Sess. (3 Mar. 1824) pp. 1734-1735. Favorable report of the Committee on Military Affairs recommends the authorization of the issue of ammunition to the American Literary, Scientific, and Military Academy to improve the pupils in practical gunnery. Also printed in H.rp.82 (18-1) 106 (entry **3666**) and Mil.aff.254 (18-1) ASP 017 (entry **3665**).

3663. Mallary, Rollin C. (Vt.). "Surveys for Roads and Canals," *Annals of Congress.* 18th Cong., 1st Sess. (15 Jan. 1824) pp. 1057-1063. Opposes the federal government constructing roads and canals throughout the states. Contends that the Constitution does not grant that authority which would violate states' rights and undermine their authority.

3664. Mallary, Rollin C. (Vt.). "The Tariff Bill," *Annals of Congress.* 18th Cong., 1st Sess. (12 Feb., 28 Feb. 1824) pp. 1490-1492; 1712-1731. Opposes increasing duties on spirits, which benefit the West at the expense of the eastern states; favors other tariffs. Illustrates the experience and success of tariffs in various European countries and examines the current tariff situation.

3665. "Ammunition for Captain Partridge's Academy," *American State Papers: Military Affairs*, Vol. II (Doc. 254) pp. 625-626. (ASP 017). Favorable report of the Committee on Military Affairs recommends the authorization of the issue of ammunition to the American Literary, Scientific, and Military Academy to improve the pupils in practical gunnery. Includes letter from the War Department estimating the cost of supplying the ammunition. Same as H.rp.82 (18-1) 106 (entry **3666**). Report, without letter, also printed in the *Annals of Congress*, (18th Cong., 1st Sess.) "Partridge's Military Academy" pp. 1734-1735 (entry **3662**).

3666. U.S. House. *Report of the Committee on Military Affairs on the Resolution Instructing It to Inquire into the Expediency of Issuing Ammunition to Captain Alden Partridge, for the Instruction of His Pupils in Practical Gunnery, Accompanied with a Bill, &c.* 18th Cong., 1st Sess. (H.Rpt.82). [Washington: 1824]. 4 pg. (Serial Set 106). Same as Mil.aff.254 (18-1) ASP 017. See entry **3665**. Report, without letter, also printed in the *Annals of Congress*, (18th Cong., 1st Sess.) "Partridge's Military Academy," pp. 1734-1735 (entry **3662**).

18TH CONGRESS, 2ND SESSION

3667. Mallary, Rollin C. (Vt.). "Chesapeake and Delaware Canal," *Register of Debates.* 18th Cong., 2nd Sess. (20 Jan., 21 Jan. 1825) pp. 297-298; 323-324. Supports the proposed canal. Position varies from previous speech in that request originated from the states themselves instead of from the President

3668. Mallary, Rollin C. (Vt.). "Georgia Militia Claims," *Register of Debates.* 18th Cong., 2nd Sess. (14 Feb. 1825) pp. 572-577. Advocates support of the claims of the Georgia militia, called into action from 1792-1794 to defend the Georgia frontier against Indian aggressions. Documents that the federal government conducted the military operations, thus making them financially responsible, and that the claims were never embraced in the articles of cession by which the Western Territory of Georgia was transferred to the nation.

3669. "Smuggling on the Northwestern Frontier," *American State Papers: Finance*, Vol. V (Doc. 724) pp. 220-225. (ASP 013). Treasury Dept. provides information on measures necessary to prevent smuggling on the northwestern frontier; provides relevant correspondence from collectors on that frontier.

19TH CONGRESS, 1ST SESSION

3670. Bradley, William C. (Vt.). "Weights and Measures," *Register of Debates.* 19th Cong., 1st Sess. (16 May 1826) pp. 2633-2634, 2648-2652. Supports resolution to ascertain the true length of the pendulum at New York City and Washington, and to compare the lengths toward the adoption of a standard to which weights and measures should be brought to conform. Discusses the merits of the French decimal system.

3671. Mallary, Rollin C. (Vt.). "Mission to Panama," *Register of Debates.* 19th Cong., 1st Sess. (20 Apr. 1826) pp. 2408-2410. Supports a modified resolution that the United States would be represented at the Congress of Panama only in diplomatic character and would incur no political entanglements.

3672. "Claim of William Hunt, Administrator of Ira Allen," *American State Papers: Foreign Relations*, Vol. VI (Doc. 434) p. 2. (ASP 06). Claim of Ira Allen upon the U.S. Treasury for redress of damages for losses incurred during his 1796 capture and detention by the British government is rejected. Same as H.rp.218 (19-1) 142 (entry **3673**).

3673. U.S. House. *Ira Allen.* 19th Cong., 1st Sess. (H.Rpt.218). [Washington: 1826]. 1p. (Serial Set 142). Same as For.rel.434 (19-1) ASP 06. See entry **3672**.

3674. U.S. House. *Letter from the Secretary of War, Transmitting a Report of a Survey of Connecticut River, from Barnet, in Vermont, to Lake Connecticut, and, Also, a Canal Route from Memphrymagog to Connecticut River.* 19th Cong., 1st Sess. (H.Doc.154). Washington: Gales & Seaton, 1826. 65 pg. (Serial Set 139). Includes report of surveys, cost estimates, and detailed topographic descriptions for the Black River and Joe's Brook route, Barton and Passumpsic route, Clyde and Nulhegan route, and the Connecticut River.

19TH CONGRESS, 2ND SESSION

3675. Mallary, Rollin C. (Vt.). "British Colonial Trade," *Register of Debates*. 19th Cong., 2nd Sess. (27 Feb., 28 Feb. 1827) pp. 1451-1460; 1494-1496. Opposes regulating the commerce between the United States and Great Britain, particularly as it restricts trade with Canada, Vermont's access to European ports. Strongly objects to limiting trade to Lower Canada (Lake Champlain region), while Upper Canada (western New York region) is untouched.

3676. Mallary, Rollin C. (Vt.). "Duties on Wool and Woollens," *Register of Debates*. 19th Cong., 2nd Sess. (17 Jan., 23 Jan., 15 Jan. 1827) pp. 733-744; 794-801; 823-824. Supports increased duties on wool and woolens. Presents overview of the industry, including the number of people, amount of capital and agricultural interest involved. Discusses causes of present problems and how the proposed tariff would offer relief. Second speech and further remarks address questions from the floor, further clarifying the wool industry and the effects of the proposed tariff.

20TH CONGRESS, 1ST SESSION

3677. Hunt, Jonathan (Vt.). "Tariff Bill," *Register of Debates*. 20th Cong., 1st Sess. (6 Mar. 1828) pp. 1784-1789. Opposes increasing the duty upon foreign molasses and repealing the drawback upon the exportation of spirits distilled from molasses. Argues that it targets the poor and the industries dependent on distilling molasses.

3678. Hunt, Jonathan (Vt.). "Tariff Bill," *Register of Debates.* 20th Cong., 1st Sess. (14 Apr. 1828) pp. 2329-2332. Supports an increased tariff upon slate; provides brief overview of the slate industry.

3679. Mallary, Rollin C. (Vt.). "Protection to Manufactures," *Register of Debates.* 20th Cong., 1st Sess. (31 Dec. 1827) pp. 869-871. Defends the tariff bill of the last session.

3680. Mallary, Rollin C. (Vt.). "Tariff Bill," *Register of Debates.* 20th Cong., 1st Sess. (4 Mar. 1828) pp. 1729-1749. Supports tariffs, but opposes parts of the proposed bill. Addresses iron, steel, and wool tariffs in detail.

3681. "In Favor of Increase of Duties on Imports," *American State Papers: Finance,* Vol. V (Doc. 800) pp. 692-694. (ASP 013). Vermont inhabitants plea for protection of agriculturist industries by increasing duties on imports. Discuss the philosophy of protectionism. Same as H.doc.31 (20-1) 170 (entry **3683**).

3682. U.S. House. *Letter from the Secretary of War, Transmitting a Report of the Surveys of the Kennebec River, and of Contemplated Routes for Canals, Connected with the Waters of the Said Rivers.* 20th Cong., 1st Sess. (H.Doc.173). Washington: Gales & Seaton, 1828. 57 pg. (Serial Set 173). Reports of the various surveys in the States of Maine, New Hampshire, and Vermont. Surveys include: the Kennebec River, from its mouth up to Augusta; the Brunswick Canal, to join the waters of Merrymeeting and Casco Bays (reviews three possible routes); Cobbisecontee Canal, to connect the waters of the Kennebec at Gardner, with those of the Androscoggin at Leeds; Ammonoosuck Canal, to unite the waters of the Connecticut with those of the Androscoggin; Oliverian Canal, to connect the waters of the Connecticut with those of the Pemigawasset or Merrimac; Sunapee Canal, to connect the Connecticut River with the Merrimac; Pasumpsic Canal, to unite the waters of the Connecticut with those of Lake Memphremagog; Montpelier Canal, to connect the waters of Lake Champlain with those of Connecticut River; Rutland Canal, to connect the town of Rutland, Vt. with the northern canal at Whitehall, N.Y.; and La Moille Canal, to connect Lake Memphremagog with Lake Champlain.

3683. U.S. House. *Memorial of Samuel C. Crafts and Others, Citizens of the State of Vermont, Praying for Further Protection to Domestic Industry.* 20th Cong., 1st Sess. (H.Doc.31). Washington: Gales & Seaton, 1828. 6 pg. (Serial Set 170). Same as Finance 800 (20-1) ASP 013. See entry **3681**.

20TH CONGRESS, 2ND SESSION

3684. Mallary, Rollin C. (Vt.). "Drawback on Refined Sugar," *Register of Debates.* 20th Cong., 2nd Sess. (17 Dec. 1828) p. 118. Supports the drawback.

3685. Mallary, Rollin C. (Vt.). "Tonnage Duties," *Register of Debates.* 20th Cong., 2nd Sess. (26 Feb. 1829) p. 384. Opposes a tax on navigation.

3686. U.S. House. *Letter from the Secretary of War, Transmitting a Report and Survey of a Canal from Connecticut River to Lake Memphremagog, and the Report of a Survey from the Same River to Lake Champlain.* 20th Cong., 2nd Sess. (H.Doc.118). [Washington: Gales & Seaton, 1829]. 12 pg. (Serial Set 186). Geographical description of proposed canal route; no maps.

21ST CONGRESS, 1ST SESSION

3687. Hunt, Jonathan (Vt.). "Distribution of Public Lands," *Register of Debates.* 21st Cong., 1st Sess. (7 Jan. 1830) pp. 501-503. Supports the distribution of public lands according to the principle of apportionment.

3688. Mallary, Rollin C. (Vt.). "Collection of the Imposts, etc.," *Register of Debates.* 21st Cong., 1st Sess. (15 April 1830) pp. 795-803. Supports the bill to close loopholes in the tariff law of 1828 that interfere with enforcement of the collection of duties. Discusses abuses and customhouse procedures in detail.

3689. Mallary, Rollin C. (Vt.). "Navigation and Impost Law," *Register of Debates.* 21st Cong., 1st Sess. (30 Apr. 1830) pp. 863-865. Agrees with the necessity of import duties.

3690. "Application of Vermont for the Construction of Certain Fortifications, and that Persons under Twenty-One and over Thirty-Five Years of Age Be Exempted from Militia Duty in Time of Peace," *American State Papers: Military Affairs*, Vol. IV (Doc. 414) p. 209. (ASP 019). Presents resolutions on age of military personnel, and in support of fortifications at Isle la Motte, Vermont and Point Au Fer, New York.

21ST CONGRESS, 2ND SESSION

3691. U.S. House. *Memorial of Citizens of Windham County, Vermont, against the Passage of Any Act of Congress Prohibiting the Transportation of the Mail, Etc., on the Sabbath Day.* 21st Cong., 2nd Sess. (H.Doc.115). Washington: Duff Green, 1831. 6 pg. (Serial Set 209-1). Debate of Church vs. State in regards to right of Congress to prohibit delivery of mail on the Sabbath Day in preference to certain religious beliefs.

22ND CONGRESS, 1ST SESSION

3692. Everett, Horace (Vt.). "Revolutionary Pensions," *Register of Debates.* 22nd Cong., 1st Sess. (3 Apr. 1832) pp. 2370-2372. Contends that there should be no property restriction limiting those entitled to a pension.

3693. Everett, Horace (Vt.). "The Tariff," *Register of Debates.* 22nd Cong., 1st Sess. (18 June 1832) pp. 3665-3671. Addresses the effects of the tariff on wool and woolens. Reviews the status of the wool industry.

3694. Everett, Horace (Vt.). "The Tariff," *Register of Debates.* 22nd Cong., 1st Sess. (22 June 1832) pp. 3716-3717. Opposes the proposed reduced duty on salt; maintains that the protection of salt is beneficial to the agricultural interest and that reducing the duty would not reduce the price.

3695. Hunt, Jonathan (Vt.). "Apportionment Bill," *Register of Debates.* 22nd Cong., 1st Sess. (25 Jan. 1832) pp. 1630-1635. Opposes the proposed ratio of 48,000 as particularly detrimental to the old states. Contends that a ratio of 44,000, with the resulting increased size of the House, would be better for all.

3696. Slade, William (Vt.). "Apportionment Bill," *Register of Debates.* 22nd Cong., 1st Sess. (31 Jan. 1832) pp. 1686-1697. Opposes the proposed apportionment ratio of 48,000 as unjust and unequal. Supports a ratio of 44,000 with its increased number of Representatives.

3697. Slade, William (Vt.). "Wiscasset Collector," *Register of Debates.* 22nd Cong., 1st Sess. (5 May 1832) pp. 2754-2799. Discusses the case of the collector of customs at Wiscasset, Maine, accused of extortion and solicitation to commit perjury. Touching on his distrust of the Executive to do his duty, he focuses on attacking the present administration. Defends his own removal from office in the State Department.

3698. "Application of Vermont for a More Perfect Organization of the Militia of the United States," *American State Papers: Military Affairs*, Vol. IV (Doc. 491) p. 806. (ASP 019).

3699. U.S. House. *Matthew Lyon - Heirs of.* 22nd Cong., 1st Sess. (H.Rpt.218). Washington: Duff Green, 1831. 2 pg. (Serial Set 224). Committee on the Judiciary reports on the petition of heirs of Matthew Lyon, supporting the unconstitutionality of the sedition law and recommending the return of the fine, with interest, to the legal representatives of Matthew Lyon.

3700. U.S. House. *Memorial of Citizens of Rutland County, Vermont, on the Subject of the Tariff.* 22nd Cong., 1st Sess. (H.Doc.283). Washington: Duff Green, 1832. 2 pg. (Serial Set 221). Statement supports the tariff of 1828 and objects to proposed changes, particularly as they would affect wool.

3701. U.S. House. *Memorial of Citizens of the State of Vermont, in Public Meeting at Windsor [on the Subject of the Tariff].* 22nd Cong., 1st Sess. (H.Doc.251). Washington: Duff Green, 1832. 8 pg. (Serial Set 221). Responds to the report of the Secretary of the Treasury, and the appended bill; opposes the proposed reduction of the tariff. Discusses the wool industry and the consequent effects of the proposed action.

3702. U.S. House. *Memorial of Citizens of Vermont, on the Subject of the Tariff.* 22nd Cong., 1st Sess. (H.Doc.276). Washington: Duff Green, 1832. 2 pg. (Serial Set 221). Citizens of Bennington, Vt., oppose the proposed tariff changes, particularly as they relate to wool and woolen goods.

3703. U.S. House. *Memorial of His Excellency Governor Palmer, of the Bank of Caledonia, and the Citizens of Danville, in Vermont, Praying that the Charter of the Bank of the United States May Be Renewed.* 22nd Cong., 1st Sess. (H.Doc.158). Washington: Duff Green, 1832. 1 pg. (Serial Set 219).

3704. U.S. House. *Memorial of Inhabitants of Brattleborough and Vicinity, Praying for the Renewal of the U.S. Bank Charter.* 22nd Cong., 1st Sess. (H.Doc.168). Washington: Duff Green, 1832. 1 pg. (Serial Set 219).

3705. U.S. House. *Memorial of the Hon. Elijah Paine, and the Citizens of Montpelier, in Vermont, Praying that the Bank of the United States May Be Rechartered.* 22nd Cong., 1st Sess. (H.Doc.157). Washington: Duff Green, 1832. 1 pg. (Serial Set 219).

3706. U.S. Senate. [Petition of Heman Allen, Late Marshal of Vermont]. 22nd Cong., 1st Sess. (S.Doc.19). Washington: Duff Green, 1832. 1 pg. (Serial Set 212). Favorable report of the Committee of Claims to grant the petitioner his claim for poundage fees.

22ND CONGRESS, 2ND SESSION

3707. "Matthew Lyon's Fine," *Register of Debates.* 22nd Cong., 2nd Sess. (12 Jan. 1833) pp. 1010-1022. Debate in the House on the bill to refund to the heirs of Matthew Lyon the fine (with interest) paid by him under the sedition law. Debate focuses on the authority of the House to reconsider a judicial decision of the Supreme Court.

3708. "Matthew Lyon," *Register of Debates.* 22nd Cong., 2nd Sess. (8 Feb. 1833) p. 1654. Review of the debate for the relief of the heirs of Matthew Lyon; some contend that Lyon's friends paid the fine.

3709. Everett, Horace (Vt.). "The Tariff Bill," *Register of Debates.* 22nd Cong., 2nd Sess. (23 Jan., 25 Feb. 1833) pp. 1228-1249; 1778-1779. Opposes the tariff bill proposing the gradual abandonment of the protective system until 1842. Addresses the bill in relation to the revenue, the agricultural and manufacturing interests of the country, and the complaints of South Carolina. Briefly remarks on the distribution of the proceeds from public lands.

3710. Slade, William (Vt.). "The Tariff Bill," *Register of Debates.* 22nd Cong., 2nd Sess. (29 Jan. 1833) pp. 1454-1477. Opposes the abandonment of the protective policy and the American system. Discusses the alleged unequal burden on the South, the effect of various duties, and nullification and South Carolina's threat to secede.

3711. "Application of Vermont for a Division of the Proceeds of the Sales of the Public Lands Among the Several States," *American State Papers: Public Lands*, Vol. VI (Doc. 1103) p. 604. (ASP 033).

3712. U.S. House. *Tariff - Memorial of Citizens of Vermont.* 22nd Cong., 2nd Sess. (H.Doc.111). Washington: Duff Green, 1832. 11 pg. (Serial Set 235). Memorial strongly opposes the proposed reduction of the tariffs. Discusses protectionism, with particular reference to South Carolina. Same as S.doc.64 (22-3) 230 (entry **3714**).

3713. U.S. House. *Vermont Resolutions - Legislature.* 22nd Cong., 2nd Sess. (H.Doc.21). Washington: Duff Green, 1832. 3 pg. (Serial Set 233). Resolutions support proper division of moneys from sale of the public lands, oppose a change to the tariff laws, support internal improvements and the Bank of the United States, and support the authority of the Supreme Court. Same as S.doc.51 (22-2) 230 (entry **3715**).

3714. U.S. Senate. *Memorial of Inhabitants of Windsor County, Vermont, in Favor of the Protective System.* 22nd Cong., 2nd Sess. (S.Doc.64). Washington: Duff Green, 1832. 12 pg. (Serial Set 230). Same as H.doc.111 (22-2) 235. See entry **3712**.

3715. U.S. Senate. *Resolutions of the Legislature of Vermont, on the Subject of the Disposition of the Public Lands, the Tariff, Internal Improvements, Bank U.S., and Supreme Court.* 22nd Cong., 2nd Sess. (S.Doc.51). Washington: Duff Green, 1832. 3 pg. (Serial Set 230). Same as H.doc.21 (22-2) 233. See entry **3713**.

23RD CONGRESS, 1ST SESSION

3716. Allen, Heman (Vt.). "Burlington (Vt.) Memorial," *Register of Debates.* 23rd Cong., 1st Sess. (5 May 1834) pp. 3951-3952. Supports the memorialists and their memorial and resolutions requesting that the deposits be restored and the Bank of the United States be re-chartered.

3717. Allen, Heman (Vt.). "Commutation Pension Bill," *Register of Debates.* 23rd Cong., 1st Sess. (13 May 1834) pp. 4049-4054. Opposes the bill, which enlarges the pool of those entitled to Revolutionary claims, because it departs from established rules of evidence and relies on presumptive evidence. Also opposes payment of interest on the claims. Reviews intent of past resolutions of Congress on pensions and the rights of heirs.

3718. Everett, Horace (Vt.). "The General Appropriation Bill," *Register of Debates.* 23rd Cong., 1st Sess. (25 Apr. 1834) pp. 3796-3799. Remarks on the expenses of the Post Office Department; contends that the Postmaster General should not be able to appoint clerks and determine salaries as he pleases.

3719. Everett, Horace (Vt.). "The General Appropriation Bill," *Register of Debates.* 23rd Cong., 1st Sess. (1 May 1834) pp. 3894-3895. Questions appropriations for a minister to Great Britain.

3720. Everett, Horace (Vt.). "Harbor Bill," *Register of Debates.* 23rd Cong., 1st Sess. (19 June 1834) pp. 4567-4569. Supports continued surveys for internal improvements. Regrets that internal improvements have not been uniformly supported beyond the seaboard to the interior; asks for equal justice.

3721. Everett, Horace (Vt.). "Western (Indian) Territory," *Register of Debates.* 23rd Cong., 1st Sess. (25 June 1834) pp. 4764-4768. Explains and defends the bill for the establishment of the Western Territory and the security and protection of the Indian tribes therein. Discusses its provisions; answers opponents' objections. Maintains that entering the plan, or confederation, is voluntary, and that this confederation is intended as the beginning of self-government among the Indians.

3722. Everett, Horace (Vt.). "Woodstock (Vt.) Resolutions," *Register of Debates.* 23rd Cong., 1st Sess. (17 Mar. 1834) pp. 3021-3022. Presents and supports resolutions from Woodstock asking to restore the deposits and to establish a national bank; describes the character of these constituents.

3723. Hall, Hiland (Vt.). "Windham (Vt.) Memorial," *Register of Debates.* 23rd Cong., 1st Sess. (5 May 1834) pp. 3943-3948. Supports the character of the memorialists and their memorial opposed to the removal of the deposits and in favor of the Bank of the United States. Discusses the effect of removing the deposits on the economy and the Executive's usurpation of legislative power.

3724. Prentiss, Samuel (Vt.). "Burlington (Vt.) Memorial," *Register of Debates.* 23rd Cong., 1st Sess. (11 Mar. 1834) pp. 855-858. Presents memorial from Burlington, Vt., praying for a restoration of the public deposits. Supports the character of the memorialists and the positions of the memorial.

3725. Prentiss, Samuel (Vt.). "Chittenden (Vt.) Memorial," *Register of Debates.* 23rd Cong., 1st Sess. (3 Apr. 1834) pp. 1240-1241. Supports the memorialists and their request for a restoration of the deposits to relieve the financial distress of the country.

3726. Prentiss, Samuel (Vt.). "Vermont Memorial," *Register of Debates.* 23rd Cong., 1st Sess. (11 Apr. 1834) pp. 1289-1290. Presents resolutions and a memorial from Rutland praying for a restoration of the public deposits and a re-chartering of the Bank of the United States. Maintains that the removal of the deposits was impolitic, unnecessary and unauthorized.

3727. Prentiss, Samuel (Vt.). "Vermont Resolutions," *Register of Debates.* 23rd Cong., 1st Sess. (14 Mar. 1834) p. 958. Presents and supports resolutions from a convention in Windsor, Vt., requesting a restoration of the public deposits and advocating a national bank.

3728. Slade, William (Vt.). "Addison County (Vt.) Memorial," *Register of Debates.* 23rd Cong., 1st Sess. (5 May 1834) pp. 3948-3951. Supports the character of the memorialists and their memorial and resolutions requesting that the deposits be restored and the Bank of the United States be re-chartered.

3729. Slade, William (Vt.). "Vermont Memorials," *Register of Debates.* 23rd Cong., 1st Sess. (7 Apr. 1834) pp. 3517-3521. Supports the character of the memorialists from Rutland and their resolutions against the removal of the public deposits from the Bank of the United States.

3730. Swift, Benjamin (Vt.). "Burlington (Vt.) Memorial," *Register of Debates.* 23rd Cong., 1st Sess. (11 Mar. 1834) pp. 858-860. Supports the memorial praying to restore the public deposits. Discusses the economic distress of Vermont.

3731. Swift, Benjamin (Vt.). "Vermont Memorials," *Register of Debates.* 23rd Cong., 1st Sess. (1 May 1834) pp. 1594-1596. Supports the character of the memorials and their memorial and resolutions remonstrating against the removal of the deposits and the consequent derangement of the currency.

3732. U.S. House. *Matthew Lyon - Heirs of [To accompany bill H.R. No.498].* 23rd Cong., 1st Sess. (H.Rpt.491). [Washington: 1834]. 3 pg. (Serial Set 263). The Committee on the Judiciary reports a bill supporting the relief sought by the heirs of Matthew Lyon. Reprints earlier report of Jan. 20, 1832, H.rp.218 (22-1) 224 (entry **3699**).

3733. U.S. House. *Meeting and Memorial of Inhabitants of Rutland County, in Relation to the Removal of the Deposites from the Bank of the United States.* 23rd Cong., 1st Sess. (H.Doc.300). [Washington: Gales & Seaton, 1834]. 8 pg. (Serial Set 257). Presents thirteen resolutions disapproving of the removal of the deposits from the Bank of the United States; memorial elaborates on the subsequent adverse effects on the economy.

3734. U.S. House. *Memorial and Resolutions of a Meeting of Citizens of the County of Chittenden, Vermont, Remonstrating against the Removal of the Public Money from the Bank of the United States, and Praying that Such Measures May Be Taken As to Restore the Currency to Its Former Sound State.* 23rd Cong., 1st Sess. (H.Doc.266). [Washington: Gales & Seaton, 1834]. 8 pg. (Serial Set 257). Same as S.doc.241 (23-1) 240 (entry **3744**), but also includes the names of citizens.

3735. U.S. House. *Memorial of Citizens of Addison County, Opposed to the Late Removal of the Public Deposites, etc.* 23rd Cong., 1st Sess. (H.Doc.381). [Washington: Gales & Seaton, 1834]. 2 pg. (Serial Set 258). Memorial and resolutions; same as S.doc.336 (23-1) 241 (entry **3741**), but without the names of the memorialists.

3736. U.S. House. *Memorial of Citizens of Burlington and Its Vicinity, in Relation to the Currency.* 23rd Cong., 1st Sess. (H.Doc.156). [Washington: Gales & Seaton, 1834]. 3 pg. (Serial Set 256). Memorial disapproves of the measures of the Executive in removing the deposits from the Bank of the United States. Discusses the "interference of the President" in the powers of Congress to maintain a sound currency. Same as S.doc.159 (23-1) 240 (entry **3742**).

3737. U.S. House. *Memorial of Citizens of Rutland County, Praying for a Restoration of the Deposites to the Bank of the United States.* 23rd Cong., 1st Sess. (H.Doc.329). [Washington: 1834]. 4 pg. (Serial Set 257). Discusses the harmful effects of the removal of deposits on the economy; includes names of citizens supporting memorial.

3738. U.S. House. *Memorial of the Inhabitants of Windham County, Vermont, Relative to the Currency.* 23rd Cong., 1st Sess. (H.Doc.380). [Washington: Gales & Seaton, 1834]. 11 pg. (Serial Set 258). Body of the report consists of the names of the memorialists.

3739. U.S. House. *Proceedings of a Meeting of Citizens of Vermont, Held at Woodstock, in Relation to the Public Deposits.* 23rd Cong., 1st Sess. (H.Doc.177). [Washington: Gales & Seaton, 1834]. 2 pg. (Serial Set 256). Resolutions disapprove of the removal of the deposits from the Bank of the United States. Same as S.doc.180 (23-1) 240 (entry **3745**).

3740. U.S. House. *Resolutions Adopted at a Meeting of Young Men of Burlington, Praying for a Restoration of the Deposites, and a Recharter of the Bank of the United States.* 23rd Cong., 1st Sess. (H.Doc.385). [Washington: Gales & Seaton, 1834]. 5 pg. (Serial Set 258). Reports ten resolutions and a memorial. Memorial focuses on the abuse of power of the Executive Branch in removing the deposits.

3741. U.S. Senate. *Memorial and Resolutions of the Citizens of Addison County, Vermont, for the Restoration of the Deposites, and Recharter of the Bank of the United States.* 23rd Cong., 1st Sess. (S.Doc.336). Washington: Duff Green, 1834. 21 pg. (Serial Set 241). Brief memorial with eight resolutions relating to the restoration of the deposits and the Bank of the United States. Contains 19 pg. of names of memorialists. Same text as H.doc.381 (23-1) 258 (entry **3735**), but includes names.

3742. U.S. Senate. *Memorial of One Hundred and Thirty of the Inhabitants of Burlington, Vermont, Disapproving the Measures of the Executive in Removing the Deposites from the Bank of the United States.* 23rd Cong., 1st Sess. (S.Doc.159). Washington: Duff Green, 1834. 3 pg. (Serial Set 240). Same as H.doc.156 (23-1) 256. See entry **3736**.

3743. U.S. Senate. *Memorial of the Citizens of Windsor County, Vermont, Opposed to the Removal of the Deposites, and in Favor of the Bank of the United States.* 23rd Cong., 1st Sess. (S.Doc.335). Washington: Duff Green, 1834. 38 pg. (Serial Set 241). Discusses the economy and the effects of the removal of the deposits as well as the right of the people to protest such an action. Contains 33 pages of names with occupations.

3744. U.S. Senate. *Resolutions and Memorial of the People of Chittenden County, Vermont, Opposed to the Measures of the Executive in Removing the Deposites from the Bank of the United States.* 23rd Cong., 1st Sess. (S.Doc.241). Washington: Duff Green, 1834. 5 pg. (Serial Set 240). Resolution and discussion of the power of the Executive branch vs. Congress to withdraw deposits. Same as H.doc.266 (23-1) 257 (entry **3734**), without the names.

3745. U.S. Senate. *Resolutions Passed at a Meeting of a Convention of Delegates from the Several Towns of the County of Windsor, Vermont, Disapproving of the Removal of the Deposits from the Bank of the United States.* 23rd Cong., 1st Sess. (S.Doc.180). Washington: Duff Green, 1834. 2 pg. (Serial Set 240). Same as H.doc.177 (23-1) 256 (entry **3739**).

23RD CONGRESS, 2ND SESSION

3746. Debate on the Resolutions of the Vermont Legislature, *Congressional Globe.* 23rd Cong., 2nd Sess. (18 Feb., 23 Feb. 1835) pp. 261; 281. Debate on the reception of resolutions of the Vermont Legislature in favor of the distribution of the proceeds of the sales of the public lands, in favor of a national bank, and opposed to the removal of the deposits. Different version of the same debate is reported in the *Register of Debates*, "Vermont Resolutions," pp. 1415-1418; 1462-1463. *Register of Debates* version includes lengthier remarks by William Slade (Vt.) and a copy of the resolutions.

3747. Everett, Horace (Vt.). "The Western Territory," *Congressional Globe.* 23rd Cong., 2nd Sess. (20 Feb. 1835) p. 274. Remarks on a bill to provide for the security and protection of the Indian tribes. Advocates sending an Indian delegate to Congress and establishing a confederation of tribes with their own regulations. Also printed in the *Register of Debates*, "Indian Territory," pp. 1445-1446.

3748. Janes, Henry F. (Vt.). "Hon. Benjamin F. Deming," *Congressional Globe.* 23rd Cong., 2nd Sess. (3 Dec. 1834) p. 9. Memorial statement for the Hon. Benjamin F. Deming. Also printed in the *Register of Debates*, "Death of Mr. Deming," p. 752.

3749. Prentiss, Samuel (Vt.). "French Spoliations," *Register of Debates.* 23rd Cong., 2nd Sess. (13 Jan. 1835) pp. 195-199. Supports the claims for French spoliations prior to 1800. Provides a short history of the negotiations, and a summary of the circumstances whereby the government released France from these claims. Provides documentary evidence.

3750. Prentiss, Samuel (Vt.). "Lucy Bond," *Register of Debates*. 23rd Cong., 2nd Sess. (3 Feb. 1835) pp. 283-285. Opposes paying interest on the claim allowed the heirs of Lucy Bond.

3751. Slade, William (Vt.). "Abolition of Slavery," *Register of Debates*. 23rd Cong., 2nd Sess. (23 Feb. 1835) pp. 1463-1464. Supports the character of the Addison memorialists.

3752. U.S. House. *Resolutions of the Legislature of the State of Vermont, in Relation to the Bank of the United States*. 23rd Cong., 2nd Sess. (H.Doc.170). [Washington: Gales & Seaton, 1835. 2 pg. (Serial Set 274).

24TH CONGRESS, 1ST SESSION

3753. Everett, Horace (Vt.). "Indian Annuities," *Congressional Globe, Appendix*. 24th Cong., 1st Sess. (3 June 1836) pp. 573-578. Opposes an amendment for appropriations for the removal of the Creek nation, which would violate an existing treaty. Discusses Indian policy of the government, the history of the treaties with the Creeks, and the causes of the Seminole war. Also printed in the *Register of Debates*, "Indian Annuities, &c.," pp. 4141-4162.

3754. Everett, Horace (Vt.). "Navy Appropriations," *Congressional Globe, Appendix*. 24th Cong., 1st Sess. (10 Feb. 1836) pp. 678-679. Supports reducing appropriations for the navy yard at Portsmouth, N.H., with a view to ultimately discontinuing it. Same speech printed in the *Register of Debates*, "Naval Appropriation Bill," pp. 2509-2512.

3755. Everett, Horace (Vt.). "Ohio and Michigan," *Congressional Globe, Appendix*. 24th Cong., 1st Sess. (9 June 1836) pp. 559-564. Opposes the admission of Michigan into the Union on the basis of its assumed boundaries with Ohio, its constitution, and the provisions of the bill. Same speech printed in the *Register of Debates*, "Michigan and Arkansas," pp. 4214-4232.

3756. Everett, Horace (Vt.). Remarks on Relief for Sufferers from the Creek War, *Congressional Globe*. 24th Cong., 1st Sess. (25 May 1836) pp. 499-500. Opposes relief for sufferers in Alabama who had been driven from their homes by the Creek.

3757. Everett, Horace (Vt.). Remarks on the Western Boundary of Arkansas, *Congressional Globe, Appendix*. 24th Cong., 1st Sess. (13 June 1836) p. 482. Opposes extending the Arkansas boundary to include land now possessed by the Cherokees under guarantee of treaty; establishes that the Missouri extension was not a precedent.

3758. Everett, Horace (Vt.). "Sufferers by New York Fire," *Congressional Globe, Appendix.* 24th Cong., 1st Sess. (8 Mar. 1836) pp. 150-152. Supports an amendment offering relief to those who suffered loss in the 16 Dec. 1835 fire. Same speech printed in the *Register of Debates*, "Sufferers by Fire in New York," pp. 2705-2710.

3759. Hall, Hiland (Vt.). "Fortification Bill," *Register of Debates.* 24th Cong., 1st Sess. (13 June 1836) pp. 4314-4318. Maintains that the proposed appropriations for fortifications are unnecessary. Compares the request against the appropriations approved for the past five years; discusses unexpended appropriations and the past inaccurate estimates of necessary expenses.

3760. Hall, Hiland (Vt.). "Policy of the Government," *Congressional Globe, Appendix.* 24th Cong., 1st Sess. (24 May 1836) pp. 717-722. Supports appropriations for necessary fortifications for national defense, but questions the multitude of requests originating due to the surplus money in the Treasury. Reviews the condition of the Treasury, ascertaining and strongly advocating the ability to distribute the proceeds of the public lands among the states. Same speech printed in the *Register of Debates*, "Fortification Bill," pp. 3973-3989.

3761. Hall, Hiland (Vt.). "Post Office Department," *Register of Debates.* 24th Cong., 1st Sess. (20 May 1836) pp. 3808-3809. Opposes prohibiting the Post Office from distributing incendiary publications; contends that it would be a violation of freedom of the press.

3762. Prentiss, Samuel (Vt.). "Slavery in the District of Columbia," *Congressional Globe, Appendix.* 24th Cong., 1st Sess. (1 Mar. 1836) pp. 619-620. Advocates the right of all petitions presented before Congress to receive respectful consideration of the subject matter; addresses and supports the authority of Congress to abolish slavery in the District; supports states' rights to legislate slavery within their boundaries. Same speech printed in the *Register of Debates*, "Abolition of Slavery," pp. 664-671.

3763. Slade, William (Vt.). "Abolition Report," *Register of Debates.* 24th Cong., 1st Sess. (26 May 1836) p. 4054. Reprint of his letter to the *Intelligencer* explaining his negative votes on the slavery resolutions.

3764. Slade, William (Vt.). Remarks on Slavery Petitions, *Congressional Globe.* 24th Cong., 1st Sess. (16 Dec. 1835) pp. 24-25. Supports consideration of the petitions to abolish slavery within the District of Columbia. Different version of these remarks printed in the *Register of Debates*, "Slavery in the District of Columbia," pp. 1962-1963.

3765. Slade, William (Vt.). "Slavery in the District of Columbia," *Congressional Globe, Appendix.* 24th Cong., 1st Sess. (23 Dec. 1835) pp. 82-87. Supports the right of the petitioners to receive serious consideration, the right of Congress to legislate on slavery in the District, and the gradual abolition of slavery and immediate end to the slave trade in the District.

Discusses slavery; addresses many of the objections of the Southern Representatives. Same speech printed in the *Register of Debates*, "Slavery in the District of Columbia," pp. 2042-2062. Partial summary of speech in *Congressional Globe*, pp. 47-48.

3766. Swift, Benjamin (Vt.). "The Quaker Memorial," *Congressional Globe.* 24th Cong., 1st Sess. (7 Mar. 1836) p. 230. States that the people of Vermont feel that Congress has the power, which it ought to apply, to abolish slavery in the District of Columbia.

3767. Swift, Benjamin (Vt.). "Slavery in the District," *Congressional Globe.* 24th Cong., 1st Sess. (28 Jan. 1836) p. 147. Presents a petition by Vermont citizens to abolish slavery in the District of Columbia. While giving no personal opinion on the topic, supports serious consideration of the petition. Different version of his remarks and the debate printed in the *Register of Debates*, "Slavery in the District of Columbia," pp. 300-303.

3768. U.S. House. *Letter from the Secretary of War, Transmitting a Report of a Canal Route from Wells's River to Burlington, in Vermont.* 24th Cong., 1st Sess. (H.Doc.190). [Washington]: Blair & Rives, Printers, [1836]. 25 pg. (Serial Set 289). Report of a survey to determine the practicality of a canal connecting Lake Champlain and the Connecticut River by way of the valleys of the Onion [a.k.a. Winooski] and Wells's rivers; executed in 1829 and 1830.

3769. U.S. House. *Matthew Lyon - Heirs of [To accompany bill H.R.No.318].* 24th Cong., 1st Sess. (H.Rpt.304). [Washington]: Blair & Rives, Printers, [1836]. 3 pg. (Serial Set 293). Brief history of the petitions for relief of Matthew Lyon, again supporting the petitioners claims. Includes reprint of Jan. 20, 1832 report, H.rp.218 (22-1) 224 (entry **3699**).

3770. U.S. Senate. *Report from the Secretary of War, in Compliance with a Resolution of the Senate, Transmitting a Report of the Survey of a Channel Between the Islands of North and South Hero, in Lake Champlain.* 24th Cong., 1st Sess. (S.Doc.85). Washington: Gales & Seaton, 1836. 3 pg. (Serial Set 280). Reports advantages and cost estimates for both an eight-foot and a six-foot channel to facilitate traffic between St. Albans, Vt., and Plattsburg, N.Y.

24TH CONGRESS, 2ND SESSION

3771. Everett, Horace (Vt.). "Appropriations for the Indian Department," *Congressional Globe, Appendix.* 24th Cong., 2nd Sess. (1 Feb. 1837) pp. 305-306, 307. Deplores the inhumane removal and treatment of the Creeks. Includes a reprint of an article published in the *Arkansas Gazette,* describing their sufferings. Remarks also printed in the *Register of Debates*, "Indian Appropriation Bill," pp. 1537-1541, 1549-1550.

3772. Everett, Horace (Vt.). "Banking Institutions," *Congressional Globe, Appendix.* 24th Cong., 2nd Sess. (29 Dec. 1836) p. 51. Requests the specifics of the administration's banking policy.

3773. Everett, Horace (Vt.). "Indian Appropriation Bill," *Register of Debates.* 24th Cong., 2nd Sess. (2 Feb. 1837) pp. 1561-1563. Continued remarks on the frauds committed against the Creeks; presents letter from the chiefs of the Creek nations objecting to the emigration company.

3774. Everett, Horace (Vt.). "William Anderson," *Register of Debates.* 24th Cong., 2nd Sess. (6 Jan. 1837) pp. 1300-1304. Opposes the claim of William Anderson for losses suffered by the Cherokees. Establishes that no rights secured by treaty were violated, and that the government is not bound by any principle or right to indemnify the claimant.

3775. Slade, William (Vt.). "Right of Petition," *Register of Debates.* 24th Cong., 2nd Sess. (11 Feb. 1837) pp. 1734-1738. Reprint of his letter to the *National Intelliegncer* on the right of slaves to petition Congress. Maintains that the House can receive petitions from slaves without disregarding anyone's dignity or rights, and that slaves do possess the right of petition.

25TH CONGRESS, 1ST SESSION

3776. Everett, Horace (Vt.). "Postponement of Fourth Instalment," *Congressional Globe, Appendix.* 25th Cong., 1st Sess. (Sept. 1837) pp. 317-318. Opposes postponing the fourth installment; maintains that the states, including Vermont, have based their business upon anticipation of the money. Discusses the public finances. Same speech printed in the *Register of Debates,* "Fourth Instalment Bill," (29 Sept. 1837) pp. 1129-1132.

3777. Slade, William (Vt.). "Mississippi Contested Election," *Register of Debates.* 25th Cong., 1st Sess. (3 Oct. 1837) pp. 1735-1740. Discusses the Mississippi contested election concerning the vacancies filled by Messrs. Claiborne and Gholson. Maintains that the law of Mississippi rules that the members have only been elected to fill the vacancies until the Nov. election.

3778. U.S. House. *Memorial of Sundry Citizens of Vergennes and its Vicinity, in the State of Vermont, Praying for the Establishment of a National Bank.* 25th Cong., 1st Sess. (H.Doc.10). Washington: Thomas Allen, 1837. 2 pg. (Serial Set 311). Advocates establishment of a national bank as a solution to the financial problems of the country.

25TH CONGRESS, 2ND SESSION

3779. "Vermont Resolutions," *Congressional Globe.* 25th Cong., 2nd Sess. (19 Dec. 1837, 16 Jan. 1838) pp. 39-40; 107-109. Debate on resolutions from the

Vermont Legislature exerting Congress to abolish slavery in the District of Columbia and prevent its further extension into the territories. Remarks by Heman Allen (Vt.), Benjamin Swift (Vt.) and Samuel Prentiss (Vt.), defending Vermont's right to express her opinions.

3780. Fletcher, Isaac (Vt.). "Army Bill," *Congressional Globe.* 25th Cong., 2nd Sess. (28 June 1838) p. 484. Remarks in defense of Vermont.

3781. Hall, Hiland (Vt.). Remarks Correcting the Congressional Globe, *Congressional Globe.* 25th Cong., 2nd Sess. (23 Mar. 1838) pp. 253-254. Corrects statements in the *Congressional Globe* concerning his vote in 1835 on regulating the deposits in local banks.

3782. Prentiss, Samuel (Vt.). Remarks against Duelling, *Congressional Globe.* 25th Cong., 2nd Sess. (2 Mar. 1838) pp. 206-207. Introduces and supports a bill to prohibit and suppress dueling.

3783. Prentiss, Samuel (Vt.). "Slavery in the District," *Congressional Globe.* 25th Cong., 2nd Sess. (18 Dec. 1837) p. 35. Remarks on public opinion in Vermont concerning the reception of the abolition petitions.

3784. "On Claim of a Company of Vermont Militia, Not Mustered into the Service of the United States, for Compensation for Services at the Battle of Plattsburg, in 1814," *American State Papers: Military Affairs,* Vol. VII (Doc. 751) pp. 775-776. (ASP 022). Claim denied as no muster rolls or other verification available.

3785. U.S. House. *Matthew Lyon - Heirs of [To accompany bill H.R.No.461].* 25th Cong., 2nd Sess. (H.Rpt.377). [Washington]: Thomas Allen, Print., [1838]. 2 pg. (Serial Set 334). Brief history of the petition for relief of Matthew Lyon, supporting earlier recommendations for passage. Reprints Jan. 20, 1832 report, H.rp.218 (22-1) 224 (entry **3699**).

3786. U.S. House. *Petition and Protest of 187 Inhabitants of Montpelier, Vermont, Protesting against the Passage of Buchanan's Neutrality Bill; Praying for a Recall of All Orders for the Seizure of Arms and Ammunition; Also, that Congress Intercede in Behalf of the Prisoners at Montreal, Toronto, and Other Places.* 25th Cong., 2nd Sess. (H.Doc.193). [Washington]: Thomas Allen, Print., [1838]. 2 pg. (Serial Set 327).

3787. U.S. House. *Petition and Remonstrance of E.P. Walton and 215 Other Legal Voters of Washington County, in the State of Vermont, against the Passage of Any Law Prohibiting the Selling, Transporting, or Giving to the Canadians, Arms, Ammunition, or Provisions, or Giving Any Authority to Seize or Detain the Same, beyond What Is Given by Existing Laws.* 25th Cong., 2nd Sess. (H.Doc.194). [Washington]: Thomas Allen, Print., [1838]. 1 pg. (Serial Set 327).

3788. U.S. House. *Report and Resolutions of the Legislature of Vermont, on the Subject of Texas, Slavery, the Slave Trade, etc.* 25th Cong., 2nd Sess. (H.Doc.182). [Washington]: Thomas Allen, Print., [1838]. 4 pg. (Serial Set 327). Vermont resolutions oppose annexation of Texas, or any new state whose constitution tolerates domestic slavery, and advocate giving Congress the power to abolish slavery and the slave trade in the District of Columbia, the territories of the U.S., and the states.

3789. U.S. Senate. *Petition of a Number of Citizens of Dorset, Vermont, Praying that the Treaty with the Cherokee Indians, Providing for Their Removal, May Not Be Enforced.* 25th Cong., 2nd Sess. (S.Doc.416). Washington: Blair and Rives, 1838. 2 pg. (Serial Set 318). Advocates sympathy for the Cherokee Indians in not enforcing their removal if the treaty requiring their removal never received their sanction; list of petitioners' names includes separate "ladies" section.

3790. U.S. Senate. *Petition of a Number of Members of the Vermont Peace Society, Praying Congress to Propose the Establishment of a Congress of Nations for the Adjustment of International Disputes.* 25th Cong., 2nd Sess. (S.Doc.307). Washington: Blair and Rives, 1838. 8 pg. (Serial Set 317). Petition advocates that the United States lead in the establishment of an impartial international board of arbitration to resolve international disputes. A similar gathering is proposed to digest and prepare an international code of law. Four resolutions presented; names of petitioners included.

25ᵀᴴ CONGRESS, 3ᴿᴰ SESSION

3791. Debate on Slavery Resolutions from the Vermont Legislature, *Congressional Globe.* 25th Cong., 3rd Sess. (9 Jan. 1839) pp. 102-103. Debate on the resolutions of the Legislature of Vermont opposed to the annexation of Texas, and in support of the abolition of slavery and the slave trade in the District of Columbia and the territories. Remarks by Samuel Prentiss (Vt.).

3792. Everett, Horace (Vt.). "Indian Affairs," *Congressional Globe, Appendix.* 25th Cong., 3rd Sess. (24 Jan. 1839) pp. 321-323. Remarks on the President's message concerning the government's Indian policy.

3793. Everett, Horace (Vt.). "Maine Boundary Question," *Congressional Globe, Appendix.* 25th Cong., 3rd Sess. (26 Feb., 2 Mar. 1839) pp. 232, 233; 285-286. Remarks on the message of the President relating to the difficulties between Maine and New Brunswick. Opposes the bill giving the President additional power for the defense of the U. S. in case of invasion (of Maine).

3794. Fletcher, Isaac (Vt.). Remarks on a Pension Agency at Montpelier, *Congressional Globe.* 25th Cong., 3rd Sess. (9 Feb. 1839) p. 171. Supports establishing a pension agency at Montpelier, Vermont, in addition to the ones at Windsor and Burlington.

3795. Slade, William (Vt.). "Executive Power," *Congressional Globe, Appendix.* 25th Cong., 3rd Sess. (22 Feb. 1839) pp. 323-333. Reviews the policy of the government, particularly of Andrew Jackson's administration, and discusses the struggle between executive power and constitutional freedom.

3796. U.S. House. *Memorial of Alden Partridge and Edward Burke, Appointed a Committee to Memorialize Congress on the Subject of the Militia.* 25th Cong., 3rd Sess. (H.Doc.140). Thomas Allen, Print., [1839]. 19 pg. (Serial Set 347). Reprint of the invitation to the State Military Convention to be held at Norwich, Vt. on 4 July 1838, includes the minutes and resolutions of the Convention and its adjourned sessions, the plan reported for the discipline of the militia, and an address to the people. Same as S.Doc.197 (25-3) 340 (entry **3801**).

3797. U.S. House. *Memorial of Inhabitants of St. Alban's, Vermont, upon the Subject of the Attack on the Steamer Caroline, the Neutrality Law, and the Disturbances on the Canadian Frontier.* 25th Cong., 3rd Sess. (H.Doc.214). [Washington]: Thomas Allen, Print., [1839]. 2 pg. (Serial Set 348). Statement objects to the Neutrality Law and its unconstitutional violation of personal rights; requests revenge and atonement for the destruction of the Caroline.

3798. U.S. House. *Memorial of Inhabitants of Washington County, Vermont, in Relation to the Neutrality Law.* 25th Cong., 3rd Sess. (H.Doc.250). [Washington]: Thomas Allen, Print., [1839]. 2 pg. (Serial Set 349). Statement objects to the law that violates citizens' rights and liberties and aids a foreign power against citizens at the border.

3799. U.S. House. *Resolution of the Legislature of the State of Vermont, for a More Thorough Organization of the Militia of the United States.* 25th Cong., 3rd Sess. (H.Doc.89). [Washington: 1839]. 1 pg. (Serial Set 346). Same as S.doc.59 (25-3) 339 (entry **3803**), without transmittal note.

3800. U.S. Senate. *Memorial of a Number of Citizens of Addison County, Vermont, Praying the Establishment of a National Foundry at Vergennes, in That State.* 25th Cong., 3rd Sess. (S.Doc.260). Washington: Blair and Rives, 1839. 2 pg. (Serial Set 341). Presents the advantages of Vergennes as a location.

3801. U.S. Senate. *Memorial of Alden Partridge and Edmund Burke, in Behalf of the State Military Convention of Vermont, Praying the Adoption of a Plan Proposed by Them for the Reorganization of the Militia of the United States.* 25th Cong., 3rd Sess. (S.Doc.197). Washington: Blair and Rives, 1839. 19 pg. (Serial Set 340). Same as H.Doc.140 (25-3) 347. See entry **3796**. Parts reproduced in later report of the committee, S.doc.238 (26-1) 358 (entry **3812**).

3802. U.S. Senate. *Resolution of the Legislature of Vermont, in Favor of Granting a Tract of Land to Each of the Colleges in That State.* 25th Cong., 3rd Sess. (S.Doc.60). Washington: Blair and Rives, 1839. 1 pg. (Serial Set 339).

3803. U.S. Senate. *Resolutions of the Legislature of Vermont, in Favor of a More Thorough Organization of the Militia of the United States.* 25th Cong., 3rd Sess. (S.Doc.59). Washington: Blair and Rives, 1839. 1 pg. (Serial Set 339). Same as H.doc.89 (25-3) 346 (entry **3799**), but with additional transmittal note.

26TH CONGRESS, 1ST SESSION

3804. Debate on Petition of Heirs of Matthew Lyon, *Congressional Globe.* 26th Cong., 1st Sess. (23 May 1840) pp. 410-414. House debate on the petition includes reprint of 1832 report of the Judiciary Committee.

3805. Everett, Horace (Vt.). "Independent Treasury Bill," *Congressional Globe.* 26th Cong., 1st Sess. (11 Mar. 1840) p. 261. Remarks and amendment to determine the bill's true intent concerning the powers of the Treasury.

3806. Hall, Hiland (Vt.). Remarks in Support of Abolishing the Committee on Public Expenditures, *Congressional Globe.* 26th Cong., 1st Sess. (18 Apr. 1840) p. 338.

3807. Slade, William (Vt.). "Abolition of Slavery," *Congressional Globe, Appendix.* 26th Cong., 1st Sess. (18 Jan., 20 Jan. 1840) pp. 888-907. Addresses the right of petition, the power of Congress to abolish slavery and the slave trade in the District of Columbia, the implied faith of the North and the South to each other in forming the Constitution, and the principles, purposes, and prospects of abolition. Summary of speech in *Congressional Globe*, pp. 129, 130.

3808. Slade, William (Vt.). "New Jersey Contested Election," *Congressional Globe, Appendix.* 26th Cong., 1st Sess. (10 Dec. 1839) pp. 32-36. Remarks on whom should be allowed to vote from New Jersey on the right of claimants from New Jersey to seats in the House.

3809. Smith, John (Vt.). "Independent Treasury," *Congressional Globe, Appendix.* 26th Cong., 1st Sess. (4 June 1840) pp. 556-560. Supports a bill for an Independent Treasury to provide for the collection, safekeeping, transfer, and disbursement of the public revenue. Presents arguments and a history of the opposition to a national bank. Summary of remarks printed in *Congressional Globe*, pp. 443-444.

3810. U.S. House. *Matthew Lyon - Heirs of [To accompany bill H.R.No.80].* 26th Cong., 1st Sess. (H.Rpt.86). [Washington]: Blair & Rives, Printers,

[1840]. 3 pg. (Serial Set 370). Brief history of petition for relief of Matthew Lyon, again recommending passage of the bill. Includes reprint of the Jan. 20, 1832 report, H.rp.218 (22-1) 224 (entry **3699**).

3811. U.S. House. *Resolutions of the General Assembly of Vermont, in Favor of a Distribution of the Proceeds of the Public Lands Among the Several States.* 26th Cong., 1st Sess. (H.Doc.53). [Washington]: Blair and Rives, [1840]. 1 pg. (Serial Set 364). Same as S.doc.133 (26-1) 357 (entry **3813**).

3812. U.S. Senate. *Memorial of a Committee of the Military Convention at Norwich, Vermont, Praying the Revision and Alteration of the System of the Military Defences of the United States.* 26th Cong., 1st Sess. (S.Doc.238). Washington: Blair and Rives, 1840. 26 pg. (Serial Set 358). Report of a committee formed at the State Military Convention at Norwich presenting a plan for the military defense of the United States, covering a standing army, the militia, fortifications, and marine defenses. Also includes an extract from Capt. Alden Partridge's lecture on national defense. Reproduces parts of S.doc.197 (25-3) 340 (entry **3801**), including minutes of the adjourned meeting and an address to the people.

3813. U.S. Senate. *Resolutions of the Legislature of Vermont, in Favor of the Distribution of the Proceeds of the Sales of the Public Lands Among the Several States.* 26th Cong., 1st Sess. (S.Doc.133). Washington: Blair and Rives, 1840. 1 pg. (Serial Set 357). Same as H.doc.53 (26-2) 364 (entry **3811**).

26ᵀᴴ CONGRESS, 2ᴺᴰ SESSION

3814. Everett, Horace (Vt.). "Case of the Caroline," *Congressional Globe, Appendix.* 26th Cong., 2nd Sess. (13 Feb. 1841) pp. 374-376. Disagrees with the report of the Committee on Foreign Relations on the Caroline affair. General points of argument also printed in *Congressional Globe*, pp. 173-174.

3815. Prentiss, Samuel (Vt.). "Debate on the Treasury Note Bill," *Congressional Globe, Appendix.* 26th Cong., 2nd Sess. (12 Feb. 1841) pp. 283-284. Favors granting half-pay and pensions to certain widows.

3816. Prentiss, Samuel (Vt.). "Pre-emption Law," *Congressional Globe, Appendix.* 26th Cong., 2nd Sess. (8 Jan., 20 Jan. 1841) pp. 47; 194-196. Opposes the presented bill for preemption; considers it too extensive in operation, prospective and permanent.

3817. U.S. House. *Memorial of Alden Partridge, Praying Congress to Adopt Measures with a View to the Establishment of a General System of Education for the Benefit of the Youth of This Nation.* 26th Cong., 2nd Sess. (H.Doc.69). [Washington: 1841]. 8 pg. (Serial Set 383). Memorial supports using the proceeds of the sales of the public lands to establish a system of education. Discusses the importance of education; deplores the present system of education as anti-republican. Outlines his proposed plan to establish a better system. Same as S.doc.80 (26-2) 377 (entry **3821**).

3818. U.S. House. *Memorial of Alden Partridge, Relating to the Military Academy at West Point, and Praying that Young Men Educated at Other Military Schools May Have an Equal Chance for Admission to the Army as Those Young Men Have Who Are Educated at West Point.* 26th Cong., 2nd Sess. (H.Doc.68). [Washington: 1841]. 5 pg. (Serial Set 383). Opposes the Academy at West Point as unconstitutional, unnecessary, and calculated to promote executive patronage and a military aristocracy. Particularly objects that men from other military schools do not have an equal chance to become commissioned officers in the army. Praises the students of Norwich University, at Norwich, Vermont. Same as S.doc.79 (26-2) 377 (entry **3822**).

3819. U.S. House. *Reimburse Vermont for Militia Services.* 26th Cong., 2nd Sess. (H.Rpt.126). [Washington: 1841]. 6 pg. (Serial Set 388). Favorable report on the claims of Vermont for reimbursement of services of her militia during the years 1838 and 1839 for the protection of the Canadian frontier. Includes letter from Governor Silas H. Jenison detailing the course of events.

3820. U.S. House. *Resolutions of the Legislature of the State of Vermont, on the Subject of the New Jersey Election.* 26th Cong., 2nd Sess. (H.Doc.100). [Washington: 1841]. 1 pg. (Serial Set 384). Resolution supports the five Representatives commissioned by the Governor of New Jersey.

3821. U.S. Senate. *Memorial of Alden Partridge, Praying the Application of a Portion of the Proceeds of the Sales of the Public Lands to the Establishment of a System of Education.* 26th Cong., 2nd Sess. (S.Doc.80). Washington: Blair and Rives, Printers, 1841. 8 pg. (Serial Set 377). Same as H.doc.69 (26-2) 383. See entry **3817**.

3822. U.S. Senate. *Memorial of Alden Partridge, Praying the Discontinuance of the Military Academy at West Point.* 26th Cong., 2nd Sess. (S.Doc.79). Washington: Blair & Rives, Printers, 1841. 5 pg. (Serial Set 377). Same as H.doc.68 (26-2) 383. See entry **3818**.

3823. U.S. Senate. *Resolutions of the Legislature of Vermont, in Favor of Restricting the Eligibility of the President of the United States to a Single Term.* 26th Cong., 2nd Sess. (S.Doc.45). Washington: Blair and Rives, 1841. 1 pg. (Serial Set 376).

27TH CONGRESS, 1ST SESSION

3824. Everett, Horace (Vt.). "Case of McLeod," *Congressional Globe, Appendix.* 27th Cong., 1st Sess. (3 Sept. 1841) pp. 425-429. Addresses the report of the Committee on Foreign Affairs on the case of Alexander McLeod, a British subject captured as one of the participants in the Caroline affair.

3825. Everett, Horace (Vt.). "Reports from Committees," *Congressional Globe.* 27th Cong., 1st Sess. (24 June 1841) p. 112. Defends Mr. Hassler and his reports of the coast surveys.

3826. Slade, William (Vt.). "Rules of the House," *Congressional Globe.* 27th Cong., 1st Sess. (3 June 1841) pp. 17-18. Remarks on the 21st rule concerning the reception of abolition petitions; recommends that petitions be sent at the next regular session of Congress, not the extra session, requesting that the rule not be adopted.

27ᵀᴴ CONGRESS, 2ᴺᴰ SESSION

3827. Everett, Horace (Vt.). "Apportionment Bill," *Congressional Globe.* 27th Cong., 2nd Sess. (2 May 1842) p. 464. Supports the district system as the proper mode of electing Representatives. Discusses the impact on the larger and smaller states.

3828. Everett, Horace (Vt.). "General Appropriation Bill," *Congressional Globe.* 27th Cong., 2nd Sess. (12 May 1842) p. 494. Questions the authority for the appointments of the dispatch agents.

3829. Everett, Horace (Vt.). "Treasury Note Bill," *Congressional Globe.* 27th Cong., 2nd Sess. (13 Jan. 1842) p. 129. Opposes all debts, whether by Treasury notes or a loan; concerned that the notes would become a permanent means of revenue. Reviews the causes for the scarcity of money and the difficulty of obtaining a loan.

3830. Hall, Hiland (Vt.). Remarks on Claim of Colonel Francis Eppes, *Congressional Globe.* 27th Cong., 2nd Sess. (19 Mar. 1842) p. 339. Opposes the claim for pay due Eppes, of the Virginia Continental Line in the Revolutionary War.

3831. Hall, Hiland (Vt.). "Virginia Bounty Land Claims," *Congressional Globe, Appendix.* 27th Cong., 2nd Sess. (16 June, 25 June 1842) pp. 936-943. Objects to the government satisfying Virginia land claims when the deed of cession of Virginia already reserved to Virginia land on which the warrants might be satisfied.

3832. Prentiss, Samuel (Vt.). Letter of Resignation from the Senate, *Congressional Globe.* 27th Cong., 2nd Sess. (11 Apr. 1842) p. 408.

3833. Slade, William (Vt.). "Protective Tariff," *Congressional Globe, Appendix.* 27th Cong., 2nd Sess. (20 Dec. 1841) pp. 168-177. Supports protective tariffs. Presents a history of the protective policy in this country. Partial summary of speech in *Congressional Globe*, pp. 33-34.

3834. Slade, William (Vt.). "The Tariff Bill," *Congressional Globe, Appendix.* 27th Cong., 2nd Sess. (11 July, 12 July 1842) pp. 945-951. Discusses tariffs in general, and those on wool and woolens in detail. Presents a history and discussion of the wool industry.

3835. U.S. House. *Resolutions of the Legislature of Vermont, on the Subject of the Tariff.* 27th Cong., 2nd Sess. (H.Doc.52). [Washington: 1842]. 2 pg. (Serial Set 402). Resolutions favor protective tariffs. Same as S.doc.33 (27-2) 396 (entry **3837**), without transmittal note.

3836. U.S. Senate. *Resolutions of the General Assembly of Vermont, Relative to the Election of the President and Vice President of the United States.* 27th Cong., 2nd Sess. (S.Doc.35). [Washington: 1842]. 1 pg. (Serial Set 396). Resolutions advocate designating the same day for the choice of electors of President and Vice President of the United States.

3837. U.S. Senate. *Resolutions of the General Assembly of Vermont, in Favor of the Establishment of a Protective Tariff.* 27th Cong., 2nd Sess. (S.Doc.33). [Washington]: Thomas Allen, Print., [1842]. 1 pg. (Serial Set 396). Same as H.doc.52 (27-2) 402 (entry **3835**), but with additional transmittal note.

3838. U.S. Senate. *Resolutions of the General Assembly of Vermont, Relative to the Re-elegibility of the President of the United States.* 27th Cong., 2nd Sess. (S.Doc.34). [Washington: 1842]. 1 pg. (Serial Set 396). Resolutions to restrict the office of President to a single term.

27TH CONGRESS, 3RD SESSION

3839. Everett, Horace (Vt.). "The Exchequer," *Congressional Globe.* 27th Cong., 3rd Sess. (11 Jan. 1843) p. 152. Opposes the bill as enlarging the power of the Executive and resulting in the creation of a government bank.

3840. Everett, Horace (Vt.). "Treaty of Washington," *Congressional Globe.* 27th Cong., 3rd Sess. (28 Feb. 1843) pp. 369-370. Supports the treaty as he does not support Maine's claims for the territory. Offers and justifies an amendment for the purpose of suppressing the slave trade.

3841. U.S. House. *Resolutions of the Legislature of the State of Vermont, for Continuing for Five Years the Pensions to Widows.* 27th Cong., 3rd Sess. (H.Doc.34). [Washington: 1842]. 1 pg. (Serial Set 420).

3842. U.S. House. *Resolutions of the Legislature of the State of Vermont, for the Repeal of the Bankrupt Law.* 27th Cong., 3rd Sess. (H.Doc.33). [Washington: 1842]. 1 pg. (Serial Set 420).

28TH CONGRESS, 1ST SESSION

3843. Black, Edward J. (Ga.). "Report of the Committee of Elections," *Congressional Globe, Appendix.* 28th Cong., 1st Sess. (12 Feb. 1844) pp. 203-

204. Summary of the attempts of the House to expel members; includes the attempts to expel Matthew Lyon (Vt.) for his attack on Roger Griswold (Conn.) and for violation of the sedition law.

3844. Collamer, Jacob (Vt.). "The Rules," *Congressional Globe.* 28th Cong., 1st Sess. (15 Dec. 1843) p. 38. Opposes a proposed House rule that would limit what is entered in the journal of its proceedings.

3845. Collamer, Jacob (Vt.). "Wool and Woollens," *Congressional Globe, Appendix.* 28th Cong., 1st Sess. (29 Apr. 1844) pp. 467-471. Addresses the origin, history, extent, importance and present condition of the wool industry of the country, and the negative consequences of reducing tariffs on that industry.

3846. Dillingham, Paul, Jr. (Vt.). "Report of the Committee of Elections," *Congressional Globe, Appendix.* 28th Cong., 1st Sess. (7 Feb. 1844) pp. 115-117. Supports the right of the members elected by general ticket to their seats, and also the power of Congress over federal elections, particularly apportionment. Main points of speech also printed in *Congressional Globe,* pp. 247-248.

3847. Marsh, George P. (Vt.). "The Tariff," *Congressional Globe, Appendix.* 28th Cong., 1st Sess. (30 Apr. 1844) pp. 637-641. Presents general considerations in support of tariffs and protectionism. Examines some of the politics involved in the issue; briefly describes life in Vermont.

3848. Phelps, Samuel S. (Vt.). "Postage - Franking Privilege," *Congressional Globe.* 28th Cong., 1st Sess. (1 Apr. 1844) p. 479. Supports a bill to reduce the postage rates, but opposes limiting the use of franking privileges.

3849. Phelps, Samuel S. (Vt.). "The Tariff," *Congressional Globe, Appendix.* 28th Cong., 1st Sess. (16 Feb., 19 Feb. 1844) pp. 337-345. Supports the tariff and opposes reducing the rates of duties under the present tariff to the standard of the Compromise Act. Summary of speech printed in *Congressional Globe,* pp. 292-293, 300-301.

3850. U.S. House. *Resolution of the Legislature of Vermont Relative to Pensions to Widows of Officers and Soldiers of the Revolutionary War.* 28th Cong., 1st Sess. (H.Doc.101). [Washington: 1844]. 2 pg. (Serial Set 442).

3851. U.S. House. *Resolutions of the Legislature of Vermont, Asking Compensation for Services of Her Militia and Volunteers before and at the Battle of Plattsburg.* 28th Cong., 1st Sess. (H.Doc.102). [Washington: 1844]. 2 pg. (Serial Set 442).

3852. U.S. House. *Resolutions of the Legislature of Vermont, Remonstrating against Any Effort on the Part of the Present Congress to Repeal the Tariff Law.* 28th Cong., 1st Sess. (H.Doc.103). [Washington: 1844]. 2 pg. (Serial Set 442). Same as S.doc.56 (28-1) 432 (entry **3855**).

3853. U.S. Senate. [Report of a Petition of James Smalley for Compensation of Services at the Battle of Plattsburg]. 28th Cong., 1st Sess. (S.Doc.101). Washington: Gales and Seaton, 1844. 1 pg. (Serial Set 433). Report supports the petition for compensation. Reprinted later in S.doc.55 (28-2) 450 (entry **3864**) and S.doc.379 (29-1) 477 (entry **3875**).

3854. U.S. Senate. [Report of the Petition for Compensation for Services at the Battle of Plattsburg]. 28th Cong., 1st Sess. (S.Doc.103). Washington: Gales and Seaton, 1844. 1 pg. (Serial Set 433). Report recommends not granting the petition. Citizens were not mustered and therefore length and value of service cannot be ascertained.

3855. U.S. Senate. *Resolution of the General Assembly of Vermont, Adverse to the Repeal of the Present Revenue Laws, and in Favor of a Protective Tariff.* 28th Cong., 1st Sess. (S.Doc.56). Washington: Gales and Seaton, 1844. 1 pg. (Serial Set 432). Same as H.doc.103 (28-1) 442 (entry **3852**).

3856. U.S. Senate. *Resolutions Passed by the Legislature of the State of Vermont, against the Annexation of Texas to the Union.* 28th Cong., 1st Sess. (S.Doc.166). Washington: Gales and Seaton, 1844. 1 pg. (Serial Set 433).

28TH CONGRESS, 2ND SESSION

3857. Collamer, Jacob (Vt.). "Annexation of Texas," *Congressional Globe, Appendix.* 28th Cong., 2nd Sess. (23 Jan. 1845) pp. 402-406. Objects to the resolution for the annexation of Texas because 1) the United States would become responsible for her debts, 2) Texas was a revolted colony of Mexico, and that a war currently exists between Texas and Mexico, and 3) it was a slave-holding country. Summary of speech in *Congressional Globe*, p. 181.

3858. Collamer, Jacob (Vt.). "The Public Lands," *Congressional Globe.* 28th Cong., 2nd Sess. (14 Dec. 1844) pp. 21-22. Opposes the graduation land bill; maintains that it would not benefit the poor settler and would reduce the revenue from the public lands.

3859. Dillingham, Paul (Vt.). "The Independent Treasury," *Congressional Globe.* 28th Cong., 2nd Sess. (21 Dec. 1844) p. 60. Addresses objections to giving the Treasury a physical locality; maintains that it would be in conformance with the Constitution.

3860. Marsh, George P. (Vt.). "Annexation of Texas," *Congressional Globe, Appendix.* 28th Cong., 2nd Sess. (20 Jan. 1845) pp. 314-319. Opposes the annexation of Texas. Addresses arguments, including the danger to the South of confining the black race within their present boundaries, that the admission of Vermont was parallel in nature, and that it is necessary from a military point of view. Summary of remarks in *Congressional Globe*, pp. 160-161.

3861. Phelps, Samuel S. (Vt.). "Post Office Reform," *Congressional Globe.* 28th Cong., 2nd Sess. (30 Jan., 4 Feb. 1845) pp. 220; 238-239. Opposes the proposed reform as not radical enough to effect its desired results. Objects to the proposal that deficiencies of the Post Office Department be supplied from the public Treasury; advocates reducing compensation to mail contractors.

3862. Upham, William (Vt.). "Annexation of Texas," *Congressional Globe.* 28th Cong., 2nd Sess. (26 Feb. 1845) p. 352. Summary of speech reviewing the opposition of the people of Vermont to the annexation of Texas on the basis of expediency and constitutionality.

3863. U.S. House. *Resolutions of the Legislature of Vermont, Relative to the Annexation of Texas to the Union.* 28th Cong., 2nd Sess. (H.Doc.70). [Washington]: Blair & Rives, Print., [1845]. 2 pg. (Serial Set 464). Resolutions against the annexation of Texas and the institution of slavery.

3864. U.S. Senate. [Report of a Petition of James Smalley for Compensation of Services at the Battle of Plattsburgh]. 28th Cong., 2nd Sess. (S.Doc.55). Washington: Gales and Seaton, 1845. 2 pg. (Serial Set 450). Though much of the supporting evidence has been lost, supports two earlier reports of Congress favoring the petition. Reprints 7 Feb. 1844 report, S.Doc.101 (28-1) 433 (entry **3853**), and is itself reprinted in S.doc.379 (29-1) 477 (entry **3875**).

3865. U.S. Senate. *Resolution of the General Assembly of Vermont, in Favor of Reducing the Rates of Postage, and of Curtailing the Franking Privilege.* 28th Cong., 2nd Sess. (S.Doc.70). Washington: Gales and Seaton, 1845. 1 pg. (Serial Set 451).

3866. U.S. Senate. *Resolutions of the General Assembly of Vermont, Adverse to the Repeal of the Tariff Act of 1842, and in Favor of the Distribution of the Proceeds of the Public Lands.* 28th Cong., 2nd Sess. (S.Doc.71). Washington: Gales and Seaton, 1845. 1 pg. (Serial Set 451).

29TH CONGRESS, 1ST SESSION

3867. Collamer, Jacob (Vt.). "The Tariff," *Congressional Globe, Appendix.* 29th Cong., 1st Sess. (26 June 1846) pp. 960-964. Supports the current tariff, which raises revenue while discriminating for protection, and opposes the proposed tariff, which amounts to absolute free trade. Maintains that if this is a permanent system of domestic national policy, as proclaimed, the temporary revenue needs of the war should be irrelevant. Discusses the general principles on which the bill was framed. Summary of speech in *Congressional Globe,* pp. 1018-1020.

3868. Foot, Solomon (Vt.). "The Mexican War," *Congressional Globe, Appendix.* 29th Cong., 1st Sess. (16 July 1846) pp. 1098-1101. Opposes the Mexican War. Examines the origin of the war. Maintains that the war was brought about by unauthorized and unconstitutional acts of the administration and that the direct cause was the unnecessary order to remove the army from Corpus Christi to the banks of the Rio Grande. Presents a detailed rebuttal of the President's defense as stated in his special message to Congress.

3869. Foot, Solomon (Vt.). "Oregon Question," *Congressional Globe, Appendix.* 29th Cong., 1st Sess. (6 Feb. 1846) pp. 248-253. Opposes terminating the joint occupation of Oregon; maintains that as the title is vague and inconclusive, the proper course of action is negotiation and compromise. Contends that war would be the consequence of claiming exclusive rights. Summary of speech in *Congressional Globe*, p. 330.

3870. Marsh, George P. (Vt.). "Smithsonian Institution," *Congressional Globe, Appendix.* 29th Cong., 1st Sess. (22 Apr. 1846) pp. 850-854. Supports the bill establishing the Smithsonian Institution. To meet the directives that the bequest be used for the "increase and diffusion of knowledge among men," the bill's proposals include building public collections of nature, art, and literature. Maintains that a library would both collect and diffuse knowledge; generally discusses libraries and their value.

3871. Marsh, George P. (Vt.). "The Tariff," *Congressional Globe, Appendix.* 29th Cong., 1st Sess. (30 June 1846) pp. 1009-1014. Opposes the proposed tariff bill. Maintains that the protective system is advantageous not only to the manufacturer, but also to the laborer, agriculturist, and the country. Discusses the Secretary of the Treasury's report, the organization of the manufacturing industry, and the advantages of maintaining the present system.

3872. Phelps, Samuel S. (Vt.). "Claims of New Hampshire," *Congressional Globe.* 29th Cong., 1st Sess. (12 Jan. 1846) pp. 183, 184. Remarks concerning New Hampshire's claims for expenses incurred in defending her jurisdiction at the Indian Stream settlement. Maintains that Canada did not attempt to exercise authority over the territory, that it was merely New Hampshire asserting her jurisdiction against the opposition of her own citizens.

3873. U.S. House. *Resolution of the Legislature of Vermont, Relative to the Brass Cannon Taken by the Green Mountain Boys at Bennington.* 29th Cong., 1st Sess. (H.Doc.65). [Washington: 1846]. 1 pg. (Serial Set 483).

3874. U.S. Senate. [Petition of Nathaniel Stafford, of Vermont]. 29th Cong., 1st Sess. (S.Doc.351). Washington: Ritchie & Heiss, 1846. 2 pg. (Serial Set 476). Favorable report to grant the request for arrearage of his pension as an invalid soldier. Reviews the circumstances surrounding his disability.

3875. U.S. Senate. [Report on the Petition of James Smalley Seeking Compensation for the Battle of Plattsburg]. 29th Cong., 1st Sess. (S.Doc.379). Washington: Ritchie & Heiss, 1846. 2 pg. (Serial Set 477). Another favorable report on the petition. Reprints the 22 Jan. 1845 report (S.doc.55 (28-2) 450 (entry **3864**)) and the 7 Feb. 1844 report (S.doc.101 (28-1) 433 (entry **3853**).

3876. U.S. Senate. *Resolutions of the Legislature of Vermont, against the Admission of Texas into the Union without the Consent of All the Other States of the Union.* 29th Cong., 1st Sess. (S.Doc.25). Washington: Ritchie & Heiss, 1846. 1 pg. (Serial Set 472).

29TH CONGRESS, 2ND SESSION

3877. Collamer, Jacob (Vt.). Remarks on the Mexican War, *Congressional Globe.* 29th Cong., 2nd Sess. (22 Feb. 1847) p. 478. Opposes the bill for support of the army in Mexico.

3878. Foot, Solomon (Vt.). "The Mexican War," *Congressional Globe, Appendix.* 29th Cong., 2nd Sess. (10 Feb. 1847) pp. 335-340. Strongly opposes the Mexican War. Claims that it ought to have been avoided, that the war resulted from the unauthorized and unconstitutional acts of our own government rather than acts of Mexico, and that it is a war of invasion and conquest. Also strongly opposes the acquisition of any territory, either by conquest or treaty.

3879. Upham, William (Vt.). "Increase of the Army," *Congressional Globe.* 29th Cong., 2nd Sess. (22 Jan. 1847) p. 239. Opposes increasing the regular army; maintains that a volunteer force is sufficient.

3880. Upham, William (Vt.). Remarks on Slavery and the Mexican War, *Congressional Globe.* 29th Cong., 2nd Sess. (1 Mar. 1847) pp. 546-551. Supports and defends the resolutions of the Vermont Legislature in opposition to the acquisition of foreign territory to be created into slave states, and, as such, admitted into the Union.

3881. U.S. House. *Resolutions of the Legislature of Vermont, Relative to Slavery and the Mexican War.* 29th Cong., 2nd Sess. (H.Doc.81). [Washington: Ritchie & Heiss, Printers, 1847]. 1 pg. (Serial Set 500). Resolutions oppose the Mexican War and request a speedy conclusion. Also oppose admitting into the Union any new state whose constitution tolerates slavery. Same as S.Doc.97 (29-2) 494 (entry **3883**).

3882. U.S. Senate. [Report Recommending Passage of the Bill Changing the Places and Fixing the Times for Holding the Circuit and District Courts in Vermont]. 29th Cong., 2nd Sess. (S.Doc.38). Washington: Ritchie and Heiss, 1847. 1 pg. (Serial Set 494).

3883. U.S. Senate. *Resolutions of the Legislature of Vermont in Relation to Slavery and the Mexican War.* 29th Cong., 2nd Sess. (S.Doc.97). Washington: Ritchie and Heiss, 1847. 1 pg. (Serial Set 494). Same as H.Doc.81 (29-2) 500. See entry **3881**.

30TH CONGRESS, 1ST SESSION

3884. Collamer, Jacob (Vt.). "Admission of Wisconsin," *Congressional Globe.* 30th Cong., 1st Sess. (10 May 1848) pp. 748-749. Objects to the bill to admit Wisconsin as a state and to the proposed distribution of public lands and revenue from such lands.

3885. Collamer, Jacob (Vt.). "Bounty-Land Bill," *Congressional Globe.* 30th Cong., 1st Sess. (8 May 1848) pp. 733-735. Addresses the responsibilities and financial implications of promising bounty lands to soldiers in the Mexican War.

3886. Collamer, Jacob (Vt.). "The Mexican War," *Congressional Globe, Appendix.* 30th Cong., 1st Sess. (1 Feb. 1848) pp. 217-221. Opposes the war and the territorial conquest of Mexico in whole or in part. Summary in *Congressional Globe*, pp. 282-283.

3887. Collamer, Jacob (Vt.). "New Mexico, California, and Oregon," *Congressional Globe, Appendix.* 30th Cong., 1st Sess. (27 July 1848) pp. 966-968. Questions the message of the President and his discussion of "peace" and using "indemnity for the past," for the acquisition of territory; strongly supports a law forbidding slavery in the territories.

3888. Collamer, Jacob (Vt.). "Oregon," *Congressional Globe.* 30th Cong., 1st Sess. (29 May 1848) p. 790. Maintains that a territorial government in Oregon would not protect the inhabitants against the Indians; supports a bill to raise troops to be sent to that country. Discusses the fate of previous acts passed for that purpose.

3889. Collamer, Jacob (Vt.). "Return of Santa Anna to Mexico," *Congressional Globe.* 30th Cong., 1st Sess. (13 Jan. 1848) p. 170. Maintains that Congress need not give control of the war to the President but rather should manifest its will.

3890. Collamer, Jacob (Vt.). "Revolutionary Trophies," *Congressional Globe.* 30th Cong., 1st Sess. (3 July 1848) p. 891. Presents a resolution to give two brass field-pieces captured at the battle of Bennington, Vt., in 1777, to Vermont. Offers a brief history of the two field-pieces and the claim of Vermont to them.

3891. Marsh, George P. (Vt.). "The Mexican War," *Congressional Globe, Appendix.* 30th Cong., 1st Sess. (10 Feb. 1848) pp. 337-341. Addresses the causes, character, and objects of the war. Opposes the loan bill, designed to prosecute hostilities professedly commenced for defense but which were in reality for purposes of aggression, invasion, and conquest. Summary of speech in *Congressional Globe*, pp. 331-333.

3892. Marsh, George P. (Vt.). "Slavery in the Territories," *Congressional Globe, Appendix.* 30th Cong., 1st Sess. (3 Aug. 1848) pp. 1072-1076. Supports

Congress prohibiting slavery in the territories. Maintains that it is a matter of doubt whether slavery had ever been legally abolished in Oregon, California, or New Mexico.

3893. Phelps, Samuel S. (Vt.). "California Claims," *Congressional Globe, Appendix.* 30th Cong., 1st Sess. (26 Apr. 1848) p. 567. Opposes the proposal that takes away responsibilities established by law upon certain officers and confers them upon the nominees of Congress.

3894. Phelps, Samuel S. (Vt.). "California Claims," *Congressional Globe.* 30th Cong., 1st Sess. (13 Apr. 1848) p. 631. Opposes the creation of the proposed office to settle the claims; reviews alleged precedents.

3895. Phelps, Samuel S. (Vt.). "The French Revolution," *Congressional Globe, Appendix.* 30th Cong., 1st Sess. (6 Apr. 1848) pp. 463-464, 466-467. Remarks on reservations concerning the resolutions of congratulation to the French people.

3896. Phelps, Samuel S. (Vt.). "The Loan Bill," *Congressional Globe, Appendix.* 30th Cong., 1st Sess. (28 Mar. 1848) pp. 493-496. Discusses three aspects of the bill: 1) how do expenditures agree with income, 2) what is the condition of the Treasury in reference to its means and resources, and 3) what are the available means in the Treasury to meet its obligations. Summary of speech in *Congressional Globe*, p. 549.

3897. Phelps, Samuel S. (Vt.). "Supreme Court Bill," *Congressional Globe.* 30th Cong., 1st Sess. (7 Apr. 1848) p. 597. Supports a temporary measure of relief for the Court.

3898. Phelps, Samuel S. (Vt.). "Territorial Government of Oregon," *Congressional Globe, Appendix.* 30th Cong., 1st Sess. (29 June, 22 July, 24 July 1848) pp. 880-883; 1143-1144; 1153-1157. Addresses the slave question. As the only Senator from the North supporting the bill, he defends continuing existing laws in Oregon and the power of the legislature to change or continue them, which he considers to be an effectual prohibition of slavery in the territory without the assent of Congress. Summary of remarks in *Congressional Globe*, pp. 883, 988, 993.

3899. Phelps, Samuel S. (Vt.). "The War and the Public Finances," *Congressional Globe, Appendix.* 30th Cong., 1st Sess. (27 Jan., 28 Jan. 1848) pp. 231-238. Discusses the financial aspects of the war upon the Treasury and the economy in general. Examines the costs and effects thus far, and makes estimates of future expenses and the effects of continuing and terminating the war. Considers desired treaty results.

3900. Upham, William (Vt.). "The Mexican War," *Congressional Globe, Appendix.* 30th Cong., 1st Sess. (15 Feb. 1848) pp. 445-453. Opposes the "Ten-Regiment Bill," that would raise a temporary additional military force; also opposes those desiring to annex Mexico. Compares the War of 1812 to the current war; discusses the history of events leading to the war and actions following. Summary of speech in *Congressional Globe*, p. 362.

3901. Upham, William (Vt.). "Territorial Government of Oregon," *Congressional Globe, Appendix.* 30th Cong., 1st Sess. (26 July 1848) pp. 1185-1188. Discusses the question of slavery in the territories. Demonstrates, using various authorities and legislative precedents, that Congress has exclusive power over the territories, that justice and expediency demand the exclusion of slavery from the free territories, and that this bill is not sufficient to exclude slavery. Addresses the arguments of the southern Senators and the question of slaves as property. Examines the practical operation of the measure.

3902. "An Act for the Payment of the Fourth Regiment in the Second Brigade of the Third Division of the Vermont Militia, for Services at the Battle of Plattsburg," *Statutes at Large*, Vol. IX (14 Aug. 1848) p. 331.

3903. U.S. House. *Resolutions of the Legislature of Vermont, in Favor of Asa Whitney's Plan of a Railroad from Lake Michigan to the Pacific Ocean.* 30th Cong., 1st Sess. (H.Misc.Doc.75). Washington: Tippin & Streeper, 1848. 1 pg. (Serial Set 523).

3904. U.S. Senate. *Response of the Legislature of Alabama, in Answer to the Resolutions of the State of Vermont on the Subject of Slavery and the War with Mexico.* 30th Cong., 1st Sess. (S.Misc.Doc.85). Washington: Tippin & Streeper, 1848. 1 pg. (Serial Set 511). Resolutions in response to S.doc.97 (29-2) 494 (entry **3892**). Alabama supports the Mexican War, though also supports its peaceful resolution, and states that its opinions on slavery, which have not changed since admission to the Union, will not be retracted.

30TH CONGRESS, 2ND SESSION

3905. Collamer, Jacob (Vt.). "The Contingent Fund," *Congressional Globe.* 30th Cong., 2nd Sess. (12 Dec. 1848) p. 30. Requests further inquiry into the improper expenditures of the fund before final consideration of the bill.

3906. Collamer, Jacob (Vt.). "Payment for a Slave," *Congressional Globe.* 30th Cong., 2nd Sess. (13 Jan. 1849) pp. 245-247. Remarks on the bill to indemnify Antonio Pacheco for loss of a slave. Compares the status of fugitive slaves to those captured by the enemy in time of war.

3907. Collamer, Jacob (Vt.). Remarks on a Public Lands Bill, *Congressional Globe.* 30th Cong., 2nd Sess. (13 Feb. 1849) p. 532. Supports granting the right of way over public lands for the construction of railroads, including preemption claims on land within ten miles of the railroad route.

3908. Phelps, Samuel S. (Vt.). "Deficiencies in Appropriations," *Congressional Globe.* 30th Cong., 2nd Sess. (12 Jan. 1849) p. 232. Opposes further appropriations for astronomical observations in the South Seas; claims that Congress should not fund these appropriations forced upon it by improper calculations.

3909. Phelps, Samuel S. (Vt.). "Extension of a Patent," *Congressional Globe.* 30th Cong., 2nd Sess. (11 Jan. 1849) p. 219. Remarks on a bill proposing to prolong the rights of the assignees at the expense of the patentee.

3910. Phelps, Samuel S. (Vt.). "John P. Baldwin," *Congressional Globe.* 30th Cong., 2nd Sess. (2 Jan. 1849) p. 131. Maintains that the officer, not the government, is responsible for the losses John P. Baldwin incurred when his brig was ordered to be burnt.

3911. Phelps, Samuel S. (Vt.). "Reciprocity with Canada," *Congressional Globe.* 30th Cong., 2nd Sess. (8 Jan. 1849) p. 185. Objects to the proposed list of goods for which reciprocity of trade is intended; recommends adding items manufactured in New England.

3912. Phelps, Samuel S. (Vt.). "United States Courts in Louisiana," *Congressional Globe.* 30th Cong., 2nd Sess. (1 Mar. 1849) p. 626. Opposes changing the practice of the U.S. courts in Louisiana; favors a uniform practice in the courts throughout the United States.

3913. Phelps, Samuel S. (Vt.). "Liability of Government for Debts of Texas," *Congressional Globe.* 30th Cong., 2nd Sess. (19 Jan., 26 Jan. 1849) pp. 299; 373-375. Objects to the government being liable; states admitted to the Union are left with all the powers of a sovereign state (contracting of debts, providing a revenue, etc.), enabling them to maintain their responsibilities.

3914. U.S. House. [Report on Loaning Two Pieces of Field Artillery to Norwich University]. 30th Cong., 2nd Sess. (H.Rpt.61). [Washington: 1849]. 1 pg. (Serial Set 545). Report opposes loaning the artillery directly to Norwich University. The law provides for artillery to be lent only to the states themselves, who may in turn lend it to the desired institutions.

3915. U.S. Senate. [Report on Loaning Two Pieces of Field Artillery to Norwich University]. 30th Cong., 2nd Sess. (S.Rpt.272). Washington: [Tippin & Streeper], 1849. 1 pg. (Serial Set 535). The report opposes lending the artillery directly to Norwich University. The law provides for artillery to be lent only to the states themselves, who may in turn lend it to the desired institutions.

NEW ENGLAND

1ST CONGRESS, 1ST SESSION

[no references]

1ST CONGRESS, 2ND SESSION

[no references]

1ST CONGRESS, 3RD SESSION

[no references]

2ND CONGRESS, 1ST SESSION

[no references]

2ND CONGRESS, 2ND SESSION

3916. "An Act to Alter the Times and Places of Holding the Circuit Courts, in the Eastern District, and in North Carolina, and for Other Purposes," *Statutes at Large*, Vol. I (2 Mar. 1793) pp. 335-336.

3RD CONGRESS, 1ST SESSION

[no references]

3RD CONGRESS, 2ND SESSION

[no references]

4TH CONGRESS, 1ST SESSION

[no references]

4TH CONGRESS, 2ND SESSION

[no references]

5TH CONGRESS, 1ST SESSION

[no references]

5TH CONGRESS, 2ND SESSION

3917. "Great Britain," *American State Papers: Foreign Relations*, Vol. II (Doc. 141) pp. 183-185. (ASP 02). Communications concerning an exemption to the fifth article of the Treaty of Peace to establish the exact latitude and longitude of the source of the St. Croix River.

5TH CONGRESS, 3RD SESSION

[no references]

6TH CONGRESS, 1ST SESSION

[no references]

6TH CONGRESS, 2ND SESSION

[no references]

7TH CONGRESS, 1ST SESSION

[no references]

7TH CONGRESS, 2ND SESSION

[no references]

8TH CONGRESS, 1ST SESSION

3918. "Great Britain," *American State Papers: Foreign Relations*, Vol. II (Doc. 183) pp. 584-591. (ASP 02). Convention between the United States and Great Britain for settling their northeastern and northwestern boundaries is presented to the Senate for ratification. Includes copies of the convention, instructions to the minister of the United States to Great Britain, and other correspondence on the boundary.

8TH CONGRESS, 2ND SESSION

3919. "Relations with Great Britain," *Annals of Congress.* 8th Cong., 2nd Sess. (1802) pp. 1235-1255. Reprints of a convention with Great Britain (never ratified) and other official correspondence concerning the establishment of the northeastern boundary between the United States and Canada in accordance with the treaty of 1783.

9TH CONGRESS, 1ST SESSION

[no references]

9TH CONGRESS, 2ND SESSION

[no references]

10TH CONGRESS, 1ST SESSION

[no references]

10TH CONGRESS, 2ND SESSION

3920. "Insurrectionary Combinations in the Neighborhood of Lake Champlain," *American State Papers: Miscellaneous*, Vol. I (Doc. 257) p. 940. (ASP 037). Proclamation by Pres. Jefferson commands insurgents to disperse and those with authority to assist in subduing such insurrections.

11TH CONGRESS, 1ST SESSION

[no references]

11TH CONGRESS, 2ND SESSION

[no references]

11TH CONGRESS, 3RD SESSION

[no references]

12TH CONGRESS, 1ST SESSION

[no references]

12TH CONGRESS, 2ND SESSION

[no references]

13TH CONGRESS, 1ST SESSION

[no references]

13TH CONGRESS, 2ND SESSION

[no references]

13TH CONGRESS, 3RD SESSION

3921. "Application to Purchase Twenty-five Townships of Land, Payable in Twelve Years," *American State Papers: Public Lands*, Vol. II (Doc. 232) p. 898. (ASP 029). Application by the New England Emigration Society to purchase lands in the west to be settled by them; discusses the terms of payment.

3922. "Revenue Laws," *American State Papers: Finance*, Vol. II (Doc. 435) pp. 881-882. (ASP 010). Report from Treasury Department on defects of the present revenue laws regarding trade and intercourse with the enemy across the northern border; discusses the authority of the Inspectors and customs officers, existing means to execute the laws, and suggestions for improvements.

14TH CONGRESS, 1ST SESSION

[no references]

14TH CONGRESS, 2ND SESSION

[no references]

15TH CONGRESS, 1ST SESSION

3923. "Disputed Boundary with Great Britain," *American State Papers: Miscellaneous*, Vol. II (Doc. 456) pp. 512-518. (ASP 038). Report on the expenses incurred under the fourth, fifth, sixth, and seventh articles of the Treaty of Ghent. Reviews the course pursued by the commissioners of the sixth and seventh articles in determining the boundaries; maintains that it is slow, expensive and unnecessary. Also maintains that a map is unnecessary. Recommends that the commissioners ascertain the best navigable channel instead. Reviews the expenses incurred in the execution of the various articles; includes relevant correspondence.

15TH CONGRESS, 2ND SESSION

[no references]

16TH CONGRESS, 1ST SESSION

[no references]

16TH CONGRESS, 2ND SESSION

3924. "Great Britain: Execution of the Treaty of Ghent," *American State Papers: Foreign Relations*, Vol. IV (Doc. 320) pp. 647-650. (ASP 04). Report on the progress and expenditures of the commissioners under the fifth, sixth, and seventh articles of the Treaty of Ghent. Reports that no information on the fifth article has been received; that the surveys under the sixth article will be completed during the next season. Concerned that the commissioners have not accounted for moneys drawn from the Treasury; recommends reducing their salaries and requiring them to account for all public moneys received.

17TH CONGRESS, 1ST SESSION

3925. "Boundary Line under Fifth Article Treaty of Ghent," *American State Papers: Foreign Relations*, Vol. V (Doc. 350) pp. 138-139. (ASP 05). Report on the progress made in ascertaining and establishing that part of the boundary from the source of the St. Croix to the northwesternmost head of the Connecticut River. Same as H.doc.58 (17-1) 66 (entry **3926**).

3926. U.S. House. *Message from the President of the United States, Transmitting the Information Required (By a Resolution of the House of Representatives of the 22d Ultimo,) in Relation to the Progress Made by the Commissioners under the Fifth Article of the Treaty of Ghent.* 17th Cong., 1st Sess. (H.Doc.58). Washington: Gales & Seaton, 1822. 8 pg. (Serial Set 66). Report on the progress made in ascertaining and establishing that part of the boundary from the source of the St. Croix to the northwesternmost head of the Connecticut River. Same as For.rel.350 (17-1) ASP 05 (entry **3925**).

17TH CONGRESS, 2ND SESSION

[no references]

18TH CONGRESS, 1ST SESSION

[no references]

18TH CONGRESS, 2ND SESSION

3927. "Correspondence with Great Britain on the Various Topics of Discussion Between the United States and That Government, Viz:...," *American State Papers: Foreign Relations*, Vol. V (Doc. 396) pp. 510-582. (ASP 05). Correspondence on commercial intercourse with the British colonies of the West Indies and Canada, the northeastern boundary under the Treaty of Ghent, navigation of the St. Lawrence River, the Newfoundland fishery, maritime questions, and the northwest coast of America. Also includes copies of the American and British papers on the navigation of the St. Lawrence and a report of negotiations on the boundary line (pp. 543-546).

3928. "Smuggling on the Northwestern Frontier," *American State Papers: Finance*, Vol. V (Doc. 724) pp. 220-225. (ASP 013). Treasury Dept. provides information on measures necessary to prevent smuggling on the northwestern frontier by providing relevant correspondence from collectors on that frontier.

19ᵀᴴ CONGRESS, 1ˢᵀ SESSION

3929. "Revised Report of the Board of Engineers on the Defence of the Seaboard," *American State Papers: Military Affairs*, Vol. III (Doc. 327/2) pp. 283-302. (ASP 018). Discusses the various means of defense that could be utilized to defend the maritime frontier. Examines the various sections of the coast, including the northeastern (Nova Scotia to Cape Cod) and the middle (Cape Cod to Cape Hatteras). Includes a classification of the proposed fortifications, estimates of cost for those fortifications and the necessary forces, and statistics on the available militia force. Same as H.Doc.153 (19-1) 139 (entry **3930**).

3930. U.S. House. *Revised Report of the Board of Engineers on the Defence of the Sea Board.* 19th Cong., 1st Sess. (H.Doc.153). Washington: Gales & Seaton, 1826. 51 pg. (Serial Set 139). Same as Mil.aff.327/2 (19-1) ASP 018. See entry **3929**.

19ᵀᴴ CONGRESS, 2ᴺᴰ SESSION

[no references]

20ᵀᴴ CONGRESS, 1ˢᵀ SESSION

3931. "An Act Authorizing the President of the United States to Appoint Certain Agents Therein Mentioned," *Statutes at Large*, Vol. IV (17 Apr. 1828) pp. 262-263. Authorizes agents to assist in the designation and settlement of the northeastern boundary line.

3932. "Convention with Great Britain for Continuing in Force the Commercial Convention of the Third of July, 1815... Convention with Great Britain for the Reference to a Friendly Sovereign the Points of Difference Relating to the Northeastern Boundary of the United States," *American State Papers: Foreign Relations*, Vol. VI (Doc. 458) pp. 639-706. (ASP 06). Treaty presented to the Senate for ratification on the boundary begins on p. 643. Includes copies of the conventions, together with the correspondence and documents illustrative of their negotiations.

3933. "Conventions with Great Britain...3. Convention for Carrying into Effect the Fifth Article of the Treaty of Ghent Relative to the Northeastern Boundary of the United States," *American State Papers: Foreign Relations*, Vol. VI (Doc. 492) pp. 999-1002. (ASP 06). Convention for the settlement of the boundary line is stated, giving the conditions of the deliberations.

3934. "Instructions for the Settlement of the Boundaries of the United States with Great Britain by the Government of the Confederation," *American State Papers: Foreign Relations*, Vol. VI (Doc. 481) pp. 866-882. (ASP 06). The

Secretary of State reports that the only instructions and correspondence relating to the settlement of the boundary line of the treaty of 1783 were printed in the second and third volumes of the *Secret Journals of Congress*. Reprints of the relevant proceedings of Congress and instructions to ministers relating to the settlement of the boundary line are included.

3935. "Mitchell's Map and Map A of the Northeastern Boundary of the United States," *American State Papers: Foreign Relations*, Vol. VI (Doc. 466) p. 821, 2 maps. (ASP 06). Includes Mitchell's map, "Extract from a Map of the British & French Dominions in North America," dated 1755, and Map A, "Map of the Northern Part of the State of Maine and of the Adjacent British Provinces," dated 1830.

3936. U.S. House. *Message from the President of the United States, in Reply to a Resolution of the House of Representatives, of the 25th Ultimo, Requesting Copies of Instructions Given by the Government of the Confederation to Its Ministers, in Relation to the Settlement of Boundaries with Great Britain, &c.* 20th Cong., 1st Sess. (H.Doc.217). Washington: Gales & Seaton, 1828. 4 pg. (Serial Set 173). The Sec. of State reports that the only instructions given were published in the second and third volumes of the *Secret Journals of Congress*.

3937. U.S. House. *Letter from the Secretary of State, Transmitting, Pursuant to a Resolution of the House of Representatives, of the 19th Ultimo, a Copy of the Maps and Report of Commissioners under the Treaty of Ghent, for Ascertaining the Northern and Northwestern Boundary, Between the U. States and Great Britain.* 20th Cong., 1st Sess. (H.Doc.218). Washington: Gales & Seaton, 1828. 3 pg. (Serial Set 173). No maps included.

20TH CONGRESS, 2ND SESSION

[no references]

21ST CONGRESS, 1ST SESSION

3938. "Indian Affairs," *Register of Debates.* 21st Cong., 1st Sess. (1 Mar. 1830) pp. 590-594. Debate on printing the memorial from the Society of Friends in New England opposing the removal of the southern Indian tribes to the west of the Mississippi River. Includes comments by Tristam Burges (R.I.), Henry Hubbard (N.H.), and John Reed (Mass.).

3939. U.S. House. *Petition of the Yearly Meeting of Friends in New England.* 21st Cong., 1st Sess. (H.Rpt.246). [Washington: 1830]. 3 pg. (Serial Set 200). Petition opposes the removal of the southern Indian tribes to the west of the Mississippi River. Reminds Congress that the Indians had original ownership and jurisdiction of the country and that the consent of the rightful owners was always necessary to obtain possession of their lands. Requests that Congress honors the pledges and treaties made with the Cherokee and other neighboring Indian nations.

3940. U.S. House. *Survey of Connecticut River.* 21st Cong., 1st Sess. (H.Rpt.294). [Washington: 1830]. 1 pg. (Serial Set 200). Recommendation to survey a route for a canal, or railroad, or improvement of the navigation of the Connecticut River.

21ST CONGRESS, 2ND SESSION

3941. U.S. House. *Letter from the Secretary of War, Transmitting a Report of the Survey of Connecticut River, under the Provisions of the Act of 30th April, 1824.* 21st Cong., 2nd Sess. (H.Doc.121). Washington: Duff Green, 1831. 39 pg. (Serial Set 209-1). Survey of the valley of the Connecticut River to evaluate the advantages and disadvantages of improving the river, building a canal, or constructing a railroad. Briefly describes the area; examines the sections involved, current means of navigation, and existing locks and canals. Discusses the involvement and contributions of the contiguous states. Utilizes the 1825 survey of Holmes Hutcherson. Estimates probable expenses. Recommends the adoption of a railroad or canal, but not the river project.

22ND CONGRESS, 1ST SESSION

[no references]

22ND CONGRESS, 2ND SESSION

[no references]

23RD CONGRESS, 1ST SESSION

3942. U.S. House. *Letter from the Secretary of War, Transmitting a Copy of the Report and Estimates for the Improvement of the Harbors of Plattsburg, Port Kent, and Burlington Bay, on Lake Champlain.* 23rd Cong., 1st Sess. (H.Doc.131). [Washington: Gales & Seaton, 1834]. 8 pg. (Serial Set 256). Topographic report and estimates for the erection of piers and breakwaters in the harbors of Burlington, Port Kent, and Plattsburg.

23RD CONGRESS, 2ND SESSION

3943. U.S. House. *Message from the President of the United States, Transmitting Information in Relation to the Establishment and Settlement of the Northeastern Boundary of the United States.* 23rd Cong., 2nd Sess. (H.Doc.62). [Washington: Gales & Seaton, Print., 1835]. 2 pg. (Serial Set 272). Jackson responds that while the settlement of the northeastern boundary is in progress it would be incompatible with the public interest to make available any communications between the United States and Great Britain on that topic.

24TH CONGRESS, 1ST SESSION

3944. U.S. Senate. *Message from the President of the United States, Transmitting Sundry Documents Relating to the Northeastern Boundary of the United States.* 24th Cong., 1st Sess. (S.Doc.414). Washington: Gales & Seaton, 1836. 64 pg. (Serial Set 284). Correspondence requested and denied at last session of Congress now sent to the Senate to decide whether it is expedient to publish before negotiations have been closed. Includes correspondence between the Secretary of State and the diplomatic representatives of Great Britain at Washington.

24TH CONGRESS, 2ND SESSION

[no references]

25TH CONGRESS, 1ST SESSION

[no references]

25TH CONGRESS, 2ND SESSION

3945. U.S. Senate. *Report from the Secretary of War, in Compliance with a Resolution of the Senate of the 14th October, 1837, Relative to a Plan for the Protection of the North and Eastern Boundary of the United States.* 25th Cong., 2nd Sess. (S.Doc.88). Washington: Blair and Rives, 1838. 7 pg. (Serial Set 314). Report reviews the minimum force required at various posts and stations to protect the northern and eastern frontiers.

3946. U.S. Senate. [Report on the Northeastern Boundary of the United States]. 25th Cong., 2nd Sess. (S.Doc.502). Washington: Blair and Rives, 1838. 16 pg., 2 maps. (Serial Set 319). Report of the Committee on Foreign Relations opposes the bill to survey the northeastern boundary line of the United States until all reasonable means of effecting resolution have been exhausted. Reviews the boundary controversy; establishes the validity of the title of the United States to the territory in dispute. Includes John Mitchell's map, "Extract from a Map of the British and French Dominions in North America" and Map A, "Map of the Northern Part of the State of Maine and of the Adjacent British Provinces."

25TH CONGRESS, 3RD SESSION

3947. U.S. Senate. [Report on the Northeastern Boundary of the United States]. 25th Cong., 3rd Sess. (S.Doc.287). Washington: Blair and Rives, 1839. 16 pg., 2 maps. (Serial Set 342). Reprint of report of last session of Congress, S.doc.502 (25-2) 319. See entry **3946**.

26TH CONGRESS, 1ST SESSION

3948. "An Act to Provide for the Expenses of Making an Exploration and Survey of That Part of the Northeastern Boundary Line of the United States Which Separates the States of Maine and New Hampshire from the British Provinces," *Statutes at Large*, Vol. V (20 July 1840) p. 402.

3949. U.S. House. *Message from the President of the United States, Transmitting the Information Required by the Resolution of the House of Representatives of the United States of the 6th of April Last, Respecting the Military Preparation of Great Britain on the Northern and Northeastern Frontier of the United States, &c.* 26th Cong., 1st Sess. (H.Doc.245). [Washington: 1840]. 4 pg. (Serial Set 369). Report of various officers on the frontier as to the status of British military defenses in their regions.

26TH CONGRESS, 2ND SESSION

3950. "An Act to Make Further Provision for the Expenses of an Exploration and Survey of That Part of the Northeastern Boundary Line of the United States Which Separates the States of Maine and New Hampshire from the British Provinces," *Statutes at Large*, Vol. V (27 Feb. 1841) pp. 413-414.

3951. U.S. House. *Message from the President of the United States, Transmitting a Communication from the Secretary of State upon the Subject of the Northeastern Boundary of the United States.* 26th Cong., 2nd Sess. (H.Doc.93). [Washington: 1841]. 6 pg. (Serial Set 384). Report and correspondence on expenses for the exploration and survey of the northeastern boundary.

3952. U.S. House. *Message from the President of the United States, Transmitting a Copy of the Commissioners for the Exploration and Survey of* *the Northeastern Boundary, &c. &c.* 26th Cong., 2nd Sess. (H.Doc.102). [Washington: 1841]. 13 pg. (Serial Set 384). Report of the exploration of the boundary line; due to insufficient time to complete the survey, commissioners contend it is premature to present their findings. Same as S.doc.173 (26-2) 378 (entry **3953**).

3953. U.S. Senate. *Message from the President of the United States, Transmitting a Copy of the Report of the Commissioners for the Exploration and Survey of the Northeastern Boundary.* 26th Cong., 2nd Sess. (S.Doc.173). Washington: Blair and Rives, 1841. 13 pg. (Serial Set 378). Same as H.doc.102 (26-2) 384. See entry **3952**.

27TH CONGRESS, 1ST SESSION

[no references]

27TH CONGRESS, 2ND SESSION

3954. U.S. House. *Message from the President of the United States, Transmitting a Report of the Commissioners for the Exploration and Survey of the Boundary Line Between the States of Maine and New Hampshire, and the Conterminous British Provinces, &c.* 27th Cong., 2nd Sess. (H.Doc.70). [Washington: 1842]. 11 pg. (Serial Set 402). Report of progress and estimate of needed funds to complete the surveys. Same as S.doc.97 (27-2) 396 (entry **3955**).

3955. U.S. Senate. *Message from the President of the United States, Communicating Copies of a Report and Letter from the Commissioners Appointed for the Exploration and Survey of the Northeastern Boundary.* 27th Cong., 2nd Sess. (S.Doc.97). [Washington]: Thomas Allen, Print., [1842]. 10 pg. (Serial Set 396). Report of progress and estimate of needed funds to complete the surveys. Same as H.doc.70 (27-2) 402 (entry **3954**).

27TH CONGRESS, 3RD SESSION

3956. "Correspondence with the British Special Mission - Northeastern and Northwestern Boundary," *Congressional Globe.* 27th Cong., 3rd Sess. (1842) pp. 4-12. Copies of the correspondence between Lord Ashburton and Daniel Webster on the boundary dispute between Canada and Maine that resulted in the Webster-Ashburton Treaty.

3957. "Correspondence with State Authorities - North Eastern Boundary," *Congressional Globe.* 27th Cong., 3rd Sess. (1842) pp. 12-22. Copies of various correspondences relating to the northeastern boundary negotiations.

Includes correspondence from the states of Massachusetts, Maine and New Hampshire, correspondence between Mr. Webster and the Maine Commissioners, and correspondence between Mr. Webster and the Massachusetts Commissioners.

3958. Benton, Thomas H. (Mo.). "The British Treaty," *Congressional Globe, Appendix.* 27th Cong., 3rd Sess. (18 Aug. 1842) pp. 1-27. Secret Session. Lengthy speech opposes the proposed treaty. Reviews the various disputes which were to be resolved and his objections to proposed settlements. Maintains that all the issues were not settled and that the treaty makes a sectional distinction between the states. Discusses the proposed boundary settlement, reviewing the grants and compensations on each side. Discusses the Maine boundary dispute and the map from Mr. Jefferson's collection. Includes copy of the map, "Map of the North Eastern Boundary."

3959. Buchanan, James (Pa.). "British Treaty," *Congressional Globe, Appendix.* 27th Cong., 3rd Sess. (19 Aug. 1842) pp. 101-110. Secret Session. Presents his reasons for voting against the ratification of the treaty. Believes that the proposed treaty is unjust and dishonorable. Addresses each of the subjects of the treaty, examining the terms of the treaty and the various concessions made. Discusses the northeastern boundary questions and the pretexts of the British government. Reviews the history of the negotiation between Mr. Webster and Lord Ashburton in relation to the Maine boundary.

3960. Calhoun, John C. (S.C.). "British Treaty," *Congressional Globe, Appendix.* 27th Cong., 3rd Sess. (Aug. 1842) pp. 49-53. Secret Session. States his reasons in favor of and against the ratification of the proposed treaty. Discusses the settlement of the northeastern boundary. Maintains that this dispute can only be settled by a compromise or conventional line. Reviews the provisions of the treaty in reference to the proposed line.

3961. Rives, William C. (Va.). "British Treaty," *Congressional Globe, Appendix.* 27th Cong., 3rd Sess. (17 August, 19 Aug. 1842) pp. 59-67. Secret Session. Gives the background behind the recommendation of the Committee on Foreign Relations to ratify the proposed treaty. Reviews the stipulations of the treaty, including those regarding the northeastern boundary. Gives a brief history of the controversy and the actions of the two governments; analyzes the details of the arrangement. Maintains that the boundary is open to controversy, and thus subject to arbitration. Discusses the relevance of the maps offered.

3962. U.S. House. *Message from the President of the United States, Transmitting a Report of the Board of Commissioners Appointed to Survey the Northeastern Boundary.* 27th Cong., 3rd Sess. (H.Doc.31). [Washington: 1842]. 49 pg., 1 profile. (Serial Set 420). Report of the commission on the exploration and survey of the disputed lines, and report upon the arguments contained in the report of Messrs. Featherstonhaugh and Mudge. Includes a profile of the meridian line from the source of the St. Croix River to the St. John River.

28TH CONGRESS, 1ST SESSION

3963. U.S. House. *Letter from the Secretary of State, Transmitting to the Committee of Ways and Means the Letter of Albert Smith, Esq., Relative to the Northeastern Boundary.* 28th Cong., 1st Sess. (H.Doc.169). [Washington]: Blair & Rives, Print., [1844]. 6 pg. (Serial Set 442). Report of the progress of the commissioner concerning the disputed boundary-line described in the 1st article of the Treaty of Washington; requests further appropriations for reimbursement of funds and to complete the work.

28TH CONGRESS, 2ND SESSION

3964. U.S. Senate. *Memorial of the Yearly Meeting of the Society of Friends in New England Praying that Texas May Not Be Annexed to the United States.* 28th Cong., 2nd Sess. (S.Doc.127). Washington: Gales & Seaton, 1845. 2 pg. (Serial Set 456). Maintains that the annexation would perpetuate slavery and probably result in war.

29TH CONGRESS, 1ST SESSION

3965. Dickinson, Daniel S. (N.Y.). "Treaty of Washington," *Congressional Globe, Appendix.* 29th Cong., 1st Sess. (9 Apr. 1846) pp. 537-545. Responds to Mr. Webster (Mass.) on the northeastern boundary. Maintains that the Ashburton treaty gave Great Britain the entire territory in dispute plus 700,000 acres - more than she was entitled to by her own maps. Discusses Maine's consent to the arrangement. Examines the concessions of the treaty. Remainder of speech addresses the right of search and the destruction of the Caroline.

3966. U.S. Senate. *Message from the President of the United States, in Answer to a Resolution of the Senate, Communicating the Correspondence Which Took Place Between the Government of Great Britain and That of the United States Between the 20th of June, 1840, and the 4th of March, 1841, Relative to the Northeastern Boundary.* 29th Cong., 1st Sess. (S.Doc.274). Washington: Ritchie & Heiss, 1846. 22 pg. (Serial Set 474). Correspondence includes discussion and modifications of draft of convention between Great Britain and the United States to ascertain and determine the northeastern boundary.

3967. U.S. Senate. *Memorial of a Committee of a Meeting of Paper Manufacturers of New England, Praying that the Present Duties on Foreign Paper and Books May Not Be Changed.* 29th Cong., 1st Sess. (S.Doc.450). Washington: Ritchie & Heiss, 1846. 3 pg. (Serial Set 478). Memorial describes the paper manufacturing business; details why the proposed reduction of duties would seriously injure their business.

3968. U.S. Senate. *Memorial of the Representatives of the Yearly Meeting of the Society of Friends for New England, on the Subject of War, and Praying the Adoption of Measures that Will Tend to Perpetuate Peace.* 29th Cong., 1st Sess. (S.Doc.386). Washington: Ritchie & Heiss, 1846. 3 pg. (Serial Set 477). Memorials from the Society of Friends for New England and the Religious Society of Friends for the States of New York, Vermont, and Michigan, oppose war and maintain that it can never be justified.

29TH CONGRESS, 2ND SESSION

3969. Debate on the Memorial of the Society of Friends, *Congressional Globe.* 29th Cong., 2nd Sess. (29 Dec. 1846) pp. 95-96. Debate in the House on printing the memorial of the Society of Friends for New England asking for the termination of the Mexican War. Includes remarks by Daniel King (Mass.).

3970. "Memorial of the Society of Friends," *Congressional Globe.* 29th Cong., 2nd Sess. (23 Dec., 29 Dec. 1846) pp. 69-71; 95-96. Debate in the Senate on printing the memorial from the Society of Friends for New England asking for the termination of the Mexican War. Reprints text of memorial. Includes remarks by John Davis (Mass.), Charles Atherton (N.H.), James Simmons (R.I.), and John Niles (Conn.).

30TH CONGRESS, 1ST SESSION

3971. "Peace Memorial from the Quakers," *Congressional Globe.* 30th Cong., 1st Sess. (10 Feb. 1848) pp. 329-331. Presents the memorial from the Society of Friends for New England requesting the speedy termination of the war with Mexico. Remarks by Daniel P. King (Mass.) and John G. Palfrey (Mass.) support the character and petition of the memorialists. Debate focuses on the printing of memorials from individual citizens. Includes reprint of the memorial.

3972. U.S. House. *Memorial of the Representatives of the Yearly Meeting of the Society of Friends for New England, for the Adoption of Measures for the Speedy Termination of the War.* 30th Cong., 1st Sess. (H.Misc.Doc.21). Washington: Tipping & Streeper, 1848. 2 pg. (Serial Set 523). Memorial opposes the war as contrary to the gospel of Christ.

30TH CONGRESS, 2ND SESSION

[no references]

AUTHOR INDEX: INDIVIDUALS, ORGANIZATIONS, AND PLACES

SUBJECT INDEX

About the Author

SUZANNE M. CLARK has had an extensive career as a librarian and researcher. She has been Head of Public Service at Hawaii Medical Library, Head of the Documents and Maps Department of the University of Vermont library, and a Research Associate with PROMIS Laboratory, a problem-oriented medical record information system. Her publications have appeared in journals such as *Government Publications Review* and *Journal of Education for Library and Information Science*.

ISBN 0-313-28128-9

90000>

EAN

9 780313 281280

HARDCOVER BAR CODE